PRICEWATERHOUSE COOPERS 🅿️

# Manual of Accounting
## Management Reports and Governance – 2009

UK Accounting Consulting Services
PricewaterhouseCoopers LLP, Chartered Accountants

Published by

 CCH
a Wolters Kluwer business

145 London Road
Kingston-upon-Thames
Surrey
KT2 6SR
Tel: +44 (0) 844 561 8166
Fax: +44 (0) 208 247 1184
E-mail: info@cch.co.uk
Website: www.cch.co.uk

This book has been prepared for general guidance on matters of interest only, and does not constitute professional advice. You should not act upon the information contained in this book without obtaining specific professional advice. Accordingly, to the extent permitted by law, PricewaterhouseCoopers LLP (and its members, employees and agents) and publisher accept no liability, and disclaim all responsibility, for the consequences of you or anyone else acting, or refraining from acting, in reliance on the information contained in this document or for any decision based on it, or for any consequential, special or similar damages even if advised of the possibility of such damages.

ISBN 978-1-84798-112-7.

Printed and bound in Italy by Legoprint.
Typeset by YHT, London.

British Library Cataloguing-in-Publication Data.

A catalogue record for this book is available from the British Library.

# Authors

PricewaterhouseCoopers' Manual of Accounting – Management Reports and Governance is written by the PricewaterhouseCoopers LLP's UK Accounting Consulting Services team.

Writing team led by

Barry Johnson
Peter Holgate

**Authors, contributors and reviewers**

Zoe Anderson
Gary Berckowitz
Nicola Bruyns
Dasa Brynjolffssen
Karen Burrows
Clare de Arostegui
Nigel Dealy
Margaret Cassidy
Fredré Ferreira
Michael Gaull
Jyoti Ghosh
Marek Grabowski
Angela Green
Margaret Heneghan
Eddie Hodgson
Peter Hogarth
Mary Holden
Hannah King
Sabine Koch
Stephen Lomax
Joanna Malvern

Helen McCann
Susannah McKay
Janet Milligan
Monica Peters
Marian Lovelace
Iain Selfridge
Anjani Shah
Anne Simpson
Laura Taylor
Julie Thomas
Sandra Thompson
Sarah Troughton
Gail Tucker
Stanislav Varkalov
Andrew Walker
Dave Walters
Barbara Willis
Michelle Winarto
Katie Woods

# Preface

PricewaterhouseCoopers' Manual of Accounting – Management reports and governance is a practical guide to the legal and other regulatory requirements that impact elements of financial statements that are common to users of both IFRS and UK GAAP, often referred to as the 'front half' of the financial statements, together with other legal issues. The Manual includes practical advice based on our work in the PricewaterhouseCoopers LLP's UK Accounting Consulting Services team in advising the firm's clients, partners and staff.

The Manual deals with the requirements of the Combined Code on corporate governance and looks at the rules for the business review and guidance for the operating and financial review. Also explained are the directors' report and their remuneration report, together with the legality of directors' loans. The legal aspects concerning areas such as company reporting periods and purchase of own shares, together with their accounting implications, are fully explored. It also deals with the implications of the Companies Act 2006.

This book supplements our two books which deal with the latter half of the financial statements: 'PricewaterhouseCoopers' Manual of Accounting – IFRS for the UK' and 'PricewaterhouseCoopers' Manual of Accounting – UK GAAP'.

Even in a work of this size it is not possible to cover every aspect of company reporting.

We hope that finance directors, accountants, legal practitioners, company administrators, financial advisers and auditors will find this manual useful.

Barry Johnson, Peter Holgate
PricewaterhouseCoopers LLP
London
November 2008

# Contents

|  |  | Page |
|---|---|---|
| *Abbreviations and terms used* | | P009 |
| 1 | Introduction | 1001 |
| 2 | Operating and financial review | 2001 |
| 3 | Directors' report | 3001 |
| 4 | Corporate governance | 4001 |
| 5 | Disclosure of directors' remuneration | 5001 |
| 6 | Loans and other transactions involving directors | 6001 |
| 7 | Acquisition of own shares | 7001 |
| 8 | Secretarial matters | 8001 |

# Abbreviations and terms used

| | |
|---|---|
| AAPA | Association of Authorised Public Accountants |
| ABI | Association of British Insurers |
| AC | Appeal Cases, law reports |
| Accounts | financial statements |
| ADR | American depositary receipts |
| AESOP | all employee share ownership plan |
| the 1985 Act | the Companies Act 1985 (as amended by the Companies Act 1989) |
| the 1989 Act | the Companies Act 1989 |
| the 2006 Act | the Companies Act 2006 |
| ACCA | Association of Chartered Certified Accountants |
| ACT | advance corporation tax |
| AFS | available-for-sale |
| AG | Application Guidance |
| AGM | Annual General Meeting |
| AIM | Alternative Investment Market |
| AIMR | Alternative Investment Market Rules |
| AITC | Association of Investment Trust Companies |
| All ER | All England Law Reports |
| AMPS | auction market preferred shares |
| APB | Auditing Practices Board |
| APC | Auditing Practices Committee |
| App | Application note of a Financial Reporting Standard |
| app | appendix |
| ARC | Accounting Regulatory Committee |
| ASB | Accounting Standards Board |
| ASC | Accounting Standards Committee |
| | |
| BBA | British Bankers' Association |
| BC | Basis for Conclusions (to an accounting standard) |
| BCLC | Butterworths Company Law Cases |
| BERR | Department for Business, Enterprise and Regulatory Reform (formerly the Department of Trade and Industry (DTI)) |
| BES | business expansion scheme |
| BNA 1985 | Business Names Act 1985 |
| | |
| CCA | current cost accounting |
| CCAB | Consultative Committee of Accountancy Bodies Limited |
| CC | The Combined Code – Principles of good governance and code of best practice |
| CC(CP) | Companies Consolidation (Consequential Provisions) Act 1985 |
| CEO | chief executive officer |
| CESR | Committee of European Securities Regulators |

## Abbreviations and terms used

| | |
|---|---|
| CGAA | Co-ordinating Group on Audit and Accounting Issues |
| CGU | cash-generating unit |
| Ch | Chancery Division, law reports |
| chp | Chapter |
| chapter (1) | 'PricewaterhouseCoopers' Manual of accounting' – chapter (1) |
| CIF | cost, insurance, freight |
| CIMA | Chartered Institute of Management Accountants |
| CIPFA | Chartered Institute of Public Finance and Accountancy |
| CISCO | The City Group for Smaller Companies |
| Cmnd | Command Paper |
| CBO | collateralised bond obligation |
| CDO | collateralised debt obligation |
| CLO | collateralised loan obligation |
| CMO | collateralised mortgage obligation |
| COSO | Committee of Sponsoring Organisations of the Treadway Commission |
| CPP | current purchasing power |
| CR | Report of the committee on The Financial Aspects of Corporate Governance (the 'Cadbury Report') |
| CSR | corporate social responsibility |
| CTD | cumulative translation difference |
| CUV | continuing use value |
| | |
| DG XV | Directorate General XV |
| the 7th Directive | EC 7th Directive on Company Law |
| DP | discussion paper |
| DRC | depreciated replacement cost |
| DTI | Department of Trade and Industry |
| DTR | double taxation relief |
| | |
| EASDAQ | European Association of Securities Dealers Automated Quotation |
| EBIT | earnings before interest and tax |
| EBITDA | earnings before interest, tax, depreciation and amortisation |
| EC | European Community |
| ECU | european currency unit |
| ED | exposure draft |
| EFRAG | European Financial Reporting Advisory Group |
| EGM | extraordinary general meeting |
| EITF | Emerging Issues Task Force (US) |
| EPS | earnings per share |
| ESOP | employee share ownership plan |
| ESOT | employee share ownership trust |
| EU | European Union |
| EU 2005 Regulation | Regulation (EC) No 1606/2002 on the application of International Accounting Standards |
| EUV | existing use value |
| | |
| FASB | Financial Accounting Standards Board (US) |
| FEE | The European Federation of Accountants |
| FIFO | first-in, first-out |
| financial statements | Accounts |

| | |
|---|---|
| FLA | Finance and Leasing Association |
| FM | facilities management |
| FOB | free on board |
| FPI | foreign private investors (US-listed) |
| FRAG | Financial Reporting and Auditing Group of the ICAEW |
| Framework | Framework for the preparation and presentation of financial statements |
| FRED | Financial Reporting Exposure Draft |
| FRA | forward rate agreement |
| FRC | Financial Reporting Council |
| FRN | floating rate note |
| FRRP | Financial Reporting Review Panel |
| FRS | Financial Reporting Standard |
| FRSSE | Financial Reporting Standard for Smaller Entities |
| FSA | Financial Services Authority |
| FVTPL | at fair value through profit or loss |
| | |
| GAAP | generally accepted accounting principles (and practices) |
| GAAS | generally accepted auditing standards |
| GB | Great Britain |
| GCFR | Going Concern and Financial Reporting - published by the joint working group of the Hundred Group of finance directors, ICAEW and ICAS |
| GRI guidelines | Global Reporting Initiative guidelines |
| | |
| HMSO | Her Majesty's Stationery Office |
| HP | hire purchase |
| HMRC | HM Revenue & Customs |
| | |
| IAASB | International Auditing and Assurance Standards Board |
| IAS | International Accounting Standard (see also IFRS) |
| IASB | International Accounting Standards Board |
| IASC | International Accounting Standards Committee |
| IBF | Irish Bankers' Federation |
| IBNR | incurred but not reported |
| ICAEW | Institute of Chartered Accountants in England and Wales |
| ICAI | Institute of Chartered Accountants in Ireland |
| ICAS | Institute of Chartered Accountants of Scotland |
| ICFR | Internal Control and Financial Reporting - published by the joint working group of the Hundred Group of finance directors, ICAEW and ICAS |
| ICR | Industrial Cases Reports |
| ICSA | Institute of Chartered Secretaries and Administrators |
| IFAC | International Federation of Accountants |
| IFRIC | International Financial Reporting Interpretations Committee |
| IFRS | International Financial Reporting Standard (see also IAS) |
| IG | Implementation Guidance (to an accounting standard) |
| IGU | income-generating unit |
| IIMR | Institute of Investment Management and Research (see SIP) |
| IoD | Institute of Directors |
| IOSCO | International Organisation of Securities Commissions |
| IPO | initial public offering |

| | |
|---|---|
| IPR&D | in-process research and development |
| IR | Statement on interim reporting issued by ASB |
| ISA | International Standard on Auditing |
| ISA (UK & Ire) | International Standard on Auditing (UK and Ireland) |
| ISDA | International Swap Dealers Association |
| ISP | internet service provider |
| IVSC | International Valuation Standards Committee |
| | |
| JANE | joint arrangement that is not an entity |
| JWG | Joint Working Group |
| | |
| LIBID | London inter-bank bid rate |
| LIBOR | London inter-bank offered rate |
| LIFFE | the London International Financial Futures and Options Exchange |
| LIFO | last-in, first-out |
| LR | UK Listing Authority's Listing Rules |
| | |
| MBO | management buy-out |
| MD&A | management's discussion and analysis |
| MR | Master of the Rolls |
| | |
| NASDAQ | National Association of Securities Dealers Automated Quotations |
| NCU | national currency unit |
| NIC | national insurance contributions |
| NPAEs | non-publicly accountable entities |
| | |
| OFR | operating and financial review |
| OEICs | open-ended investment companies |
| OIAC | Oil Industry Accounting Committee |
| OTC | over-the-counter market |
| | |
| PA | preliminary announcement |
| para(s) | paragraph(s) of Schedules to the Companies Acts, or IFRSs or IASs or FRSs, or SSAPs, or FREDs, or EDs, or DPs, or text |
| PCAOB | Public Company Accounting Oversight Board (US) |
| PE | price-earnings |
| PFI | Private Finance Initiative |
| PPE | property, plant and equipment |
| PPERA | Political Parties, Elections and Referendums Act 2000 |
| PPF | Pension Protection Fund |
| PRAG | Pensions Research Accountants Group |
| PS | Practice Statements |
| | |
| QC | Queen's Counsel |
| QUEST | qualifying employee share ownership trust |
| | |
| R&D | research and development |
| RDG | regional development grant |

| | |
|---|---|
| Reg | regulation of a statutory instrument (for example, SI 1995/2092 Reg 5 = regulation 5 of The Companies (Summary Financial Statements) Regulations 1995) |
| RICS | Royal Institution of Chartered Surveyors |
| RS | Reporting Standard |
| | |
| SAC | the Standards Advisory Council |
| SAS | Statement of Auditing Standards |
| SC | Session Cases |
| Sch | Schedule to the Companies Act 1985 (eg 4A Sch 85 = Schedule 4A, paragraph 85) |
| SDC | Standards Development Committee |
| SEC | Securities and Exchange Commission (US) |
| Sec(s) | Section(s) of the Companies Act 1985/the Companies Act 2006 Act |
| SEE | social, environmental and ethical |
| SERPS | State earnings related pension scheme |
| SFAC | Statement of Financial Accounting Concepts issued in the US |
| SFAS | Statement of Financial Accounting Standards issued in the US |
| SI | Statutory Instrument |
| SIC | Standing Interpretation Committee of the IASC (see IFRIC) |
| SIP | Society of Investment Professionals (formerly IIMR) |
| SIPs | share incentive plans |
| SMEs | small and medium-sized entities |
| SOI | Statement of Intent |
| SoP | Statement of principles |
| SORIE | statement of recognised income and expense |
| SORP | Statement of Recommended Practice |
| SPE | special purpose entity |
| SPV | special purpose vehicle |
| SSAP | Statement of Standard Accounting Practice |
| Stock Exchange (or LSE) | the London Stock Exchange |
| STRGL | statement of total recognised gains and losses |
| | |
| TR | Technical Release of the ICAEW |
| TUPE | Transfer of Undertakings (Protection of Employment) Regulations |
| | |
| UITF | Urgent Issues Task Force |
| UK | United Kingdom |
| US | United States of America |
| | |
| VAT | value added tax |
| VIE | variable interest entity |
| | |
| WACC | weighted average cost of capital |
| WLR | Weekly Law Reports |

# Chapter 1

# Introduction

|                                | Page |
| ------------------------------ | ---- |
| Corporate reporting today      | 1001 |
| International developments     | 1002 |
| The approach in this Manual    | 1003 |

**Chapter 1**

# Corporate reporting today

**1.1**  Recent years have seen major changes in financial reporting worldwide. It would be difficult to argue with the assertion that the biggest single change has been the process of global harmonisation around international financial reporting standards (IFRS), including their adoption for the consolidated financial statements of listed companies in the UK and the rest of the EU. But an important further trend has been the increasing importance and role of the various constituents of what is often called the 'front half' of the annual report, that is: management's commentary on how the business has fared since the last report; governance reports; reports on directors' remuneration; and indeed the statutory directors' report. This second trend is the subject of this book.

**1.2**  While the directors' report has long been a legal requirement for UK companies, the other parts of the front half are more recent. They are part of a trend that recognises that pure accounting numbers, however good the accounting policies and however extensive the footnote disclosure, are only part of the story. To be really useful to investors and other users, they need to be supplemented by additional disclosure – often in narrative form – that seeks to give a sense of context, an explanation of what is going on and a sense of what might happen in the future. This, taken in aggregate, can be described as 'corporate reporting', as opposed to financial reporting.

**1.3**  The emphasis on a broader notion of corporate reporting is to some extent a social and political trend. There has been much debate in the last five years during the work leading up to the current company law reform, culminating in the recent enactment of the Companies Act 2006 about whether directors should have as their, and their companies', objectives a narrow focus on the shareholders or a wider focus on a range of stakeholders. However, what is clear is that both the government and a wide range of opinion believe, as a general principle, that narrative reporting is increasingly important.

**1.4**  The Companies Act 206 requires management to provide a fair review of the company's business along with a description of its principal risks and uncertainties, in other words a business review. The requirement to present a business review is noteworthy in two respects. First, it applies to all companies, except those that are 'small' according to the definitions in the Companies Act. Thus many medium-sized private companies, including wholly-owned subsidiaries of groups, have to produce business reviews. Secondly, the requirements are flexible and tailored to the circumstances. For example, the review should be *"a balanced and comprehensive analysis of the development and performance of the business of the company during the financial year, and the position of the company at the end of that year, consistent with the size and complexity of the business"*. Also, key performance indicators need to be disclosed *"to the extent necessary for an* *understanding of the development, performance or position of the business of the company"*. This is sensible, in that it expects more when there is more to tell and where, in practice, there is a significant public interest to satisfy.

**1.5** Little guidance is available on the practical aspects of preparing a business review, which, for a large diverse company, could be detailed and complex. In fact, most UK listed and public interest entities provide the business review information in the form of an operating and financial review (OFR) and consider it a key mechanism for communicating with investors. The ASB has issued non-mandatory guidance to assist companies preparing OFRs, which although not written with the business review specifically in mind, does deal with a number of its required disclosures. The guidance is principles based, ie information should be presented through the eyes of management focussing on matters relevant to members in a way that is comprehensive, understandable and forward looking as well as being balanced, neutral and comparable over time.

**1.6** As a sign of its importance, the Financial Review Panel now has responsibility for reviewing directors' reports (including business reviews) to ensure compliance with the Companies Act.

**1.7** Some aspects of the front half owe more to politics than to financial reporting. Politics, rather than accounting as such, lies behind the extensive disclosures required in the UK of directors' remuneration. Politics, in a broad sense, is already taking narrative reporting into more fields. Corporate reporting is starting to encompass environmental reporting and social reporting of various kinds, some of which are new requirements of the Companies Act 2006.

## International developments

**1.8** The developments in narrative reporting are to a degree domestic matters, some resulting from UK legal requirements.

**1.9** Although it is seen in the UK as part of the directors' report, the requirement for a business review has an EU origin, namely a 2003 amendment to the earlier 4th and 7th accounting directives. The recitals to the 2003 directive say: *"The annual report and consolidated annual report are important elements of financial reporting. Enhancement, in line with current best practice, of the existing requirement for these to present a fair review of the development of the business and of its position, in a manner consistent with the size and complexity of the business, is necessary to promote greater consistency and give additional guidance concerning the information a "fair review" is expected to contain. The information should not be restricted to the financial aspects of the company's business ….."*. In the UK, this type of thinking is reasonably well established. This appears to be less the case in some other EU member states, so it is reasonable to assume that the business review will be implemented with a variety of speeds and degrees of enthusiasm.

**1.10** There are also further international comparisons that can be made. For example, both Australia and Canada have similar guidance and principles to those used by the ASB in their OFR guidance. The US SEC requires a Management Discussion and Analysis (MD&A), which while differing in detail, is largely based on the same objectives and principles as used by the ASB.

**1.11** The IASB is also involved in the debate, their discussion paper entitled 'Management commentary' in 2005 received 117 comment letters with 92 per cent of respondents agreeing that management commentary is an integral part of financial reports. The Chairmen of the FASB and IASB appear to agree, with Rober Herz (Chairman of the FASB) stating:

> *"Businesses are complex and numbers on their own are never going to tell the full story. Narrative reporting is a vital complement to the figures."*

In addition, Sir David Tweedie (Chairman of the IASB) has said:

> *"The narrative statement is not an adjunct. It is a key component."*

**1.12** The management commentary project is now on the IASB's active agenda. An exposure draft is expected in late 2008/early 2009.

## The approach in this Manual

**1.13** Considerations relating to the front half apply to all UK companies at least to some extent. Even the smallest company has to prepare a directors' report. Other requirements come into play once a company achieves a certain size, becomes listed or pays its directors above a certain amount. For these various reports, we give our views on what the requirements or recommendations mean and on what is good disclosure in the areas in which there are no rules or guidance. As part of that approach, this Manual contains many examples and extracts from financial reports.

**1.14** This Manual can be viewed as a supplement to two other works. One is the 'PricewaterhouseCoopers' Manual of Accounting – UK GAAP', which gives guidance to the many UK companies that still follow UK GAAP. The second is the 'PricewaterhouseCoopers' Manual of Accounting – IFRS for the UK', which applies to those UK listed groups that have to follow IFRS and other entities that have opted to apply IFRS. The issues described in this Manual relating to the 'front half' apply to some extent to both categories of company, though the requirements and expectations for listed companies are greater than for others.

Chapter 2

# Operating and financial review

|                                                                           | Page |
| ------------------------------------------------------------------------- | ---- |
| Introduction                                                              | 2001 |
| Interaction with Company Law                                              | 2002 |
| Business review requirements                                              | 2003 |
| ASB's view of the business review requirements for listed companies       | 2004 |
| Location of the OFR within the annual report                              | 2005 |
| ASB's reporting statement: operating and financial review                 | 2006 |
| Scope and definitions                                                     | 2006 |
| Objective                                                                 | 2006 |
| Principles                                                                | 2007 |
| Principle 1 – Business analysis through the board's eyes                  | 2007 |
| Principle 2 – Focus on matters relevant to members                        | 2008 |
| Principle 3 – Forward looking                                             | 2009 |
| Principle 4 – Complement and supplement the financial statements          | 2012 |
| Principle 5 – Comprehensive and understandable                            | 2016 |
| Principle 6 – Balanced and neutral                                        | 2020 |
| Principle 7 – Comparable                                                  | 2021 |
| Disclosure framework                                                      | 2022 |
| Detailed guidance within the disclosure framework                         | 2025 |
| The business' nature, objectives and strategies                           | 2025 |
| Current and future development and performance                            | 2042 |
| Development and performance in the year                                   | 2042 |
| Resources                                                                 | 2059 |
| Principal risks and uncertainties                                         | 2063 |
| Relationships                                                             | 2068 |
| Financial position                                                        | 2074 |
| General                                                                   | 2074 |
| Accounting policies                                                       | 2076 |
| Capital structure and treasury policies                                   | 2077 |
| Cash flows                                                                | 2080 |
| Liquidity                                                                  | 2082 |
| Going concern                                                              | 2089 |
| Key performance indicators                                                | 2090 |
| Other performance indicators                                              | 2095 |
| 'Seriously prejudicial'                                                   | 2096 |
| Statement of compliance                                                   | 2097 |
| International developments                                                | 2097 |

Chapter 2

# Operating and financial review

## Introduction

**2.1**  There is no UK requirement for an entity to prepare an operating and financial review (OFR). Many UK listed and public interest entities produce one voluntarily and consider it a key mechanism for communicating with investors.

**2.2**  To assist directors in preparing OFRs, the ASB has issued a non-mandatory reporting statement, 'Operating and financial review' (RS (OFR)). Although non-mandatory, is it generally accepted that directors of a company preparing an OFR will give due regard to it.

**[The next paragraph is 2.4].**

**2.4**  Further publications that may provide additional guidance to companies in preparing an OFR include:

| Title of publication | Description |
|---|---|
| Guide to forward-looking information – Don't fear the future: communicating with confidence | This guide provides practical guidance on how the reporting of forward-looking information can be achieved, together with examples from progressive companies, both in the UK and elsewhere, who are already adopting a forward-looking orientation in their narrative reporting. |
| Guide to key performance indicators – Communicating the measures that matter | A practical publication that has been developed to highlight the increasing demand for reporting of key performance indicators (KPIs). It addresses many of the questions posed by these demands and demonstrates what good reporting of KPIs looks like with a collection of examples drawn from the UK and elsewhere. |
| Report Leadership: Tomorrows reporting today | Provides a framework, strategic thinking and practical ideas for improving the content of annual reports, including the narrative section. |

> These publications are equally relevant to companies preparing a Business Review to form part of a directors' report (see further chapter 3). All of these publications can be found at www.corporatereporting.com, which also provides further examples of good narrative reporting. The publications are located under the 'Toolkit' tab, followed by 'Practical Guides'. Many illustrative examples of OFR reporting can be found on www.pwcinform.com.

## Interaction with Company Law

**2.5** Directors of all UK companies (except small companies) are required, by the Companies Act to provide a business review in their directors' report.

**2.6** The underlying purpose of the business review is to provide investors with information that will supplement the financial statements and enable them to make informed investment decisions. For smaller owner-managed businesses or wholly-owned subsidiaries, it is likely that the owners of the business are sufficiently well informed without the need for an in-depth business review. But for the larger listed companies with a diverse shareholder population, the information need is far greater and more detail should be given.

**2.7** Company law requires a company to publish its business review within the directors' report. If companies that prepare an OFR also give this information in their directors' reports, there would be considerable duplication.

**2.7.1** To avoid such duplication BERR, in its 'Guidance on the changes to the directors' report requirements in the Companies Act 1985' confirms that if a company publishes an OFR, it is acceptable to cross-refer to it in the business review, provided that the following conditions are met:

- The directors' report and the OFR are published together in such a way that users can easily refer to both documents.

- The cross-reference must clearly indicate which specific sections of the OFR are relevant, whether by page numbers, paragraph numbers or headings. An example of suitable working to meet this condition is provided in the BERR's guidance as follows:

  > *"The information that fulfils the requirements of the business review can be found in the OFR on pages x to y, which are incorporated in this report by reference."*

**2.8** Little guidance is available on the practical aspects of preparing a business review, which, for a large diverse company, could be detailed and complex. Although not written with the business review specifically in mind, the ASB's RS (OFR) does deal with a number of its required disclosures. Thus, it is common for those preparing an OFR that will incorporate the business review disclosures, or those preparing a business review as part of the directors' report to comply with the ASB's RS (OFR) to ensure that investors receive the most appropriate information set.

**[The next paragraph is 2.10.]**

## Business review requirements

**2.10**  The Companies Act requirements for a business review set out the purpose of the review, which is *"to inform the members of the company and help them assess how the directors have performed their duty under section 172 (duty to promote the success of the company)."* [CA06 Sec 417(2)].

**2.11**  The requirements are considered in detail in chapter 3 but, in summary, management must provide a business review comprising:

■  A fair review of the company's business.

■  A description of the principal risks and uncertainties facing the company.

[CA06 Sec 417(3)].

**2.12**  The review requires a balanced and comprehensive analysis of:

■  The development and performance of the company's business during the financial year,

■  The position of the company's business at the end of that year,

consistent with the size and complexity of the business.

[CA06 Sec 417(4)].

**2.13**  The review also requires the following, to the extent necessary for an understanding of the development, performance and position of the company:

■  Analysis using financial key performance indicators (KPIs).

■  Where appropriate, analysis using other key performance indicators, including information relating to environmental matters and employee matters.

[CA06 Sec 417(6)].

**2.14**  In addition there are additional requirements relating to quoted companies. To the extent necessary for *"an understanding of the development, performance or position of the company's business, quoted companies must include the main trends and factors likely to affect the future development, performance and position of the company's business".* [CA06 Sec 417(5)(a)].

**2.15** Also to the extent necessary, quoted companies are also required to provide information about:

- Environmental matters (including the impact of the company's business on the environment).

- The company's employees.

- Social and community issues.

This includes information about any policies of the company in relation to those matters and the effectiveness of those policies and information about persons with whom the company has contractual or other arrangements which are essential to the business of the company. [CA06 Sec 417(5)(b)(c)].

**2.16** Where the review does not contain information referred to in paragraph 2.15, the review *"must state which of those kinds of information it does not contain"*. [CA06 Sec 417(5)].

**2.17** The review must also contain, where appropriate, references to and additional explanation of amounts included in the financial statements. [CA06 Sec 417(8)].

**[The next paragraph is 2.21.]**

**ASB's view of the business review requirements for listed companies**

**2.21** In January 2007 the ASB issued 'A review of narrative reporting by UK listed companies in 2006' with the aim of keeping the spotlight on narrative reporting and encouraging continuing improvement in this area. The report assessed 23 companies' annual reports with a year end of 31 March 2006 against both:

- the ASB's OFR reporting statement; and

- minimum compliance with the business review.

**2.22** It is the ASB's assessment of minimum compliance that provides some 'indicators' for the FRRP, which, has the business review within its scope. For example the document notes that:

> *"While the requirements to disclose KPIs is a matter of judgement for the directors, the lack of inclusion of any KPIs in a Business Review in the future will provide the Financial Reporting Review Panel (FRRP) with a possible indicator that the Review may not be compliant with the law."*

**2.23**  The ASB's views relating to the business review requirements are summarised below:

| Business review [CA06 Sec 417]. | ASB Interpretation |
|---|---|
| "a fair review of the company's business" | Description of the business and the external environment in which it operates. Discussion on the objectives of the business and the strategies to achieve those objectives. |
| "a description of the principal risks and uncertainties facing the company." | Description of principal risks rather than simply providing a list of all the possible risks they may face. |
| "The review must, to the extent necessary for an understanding of the development, performance or position of the business of the company, include: (a) analysis using financial key performance indicators, and (b) where appropriate, analysis using other key performance indicators, including information relating to environmental matters and employee matters." | Explicit identification of financial and non-financial key performance indicators. |
| "The review must, where appropriate, include references to, and additional explanations of, amounts included in the company's annual accounts." | Resources available to the business, particularly those items not reflected in the balance sheet. Financial position. |

**2.24**  In summary, a significant number of key disclosure recommendations of RS (OFR) are consistent with the requirements of the Companies Act relating to the business review.

**Location of the OFR within the annual report**

**2.25**  Historically, many listed companies have presented an OFR as a separate statement within the annual report. The business review is required to be included within the Directors' report, although BERR has indicated that cross-referencing to information contained elsewhere in the annual report (for example, in the OFR) is acceptable (see para 2.7.1).

**2.26**  However, the Companies Act 2006 introduced provisions that give directors a 'safe harbour' in respect of civil liability arising out of the content of the directors' report (see further chapter 8). Thus, companies may wish to include the OFR within the directors' report in order to benefit from the 'safe harbour' provisions.

**[The next paragraph is 2.36.]**

## ASB's reporting statement: operating and financial review

### Scope and definitions

**2.36**  The reporting statement has been written with quoted companies in mind, but applies to any entity that purports to prepare an OFR.

**2.37**  The term 'quoted company' is defined in the Companies Act as a company whose equity share capital:

- has been included in the official list in accordance with the provisions of Part VI of the Financial Services and Markets Act 2000;

- is officially listed in an EEA State; or

- is admitted to dealing on either the New York Stock Exchange or the exchange known as NASDAQ.

[CA85 Sec 262; CA06 Sec 474].

**2.38**  This means, for instance, that companies traded on AIM and other public companies, that are not 'quoted' as defined in the Act, are not specifically covered by the reporting statement's scope. Nor are large private companies. However, many such companies may voluntarily prepare an OFR. The reporting statement applies to them if they 'purport' to prepare an OFR. [RS (OFR) para 2]. 'Purporting' to prepare an OFR would normally mean that the entity uses the words 'operating and financial review'.

**2.39**  An OFR is defined as *"a narrative explanation, provided in or accompanying the annual report, of the main trends and factors underlying the development, performance and position of an entity during the financial year covered by the financial statements, and those which are likely to affect the entity's future development, performance and position"*. [RS (OFR) para 3].

**[The next paragraph is 2.41.]**

### Objective

**2.41**  The objective of an OFR is to provide a balanced and comprehensive analysis, consistent with the business' size and complexity, of:

- The development and performance of the entity's business during the year.

- The position of the entity at the end of the year.

- The main trends and factors underlying the development, performance and position of the entity's business during the year.

- The main trends and factors that are likely to affect the entity's future development, performance and position.

The analysis should be prepared so as to assist members to assess the strategies adopted by the entity and the potential for those strategies to succeed. [RS (OFR) para 1].

**[The next paragraph is 2.44.]**

**Principles**

**2.44** The ASB's reporting statement 'Operating and financial review' adopts a principles based approach.

**2.45** Seven principles are set out in bold in the reporting statement. These are:

- The OFR should set out an analysis of the business through the eyes of the board of directors (see further from para 2.46).

- The OFR should focus on matters that are relevant to the interests of members (see further from para 2.48).

- The OFR should have a forward-looking orientation, identifying those trends and factors relevant to the members' assessment of the current and future performance of the business and the progress towards the achievement of long-term business objectives (see further from para 2.53).

- The OFR should complement as well as supplement the financial statements, in order to enhance the overall corporate disclosure (see further from para 2.64).

- The OFR should be comprehensive and understandable (see further from para 2.79).

- The OFR should be balanced and neutral, dealing even-handedly with both good and bad aspects (see further from para 2.92).

- The OFR should be comparable over time (see further from para 2.93).

*Principle 1 — Business analysis through the board's eyes*

**2.46** This principle states that *"The OFR should set out an analysis of the business through the eyes of the board of directors"*. [RS (OFR) para 4]. It ensures that the matters that are reported to the company's members are those of most interest to the board; for example, the strategies the board will implement to achieve the company's objectives, specific performance measures they regularly review and significant risks.

**2.47** The reporting statement notes that the directors should disclose appropriate elements of information used in managing the entity and its subsidiaries. More emphasis is given in a group situation to matters that are significant to the group as a whole. [RS (OFR) para 5]. Significant matters may include matters relating to a specific business segment where this is relevant to understanding the business as a whole; for example, particular emphasis on a geographical segment where developments in a new market are significant to the entity as a whole, because expansion in that area is a major part of the strategy.

### Principle 2 — Focus on matters relevant to members

**2.48**   Principle 2 states that *"The OFR should focus on matters that are relevant to the interests of members"*. [RS (OFR) para 6]. This is consistent with directors' and auditors' reporting on the financial statements.

**2.49**   The priority of the OFR is to report to members, however, it will also be of interest to other users, such as other investors, potential investors, creditors, customers, suppliers and society more widely. The directors should consider the extent to which they should report on issues relevant to these other users where they are also of importance to members because those issues influence the business' performance and its value. The OFR should not, however, be used as a replacement for other forms of reporting addressed to a wider stakeholder group. [RS (OFR) paras 7, 27, 28].

**2.50**   The interests of other OFR users may significantly affect the directors' perspective, because they also affect the members' assessment. Factors that may contribute to the relative importance include relationships with key resources (for example, reliance on skilled employees, dependence on a few large customers or suppliers) and the power of other users to affect the entity's business (for example, actions of regulators and unions).

**2.51**   These issues should be covered by the OFR where they are significant, because the actions of the other users may affect the business and thus the interests of members.

**2.52**   The example in Table 2.1 indicates that while the company limits its OFR audience to shareholders, it acknowledges that further tailoring can be made to enhance the usefulness of the report to all readers.

---

**Table 2.1 – Reporting to members**

**Stagecoach Group plc – Annual Report and Financial Statements – 30 April 2007**

**3. Operating and financial review (extract)**

**3.1 Introduction (extract)**
The Operating and Financial Review that follows is intended largely to reflect the recommendations of the Accounting Standards Board's 2006 reporting statement of best practice on the Operating and Financial Review. We continue to monitor developments in best practice with a view to further tailoring our Operating and Financial Review to enhance its usefulness to readers of the Annual Report.

**3.2 Cautionary statement (extract)**
The Operating and Financial Review has been prepared for the shareholders of the Company, as a body, and no other persons. Its purpose is to assist shareholders of the Company to assess the strategies adopted by the Company and the potential for those strategies to succeed and for no other purpose.

---

## Principle 3 — Forward looking

**2.53**  Principle 3 states that *"The OFR should have a forward-looking orientation, identifying those trends and factors relevant to the members' assessment of the current and future performance of the business and the progress towards the achievement of long-term business objectives".* [RS (OFR) para 8].

**2.54**  Issues that should be addressed are those that have affected development, performance and position during the year and those that are likely to affect the entity's future development, performance and position. [RS (OFR) para 9].

**2.55**  There are no rules dictating what information a company must provide in its OFR. Directors must decide which information to include on the basis of their own business dynamics and those of the industry sectors in which they operate.

**2.56**  Issues might include:

- An explanation of the resources, principal risks and uncertainties and relationships that may affect the entities long-term value, for example development of new products or services.

- An analysis of the trends and factors the directors believe are likely to impact future prospects, for example introduction of new technology.

- Information on future targets, for example for key performance indicators.

**[The next paragraph is 2.58.]**

**2.58**  The reporting statement acknowledges directors' concerns regarding the disclosure of forward-looking information. It notes that some forward-looking information cannot be objectively verified, even though it has been given in good faith. It states that directors may want to include a statement in the OFR that such information should be treated with caution and explain the uncertainties inherent in such information. [RS (OFR) para 10].

**2.58.1**  As noted in paragraph 2.25, directors may wish to include forward looking information in the directors' report, rather than a separate OFR in order to benefit from the 'safe harbour' provisions contained within the Companies Act 2006, protecting them from civil liability for forward-looking statements made in the directors' report.

**2.59**  An example of a cautionary statement used by a UK company that conveys a warning similar to that suggested by the reporting statement is given in Table 2.3.

---

**Table 2.3 – Cautionary statement**

**Smiths Group plc – Annual Report and Accounts – 31 July 2007**

**Operating and financial review — extract**

The purpose of this Report is to provide information to the members of the Company. The Annual Report contains certain forward-looking statements with respect to the operations, performance and financial condition of the Group. By their nature, these statements involve uncertainty since future events and circumstances can cause results and developments to differ materially from those anticipated. The forward-looking statements reflect knowledge and information available at the date of preparation of this Annual Report and the Company undertakes no obligation to update these forward-looking statements. Nothing in this Annual Report should be construed as a profit forecast.

---

**2.60** The reporting statement also recommends commentary on the impact on future performance of significant events after the balance sheet date. [RS (OFR) para 11]. An example is provided in Table 2.3A.

---

**Table 2.3A – Significant events after the balance sheet date**

**Marconi Corporation plc – Report and Accounts – 31 March 2005**

**Key Customer Overview (extract)**
In the year ended 31 March 2005, our ten largest customers were (in alphabetical order): BT, Deutsche Telekom, E-Plus, Metro City Carriers (Germany), O2, Telecom Italia, Telkom South Africa, Telstra, US Federal Government and Vodafone. In aggregate, these customers accounted for 57 per cent of sales from Continuing Operations. The ten largest customers accounted for 55 per cent of sales from Continuing Operations in the year ended 31 March 2004.

**Sales to BT**
BT was our largest customer and accounted for 25 per cent of sales from Continuing Operations for the year ended 31 March 2005 (year ended 31 March 2004 was 25 per cent).

The breakdown of our revenues from BT is as follows:

**Sales to BT, Year ended 31 March 2005**
**£ million**

| | | |
|---|---:|---:|
| Services of which: | | 173 |
| *Cable Services* | *101* | |
| *IC&M and Support* | *72* | |
| Optical | | 88 |
| Legacy Access | | 48 |
| Broadband Access | | 13 |
| **Total Sales** | | **322** |

Of our total sales revenues of £322 million with BT, £173 million were services revenues. The largest element of our services revenues for the year ended 31 March 2005 was the £101 million earned under our four-year frame services contract with BT Cable Services. The contract, which runs to 2008, involves the installation of fibre and copper services to residential and business users and is not directly associated with the BT 21CN network transformation project.

The balance of our services revenues (£72 million) was for the installation and commissioning and support of optical, access and switching equipment.

---

Our optical sales to BT are under a three-year frame contract, which guarantees Marconi a minimum of 70 per cent of BT's transmission requirements until March 2006. Optical sales to BT in the year ended 31 March 2005 were £88 million.

Broadband access rollout, which is also covered under our three-year frame contract with BT, accounted for £13 million of product sales in the current financial year, having increased to £7 million in the final quarter of the year. The contract with BT runs until August 2006.

Legacy access products made up the balance of sales to BT (£48 million).

While it has recently been announced that Marconi has not been selected as a preferred supplier for BT's next-generation 21st Century Network, we expect to continue to supply products and services to BT under existing contracts.

**OUTLOOK (extract)**
Following BT's announcement on preferred suppliers for its 21CN project, we currently expect a reduction in BT revenues from equipment sales and associated services in the order of £50 million in FY06 compared to FY05.

**2.61** OFRs should discuss forward-looking comments, both positive and negative, made in previous years' reviews, whether or not these have been borne out by events. [RS (OFR) para 12]. The discussion would usefully include the reasons why any previous predictions have not been fulfilled.

**2.62** Such comments might include previous discussions around likely trends and factors impacting the business – for example whether 'gross domestic product' (GDP) growth rates have matched forecasts. They may also include goals or targets set by the company and an explanation comparing actual performance with those goals.

**2.63** The example in Table 2.4 explains the financial goals set in previous years and how performance over a period of time compares with those goals, including high level commentary. Further detailed explanations of performance are given in subsequent pages of the annual report.

**Table 2.4 – Forward-looking comments made previously**

**Cadbury Schweppes plc – Annual Report and Accounts – 31 December 2006**

**Transforming our performance**

We set five goals to focus our energy and measure our performance, both internally and externally. Since 2003, we've made good progress against these goals. We delivered above average returns to our shareowners and improved our structure, culture and capabilities. We now have much stronger confectionery and beverages businesses and enhanced capabilities to support them.

We also set three financial goals in 2003, for sales, margin and cash flow. We delivered much improved revenue growth in line with the goals we set and improved cash flow generation.

Although we improved our margins, our margin performance was below the goal we set ourselves, because of significant increases in raw material costs in each of the last three years, events in the UK and Nigeria, and our continued investment behind revenue growth.

*Operating and financial review*

**How we've performed against our financial goals:**

|  | 2003<br>Financial goal | 2004-2006 |
|---|---|---|
| Revenue growth | 3-5% p.a. | 5.1% average p.a[1] |
| Margin growth | 50-75bps p.a. | 27bps average p.a. |
| Free Cash Flow generation[2] | £1.5bn in 2004-2007 | £1.0bn in 2004-2006 |

*Principle 4 — Complement and supplement the financial statements*

**2.64** Principle 4 states that *"The OFR should complement as well as supplement the financial statements, in order to enhance the overall corporate disclosure".* [RS (OFR) para 13].

## Supplementing the financial statements

**2.65** Supplementing the financial statements means:

- providing additional explanations of amounts recorded in the financial statements; and

- explaining the conditions and events that shaped the information contained in the financial statements.

[RS (OFR) para 15].

**2.66** The information recorded in financial statements is increasingly complex. For example, pension liabilities are significant for many companies – an understanding of these is essential for investors. The OFR (and the financial statements themselves) can be used to provide additional information to aid that understanding. Events and conditions also shape amounts recorded in the financial statements.

**2.67** Taking the example of pensions, it is difficult to truly understand the risks inherent in a scheme and the chances of increased cash contributions or other action being needed in the future.

**2.68** One company that supplements its financial statement information on pensions in this way is shown in the example in Table 2.5.

Table 2.5 – Supplementing financial statements

Tomkins RHM plc – Annual Report – 30 December 2006

**Actuarial assumptions**

Actuarial assumptions are reviewed on a regular basis and updated where appropriate. Tomkins believes that all defined benefit pension plans reflect appropriate mortality assumptions.

Of our total defined benefit pension plan liabilities of £648.9 million, £489.8 million relates to benefits that are deferred or currently being drawn, £20.5 million relates to benefits for active participants that have been frozen in respect of future service or pay-related accruals, and a further £22.9 million relates to plans with benefits based on length of service rather than changes in salary scale. Therefore, £533.2 million of liabilities are not sensitive to changes in salary scale. The majority of defined benefit pension plans are closed to new entrants and therefore the impact of changes in salary scale is limited. £115.7 million, or 17.8%, of the total defined benefit pension plans liabilities are sensitive to salary scale. The table below shows the estimated sensitivity of the liabilities of the defined benefit pension plans to changes in the mortality and salary scale. The impact of changes in the discount rate and expected return on assets is shown in note 33 to the financial statements.

| Assumption | Assumption change | Impact on | Estimated impact |
|---|---|---|---|
| Life expectancy | Increase by 1 year | Liabilities | Increase by 2.6% |
| | | Service cost | Increase by 2.4% |
| | | Interest cost | Increase by 2.7% |
| Salary scale | Increase by 0.5% | Liabilities | Increase by 1.3% |

**[The next paragraph is 2.70].**

## Complementing the financial statements

**2.70** Complementing the financial statements means providing useful financial and non-financial information about the business and its performance that is not reported in the financial statements, but which is judged by the directors to be relevant to the members in evaluating past results and assessing future prospects. [RS (OFR) para 14].

**2.71** Our ongoing research programme with investors over the past decade has clearly shown that, as investors model the future, they typically have insufficient contextual and non-financial information to underpin their cash flow projections. Traditional reporting focuses on past financial performance, which is not the only guide to future returns. The OFR's requirement to complement the financial statements addresses that need.

**2.72** Contextual information can be defined broadly and will be unique to each company and its industry sector. It may include information about the markets in which the company operates and expectation for growth. How the company plans to achieve its objectives and the resource and relationships it will need to manage to do, so are key pieces of information to allow investors to evaluate the company. The disclosure framework included in reporting statement (discussed in paras 2.96 onwards) provides guidance on the type of information to be reported, much of it contextual in nature.

**2.72.1** Similarly, an entity might use the OFR to disclose non-financial information that is relevant to business performance. Examples might include health and safety statistics, such as accident rates, environmental information such as total carbon dioxide emissions and community and social issues. Such factors may have major impacts on the business and, where they are significant, disclosure may be necessary for an assessment of the business' development, performance and position. The impacts are potentially limitless and can include regulatory penalties for underperformance, litigation, employee loyalty, reputation and customer confidence.

**Providing non-statutory financial information**

**2.73** One specific area of financial reporting that is increasingly being considered by companies is the reporting of non-GAAP information – financial figures that differ from those reported on a statutory basis.

**2.74** Where amounts from the financial statements have been adjusted for inclusion in the OFR, that fact should be highlighted and a reconciliation provided. [RS (OFR) para 15].

**2.75** This is an important recommendation and mirrors guidance issued by the Committee of European Securities Regulators (CESR) in November 2005 'Recommendations on alternative performance measures'. This contained a number of recommendations relating to alternative measures produced by companies that have adopted IFRS. More information can be found at www.cesr.eu.

**2.76** These recommendations include:

■ The principles for financial reporting contained in the IASB Framework and the qualitative characteristics of understandability, relevance, reliability and comparability in the Framework should be followed when reporting alternative measures.

■ Alternative performance measures should be defined (both the terminology and the basis of calculation).

■ Alternative performance measures should only be presented with defined measures and should be reconciled to the defined measures.

■ Comparatives should be given and alternative measures should be presented consistently over time.

■ Defined measures should be presented with greater prominence than alternative measures.

■ An explanation should be provided to explain why alternative measures are presented and how they are used internally.

**2.77** We consider that the recommendations above set out by CESR on the use of alternative performance measures should be adopted in OFRs. These recommendations extend to the 'highlights' sections, press releases and commentary sections related to both preliminary and interim announcements, interim management statements and reports and elsewhere in annual reports. See chapter 4 of the Manual of Accounting – IFRS for the UK and chapter 31 of the Manual of Accounting – UK GAAP for further information.

**2.77.1** Some companies present an analysis that uses widely accepted measures, such as profitability measured in terms of constant exchange rates, or accepted industry-specific measures, such as replacement cost profit (as used in the oil and gas industry) or the achieved profits method (used in the insurance industry). Despite being widely understood, any such measures should be defined in the annual report and the use of consistent measures across an industry will aid comparison by users.

**2.78** An example of a company providing alternative performance measures in accordance with the CESR guidelines is shown in Table 2.6. As well as discussing such measures in the OFR, this company includes non-GAAP information on the face of its primary financial statements, a practice that is acceptable under IFRS and UK company law, where the CESR guidance has been followed.

---

**Table 2.6 – Alternative performance measures**

**Diploma PLC – Annual Report – 30 September 2006**

**Operating and Financial Review (extract)**

ALTERNATIVE PERFORMANCE MEASURES
The Directors consider that there are alternative measures which are helpful in assessing the underlying operating performance of the Group. For internal management reporting purposes, the Board uses a number of financial measures (which are not defined within IFRS) to assess the underlying operational performance of the Group and its businesses. As such the Board believes these measures are important and should be considered alongside the IFRS measures. The alternative performance measures, which have been used in this Annual Report, are described in note 2 to the consolidated financial statements.

ALTERNATIVE PERFORMANCE MEASURES (note 2)

| | Note | 2006 £m | 2005 £m |
|---|---|---|---|
| Profit before tax | | 31.2 | 17.2 |
| Less: Profit on sale of property | | (11.1) | - |
| Add: Amortisation of acquisition intangible assets | | 0.3 | - |
| ADJUSTED PROFIT BEFORE TAX | | 20.4 | 17.2 |
| ADJUSTED EARNINGS PER SHARE | 10 | 62.8p | 53.7p |

**Notes to the Consolidated Financial Statements (extract)**

2. ALTERNATIVE PERFORMANCE MEASURES
The Group uses a number of alternative (non-Generally Accepted Accounting Practice ("non-GAAP")) financial measures which are not defined within IFRS. The Directors use these measures in order to assess the underlying operational performance of the Group and as such,

---

these measures are important and should be considered alongside the IFRS measures. The following non-GAAP measures are referred to in this Annual Report.

### 2.1 Adjusted profit before tax

On the face of the consolidated income statement, "adjusted profit before tax" is separately disclosed, being defined as profit before tax and before the costs of restructuring or rationalisation of operations, the profit or loss relating to the sale of property and the amortisation and impairment of acquisition intangible assets. The Directors believe that adjusted profit before tax is an important measure of the underlying performance of the Group.

### 2.2 Adjusted earnings per share

"Adjusted earnings per share" is calculated as the total of adjusted profit, less income tax costs, but excluding the tax impact on the items included in the calculation of adjusted profit and the tax effects of goodwill in overseas jurisdictions, less profit attributable to minority interests, divided by the weighted average number of ordinary shares in issue during the year. The Directors believe that adjusted earnings per share provides an important measure of the underlying earning capacity of the Group.

### 2.3 Free cash flow

On the face of the consolidated cash flow statement, "free cash flow" is reported, being defined as net cash flow from operating activities, after net capital expenditure on fixed assets (excluding business combinations), but before expenditure on business combinations and dividends paid to both minority shareholders and the Company's shareholders. The Directors believe that free cash flow gives an important measure of the cash flow of the Group, available for future investment.

### 2.4 Trading capital employed

In the segment analysis in note 5 to the consolidated financial statements, "trading capital employed" is reported, being defined as net assets less cash and cash equivalents and deferred tax assets, and after adding back retirement benefit obligations. Return on trading capital employed is defined as being adjusted profit before finance income and tax, divided by trading capital employed plus all historic goodwill and as adjusted for the timing effect of major acquisitions and disposals. Return on trading capital employed at the sector level does not include historic goodwill. The Directors believe that return on trading capital employed is an important measure of the underlying performance of the Group.

## *Principle 5 — Comprehensive and understandable*

**2.79** This principle states that *"The OFR should be comprehensive and understandable"*. [RS (OFR) para 16]. The reporting statement adds to this principle by stating that directors should consider whether the omission of information might reasonably be expected to influence significantly the assessment by members. [RS (OFR) para 17]. This is similar wording to that used in defining materiality in IAS 1 and the Statement of Principles in the UK (see further chapter 4 of the Manual of Accounting – IFRS for the UK and chapter 2 of the Manual of Accounting – UK GAAP) and is, perhaps another way of saying that all material information should be included.

**2.80** The reporting statement notes that the recommendation for the OFR to be comprehensive does not mean that it should cover all possible matters. The objective is quality not quantity. It is not possible for a reporting statement to list all of the elements that might need to be included, as these will vary depending on the nature and circumstances of the particular business and how it is run. [RS (OFR) para 18].

**2.81**  A simple example of what types of information might be relevant to one entity's OFR, but not to another's might be:

| | Company A | Company B |
| --- | --- | --- |
| | | (Operates solely in the UK, sourcing its |
| | (Operates internationally) | product and making sales in the UK) |
| Exchange rates | Relevant | Less relevant |
| Political disturbances | Relevant | Less relevant |
| Cross border tax rules | Relevant | Less relevant |
| Hyperinflation | Possibly relevant | Less relevant |
| Global market trends | Relevant | Less relevant |

**2.81.1**  The question of whether information is comprehensive may be particularly difficult to assess when dealing with the future and forward-looking statements. This is a natural consequence of the increased uncertainty inherent in predicting the future.

**2.82**  The reporting statement notes that, where relevant, directors should explain the source of information and the degree to which the information is objectively supportable, so that members can assess the reliability of the information for themselves. [RS (OFR) para 19]. Table 2.8 shows an example of disclosure of sources and provides both trend data and a forward-looking orientation to the information.

**2.83**  It is likely that directors, as well as making the 'cautionary statement' referred to above in paragraph 2.58, may, in particular, wish to explain fully the basis for predictive (forward-looking) statements and the degree of objective evidence supporting the statements. This is not to say that objective evidence does not exist for predictive statements or that uncertainty should, in itself, restrict directors' predictive statements, but rather that appropriate caveats may need to be given.

**2.84**  One type of forward-looking statement for which objective evidence should exist, is the expected growth rate for a particular country in which the entity may wish to expand its business. Such growth rates or rates of consumer spending may be based on estimates made by governments or by international organisations such as the World Bank. Another example is forecast growth rates for an industry sector where a recognised and reputable organisation provides industry specific data. An example of the latter is provided in Table 2.8, explaining the source and its objectivity.

---

**Table 2.8 – Objective evidence for forecasts**

**Emap plc – Annual Report and Accounts – 31 March 2007**

**Business review (extract)**

**UK advertising**

Advertising accounted for 45% of Continuing Group revenue in 2007, showing that the state of the UK advertising market has an effect on our performance. However, over the last five years the proportion of our revenue derived from advertising has declined from 50% to 45% and we would expect this trend to continue in the future as we reshape the Group.

In the UK, the Advertising Association (AA) is recognised as a reputable, independent source of information and estimates of growth for the advertising market. The Internet Advertising Bureau (IAB) is an independent source of information and estimates for the internet advertising market. According to the latest available AA estimates (Mar 07), in 2006 the total advertising market in the UK was broadly flat, with consumer magazine, radio, B2B magazine and TV advertising all showing declines. In this environment, our ability to grow the amount of advertising across our traditional media platforms has been challenging and the state of the advertising market will continue to affect our prospects going forward.

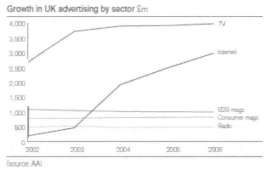

Growth in UK advertising by sector £m

(source: AA)

The internet continues to be the fastest growing medium for advertising, up 41% in 2006, driven by increasing broadband penetration and internet usage. Internet advertising accounted for 12% of total UK advertising spending in 2006, up from 8% in 2005 (source: AA).

---

**2.85** The directors should consider the key issues to be included in the OFR. The inclusion of too much information may obscure judgements and will not promote understanding. Where additional information is included elsewhere in the annual report or other reports, cross-referencing to those sources will assist members. [RS (OFR) para 20].

**2.86** However, where information, such as environmental or employee information, is included in a separate corporate social responsibility (CSR) report, the relevant information should still be included in the OFR to the extent necessary to enable members to assess the entity's development, performance and position. Any cross-referencing should be to additional information in the CSR or other report that is not essential for the purpose of the OFR.

**2.87** The example in Table 2.9 shows that only certain aspects of its CSR reporting are included in the OFR and refers readers elsewhere for more in-depth information.

---

**Table 2.9 – Cross reference to supplementary information**

**Centrica plc – Annual Report and Accounts – 31 December 2006**

**Corporate Responsibility (extract)**

Information on our corporate responsibility (CR) activities over the last year is included in the reports on each of our business units. This section provides a summary of key themes, as well as performance information on group-wide activities. More detail will be provided in our 2006 CR Report, which will be available at www.centrica.com/responsibility in May 2007.

---

**2.88** The reporting statement recommends that the OFR should be written in a clear and readily understandable style. [RS (OFR) para 21].

**2.89** Management should consider what it needs to communicate, and what investors want to know, to prevent key messages from getting lost. For example, some form of narrative sequence and clear linkage from the company's markets to their strategy to their key performance indicators and future goals. An integrated structure, where important issues are linked throughout the report, can aid the reader's retention of the information provided.

**2.90** Making the messages within the OFR understandable is imperative. Directors can help readers to navigate their reporting by explaining the critical issues for the company, highlighting them in quotes, titles, bullet points, etc. Graphical summaries can be used to present complex information visually. Use of plain English with clear explanations of technical terms and avoidance of jargon will help companies meet the aim of the principle of clarity and understandability.

**2.90.1** This may be of particular application to industries where the product is of a highly technical or scientific nature. For example, whilst use of technical terms and scientific names may be unavoidable in an explanation of a drug development pipeline, application of this principle might mean additional information being given to describe 'in layman's terms' what the drug does in relation to diseases or other conditions and how development will benefit both the company and the sufferers. Many pharmaceutical companies also include a brief description of the various stages (phases) of the approval process for new drugs.

**2.91** Helpful navigation ensures that readers can find the information they need. A clear table of contents and an index, use of colour-coded sections or tabs and clarity in titles and sub-headings will all help achieve this. Companies can also repeat information or provide cross-referencing to other areas of the report to provide context and, use box-outs to highlight key issues or figures.

## Principle 6 — Balanced and neutral

**2.92** Principle 6 states that *"The OFR should be balanced and neutral, dealing even-handedly with both good and bad aspects"*. [RS (OFR) para 22]. It means that directors should maintain a balance between good and bad news, give details of unfavourable events and include information about setbacks or misjudgements. [RS (OFR) para 23]. An example of disclosure that balances positive and negative aspects of the business is shown in Table 2.10.

---

**Table 2.10 – Balanced reporting**

**ITV plc – Report and Accounts – 31 December 2006**

**Message from the Executive Chairman** Michael Grade

On Monday, 8 January, 2007 I returned to work for ITV. From the moment I was approached by the Board last year, I had no doubt that I would accept this most stimulating and challenging position in British broadcasting.

ITV has not had an easy time in recent history, operating in the highly competitive and technology driven media sector. It faced a challenging advertising market and speculation over both its leadership and its ownership.

My brief is to restore the fortunes of the Group and thus return the business to growth.

Having been in post for two months it is too soon to conclude definitive plans for the business, but generally I have developed more positive impressions than negative ones, and the latter are mostly within our control to remedy.

On the positive side:
- There are talented and dedicated people across all areas of the Company;
- ITV Productions is a superb business of real scale with the ability to deliver outstanding content, from the Oscar winning film "The Queen" starring Dame Helen Mirren, to Coronation Street and Emmerdale, to Dancing on Ice;
- ITV remains a much-loved brand and ITV1 is still the UK's most popular television channel in peak-time with the England v Sweden game during the football World Cup achieving the highest audience (18.5 million) on any channel in 2006;
- Our strong regional presence is a greater asset than is recognised and the growth in regional advertising has been particularly buoyant against a depressed national TV advertising market. We need to find ways to sustain and even enhance this valuable public service. It is part of what binds ITV to its audiences throughout the UK and distinguishes us from our competitors.
- Our digital channels are the most successful free to air commercial family of digital channels in the UK, each with distinctive branding and programming. We must ensure that they have the investment they need to grow their leading market position as we approach digital switchover;
- The Consumer businesses represent an area of proven growth which we will seek to accelerate; and
- The Board's strategy which I inherit is essentially sound. The businesses that have been recently acquired and developed are all natural extensions of the core operations.

On the negative side:
- Whilst the strategy is sound, we are playing catch up in many areas, no doubt due to the efforts required to 'bed in' the successful Carlton/Granada merger. We have a valuable multichannel offering and exciting web opportunities – but still a long way to grow;
- 

---

There is a lack of innovation in our programming, partly resulting from a fear of ratings failure and the punitive consequences that follow under the Contract Rights Renewal (CRR) remedy (described below);

- The Company has developed a tendency towards bureaucracy. The cure for this lies with the example set by the leadership team within the businesses. I will improve delegation, and place emphasis on the need to make the ITV values (described on page 25) a reality in our actions;
- We need to continue strengthening the relationship between our commissioning teams and both internal and external producers. This is critical to ensure that the commissioning pipeline is filled with the high-quality programmes that deliver the audiences which in turn our commissioning team need to fulfil our advertisers' and viewers' aspirations; and
- Our regulatory environment needs to reflect the reality of our 21st century structure and the developing market in which we operate these days. ITV may have consolidated, but it is a long way from the advertising monopoly of yesteryear. The regulatory burden has yet fully to reflect this.

### Principle 7 — Comparable

**2.93**   Principle 7 states that *"The OFR should be comparable over time"*. [RS (OFR) para 24]. This ensures that directors do not change from one performance measure to another from year to year depending on which gives the more favourable impression of the business. Similarly, if information is given in one year about a particular aspect of the business, similar information should be given in subsequent years if that aspect of the business remains significant. The aim is for information to be sufficient for members to compare it with similar information about the entity for previous financial years. Information on particular aspects of the business given over several years enables members to identify and analyse trends and other factors over successive years. [RS (OFR) para 25].

**2.94**   The example illustrated in Table 2.11 shows how performance indicators are measured over several years and highlights that a new measure will be developed and introduced in the following period.

Table 2.11 – Comparability over time

Centrica plc – Annual Report and Accounts – 31 December 2006

Measuring our performance (extract)

Non-financial

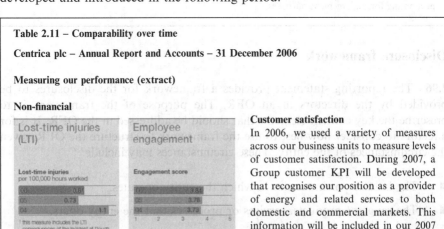

Customer satisfaction

In 2006, we used a variety of measures across our business units to measure levels of customer satisfaction. During 2007, a Group customer KPI will be developed that recognises our position as a provider of energy and related services to both domestic and commercial markets. This information will be included in our 2007 Annual Report.

**2.95** The reporting statement notes that directors may wish to consider the extent to which the OFR is consistent with reviews prepared by other entities in the same industry or geographical sector. [RS (OFR) para 25].

---

Table 2.12 – Comparability across industry sector

**Prudential plc – Annual Report and Accounts – 31 December 2006**

**Directors report: Operating and financial review (extract)**

**Other corporate information (extract)**

In May 2004, the CFO Forum, representing the Chief Financial Officers of 19 European insurers, published the European Embedded Value Principles (Principles) which are designed to improve the transparency and consistency of embedded value reporting.

Member companies, of which Prudential is one, agreed to adopt the Principles for supplementary reporting no later than the financial year end commencing 1 January 2005. Prudential fully adopted the Principles for the first time in respect of full-year 2005 results.

For Prudential, EEV reporting represents an evolution from achieved profits reporting and it welcomes the improved clarity and consistency of information that it provides to investors although there is still some way to go before achieving full consistency.

Compared to achieved profits, the principal differences are in respect of three areas:
- inclusion of an explicit allowance for the impact of options and guarantees. This typically requires stochastic calculations, under which a large number of simulations are performed that provide a representation of the future behaviour of financial markets;
- more active allowance for the combined impact of risk profile and encumbered capital in the selection of discount rates. This ensures that the risks to the emergence of shareholder cash flows are properly accounted for; and
- enhanced disclosure that enables informed investors to understand better the key risks within the business and the basis of preparation of the results.

The EEV basis not only provides a good indicator of the value being added by management in a given accounting period but it also demonstrates whether shareholder capital is being deployed to best effect. Indeed, insurance companies in many countries use comparable bases of accounting for management purposes.

---

# Disclosure framework

**2.96** The reporting statement provides a framework for the disclosures to be provided by the directors in an OFR. The purpose of the framework is to prescribe the key content elements that should be addressed in the OFR. It is for directors to consider how best to use the framework to structure the OFR, given the circumstances of the entity. These circumstances may include:

■ The industry or industries in which the entity operates.

■ The range of products, services or processes that the entity offers.

■ The number of markets served by the entity.

[RS (OFR) para 26].

**2.96.1**  Companies may also consider other criteria. For example, the company values adopted by Body Shop International PLC affect how the company presents its operating and financial review. The company's reputation and success is strongly linked to its social, environmental and ethical values on animal testing, community trade, self-esteem, human rights and protecting the planet. It aligns its business policies closely with its own and its customers' shared beliefs in these values and links the sale of its products, such as those relating to 'self esteem' with high profile campaigns, for example against domestic violence. As a result, the content and presentation of the OFR is more than usually devoted to social, environmental and ethical issues, because these are the issues that are of interest to its customers and members and which also contribute to the company's performance. This approach, 'profits with principles' is set out in Table 2.12A.

---

**Table 2.12A – Profits with principles**

**Body Shop International PLC – Report and Accounts – 26 February 2005**

**Delivering Value to Stakeholders**
The Body Shop has an established reputation as a socially and environmentally responsible company. We believe that our values are consistent with strong and sustained financial performance, and that profits with principles must be achieved in order to sustain the long-term future of the Group.

The Body Shop is committed to maintaining high standards of social and environmental performance. We believe in doing business with integrity and transparency. This means using our ethical principles to inform the way we do business, setting ourselves and our business partners clear standards of practice. It also involves engaging stakeholders with our business aims and publicly reporting on our performance within the overall context of our business strategy.

The overall strategic direction of the Group's values is reviewed periodically by the Board in consultation with the Director of Values. The Director of Values reports into the Chief Executive Officer and has overall responsibility for directing the Group's social and environmental programme. Strategic values objectives are aligned with the business objectives as well as stakeholder perceptions and expectations. These objectives are fully embraced by the senior management team, who have responsibility for balancing the interests of all key stakeholder groups. Sub-committees help direct the social and environmental approach of the business. These include an Issues Management Group, which reports into the Risk Committee; a Corporate Health and Safety Strategy Group; an Environmental Steering Group; and an Animal Protection Steering Group.

---

**2.97**  The OFR should provide information to assist members to assess the strategies adopted by the entity and the potential for those strategies to succeed. The key elements of the disclosure framework necessary to achieve this are:

- The nature of the business, including a description of the market, competitive and regulatory environment in which the entity operates and the entity's objectives and strategies.

- The business' development and performance, both in the financial year under review and in the future.

■ The resources, principal risks and uncertainties and relationships that may affect the entity's long-term value.

■ Position of the business including a description of the entity's capital structure, treasury policies and objectives, and liquidity, both in the financial year under review and the future.

[RS (OFR) para 27].

**2.98** To assist companies in structuring their OFR information more effectively, the reporting statement sets out the above disclosure framework, which can be represented in a logical flow as shown in Table 2.13.

---

**Table 2.13 – Disclosure framework**

| The nature, objectives and strategies of the business | Resources, risks and uncertainties, and relationships | Current and future development of performance | Financial position |
|---|---|---|---|
| – Description of business and external environment. <br> – Objectives to generate or preserve value over the longer term. <br> – Strategies for achieving the objectives. | – Description of resources, tangible and intangible, available and how they are managed. <br> – Description of principal risks and uncertainties and the directors' approach to them. <br> – Information about significant relationships and stakeholders other than investors who may directly impact performance. | – Significant features of the development and performance of the business. <br> – Main trends and factors likely to impact future performance. | – Analysis of the financial position and critical accounting policies. <br> – Discussion of the capital structure. <br> – Discussion of the cash inflows and outflows, ability to generate cash to meet commitments and fund growth. <br> – Discussion of current and prospective liquidity. |

**Underpinned by the financial and non-financial KPIs used to assess progress against stated objectives, as well as other measures and evidence**

---

**2.99** The OFR should also include the following information to the extent necessary to meet the recommendations set out in paragraph 27 of the reporting statement:

■ Environmental matters (including the impact of the entity's business on the environment).

■ The entity's employees.

■ Social and community issues.

■ Persons with whom the entity has contractual or other arrangements that are essential to the entity's business.

- Receipts from, and returns to, the entity's members in respect of members' shareholdings.

- All other matters the directors consider to be relevant.

[RS (OFR) para 28].

**2.100** The OFR should also include the following items relating to the environmental matters, the entity's employees and social and community issues:

- The entity's policies in each area mentioned.

- The extent to which those policies have been successfully implemented.

[RS (OFR) para 29].

## Detailed guidance within the disclosure framework

### The business' nature, objectives and strategies

**2.101** The OFR should include a description of the business and the external environment in which it operates. This is to provide a context for the discussion and analysis of the entity's development, performance and financial position. [RS (OFR) para 30].

**2.102** Depending on the nature of the business, the OFR should include discussion of matters such as:

- The industries in which the business operates.

- The entity's major markets and competitive position within those markets.

- Significant features of the legal, regulatory, macro-economic and social environment that influence the business.

- The main products and services, business processes and distribution methods.

- The business' structure and its economic model, including an overview of the main operating facilities and their location.

[RS (OFR) paras 31, 32].

**2.103** To understand and evaluate a company's strategy and performance, investors need a clear grasp of its business environment and the impact this has on the company now and in the future. Often, performance has been reported in isolation with only high level commentary on the business environment such as "...*against intensifying competition...*" or "...*prospects are good...*".

**2.104** Investors who are familiar with the company are interested in management's interpretation of market developments and trends; some may be less familiar and need the information to judge performance and the logic of strategies adopted by the company.

**2.105**    The example in Table 2.14 shows how the description of a business can be clearly presented, identifying the sectors they operate in, cross referencing to further information for ease of navigation and highlighting the key messages for each sector. It also includes information on their economic model – how they own each type of property.

---

**Table 2.14 – Description of business**

**Land Securities PLC – Annual Report – 31 March 2007**

**Report of the Directors (extract)**

**All you need to know (extract)**

Land Securities is one of the world's five largest Real Estate Investment Trusts. Our national portfolio of commercial property includes some of UK's best-known shopping centres and landmarks.

We are leading urban renaissance through our multi-billion pound development programme, transforming regional city centres and key sites in Central London. We are also one of the leading names in Property Partnerships, and are involved in long-term, large-scale regeneration projects in the south east.

**Land Securities Group**

**Retail Portfolio** *See pages 34-44*
This business unit includes shopping centres, retail warehouses, shops outside London, shops held through the Metro Shopping Fund LP, regional offices and other regional properties.

Key points:

- 29 shopping centres and 31 retail parks
- 1.8 million $m^2$ of retail accommodation
- approximately 1,700 retailer occupiers
- nearly 300 million shopper visits per year
- development pipeline for some 255,000$m^2$ of retail led space

**London Portfolio** *See pages 44–53*
This business unit includes all London offices and London retail, but excludes those assets held in the Metro Shopping Fund LP.

Key points:

- over one million $m^2$ of office and retail accommodation
- more than 50,000 people work in offices owned by us
- provides accommodation for over 400 organisations
- potential to develop 600,000$m^2$ of commercial and residential space over next 10 years

**Property Partnerships\*** *See pages 54–63*
This business unit is engaged in long-term property outsourcing partnerships with public sector organisations including DWP, DVLA and Royal Mail and with corporates including Norwich Union, Barclays and Accor Hotels. We have interests in 105 Public Private Partnership (PPP) projects in areas such as schools, hospitals, secure accommodation and offices.

Key points:

- 3.4 million $m^2$ across 2,024 properties in property outsourcing partnerships

---

- 1.4 million m$^2$ of PPP project floorspace average length of property outsourcing partnership contracts is 24 years with gross income of £794m
- Property Partnerships employs 919 people across the UK

*Land Securities Trillium, which we previously described as our property outsourcing business, is now known as Land Securities Trillium Property Partnerships as a result of our expansion into the PPP/Private Finance Initiative (PFI) markets.

**2.105.1**  From the business description, a user of the financial statements can expect to get an overall picture of the business. For example:

- Whether it operates internationally.

- Whether it operates in unstable economic and political regions.

- The entity's relative strength in the markets/industry compared to its competitors, including its strongest and weakest business and geographic areas.

- Whether the entity is highly regulated, or subject to significant legal actions against it.

- The economic performance and outlook for the economies, markets and sectors in which the business operates.

- The environmental and social factors that influence the business.

- The products or services the entity provides, whether they involve significant R&D or advertising support and the product risk involved; whether there is significant dependency on a small number of customers or suppliers or scarcity of sources of supply for raw materials that affect the business.

- Whether there are significant factors involved in manufacturing or distributing the entity's products.

- How the business is organised and monitored by the board, for example by business or geographic sectors or a combination of both. Whether the business is run centrally or if the individual units have a high degree of autonomy.

- Where the main operating facilities are located, their numbers, giving an idea of the business' size and the number of its employees.

**2.106**  The OFR should discuss the objectives of the business to generate or preserve value over the longer-term. [RS (OFR) para 33]. The reporting statement notes that objectives will often be defined in terms of financial performance, but that objectives in non-financial areas should also be discussed, where appropriate. [RS (OFR) para 34].

**2.106.1**  To some extent this understates the increasing importance to businesses of non-financial objectives. In the past such non-financial objectives have been of lesser importance. To take an extreme case, in the past a timber company might have obtained its product through flattening an area of rainforest, with little or no regard for the social, ecological or other consequences. The directors' concern would have been to make as much money as possible for the members. However, today such a policy would be extremely damaging to such an entity's reputation. In addition, it is likely that a significant number of customers would boycott the product, there would be legal action by deprived ethnic groups and environmental and regulatory authorities would impose fines or other sanctions. And that is before any action by environmental pressure groups. This is because there is a growing awareness of, and emphasis placed by both customers and members on, such non-financial elements of business operations. It is no longer just a question of making money, but also of how money is made.

**2.106.2**  For this reason the attitude of both directors and members is changing as they discover that in order to make the best return, their financial objectives and general interests are best served by having increased regard to social, environmental and other non-financial factors. As a result an entity's objectives, whilst generally continuing to focus on achieving returns for members, include or refer to non-financial objectives or factors, particularly in those industries that have the potential to significantly affect the environment in which they operate. The theme of increasing responsibility is now a trend or factor that influences the development of businesses. It emerges even more clearly in the development of strategies.

**2.106.3**  A growing number of large companies now produce separate corporate social responsibility reports. Thus, whilst in some cases the OFR may contain details of a company's policy and performance in this area, in other cases a separate report is often prepared. Sometimes such a report is separate from the annual report and accounts, with only a summary appearing in the latter document. On other occasions a full corporate social responsibility report is included with the annual report, either separate from the OFR or incorporated within it.

**2.106.4**  Whilst discussion of corporate social responsibility is outside the scope of this chapter, it is worth noting that there are a number of organisations dedicated to improving corporate reporting in this area. Among them is Business in the Community and The Business Impact Review Group, which are working together to develop a common approach to social and environmental reporting. As part of this work they have developed guidance for disclosures under five major headings: marketplace, environment, workplace, community and human rights.

**2.106.5**  In relation to the importance of non-financial objectives, the example in Table 2.14A is an example of the disclosure of a company's non-financial policies and performance.

**Table 2.14A – Social, environmental and other non-financial factors**

**Smiths Group plc – Annual Report and Accounts – 31 July 2007**

**Business Review (extract)**

**Corporate responsibility**

Smiths has six fundamental strengths. Corporate responsibility for Smiths is enshrined in the sixth strength: 'doing business the right way'. Smiths defines 'the right way' in the Code of Corporate Responsibility and Business Ethics ('the Code'), which is based on 12 principles:

1   compliance with national laws and regulations;
2   fair and vigorous competition in the marketplace;
3   integrity and ethical conduct as the standard of individual and corporate business behaviour;
4   fair and honest treatment of suppliers and customers;
5   proper and respectful treatment of employees;
6   high standards for health and safety in the workplace;
7   respect for the environment;
8   contributions to the communities in which we live and work;
9   straightforward public information and activities;
10   respect for human rights;
11   prudent and transparent public accounting and reporting; and
12   a culture of compliance throughout the entire Smiths organisation – from the Chief Executive to the newest employee.

Translated into 13 languages, the Code applies to all Smiths businesses and employees worldwide and provides the framework for policies, programmes and procedures for a range of corporate responsibility issues. It is endorsed and fully supported by the Board.

Code compliance support to Smiths businesses worldwide is provided through a number of channels (including via the legal, human resources and internal audit functions) which provide advice, export control policies, education, training, guidance materials and risk assessment tools.

**Managing corporate responsibility**

The Code is set by the Board and monitored by the Code Compliance Council, chaired by the General Counsel, which reports at least twice a year to the Audit Committee of the Board. Responsibility for managing specific issues, however, lies at different levels within the Group, depending on the nature of the issue and how it can most effectively be managed:

- health, safety and environment issues are managed through a Group-wide steering committee and organisation;
- employee issues are managed through the human resources function and by line management;
- supplier and customer programmes are managed by each business; and
- community programmes are principally managed locally, although there is also some Group-level activity.

**Environment**

Smiths is committed to ensuring that, as far as is reasonably practicable, any detrimental effects of its activities, products and services upon the environment are minimised. In practice, this means using performance-based environmental management systems to drive improvement throughout the business.

*Operating and financial review*

**Performance against targets**

| Target (set July 04) | 2007 result | 2006 result | Comment |
|---|---|---|---|
| **ISO14001 certification** for sites except small offices, with new acquisitions achieving certification within two years | **74 out of 75 currently eligible sites certified** | 83 out of 104 eligible sites | All originally targeted sites all have been certified. Ongoing certified programme in place for certification of new sites |
| **Energy consumption** target set at 180MWh/£m sales (5% reduction over three years) | **145 MWh/£m sales** | 176MWh/£m sales | Target achieved |
| **Waste to landfill** target set at 3.5 Tonnes/£m sales (6% reduction over three years) | **3.39 Tonnes/£m sales** | 2.93 Tonnes/£m sales | Target achieved |
| **Air emissions** target set at 112kg/£m sales (6% reduction over three years) | **106kg/£m sales** | 100kg/£m sales | Target achieved |
| **Water consumption** target set at 411m³/£m sales (12% reduction over three years) | **258m³/£m sales** | 398m³/£m sales | Target achieved |

*Note that the 2004 baseline data includes Smiths Aerospace whereas 2007 does not. Whilst normalisation against sales makes the figures directly comparable, the changed mix of manufacturing processes can exaggerate to some extent an already positive level of achievement.

**Health and safety**

Smiths is committed to conducting all its activities in a manner which achieves the highest practicable standards of health and safety. This year, attention has been focused on the underperforming sites and improving cross-divisional sharing of good practice.

**Performance against targets**

| Target (set July 04) | 2007 results | 2006 result | Comment |
|---|---|---|---|
| **Recordable incident rate** no target set | **1.96/200,000 man-hour** | 2.58/200,000 man-hours | Ongoing year-on-year improvement achieved |
| **Lost days rate** no target set | **25.61/200,000 man-hours** | 27.91/200,000 man-hours | Ongoing year-on-year improvement achieved |
| **Lost time incident rate** 1 incident/200,000 man-hours | **0.92/200,000 man-hours** | 1.15/200,000 man-hours | Target achieved |

**New targets**

We are pleased that the three-year targets set in 2004 have been achieved and new targets have been developed to drive improvement still further.

**Environment**

The major current public environmental issue worldwide is greenhouse gas emissions and their impact on climate change. Smiths most significant emissions source is from the generation of electrical energy purchased by and consumed in our facilities. We have in recent publications converted our energy consumption to carbon dioxide equivalent values and for the next three-year period it is appropriate to target our overall greenhouse gas emissions. This will include emissions from energy usage and VOC emissions and thus replace these former targets.

Formal international greenhouse regulatory systems do not consider normalisation. Instead, they target based on a fixed cap. It is appropriate that Smiths follows this trend and establishes a target of the same level of emissions or better in FY 2009 to 2010 as FY 2006 to 2007 for each individual facility. Additionally, total waste (net of recycled waste) and water consumption will continue to be targeted with an overall 9% improvement normalised against sales.

**Health and safety**

Building on the successful drive to reduce lost time incidents it has been decided to target 'recordable incidents'. This measure includes incidents that do not necessarily lead to lost time and thus is more challenging. Good practice is acknowledged as a recordable incident rate of better than 1.5 per 100 employees per year and this target has been set as the goal for the Group. Many parts of Smiths are already performing at this level but we will focus on those that do not whilst striving to maintain progress at all sites.

The implementation of the ISO14001 Environmental Management System plays a significant part in ensuring that our businesses have robust systems in place for managing environmental performance. Thus it has been decided to target implementation of the comparable OHSAS18001 Health and Safety Management System. At this stage the target has been set for external certification at two-thirds of our manufacturing sites with 50 or more employees within the next three years.

**Employees**

The Group's policy is to provide equal opportunities for employment. Smiths recruits, selects and promotes employees on the basis of their qualifications, skills, aptitude and attitude. In employment-related decisions, Smiths complies with anti-discrimination requirements in the relevant jurisdictions concerning matters of race, colour, national origin, gender, marital status, sexual orientation, religious belief, age, or physical or mental disability. Disabled people are given full consideration for employment and subsequent training, career development and promotion on the basis of their aptitudes and abilities.

All Smiths employees are treated with respect and dignity. Accordingly, any harassment or bullying is unacceptable. Smiths respects the right of each employee to join or not to join a trade union or other bona fide employee representative organisation. Smiths believes in good communications with employees and in promoting consultation, co-operation and teamwork on matters of mutual concern. Smiths offers all employees in the US and UK share schemes that enable employees to acquire an interest in the Company's shares and to align their interests more closely with those of shareholders.

**Reaching Full Potential**

Smiths invests in employees' skills and capabilities to help them reach their own Full Potential, which in turn helps the Company and its businesses to do likewise. Current priorities for Smiths to achieve full potential across the Group are talent development, succession planning and employee engagement.

**Talent development**

Smiths Group and the individual businesses continue to invest in identifying and developing the talents of our people. Smiths provides employees with challenging work that stretches their capabilities, backing that up with training and development activities tailored to individual needs. In 2006, Smiths introduced a new process for the most senior people, integrating the performance review with the overall 'Full Potential' goals of the business.

Smiths continues to be actively involved in all aspects of training and developing young people, including initiatives designed to ease the transition from school to work. Horizons is a two-year programme for new and recently appointed graduates. It provides an understanding of the Group and the business world in general, and develops personal and teamworking skills.

**Succession planning**

Smiths has a systematic succession management process for senior leadership roles. The Group identifies leadership talent and development needs, and follows this up with individual development plans that are monitored by senior management.

**Employee engagement**

Smiths provides information to and communicates with employees as an important part of doing business. Employees are regularly provided with a wide range of information concerning the performance and prospects of the business in which they are involved by means of employee councils, information and consultation forums, and other consultative bodies that allow their views to be taken into account.

**Communities**

Smiths is committed to contributing to the communities in which we operate. In addition to providing employment opportunities, we focus on community involvement through charitable giving, regeneration and education initiatives.

Smiths supports national and international charitable organisations from a central budget administered by the Charity and Donations Committee. This year's beneficiaries include the Royal Academy of Engineering, which helped to set up a new collaborative education initiative with Smiths in the UK – the Smiths Technology Education Programme (STEP) – which aims to provide able young people with the information and financial support they need to explore a career in technology. Individual businesses also support charity projects in a number of areas. For example, Smiths Medical supports medical research via the Smiths Medical Chair of Anaesthesia and Critical Care at University College London. In addition to corporate donations, Smiths businesses devote a time to local community projects around the world. For example, Smiths Medical recently participated in St Mungo's Putting Down Roots scheme, a gardening project for London's homeless.

For further information, please see the Corporate Responsibility Report 2007 at www.smiths.com/responsibility.

**2.106.6** Examples of where financial objectives are qualified by non-financial considerations in the extractive industry, one of the industries where such factors are most significant, are given in Tables 2.14B and 2.14C. A further example, where the objectives are extended from the most common 'increasing value for members' to inclusion of all stakeholders in that objective, together with a strong emphasis on non-financial factors is quoted in Table 2.14D.

**Table 2.14B – Social, environmental and other non-financial factors**

**Rio Tinto plc – Report and Accounts – 31 December 2006**

**Rio Tinto**

Rio Tinto is a leading international mining group headquartered in the UK, combining Rio Tinto plc, a London listed public company, and Rio Tinto Limited, which is listed on the Australian Securities Exchange.

Rio Tinto's business is finding, mining and processing mineral resources. Major products are aluminium, copper, diamonds, energy (coal and uranium), gold, industrial minerals (borax, titanium dioxide, salt, talc) and iron ore. Activities span the world but are strongly represented in

Australia and North America with significant businesses in South America, Asia, Europe and southern Africa.

The Group's objective is to maximise the overall long term return to shareholders through a strategy of investing in large, cost competitive mines, driven by the quality of each opportunity, not the choice of commodity.

Wherever Rio Tinto operates, the health and safety of its employees is the first priority. The Group seeks to contribute to sustainable development. It works as closely as possible with host countries and communities, respecting their laws and customs and ensuring a fair share of benefits and opportunities.

**Rio Tinto (extract)**

**Objective, strategy and management structure**

Our fundamental objective is to maximise the overall long term value and return to our shareholders. We do this by operating responsibly and sustainably in areas of proven expertise such as exploration, project evaluation and mining, where the Group has a competitive advantage.

Our strategy is to maximise net present value by investing in large, long life, cost competitive mines. Investments are driven by the quality of each opportunity, not by the choice of commodity.

Rio Tinto's management structure is designed to facilitate a clear focus on the Group's objective. This structure, reflected in this report, is based on the following principal product and global support groups:

- Iron Ore
- Energy
- Industrial Minerals
- Aluminium
- Copper
- Diamonds
- Exploration
- Operational and Technical Excellence (OTX).

The chief executive of each product group reports to the chief executive of Rio Tinto.

---

**Table 2.14C – Social, environmental and other non-financial factors**

**BHP Billiton plc – Report and Accounts – 30 June 2006**

**We are BHP Billiton, a leading global resources company**

Our purpose is to create long-term value through the discovery, development and conversion of natural resources, and the provision of innovative customer and market-focused solutions.

Our seven strategic drivers assist us in achieving our objectives. These drivers are our people; our licence to operate; our world-class assets; the way we do business; our financial strength and discipline; our project pipeline; and growth options.

Underpinning our strategic drivers are the values that guide us. They are:

- An overriding commitment to health, safety, environmental responsibility and sustainable development.
- Integrity and doing what we say we will do.
- A commitment to achieving superior business results and stretching our capabilities.
- Having the courage to lead change in the face of adversity.

- The embracing of diversity and showing respect for and trust in each other.

### 3. Operating and financial review and prospects (extract)

#### Strategic drivers of our business

Our core purpose is to create long-term value through the discovery, development and conversion of natural resources and the provision of innovative customer and market-focused solutions.

Fundamentally, this means that our business will have:

- a focus on the upstream extraction of natural resources
- high-quality, long-life and low-cost assets with embedded growth options
- a diversified portfolio of commodities and assets and geographic regions that reduce the volatility of cash flows
- a focus on seaborne traded commodities
- a global portfolio of employees, assets and customers.

Our strategy is based around discovering or acquiring and developing large, low-cost, high reserve assets to produce stable cash flows that support an ongoing program of exploration and development of new assets, as well as providing consistent and growing returns to shareholders. In executing this strategy, we focus on seven strategic drivers:

- People – the foundation of our business is our people. We require people to find resources, develop those resources, operate the businesses that produce our products, and then deliver that product to our customers.
- Licence to operate – we ensure that those who are impacted by our operations also benefit by the operation. Licence to operate means win-win relationships and partnerships. This includes a central focus on health, safety, environment and the community, and being valued as a good corporate citizen.
- World-class assets – our world-class assets provide the cash flows that are required to build new projects, to pay our employees, suppliers, taxes and partners, and ultimately to pay dividends to our shareholders. We maintain high-quality assets by managing them in the most effective and efficient way. Taking care of our world-class assets is absolutely critical.
- The BHP Billiton way – this concept captures a series of Business Excellence processes, knowledge sharing networks and our customer-focused marketing organisation, which is applied to all of our assets and businesses. The development of these processes and sharing of the principles behind those concepts lead to increased economies of scale and shared best practices.
- Financial strength and discipline – we have a solid single 'A' credit rating, which balances financial flexibility with the cost of finance. Strong financial management is necessary in order to support the growth initiatives we are undertaking globally across all our businesses.
- Project pipeline – we are continuously identifying, prioritising and executing the next set of growth projects. It is a critical part of our strategy to successfully deliver our growth projects on time and on budget.
- Growth options – we use exploration, technology and our global footprint to identify the next generation of opportunities where we can invest and use our skills and strengths.

#### BHP Billiton Charter

Our purpose is to create long-term value through the discovery, development and conversion of natural resources, and the provision of innovative customer and market-focused solutions.

#### To prosper and achieve real growth, we must:

- actively manage and build our portfolio of high-quality assets and services,
- continue the drive towards a high-performance organisation in which every individual accepts responsibility and is rewarded for results,

- earn the trust of employees, customers, suppliers, communities and shareholders by being forthright in our communications and consistently delivering on commitments.

**We value:**

- **Safety and the Environment** – An overriding commitment to health, safety, environmental responsibility and sustainable development.
- **Integrity** – Doing what we say we will do.
- **High Performance** – The excitement and fulfilment of achieving superior business results and stretching our capabilities.
- **Win-Win Relationships** – Having relationships which focus on the creation of value for all parties.
- **The Courage to Lead Change** – Accepting the responsibility to inspire and deliver positive change in the face of adversity.
- **Respect for Each Other** – The embracing of diversity, enriched by openness, sharing, trust, teamwork and involvement.

**We are successful in creating value when:**

- our shareholders are realising a superior return on their investment
- our customers and suppliers are benefiting from our business relationships
- the communities in which we operate value our citizenship
- every employee starts each day with a sense of purpose and ends each day with a sense of accomplishment.

---

**Table 2.14D – Non-financial factors**

**Barloworld Limited – Report and Accounts – 30 September 2006**

**"Our goal at Barloworld is sustainable value creation by focusing on a core group of businesses that demonstrate market leading characteristics."**

Tony Phillips, CEO

**VALUE BASED MANAGEMENT 4.8**

"Value Based Management (VBM) was adopted in 1999 as our philosophy in doing business."

Tony Phillips, CEO

At Barloworld, sustainability is not just a section in the annual report. It lies at the heart of how we do business. We view sustainability in a holistic manner that treats both financial and non-financial performance as part of maintaining a stable profit stream from our businesses in a manner that benefits all stakeholders. This results in a long-term view of managing businesses. We are not portfolio traders, but rather try to build a core of businesses that are able to consistently achieve top-quintile performance through market leading characteristics.

"We structure our businesses to be able to profitably endure business cycles while growing at a pace that creates sustainable shareholder value."

Tony Phillips, CEO

Value Based Management was adopted in 1999 as our philosophy in doing business. While the principles contained in the VBM doctrine were already well entrenched in the way that Barloworld operates, the VBM framework allowed us to formalise what has essentially always been the Barloworld way of doing business.

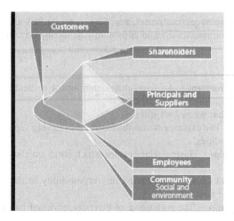

Barloworld's direct stakeholder groups are represented by the four points of a pyramid (see above). At its apex are our shareholders. At its base are our customers, our employees and our principals and suppliers. The pyramid is founded on the social and physical environment in which we operate. VBM is fundamentally different because it requires that we move beyond the traditional approach of tradeoffs between stakeholders, and search for solutions which add value for all.

**2.106.7** The OFR should set out the directors' strategies for achieving the business' objectives. Although the reporting statement refers to 'objectives' and 'strategies' neither term is defined. In practice some entities refer only in very general terms to a single broad objective, such as 'to be the best' or 'to produce sustainable and responsible growth in value', and concentrate more on the business' detailed strategies. Others simply do not mention an objective at all, but discuss only strategies.

**2.107** To assess the quality and sustainability of a company's performance, investors need to be clear about its objectives and the strategies for achieving those objectives. They need to know how management intends to address market trends and the threats and opportunities that they represent. They also need to understand the relationship between strategic objectives, management actions and executive remuneration. This enables them to judge the appropriateness and success of management actions in delivering the strategy and what to expect in the future.

**2.108** Statements of objectives and strategies should provide the detail that enables investors to understand the priorities for action or the resources that must be managed to deliver results, as well as explaining how success will be measured and over what period of time it should be assessed.

**2.109** The reporting statement notes that objectives will often be defined in terms of financial performance, but that objectives in non-financial areas should also be discussed, where appropriate. [RS (OFR) para 34].

**2.110** Many strategic objectives focus on achieving value for shareholders and financial success. However, a company's strategy should also be based on an understanding of the key areas in which a company has competitive advantage, for example, a market-leading customer base or a highly skilled workforce. The company's success in creating value will depend on management's ability to invest resources in these areas and manage them so that they deliver the financial performance investors expect.

**2.111**  The example in Table 2.15 illustrates the company's key objectives, how they will measure success, the potential challenges to achieving that success and cross-references to where additional information can be found.

**Table 2.15 – Objectives**

**Trifast plc – Report and Accounts – 31 March 2007**

**Business Review and Objectives (extract)**

| PERFORMANCE INDICATORS | POTENTIAL CHALLENGES | KEY OBJECTIVE WHAT ARE WE DOING? | KEY |
|---|---|---|---|
| To win key, large, profitable customers in Asia and Europe | New customer conversion rate | Raw material price increases Pressure from large customers to reduce prices | p.13, p.15, p.23 |
| To introduce priced catalogues for transactional customers | Improve % revenue from transactional customers | Transactional sales in the fastener industry are highly competitive and tend to be served by local companies | p.8 |
| To increase market penetration of TR branded products | Sales of TR branded products | Proprietary brands becoming commodity priced | p.9, p.17 |
| To provide customers with engineering and design data | Number of engineers registered for our web-based solution | Maintaining and informative and relevant database. | p.16 |
| To retain existing customers and strengthen customer relationships to maximise the available opportunities | Growth from existing customers and customer satisfaction results | Centrally controlled Group contracts Manufacturing migration to low-cost countries | p.8 |
| To have the best trained, most committed, inspired workforce in the industry | Staff retention Staff satisfaction results | Talent management Career development | p.22, p.23 |
| To improve the quality of our supply chain | Own manufactured spend as a % of total spend Number of quality rejects | Raw material availability Geographical spread of suppliers Meeting customer quality expectations | p.19 |

| To continue to operate as a socially conscious company | % of profits committed to CSR activities Environmental audits | Cost implications Legislation | p.28, p.29 |
|---|---|---|---|
| To generate cash | Reduction in debt funding organic growth Cash funding of acquisitions | Exchange rate risk Bad debts Working capital requirements for new accounts | p.26 |

**2.112** Strategies and objectives may also embed environmental, social and ethical values of particular importance to the company, as shown in Table 2.16.

**Table 2.16 – Embedding CRS in strategy and objectives**

**Marks and Spencer Group PLC – Annual Report and Financial Statements – 31 March 2007**

**Business Review (extract)**

Plan A

In any company, the temptation can be to focus too narrowly on short-term business performance. Responsible companies have to look to the long term.

We set ourselves very high quality and ethical standards. Last year, we used our 'Look behind the label' campaign to describe the lengths we go to to ensure everything we sell is produced responsibly.

But customers and staff wanted to understand our overall approach and our plan for the future.

The result was Plan A, our five-year, £200m 'eco plan' launched in January 2007.

We've made 100 commitments across the five areas, including becoming carbon neutral, sending no waste to landfill, cutting our packaging by a quarter and only using fish and wood from sustainable sources. As well as addressing the wider issues, we continue to work closely with local communities through our 'Marks & Start' work experience programme, for example.

All of these commitments are described in our 'How we do business' report, published alongside this document at www.marksandspencer.com/howwedobusinessreport2007. Each year we will report on how far we have got in achieving them.

To make sure Plan A is a success it is being completely integrated into our day-to-day operations. It will change how we operate forever.

**PLAN A**

Plan A is our five-year, 100-point plan to tackle some of the biggest challenges facing our business and our world.

**Climate Change** We aim to make our UK and Republic of Ireland operations carbon neutral in five years. We will minimise energy use, maximise the use of renewables and offset only as a last resort.

**Waste** We'll reduce packaging by 25%, find new ways to recycle and stop sending waste to landfill from our stores, offices and warehouses.

**Sustainable Raw Materials** From fish to forests, our goal is to make sure our key raw materials come from the most sustainable sources available.

**Fair Partner** By being a fair partner, we'll help improve the lives of hundreds of thousands of people in our worldwide supply chain and local communities.

**Health** We'll help customers and employees choose healthier lifestyles through healthy food ranges and clear labelling.

*To find out more visit*
*www.marksandspencer.com/PlanA*

**2.113** The OFR should discuss the business' objectives to generate or preserve value over the longer-term. [RS (OFR) para 33].

**2.114** The nature of the industry will affect the directors' determination of an appropriate time frame for the OFR. [RS (OFR) para 35]. The reporting statement gives, as an example, a business that focuses on long-term projects and that has to plan over the full project life cycle, which may be 20 years or more. It also states that if a project has a long-term impact on the environment, this is likely to affect long-term value and, therefore, determines the time perspective for reporting in the OFR. Industries with such long-term perspectives include, for example, the extractive industry, where the development and exploitation of a mine may extend for 20 years or more.

**2.115** This contrasts with a service industry having few physical assets and depending on the supply of particular employee skills for its competitive advantage. Such an industry, it says, will plan over a period consistent with its ability to recruit, train and develop its staff, which may be a much shorter period than the industries cited above.

**2.115.1** An example of the use of different time frames for different elements is BAA plc (see Table 2.17). BAA provides ten year forecasts, details of airport charges over five years and operating costs to be incurred over the following three years.

---

**Table 2.17 – Different time scales**

**BAA plc – Report and Accounts – 31 March 2005**

**Passengers**
Forecast growth in passenger numbers provides a critical input into capacity planning and other infrastructure decisions. The Group is forecasting average traffic growth of 3.0% per annum for its three London airports over the next ten years.

| Total Passengers | Heathrow | Gatwick | Stansted | Total London |
|---|---|---|---|---|
| 2004/05 (actual) | 67.7 | 32.0 | 21.2 | 120.9 |
| 2005/06 | 69.5 | 33.4 | 22.2 | 125.1 |
| 2006/07 | 70.9 | 34.6 | 23.4 | 128.9 |
| 2007/08 | 72.3 | 36.0 | 24.7 | 133.0 |
| 2008/09 | 75.0 | 37.0 | 26.3 | 138.3 |
| 2009/10 | 78.0 | 38.0 | 28.0 | 144.0 |
| 2010/11 | 80.0 | 38.5 | 29.6 | 148.1 |
| 2011/12 | 81.5 | 39.5 | 30.9 | 151.9 |
| 2012/13 | 83.0 | 40.0 | 32.3 | 155.3 |
| 2013/14 | 84.5 | 40.5 | 33.7 | 158.7 |
| 2014/15 | 86.0 | 41.0 | 35.0 | 162.0 |

The key drivers and assumptions underlying the forecast growth at our London airports are:

- Traffic demand growth will average about 3.9% per annum
- Capacity constraints will restrict annual throughput growth to an average of 3.0% per annum. An element of traffic demand will, therefore, be lost from the London system as a result of these constraints

---

- UK GDP will grow in line with the historical trend, ie 2.0–2.5% per annum over the course of the forecasting period
- Real air fares will decline, on average, by 0.5–1.0% per annum. However, the rate of decline will vary between markets, eg. faster rate of fares decline has been assumed for those markets facing low-cost competition
- Major capacity developments are:
  - First full-year of Terminal 5 operation in 2008/09
  - Further development of Heathrow non-Terminal 5 infrastructure
  - Gatwick develops to handle at least 40 million passengers per annum on the existing runway
  - Stansted develops to 35 million passengers per annum on the existing runway.

**Regulated Airport Charges**
Under the Airports Act, Heathrow, Gatwick and Stansted are subject to economic regulation whereby the Civil Aviation Authority (CAA) sets a price cap on airport charges for each airport every five years. The charges included within the price cap applied are the runway landing charge, the aircraft parking charge and the departing passenger charge. In February 2003, the CAA published its decision on the price caps that apply for the period 1 April 2003 until 31 March 2008:

**Maximum Allowable Yield**

|  | 2003/04 out-turn | 2004/05 out-turn | 2005/06 RPI plus | 2006/07 RPI plus | 2007/08 RPI plus |
|---|---|---|---|---|---|
| Heathrow | £6.48 | £7.08 | + 6.5% | + 6.5% | + 6.5% |
| Gatwick | £4.32 | £4.44 | + 0.0% | + 0.0% | + 0.0% |
| Stansted | £4.89 | £5.03 | + 0.0% | + 0.0% | + 0.0% |

The pricing regime at Heathrow is linked to five triggers based on the completion of Terminal 5 and at Gatwick, linked to the completion of Pier 6. The trigger is an element of the price cap formula, and each trigger is equivalent to a 2% decrease in airport charges at Heathrow and 1% at Gatwick. The first two of the five triggers related to Terminal 5 were met by the 31 March 2005 deadline and Pier 6 at Gatwick was completed ten months ahead of schedule.

**Impact of Business Developments on Operating Costs**
Over the next three years the operating cost base of the Group will be impacted by some significant developments to our business.

Firstly, the opening of Heathrow Terminal 5 will impact the Group's operating costs. Over the next three years, BAA and its partners, will be increasingly focused on ensuring the operations are ready for Terminal 5's opening on 30 March 2008. This activity is focusing on three areas: planning for the new operations with our partners (including adapting organisational structures, work practices and processes); the recruitment and training of staff; and assisting our airline partners to integrate and reorganise operations across the five terminals. Accounting rules on pre-opening costs, under both UK GAAP and IFRS, mean that certain of these non-recurring costs will be included within the profit and loss account as opposed to being capitalised. Our initial estimate indicates a potential cost related to this activity of approximately £60 million over the next three years, the majority being incurred in the final year.

Once open, these non-recurring costs will fall away, however, the fifth terminal will significantly increase Heathrow's fixed cost base. The key contributors to this will be facility related expenditure, such as additional depreciation on the new assets, maintenance, rates and utilities. In addition, the nature of the activity in 2007/08 at Terminal 5 may require depreciation and interest to be charged against profit for approximately three months.

Secondly, the significant changes being planned in the way BAA organises its operations will lead to a more efficient application of resources and people. In making these changes, the Group will incur costs of reorganisation over a three-year period. £16 million of these have been recognised in 2004/05 (see explanation above).

**2.115.2** The OFR should set out the directors' strategies for achieving the business' objectives. [RS (OFR) para 36].

**2.115.3** As noted above objectives and strategy are not clearly defined in the reporting statement and are often described as if they were the same thing. Consequently, much of the discussion above about objectives applies to strategies as well. The reporting statement says that disclosure of the directors' strategies is recommended in order for members to assess the current and past actions undertaken by directors in respect of the stated objectives. [RS (OFR) para 37].

**2.115.4** When describing an entity's strategies, directors should include descriptions of any changes in strategies. This is particularly important where past strategies have not been successful, resulting in poor performance. In such circumstances, it is important for directors, in seeking to restore lost confidence in the entity, to spell out in detail the revised strategies for the future. In doing so, they may have particular regard, when discussing past strategy, to the principle that the OFR should be balanced and neutral, dealing even-handedly with both good and bad aspects.

**2.116** When describing an entity's strategies, directors should include descriptions of any changes in strategies, for example as a result of a strategic review as shown in the example in Table 2.18.

---

**Table 2.18 – Changes in strategy**

**Imperial Chemical Industries PLC – Annual Report and Accounts – 31 December 2006**

**Statement by the Chairman and the Chief Executive (extract)**

**Major business portfolio developments**
As a result of the Quest and Uniqema disposals, ICI will have a focused portfolio of market-leading coatings, adhesives, starch and synthetic polymer businesses combined with a significantly stronger balance sheet.

The Uniqema disposal to Croda International Plc was completed in September for a gross consideration of £410m. We would like to thank all Uniqema employees for their great service to ICI, and their endeavours to improve the performance of the business during a challenging period.

In November, we announced the agreed sale of Quest to Givaudan SA for £1.2bn. The consideration obtained by ICI reflects the strategic value of Quest to Givaudan as it enables them to increase their leadership in the global flavours and fragrance industry. It also reflects the positive trend of Quest's performance in recent quarters.

We would like to thank the Quest team for their outstanding efforts in rebuilding the performance and value of the business over the past three years.

**From Turnaround to Transformation**
As a result of these recent developments combined with the performance improvements delivered through restructuring, ICI has moved from a **turnaround** strategy, which we embarked on in 2003, to one **of transformation**, which we signalled in part with our restructuring plans announced in May 2006. Delivery of our transformation strategy will focus on three important levers – **accelerating profitable growth**, sustaining our improvements in **operational effectiveness** and developing a **culture of sustainable improvement**.

---

**2.117** To the extent necessary, the OFR should include the key performance indicators, both financial and non-financial, used by the directors to assess progress against their stated objectives. [RS (OFR) para 38]. The KPIs disclosed should be those that the directors judge are effective in measuring the delivery of their strategies and managing their business. Regular measurement using KPIs will enable an entity to set and communicate its performance targets and to measure whether it is achieving them [RS (OFR) para 39]. Comparability will be enhanced if KPIs are widely used, either within the industry sector or more generally. [RS (OFR) para 40]. However, it is important that the KPIs used are appropriate for measuring the entity's performance from year to year.

**2.118** KPIs are discussed from paragraph 2.192 and examples are given in Tables 2.44 and 2.45.

**2.119** Directors should also consider the extent to which other performance indicators and evidence should be included. [RS (OFR) para 41]. Other performance indicators may be narrative evidence describing how the directors manage the business or indicators that are used to monitor the entity's external environment and/or its progress towards achieving its objectives. [RS (OFR) para 42]. Other performance indicators are discussed from paragraph 2.207 below.

**Current and future development and performance**

*Development and performance in the year*

**2.120** The OFR should describe the significant features of the business' development and performance in the financial year, focusing on business (including geographical) segments that are relevant to an understanding of the development and performance as a whole. [RS (OFR) para 43].

**2.121** Trends and factors in development and performance suggested by an analysis of current and previous financial years should be highlighted. Development and performance should be described in the context of the business' strategic objectives. [RS (OFR) para 44].

**2.122** Comparison over a number of years may be appropriate where, for example, the entity has a particular strategic objective with a duration of several years. Table 2.19 illustrates the performance achieved on a reorganisation project, tracked over several years.

Table 2.19 – Reorganisation project

Reuters Group PLC – Report and Accounts – 31 December 2004

Company information (extract)

Reuters strategy (extract)

On 18 February 2003 Reuters announced it was accelerating its transformation strategy to become a more competitive, focused and profitable information company. The three-year action plan, *Fast Forward,* is intended to strengthen Reuters core information business. It addresses the impact of structural changes in the financial services industry including consolidation, reduced headcount, growth in market data volumes and increasing regulation.

The five principal components of the *Fast Forward* plan are:

1. Supply information that customers value, by building on core strengths in providing content, analytics and trading and messaging capabilities in an open technology format. Reuters expects to; provide new company fundamental data and investment research through its pending acquisition of Multex.com, Inc. (Multex) (described below); increase its investment in analytics; continue to provide advanced tools to help customers communicate and share information; and build enhanced trading capabilities for the equities and fixed income markets into its premium information products.

2. Move to a single product delivery system, radically simplifying the way products and data are delivered by the use of a single, global technology platform.

3. Simplify and segment the product line, supplying the right product at the right price to profitable target markets, worldwide. During 2003 Reuters expects to launch a series of next generation products, offering specific data and tools required by different financial professionals. At the same time Reuters will speed up the withdrawal of numerous legacy products and platforms.

4. Focus Reuters solutions business, withdrawing from some elements of the established solutions business and actively managing Reuters portfolio of non-core investments. Going forward, Reuters solutions business will focus on three core areas of expertise – risk management, content management and treasury products – and Reuters will not seek further business from pure technology consulting or technology solutions that are not based on Reuters offerings.

See 'Operating and financial review' for information concerning the expected financial impact of the *Fast Forward* plan.

Operating and financial review (extract)

3. *Fast Forward*
As a result of the *Fast Forward* plan, the number of Reuters employees is expected to fall from 15,900 to around 13,000 by the end of 2006. Reuters expects to incur restructuring charges of £340 million between 2003 and 2005, with £160 million incurred in 2003. Reuters is targeting annualised savings from *Fast Forward* of approximately £440 million by 2006. The investment associated with *Fast Forward* measures such as building out the existing Bridge distribution system and building up Reuters content and analytics offerings is expected to come from the redirection of internal resources, rather than any incremental spend. Reuters estimates the amount of this internal investment at £120 million in each of 2003 and 2004.

## CHIEF EXECUTIVE'S REVIEW (extract)

Q You say Reuters is being transformed – from what to what?

In short, from a company at the edge to a great company again. The Reuters of three years ago was at a crisis point. Our revenues were falling rapidly, we were losing market share, our costs were too high, and our organisation was too complex. Today, two-thirds of the way through Fast Forward, I'm pleased with our progress. We have strengthened our product line, we are meeting our cost savings targets and we have done much to simplify the company and reduce our portfolio. It's a tough process, and one that will continue this year, but it's worth it because I truly believe we are on the way to making Reuters a great company again.

## COMPANY INFORMATION (extract)

### 02 STRATEGY (extract)

Reuters goal is to be the information company our customers value most, by offering indispensable content, innovative trading services and great customer service.

- First, complete and realise the benefits of Fast Forward, our business transformation programme – **'Fix it'**
- Second, complete the migration of our customers to our latest products, expand into areas of our market closely related to our current business, and make our business more resilient – **'Strengthen it'**
- Third, reposition our business over the longer term to take advantage of the structural changes and new opportunities in the global markets – **'Grow it'**.

### 'Fix it' through Fast Forward

The Fast Forward programme aims to transform Reuters into a more competitive, simpler, more customer service-driven and more efficient organisation. We have now completed two-thirds of the Fast Forward programme and have made real progress in each of these areas.

Our drive to become more competitive delivered a successful defence of our foreign exchange information and trading franchise, where the number of user positions grew in 2004 for the first time in seven years, despite increased competition.

To simplify the way we do business, we have made major changes to our product line and cut the number of products being actively sold by two-thirds, on the way to our target of 50 desktop financial information products.

We also continued to clear out our portfolio, and have now divested over 80 holdings. The most significant of these in 2004 was the sale of the majority of our stake in TIBCO Software Inc. (TSI).

To make Reuters more efficient, we exceeded our cost savings targets. At the end of 2004, we had cumulative savings of £234 million towards our goal of £440 million by the end of 2006.

We conduct an annual survey of 12,000 customers to measure their satisfaction with our products and service. Customer satisfaction continued to increase in 2004, following the trend from 2003, with users of the latest versions of our products ranking us more highly than users of our older products. However, a power disruption at our UK Docklands data centre in October caused a setback in the fourth quarter, and we immediately took corrective action to improve data centre resilience.

### OPERATING AND FINANCIAL REVIEW (extract)
### Restructuring

The Fast Forward programme resulted in a restructuring charge of £120 million in 2004 within operating profit. This compared with Fast Forward restructuring charges of £134 million, net of a £10 million release of legacy programme provisions, in 2003, and to previous business transformation plan charges of £112 million in 2002.

In 2004, Fast Forward delivered a further £159 million in cost savings leading to cumulative savings from the programme of £234 million. 900 employees were made redundant during the course of 2004, most of whom have already left the company, with the rest expected to leave in 2005.

**2.123** The OFR should cover significant aspects of the statements of financial performance and, where appropriate, should be linked to other aspects of performance. [RS (OFR) para 45]. The example in Table 2.20 shows a graphical explanation of the revenue and profit from operations included in the financial statements. There is a clear indication of reasons for changes in these figures from one period to the next. Further information on each element of the movement is given in detailed narrative explanations of financial performance.

**Table 2.20 – Explaining financial performance**

**Tomkins plc – Annual Report – 30 December 2006**

**Directors report (extract)**

**Operating and financial review (extract)**

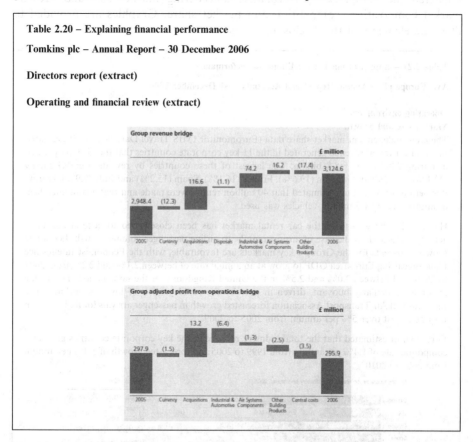

**2.124** Unusual, non-recurring or exceptional items should be discussed and fully explained. Such items may include gains and losses on sales of businesses, reorganisation costs, fines and penalties, impairments, litigation costs and other material items that have been separately disclosed in the financial statements.

**2.125** The OFR should include the directors' analysis of the effect on current development and performance of changes in the industry or external environment in which the business operates and developments within the business. Such changes include market conditions impacting the business and new products or services introduced by the company. [RS (OFR) para 46].

**2.126** Competition, regulation and macro-economics can all affect a company's current development and performance. The introduction of a new competitor may result in changes to pricing decisions, as can regulatory pressure. Macro-economics and other broad market factors such as geopolitical events can also impact how the company has performed.

**2.127** Table 2.21 provides an illustration of how market conditions have impacted the company's performance, considering market size and growth, market composition, competition and market share. Graphics are provided to illustrate elements of the disclosure.

---

Table 2.21 – Impact of market conditions on performance

Avis Europe plc – Annual Report and Accounts – 31 December 2006

**Operating environment**
**Market size and growth**
The latest independent market share data (Euromonitor IMIS Travel Database 2005) estimated the total car rental revenue generated in the 11 key corporate countries that the Group operated in during 2005 to be €8.8 billion. The largest of these countries by revenue were Germany (22.1%), the United Kingdom (19.6%), France (16.1%), Spain (15.2%) and Italy (9.9%). During this period, Euromonitor estimated that 40 million rentals were made and that a combined fleet of approximately 1.2 million vehicles was used.

Historically, the growth of the car rental market has been closely tied to general economic activity levels and, in the case of airport rentals, to airline passenger volume growth. Economic growth prospects for the Group's key markets are favourable, with the Economist Intelligence Unit forecasting Euro-area GDP to grow at an annual rate of between 2.1% and 2.2% from 2007 to 2010, and between 2.0% and 2.5% in the United Kingdom over the same period. The airline sector is particularly buoyant, driven in part by the rapid growth of low cost airlines. The International Air Transport Association forecasted growth in passenger arrivals for flights within Europe of just over 5% per annum from 2005 to 2009.

Euromonitor estimated that the total industry revenue in the key corporate countries grew at a compound rate of 1.4% per annum from 1999 to 2005 and forecasted growth of 3.0% per annum from 2005 to 2010.

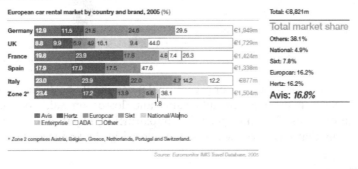

---

**Competition**

Euromonitor research shows that the Group had the highest aggregate market revenue share in its 11 largest corporate countries in 2005 at 16.8%, followed by Hertz and Europcar with 16.2% each (please see the table on page 13). The recent merger between Europcar and Vanguard has given Europcar a leading position in this European market place.

In specific markets, the Group faces competition from Sixt in Germany and Enterprise in the United Kingdom, together with a large number of smaller-scale operators, with strength in particular markets (frequently the Mediterranean), examples being Maggiore in Italy and ADA in France.

On a global scale, the Group operates two of the three truly global brands, Avis, Budget and Hertz. The merger between Europcar and Vanguard referred to above creates a fourth global brand.

**2.128**   The introduction of new products or services is often a factor that has affected a company's development and performance. The example in Table 2.22 shows how this pharmaceutical company explains its product pipeline including the investment in research and development.

---

**Table 2.22 – Effect of new products on performance**

**AstraZeneca PLC – Annual Report and Form 20-F Information – 31 December 2006**

**Business Review (extract)**

**REASEARCH AND DEVELOPMENT (extract)**

**WE HAVE A GLOBAL RESEARCH AND DEVELOPMENT ORGANISATION, WITH AROUND 12,000 PEOPLE AT 16 MAJOR CENTRES IN EIGHT COUNTRIES DEDICATED TO TRANSLATING LEADING-EDGE SCIENCE INTO INNOVATIVE, NEW MEDICINES THAT MAKE A DIFFERENCE IN THE LIVES OF PATIENTS.**

In 2006, we spent $3.9 billion on research and development (2005 $3.38 billion, 2004 $3.47 billion) and approved $300 million of R&D capital investments including announcements of major new facilities in Sweden (safety pharmacology), the US (cancer and infection) and China (cancer).

We want to be among the best in the industry in terms of the quality of our work and the speed with which we get new medicines to market. During 2006 we continued our drive to improve the efficiency of our processes and the effectiveness of our decision-making, so that we can quickly eliminate weaker candidate drugs (CDs) and concentrate on the robust, rapid progress of the ones most likely to succeed as significant advances in healthcare.

In line with our strategy, we also continued to focus on accessing external innovation that complements our in-house capabilities, and on page 39 you can read more about our externalisation activities during the year.

PIPELINE STRATEGY

Our R&D strategy is geared to maintaining a flow of new products that will deliver sustained business growth in the short, medium and long term.

In the short term, our business needs will be met through successful delivery of the Phase III programmes and optimised life-cycle management for our key products.

In 2006, we experienced some setbacks with our Phase III portfolio with the termination of the programmes for Galida and NXY-059, as described in more detail on pages 18 and 25 respectively. Despite these setbacks, as at 1 February 2007 we still have 28 Phase III programmes compared with 29 at the end of January 2006.

Notable successes in the life-cycle management of our key marketed brands during the year included nine submissions and nine approvals in the US or EU and are described in the Therapy Area Review (pages 16 to 32).

In the mid term we will drive our pre-clinical and clinical Phase I and II projects towards proof of concept as rapidly as possible whilst recognising that we will need to continue our emphasis on externalisation to complement our internal R&D efforts. Our drug discovery effort is now a process that is much wider than our own laboratories, as we actively seek to make alliances and acquisitions with external partners to gain access to leading drug projects or technology platforms.

The progress we are making in our drive to increase productivity is reflected in the growth of our early development portfolio: during 2006 21 CDs were selected (compared with 25 in 2005 and 18 in 2004), and we have 92 development projects in the proof of principle phase (before Phase III, latestage development).

During 2006 we progressed 12 compounds into man.

In the long term, in addition to our current capabilities, we are also seeking to transform the AstraZeneca pipeline through a strategic move into biopharmaceuticals and by using biomarkers to help identify winning projects much earlier.

**2.128.1**   Where a company operates in a number of different territories and has a number of different product lines that are affected by different trends and factors (either economic or non-economic), analysis of performance that showing this level of detail may be useful. Table 2.22A discloses changes in sales and sales volumes global and local brands.

**Table 2.22A – Market analysis for brand and geographic segment**

**Diageo plc – Report and Accounts – 30 June 2006**

**Operating and financial review (extract)**

**Europe (extract)**

Summary:
- Net sales, after deducting excise duties, were unchanged year on year as growth in core spirits offset tough market conditions in beer and ready to drink
- Spirits demonstrated healthy volume growth at 3%
- Innovation is increasing brand visibility with new and existing customers
- Marketing spend was reduced by 4% and prioritised against specific opportunities such as Johnnie Walker throughout Europe and J&B in France

| Key measures | 2006 £ million | 2005 £ million | Reported movement % | Organic movement % |
|---|---|---|---|---|
| Volume | | | 2 | 1 |
| Net sales after deducting excise duties | 2,455 | 2,499 | (2) | – |
| Marketing | 389 | 403 | (4) | (4) |
| Operating profit before exceptional items | 737 | 702 | 5 | 6 |

**Reported performance** Net sales, after deducting excise duties, were £2,455 million in the year ended 30 June 2006, down by £44 million from the prior year. Operating profit before exceptional items increased by £35 million from £702 million to £737 million.

**Organic performance** Disposals net of the impact of acquisitions decreased net sales, after deducting excise duties, by £16 million and there was an organic decrease in net sales, after deducting excise duties, of £4 million and an adverse impact of exchange of £1 million. Transfers between business segments decreased prior year net sales, after deducting excise duties, by £23 million. Operating profit before exceptional items decreased by £5 million as a result of foreign exchange impacts. Acquisitions increased operating profit before exceptional items by £4 million and organic growth of £39 million was achieved. Transfers between business segments decreased prior year operating profit before exceptional items by £3 million.

| | Reported volume movement % | Organic volume movement % | Reported net sales movement % | Organic net sales* movement % |
|---|---|---|---|---|
| **Organic brand performance** | | | | |
| Global priority brands | 1 | 1 | (1) | (1) |
| Local priority brands | (2) | (2) | (1) | (1) |
| Category brands | 6 | 2 | (3) | 2 |
| **Total** | 2 | 1 | (2) | - |
| **Key brands** | | | | |
| Smirnoff vodka | | 8 | 8 | 7 |
| Smirnoff ready to drink | | (22) | (21) | (21) |
| Johnny Walker | | 3 | 6 | 6 |
| Baileys | | 1 | - | - |
| J&B | | (3) | (5) | (5) |
| Guinness | | (3) | - | - |
| * after deducting excise duties | | | | |

Spirits demonstrated resilient growth with volume and net sales, after deducting excise duties, up 3%, while beer, volume down 3%, and ready to drink, volume down 22%, held back total performance. The shift from the on to the off trade in Ireland again negatively impacted overall beer performance. Wine volume grew 7% driven by Blossom Hill's robust growth in Great Britain and Ireland.

Smirnoff vodka, excluding ready to drink, continued to grow strongly, delivering volume growth of 8% and growth of net sales, after deducting excise duties, of 7%. A pan-European advertising campaign, focusing on the quality credentials of Smirnoff, continued to build the distinctiveness of the brand, although marketing spend was reduced by 9%.

Johnnie Walker Red Label volume grew 1% while net sales, after deducting excise duties, were flat. However, very strong volume growth of Johnnie Walker Black Label, up 14%, and Johnnie Walker Super Deluxe, up 21%, delivered overall growth in Johnnie Walker, with volume up 3%, and had a positive mix impact as net sales, after deducting excise duties, increased 6%. Growth was driven mainly by increased demand in Southern Europe, Russia and Eastern Europe and the favourable impact of advertising, especially the sponsorship of Team McLaren Mercedes Formula One. Marketing spend was up 19% as a result of increased activities in sports sponsorship.

Europe accounts for over half of Baileys volume worldwide and brand volume was up a further 1% year on year, driven by growth in France, Italy, Russia and Central and Eastern Europe. Net sales, after deducting excise duties, were flat. Excluding ready to drink, both volume and net sales, after deducting excise duties, grew by 1%.

*Operating and financial review*

The majority of J&B's volume in Europe is sold in Spain, where the decline of the scotch category led to a 3% decrease in overall volume of J&B. However, elsewhere in Europe, especially in France and Eastern Europe, J&B performed well.

Guinness volume declined 3% although pricing offset weak volumes and net sales, after deducting excise duties, were flat year on year. Guinness sales progressed well in Russia during the year following Diageo's agreement in July 2005 with Heineken NV for the production and distribution of Guinness in Russia.

Despite a year on year decline in ready to drink, Diageo has managed costs and increased the margin on ready to drink, even though contribution in absolute terms was down.

Total local priority brand performance was negatively impacted by the decline of Diageo's beer volume in Ireland.

Marketing spend was reduced by 4%, driven by a 23% reduction in spending on ready to drink.

**Great Britain**
Volume was flat and net sales, after deducting excise duties, were down 1% as the decline in ready to drink continued to cause a negative mix impact.

The total spirits market in Great Britain was broadly flat as growth in the off trade offset declines in the on trade. Diageo maintained leadership across all key categories and, excluding ready to drink, grew spirits volume by 2%.

Growth in spirits was attributable to Smirnoff vodka in particular, which continued to gain share as volume grew 6% and net sales, after deducting excise duties, grew 8%. Smirnoff performance was driven by marketing programmes focused on quality and on trade activity around signature cocktails. Smirnoff ready to drink volume declined 19%, a rate similar to the prior year.

Total Baileys volume declined 2% and net sales, after deducting excise duties, declined by 4%. Excluding Baileys Glide, Baileys volume declined 1% whilst net sales, after deducting excise duties, grew 1%. The majority of Baileys is sold in the off trade where there has been increased competition from value brands, however while volume declined, the brand maintained its value share. Baileys grew in the on trade driven by distribution gains and price increases.

Total Guinness volume declined 1% whilst net sales, after deducting excise duties, grew 1% driven by a price increase on Guinness Draught. While volume in the on trade beer market in Great Britain declined 3% as consumers shifted to consumption at home, Guinness Draught gained share in the on trade, growing volume 1% and net sales, after deducting excise duties, by 4%. Media activities were focused on quality attributes and Dublin brewed Guinness, as well as the first year of a four-year sponsorship of the rugby premiership. This helped to generate growth in the second half and increase share.

Local priority brand volume declined 2% and net sales, after deducting excise duties, fell 6%, mainly due to the decline in Archers ready to drink. Gordon's volume grew 1% and net sales, after deducting excise duties, were up 4%. Bell's Extra Special volume grew 2% although net sales, after deducting excise duties, were down.

Category brand volume grew 4% and net sales, after deducting excise duties, increased 2% driven by Blossom Hill, which continued to grow strongly with volume up 13%, and the launch in May 2006 of a new product, Quinn's, an alcoholic fruit ferment blended drink, into the on and off trade.

**Ireland**
The performance in Ireland reflects the continuing change in market dynamics from on to off trade, high levels of competitor investment, and consumer migration to value brands. While the

total beverage alcohol market grew 2%, the on trade was down 3% and the off trade was up 7%. The on trade now represents 51% of the total market.

Volume declined 3% and net sales, after deducting excise duties, were down 1%. This was due to weak performance in beer, where volumes were down 6%, partly offset by growth in wine and spirits, where volume grew 18% and 7% respectively. The impact on net sales, after deducting excise duties, of declining beer volume was partly offset by price increases.

Guinness volume declined 8% whilst net sales, after deducting excise duties, declined 3% as a result of price increases introduced in June 2005 and May 2006. Guinness was impacted by increased levels of competitor investment and the movement to the off trade where Guinness' share is lower. In the year there was innovation on the Guinness brand with positive consumer response to the launch of the limited edition Brewhouse Series. In the second half, Guinness Mid-Strength, a lower alcohol by volume format, began consumer trials in 80 outlets.

The introduction of new packaging on Harp, new marketing executions on Carlsberg and Harp and increased distribution have helped reinvigorate both brands. As a result both Carlsberg and Harp have maintained volume year on year and net sales, after deducting excise duties, have increased 7% and 2% respectively.

Smirnoff continued to be the number one vodka in Ireland and outperformed the vodka category in both the on and off trade.

Baileys volume declined 2% and net sales, after deducting excise duties, fell 8% due to increased competition from lower value brands.

**Iberia**
In Iberia, volume and net sales, after deducting excise duties, both declined 3%. In Spain, spirits penetration is declining in all age groups versus other leisure categories and this has negatively impacted the Spanish business, whilst in Portugal trading conditions continued to be tough as a result of tightening consumer expenditure.

J&B faced increased pressure as the standard whisky segment in Spain continued to decline as consumers continued to switch to dark rums. Therefore, while J&B gained share in the Spanish on trade, overall Iberian volume declined 7% and net sales, after deducting excise duties, fell 10%. Marketing spend increased 3% behind J&B driven by investment in Spain.

Johnnie Walker volume declined 2%, however net sales, after deducting excise duties, were up 2% driven by the growth of Johnnie Walker Black Label, Super Deluxe and price increases throughout Iberia. Johnnie Walker Black Label and Super Deluxe combined grew volume by 4% and net sales, after deducting excise duties, by 11%. Johnnie Walker Red Label volume declined 3% despite a good performance in Spain, where it is the only standard whisky brand growing volume and share in the on trade. Total Diageo share in the standard scotch segment in Spain increased by 0.3 percentage points.

Across Iberia, Baileys volume was down 6% and net sales, after deducting excise duties, declined 5% driven by contraction in the on trade. José Cuervo volume grew 13% and net sales, after deducting excise duties, were up 15% due to continued consumer interest in the tequila category.

Local priority brand volume grew 5% and net sales, after deducting excise duties, were up 7%. Dark rums grew robustly in the on and off trade with Cacique volume up 6% and net sales, after deducting excise duties, up 9% as a result of repositioning the brand.

Category brand volume declined 8% and net sales, after deducting excise duties, fell 9%. Pampero volume declined 14% with net sales, after deducting excise duties, down 12% as marketing spend was focused on Cacique. In total, Diageo's rum brands grew volume 2% and net sales, after deducting excise duties, grew 5%.

**Rest of Europe**

In the rest of Europe, solid performances in Italy and Central and Eastern Europe and the growth of super premium brands in Russia drove volume growth of 6% and growth in net sales, after deducting excise duties, of 4%.

Johnnie Walker Red Label volume in the rest of Europe was up 2% and net sales, after deducting excise duties, were up 1%. Johnnie Walker Black Label and Super Deluxe experienced strong growth with volume up 25% and net sales, after deducting excise duties, up 28% from key markets such as Greece, Russia and Northern Europe.

Captain Morgan delivered volume growth of 29% driven by Northern Europe and Russia with net sales, after deducting excise duties, up 23%.

J&B performed well in France, its second largest market, with volume up 9% benefiting from effective on trade advertising and promotion. Baileys enjoyed strong sales in France and Italy.

Ready to drink volume in the rest of Europe declined by 27%, as a result of the continued decline in the segment in France.

Russia continued its momentum with robust volume growth of 25% and net sales, after deducting excise duties, up 26% driven by Johnnie Walker, as the trend towards premium products in Russia continued. Johnnie Walker is the number one scotch in Russia and Baileys holds the same position in the imported liqueur category.

Diageo has announced the acquisition of the Smirnov brand in Russia through a company in which Diageo holds a 75% stake. This company will unite the Smirnoff/Smirnov brands under common ownership and will be the exclusive distributor of Diageo spirits brands and the Smirnov vodka brand in Russia.

**2.129**  Another factor that can have significant impact on a company's current development and performance is changes in the business from acquisitions or disposals. The example in Table 2.23 clearly illustrates the impact of two significant acquisitions for this mining company, including the savings from synergies that have been achieved.

**Table 2.23 – Trends in performance**

**Xstrata plc – Annual Report – 31 December 2006**

**Operational Review (extract)**

**Copper (extract)**

Operations
The highlight of the 2006 financial year has been the acquisition and integration of the Tintaya and Falconbridge copper assets within the Xstrata Copper business unit, contributing 74% or $2.7 billion to the business unit's EBIT growth of $3.6 billion for the year.

During the Falconbridge integration planning process, Xstrata Copper identified approximately $60 million of annual synergy benefits from the integration of the former Falconbridge copper assets. The progressive implementation of integration plans will see these benefits fully realised during 2007. In addition, a once-off finance re-structuring benefit of $58 million was achieved as a result of the copper asset integration.

The synergies identified through the integration of the Tintaya operation into Xstrata Copper Peru, of $110 million of additional value, have been confirmed and are being progressively realised. A further $50 million of value uplift has already been realised through ongoing operational management initiatives, with a range of other significant initiatives being actively pursued in 2007.

**2.129.1** Similarly, the disposal of operations will affect the company's development and performance. Table 2.23A discusses discontinued activities.

---

**Table 2.23A – Disposal of significant operation**

**GKN plc – Report and Accounts – 31 December 2004**

**Discontinued operations**

*AgustaWestland*

The Group completed the sale of its 50% shareholding in AgustaWestland on 30 November 2004. Figures for 2004 therefore reflect our share for the 11 months ended on that date and are based on accounts which reflect the contract margin and provision reviews which normally take place as part of the year-end procedures.

GKN's share of sales revenue in 2004 of £740 million was £136 million below the 2003 figure, reflecting the loss of one month's revenue, together with lower underlying sales largely as a consequence of the completion of the EH101 contract for the UK Ministry of Defence during the early part of 2003 and delivery of the final six Apaches for the British Army in 2004.

As a consequence, GKN's share of operating profit of £86 million was £16 million below last year.

As noted earlier, the Group also booked an exceptional profit of £652 million on disposal of the business.

---

**2.129.2** Table 2.23B illustrates the effect of changes in exchange rates and inflation.

---

**Table 2.23B – Exchange rate movements and inflation**

**Cadbury Schweppes plc – Report and Accounts – 31 December 2004**

**10 Effect of exchange rates and inflation on 2004 reported results**

Over 80% of the Group's sales and profits in 2004 were generated outside the United Kingdom. The Group's reported results have been affected by changes in the exchange rates used to translate the results of non-UK operations. In 2004 compared with 2003, the biggest exchange rate impact on the Group's results was the 12% weakening of the US dollar followed by the weakening Mexican Peso, which fell by 16%. The weakness in the US dollar was partially offset by the Canadian dollar (up 4%) and the Australian dollar (up 2%).

The overall impact of exchange rate movements on the Group's Profit and Loss statement and free cash flow generation was adverse and is shown separately. In 2004, movements in exchange rates, primarily the US dollar reduced the Group's sales by 4%, underlying pre-tax profit by 7% and underlying earnings per share by 7%. There was a greater impact on underlying operating profit than turnover as the Group generated higher profits in the currencies that have weakened during the year compared to those that have strengthened.

---

> The adverse impact of currency movements on free cash flow was 16%. The reason for the greater impact on free cash flow relative to profits was due to the higher margin generation of US Dollar sales in the Americas beverages region
>
> General price inflation in countries where the Group has its most significant operations remained at a low level throughout the year and in general terms was within the 1% to 3% range. In certain developing markets, notably Venezuela, Turkey, Brazil, Russia and Argentina, the rate of inflation was significantly higher than this range, but the impact was not material to the Group results.

**2.129.3** Many companies express figures in the OFR in terms of constant currency, so as to show the trends in performance, excluding the effect of exchange rates. Where this is done, the reporting statement recommends that a reconciliation to reported figures is given.

**2.130** The discussion and analysis should also include any other factors that have affected performance in the period under review. This includes those for which the effect cannot be specifically quantified, as well as any specific exceptional items that are quantified and disclosed in the financial statements. Events range from natural disasters that may affect entities operating in the geographical regions affected, to wars and terrorist attacks, fraud and other irregularities, major strategy changes involving acquisitions and disposals or major reorganisations, regulatory fines and sanctions and so on.

**2.131** The OFR should analyse the main trends and factors that the directors consider are likely to affect future prospects. [RS (OFR) para 47]. The directors will, therefore, need to consider the potential future significance of issues in deciding whether or not to include an analysis of them in the OFR. [RS (OFR) para 49].

**2.132** An example of disclosure relating to trends and factors likely to affect future prospects is given in Table 2.24. Market conditions are described for each segment, with an indication of the key parameters that the directors consider of potential significance for the company's future development and performance.

**Table 2.24 – Future trends and factors**

**AMEC plc – Annual Report and Accounts – 31 December 2006**

**Business Review (extract)**

**Oil and gas services (extract)**

**Markets**

Oil and gas are expected to remain the dominant sources of global energy supply for the foreseeable future, as shown in the chart below.

Projected global energy supply
1990-2025

Source: International Energy Outlook 1997, 1999, 2002, 2004, 2005 – Washingrton, DC, US Department of Energy, Energy Information Administration

Major oil and gas company plans point to an investment increase of over 57 per cent in 2006-2010 compared to 2001-2005. If those plans are fully implemented and their spending forecasts prove accurate, oil and gas investment would rise from US$340 billion in 2005 to US$470 billion in 2010. The upstream sector will absorb almost two-thirds of total capital spending of which two-thirds will go towards maintaining or enhancing production from current fields. Beyond the current decade, higher investment in real terms will be needed to maintain growth in production capacity, with future projects likely to be more complex and remote, involving a higher unit cost. Slowing production declines at mature giant fields will require increased investment and enhanced recovery. (Source: IEA World Energy Outlook).

**Building and Civil Engineering (extract)**

AMEC offers integrated design, project management and construction services for hospitals, schools, rail, airports and commercial and government buildings. Clients include BAA, Transport for London, Defence Estates, South Lanarkshire Schools, Greater Manchester County Council, Marks & Spencer, Scottish Water and Welsh Water. This area of activities has synergies with the Building and Facilities Services and Investment businesses, both in relation to project tenders and in the construction phase of asset delivery. This business reported substantial losses in 2006, and significant actions have been taken to strengthen management and internal processes, together with increasing focus on higher quality work. The management team is committed to making a small profit in 2007 and the business is capable of achieving average margins of 1-3 per cent through the cycle.

**Markets**

This business is focused on UK markets which offer sound growth prospects (source: AMEC assessments) together with the right balance of risk and reward:

- Defence: The market available to AMEC is assessed at some £3 billion per annum and is expected to remain relatively stable.
- Healthcare: The UK Government is aiming to deliver 100 new hospitals by 2010; annual spending 2007/8 £4-5 billion.

- Education: The UK is committed to its largest schools capital investment programme for 30 years, with spending rising to £8 billion in 2008.
- Manufacturing: The UK market is stable, but growth opportunities exist with key clients as they invest overseas. Annual spending c. £3-4 billion.
- Transport: Growth in AMEC's available market in this sector is expected to be tempered as a result of the completion of the large terminal 5 project at London Heathrow Airport in 2007. AMEC has exited lump-sum roads contracts as this procurement route is unattractive.

**2.133**    Paragraph 48 of the reporting statement says:

*"The main trends and factors likely to affect the future development and performance will vary according to the nature of the business, but could include the development of known new products and services or the benefits expected from capital investment. The OFR should discuss the current level of investment expenditure together with planned future expenditure and shall explain how that investment is directed to assist the achievement of business objectives. Any assumptions underlying the main trends and factors should be disclosed."* [RS (OFR) para 48].

**2.133.1**    Investment expenditure is not defined in the reporting statement. The definition used by a company should be disclosed in the OFR to avoid ambiguity and should be wide enough that it enables users of financial statements to obtain an understanding of its impact on the company's future. The definition used may be wider than the definition of 'investing cash flows' used in the preparation of the cash flow statement (see further chapter 30 of the Manual of Accounting — IFRS for the UK and the Manual of Accounting — UK GAAP) and may include:

- Personnel policies and practices, including employee training.

- Pure and applied research that may lead to potential new products, services or processes.

- Development of new products and services.

- Investment in brand equity, for example through advertising and marketing activities.

- Refurbishment and maintenance programmes.

- Technical support to customers.

**2.133.2**    Discussion should also include explanations of variations in expenditure from year to year.

**2.133.3**    Table 2.24A shows discussion of movements in marketing and capital expenditure.

---

**Table 2.24A – Investment expenditure**

**Cadbury Schweppes plc – Report and Accounts – 31 December 2004**

**Operating and Financial Review (extracts)**

**Marketing**
Total marketing expenditure in 2003 was £702 million, an increase of 28% over 2002 (£547 million) and an increase of 30% at constant exchange rates. This represents a marketing to turnover ratio of 10.9% compared to 10.3% in 2002, with the increase being due to the acquisition of Adams, which had a higher marketing to turnover ratio.

Prior to acquisitions, the marketing to turnover ratio was 9.9%, with the year-on-year reduction reflecting the combination of exchange rate movements and lower spend during periods of unfavourable weather conditions in Americas Beverages and EMEA.

**Capital Structure and Resources (extract)**
**(c) Capital Expenditure**
Capital expenditure in 2004 was £285 million, a decrease of 6% from the level of expenditure in 2003 with key areas of expenditure being related to Fuel for Growth cost reduction programmes and IT spend related to the continued roll out of project Probe and the costs associated with transferring Adams businesses from Pfizer to Cadbury systems. All these projects were funded from internal resources.

For 2005, the Group expects capital spend to be in the region of £300 million, driven by investments behind the Fuel for Growth initiatives. The Group expects to continue to fund this from internal resources.

Capital expenditure in 2003 was £302 million, an increase of 8% over the level of expenditure in 2002 with key areas of expenditure being acquisition related capital expenditure in Adams in the Americas, capital expenditure related to Fuel for Growth cost reduction programmes in the UK, Irish and French confectionery businesses and IT spend related to the continued roll out of Probe, and the costs associated with transferring Adams businesses from Pfizer to Cadbury systems. All these projects were funded from internal resources.

Capital expenditure in 2002 was £279 million, an increase of 16% over the level of expenditure in 2001. The Group continued to implement project Probe. This project was a significant contributor to the increased level of capital expenditure in 2002. The Group also carried out specific projects to increase production capacity in Mott's, Schweppes Spain and Cadbury Trebor Bassett. All these projects were funded from internal sources.

At 2 January 2005, the Group had capital commitments of £15 million. It is anticipated that these commitments will be financed out of the Group's operational free cash flow.

---

**2.134** Table 2.25 illustrates how investing in training and development for employees helps this company to achieve its objectives around its key resource, its people.

**Table 2.25 – Investing to meet objectives**

**Amlin plc – Annual Report – 31 December 2006**

**Operating and Financial Review (extract)**

**People – retaining, motivating and building skills (extract)**

With regard to Amlin's employees our key objectives remain:
> A working environment where employees are well motivated and have a strong belief in the Company, its strategy and core values.
> The development of loyalty between the Company and employees.
> Continual improvement in the effective management of people and the skills and competency of staff at all levels and across all disciplines.
> The retention and growth of key skills which are critical to the business.
> Well constructed and fair reward systems which help drive superior performance and align employee and shareholder interests.
> The development and use of first class employment practices throughout the Group.

**Training and development (extract)**

Amlin Academy, now in its sixth year, provides training and development programmes for Group employees and selected open courses for others. The Academy's objective is to provide a core curriculum of training, while encouraging professional and personal development at every level throughout the organisation.

The Academy supports regulatory and compliance requirements and also provides a broad range of initiatives including technical training and management and personal development, to help staff realise their full potential. The number of employee days devoted to training increased by 21% to 1,252 days in 2006 as a result of increased personal development, much of which was associated with the roll out of our core values programme as referred to overleaf.

During 2006 a bespoke workshop was designed to educate all underwriting staff on the requirements of "Contract Certainty" with the primary objective of maintaining Amlin's position as a market leader in best practice and customer service.

A key initiative during 2006 was the development of a claims competency framework which incorporates a set of key behaviours specifically identified for claims staff, together with a technical know-how and skills matrix which categorises the skills required to perform the day job at various levels. This took longer to complete than originally envisaged, and is a high quality piece of work which will be used as a template for developing other competency frameworks across the business.

While fewer days in 2006 were devoted to management development than in 2005, Amlin continued to work closely with The Roffey Park Institute and The Coverdale Organisation in providing management development training. Both training providers have a good insight into the culture of Amlin, which adds a huge benefit when delivering their programmes.

Work commenced in 2006 on the design of a leadership development programme to provide directors and senior managers with tailored personal development and to raise the level of leadership capability across the Group. Completion of this in 2007 is a key priority.

## *Resources*

**2.135**   The OFR should include a description of the resources available to the entity and how they are managed. [RS (OFR) para 50]. It should set out the key strengths and resources, tangible and intangible, available to the business that will assist it in pursuing its objectives. This should include, in particular, resources that are not reflected in the balance sheet. Depending on the business' nature, these may include:

- Corporate reputation.
- Brand strength.
- Natural resources.
- Employees.
- Research and development.
- Intellectual capital.
- Licences, patents, copyright and trademarks.
- Market position.

[RS (OFR) para 51].

Other examples not specifically referred to in the standard, include:

- Customer/supplier relationships.
- Strength of proprietary business processes, such as distribution systems.
- Web sites and databases.
- Non-financial aspects of reputation, such as environmental reputation or strength of involvement in and identification with the community.
- Strength of geographical spread or product range.

**2.136**   As noted in the reporting statement, resources to be disclosed will depend on the nature of the business and the industry the company operates in. The example in Table 2.26 shows how the company sees its brands as key assets and explains how it has developed them during the year.

*Operating and financial review*

**Table 2.26 – Resources – brands**

**Diageo plc – Annual Report – 30 June 2008**

**Business review (extract)**

**Premium drinks (extract)**

The collection of premium drinks comprises brands owned by the company as a principal and brands held by the company under agency or distribution agreements. They include:

**Global priority brands**

Smirnoff vodka and Smirnoff ready to drink products
Johnnie Walker scotch whiskies
Captain Morgan rum
Baileys Original Irish Cream liqueur
J&B scotch whisky
José Cuervo tequila (agency brand in North America and many other markets)
Tanqueray gin
Guinness stout

**Other spirits brands include:**

Crown Royal Canadian whisky
Buchanan's De Luxe whisky
Gordon's gin and vodka
Windsor Premier whisky
Bell's Extra Special whisky
Seagram's whiskey
Old Parr whisky
Bushmills Irish whiskey
Bundaberg rum
Cacique rum
Ketel One vodka (exclusive worldwide distribution rights)

**Wine brands include:**

Beaulieu Vineyard
Sterling Vineyards
Rosenblum Cellars
Chalone Vineyard
Blossom Hill
Piat d'Or

**Other beer brands include:**

Harp lager
Smithwick's ale
Malta Guinness non-alcoholic malt
Red Stripe lager
Tusker lager

Diageo's agency agreements vary depending on the particular brand, but tend to be for a fixed number of years. Diageo's principal agency brand is José Cuervo in North America and many other markets (with distribution rights extending to 2013). In the year ended 30 June 2008, Diageo signed a three-year agency agreement with Inversiones de Guatemala to distribute

Zacapa ultra premium rums globally, other than in Central America (Guatemala, Guatemalan duty free, El Salvador, Honduras, Nicaragua, Costa Rica, and Panama), where Industrias Licoreras de Guatemala will retain the right to distribute the Zacapa brands. There can be no assurances that Diageo will be able to prevent termination of distribution rights or rights to manufacture under licence, or renegotiate distribution rights or rights to manufacture under licence on favourable terms when they expire.

Diageo also brews and sells other companies' beer brands under licence, including Budweiser and Carlsberg lagers in Ireland, Heineken lager in Jamaica and Tiger beer in Malaysia.

**Global priority brands** Diageo has eight global priority brands that it markets worldwide. Diageo considers these brands to have the greatest current and future earnings potential. Each global priority brand is marketed consistently around the world, and therefore can achieve scale benefits. The group manages and invests in these brands on a global basis. Figures for global priority brands include related ready to drink products, unless otherwise indicated. Net sales are sales after deducting excise duties.

In the year ended 30 June 2008, global priority brands accounted for 59% of total volume (86.3 million equivalent units) and contributed net sales of £4,614 million.

Smirnoff achieved sales of 29.6 million equivalent units in the year ended 30 June 2008. Smirnoff vodka volume was 25.1 million equivalent units. It was ranked, by volume, as the number one premium vodka and the number one premium spirit brand in the world. Smirnoff ready to drink volume totalled 4.5 million equivalent units.

Johnnie Walker scotch whiskies comprise Johnnie Walker Red Label, Johnnie Walker Black Label and several other brand variants. During the year ended 30 June 2008, Johnnie Walker Red Label sold 10.0 million equivalent units, Johnnie Walker Black Label sold 5.5 million equivalent units and the remaining variants sold 0.8 million equivalent units. The Johnnie Walker franchise was ranked, by volume, as the number one premium scotch whisky and the number three premium spirit brand in the world.

Captain Morgan was ranked, by volume, as the number two premium rum brand in the world with sales of 8.3 million equivalent units in the year ended 30 June 2008.

Baileys was ranked, by volume, as the number one liqueur in the world, having sold 7.5 million equivalent units in the year ended 30 June 2008.

Guinness is the group's only global priority beer brand, and for the year ended 30 June 2008 achieved volume of 11.4 million equivalent units.

Other global priority brands were also ranked, by volume, among the leading premium distilled spirits brands by Impact Databank. These include: J&B scotch whisky (comprising J&B Rare, J&B Reserve, J&B Exception and J&B Jet), ranked the number three premium scotch whisky in the world; José Cuervo, ranked the number one premium tequila in the world; and Tanqueray, ranked the number four premium gin brand in the world. During the year ended 30 June 2008, J&B, José Cuervo and Tanqueray sold 6.1 million, 5.0 million and 2.1 million equivalent units, respectively.

**Other brands** Diageo manages its other brands by category, analysing them between local priority brands and category brands. Local priority brands represent the brands, apart from the global priority brands, that make the greatest contribution to operating profit in a business area (North America, Europe, International or Asia Pacific), rather than worldwide. Diageo has identified 25 local priority brands. Diageo manages and invests in these brands within its business areas and, unlike the global priority brands, may not have a consistent marketing strategy around the world for such brands. For the year ended 30 June 2008, local priority brands contributed volume of 26.0 million equivalent units, representing 18% of total volume, and net sales of £1,734 million. Examples of local priority brands include Crown Royal Canadian whisky in North America, Buchanan's De Luxe whisky in International, Windsor Premier whisky in Asia Pacific, Gordon's gin in Europe, Bundaberg rum in Asia Pacific, Cacique rum in Europe, Malta Guinness non-alcoholic malt in International, Tusker lager in International, Seagram's 7 Crown whiskey and Seagram's VO whisky in North America, Bell's Extra Special whisky in Europe and Sterling Vineyards wines in North America.

The remaining brands are grouped under category brands. Category brands include spirits, beer and wine brands and for the year ended 30 June 2008, these category brands contributed volume of 32.8 million equivalent units, representing 23% of total volume, and net sales of £1,742 million. Of this, spirits achieved volume of 23.9 million equivalent units and contributed £1,120 million to Diageo's net sales in the year ended 30 June 2008. Examples of category spirits brands are Gordon's gin (all markets except Europe in which it is a local priority brand), Gordon's vodka, The Classic Malt whiskies and White Horse whisky.

In the year ended 30 June 2008, Diageo sold 13.2 million equivalent units of beers other than Guinness, achieving net sales of £765 million. Other beer volume was mainly attributable to owned brands, such as Red Stripe, Pilsner, Tusker and Harp lager, with a minority being attributable to beers brewed and/or sold under licence, such as Tiger beer in Malaysia and Heineken lager in Jamaica.

In addition, Diageo produces and markets a wide selection of wines. These include well known labels such as Beaulieu Vineyard, Sterling Vineyards, Rosenblum Cellars and Chalone Vineyard in the United States, Blossom Hill in the United Kingdom, and Barton & Guestier and Piat d'Or in Europe. For the year ended 30 June 2008, other wine volume was 2.3 million equivalent units, contributing net sales of £275 million.

**2.137**   A further example is given in Table 2.27 where the company reports on four key resources it must manage in order to achieve profitable growth.

---

**Table 2.27 – Resources – brands**

**The Capita Group Plc – Annual Report and Accounts – 31 December 2006**

**Business review (extract)**

**Our business strategy** How do we manage and measure our growth? (extract)

**c) Resource and operational controls**

Our continued growth and financial performance depends on having the right resources in place. To sustain our high contract win and retention rates, we have to satisfy clients that we have the operational scale and capability to deliver our promises – whether on relatively simple contracts or large scale, multi-service packages. Through the MOB process we continuously assess the needs of each business unit to ensure that we have the necessary people, infrastructure and resources for current and future development.

Each month, we monitor and review comprehensive operational management information enabling us to manage the business in a way that delivers our key financial aims.

---

**4 key areas of attention:**

| Core operational indicators | Aim | Progress | |
|---|---|---|---|
| | | **Year end 2006** | Year end 2005 |
| **Retaining the right people** | Senior management retention (top 250 earning over £90k) – attract and retain the appropriate level of senior management to drive the strategic direction of the Group | **91%** | 92% |
| | Overall employee retention – attract and retain the right people to deliver Group strategy, maintaining employee retention at or above industry average (81.7%) | **82%** | 81% |
| **Creating extensive infrastructure** | Continue to grow our infrastructure of business centres to meet the needs of our growing business | **52 business centres: Onshore 46 Nearshore 4 Offshore 2** | 47 business centres: Onshore 42 Nearshore 3 Offshore 2 |
| | Extend our offshore capability – have at least 10% of our people based in India by 2009 | **3%** | 1.6% |
| **Using ICT and innovation to add value** | Generate economies of scale by maximising use and growing number of shared technology platforms | **11 shared platforms** | 9 shared platforms |
| **Ensuring effective procurement** | Monitor and build relationships with key strategic suppliers through our Supplier Development Programme | **Introduced comprehensive Supplier Development Programme** | – |
| | Continue to audit all existing suppliers against Capita's standards of business – 50% of all suppliers to be audited by December 2007 | **Supplier audit commenced – targets set** | Supplier profiling project undertaken |

## *Principal risks and uncertainties*

**2.138** The OFR should include a description of the principal risks and uncertainties facing the entity, together with a commentary on the directors' approach to them. [RS (OFR) para 52].

**2.139** It is important that companies distinguish their principal risks and uncertainties rather than listing all possible risks without highlighting to the reader which are the most important in assessing the potential success of the company's strategy.

**2.140**  The example in Table 2.28 clearly illustrates four principal risks and uncertainties, providing further commentary on them elsewhere.

---

**Table 2.28 – Principal risks and uncertainties**

**Rentokil Initial plc – Annual Report – 31 December 2006**

**A Letter from the Chairman & CEO (extract)**

The principal risks and uncertainties relating to our strategy are summarised below and discussed at greater length in the relevant parts of this review.
- Disruption in the businesses undergoing extensive organisational change.
- Ensuring acquisitions are integrated properly and meet the investment case.
- Resolving the challenges in the Textiles and Washroom Services division in some of its continental European markets.
- Retaining the management team.

---

**2.140.1**  Significant risks and uncertainties include both financial risks and non-financial risks. Indeed the two types are often indistinguishable because non-financial risk, such as the risk that a product may be faulty, may have serious financial consequences, such as the cost of withdrawing the product, penalties on long-term contracts, damage to the entity's reputation and so on. Other non-financial risks, which are increasingly referred to, reflect trends in consumer and social behaviour and potential regulatory actions. Examples include the health hazards of cigarettes, obesity risk and possible health risks from the use of mobile phones. Product risk is, therefore, often significant.

**2.141**  Entities should disclose the strategic, commercial, operational and financial risks where these may significantly affect the entity's strategies and development of the entity's value. [RS (OFR) para 53]. Specific risks facing entities will vary according to the nature of the business, but some risks, such as reputational risks, will be common to all. [RS (OFR) para 54]. Description of the principal risks should cover both exposures to negative consequences as well as potential opportunities. The directors' policy for managing principal risks should also be disclosed. [RS (OFR) para 55]. The OFR should cover the principal risks and uncertainties necessary to understand the business' objectives and strategy both where they constitute a significant external risk to the entity and where the entity's impact on other parties through its activities, products or services, affects its performance. Directors will need to consider the full range of business risks. [RS (OFR) para 56].

**2.142**  Table 2.29 illustrates a company reporting its key external and internal risks, encompassing strategic and commercial areas such as its business environment, operational issues such as customer service and financial risks such as diversifying revenue sources. Management also explains the actions the company is taking to manage the six principal risks, four of which are shown in Table 2.29.

**Table 2.29 – Principal risks and uncertainties**

**Reuters Group PLC – Annual Report and Form 20-F – 31 December 2006**

**Business review (extract)**

Our 'risk radar', reviewed by the Board, captures key external and internal risks that could affect Reuters ability to reach its full potential and the actions and plans in place to mitigate them.

| Risk | Inpact | Action |
|------|--------|--------|
| Financial markets are cyclical. | Downturn in the financial markets could make it more difficult for us to achieve our financial goals. | • Diversify revenues through emphasis on Core Plus.<br>• Prioritise initiatives that help customers achieve greater efficiency through business automation.<br><br>See 'Strategy' on pages 44–45; 'Enterprise division' on page 61. |
| The financial services industry is undergoing rapid structural and regulatory evolution. | We need to keep pace with structural changes if we are to maintain a strong market position. | • Continue to develop Core Plus electronic trading initiatives.<br>• Implement services which address MiFID and Reg NMS requirements.<br>• Monitor industry shifts closely.<br>• Engage with customers' strategies and ensure our own strategy remains aligned with theirs.<br>• Launch FXMarketSpace with CME.<br>• Experiment with new business models within our Innovation portfolio.<br><br>See 'Markets' on pages 45–47; 'Divisional performance' on pages 58–62; 'Strategy' on pages 44–45. |
| The integrity of our reputation is key to our ability to remain a trusted source of news and information. | We need to protect our brand in order to sustain our credibility as a neutral supplier of content. | • Set appropriate 'tone at the top' from senior management.<br>• Provide training on ethics and Reuters Trust Principles.<br>• Enforce clear accountability.<br>• Ensure regular Board review.<br><br>See 'Corporate governance' on pages 22–23; 'Our commitment to ethics and compliance' on pages 48–49; 'People' on pages 47–48. |

| Our customers demand high levels of service to help them perform effectively. | We need to anticipate and respond to our customers' needs if we are to improve our competitiveness. | • Measure and monitor service levels. <br> • Execute service improvement and content quality plans. <br> • Continue to promote a service-driven culture. <br> • Complete investments in data centre and capacity improvements. <br><br> See 'Strategy' on pages 44–45; 'People' on pages 47–48. |
|---|---|---|

**2.143** Table 2.30 is an example of a company quantifying its risks in a graphical format, to indicate the relationship between likelihood and impact. It also specifically assigns accountability to individual directors for managing each risk, sets targets for risk mitigation and monitors progress against these. Disclosure is also made of risks additional to the small group identified as key risks.

**Table 2.30 – Risk mitigation and quantification**

**Speedy Hire plc – Annual Report and Accounts – 30 June 2007**

**Corporate governance (extract)**

**Risk map**

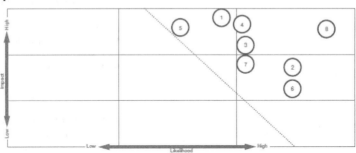

The table below summarises the small group of risks that were identified as key, together with a short description of monitoring/mitigation activities and sponsorship at Board level.

| Risk no. | Risk area | Board Sponsor | Risk monitoring/ mitigation | Progress 06/07 & target 07/08 |
|---|---|---|---|---|
| 1 | IT/business | Neil O'Brien | Detailed testing and phased, budgeted roll-out. Ongoing internal audit implementation review. Weekly call on project performance. | Third company going live. Roll-out phase to be implemented during 2007/8. Project risk analysis to be monitored on a regular basis. |
| 2 | Effective communication | Steve Corcoran | One Speedy initiative. Full review of internal/ external marketing structures and strategies. | Feedback from staff on internal communication programme to be sought. Major risks to |

| | | | | the One Speedy initiative to be identified and managed. |
|---|---|---|---|---|
| 3 | Business co-ordination | Steve Corcoran | Implementation by Executive Management Team. Sales training and in-house marketing. | Improved cross-selling through training. |
| 4 | Major acquisition: risk of poor performance | Mike McGrath | Consideration of project impact as part of all major acquisition programmes. Monitoring of performance against integration plan with reporting to the Board. | Ongoing review of impact on Senior Management resources/time. |
| 5 | Major acquisition integration | Mike McGrath | Documented procedures, with alignment of deal and integration teams. Formal review and reporting to the Board following the acquisition. | Continue to monitor and manage existing controls. |
| 6 | Employee training and development | Mike McGrath | Training and development plans in place, supported by internal communication programme. | Joint venture entered into with the leading training provider Carter & Carter. Mandatory training line to support current standard operating procedures. |
| 7 | Market competition | Neil O'Brien | Market developments continuously monitored and reported monthly to the Board. | Continue to monitor and manage existing controls. |
| 8 | Co-ordination/implementation of key strategic projects | All | Phased strategic projects, monitored by Strategy Steering Committee and overseen by CEO. | Implement key findings of integration project. Undertake talent review against strategic growth plans. |

Other risks which do not feature on the above table nevertheless are regularly reviewed. For example:

1    The Board's belief is that the outlook for the construction industry remains strong (see Stratton report and OFR).
2    The Group is aware of the risk of product obsolescence and mitigates this by continually monitoring developments in technology relevant to the industry and discussing customers' needs with its suppliers.
3    The Board is also conscious of the potential for the expansion of off-site construction reducing the demand for hired tools to site. However, this is perceived to be a medium to long-term risk.

**2.144** Management should disclose uncertainties as well as risks. These may include contingent liabilities relating to specific operational uncertainties, such as outstanding litigation; or market uncertainty, for example whether a new product will be successful. There are also inherent uncertainties that surround the preparation of the financial statements, which may require significant estimates and judgements. These may be referred to in the description of risk factors, but are more often dealt with in the description of critical accounting policies. Disclosure of critical accounting policies is addressed below under 'Accounting policies'. In addition, IAS 1 requires disclosure in the financial statements of significant judgements made by directors and of key sources of estimation uncertainty. [IAS 1 paras 113 and 116].

**2.145** As well as the recommendation in the reporting statement to disclose risks and uncertainties, including financial risks, IAS 32 and IFRS 7 and FRS 25 and FRS 29 (the UK equivalents) all require such disclosure for financial policies and risks. IAS 32, for example, requires an entity to *"describe its financial risk management objectives and policies, including its policy for hedging each main type of forecast transaction for which hedge accounting is used"*. [IAS 32 para 56]. Chapter 6 of the 'Manual of Accounting: IFRS for the UK' deals with disclosures under IAS 32 and IFRS 7.

### Relationships

**2.146** Information should be included in the OFR about significant relationships with stakeholders other than members, where they are likely to influence, directly or indirectly, the business performance and its value. This information should be given to the extent necessary to enable members to assess the entity's strategies and their potential to succeed. [RS (OFR) para 57].

**2.147** Stakeholders other than members may include customers, suppliers, employees, contractors, lenders, creditors, regulators and tax authorities. They may also include the community in which the entity operates and society generally, as well as those entities with which the entity has strategic alliances. [RS (OFR) para 58].

**2.148** The types of significant relationships that may be appropriate to disclose include:

■ Customers – this may include management of customer service, details of losses or gains of customers, in particular those on which the company has a degree of reliance, and of new business developments with customers.

■ Suppliers – including management of procurement activities, ability to source appropriate suppliers, consideration of raw material availability and prices, vetting of supplier behaviour and policy regarding child labour, fair wages etc.

- Employees – including satisfaction surveys, recruitment and retention, training and development, diversity, health and safety, employee communications, productivity, human rights, ethical trading.

- Impact on society and communities – including environmental impact (for example, noise, pollution, waste), product safety, product responsibility, charitable donations and community projects.

- Lenders and creditors – for example, negotiations of credit facilities and other arrangements with lenders, impact of macro-economic factors on availability of credit.

- Regulators – for example licences to operate, pricing restrictions, tax negotiations, government discussions on legislation impacting the company.

- Strategic alliances – such as joint ventures, sub-contractors, franchises.

**2.149** The reporting statement notes that in deciding what should be included in the OFR, directors will need to take a broad view in determining the extent to which the actions of stakeholders other than members may affect the entity's performance and value. [RS (OFR) para 58]. Each of the examples of relationships set out in the previous paragraph may impact the company more or less depending on its circumstances. The following paragraphs highlight just a few of these. Management should decide which are important to them and explain how managing those relationships contributes to the potential future success of their strategies.

**2.150** The example in Table 2.31 illustrates how customer relationships pose a key risk to the strategy of Cadbury Schweppes plc.

---

**Table 2.31 – Relationships – customers**

**Cadbury Schweppes – Annual Report and Accounts – 31 December 2007**

**Consumer demand**

Consumer demand for the Group's products may be affected by factors including changes to consumer preferences, unseasonable or unusual weather, or longer-term climatic changes. The Group has made substantial investments in understanding consumer preferences and in its ability to respond to consumer needs through innovation, and also has products appealing to a wide range of consumers. However, it may be unable to respond successfully or at reasonable cost to rapid changes in demand or consumer preferences, which may adversely affect its performance.

---

**2.151** A major change in the customer base may have a significant effect on the business, because the extent and direction of operations may have to be materially curtailed or expanded and the entity's strategy may have to be modified to meet changed circumstances.

**2.152** Table 2.33 illustrates management's efforts to manage relations with its employees, including the values underpinning the relationship and the ways in which it engages its workforce.

**Table 2.33 – Relationships – employees**

**Alfred McAlpine plc – Annual Report and Accounts – 31 December 2006**

**Business review (extract)**

**People**

Our employee strategy remains focused on supporting delivery and customer service, through a motivated and engaged workforce. The key differentiator in the service we provide to our customers is the quality and motivation of our employees. This is visibly demonstrated through their performance: through productivity, quality, safety and customer service.

To achieve a motivated and engaged workforce, we support our employees through excellent leadership, skilled management, investment in development and training, involvement through inclusive consultation and innovative internal communications as well as a reward package that motivates and supports them.

In addition, we utilise our HR, time management, routing and knowledge management systems to ensure that we provide our customers with the right person, with the right skills and motivation, at the right location, at the right time, with all the knowledge of the Company at their disposal.

**Culture and values**

We believe that a positive culture is essential to high-quality customer service. Our values of winning, passion, honesty, collaboration and enjoyment have to be reflected in all our practices and procedures. Our reputation has been built on our people and we believe that employees whose behaviours reflect our values deliver excellent customer service.

The five values are:

**Winning** Alfred McAlpine values winners – people who want to create success for themselves, their company, and their customers; people with real commitment.

**Passion** Superior performance is born out of passion. Alfred McAlpine values people who are passionate about their work and about doing the very best job for their customers.

**Honesty** Alfred McAlpine demands honesty – honesty in dealing with each other and honesty in dealing with all external stakeholders.

**Collaboration** The Company values people who work openly and productively with each other, clients and partners – people who listen, people who explore new ideas and create new value.

**Enjoyment** The Company values job satisfaction. People who enjoy what they do put more in – and get more out.

**Achieving an engaged workforce**

**Leadership**

Motivated employees require great leaders and we have continued to focus on facilitating and nurturing leadership. We have established talent management programmes covering the majority of our management team and these provide both awareness of those who will benefit from accelerated development and, more importantly, focus the development needs of participants. Our 360 degree feedback process, our performance management and our employee survey all give us insight into the behaviour of our leaders. Our employee survey demonstrates that the improvements are visible to our employees.

**Training and development**

We run a series of training and development programmes operating across the core businesses which ensure that we obtain maximum value from our employees by helping them reach their full potential.

When asked through the MORI survey whether employees felt they had a clear career path, MORI recorded the highest score that they have recorded for any company.

**Employee forums and consultation**
We consult employees and listen to their feedback through the annual employee survey and a regular employee forum in each Business Stream. We also publish a range of internal magazines and newsletters across the Group and use web-based knowledge management systems. We also hold regular team briefings and toolbox talks.

**2.153**   There are many ways in which an entity's operations may affect the community in which it operates. How the entity interacts with society generally and those who are affected by its operations, has a significant effect on its reputation and, consequently, on its business performance. The non-financial matters range widely, from the 'big issues', such as ethical trading, human rights and environment, to the smaller but valuable involvement in the community through, for example, donations and secondments of employees to charities and help given to aid organisations dealing with natural disasters. The example shown in Table 2.34 illustrates the company's approach to managing its environmental and social impacts.

Table 2.34 – Relationships – society

Royal Dutch Shell plc – Annual Report and Form 20-F – 31 December 2006

OPERATING AND FINANCIAL REVIEW (extract)

Environment and society

**INTRODUCTION**
We recognise that our continuing business success depends on finding environmentally and socially responsible ways to help meet the world's growing energy needs. Managing today's business risks, delivering our strategy and achieving our goals all critically require maintaining the trust of a wide range of stakeholders. To keep the trust of stakeholders, we must do many things, including: behaving with integrity at all times, in line with the Shell General Business Principles (Business Principles); operating our facilities safely; being a good neighbour; contributing to development in the societies where we operate; and helping to find effective solutions to the problem of growing $CO_2$ emissions. In this section we discuss our overall approach to managing environmental and social impacts, how we are addressing our main risks and opportunities and our performance in this area in 2006.

**OUR APPROACH TO MANAGING ENVIRONMENTAL AND SOCIAL IMPACTS**
We take a systematic approach to managing environmental and social impacts as part of the Shell Control Framework, through a combination of Group wide standards and processes, controls, incentives and our governance. In 2006, we took additional steps to clarify what we expect from staff, and how to increase their skills, and share our knowledge better around the Group.

**STANDARDS AND PROCESSES**
Our Business Principles include our commitment to contribute to sustainable development. This requires balancing short- and long-term interests and integrating economic, environmental and social considerations into business decision-making.

All companies and joint ventures where we have control over operations – for example as majority shareholder or operator – must apply the Business Principles, our new Code of Conduct (Code) launched in 2006, and the rest of the Shell Control Framework. The Business Principles and Code require compliance with all applicable laws and support for human rights. They forbid, among other things, bribery, fraud and anti-competitive behaviour. The commitment to contribute to sustainable development includes engaging with external stakeholders and being a good neighbour. These companies and joint ventures must also apply Shell-wide environmental and social standards. These include the Group Health, Safety and Environment (HSE) policy and commitment, requiring the systematic management of HSE, as well as our standards for animal testing, biodiversity, climate change, environmental management, health management, incident reporting, security, ship quality and our relationship with our people. We require contractors to manage HSE in line with our standards and expect them to follow our Business Principles or equivalent ones by including these expectations in our contract terms and conditions. We also encourage suppliers and ventures where we do not have a controlling interest to adopt and follow equivalent principles and HSE standards. If these contractors, suppliers and ventures cannot meet our expectations within a reasonable timeframe, we are required to review the relationship.

Our Business Principles and standards are reflected in our business processes. For example, they are included in the criteria used to assess investment proposals and in the planning and design of major new projects. All major new investments must include the expected future costs of emitting carbon in their financial calculations. We require an Impact Assessment to be carried out before we begin significant work on a project or at an existing facility. The actions identified must be part of the project's design and operation. All our major refining and chemicals facilities, and upstream operations with potential for high social impact, must also have social performance plans in line with Group guidance. These plans spell out how the operation will manage its social impacts and generate benefits for the local community.

In 2006, our Exploration & Production business clarified and tightened its requirements for identifying and managing environmental and social impacts when developing new projects – particularly at the earliest stages of project design. Experts from the business and central functions now review the top 70 new Exploration & Production prospects for environmental and social risks and opportunities. These include projects still in early concept or design phases.

**CONTROLS AND INCENTIVES**
Following our environmental and social standards is part of the duties of line managers, with support provided by HSE, social performance, security, human resources and finance specialists. Each Shell business is responsible for complying with our requirements and achieving its specific targets in this area.

We monitor compliance through an annual assurance letter process, internal audits and performance appraisals. The assurance letter process requires the relevant senior manager to report to the Chief Executive on the performance of their business or function in following our Business Principles and Group Standards. Results are reported to the Audit Committee of the Board. Sustainable development performance is an important component of appraisals and compensation, as it comprises 20% of the Group Scorecard.

**GOVERNANCE**
The Chief Executive counts sustainable development among his responsibilities. On his behalf, the Corporate Affairs Director chairs the Group Sustainable Development and HSE Executive Committee, which reviews performance and sets priorities, key performance indicators (KPIs) and targets. The Group HSE Function, central Social Performance Management Unit and issues management staff provide the needed challenge and support to our businesses to develop the necessary skills, share lessons learned and deal with issues in a consistent way. The Social Responsibility Committee is one of four committees of the Royal Dutch Shell plc Board. It reviews our policies and performance with respect to our Business Principles, Code of Conduct, HSE policy, and other relevant environmental and social standards, and major issues of public concern. It is composed of three Non-executive Directors, including its chair, Wim Kok, former Prime Minister of the Netherlands.

**2.154** Details should be given of receipts from and returns to shareholders in relation to their shareholdings. This should include a description of distributions, capital raising and repurchases of shares. The information should be given to the extent necessary to give an understanding of the business. [RS (OFR) para 59].

**2.155** An entity's dividend policy can impact which investors are interested in the company, depending on whether they are looking for income growth or capital growth. An example of disclosure of dividend policy is given in Table 2.35.

---

Table 2.35 – Relationships – shareholders

Prudential plc – Annual Report – 31 December 2006

Directors' report: Operating and financial review (extract)
Group overview (extract)

**Dividend per share**
The Board has reviewed its longer-term dividend policy in light of its expectation that the overall operating cash flow of the Group will be positive from 2008.

The directors recommend a final dividend for 2006 of 11.72 pence per share payable on 22 May 2007 to shareholders on the register at the close of business on 13 April 2007. The interim dividend for 2006 was 5.42 pence per share. The total dividend for the year, including the interim dividend and the recommended final dividend, amounts to 17.14 pence per share compared with 16.32 pence per share for 2005, an increase of five per cent. The total cost of dividends in respect of 2006 was £418 million.

The full-year dividend is covered 1.5 times by post-tax IFRS operating profit from continuing operations.

Dividend cover is calculated as operating profit after tax on an IFRS basis, divided by the current year interim dividend plus the proposed final dividend.

The Board will focus on delivering a growing dividend, which will continue to be determined after taking into account the Group's financial flexibility and opportunities to invest in areas of the business offering attractive returns. The Board believes that in the medium term a dividend cover of around two times is appropriate.

---

**2.156** Significant share issues and repurchases affect members' interests as they may dilute those interests or require members to make further investment, for example in a rights issue. The reasons for such changes in capital may include:

- The need for additional finance for acquisitions or for organic expansion of the business.

- Changing the capital structure to one that the directors consider to be more appropriate to the business' needs by increasing capital and using the proceeds to reduce debt or by repurchasing shares and increasing debt.

- Returning capital as part of cash flow management

**2.157** An example of how share buybacks and dividends are used to help achieve strategic objectives, in this case effective cash management, is shown in Table 2.36.

---

**Table 2.36 — Relationships — shareholders**

Imperial Tobacco Group PLC – Annual Report and Accounts – 30 September 2006

Operating and Financial Review (extract)

**Our Strategy**
Our strategy is to create sustainable shareholder value by growing both organically and through acquisitions.

**Our Strategic Objectives**
We actively pursue three primary objectives which underpin our strategy:
* Sales development.
* Cost optimisation and efficiency improvements.
* Effective cash management.

**Total Shareholder Return (extract)**
In the past ten years we have returned more than £2.8 billion to shareholders by way of dividends and share buybacks.

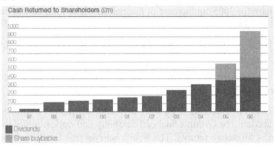

---

## Financial position

**2.158**   The OFR should include an analysis of the entity's financial position. [RS (OFR) para 60].

### *General*

**2.159**   An entity's financial position – for example, plans for future capital expenditure and acquisitions and the robustness of its funding position to achieve those plans – is often contained in a separate section of the OFR, usually called the financial review or the finance director's review. In larger entities with diversified operations, additional financial information may be given elsewhere, for example by dividing the OFR into sections covering each of the main business segments, which describe the operations and financial position of each segment. Even where that form of presentation is adopted, however, there is usually a separate financial review dealing with the group's overall financial position.

**2.160**   The analysis of financial position in the OFR, while based upon the financial statements, should supplement the disclosures required by accounting standards and comment on events that impacted the entity's financial position during the year. This is particularly relevant when a large part of the company operates in an area of economic instability. The analysis should also comment on future factors that are likely to affect the financial position going forward. The reporting statement refers specifically to supplementing disclosures required by FRS 25 (IAS 32) or FRS 29 (IFRS 7). [RS (OFR) para 61]. The use of derivatives and the requirement of the standards to fair value certain types of instrument means that there can be significant volatility in the reported results. Requirements to classify certain instruments and arrangements involving shares as debt, may also have significant effects on the balance sheet presentation. This is why particular emphasis is placed on the need to further explain the entity's policies and practices in the OFR. The guidance contained in chapter 6 of the Manual of Accounting — IFRS for the UK and the Manual of Accounting — UK GAAP may be useful when preparing disclosure in this area.

**2.161**  A number of the measures used to monitor the company's financial position may be directly taken from the financial statements, but directors often supplement these with other measures common to their industry to monitor their progress towards stated objectives. Such disclosure may reflect non-GAAP measures (see paras 2.73 to 2.78) and may include sensitivity analysis, for example in respect of financial instrument values where volatility can have a significant impact on the company's financial position.

**2.162**  Table 2.37 shows how this company supplements the disclosures required by accounting standards with those financial position measures that it uses to manage the business. In particular, it records the significant judgements that are taken in accounting for the company's financial position.

---

Table 2.37 – Financial position

Capital & Regional plc – Annual Report – 30 December 2006

Operating and financial review – Results (extract)

**Balance sheet, debt and hedging**
Balance sheet: we look at our balance sheet in three ways:
- The enterprise balance sheet shows the £6,497 million portfolio we manage, financed by £913 million of shareholder equity and a further £2,288 million of institutional equity invested directly into our funds.
- The see through balance sheet gives our economic exposure to different market segments, and is the one we use for managing the business. It is notable that we have an increasing proportion of our exposure in the German and FIX UK portfolios.
- Our statutory balance sheet follows the accounting rules. Under these rules the three funds and various joint ventures are consolidated on an equity basis. The debt on this balance sheet excludes our share of fund and JV debt.

---

| Three balance sheets | Enterprise £m | See through £m | Statutory £m |
|---|---|---|---|
| Shopping centres | 3,185 | 772 | 398 |
| Retail parks | 1,568 | 430 | 245 |
| Leisure property | 1,252 | 359 | 210 |
| German big box retail | 382 | 359 | 382 |
| FIX UK | 110 | 110 | 110 |
| Total property | 6,497 | 2,030 | 1,345 |
| Working capital | (57) | 21 | 25 |
| Debt | (3,239) | (1,138) | (457) |
| Net assets | 3,201 | 913 | 913 |
| C&R shareholders | 913 | 913 | 913 |
| Fund investors | 2,288 | – | – |
| Total equity | 3,201 | 913 | 913 |
| Loan to value | 50% | 56% | 34% |
| Gearing (debt/equity) | 101% | 125% | 50% |

**Balance sheet judgements:** the key judgements in the balance sheet relate to:

1. Property valuations; all of which are carried out by independent valuers. For 69% of our property exposure held through the three funds, there is a further layer of scrutiny by the Fund Managers, Morley and Hermes.
2. Development provisioning; it often takes some years after a development is completed before all commercial issues are resolved and judgement is therefore needed on the level of provision required for completion costs.
3. Tax provisioning; it normally takes two or more years after each year end for all tax liabilities to be settled with the Inland Revenue. Judgement is needed on the correct level of provision required.

**2.163** The reporting statement also suggests that discussion should focus on future factors that are likely to affect the position going forward. [RS (OFR) para 61]. Forward-looking statements are discussed above from paragraph 2.53.

### Accounting policies

**2.164** The OFR should highlight the entity's critical accounting policies. The critical accounting policies are key to understanding the entity's performance and financial position. The focus should be on those that require the particular exercise of judgement in their application to which the results are most sensitive. Discussion of accounting policies should include changes in accounting policies during the year. [RS (OFR) para 62].

**2.165** Often this disclosure is a lengthy list of detailed accounting policies – similar to those found in risks disclosures. However, the example above in Table 2.37 shows another approach by highlighting the key areas in which judgements that are made in applying accounting policies related to the balance sheet. As with risks, emphasising those accounting policies that are truly key to the company's performance and position can make it easier for investors to understand the context in which those results are presented.

**2.166**  The accounting policies disclosed and discussed will vary from entity to entity and from industry to industry. Critical accounting policies may include the following:

■  Revenue recognition – particularly in assessing revenue and profit to be recognised on long-term contracts and multiple component sales.

■  Impairment – where choice of discount rates and other assumptions can have significant effects on calculations.

■  Taxation – particularly where the entity has international operations and engages in significant tax planning activities.

■  Provisions – certain types of provisions, particularly for long-term environmental obligations require significant judgements and estimates.

■  Pensions – similar to provisions above, but pensions is an area where there is also additional volatility owing to the effects of stock market fluctuations.

■  Intangible assets including goodwill and development expenditure – goodwill and intangibles may comprise a large element of an entity's net assets, particularly in certain industries, such as advertising and publishing. Significant estimates and judgements are often required in assessing recoverability of such intangibles.

**2.166.1**  Although the critical accounting policies should be outlined in the OFR, it may be appropriate to cross-refer to the detailed descriptions contained in the notes to the financial statements.

### *Capital structure and treasury policies*

**2.167**  The OFR should discuss the entity's capital structure and should set out its treasury policies and objectives. [RS (OFR) paras 63, 65].

**2.168**  This could include:

■  Type of capital instruments used.

■  Balance between equity and debt.

■  Regulatory capital.

■  Maturity profile of debt.

■  Currency.

■  Interest rate structure.

**2.169**  The discussion should include comments on short-and long-term funding plans to support the directors' strategies to achieve the entity's objectives. In addition, the discussion should comment on why the entity has adopted its particular capital structure.

**2.170** For many listed companies, this section of the OFR could be relatively complex. Discussion may include reference to inter-linking issues. For example, a discussion could:

- Start with a description of the gearing and capital structure at the beginning of the year.

- Observe that the gearing level was lower or higher than normal.

- Discuss the capital expenditure plans.

- Explain that ten year debt was raised to finance that expenditure.

- Explain that long-term debt was raised because the investment was in long-term assets, but also acknowledge that:

  - The group was overly reliant on short-term debt.

  - The group wanted to take advantage of the historically low rate of interest on long-term debt.

Finally, this could lead to a discussion of the group's policy regarding fixed or floating rate finance. If interest rate swaps had been taken out as part of this policy, this fact could be explained.

**2.171** In another example, a group might have overseas subsidiaries and may have changed the way in which these subsidiaries are financed. For example, the discussion could deal with the opening position, which might be that all funding was in sterling, and explain that the directors had decided during the year that, particularly in the light of their ambitions for overseas expansion, this gave rise to unduly high exchange rate exposure. The discussion could add that the directors had, therefore, decided to finance the overseas operations by a mixture of US dollar and euro borrowings. Alternatively, it might be explained that the group had retained its sterling borrowings, but taken out derivative contracts to hedge the overseas investments.

**2.171.1** An example of disclosure relating to capital structure and treasury policy is provided in Table 2.38. This example also shows the group's market capitalisation and the highs and lows of the share price during the year. This information is commonly given by entities as part of the financial review as it enables members to assess the market's view of the entity's value at the end of, and during, the year.

Table 2.38 – Capital structure and treasury policy

Hilton Group plc – Report and Accounts – 31 December 2004

**Capital structure and treasury policy**

**Financial risk management**

The Group's treasury function provides a centralised service for the provision of finance and the management and control of liquidity, foreign exchange and interest rates. The function operates as a cost centre and manages the Group's treasury exposures to reduce risk in accordance with policies approved by the Board.

Derivative financial instruments, such as spot and forward foreign exchange contracts, currency swaps and interest rate swaps, are used to assist in the management of the Group's financial risk. These instruments are also used, where appropriate, to generate the desired effective currency and interest rate profile. It is not the policy of the Group to trade in or enter into speculative transactions.

Group operations are primarily financed from retained earnings, bank borrowings and long-term loans. Debt is principally raised centrally by the group finance company and then lent on to operating subsidiaries on commercial terms.

In addition to the primary financial instruments mentioned above, the Group also has other financial instruments, such as trade debtors, trade creditors, accruals and prepayments, that arise directly from the Group's operations.

The Group has a £2 billion Euro Medium Term Note (EMTN) programme, which is used to increase the flexibility of funding with regards to source, cost, size and maturity. As at 31 December 2004, three public Eurobond issues had been made under this programme – a £175 million 7.25% bond, maturing July 2008; a E500 million 6.5% bond, maturing July 2009; and a £250 million 7.125% bond, maturing July 2012. Several private placements have been issued under the programme in a variety of currencies. As at 31 December 2004, these private placements had an equivalent value of £36.8 million. Funds raised via the EMTN programme have been used to repay bank debt.

In October 2003, the Group issued £300 million 3.375% convertible bonds, maturing 2010. The bonds were issued by a subsidiary company and are convertible into exchangeable redeemable preference shares of the issuer, which are guaranteed by, and exchangeable for ordinary shares of, Hilton Group plc.

The main risks managed by the Group's treasury function are interest rate risk, liquidity risk, currency risk and credit risk. The Board reviews and agrees policies for each of these risks as summarised below. Note 20 to the accounts provides further disclosures with regard to these risks.

**Interest rate risk** The Group's exposure to interest rate fluctuations on its borrowings and deposits is managed by using various interest related derivatives, primarily interest rate swaps. The Group borrows in several currencies and operates a policy of fixing the interest rate of at least 25% of core debt for more than 12 months. Non-core debt and cash are kept at short-term interest rates. At 31 December 2004, after taking account of interest rate swaps, the proportion of the Group's gross borrowings at fixed rates was 40% (2003: 44%) fixed for a weighted average period of 2.7 years (2003: 3.2 years). The annual average interest rate on fixed rate debt was 5.2% (2003: 5.4%).

**Liquidity risk** The Group aims to maintain a balance between continuity and flexibility of funding through the use of borrowings with a range of maturities. The Group's policy on liquidity is to ensure that there is sufficient medium and long-term committed borrowing facilities to meet the medium-term funding requirements. At 31 December 2004, there were undrawn committed borrowing facilities of £341.4 million (2003: £588.9 million). Total committed facilities had an average maturity of 4.5 years (2003: 4.5 years)

**Currency risk** Due to the international nature of its core activities, the Group's reported profits, net assets and gearing are all affected by foreign exchange rate movements. The Group seeks to mitigate the effect of any structural currency exposure that may arise from the translation of the foreign currency assets by borrowing in foreign currencies to match at least 75% of the foreign currency assets. At 31 December 2004, foreign currency borrowings represented 93% (2003: 96%) of the net carrying value of foreign currency assets.

Although the Group carries out operations through a number of foreign enterprises, Group exposure to currency risk at a transactional level is minimal. The day to day transactions of overseas subsidiaries are carried out in local currency.

**Credit risk** Counterparty risk arises from the investment of surplus funds and from the use of derivative instruments. This risk is managed by restricting those transactions to banks that have a defined minimum credit rating and to limit the exposure to a maximum per bank. All derivative transactions are executed under agreements conforming to the International Swaps and Derivatives Association (ISDA) standards.

**Share price and market capitalisation**
The closing share price of the Group on 31 December 2004 was 284.50 pence (2003: 224.75 pence) and market capitalisation of the Group was £4.51 billion (2003: £3.56 billion). The high and low prices during the year were 285.25 pence and 214.50 pence respectively.

**Going concern**
The directors consider the Group has adequate resources to continue in operational existence for the foreseeable future and that it is therefore appropriate to adopt the going concern basis in preparing the financial statements.

## Cash flows

**2.172** The OFR should discuss the cash inflows and outflows during the financial year, together with the entity's ability to generate cash, to meet known or probable cash requirements and to fund growth. [RS (OFR) para 68].

**2.173** The discussion should supplement the information in the financial statements around operating, investing and financing cash flows. [RS (OFR) para 69]. Specific commentary should be given on cash flows by segment where this is different from profit by segment. [RS (OFR) para 70]. This would be relevant, for example, in a long-term contracting business where the agreed timing of billings and cash receipts is out of line with profit recognition.

**2.174** The OFR should comment on any special factors that have influenced cash flows in the period and that may have a significant effect on future cash flows. This could include the existence and timing of commitments for capital expenditure and other known or probable cash requirements. [RS (OFR) para 69]. An example of the latter might be the need to repay a large tranche of debt at a particular date in the future. Unusual or non-recurring cash flows should be highlighted where material, such as proceeds of a sale and leaseback or the termination of an interest rate swap.

**2.175** Where an entity has cash that is surplus to its future operating requirements and its current levels of distributions to members, the OFR should discuss the entity's plans for making use of the cash. [RS (OFR) para 69]. Table 2.35 above indicates an example of a company reporting on its use of surplus cash.

**2.176** For many users of financial statements cash flow is a key measure of performance and entities often develop KPIs that relate to cash flow. Some measures focus on cash flow from operations after meeting the entity's obligations for interest, tax and dividends and after capital expenditure, which is sometimes termed 'free cash flow'. However, definitions of 'free cash flow' (a non-GAAP measure) often vary from entity to entity and should, therefore, be fully explained. An example of disclosure of free cash flow is provided in Table 2.40, together with a reconciliation from the GAAP measures of cash flow.

---

**Table 2.40 – Free cash flow**

**Lonmin Plc – Annual Report – 30 September 2006**

**Free cash flow**

We believe that a key metric of how successful we are as a business is ultimately the amount of cash we produce. We measure this by looking at our free cash flow. We define our free cash flow as cash flow from operations less interest and tax paid, less net capital expenditure and less dividends paid to our minority. We believe this measure indicates what cash we have which is free to fund equity dividends or make returns to shareholders, to pay down debt or to make discretionary investments.

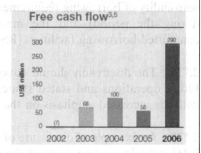

Free cash flow[3,5]

Financials for the year 2002 to 2004 are as prepared under UK GAAP. For 2005 and 2006 the financials are prepared under IFRS. Details of the nature of the changes under IFRS can be found in Note 35 to the Accounts in the Annual Report.

**Cash flow**

The following table summarises the main components of the cash flow during the year:

| | 2006 Total $m | 2005 Total $m |
|---|---|---|
| Cash flow from operations | **722** | 377 |
| Interest and finance costs | **(31)** | (27) |
| Tax | **(185)** | (79) |
| Trading cash flow | **506** | 271 |
| Capital expenditure | **(182)** | (190) |
| Proceeds from disposal of assets held for sale | **28** | - |
| Dividends received from associate | **-** | 2 |
| Dividends paid to minority | **(62)** | (27) |
| Free cash flow | **290** | 56 |
| Acquisitions* | **(14)** | (212) |

---

*Operating and financial review*

| | | |
|---|---:|---:|
| Financial investments | **(36)** | 1 |
| Shares issued | **15** | 6 |
| Equity dividends paid | **(124)** | (102) |
| Cash inflow/outflow | **131** | (251) |
| Opening net debt | **(585)** | (272) |
| Exchange | **(4)** | (2) |
| Net debt in subsidiaries acquired | **-** | (60) |
| Closing net debt | **(458)** | (585) |
| Trading cash flow (cents per share) | **354.9c** | 191.2c |
| Free cash flow (cents per share) | **203.4c** | 39.5c |

\* 2005 comparative includes $15 million on intangible non-current assets acquired in 2005.

## *Liquidity*

**2.177**   The OFR should discuss the entity's current and prospective liquidity. This should include, where relevant, a commentary on the level of borrowings, the seasonality of borrowing requirements (indicated by the peak level of borrowings during the period) and the maturity profile of borrowings and undrawn committed borrowing facilities. [RS (OFR) para 73].

**2.178**   The discussion should cover the entity's ability to fund its current and future operations and stated strategies. [RS (OFR) para 72]. This is consistent with the increased emphasis on the need for a forward-looking orientation.

**2.179**   An example of disclosure of current and future liquidity is shown in Table 2.41, including explanations of the impact of the seasonality of its business.

---

**Table 2.41 – Liquidity**

**Signet Group plc – Annual Report and Accounts – 53 weeks ended 3 February 2007**

**Financial review (extract)**

**Liquidity and capital resources**
It is the objective of the Group to maintain a strong balance sheet, after implementing its 8% – 10% new store space growth strategy in the US, the continuing programme of store refurbishments and relocations on both sides of the Atlantic, payment of dividends, and any repurchase of shares. Factors which could affect this objective would be the acquisition of a business or a change in the Group's distribution policy to shareholders or if there was a variation in the operating performance of the Group.

The cash flow performance of the Group depends on a number of factors, such as the:

- operating performance of the business;
- rate of space expansion, which influences both fixed and working capital investment;
- level of store refurbishment and relocations;
- level of inventory investment; and
- proportion of US sales made on the in-house credit card and the average monthly collection rate of the credit balances.

---

Investment in new space requires significant investment in working capital, as well as fixed capital investment, due to the slow inventory turn, and the additional investment required to fund sales in the US utilising the in-house credit card.

In years when the rate of new store space expansion in the US is towards the lower end of the planned 8% – 10% range, or the level of store refurbishment and relocation is below normal, the Group will have reduced levels of investment in fixed and working capital. In 2006/07 a faster rate of new store space growth in the US, and increased dividend payments, more than offset a lower level of refurbishment in the UK and meant that there was a cash outflow of £16.3 million (2005/06: £6.7 million) before the repurchase of shares amounting to £33.7 million (2005/06: £2.0 million) and proceeds from the issue of shares of £4.1 million (2005/06: £3.9 million).

The Group's working capital requirements fluctuate during the year as a result of the seasonal nature of its business. As inventory is purchased for the Christmas season there is a working capital outflow which reaches its highest levels in late autumn. This position then reverses over the key selling period of November and December. The working capital needs of the business are then relatively stable from January to August. The rough diamond sourcing initiative will require the Group to hold an element of its inventory for approximately an additional 60 days. The timing of the payment of the final dividend, normally in July, is also material to working capital requirements during the year.

**2.180** Beyond information on liquidity, our research has shown that investors also want a clear picture of a company's debt position in order to understand management's plans for servicing it and any risks associated with it. Companies have to give information about how they are funded, but this can be scattered throughout the annual report – both in the OFR and in the financial statements. In addition, some of the information relating to debt is not provided in the annual report at all, investors get the information outside the regulatory model.

**2.181** The problem of determining a company's credit risk profile is even greater if it has a number of subsidiaries. In this case, investors need a clear debt profile of the group and its individual business units, as well as an understanding of any restrictions on the transfer of funds between business units. Such internal sources of liquidity should be discussed. If there are restrictions on the group's ability to transfer funds from one part of the group to meet the obligations of another part of the group – for example as a result of exchange controls or tax consequences of transfers – this should be discussed. This applies where the restrictions *"...represent, or might foreseeably come to represent..."* a significant restraint on the group. [RS (OFR) para 73]. The restrictions could be in the form of legal barriers, such as exchange controls, that preclude or limit repatriation of profits, or they could be commercial obstacles, such as where funds could be repatriated, but unduly high rates of withholding or other taxes would have to be paid.

**2.182** Investors' view of debt does not stop at financial instruments or borrowings. They want to know about other debt-like liabilities. These could include revenues paid in advance by customers, operating leases, pensions, or other liabilities such as decommissioning costs that could trigger major cash outflows in the future.

**2.183** We suggest that companies should include an analysis of net debt that incorporates financial debt, operating debt in off balance sheet leases and other debt-like liabilities. Although not a requirement, investors have indicated that they value such disclosure. Investors believe all instruments that the company views as debt should be incorporated in this statement, including instruments that accounting standards classify as equity. By the same token, instruments classified by accounting standards as debt, but which the company sees as equity, should be excluded. A comprehensive maturity table of all components, analysis by currency and by subsidiary and details of any collateral or other restrictions are also highly desirable to investors.

**2.184** Examples of such financing net debt analyses are becoming more common amongst UK companies – most often within the notes to the financial statements. Table 2.42 shows a company that has included a separate 'analysis of net debt' after its 'consolidated cash flow statement' and cross references to other financial statement notes for further details of maturities, etc.

---

**Table 2.42 – Analysis of net debt**

**Home Retail Group plc – Annual Report & Financial Statements – 3 March 2007**

**Consolidated Cash Flow Statement (extract)**

**Analysis of Net Debt**
For the short period 1 April 2006 to 3 March 2007

| *Non-GAAP Measures* | *Notes* | *2007*<br>*£m* |
|---|---|---|
| **Financing net debt:** | | |
| Cash at bank and in hand | 21 | 283.8 |
| Loans and borrowings | 23 | (223.6) |
| **Total financing net debt** | | 60.2 |
| **Operating net debt:** | | |
| Property leases | | (2,920.1) |
| **Total operating net debt** | | (2,920.1) |
| **Total net debt** | | (2,859.9) |
| Deduct: | | |
| Operating leases that are off balance sheet | | 2,920.1 |
| **Total net debt reflected in balance sheet** | | 60.2 |

The Group uses the term net debt which provides the Group's aggregate net indebtedness to banks and other financial institutions together with debt-like liabilities, notably property leases.

The capitalised value of these property leases is £2,920.1m (2006: £2,795.0m) based upon discounting the current rentals at the estimated current long term cost of borrowing of 5.4%.

The analysis of net debt has not been provided for the prior year, as it is non comparable given the demerger of the Group from GUS plc in 2006.

---

**2.185** Table 2.43 illustrates a company that views its pension deficit as being 'debt-like' in nature and reports on it as such in the OFR.

Table 2.43 – Identification of 'debt-like' liabilities

Tomkins Group plc – Annual Report – 30 December 2006

Operating and Financial Review (extract)

Funding policy

The Group remains committed to funding pensions responsibly. In the UK, this means satisfying the funding agreements made with the trustees of the schemes in order to eliminate deficits over a reasonable period of time. In the US, funding objectives generally seek to avoid Pension Benefit Guaranty Corporation variable rate premiums and accelerated funding charges mandated by the Employee Retirement Income Security Act of 1974 ("ERISA"), and remain above the ERISA required minimum funding levels. Accordingly, most of the US plans are funded on the basis of reaching or exceeding a 90% funded level on a current liability basis.

The Pension Protection Act of 2006 will impact the rate at which the deficit of the US plans is eliminated, with deficits generally required to be eliminated over a period of seven years from the 2008 plan year. Tomkins is assessing the impact of the funding provisions of The Pension Protection Act and will adapt its funding policy accordingly.

Tomkins recognises its responsibility to fund defined benefit pension plan deficits and views these deficits as being debt-like in nature. Accordingly, where beneficial, Tomkins plc issues guarantees in respect of certain UK defined benefit pension plan deficits in order to improve the credit standing of these plans. This also has the effect of minimising the cost of the Pension Protection Fund's risk-based levy.

**2.185.1** Another example of disclosure of current and future liquidity is shown in Table 2.43A. This example also gives details of cash flows and of funding, such as operating leases that are not treated as debt.

Table 2.43A – Current and future liquidity

Tate & Lyle PLC – Report and Accounts – 31 March 2004

Cash Flow and Balance Sheet

Cash flow and debt

Operating cash flow totalled £289 million compared with £323 million in the previous year. There was an operating working capital outflow of £31 million (2003 – £6 million outflow). Contributions to the Group's pension funds, both regular and supplementary, reduced from £61 million in the previous year to £34 million. A net £115 million (2003 – £97 million) was paid to providers of finance as dividends and interest. Net taxation paid increased from £7 million, which included a number of refunds, to £74 million, reflecting higher payments in the UK and North America.

Plant replacement, improvement and expansion expenditure of £118 million was above depreciation of £106 million. Investment expenditure was £26 million, being primarily an investment of £15 million in the astaxanthin joint venture and an injection of funds into the Tate & Lyle Employee Benefit Trust which purchases shares to satisfy options granted under the Executive Share Option Scheme. Disposals of fixed assets and businesses generated cash of £63 million. Exchange translation, and other non-cash movements, reduced net debt by £64 million.

The Group's net borrowings fell from £471 million to £388 million.

The ratio of net borrowings to earnings before exceptional items and before interest, tax, depreciation and goodwill amortisation (EBITDA) improved from 1.4 times to 1.2 times and the gearing ratio reduced to 38% at 31 March 2004 (2003 – 45%). During the year net debt peaked at £498 million in April 2003 (April 2002 during the year ended 31 March 2003 – £605 million).

**Funding and liquidity management**
The Group funds its operations through a mixture of retained earnings and borrowing facilities, including capital markets and bank borrowings.

In order to ensure maximum flexibility in meeting changing business needs the Group seeks to maintain access to a wide range of funding sources. Capital markets borrowings include the €300 million 5.75% bond maturing in 2006, the €150 million Floating Rate Note maturing in 2007 and the £200 million 6.5% bond maturing in 2012. At 31 March 2004 the Group's long-term credit ratings from Moody's and Standard and Poor's were Baa2 and BBB respectively.

The Group ensures that it has sufficient undrawn committed bank facilities to provide liquidity back-up for its US commercial paper and other short-term money market borrowing for the foreseeable future. The Group has committed bank facilities of US$510 million which mature in 2008 with a core of highly rated banks. These facilities are unsecured and contain common financial covenants for Tate & Lyle PLC and its subsidiary companies that the interest cover ratio should not be less than 2.5 times and the ratio of net debt to EBITDA should not be greater than four times. The Group monitors compliance against all its financial obligations and it is Group policy to manage the consolidated balance sheet so as to operate well within covenanted restrictions at all times.

The majority of the Group's borrowings are raised through the Group treasury company and are then on-lent to the business units on an arm's-length basis.

The Group manages its exposure to liquidity risk by ensuring a diversity of funding sources and debt maturities. Group policy is to ensure that, after subtracting the total of undrawn committed facilities, no more than 30% of gross debt matures within 12 months and at least 50% has a maturity of more than two and a half years. At the end of the year, after subtracting total undrawn committed facilities, there was no debt maturing within 12 months and all debt had a maturity of two and a half years or more (2003 – 0% and 100%). The average maturity of the Group's gross debt was 4.9 years (2003 – 5.4 years).

At the year-end the Group held cash and current asset investments of £154 million (2003 – £172 million) and had undrawn committed facilities of £277 million (2003 – £348 million). These resources are maintained to provide liquidity back-up and to meet the projected maximum cash outflow from debt repayment and seasonal working capital needs foreseen for at least a year into the future at any one time.

**Funding not treated as debt**
In respect of all financing transactions, the Group seeks to optimise its financing costs. The following items are not included in net debt under UK accounting conventions.

At Amylum, the Group receives cash from selling amounts receivable from customers. The facility allows the sale of up to US$85 million (£46 million) of receivables, and was fully utilised at both 31 March 2004 and 31 March 2003. Where financially beneficial, operating leases are undertaken in preference to purchasing assets. Commitments under operating leases to pay rentals in future years totalled £180 million (2003 – £209 million) and related primarily to railcar leases in the USA.

Net debt of joint ventures and associates totalling £66 million at 31 March 2004 (2003 – £60 million) is not consolidated in the Group balance sheet. After counter indemnities, £22 million of this debt was subject to recourse to the Group. Tate & Lyle's share of net debt of joint ventures and associates totalled £32 million.

**2.186** Management should disclose when borrowing covenants are in place that restrict the use of financing arrangements or credit facilities and *"...negotiations with the lenders on the operation of these covenants are taking place or are expected to take place"*. The reporting statement also states that *"where a breach of a covenant has occurred or is expected to occur, the OFR should give details of the measures taken or proposed to remedy the situation"*. [RS (OFR) para 74].

**2.186.1** The meaning of the second quote is clear, although there is some judgement involved in addressing whether a breach of covenant is expected to occur. But the meaning of the first quote is clear. It recommends disclosure when negotiations are being held, perhaps to change the covenants, in a situation where there is neither a breach nor any expectation of a breach. An example might be where a covenant is being renegotiated, not because of financial difficulty, but following the introduction of a new accounting standard that alters the ratios without any change in the underlying economic position.

**2.186.2** Take an example where the company's year end borrowings were £450,000, peak borrowings were £550,000 and its facilities were £500,000, that is, it had temporarily exceeded its borrowing facilities and breached its covenants. The RS (OFR)'s recommendation in such circumstances would have the company give details about *"...measures taken or proposed to remedy the situation"*. This could lead to awkward disclosures if the company and its bankers have not agreed what the remedial measures might be. Disclosure in these circumstances is of course exactly what the reporting statement is aiming for and exactly what investors would welcome. An example of disclosure of a breach of covenant is given in Table 2.43B.

---

**Table 2.43B – Breach of covenant**

**Regent Inns plc – Report and Accounts – 3 July 2004**

**Chairman's Statement (extract)**

**Discussions with Banks**

Just prior to the scheduled preliminary results announcement on 14 September 2004, it came to the attention of the Board that the calculation of one of the covenant tests under the banking facility had not been performed in strict accordance with the terms of the facility agreement. As a result we decided to delay the announcement until today to enable us to clarify this issue with our bankers.

On 15 September 2004, we appointed Paul Felton-Smith as Interim Finance Director, and he has led discussions with our lending banks. The Company has now notified its banks that on the basis of the strict application of the agreement, it will, on delivery to them of these financial statements, be in breach of its interest cover covenant and that therefore an event of default will occur. The banks have confirmed that they are supportive of the Company in its current situation and have indicated (whilst reserving their rights) that it is their current intention to enter into negotiations in respect of the facilities with the objective of having in place facilities sufficient for the Group's currently estimated needs. The banks have agreed to waive temporarily the default while they consider the Company's financial position generally. The Board is confident that the negotiations will result in a successful outcome.

---

> **Financial Review (extract)**
>
> **Post Balance Sheet Event**
> As referred to in the Chairman's statement, on 14 September 2004 the Company delayed the preliminary announcement of its results pending clarification of the strict terms of the facility agreement in calculating the interest cover covenant. Subsequently it has been clarified that on the basis of the strict application of the agreement, the Company will, on delivery to the banks of these financial statements, be in breach of its interest cover covenant and that therefore an event of default will occur. However, notwithstanding the above, the banks have indicated (whilst reserving their rights) that it is their current intention to enter the negotiations with the Company with the objective of having in place facilities sufficient for the Group's currently estimated needs. Furthermore, the banks have agreed to waive temporarily the default while they consider the Company's financial position generally.

**2.186.3** FRS 18, 'Accounting policies', and IAS 1, 'Presentation of financial statements', require disclosure (by all companies) of any material uncertainties, of which directors are aware, that may cast significant doubt on the entity's ability to continue as a going concern. [FRS 18 para 61; IAS 1 para 23]. In addition, both IAS 32 and IFRS 7 require disclosures of any defaults and breaches of principal, interest, sinking fund or redemption provisions on loans payable and of any other breaches of loan agreements where the breaches can permit the lender to demand repayment (except where the breaches have remedied before the balance sheet date). [IAS 32 para 94(j), IFRS 7 paras 18, 19].

**2.187** Management should discuss any seasonality in its liquidity position. If the level of borrowings at the year end is not representative of the normal level during the year, this should be disclosed. If the level of cash is unrepresentative of the year as a whole this should also be disclosed. An examples of disclosure of seasonality of borrowings and of cash levels is provided in Table 2.43C.

> **Table 2.43C – Seasonality of cash and borrowings**
>
> **Imperial Chemical Industries plc – Report and Accounts – 31 December 2006**
>
> **Liquidity and investments (extract)**
> The Group's net debt position has historically changed over the course of a year, and, in particular, short-term debt has generally increased in the early part of the year to fund working capital requirements. These working capital needs arise principally from the seasonality of the Paints business, which experiences higher sales of products used on the exterior of buildings, and thus working capital, during the North American and European summer (the second and third quarters of the year). The Group's commercial paper programmes and other short-term borrowings are normally used to fund these working capital fluctuations. At 31 December 2006, the Group had £16m of short-term borrowings outstanding (as shown in note 23 relating to the Group accounts).

### 23 Financial liabilities (extract)

#### (a) Short-term borrowings

| | 2006 £m | 2005 £m | Average interest rate * 2006 £m | 2005 £m |
|---|---|---|---|---|
| **Bank borrowings** | | | | |
| Secured – by floating charge | 3 | – | | |
| Unsecured | 13 | 14 | | |
| | 16 | 14 | 2.6 | 2.5 |
| **Other borrowings** | | | | |
| Unsecured | – | – | | |
| | – | – | – | – |
| | 16 | 14 | | |
| Maximum short-term borrowings outstanding during year | 277 | 455 | | |

\* Based on borrowings outstanding at 31 December.

Various short-term lines of credit, both committed and uncommitted, are available to the Group and are reviewed regularly. There are no facility fees payable on uncommitted lines nor is there a requirement for an equivalent deposit to be maintained with any of the banks.

## Going concern

**2.188**  The FSA's Listing Rules require listed companies to make a statement as part of it corporate governance disclosures that it is a going concern as part of their corporate governance disclosures. [LR 9.8.6R(3)]. Often the required statement is made in the OFR, usually in the financial review section.

**2.189**  Guidance on the form of going concern statement that companies might use was published in November 1994 in a document entitled 'Going concern and financial reporting — guidance for directors of listed companies registered in the UK'. An example of disclosure given in the document was:

> *"After making enquiries, the directors have a reasonable expectation that the company has adequate resources to continue in operational existence for the foreseeable future. For this reason, they continue to adopt the going concern basis in preparing the accounts."*

**2.190**  Most going-concern statements do no more than reproduce with minor variations the suggested wording of the guidance. Table 2.43D shows an example that points out that in the business' particular circumstances, there are a number of fundamental uncertainties in relation to going concern. Details of the uncertainties are further described in the chairman's statement, the notes to the financial statements and are also referred to in the auditors' report.

---

**Table 2.43D – Fundamental uncertainties**

**Jarvis plc – Report and Accounts – 31 March 2004**

**8. Going concern**

After making appropriate enquiries, the Directors have a reasonable expectation that the Company and the Group have adequate resources to continue in operational existence for the foreseeable future. For this reason they continue to adopt the going concern basis in preparing the financial statements. However, Note 1(a) to the financial statements includes a number of fundamental uncertainties which might affect the basis on which the financial statements have been prepared.

---

**[The next paragraph is 2.192]**

# Key performance indicators

**2.192** To the extent necessary to meet the requirements set out in paragraph 2.114 above, the OFR should disclose the key performance indicators (KPIs), both financial and non-financial, used by the directors to assess progress against their stated objectives. [RS (OFR) para 38].

**2.193** Key performance indicators are those the directors judge are effective in measuring the entity's development, performance or position. They are quantified measurements that reflect the entity's critical success factors and disclose progress towards achieving a particular objective or objectives. [RS (OFR) para 3].

**What is key?**

**2.194** The reporting statement does not prescribe specific KPIs that entities should disclose. However, comparability will be enhanced if the KPIs are accepted and widely used, either within an industry sector or more generally. [RS (OFR) para 40]. The performance indicators that are key to a particular company are those that the directors use to manage the business.

**2.195** A challenge is whether the KPIs currently presented to the board are those that allow them to assess progress against stated strategies, and when reported externally, allow readers to make a similar assessment. If not, is this because the information is simply not available or because it is not yet escalated to the board but may instead be assessed by management of individual business units?

**2.196** In addition, the KPIs will to a degree be conditioned by the industry in which a company operates. Comparability will be enhanced if the KPIs are accepted and widely used, either within an industry sector or more generally. [RS (OFR) para 40]. However, management should not feel compelled to create KPIs to match those reported by their peers. The overriding need is for the KPIs to be relevant to that particular company. Management should explain its choice in the context of the chosen strategies and objectives and provide sufficient detail on measurement methods to allow readers to make comparisons to other companies' choices where they want to.

## How many KPIs?

**2.197** Where multiple performance measures are disclosed, management should explain which are key to managing the business. The choice of which ones are key is unique to each company and its strategy; it is impossible to specify how many KPIs a company should have. However, between four and ten measures are likely to be key for most types of company.

## Segmental or group KPIs?

**2.198** Management should consider how KPIs are collated and reported internally; whether they make sense when aggregated and reported at a group level, or would be more usefully reported at business segment level. In some instances it may be more appropriate to report KPIs for each business segment separately if the process of aggregation renders the output meaningless. For example, it is more informative to report a retail business segment separately rather than combining it with a personal financial services segment.

## How flexible is the choice of KPIs?

**2.199** Management should reflect on whether the KPIs chosen continue to be relevant over time. Strategies and objectives develop over time, making it inappropriate to continue reporting on the same KPIs as in previous periods. Equally, more information may become available to management, facilitating reporting of new KPIs that provide a deeper understanding of the business, or changing how an existing KPI is calculated.

## Does reliability matter?

**2.200** Management may sometimes be concerned about the reliability of some of the information reported on KPIs, particularly as they are encouraged to move beyond the more traditional financial KPIs that are usually the output of established systems and controls processes and routine audit. There is no specific narrative reporting requirement for KPIs to be reliable, but the nature of the information should be clear to the users of narrative reports.

**2.201** In order to address this issue and provide readers with useful information, it is more important that the limitations of the data and any assumptions made in providing it are clearly explained. Readers can then judge the reliability for themselves and make any necessary adjustments in their own analysis. Where data has been specifically assured by independent third parties, identifying this may also assist the reader.

**2.202** Readers are often as interested in the trend of a KPI as the absolute performance being reported.

**Reporting KPIs – a model for effective communication**

**2.203**    The reporting statement does not prescribe either the types or the methods of calculating KPIs. However, to ensure that the KPIs can be understood by readers and properly used by them to assess the strategies adopted by the entity and the potential for those strategies to succeed, it sets out a model for effective communication of KPIs, recommending certain disclosures to be given for each KPI reported in the OFR, as follows:

■   The KPI definition and its calculation method. Given the rapidly increasing usage of industry-specific terminology, clear definitions of performance indicators add greatly to the reader's understanding of exactly what is being measured and allows comparisons between companies within an industry. An explanation of a metric's components and how it is calculated should be included, given the absence of standards for the measurement of many industry-specific indicators and with many companies also applying their own indicators.

■   The KPI's purpose. Management should explain why it believes a performance indicator is relevant. This may be because it measures progress towards achieving a specific strategic objective.

■   The source of underlying data and, where relevant, assumptions. To enable readers to make their own assessment of the reliability of the information, management should identify the sources of the data used in calculating performance indicators and any limitations on that data. Any assumptions made in measuring performance should be explained so that readers can reach an informed view of judgements made by management. An indication of the level, if any, of independent assurance of the data would also be valuable.

■   Quantification or commentary on future targets. Some performance indicators are best suited to a quantification of future targets. Expectations and aims for other indicators may be better explained in commentary. Either way, a forward-looking orientation is essential for readers to assess the potential for strategies to succeed and to give them a basis against which to assess future performance.

■   Where information from the financial statements has been adjusted for inclusion in the OFR, that fact and a reconciliation should be provided. Performance indicators may be financial or non-financial. Where the amounts measured are financial, but are not 'traditional' measures required by accounting standards (that is, GAAP measures), it is good practice to explain any differences. A reconciliation should, therefore, be provided between accounting measures and non-GAAP measures.

■   Corresponding amounts, where available, should be given for the previous year. Measurement of performance in isolation over a single period does not provide the reader with useful information. An indication of how performance has improved or worsened over time is much more valuable in assessing the success of management's strategies. It is also beneficial to explain to the reader what a particular trend in the data means (for example, an increasing measure is not always a sign of strength) and to explain management's actions to address or maintain such trends.

■ Any changes to KPIs and the calculation method used compared to previous years should be identified and explained, including significant changes in the underlying accounting policies adopted in the financial statements. Comparability over time is a key principle of good corporate reporting. It is recognised that KPIs may evolve over time as strategies change or more information becomes available. When such changes are made to the KPIs being monitored, either in terms of the KPIs used or how they are calculated, these changes should be explained.

[RS (OFR) paras 75, 76, 77].

**2.204** The following information is also useful to investors and management when considering reporting around KPIs:

■ Link to strategy: the primary reason for including performance indicators in corporate reporting is to enable readers to assess the strategies adopted by the company and their potential to succeed. KPIs presented in isolation from strategies and objectives, or *vice versa*, cannot fulfil this requirement and will fail to provide the reader with the level of understanding they need.

■ Segmental: often KPIs make little sense when consolidated at group level. Corporate reporting users may want more detailed segmental information to assess progress towards specific segmental strategic aims. Performance indicators that are relevant to a specific segment's industry or strategy should, therefore, be provided in addition to those with a more group-wide focus.

■ Benchmarking: performance benchmarked against a relevant peer group, with an explanation of why these peers were chosen, is valuable to users. It provides a clear indication of who management believes the company's competitors to be, as well as setting the company's own performance in the context of a well defined peer group.

**2.205** The implementation guidance contains 23 examples of types of KPI. Each of the examples in the guidance follows the disclosure recommendations described above. But the layout shown in the examples is not prescriptive and directors should decide how best to present the information, perhaps by presenting some of the details in footnotes or in a separate section of the OFR.

**2.206** Many companies in the UK are now reporting their KPIs. The following examples shown in Tables 2.44 and 2.45 were chosen on the basis of their ability to align their KPIs with specific group strategies and objectives and to illustrate a variety of content aspects from the model for effective communication set out above and a variety of presentation styles.

---

**Table 2.44 – Key performance indicators**

**HBOS Plc – Annual Report and Accounts – 31 December 2006**

**Who we are**

HBOS is a diversified financial services group with powerful brands, strong distribution and a substantial customer base. We're the UK's largest provider of mortgages and savings; together with significant and growing market shares in key retail, corporate, international, treasury and insurance and investment markets.

**Our Strategy**

Our strategy has five key elements to create value. These are described in more detail in the Chief Executive's Strategy Overview on page 9.

**Key Performance Indicators**

Our Key Performance Indicators help us to measure our progress against each element of our strategy.

**Growing the UK franchise**

The power of our brands, distribution and customer base demonstrates the potential we have for further market share growth in the UK. Our goal, over time, is to grow the market shares of our main products to 15%-20%.

UK Market shares

**Insurance & Investment**

**Who we are**

Insurance & Investment is one of the UK's largest providers of investment products, offering multi-brand life, pensions, mutual funds and general insurance products.

**Our Strategy**

Our strategy is to be the UK's leading insurance and investment group using our multi-channel, multi-brand operating model and accessing the significant HBOS customer base to grow profitable market share.

**Key Performance Indicators**

Our Key Performance Indicators help us to measure our progress against each element of our strategy.

**Growing market share of personal lines insurance**

There are significant opportunities through the Group's Retail network, through intermediaries and our joint venture with esure to grow market share in Household, Motor and Repayment Insurance. In particular, we will use HBOS's market leading position in mortgages to grow market share of Household Insurance.

% of Group Mortgage customers who have our Household Insurance

General Insurance sales (Gross Written Premiums £m)

---

**2.206.1**   Table 2.45 illustrates the type of information that can be provided for each KPI, as well as providing an example of how to communicate a new KPI that will be introduced during the year.

**Table 2.45 – Key performance indicators**

**Centrica Plc – Annual Report and Accounts – 31 December 2006**

**Group Key Performance Indicators**

In this section, as part of our commitment to enhanced narrative reporting, the Board and the Executive Committee have set out the key performance indicators (KPIs) that we use to monitor progress against our strategy.

**Measuring our performance**

**Non-financial (extract)**

**Lost-time injuries (LTI)**

Lost-time injuries
per 100,000 hours worked

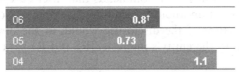

† this measure includes the LTI consequences of the incident at Rough. See the Corporate responsibility section for commentary.

**Description**

We measure lost time injuries per 100,000 hours worked. The majority of these are incurred through slips, trips, falls and manual handling. We use both incidence rates and active indicators to monitor the effectiveness of the health and safety (H&S) preventative programmes that we run throughout the Group.

**Target**

Continue to target the reduction and elimination of lost time injuries across our business and have increasingly sought to adopt a 'zero tolerance' approach on prevention.

**Analysis/comment**

We have established a solid track record of continual improvement and our underlying performance in 2006 continues to indicate the beneficial impact of our H&S strategy.

**Source/verification**
Measured internally.

**Customer satisfaction**
In 2006, we used a variety of measures across our business units to measure levels of customer satisfaction. During 2007, a Group customer KPI will be developed that recognises our position as a provider of energy and related services to both domestic and commercial markets. This information will be included in our 2007 Annual Report.

# Other performance indicators

**2.207** Management may also disclose other quantified measures that they use to monitor trends and factors and that can provide further context to their narrative reporting. However, if they are not considered by management to be KPIs and/or are outside the entity's control, the level of information about each one should be less than for a KPI.

**2.208** The reporting statement includes less stringent disclosure recommendations for other performance indicators that are not KPIs. It states that where quantified measures other than KPIs are included, the OFR should disclose:

- The definition and calculation method.

- Where available, corresponding amounts for the previous financial year.

[RS (OFR) para 78].

**'Seriously prejudicial'**

**2.209** The reporting statement recommends that disclosure should not be made in the OFR of information about impending developments or about matters in the course of negotiation if the disclosure would, in the directors' opinion, be seriously prejudicial to the entity's interests. [RS (OFR) para 79].

**2.210** The reporting statement notes that this is consistent with existing practice in informing the markets on such matters. This is a reference to the UK Listing and Prospectus Rules, which contain exemptions from disclosure of information that would be seriously detrimental to a company. [PR 2.5.2].

**2.211** Instances where non-disclosure is justified tend to include those where the omission is unlikely to mislead investors with regard to facts and circumstances that are essential for an informed assessment. This means that for information to be excluded on 'seriously prejudicial' grounds, the omission itself should not give rise to a misleading impression.

**2.212** Situations where non-disclosure on seriously prejudicial grounds might apply are likely to be rare. They include those where a company's position might be seriously prejudiced in relation to disputes with other parties on the subject matter of a provision, contingent liability or contingent asset. FRS 12 and IAS 37 contain an exemption from disclosure of some of the information otherwise required by those standards but require disclosure of the general nature of the dispute, together with the fact that the information has not been disclosed and the reason why. [FRS 12 para 97; IAS 37 para 92].

**[The next paragraph is 2.214.]**

**2.214** Although not mentioned in the reporting statement, disclosure of the fact that information on a particular matter has not been disclosed and the reasons for non-disclosure may be useful to shareholders, where such disclosure would not itself be prejudicial. For example, an entity may have let it be known that it would welcome offers for a particular segment of its business that it wishes to dispose of. It may be in negotiation with several parties who may be unaware of each other's interest. The company might disclose in the OFR that the segment is for sale, but it may consider that it would be seriously prejudicial to disclose that it is negotiating with more than one party. Non-disclosure of that information would be unlikely to mislead investors. It might instead (voluntarily) state that details of the negotiations have not been disclosed, but the outcome will be announced when the negotiations have been concluded.

## Statement of compliance

**2.215** Although not required, the OFR should, as good practice, include a statement as to whether it has been prepared in accordance with the reporting statement. [RS (OFR) para 80]. An example of such a statement is Table 2.46.

---

**Table 2.46 – Statement of compliance with OFR reporting statement**

**Xstrata plc – Annual Report and Accounts – 31 December 2007**

**Cautionary note regarding forward-looking statements (extract)**

The Business Review section of this report, comprising the Business, Markets, Financial and Operating Reviews, has been prepared in accordance with the Accounting Standards Board Reporting Statement on Operating and Financial Review (January 2006), as applicable best practice guidance for UK companies required to prepare a business review.

---

**[The next paragraph is 2.222.]**

## International developments

**2.222** In October 2005, the IASB published a discussion paper on management commentary (MC).

**2.223** It was prepared after a review of the existing requirements and guidance in place relating to contextual and non-financial reporting. The primary focus was on MC requirements and guidance in place in Canada, Germany, the UK, the US and guidance issued by the International Organisation of Securities Commissions (IOSCO).

**2.224** An appendix to the discussion paper includes proposals for a draft MC standard. Many of the principles and proposed disclosures in the draft standard are consistent with those of the ASB's reporting statement on the OFR. For example, the MC should *"supplement and complement the information in the financial statements"*, should *"provide an analysis through the eyes of management"* and should *"have an orientation to the future"*.

**2.225** The proposed standard states that information should be provided about:

- The nature of the business.
- Objectives and strategies.
- Key resources, risks and relationships.

- Results and prospects.

- Performance measures and indicators.

**2.226** The discussion paper received favourable responses and the IASB has added the project to its active agenda.

**Chapter 3**

# Directors' report

|  | Page |
|---|---|
| Introduction | 3001 |
| Companies reporting under IFRS | 3002 |
| Consolidated financial statements | 3002 |
| Matters to be dealt with in the directors' report | 3002 |
| Principal activities | 3002 |
| Business review | 3004 |
| Applying the requirements to different sizes of company | 3006 |
| Key performance indicators | 3008 |
| Interaction between the directors' report and OFR | 3008 |
| Additional matters for quoted companies | 3009 |
| Likely future developments | 3009 |
| Environmental and social matters | 3009 |
| Seriously prejudicial | 3010 |
| Additional matters for listed companies | 3010 |
| Dividends | 3012 |
| Post balance sheet events | 3012 |
| Research and development activities | 3014 |
| Differences between market and balance sheet value of land | 3014 |
| Details of directors | 3015 |
| Directors' interests in contracts | 3015 |
| Purchase of own shares and sales of treasury shares | 3016 |
| Employee information | 3018 |
| Employment of disabled persons | 3018 |
| Employee involvement | 3019 |
| Creditor payment policy | 3020 |
| Political and charitable donations | 3023 |
| Summary of the provisions for disclosure and control | 3023 |
| Definitions | 3023 |
| Prohibition on political donations and expenditure | 3025 |
| Exemptions for donations | 3025 |
| Subsidiaries incorporated in Great Britain and Northern Ireland | 3026 |
| Directors' liability | 3026 |
| Disclosure of political donations and expenditure – financial years beginning before 6 April 2008 | 3027 |
| Stand alone company – not wholly-owned by a GB parent | 3027 |
| Company with subsidiary – not wholly-owned by a GB parent | 3028 |
| Company that is a wholly-owned subsidiary of a GB parent | 3028 |
| Disclosure of political donations and expenditure – financial years beginning on or after 6 April 2008 | 3028 |
| Stand alone company – not wholly-owned by a UK parent | 3028 |

*Directors' report*

Company with subsidiary – not wholly-owned by a UK parent .. 3029
Company that is a wholly-owned subsidiary of a UK parent .... 3029
Disclosure of charitable gifts – accounting periods beginning before
6 April 2008 .................................................. 3029
Disclosure of charitable gifts – accounting periods beginning on or
after 6 April 2008 ........................................... 3030
Financial instruments ......................................... 3031
Disclosure of overseas branches ............................... 3032
Directors' responsibility statements .......................... 3032
Statement on disclosure of information to the auditors ........ 3035
Re-appointment of auditors ................................ 3036
Disclosure of qualifying third party indemnity provisions ..... 3036
Additional matters for publicly traded companies .............. 3037
Control and share structures .................................. 3037
Agreements affected by a change of control ................... 3038
Matters for listed companies .................................. 3040
Major interest in company's shares ............................ 3040
Transactions with a controlling shareholder .................. 3042
Directors' service contracts .................................. 3043
Disclosure of directors' interests ............................ 3046
Connected persons ......................................... 3047
Directors' interests in contracts of significance ............. 3048
Waiver of dividends ........................................... 3049
Corporate governance .......................................... 3049
Special business .............................................. 3049
Additional disclosures for listed companies purchasing own share or
selling treasury shares ....................................... 3052
Directors' liability: safe harbour ............................ 3052
Filing exemption for small companies .......................... 3052
Approval and signing of directors' report ..................... 3053
Liability for contravention ................................ 3054
Position of the auditor ....................................... 3054
Enforcement ................................................... 3055

# Chapter 3

# Directors' report

## Introduction

**3.1** The directors' report is one of the mandatory components of a company's annual financial statements and reports for members. It must also be delivered to the Registrar of Companies by all companies except those entitled to the small companies exemption. [CA85 Sec 242(1); CA06 Secs 445(1), 446(1), 447(1)].

**3.2** The duty to prepare a directors' report is contained in section 234 of the 1985 Act (section 415 of the 2006 Act). However, neither the 1985 Act, nor the 2006 Act contains all the disclosure requirements: many of the detailed requirements are contained in Schedule 7 to the Companies Act 1985. For directors' reports for financial years to which the 2006 Act applies, the detailed requirements are found in Schedule 5 to SI 2008/409, 'The Small Companies and Groups (Accounts and Reports) Regulations 2008', for companies or groups falling within the definition of 'small' (see chapter 31 of the Manual of Accounting — UK GAAP) and Schedule 7 to SI 2008/410, 'The Large and Medium-sized Companies and Groups (Accounts and Reports) Regulations 2008' for all other companies.

**3.2.1** Most of the provisions in the 2006 Act regarding the Director's report are in force for financial years commencing on or after 6 April 2008 (for financial years commencing prior to that, the 1985 Act applies). However, section 417 (contents of directors' reports: business review) came into effect for reports for financial years beginning on or after 1 October 2007 and, in this area, the guidance in this chapter has been fully updated to reflect the requirements of the 2006 Act (see from para 3.23).

**3.3** Directors have a responsibility to prepare the report even if none of the directors at the time the report is produced were directors during the period covered by the report. They cannot avoid this responsibility simply because they were not responsible for all or some of the activities that are being reported on.

**3.4** The principal objective of the directors' report is not only to supplement the financial information in the profit and loss account and the balance sheet with discussions and explanations about the company's activities and its future, but also to provide details of other non-financial matters. The purpose of the narrative information is to give the user of the financial statements a more complete picture of the company than would otherwise be obtained.

**3.5** Listed companies regard the annual financial statements as an important mode of communication with shareholders. They, therefore, take the opportunity to provide the shareholders with information about all aspects of the company's activities and the environment in which it operates, the company's objectives and its values. Such voluntary information may be presented outside the statutory directors' report, for example, in the chairman's statement or in a separate operating and financial review (see further chapter 2). However, the Companies Act 2006 introduces provisions that give directors a 'safe harbour' in respect of civil liability arising out of the content of the directors' report and the directors' remuneration report. (See further from para 3.143.) Thus, companies may wish to include the voluntary disclosures within the directors' report in order to benefit from the 'safe harbour' provisions.

**[The next paragraph is 3.11.]**

## Companies reporting under IFRS

**3.11** The requirements relating to the directors' report are contained within the body of the Companies Acts and, thus, apply to all companies, regardless of whether the financial statements are prepared under IFRS or UK GAAP.

## Consolidated financial statements

**3.12** The 1985 and 2006 Acts require that, where an entity is a parent company and the directors prepare consolidated financial statements, the directors' report must be a consolidated report covering the company and its subsidiary undertakings included in the consolidation. [CA85 Sec 234(2); CA06 Sec 415(2)].

**3.13** Where appropriate, the consolidated report should give greater emphasis to matters that are significant to the company and its subsidiary undertakings included in the consolidation, taken as a whole. [CA85 Sec 234(3); CA06 Sec 415(3)].

**[The next paragraph is 3.16.]**

## Matters to be dealt with in the directors' report

### Principal activities

**3.16** The principal activities of both the company and of its subsidiaries during the year, and details of any significant change in those activities, should be stated. [CA85 Sec 234ZZA(1)(b); CA06 Sec 416(1)].

**3.17** The term 'principal activities' is not defined in either Act, but is generally taken to mean the diverse industry segments or classes of business in which the entity operates. Guidance is provided in SSAP 25, 'Segmental reporting', which defines a separate class of business as the distinguishable component of the entity that provides a separate product or service or a separate group of related products or services. [SSAP 25 para 11]. Similarly, IAS 14, 'Segment reporting', defines a business segment as a distinguishable component of the entity that provides an individual product or service or group of related products and services and that has risks and returns that are different from those of other business segments. [IAS 14 para 9]. IFRS 8, 'Operating segments', (applicable for financial years beginning on or after 1 January 2009) considers segments entirely differently and uses a 'through the eyes of management' approach. Thus, directors applying that standard may find that some distinction appears between the company's operating segments and its principal activities. The decision to separate the two should not, however, be taken lightly. Distinguishable components of an entity may include, for example, mining, textiles, electrical etc. Broad categories such as manufacturing, wholesaling and retailing are not indicative of the industries in which the entity operates. Those terms should not generally be used to describe an entity's industry segments without identification of the products or services.

**3.18**   Therefore, the categories of principal activities described in the directors' report should, as far as possible, be consistent with the information that is provided for segmental reporting purposes. There are various factors that should be taken into account when deciding whether or not an entity operates in different industry segments and these are discussed further in chapter 10 on segmental reporting in both the Manual of Accounting – UK GAAP and the Manual of Accounting – IFRS for the UK. However, no single set of characteristics is universally applicable in determining industry segments of all entities, nor is any single set of characteristics likely to be relevant in all cases. Consequently, determining the industry segments in which the entity operates must depend to a considerable extent on the directors' judgement.

**3.19**   Furthermore, judgement is required in deciding whether differing types of business are sufficiently significant to require separate disclosures. Although no precise rules have been laid down in this respect, it is suggested that where there are significant differences between categories of activity, such that they cannot reasonably be treated as a single class, entities should follow the size criterion (the ten per cent thresholds) discussed in chapter 10 of the UK Manual of Accounting – UK GAAP, in determining whether an activity is significant enough to require separate disclosure.

**3.20**   A change in activity should be reported whenever there has been a commencement of a new activity or a complete withdrawal from a previous activity rather than a change in the degree of the activity undertaken. Such a change may be brought about by the acquisition or disposal of a subsidiary undertaking. In order to provide meaningful disclosure of the changes in activities, the extent to which the acquisition or disposal has impacted on any resultant change in the group's activities should be considered. Indeed, FRS 3, 'Reporting financial performance', requires that if an acquisition, a sale or a termination has a material impact on a major business segment, this impact should be disclosed and explained. [FRS 3 para 53]. Similarly, under IAS 14, 'Segment reporting', entities are encouraged to disclose the nature and amount of any items of segment revenue and segment expense that are of such size, nature or incidence that their disclosure is relevant to explain the performance of each reportable segment for the period. [IAS 14 para 59]. Although there are no equivalent requirements in IFRS 8 or in UK GAAP, we consider such disclosure to be strongly recommended.

**3.21** The degree of detail that should be given under principal activities will obviously depend upon the nature of the company's business. For companies operating in one or two business segments, the relevant information is normally given in the directors' report. Multinational corporations engaged in a wide range of business activities tend to include the relevant details elsewhere in the financial statements, for example, in a separate statement that sets out a detailed review of their operations. Where this is done, a reference should be given in the directors' report to where the necessary information can be found. Table 3.1 provides an illustration of the disclosure of principal activities.

---

**Table 3.1 — Principal activities**

**Smiths Group plc — Annual report and accounts — 31 July 2005**

**Directors' report (extract)**

**Principal activities**

The principal activities of the Company and its subsidiaries are the development, manufacture, sale and support of:

- aerospace systems, including integrated electronic and mechanical systems and precision components, for commercial and military aircraft;
- advanced security equipment, using trace detection and x-ray imaging to detect and identify explosives, chemical and biological agents, weapons and contraband;
- medical devices aligned to specific therapies, principally airway, pain and temperature management, infusion, needle protection, critical care monitoring and vascular access;
- mechanical seals used in industries ranging from petrochemical processing to aerospace; interconnect products to connect and protect safety-critical electrical and electronic equipment; marine navigation; ducting and hose assemblies.

The main manufacturing operations are in the UK , the Americas and Continental Europe. A review of the development of the Company and its subsidiary undertakings during the 2004/05 financial year is provided in the Operating and Financial Review within this Report.

---

**[The next paragraph is 3.23.]**

**Business review**

**3.23** The directors should include in their report a review of the business of the company and its subsidiaries. [CA85 Sec 234(1)(a); CA06 Sec 417(1)]. Unless the company is entitled to the small companies' exemption (see from para 3.147), the directors' report must contain a business review.

**3.24** The purpose of the business review is to inform the company's members and help them assess how the directors have performed their duty to promote the company's success. [CA06 Sec 417(2)].

**3.24.1** In promoting the company's success, directors must, in particular, have regard to:

■ The likely consequences of any decision in the long term.

■ The interests of the company's employees.

■ The need to foster the company's business relationships with suppliers, customers and others.

■ The impact of the company's operations on the community and the environment.

■ The desirability for the company maintaining a reputation for high standards of business conduct.

■ The need to act fairly as between the company's members.

[CA06 Sec 172].

**3.24.2** The business review must contain, at a minimum:

■ A fair review of the entity's business.

■ A description of the principal risks and uncertainties facing the entity.

[CA06 Sec 417(3)].

**3.24.3** The review should be consistent with the business' size and complexity and provide a balanced and comprehensive analysis, of:

■ The development and performance of the entity's business during the financial year.

■ The entity's position at the end of the year.

[CA06 Sec 417(4)].

**3.24.4** The review should also include the following, to the extent necessary for an understanding of the development, performance or position of the entity's business:

■ Analysis using financial key performance indicators (KPIs).

■ Where appropriate, analysis using other KPIs, including information on environmental and employee matters.

[CA06 Sec 417(6)].

**3.24.5** The review must contain, where appropriate, references to and additional explanation of amounts included in the financial statements. [CA06 Secs 415(1), 417(1), 418(2), 417(8)].

**3.25** Where a company qualifies as medium-sized in relation to a financial year (see chapter 31 of the Manual of Accounting — UK GAAP), the directors' report for the year need not comply with the requirements of section 417(6) of the 2006 Act (see para 3.24.4) so far as they relate to non-financial information.

**3.26** Where an entity is a parent company and prepares consolidated financial statements, the business review should be a consolidated review covering the company and its subsidiary undertakings included in the consolidation. [CA06 Sec 417(9)]. There is no requirement for the parent company to prepare a separate review for the company alone.

### Applying the requirements to different sizes of company

**3.27** All companies must prepare a business review, other than those entitled to the small companies exemption (see para 3.23). The ASB's Reporting Statement 'Operating and Financial Review' (considered in detail in chapter 2) offers some guidance on practically implementating of the various business review requirements, although this is of more relevance to listed companies. Guidance to assist directors in preparing a business review is limited for private entities.

**3.27.1** Many of the requirements of the business review are preceded with the words *"to the extent necessary for an understanding of the development, performance or position of the company's business"*, thus giving directors some discretion over the level of detail that should be presented in the business review.

**3.27.2** Bearing in mind that the overriding purpose of the business review is as a tool for communicating with members, (see further para 3.24), we believe that the type and extent of disclosure required depends on the extent to which an entity's share ownership structure is dispersed. This distinction can be summarised as follows:

- For owner-managed companies, members already have a good understanding of the company's development, performance and position. Consequently, the minimum information to comply with the legislation is all that is needed to present a clear picture to members.

- The position for wholly-owned subsidiaries of a parent company that actively monitors the performance of the business on an ongoing basis is similar to that for owner-managed companies. Often both the management and reporting of risk and key performance indicators for wholly-owed subsidiaries are undertaken at the group level. In such circumstances, it is appropriate to refer to further information available in the group annual report. The cross-reference should be to a specific paragraph, heading, or page in the group annual report.

- For public interest companies, AIM-listed (or PLUS-quoted) companies and private companies (including wholly-owned subsidiaries) where ownership is distinct from those who manage the entity on members' behalf, the minimum disclosures described for owner-managed entities should be supplemented by additional contextual information around risk and key performance indicators, as well as a description of the entity's strategy and business environment.

- Fuller disclosure is necessary for quoted companies, to assist members in understanding the entity's development, performance and position. The most appropriate guidance is in the recommendations of the ASB's Reporting Statement, 'Operating and Financial Review'. (See chapter 2.)

**3.27.3**  Illustrative examples of business reviews for each category of company can be found in full at www.corporatereporting.com/practical-guides.html. Examples of good disclosure by listed companies are available on www.pwcinform.com.

**3.27.4**  The table below provides a guide to the type of information that should be included in a business review for private entities with dispersed ownership and public interest entities (other than those for whom compliance with the ASB's reporting statement is more relevant).

| Heading | Suggested type of content |
|---|---|
| Principal activities | Nature of the business, extent of operations. Results in terms of revenues and profits. Net debt position and net cash inflow. |
| Business environment | Description of the market and competitive environment – market factors and dynamics that can affect the business environment, for example, competitors and market outlook. Regulatory environment – legal, agency or other regulatory factors that impose requirements on the conduct of business activities; for example, deregulation and privatisation. Macro environment – factors that could have a material impact on corporate performance, for example; interest rates, demographics and economic outlook. |
| Strategy | Overriding objectives of the company and, where relevant, the group. The company's and, where relevant, the group's strategy for achieving these objectives and an explanation of each strategy, as well as how successful implementation of the strategy is measured. |
| Research and development (R&D) | Actions taken in the area of R&D and how these link into the group's strategy. |
| Future outlook | Expected development of the business environment and any planned actions to address these developments. |
| Principal risks and uncertainties | The principal risks and uncertainties that have the focus of the directors' attention – not simply a list of all risk factors that the group faces – as well as the approach taken by management to these risks. |
| Key performance indicators | The measures used to assess progress against objectives and strategies – including quantifying of these measures, trend data, definition, method of calculation and any relevant narrative. |

### Key performance indicators

**3.28**  Key performance indicators (KPIs) are defined as *"factors by reference to which the development, performance or position of the business of the company can be measured effectively"*. [CA06 Sec 417(6)]. The ASB's, 'Reporting statement: Operating and financial review', provides a more detailed definition, describing KPIs as *"...quantified measurements that reflect the critical success factors of an entity and disclose progress towards achieving a particular objective or objectives"*. [RS (OFR) para 3].

**3.29**  The 2006 Act does not prescribe specific KPIs that entities should disclose. Entities use a variety of different KPIs and the relevance of a particular KPI varies from industry to industry and even from one entity to another within an industry. In addition, methods of calculation of particular KPIs may vary from one entity to another. Directors will, therefore, need to decide which KPIs and how many best reflect their judgement of what is needed for an understanding of the business. This approach will reflect the view that KPIs are principally of use in measuring an entity's performance and the position of an entity, rather than measuring the entity's performance against other entities.

**3.30**  Directors may look to the ASB's reporting statement on the OFR for further guidance on disclosure of KPIs. The reporting statement sets out the recommendations for disclosure for each KPI. In addition, the reporting statement's implementation guidance contains examples of disclosure of KPIs. Chapter 2 discusses the reporting statement and KPIs in further detail.

### Interaction between the directors' report and OFR

**3.31**  If companies that prepare an OFR (recommended for quoted companies and any other companies that purport to prepare an OFR) were also required to give information to meet the business review requirements in their directors' report, there would be considerable duplication.

**3.32**  The DTI's (now known as BERR) 'Guidance on changes to the directors' report requirements in the Companies Act 1985 – April and December 2005' clarifies that where the directors' report and a voluntary OFR are published together, it is acceptable to cross refer from the directors' report to a business review in the OFR. This guidance is considered to be relevant to similar provisions of the 2006 Act. The cross reference must clearly refer (by page numbers, paragraph numbers or headings) to the specific section in the OFR. The guidance provides example wording for such a cross reference as follows:

> *"The information that fulfils the requirements of the business review can be found in the OFR on pages x to y, which are incorporated in this report by reference."*

**[The next paragraph is 3.42.1.]**

**Additional matters for quoted companies**

*Likely future developments*

**3.42.1**   Section 417(5)(a) of the 2006 Act requires the directors' report of a quoted company to contain an indication of the main trends and factors likely to affect the future development, performance and position of the company's business. As with the provisions relating to a review of the company's business during the year, the 2006 Act contains no amplification as to the extent and the scope of this commentary. In practice, directors tend to interpret this requirement by providing information that will have a significant impact on future earnings and profitability of the company or the group. For example, information on such matters as development of new products or services, business expansion or rationalisation plans, capital expenditure plans and proposed disposals and acquisitions, is fairly common.

**3.42.2**   The ASB's reporting statement on the operating and financial review provides some guidance in this area. (See further chapter 2.)

**3.42.3**   As stated in paragraph 3.32, it is acceptable to cross refer from the directors' report to a business review in the OFR, provided that the cross reference clearly refers (by page numbers, paragraph numbers or headings) to the specific section in the OFR.

*Environmental and social matters*

**3.42.4** The 2006 Act requires the directors of quoted companies to disclose the following in their directors' report:

- The main trends and factors likely to affect the future development, performance and position of the company's business.

- Information about persons with whom the company has contractual or other arrangements that are essential to the company's business (but see para 3.42.11).

- Information about:

    - environmental matters (including the impact of the company's business on the environment),

    - the company's employees; and

    - social and community issues,

including information about any policies of the company in relation to those matters and the effectiveness of those policies. [CA06 Sec 417(5)].

**3.42.5**   The disclosures are required *"to the extent necessary for an understanding of the development, performance or position of the company's business"*. If the review does not contain information on the items listed in the second bullet point above, it must state so.

**3.42.6** The government expressed the view that the additional disclosures would add value to the quality of reporting without imposing unnecessary costs. These provisions have effectively reinstated a number of the requirements of the (now withdrawn) OFR regulations, albeit for disclosure within the directors' report as opposed to the OFR. Further guidance on making disclosures in these areas is included in chapter 2.

**[The next paragraph is 3.42.10.]**

### Seriously prejudicial

**3.42.10** A limited exemption has been provided under the Companies Act 2006 such that disclosure of information is not required regarding *"information about impending developments or matters in the course of negotiation if the disclosure would, in the opinion of the directors, be seriously prejudicial to the interests of the company"*. [CA06 Sec 417(10)].

**3.42.11** In addition, quoted companies need not disclose information about essential contractual or other arrangements if such disclosure would, in the directors' opinion, be seriously prejudicial to the counterparty of those arrangements or contrary to the public interest. [CA06 Sec 417(11)].

### Additional matters for listed companies

**3.42.12** Companies traded on a regulated market in the UK (for example, the main market of the LSE or the Plus Market's PLUS-listed market) are required to comply with the requirements of the UKLA's Listing Rules.

**3.42.13** For listed companies, the wording for the note on future developments (considered from para 3.42.1) will have to be chosen very carefully. Otherwise, there is the danger that the note could, at some later stage, be construed as a profit forecast. Appendix 1 of the UKLA's Listing Rules defines 'profit forecast' as follows:

> *"A form of words which expressly states or by implication indicates a figure or a minimum or maximum figure for the likely level of profits or losses for the current financial period and/or financial periods subsequent to that period, or contains data from which a calculation of such a figure for future profits or losses may be made, even if no particular figure is mentioned and the word 'profit' is not used."*

It defines a profit estimate as:

> *"a profit forecast for a financial period which has expired and for which results have not yet been published."*

**3.42.14** The requirement that a business review should incorporate forward-looking information and KPIs has led many companies to believe, erroneously, that they will be expected to report profit forecasts. The business community's overriding concern with the business review, that it will expose Directors to the rigorous policing of published prospective financial information (PFI) is misplaced. Forward-looking information, properly presented, can be used to provide investors with a broad-based view of corporate performance without having to disclose sensitive PFI. The real issue is not whether forward-looking statements turn out to be accurate, but whether they were made in good faith and with due care and attention. The Companies Act 2006 introduced 'safe harbour' to Directors financial liability for statements in the Director's report (see from para 3.143).

**3.42.15** The City Code on Takeovers and Mergers states that, if a company has issued any statement that constitutes a profit forecast and that forecast relates to a period during which a takeover bid arises, then that forecast must be repeated in any offer or defence document and accountants must report on it. [City Code rule 28.3(d)].

**3.42.16** The UKLA's Listing Rules state that, if a listed company has published a forecast or estimate for a financial period for which the results have not yet been published and subsequently it is required to produce a Class 1 acquisition circular or any circular, then the issuer must either repeat or update the forecast in the listing particulars or the relevant circular or include an explanation of why the profit forecast is no longer valid. The same rules apply if a company is the subject of a Class 1 acquisition by a listed company. [LR 13.5.33R].

**3.42.17** CESR's recommendations for the consistent implementation of the Prospectus Regulation, which have been adopted by the FSA through the Prospectus Rules, state that there is a presumption that an outstanding forecast will be material in the case of share issues. Accordingly, the issuer of a prospectus would either have to include a profit forecast in the prospectus or a statement that it is no longer valid. [CESR recommendations para 44].

**3.42.18** In the circumstances described in paragraphs 3.39 and 3.40, if the directors' report of a listed company is construed as including a profit forecast or an estimate, it would have the following consequence:

■ Accountants would be required to report that the forecast or estimate has been properly compiled on the basis stated and that it is presented on a basis consistent with the accounting policies of the company or group in question. [City Code rule 28.3(b), PR Annex 1 item 13.2].

■ The directors would have to state in the circular that any profit forecast or estimate had been properly compiled on the basis stated and presented on a basis consistent with the company's accounting policies. [LR 13.5.32R(2)].

■ Whenever a listed company has published a profit forecast or estimate, whether in a City Code, Listing Rules or Prospectus Rules document, the following year's financial statements will have to explain any differences if the actual results for the period reported in those financial statements differ by ten per cent or more from any published forecast or estimate made by the company for that period. [LR 9.2.18R(2)(c)].

## Dividends

**3.43** The amount (if any) that the directors recommend should be paid as dividend must be stated except in the case of a company that is entitled to the small companies exemption under the 2006 Act. [CA06 Sec 416(3)]. Where the directors do not propose a dividend, then it is customary to state this fact. An example of the relevant disclosure is given in Table 3.3 below.

---

**Table 3.3 — Dividend payment**

**Cadbury Schweppes — Annual Report — 2 January 2005**

**Report of the Directors (extract)**

**Dividends**

The Directors recommend a final dividend of 8.70 pence per ordinary share (2003: 8.35p) to be paid on 27 May 2005 to ordinary shareowners on the register on 29 April 2005. An interim dividend of 3.80 pence was paid on 15 October 2004, which makes a total of 12.50 pence per ordinary share for the year (2003: 12.00p). Ordinary dividends paid and recommended for the year will amount to £255 million (2003: £242 million).

---

## Post balance sheet events

**3.44** Particulars of any *important* events affecting the reporting entity that have occurred since the end of the financial year must be disclosed by all companies other than those subject to the small companies regime under the 2006 Act. [CA85 7 Sch 6(1)(a); SI 2008/410 7 Sch 7(1)(a)]. This requirement gives rise to two potential conflicts between the law and FRS 21 and IAS 10, 'Events after the balance sheet date'. These standards are considered further in chapters 22 of the Manual of Accounting – UK GAAP and the Manual of Accounting – IFRS for the UK.

■  FRS 21 and IAS 10 distinguish between events that require adjustments to the amounts reported in the financial statements ('adjusting events') and events that are only required to be noted ('non-adjusting events' and the reversal of window dressing transactions). However, the law does not make such a distinction and requires disclosure of important post balance sheet events whether adjusting or non-adjusting. In practice, disclosure in the directors' report of the financial effects of material non-adjusting post balance sheet as *pro forma* information is not uncommon as indicated in Table 3.4 below.

■  The law requires material events after the balance sheet date to be disclosed in the directors' report, whereas FRS 21 and IAS 10 require disclosure of non-adjusting events in the notes to the financial statements. Where a post balance sheet event requires disclosure under both the Act and the standard, then theoretically disclosure ought to be made both in the directors' report as well as in the notes to the financial statements. In practice, however, companies normally disclose the information only in one place – usually the notes – so as to avoid duplication. A cross-reference should be given in the directors' report to the precise location of the information. The example in Table 3.4 below illustrates disclosure given in both the directors' report and the notes.

---

**Table 3.4 — Post balance sheet event**

**J Sainsbury plc — Report and Accounts — 27 March 2004**

**Report of the Directors (extract)**

**Post balance sheet events**
On 30 April 2004, the Company announced that it had completed the sale of Shaw's, its US supermarkets business, to Albertson's Inc. for $2,475 million. Subject to obtaining shareholder approval, the Company intends to return 35 pence per share to shareholders, representing approximately £680 million. This return of capital will be made by way of a B share scheme, providing shareholders with maximum flexibility in terms of tax treatment by allowing them to choose whether to receive the return as either income or capital.

The B share scheme will be accompanied by a share capital consolidation. A resolution to effect the B share scheme and the share consolidation will be proposed at an EGM to be held immediately following the AGM on 12 July 2004. A circular explaining the details of the B share scheme and the consolidation has been sent to shareholders with this Report, together with the notice of the EGM.

**36 Post balance sheet event**
Sale of Shaw's Supermarkets Inc.
On 26 March 2004 the Group signed a conditional contract to sell its US supermarkets business (Shaw's) to Albertson's Inc. for a consideration of $2,475 million, including $368 million in assumed lease liabilities.

The sale, which was subject to a price adjustment mechanism and competition clearance, completed on 30 April 2004, when proceeds of £1,177 million (net of expenses) were received by the Group.

The profit on disposal is estimated to be in excess of £250 million and will be recognised in the 2004/05 accounts.

Of the total proceeds, the Company proposes to return 35 pence per share to shareholders, representing approximately £680 million.

The trading results of Shaw's have been included within discontinued operations (note 3 on page 29), as under FRS 3, the sale of Shaw's represents a material reduction in the Group's operating facilities in the US market.

---

## Research and development activities

**3.45** An indication of the activities (if any) of the reporting entity in the field of research and development should be provided in the directors' report by all companies except those subject to the small companies regime. [CA85 7 Sch 6(1)(c); SI 2008/410 7 Sch 7(c)].

**3.46** As the law does not indicate how much detail needs to be given, the extent of disclosure varies considerably in practice. Some companies, particularly those in the pharmaceutical sector, give significant details about their research and development activities whilst others give a fairly minimal amount of disclosure on the subject. As research and development activities are particularly sensitive matters, companies are understandably reluctant to disclose too much information on the subject. However, in order to meet the requirements, the statement need not be technically elaborate or esoteric. A broadly-based note that considers the commercial aspects of the research and development activities and their impact on the activities of the company or group would be sufficient in most situations. An illustration of this disclosure is shown in Table 3.5.

---

**Table 3.5 — Research and development**

**BPB plc — Annual report and accounts — 31 March 2005**

**DIRECTORS' REPORT (extract)**

**RESEARCH AND DEVELOPMENT**
The group's research and development programme plays a key role in supporting BPB's activities. During the year, the group spent £5.3 million (2004: £5.4 million) on increasing manufacturing efficiency, improving product quality and introducing new products. BPB's acoustic, fire, systems-development and structural testing facilities are accredited to a range of international standards through UKAS; such accreditation is also recognised by a variety of international standards authorities. In addition, the facilities hold notified body status allowing tests to be conducted in support of CE marking in accordance with the Construction Products Directive.

---

**3.47** The requirement to give an indication of the research and development activities of the company and its subsidiaries does not mean that the accounting policy for research and development should be disclosed in the directors' report. It should, instead, supplement the accounting policy and the other disclosure requirements of SSAP 13, 'Accounting for research and development' (see also chapter 15 of the Manual of Accounting – UK GAAP), and IAS 38, 'Intangible assets', (see also chapter 15 of the Manual of Accounting – IFRS for the UK).

## Differences between market and balance sheet value of land

**3.48** Substantial differences between the market value and the balance sheet value of any interest in land held by the reporting entity should be disclosed in the report of any company other than one subject to the small companies regime if, in the opinion of the directors, the difference is of such significance that it should be brought to the shareholders' or debenture holders' attention. 'Land' includes the buildings and other structures. [Sch 1 Interpretation Act 1978]. The difference has to be shown with such degree of precision as is practicable. [CA85 7 Sch 1(2); SI 2008/410 7 Sch 2]. Although there is no requirement to make a negative statement that the difference is not significant, many companies do make this statement where there might otherwise be doubt.

**3.49** It is recommended that, where there are several interests in land, the aggregate market value and the aggregate book value should be compared to see if the difference is substantial. When it is considered that a substantial difference exists, it is preferable to state both the aggregate market value and the basis on which the market value has been arrived at. In this regard, for financial statements prepared in accordance with UK GAAP, FRS 19 also requires disclosure of the tax effects, if any, that would arise if the asset were realised at a price equal to the estimated market value. [FRS 19 para 64(b)]. There is no equivalent requirement in IAS 12, 'Income taxes', for financial statements prepared in accordance with IFRS. An independent professional valuation is not required if the directors are competent to arrive at the market value themselves, but the wording should make the position clear in this respect. Where property is situated overseas, especially in territories subject to political unrest or where the remittance of currencies is restricted, it may not always be practicable, and may be misleading, to give the information required. In such circumstances, the wording should make this clear.

**Details of directors**

**3.50** Disclosure is required of the names of the persons who were directors of the company at any time during the financial year. [CA85 Sec 234ZZA(1)(a); CA06 Sec 416(1)(a)]. This can be achieved either by listing the names of the directors in the report or by referring to the page where this information may be found (for example, see Table 3.17 below). In group financial statements, disclosure is required of the names of the parent company's directors only.

**3.51** Although not required by law, it has become customary to include the following information:

■   The dates of appointments or resignations of directors occurring during the financial year.

■   Changes in the directors since the end of the financial year.

■   Retirement of directors at the AGM and whether they offer themselves for election.

**[The next paragraph is 3.69.]**

**Directors' interests in contracts**

**3.69** Disclosure is required of transactions and arrangements in which the director of a company has, directly or indirectly, a material interest (for example, contracts between a director and a company for the sale of non-cash assets). The disclosure requirements of contracts or substantial property transactions in which a director has a material interest are considered in detail in chapter 6.

**[The next paragraph is 3.75.]**

## Purchase of own shares and sales of treasury shares

**3.75** Where the company has an interest in its own shares, the directors' report is required to include certain information. The directors' report must contain the details set out in paragraph 3.76 below where any of the following circumstances occur:

*Acquisition of shares by the company*

- A company purchases its own shares (including treasury shares) or otherwise acquires them by forfeiture, or by surrender in lieu of forfeiture, or by way of a gift, or redemption, or in a reduction of capital duly made, or by order of the Court. [CA85 7 Sch 7(a), Sec 143(3); SI 2008/409 5 Sch 6(1)(a); SI 2008/410 7 Sch 8(a); CA06 659(1)(2)].

*Acquisition of shares in a public company by another person*

- A nominee of a public company acquires shares in the company from a third party without the company providing any financial assistance directly or indirectly and the company has a beneficial interest in those shares. [CA85 7 Sch 7(b), Sec 146(1)(c); SI 2008/409 5 Sch 6(1)(b); SI 2008/410 7 Sch 8(b); CA06 Sec 662(1)(e)].

- Any person acquires shares in a public company with the financial assistance of the company and the company has a beneficial interest in those shares. [CA85 7 Sch 7(b), Sec 146(1)(d); SI 2008/409 5 Sch 6(1)(b); SI 2008/410 7 Sch 8(b); CA06 Sec 662(1), 671].

*Lien or charges on own shares held by the company*

- A company takes a lien or a charge (either express or implied) on its own shares for any amount that is payable in respect of those shares. [CA85 7 Sch 7(c), Sec 150(2); CA06 Sec 670(1)].

- For a financial period beginning before 6 April 2008, a company that remained an 'old public company' after 22 March 1982, and did not apply before that date to be re-registered under section 8 of the Companies Act 1980 as a public company, holds a lien or a charge (either express or implied) on its own shares, and that lien or charge existed on 22 March 1982. [CA85 7 Sch 7(c); CC(CP) Sec 6(3)]. This has not been carried forward into SI 2008/410 or SI 2008/409 for later periods.

- A company that either existed on 2 November 1862 or was formed after that date in pursuance of either any Act of Parliament (other than the 1985 or

2006 Acts) or letters patent, or was otherwise legally constituted and has registered or re-registered under section 680 of the 1985 Act as a public company (section 1040 of the 2006 Act), holds a lien or a charge (either express or implied) on its own shares, and that lien or charge existed immediately before the company applied to be re-registered or registered as a public company. [CA85 7 Sch 7(c), Sec 150(4); SI 2008/409 5 Sch 6(1)(c); SI 2008/410 7 Sch 8(c); CA06 Sec 670(4)].

**3.76** Where any of the above circumstances has occurred, the directors' report must state the following details:

*In respect of shares purchased*

- The number and the nominal value of the shares that have been purchased in the financial year and the percentage of the called-up share capital which shares of that description represent.

- The aggregate amount of consideration paid and the reasons for their purchase.

An example is given in Table 3.8 below.

*In respect of shares acquired other than by purchase or charged*

- The number and the nominal value of any shares that have been otherwise acquired (whether by the company or by its nominee or any other person) or charged at any time during the financial year.

- The maximum number and the nominal value of shares which, having been so acquired or charged (whether or not during the year) are held at any time during the financial year.

- The number and the nominal value of such shares that were disposed of by the company (or any other person holding them on behalf of the company) during the year, or that were cancelled by the company during the year.

- The percentage of the called-up share capital which shares of that description represent.

- The amount of any charge.

In addition to the above, there should be disclosed the amount or the value of any consideration for any shares that either the company or the other person disposed of during the financial year that the company or the other person acquired for money or money's worth.

[CA85 7 Sch 8; SI 2008/409 5 Sch 6(2); SI 2008/410 7 Sch 9].

---

**Table 3.8 – Repurchase of own shares**

British American Tobacco p.l.c. – Annual Report and Accounts – 31 December 2004

**Directors' Report (extract)**

**Purchase of own shares**

From February 2004, the Board continued its on-market programme of buying back the Company's ordinary shares of 25p each in order to enhance its earnings under the authority granted by shareholders in 2003. At the Annual General Meeting of the Company held on 21 April 2004, the Company was given authority to purchase up to 207,700,000 of its ordinary shares. During the year ended 31 December 2004, the Company made on-market repurchases totalling 59,000,000 of its own ordinary shares, representing 2.84 per cent of the issued share capital, for an aggregate consideration of £492,560,324. The repurchased shares were cancelled. The present authority for the Company to purchase its own shares will expire at the Annual General Meeting to be held on 28 April 2005. The Directors will be seeking fresh authority for the Company to purchase its own ordinary shares as part of the planned continuation of the share buy-back programme. The current intention is for any shares purchased to be cancelled.

---

**[The next paragraph is 3.79.]**

## Employee information

**3.79** All companies are required to include in the directors' report information regarding the company's policy in respect of the employment of disabled persons. In addition, companies other than those subject to the small companies regime must include information regarding the health, safety and welfare at work of employees, and the involvement of employees in the management of the company.

### Employment of disabled persons

**3.80** If the company employed, on average, more than 250 employees in the UK in each week of the financial year, the directors' report must contain a statement that describes the company's policy during the year in respect of the following:

- Giving full and fair consideration (having regard to the persons' particular aptitudes and abilities) to applications for employment that disabled persons (as defined in the Disabled Persons (Employment) Act 1944 for financial years beginning before 6 April 2008 and the Disability Discrimination Act 1995 for financial years thereafter) make to the company. It should be noted that the definitions of 'disabled person' differs between the 1944 and 1995 Acts, with the latter being a person who has a physical or mental impairment that has a substantial and long term adverse effect on their ability to carry out normal day-to-day activities. [Disability Discrimination Act 1995 Sec 1.]

- Continuing the employment of, and arranging appropriate training for, any of the company's employees who have become disabled during the period in which the company employed them.

- Otherwise providing for the training, the career development and the promotion of those disabled persons the company employs.

[CA85 7 Sch 9; SI 2008/409 5 Sch 5; SI 2008/410 7 Sch 10].

An illustration of this disclosure is given in Table 3.9 below.

---

**Table 3.9 — Employment of disabled persons**

**Yell Group plc — Annual report — 31 March 2005**

**Directors' Report (extract)**

**Applications for Employment by Disabled People**
Yell has a Recruitment and Selection Policy that states we are committed to the employment of people with disabilities. We guarantee an interview to people with disabilities who meet the minimum selection criteria for any vacancy. Yell UK is registered as a Two Tick employer as it satisfies the UK government's criteria on the employment of people with disabilities.

**Policy on Arrangements for Able Bodied People that Develop Disabilities**
Our Equal Opportunities Policy contains a code of good practice on disability which states that an individual who becomes disabled whilst in employment will receive support to ensure, wherever possible, they are able to continue in their role. This will involve whatever reasonable adjustments that can be made, in consultation with the individual. Again, in consultation with the individual, other positions will be considered where the individual's skills and abilities match the requirements of the role, making reasonable adjustments wherever possible.

**Policy on Training/Career Development of Disabled People**
We ensure that training and career development is equally available to people with disabilities, tailored where practicable for their specific needs.

---

## Employee involvement

**3.81** The directors' report of any company other than one entitled to the small companies exemption should describe the action the company has taken during the financial year to introduce, maintain, or develop arrangements aimed at:

- Providing employees systematically with information on matters of concern to them as employees.

- Consulting employees or their representatives on a regular basis, so that the company can take the views of employees into account in making decisions that are likely to affect their interests.

- Encouraging the involvement of employees in the company's performance through (for example) an employees' share scheme.

- Achieving a common awareness on the part of all employees of the financial and the economic factors that affect the company's performance.

[CA85 7 Sch 11(3); SI 2008/410 7 Sch 11].

**3.82** The above requirements apply only to the directors' report of a reporting entity that employs, on average, more than 250 employees in the UK each week during the financial year. [CA85 7 Sch 11(1); SI 2008/410 7 Sch 11(1)]. Table 3.10 gives an example of the information to be shown.

---

**Table 3.10 – Employee involvement**

**Marks and Spencer – Annual Report & Accounts – 2 April 2005**

**Employee involvement**

We have maintained our commitment to employee involvement throughout the business.

Employees are kept well informed of the performance and objectives of the Group through personal briefings, regular meetings and e-mail. These are supplemented by our employee publication, On Your Marks, and video presentations. Business Involvement Groups in stores, distribution centres and head office represent employees in two-way communication and are involved in the delivery of change and driving business improvement.

The tenth meeting of the European Council took place last September. This council provides an additional forum for communicating with employee representatives from the countries in the European Community.

Directors and senior management regularly visit stores and discuss, with employees, matters of current interest and concern to the business.

We continue to support employee share ownership through long-established employee share schemes, membership of which is service-related, details of which are given on pages 40 to 41.

**Equal opportunities**

The Group is committed to an active Equal Opportunities Policy from recruitment and selection, through training and development, appraisal and promotion to retirement.

It is our policy to promote an environment free from discrimination, harassment and victimisation, where everyone will receive equal treatment regardless of gender, colour, ethnic or national origin, disability, age, marital status, sexual orientation or religion. All decisions relating to employment practices will be objective, free from bias and based solely upon work criteria and individual merit.

The Group is responsive to the needs of its employees, customers and the community at large and we are an organisation that endeavours to use everyone's talents and abilities to the full.

---

## Creditor payment policy

**3.83** Company law requires a reporting entity to disclose its payment policy for its suppliers. The provision applies to public companies and large private companies (that is, neither small nor medium-sized companies) that are members of a group whose parent is a public company. [CA85 7 Sch 12(1); SI 2008/410 7 Sch 12(1)(a)(b)]. The provisions apply at a company level and not to the group as a whole. The requirement is for the directors to state with respect to the financial year *following* that covered by the annual report whether it is the company's policy to follow any code or standard on payment practice. Only where a company follows a particular code does it have to give the name of the code or standard together with an indication of where information about, and copies of, the code or standard can be obtained. [CA85 7 Sch 12(2)(a); SI 2008/410 7 Sch 12(2)(a)]]. The directors also have to state whether it is the company's policy in respect of some or all of its suppliers:

■ To settle the terms of payment with those suppliers when agreeing the terms of each transaction.

■ To ensure that those suppliers are made aware of the terms of payment.

■ To abide by the terms of payment.

[CA85 7 Sch 12(2)(b); SI 2008/410 7 Sch 12(2)(b)].

**3.84** Where the company's policy is different in respect of some or all of its suppliers from that outlined above, the directors must also state the company's policy in respect of those suppliers. In addition, where the company's policy is different for different suppliers or classes of suppliers, the directors must identify in their report the suppliers or classes of suppliers to which the different policy applies. [CA85 7 Sch 12(2); SI 2008/410 7 Sch 12(2)]. Examples of payment policies are given in Tables 3.11 and 3.12.

**3.85** The directors' report is also required to state the number of days represented by trade creditors falling due for payment within one year at the year end (for example, UK GAAP balance sheet Format 1 item E4) compared to the total amounts invoiced to suppliers during the year. The requirement is to disclose the number of days that bears to the number of days in the financial year in the same proportion as X bears to Y where:

■ X = the aggregate of the amounts that were owed to trade creditors at the end of the year.

■ Y = the aggregate of the amounts invoiced by suppliers during the year.

[CA85 7 Sch 12(3); SI 2008/410 7 Sch 12(3)].

**3.86** The calculation of the number of creditor days is illustrated in the example below.

**Example**

Trade creditors at the end of the year are £30 million. Amounts invoiced during the year by suppliers are £300 million. Number of days in the financial year is 365.

$$\frac{30}{300} \times 365 \text{ days} = 36.5$$

**3.87** For the purposes of the above provisions, a person will be a supplier of the company at any time if:

■ At the time, the person is owed an amount in respect of the goods and services supplied.

■ The amount owed would be included within trade creditors (item E4 in Format 1) if the financial statements were prepared at that time, were prepared in accordance with Schedule 4 to the 1985 Act or Schedule 1 to SI 2008/410 and that format was adopted.

[CA85 7 Sch 12(4); SI 2008/410 7 Sch 12(4)].

**3.88** If a company does not draw up its accounts under balance sheet Format 1 in Schedule 4 to the 1985 Act (Schedule 1 to SI 2008/410), it still has to comply with the disclosures outlined above. If, for example, the company prepares its financial statements in accordance with IFRS or is a banking or insurance company, the disclosure has to be given in respect of creditors for goods and services that would have been included under trade creditors, had the company drawn up its financial statements in accordance with Schedule 4 (or Schedule 1). Therefore, for an insurance company, although insurance and reinsurance creditors would not be classified as trade creditors, creditors for stationery and rent would be and the required disclosure has to be given in respect of these creditors.

**3.88.1** There is no requirement to disclose comparative information in the directors' report but it is common and best practice to do so.

---

**Table 3.11 — Creditor payment policy**

**Alliance & Leicester plc — Annual report and accounts — 31 December 2007**

**Creditor payment policy**

The Group continues to be a signatory of the Department of Business Enterprise & Regulatory Reform's Better Payment Practice Code, more details on which can be found at www.payontime.co.uk. Our policy is to:

- Agree the terms of payment at the start of business with a supplier;
- Ensure suppliers are aware of the payment terms;
- Pay in accordance with any contractual and other legal obligations.

Trade creditors of the Company for the year ended 31 December 2007 were 12 days (2006 restated: 16 days), based on the ratio of Company trade creditors at the end of the year to the amounts invoiced during the year by trade creditors.

---

**Table 3.12 — Creditor payment policy**

**Marks and Spencer Group plc — Annual report and financial statements — 29 March 2008**

**Group Directors' report (extract)**

**Creditor payment policy**
For all trade creditors, it is the Group's policy to:

- agree the terms of payment at the start of business with that supplier;
- ensure that suppliers are aware of the terms of payment; and
- pay in accordance with its contractual and other legal obligations.

The main trading company, Marks and Spencer plc, has a policy concerning the payment of trade creditors as follows:

- general merchandise payments are received between 16 and 23 days after the stock was delivered;
- food payments are received between 18 and 25 days after the stock was delivered; and

---

- distribution suppliers are paid monthly, for costs incurred in that month, based on estimates, and payments are adjusted quarterly to reflect any variations to estimate.

Trade creditor days for Marks and Spencer plc for the year ended 29 March 2008 were 15.3 days, or 10.2 working days (last year 14.7 days, or 9.8 working days), based on the ratio of Company trade creditors at the end of the year to the amounts invoiced during the year by trade creditors.

**3.89**  To assist companies to honour their contract payment terms the DTI (now known as BERR) issued the Better Payment Practice Code, which is available on http://www.payontime.co.uk/.

**[The next paragraph is 3.100.]**

**Political and charitable donations**

*Summary of the provisions for disclosure and control*

**3.100**  Company law requires a company to make disclosure in the directors' report of political donations and expenditure in the UK/EU and outside the EU. [CA85 7 Sch 3, 4, 5; SI 2008/409 5 Sch 2, 3, 4; SI 2008/410 7 Sch 3, 4, 5]. It also requires a company to control its political donations and expenditure in the UK and in other EU Member States by requiring directors to seek prior shareholder authorisation.

*Definitions*

**3.101**  Sections 362 to 379 of the Companies Act 2006 (political donations and expenditure) apply to donations made or expenditure incurred on or after 1 October 2007. However, the provisions that concern the control of political donations and expenditure to independent election candidates come into force on 1 October 2008. The new provisions also apply to Northern Ireland.

**3.101.1**  The legislation relates to political expenditure and to political donations made by companies to:

- Political parties (both those registered in the UK and those acting in connection with any election to public office in any other EU Member State).

- Political organisations other than political parties, which are any organisation:

  - Carrying on, or proposing to carry on, activities capable of being reasonably regarded as intended to affect public support for any political party (as defined) or for independent candidates at elections to public office held in an EU Member State other than the UK.

  - Carrying on, or proposing to carry on, activities capable of being reasonably regarded as intended to influence voters in national or regional referendums held under the law of any EU Member State.

- Independent election candidates at any election to public office in the UK or another EU Member State (from 1 October 2008).

[CA06 Sec 363].

**3.101.2** The definition of a political donation is wide. It includes:

- Any gift of money or other property.

- Any sponsorship provided to cover expenses relating to any party conference, meeting or event, the preparation, publication or dissemination of any party publication or any party political study or research (or to ensure that such expenses are not incurred).

- Any fee or subscription paid for membership of or affiliation to a political party or organisation.

- Any money spent in paying expenses incurred directly or indirectly by a political party, organisation or election candidate.

- Any money lent to a political party, organisation or election candidate otherwise than on a commercial basis.

- The provision (other than on a commercial basis) of property, services or facilities, (including the services of any person).

The definition includes donations to any officer, member, trustee or agent of a political party, in his/her capacity as such. Further, it includes any donation made through a third party. [CA06 Sec 364].

**3.101.3** Section 364 of the 2006 Act defines a 'political donation' by reference to sections 50 to 52 of the Political Parties, Elections and Referendums Act 2000 (disregarding amendments made by the Electoral Administration Act 2006, which remove from the definition of 'donation' loans made otherwise than on commercial terms).

**3.101.4** Political expenditure means any expenditure incurred by a company in respect of:

- the preparation, publication or dissemination of advertising, promotional or publicity material of any kind that is capable of being reasonably regarded as intended to affect public support for a political party or other political organisation, or an independent election candidate; or

- any of the company's activities of the kind referred to in the third and fourth bullet points of the definition of 'political organisation'.

[CA06 Sec 365].

### Prohibition on political donations and expenditure

**3.102**  A company is prohibited from making any political donation to a political party, political organisation or (from 1 October 2008) independent election candidate, or incurring any political expenditure unless the donation or EU political expenditure has been authorised by the company using an 'approval resolution' (see para 3.105). [CA06 Sec 366(1)].

**3.103**  This resolution must be passed before the donation or political expenditure is made or incurred or, if earlier, any relevant contract entered into. See also the special rules for subsidiaries in paragraph 3.107. Shareholder approval is not required of donations or expenditure for purposes that are not connected with party politics in any EU Member State, but these still require disclosure.

**[The next paragraph is 3.105.]**

**3.105**  An approval resolution is a resolution passed by the company that:

■  Authorises the company to make donations not exceeding a specified total or incur political expenditure (including EU political expenditure) not exceeding a specified total for a period of not more than four years beginning with the date of the resolution.

■  Is expressed in general terms (accordingly, it must not purport to authorise particular donations or expenditure).

[CA06 Sec 367].

### Exemptions for donations

**3.106**  Sections 374 to 378 of the Companies Act 2006 set out five exemptions from the requirement for prior shareholder authorisation:

■  Donations to trade unions (including those in countries other than the UK). The exemption covers donations such as the provision of company rooms for trade union meetings, the use of company vehicles by trade union officials and paid time off for trade union officials to act in that capacity. However, a donation to a trade union's political fund is not covered by the exemption. [CA06 Sec 374].

■  Subscriptions paid to EU trade associations for membership (including trade associations that carry out their activities outside the EU). [CA06 Sec 375].

■  Donations to all-party parliamentary groups. [CA06 Sec 376].

■  Political expenditure that is exempt by virtue of an order by the Secretary of State. [CA06 Sec 377].

■  Small political donations: authorisation is not required unless the political donation or aggregate amount of the political donations by the company in the 12 months ending on the date of the donation exceeds £5,000. Donations by other group companies (including subsidiaries) must be taken into account in calculating whether the £5,000 threshold has been exceeded. [CA06 Sec 378].

## Subsidiaries incorporated in Great Britain and Northern Ireland

**3.107** If the company is a subsidiary of another company (its holding company), an approval resolution may need to be passed by the holding company's shareholders as well as or instead of those of the company. This is relevant where the company is not a wholly-owned subsidiary of a UK-registered company. In addition to the resolution of the company, a resolution must be passed by its 'relevant holding company'. The relevant holding company is the ultimate holding company or, where such a company is not a UK-registered company, the holding company highest up the chain that is a UK-registered company. [CA06 Sec 366].

**3.108** A wholly-owned subsidiary of a UK-registered company is not required to pass a resolution approving political donations or expenditure, although its relevant holding company is required to do so. [CA06 Sec 366(3)].

**Example 1**

X limited wishes to make a political donation. It is an 80% subsidiary of Y limited, which is a subsidiary of Z plc. Approval resolutions must be passed by X limited (the company) and Z plc (the ultimate holding company).

**Example 2**

The facts are the same as in example 1 except that entity Z is incorporated outside the UK. Approval resolutions must be passed by X limited and Y limited (the highest UK-registered holding company of X limited).

**Example 3**

The facts are the same as in example 2 except that X limited is a 100% subsidiary of Y limited. An approval resolution must be passed by Y limited, but need not be passed by X limited.

## Directors' liability

**3.109** There are no criminal sanctions in relation to making unauthorised political donations or incurring unauthorised political expenditure. Civil remedies are available to a company in the event of a breach of the prohibitions and may be pursued in the normal manner by the company.

**3.110** If the company makes an unauthorised payment, the directors and (unless they took all available steps to prevent the political donation being made or the political expenditure being incurred), the directors of the relevant holding company are liable to reimburse the company for the amount of the political donation or political expenditure and damages for any loss it suffers together with interest until the amount is repaid to the company. [CA06 Sec 369].

**3.111** Action may be taken against the directors for reimbursement by not less than 50 members or members holding not less than five per cent of the issued share capital. In addition, in any such action, the members are entitled to require the company to provide all relevant information. If the company refuses to do so, the court may make an order directing the company or its officers or employees to provide the information. [CA06 Secs 370(3), 373(1)].

***Disclosure of political donations and expenditure — financial years beginning before 6 April 2008***

**3.112** There are separate disclosure regimes for:

■ Political donations and expenditure within the UK/EU area.

■ Contributions to political parties in the rest of the world.

*Stand alone company — not wholly-owned by a GB parent*

**3.113** If the company has made any donation to a registered party (that is, a UK political party) or other EU political organisation and/or incurred any EU political expenditure exceeding in aggregate £200 in a financial year, it must disclose the following particulars in the directors' report for the year:

■ For donations, the name of each registered party or other EU political organisation and the total amount given in the financial year.

■ For EU political expenditure, the total amount incurred in the financial year.

[CA85 7 Sch 3(1)(2)].

**3.114** All contributions made by the company to non-EU political parties also require disclosure (although there is no requirement to name the parties). There is no threshold for these disclosures. Therefore, if the company has in the financial year made any contribution to a non-EU political party the directors' report for the year must contain:

■ A statement of the amount contributed.

■ If it has made more than one contribution in the year, a statement of the total contribution.

[CA85 7 Sch 4].

*Company with subsidiary — not wholly-owned by a GB parent*

**3.115** The following applies where the company has subsidiaries that have made donations or incurred EU political expenditure in that financial year. If the amount of combined donations and EU political expenditure of the company and its subsidiaries exceeds £200, the directors' report for the year must disclose the particulars mentioned in paragraph 3.113 above in relation to the company and each subsidiary by whom any such donation or EU political expenditure has been made or incurred. [CA85 7 Sch 3(3)].

**3.116** Where the company has subsidiaries that have made any contributions to a non-EU political party in the financial year the following applies. The directors' report of the company is not required to disclose the amount of the company's own contributions, but shall instead contain a statement of the total amount of the contributions made by the company and its subsidiaries in the year. There is no threshold for these disclosures.

*Company that is a wholly-owned subsidiary of a GB parent*

**3.117** The effect of the rules described in paragraphs 3.113 to 3.116 above to a company that is a wholly-owned subsidiary of a company incorporated in Great Britain is as follows. Such a subsidiary does not have to disclose its donations, expenditure or contributions in its own directors' report, but these must be disclosed by its holding company as mentioned above.

***Disclosure of political donations and expenditure — financial years beginning on or after 6 April 2008***

*Stand alone company — not wholly-owned by a UK parent*

**3.117.1** If the company has made any donation to a political party, other political organisation or (for financial years beginning on or after 1 October 2009) independent election candidate or has incurred any political expenditure, and the aggregate of those exceeds £2,000 in a financial year, it must disclose the following particulars in the directors' report for the year:

- For political donations, the name of each political party, political organisation or (for financial years beginning on or after 1 October 2009) independent election candidate and the amount given to each in the financial year.

- The total amount of political expenditure incurred in the financial year.

[SI 2008/409 5 Sch 2(2); SI 2008/410 7 Sch 3(2)].

**3.117.2** All contributions made by the company to non-EU political parties also require disclosure (although there is no requirement to name the parties). There is no threshold for these disclosures. Therefore, if the company has in the financial year made any contribution to a non-EU political party the directors' report for the year must contain:

- A statement of the amount contributed.

- If it has made more than one contribution in the year, a statement of the total contributions.

[SI 2008/409 5 Sch 3(1); SI 2008/410 7 Sch 4(1)].

*Company with subsidiary — not wholly-owned by a UK parent*

**3.117.3**   The following applies where the company has subsidiaries that have made political donations or incurred political expenditure in the financial year. If the amount of the combined political donations and the political expenditure of the company and its subsidiaries exceeds £2,000, the directors' report for the year must disclose the particulars mentioned in paragraph 3.117.2 above in relation to the company and each subsidiary by whom any such political donation or political expenditure has been made or incurred. [SI 2008/409 5 Sch 2(3); SI 2008/ 410 7 Sch 3(3)].

**3.117.4**   Where the company has subsidiaries that have made any contributions to a non-EU political party in the financial year the following applies. The directors' report of the company is not required to disclose the amount of the company's own contributions, but should instead contain a statement of the total amount of the contributions made by the company and its subsidiaries in the year. There is no threshold for these disclosures. [SI 2008/409 5 Sch 3(2); SI 2008/410 7 Sch 4(2)].

*Company that is a wholly-owned subsidiary of a UK parent*

**3.117.5**   A wholly-owned subsidiary of a company incorporated in the UK does not have to disclose its donations, expenditure or contributions in its own directors' report, but these must be disclosed by its holding company as mentioned above.

**Disclosure of charitable gifts — accounting periods beginning before 6 April 2008**

**3.118**   Paragraph 5 of Schedule 7 to the 1985 Companies Act deals solely with charitable gifts. The disclosures required are as follows:

- *By a company (that is not a wholly-owned subsidiary of a company incorporated in Great Britain).*

    If such a company has given money exceeding £200 for charitable purposes in a financial year, its directors' report for the year must contain, for each of the purposes for which money has been given, a statement of the amount of money given for that purpose.

- *By a company with subsidiaries (that is not a wholly-owned subsidiary of a company incorporated in Great Britain).*

  In this case, the requirements in the bullet point above do not apply to the company. But if the amount given in the year for charitable purposes by the company and its subsidiaries exceeds £200, the following will apply. The directors' report for the year must contain, for each of the purposes for which money has been given by the company and its subsidiaries between them, a statement of the amount given for that purpose.

**3.119**   For these disclosures required by paragraph 5 of Schedule 7, 'charitable purposes' means purposes that are exclusively charitable and in Scotland, 'charitable' is defined in section 7(2) of the Charities and Trustee Investment (Scotland) Act 2005. Money given for charitable purposes to a person, who at the time of the gift, was ordinarily resident outside the UK is to be left out of account for these purposes.

**3.120**   Money given for purposes that include either a political or a commercial element would not come within the disclosure required by paragraph 5 of Schedule 7. However, a donation with a political element may be disclosable as a political donation and require shareholder approval. Some companies may consider it good practice to seek shareholders' approval for charitable gifts, although, unlike political donations, this is not a statutory requirement.

---

**Table 3.13A – Political and charitable donations**

**British American Tobacco p.l.c. – Report and Accounts – 31 December 2004**

**Charitable and political contributions**

Payments for charitable purposes in 2004 amounted to £14.6 million, £1.1 million of which was paid in the UK. No donation was made to any political party registered in the UK under the Political Parties, Elections and Referendums Act 2000 (the Act) but the Company gave £25,000 to Britain in Europe, which is regarded as an 'EU political organisation' for the purposes of that Act. The Company made donations in Germany to the Christlich Soziale Union and the Freie Demokratische Partei, both of which are considered to be EU political organisations for the purposes of the Act, totalling £678 and £8,488 respectively. Subsidiaries of the Company in Australia, Canada and the US made contributions to non-EU political parties in their respective countries of incorporation totalling £89,253. In addition, in the US, contributions of £17,627 were made to individual candidates.

---

***Disclosure of charitable gifts — accounting periods beginning on or after 6 April 2008***

**3.121**   The disclosures required are as follows:

- *By a company that is not a wholly-owned subsidiary of a company incorporated in the UK.*

  If such a company has given money exceeding £2,000 for charitable purposes in a financial year, its directors' report for the year must contain, for each of the purposes for which money has been given, a statement of the amount of money given for that purpose. [SI 2008/409 5 Sch 4(1); SI 2008/410 7 Sch 5(1)].

■ *By a company with subsidiaries that is not a wholly-owned subsidiary of a company incorporated in the UK.*

In this case, the requirements in the bullet point above do not apply to the company. But if the amount given in the year for charitable purposes by the company and its subsidiaries exceeds £2,000, the directors' report for the year must contain, for each of the purposes for which money has been given by the company and its subsidiaries between them, a statement of the amount given for that purpose. [SI 2008/409 5 Sch 4(2); SI 2008/410 7 Sch 5(2)].

**3.121.1** For these disclosures 'charitable purposes' means purposes that are exclusively charitable and in Scotland, 'charitable' is defined in section 7(2) of the Charities and Trustee Investment (Scotland) Act 2005. Money given for charitable purposes to a person, who at the time of the gift, was ordinarily resident outside the UK is to be left out of account for these purposes. [SI 2008/409 5 Sch 4(4); SI 2008/410 7 Sch 5(4)].

**3.121.2** Money given for purposes that include either a political or a commercial element would not come within the disclosure of charitable donations. However, a donation with a political element may be disclosable as a political donation and require shareholder approval. Some companies may consider it good practice to seek shareholders' approval for charitable gifts, although, unlike political donations, this is not a statutory requirement.

**Financial instruments**

**3.122** Companies (other than those subject to the small companies regime) are required provide the following disclosures in the directors' report in relation to the entity as a whole:

■ The entity's financial risk management objectives and policies, including the policy for hedging each major type of forecasted transaction for which hedge accounting is used.

■ The entity's exposure to price risk, credit risk, liquidity risk and cash flow risk.

The disclosure is not required where such information is not material for the assessment of the entity's assets, liabilities, financial position and profit or loss. [CA85 7 Sch 5A(1); SI 2008/410 7 Sch 6(1)].

**3.123** These requirements are consistent with IFRS 7 and FRS 29, both called 'Financial instruments: Disclosures'. Although not all companies preparing Companies Act financial statements are required to comply with FRS 29, it provides additional guidance as to appropriate disclosure.

**3.124** FRS 29 and IFRS 7 require an entity to *"provide disclosures that enable users to evaluate: (a) the significance of financial instruments for the entity's financial position and performance; and (b) the nature and extent of risks arising from financial instruments to which the entity is exposed during the period and at the reporting date, and how the entity manages those risks"*. [FRS 29 para 1; IFRS 7 para 1]. Extensive quantitative and qualitative disclosures of each type of risk arising from financial instruments (credit risk, market risk and liquidity risk) are required. [FRS 29 paras 31-42; IFRS 7 paras 31-42]. (See further chapter 6 of the Manual of Accounting — UK GAAP and the Manual of Accounting – IFRS for the UK.)

**3.125** Both IFRS 7 and FRS 29 require the disclosures to be given in the notes to the financial statements. For companies that comply with either IFRS 7 or FRS 29, to avoid the need for duplication, a specific cross-reference may be included in the directors' report to the relevant note.

**Disclosure of overseas branches**

**3.126** Companies (other than unlimited companies and those subject to the small companies regime) must give an indication of the existence of branches that they operate outside the UK. [CA85 7 Sch 6(d); SI 2008/410 7 Sch 7(1)(d)]. For this purpose, a branch is defined in section 698 of the 1985 Act (section 1046(3) of the 2006 Act) to mean only branches within the EU (see further chapter 33 of the Manual of Accounting – UK GAAP). Therefore, branches operated in the US, for example, would not require disclosure. It should be noted that disclosure is required only of the company's branches, not those of its subsidiaries. This means that the directors' report of a parent company need only refer to the existence of branches that it operates outside the UK and not to those that are operated outside the UK by its subsidiaries. Branches operated by its subsidiaries would fall to be disclosed in the subsidiaries' directors' reports.

**Directors' responsibility statements**

**3.127** There is no Companies Act requirement for a company's directors to include a statement of their responsibilities anywhere in the annual report. There is, however, a requirement that is derived from auditing standards and applies to all companies. For listed companies, however, there has been a recommendation since 1992, now incorporated into the Combined Code 2006, for directors to make a statement of their responsibilities. [CC C.1.1]. In addition, for accounting periods beginning on or after 20 January 2007, the Disclosure and Transparency Rules of the FSA require listed companies to make certain disclosures about directors' responsibilities (see further from para 3.127.6).

**3.127.1** ISA (UK&I) 700, 'The auditor's report on the financial statements', has, in substance, imposed the requirement for a director's responsibility statement on all companies. It does not impose a requirement on directors, but imposes one on auditors if such a statement is not made by the directors. It refers to the responsibilities of those charged with governance (which, in a UK context, is the company's directors) and states that:

*"(a) the auditor should distinguish between the auditor's responsibilities and the responsibilities of those charged with governance by including in the auditor's report a reference to a description of the relevant responsibilities of those charged with governance when that description is set out elsewhere in the financial statements or accompanying information; or*

*(b) where the financial statements or accompanying information do not include an adequate description of the relevant responsibilities of those charged with governance, the auditor's report should include a description of those responsibilities."*

[ISA (UK&I) 700 para 9-1].

**3.127.2**  To complement ISA (UK&I) 700, the APB has included specimen wording describing the directors' responsibilities for inclusion in an annual report where the parent company and the group apply the same accounting framework. This wording is found in Appendix 5 of Bulletin 2006/06, 'Auditor's reports on financial statements in the United Kingdom'. In addition, the example financial statements for GAAP UK plc, IFRS GAAP plc and UK GAAP Limited (see 'Illustrative financial statements: IFRS and UK GAAP 2008') each contain example wording for directors' responsibility statements.

**3.127.2.1**  In more complicated situations, for example, where the company is listed in a market outside the UK where different requirements may apply, the directors may need to take legal advice on what to include in the statement of directors' responsibilities.

**3.127.2.2**  It is now usual for a company to post its financial reports on its web site (indeed, it is a requirement for quoted companies for years beginning on or after 6 April 2008 — see further chapter 8). [CA06 Sec 430]. The example in the APB's Bulletin includes a statement that the directors take responsibility for the maintenance and integrity of financial information contained on the company's web site, which should be included where that web site includes financial reports. Table 3.13B shows an example from published financial statements that reflects such responsibility. The inclusion of this responsibility in the directors' responsibilities statement negates the requirement to include it in the audit report.

*Directors' report*

---

**Table 3.13B – Directors' responsibilities**

**BT Group plc – Annual report – 31 March 2008**

**Statement of directors' responsibilities**

The directors are responsible for preparing the group's financial statements in accordance with applicable law and International Financial Reporting Standards (IFRS) as adopted by the European Union (EU) and issued by the IASB, and for preparing the parent company financial statements in accordance with applicable law and United Kingdom Accounting Standards (United Kingdom Generally Accepted Accounting Practice).

The directors are responsible for preparing financial statements for each financial year which give a true and fair view, in accordance with IFRS as adopted by the EU and issued by the IASB, of the state of affairs of the group and of the profit or loss of the group and a true and fair view, in accordance with United Kingdom Generally Accepted Accounting Practice (UK GAAP), of the state of affairs of the company and of the profit or loss of the company for that period. In preparing those financial statements, the directors are required to:

- select suitable accounting policies and then apply them consistently;
- make judgments and estimates that are reasonable and prudent;
- state whether the consolidated financial statements comply with IFRS as adopted by the EU and issued by the IASB, and with regard to the parent company financial statements whether applicable accounting standards have been followed, subject to any material departures disclosed and explained in the financial statements; and
- prepare the consolidated and parent company financial statements on the going concern basis unless it is inappropriate to presume that the group will continue in business.

The directors confirm that they have complied with the above requirements in preparing the financial statements. The directors are responsible for keeping proper accounting records that disclose with reasonable accuracy at any time the financial position of the company and the group and to enable them to ensure that the group financial statements comply with the Companies Act 1985 and Article 4 of the IAS Regulation and the parent company financial statements comply with the Companies Act 1985. They are also responsible for the preparation of the Report on directors' remuneration, safeguarding the assets of the company and the group and hence for taking reasonable steps for the prevention and detection of fraud and other irregularities.

The directors are responsible for the maintenance and integrity of the corporate and financial information included on the group's website. Legislation in the United Kingdom governing the preparation and dissemination of financial statements may differ from legislation in other jurisdictions.

The directors confirm, to the best of their knowledge:

- that the consolidated financial statements, which have been prepared in accordance with IFRS as adopted by the EU and issued by the IASB, give a true and fair view of the assets, liabilities, financial position and profit or loss of the group; and
- that the Report of the Directors includes a fair review of the information required by Rules 4.1.8-4.1.11 of the Disclosure and Transparency Rules of the United Kingdom Financial Services Authority.

The names and functions of all of the directors are under Board of Directors and Operating Committee.

---

**3.127.2.3**   For entities that are included in the official list maintained by the FSA, the Disclosure and Transparency Rules of the FSA require the annual financial report to include a responsibility statement. [DTR para 4.1.5]. The DTR require that the persons responsible within the listed company (that is, the directors) state that, to the best of their knowledge:

■   The financial statements, prepared in accordance with the applicable set of accounting standards, give a true and fair view of the assets, liabilities, financial position and profit or loss of the listed company and the undertakings included in the consolidation taken as a whole.

■   The management report includes a fair review of the development and performance of the business and the position of the company and the undertakings included in the consolidation taken as a whole, together with a description of the principal risks and uncertainties that they face (the same wording as is used in the directors' report business review requirements in Section 417 of the 2006 Act).

[DTR 4.1.12].

This requirement does not extend to companies traded on AIM or the Plus Market's PLUS-quoted market.

**3.127.2.4**   The directors already have a responsibility to provide financial statements, prepared in accordance with applicable accounting standards that give a true and fair view. For financial years beginning prior to 6 April 2008, this was contained in section 226A of the 1985 Act for Companies Act financial statements and in IAS 1 for IAS financial statements. For subsequent financial years, this is contained in section 393 of the 2006 Act. They are also responsible for preparing of a business review (see further from para 3.23). The DTR simply require the directors to make positive statements regarding their responsibilities.

**3.127.2.5**   The name and function of each person making a responsibility statement under the DTR must be clearly indicated in the responsibility statement. [DTR 4.1.12]. If the responsibility statement is provided collectively by the board (and, for example, signed by the company secretary or a director on its behalf), all directors are, in substance, making the responsibility statement. It is not usual for the directors' names and job titles to be listed elsewhere in the annual report and it would seem appropriate, to avoid duplication, hence a specific cross-reference from the directors' report would fulfil the DTR requirements.

**[The next paragraph is 3.127.5.]**

**Statement on disclosure of information to the auditors**

**3.127.5**   The directors' report must contain a statement to confirm, for all directors in office at the time the report is approved, the following:

■   So far as each director is aware, there is no relevant audit information of which the company's auditors are unaware. Relevant information is defined as *"information needed by the company's auditors in connection with preparing their report".*

■ Each director has taken all the steps that he ought to have taken in his duty as a director in order to make himself aware of any relevant audit information and to establish that the company's auditors are aware of that information.

Steps that a director ought to have taken would include making enquiries of other directors and the auditors and any other steps required by the director's duty to exercise due care, skill and diligence.

[CA85 Sec 234ZA(2) to (4); CA06 Secs 418(1) to (4)].

**3.127.6** In determining the extent of each director's duty, the Act states that the following considerations are relevant:

■ The knowledge, skill and experience that may reasonably be expected of a person carrying out the functions of a company director.

■ The knowledge, skill and experience that a director actually has.

[CA85 Sec 234ZA(5); CA06 Sec 174].

**3.127.7** The penalty for *'knowingly or recklessly'* making a false statement in this regard, or failing to take reasonable steps to prevent the directors' report being approved, may be imprisonment or a fine, or both, for each director indicted. [CA85 Sec 234ZA(6); CA06 Sec 418(5)(6)].

### Re-appointment of auditors

**3.128** It is customary, but not a statutory requirement, to state at the end of the directors' report that a resolution will be put to the general meeting, regarding the appointment or re-appointment of the auditors. Where a private company has elected to dispense with the requirement to appoint auditors annually in accordance with section 386 of the 1985 Act (or is deemed to have reappointed its auditors in accordance with section 487(2) of the 2006 Act), such a statement will of course not be relevant. In that situation, companies may wish to include a statement indicating that in the absence of a notice proposing that the appointment be terminated, the auditors will be deemed to be re-appointed for the next financial year.

### Disclosure of qualifying third party indemnity provisions

**3.128.1** Where a qualifying third party indemnity provision (made by the company or otherwise) was in force for the benefit of one or more directors at any time during the financial year, or at the time when the report is approved, a statement should be made in the directors' report to confirm this fact. [CA85 Sec 309C; CA06 Sec 236(2),(3)].

**3.128.2** A statement is also required in the directors' report where a qualifying indemnity provision has been made during the year, or at the time when the report is approved, by the company for the benefit of one or more directors of an associated company. [CA85 Sec 309C(4); CA06 Sec 236(4),(5)]. An associated company is defined in section 309A of the 1985 Act (section 256 of the 2006 Act). A holding company is associated with all its subsidiaries and a subsidiary is associated with its holding company and all the other subsidiaries of its holding company.

**3.128.3** Section 309B of the 1985 Act (section 232(2) of the 2006 Act) define a qualifying third-party indemnity provision as one where the provision does not provide indemnity for any liability incurred by the director in respect of each of the following:

- An amount due to the company or any associated company.

- A fine imposed by criminal proceedings.

- A penalty payable to a regulatory authority in respect of non-compliance with any requirement of a regulatory nature.

- An amount payable:

  - in defending criminal proceedings in which the director is convicted;

  - in defending civil proceedings brought by the company (or an associated company) in which judgement is given against the director; or

  - in connection with any application in which the court refused to grant the director relief.

## Additional matters for publicly traded companies

**3.129** The directors' report of companies with publicly traded securities should give information on further matters in addition to those already discussed above. These additional matters are considered in the paragraphs that follow.

### Control and share structures

**3.129.1** These are general requirements designed to bring greater transparency to the market and apply to companies whether or not they are involved in a takeover. The disclosure requirements apply to companies with voting shares that were admitted to trading on a regulated market at the end of the year. [CA85 7 Sch 13(1); SI 2008/410 7 Sch 13(1)].

**3.129.2** The specific disclosure requirements are set out in Part VII of Schedule 7 to the 1985 Act (Part 6 of Schedule 7 to SI 2008/410) and include:

- The structure of the company's capital, including the rights and obligations attached to the shares.

- Any restrictions on the transfer of securities.

- Any restriction on voting rights.

- Where a person has a significant direct or indirect holding, the identity of the person, the size of the holding and the nature of the holding (see further from para 3.131).

- Where any person holds shares with specific rights regarding control of the company:

  - the identity of the person; and

  - the nature of those rights.

- Where the company has an employees' share scheme but shares relating to that scheme have rights regarding the control of the company that are not directly exercisable by the employees, how those rights are exercisable.

- Agreements between holders of securities known to the company that may result in restrictions on the transfer of securities or voting rights.

- Any rules that the company has about the appointment of directors, powers of directors or amendments to the company's articles of association.

- Significant agreements that the company is a party to that will be affected by a change in control of the company, together with the affects of such agreements (see further from para 3.129.9).

- Any agreements with employees (including directors) of the company providing for compensation for loss of office on the takeover of the company.

**[The next paragraph is 3.129.5.]**

**3.129.5**   The information required must be set out in the directors' report.

**3.129.6**   Failure to include either the information concerning control and share structures or explanatory material in the annual report will attract existing criminal sanctions under section 234(5) of the 1985 Act (sections 415 (4), (5), and 419 (3), (4) of the 2006 Act) (directors responsible for the failure to comply with provisions related to the directors' report are liable to a fine).

**Agreements affected by a change of control**

**3.129.7**   The extent to which agreements that a company has entered into will be affected by a change of control will vary, as will the nature of those contracts. Examples of agreements that may be affected (other than those specifically mentioned by the Act) are:

- Bank loan/facility agreements.

- Convertible and listed debt.

- Sale/supply agreements.

- Leases.

- Joint venture agreements.

An example showing both disclosure of agreements that would be affected by a change of control and a restriction of voting rights (that is also affected by a change of control) is given in Table 3.14.

---

**Table 3.14 – Disclosure of agreements affected by change of control**

**BSkyB Group plc – Annual Report – 30 June 2007**

**Directors' report (extract)**

**Significant agreements**
Details of any significant agreements that take effect, alter or terminate on a change of control of the Company, are disclosed in the Review of the business on page 15.

**The business, its objectives and its strategy (extract page 15)**

**Significant agreements**
The Companies Act 2006 requires us to disclose the following significant agreements that take effect, alter or terminate on a change of control of the Company:

**FAPL**
In May 2006, British Sky Broadcasting Limited entered into an agreement (the 'FAPL Licence') with The Football Association Premier League Limited (the 'FAPL') pursuant to which, the Group was awarded four of six available packages of live audio-visual rights for F.A. Premier League football (the six packages are together the 'Live Packages').

The FAPL will not award all of the Live Packages to a single licensee (either on its own or as part of a consortium or through one or more of its related parties) (the 'Single Buyer Rule').

Pursuant to the FAPL Licence, the FAPL can suspend and/or terminate all of the rights which are included in, or exercisable as part of, one of the six available Live Packages in the event that a change of control of the Company occurs at any time prior to the expiry of the FAPL Licence which, if it had occurred prior to the award of the Live Packages to the Group, would have resulted in a breach of the Single Buyer Rule.

**RCF**
On 3 November 2004, the Company, British Sky Broadcasting Limited and Sky Subscribers Services Limited entered into a revolving credit facility agreement with Barclays Capital, Citigroup Global Markets Limited, Deutsche Bank AG London, JP Morgan plc and the Royal Bank of Scotland plc (as mandated lead arrangers) and certain other financial institutions (as 'Lenders') pursuant to which the Lenders agreed to make available to the Company £1 billion to refinance existing facilities and for general corporate purposes (the 'RCF').

Pursuant to the RCF, the Lenders can require all amounts outstanding under the RCF to be repaid in the event of a change of control of the Company (other than where The News Corporation or any subsidiary or holding company thereof acquires such control).

**News Corporation voting agreement**
On 21 September 2005, the Company, BSkyB Holdco Inc., News UK Nominees Limited and News Corporation entered into a voting agreement which became unconditional on 4 November 2005 pursuant to which News UK Nominees Limited's voting rights at any general meeting are

---

capped at 37.19% (the 'Voting Agreement'). The provisions of the Voting Agreement cease to apply inter alia, on a change of control of the Company.

**EMTN bond issue**

On 3 April 2007, the Group established a Euro medium term note programme (the 'EMTN Programme') which provides the Group with a standardised documentation platform to allow for senior debt issuance in the Eurobond markets. The maximum potential issuance under the EMTN Programme is £1 billion.

On 14 May 2007, the Company issued Eurobonds consisting of £300 million guaranteed notes paying 6.000% interest and maturing on 14 May 2027 (the 'Notes'). The Notes were issued under the Group's EMTN Programme.

Pursuant to the final terms attaching to the Notes, a holder of the Notes has the option to require the Company to redeem or (at the Company's option) purchase its Notes at its principal amount plus interest for the relevant period if there is a change of control of the Company (i) which, if the Notes carry an investment grade credit rating, results in a downgrade to a non-investment grade rating or a withdrawal of that rating; or (ii) where, if the Notes carry a non-investment grade rating, results in a downgrade by one or more notches or a withdrawal of that non-investment grade rating; or (iii) where, if the Notes do not carry a credit rating, the Company does not seek such a rating or is unable to achieve such a rating.

**UK broadcasting licences**

The Group is party to a number of Ofcom broadcasting licences for the broadcast of the Sky Channels.

The Broadcasting Act 1990 (as amended by the Broadcasting Act 1996 and the Communications Act) lays down a number of restrictions on who may hold Ofcom broadcasting licences. Among those restricted from holding Ofcom broadcasting licences or from controlling a licensed Company are (a) local authorities, (b) political bodies, (c) religious bodies, (d) any company controlled by any of the previous categories or by their officers or associates, (e) advertising agencies or any company controlled by such an agency or in which it holds more than a 5% interest.

Licensees are obliged to comply with these ownership restrictions. Failure by a licensee to do so (either by the licensee becoming a 'disqualified person' or any change affecting the nature, characteristics or control of the licensee which would have precluded the original grant of the licence) may constitute a breach of the licence and, if not rectified, could result in revocation of the licence.

## Matters for listed companies

**3.129.7.1**  The following requirements apply to those companies that are subject to the UKLA's Listing Rules (for example, companies traded on the main market of the LSE or the Plus Market's PLUS-listed market).

### Major interest in company's shares

**3.130**  A statement should be given of particulars of the nature and extent of the interests of any person, in any holding of three per cent or more of the nominal value of any class of capital carrying rights to vote in all circumstances at general meetings of the company. The statement must be made at a date not more than one month prior to the date of notice of the annual general meeting. [LR 9.8.6R(2)].

**3.131** The particulars to be disclosed include the names of the persons and the amount of their interests. This information should be consistent with that contained in the register the company maintains under section 211 of the 1985 Act (section 808 of the 2006 Act). If there is no such interest, that fact should also be stated. [LR 9.8.6R(2)]. It is customary to give this information in the directors' report. An example is given in Table 3.15 below.

---

**Table 3.15 — Major interest in company's shares**

**Smiths Group plc — Report and Accounts — 31 July 2005**

**Directors' report (extract)**

**Interests in shares**
As at 21 September 2005 the Company had been notified, pursuant to the Companies Act 1985, of the following material or notifiable interests in its issued share capital:

| | No. of shares | Percentage of issued share capital[†] |
|---|---|---|
| Barclays PLC | 22.6m | 4.0% |
| Franklin Resources, Inc. | 60.3m | 10.7% |
| Legal & General Group plc | 20.7m | 3.7% |
| Janus Capital Management LLC | 22.2m | 3.9% |
| FMR Corp/Fidelity International Limited | 39.7m | 7.0% |

[†] percentage of share capital in issue on 21 September 2005.

---

**3.132** Although there is no requirement in the Companies Act 2006 for a company to maintain a shareholders' register (the requirement contained in the Companies Act 1985 having been repealed), it will be necessary to do so in order to meet this Listing Rule disclosure requirement. In order to ensure that the register is up to date, the Companies Act 2006 gives listed companies the right to write to any person who it believes is (or has been during the previous three years) interested in the company's shares and ask them to confirm that fact, or to state the person to whom the interest was transferred, [CA06 Sec 793]. Further, the DTR requires holders of more than three per cent of a company's qualifying financial instruments to notify the company if that holding increases above or falls below any integer percentage holding equal to or higher than three percent (see further chapter 8).

**[The next paragraph is 3.135.]**

*Directors' report*

## Transactions with a controlling shareholder

**3.135** The directors' report should disclose particulars of any contract of significance between the company (or one of its subsidiary undertakings) and a controlling shareholder subsisting during the year. [LR 9.8.4R(10)(b)]. For this purpose, a 'contract of significance' is one which is determined in accordance with the rules set out in paragraph 3.72 above. An example is given in Table 3.16 below.

**3.135.1** A 'controlling shareholder' is defined within the definition of an associate in the Listing Rules and is taken to mean any person who is:

■ entitled to exercise, or control the exercise of, at least 30 per cent of the voting power at the company's general meetings; or

■ is in a position to control the composition of a majority of the company's board of directors.

[LR App 1.1].

**3.135.2** In addition, the directors' report should disclose details of any contract with a controlling shareholder (as defined above) to provide services to the company or to one of its subsidiaries (see Table 3.16 below). This information is not required if the shareholder is providing services that it normally provides as part of its principal business and it is not a contract of significance that is required to be disclosed. [LR 9.8.4R(11)].

---

**Table 3.16 — Contract with a controlling shareholder**

**Premier Foods plc — Annual Report and Accounts — 31 December 2004**

**Directors' Report (extract)**

**Contracts of significance with controlling shareholder**
Details of related transactions with related parties are set out in notes 24 and 29 to the financial statements on pages 71 to 73.

**29. Related party transactions (extract)**
Prior to the IPO HMTFPL had a controlling interest in the Group. As a consequence of which a number of related party arrangements existed between the Group and HMTFPL and its affiliates, which included Hicks, Muse & Co Partners L.P. ("Hicks, Muse & Co."). Save as disclosed elsewhere in these financial statements, details of these arrangements with HMTFPL and its affiliates are shown below:

**Monitoring and Oversight agreement**
In 1999, Premier Foods Holdings Limited and Premier Financing Limited entered into a 10-year agreement (the "Monitoring and Oversight agreement") with Hicks, Muse & Co. pursuant to which the Group pays Hicks, Muse & Co. an annual fee of £1.2m for providing financial oversight and monitoring services to the Group. The annual fee is adjustable at the end of each financial year to an amount equal to one tenth of one per cent of the Group's budgeted consolidated annual net sales, but in no event may the fee be less than £1.2m. In addition, the Group has agreed to indemnify Hicks, Muse & Co. and its shareholders and their respective directors, officers, agents, employees and affiliates from and against all claims, actions, proceedings, demands, liabilities, judgements, assessments, losses and costs, including fees and expenses, arising out of or in connection with the services rendered by Hicks, Muse & Co. under

---

the Monitoring and Oversight agreement. The Monitoring and Oversight agreement makes available to the Group the resources of Hicks, Muse & Co. concerning a variety of financial and operational matters. The services that had been provided until IPO, when the agreement was terminated, could not otherwise be obtained by the Group without the addition of personnel or the engagement of outside professional advisers. In management's opinion, the fees provided for under the agreement reasonably reflect the benefits received by the Group. The Group paid £0.6m and £1.2m in the years ended 31 December 2004 and 2003 respectively under the Monitoring and Oversight agreement.

The Monitoring and Oversight agreement was terminated on 23 July 2004.

**Financial Advisory agreement**
In 1999, Premier Brands Foods Limited, Premier Financing Limited and Hicks, Muse & Co. entered into an agreement ("the Financial Advisory agreement") pursuant to which Hicks, Muse & Co. will be entitled to receive a fee equal to 1.5% of the transaction value for each acquisition, sale, merger, recapitalisation, restructuring or other similar transaction involving the Group. The Financial Advisory agreement makes available to the Group the resources of Hicks, Muse & Co. concerning a variety of financial and operational matters. The services that had been provided until IPO, when the agreement was terminated, could not otherwise be obtained by the Group without the addition of personnel or the engagement of outside professional advisers. In management's opinion, the fees provided for under the Financial Advisory agreement reasonably reflect the benefits received by the Group. The Group paid £nil and £1.6m in the years ended 31 December 2004 and 2003 respectively under the Financial Advisory agreement.

The Financial Advisory agreement was terminated on 23 July 2004.

**Golden Share**
A Golden Share was issued by Premier Financing Limited with voting rights, which entitled the holder of the Golden Share to block the passing of resolutions for the winding-up or administration of Premier Financing Limited or resolutions approving other matters that would constitute a breach of the Senior Credit Facility. Upon repayment of the Senior Credit Facility during the year (see note 19(b)), the Golden Share was automatically converted at IPO into a deferred ordinary share of Premier Financing Limited with limited rights.

At the date of the IPO HMTFPL reduced its stake in the ordinary share capital of the Company to approximately 20%. In addition, they appointed Mr. Lyndon Lea as a non-executive director of the Company.

On 15 October 2004 HMTFPL sold all its interests in the ordinary share capital of the Company.

## Directors' service contracts

**3.136** The directors' report for listed companies must state the unexpired term of the directors' service contracts of any director who is proposed for re-election at the forthcoming AGM (see Table 3.17 below). If the directors proposed for re-election do not have service contracts, the directors' report must state that fact. [LR 9.8.8R(9)]. Directors' service contracts for this purpose are defined by reference to section 318 of the 1985 Act (section 227 of the 2006 Act) and exclude contracts expiring or determinable within one year by the employing company without payment or compensation other than statutory compensation. In practice information on service contracts is usually given in the directors' remuneration report with a cross reference from the directors' report as in the example in Table 3.17.

*Directors' report*

---

Table 3.17 – Directors' service contracts

Cookson Group plc – Annual Report – 31 December 2004

**The Board (extract)**

The Articles of Association of the Company require that Directors should submit themselves for re-election at least every three years. Messrs G C Cozzani, B W Perry and D H Millard will therefore be retiring and offering themselves for re-election at this year's AGM as set out in the Notice of AGM and on page 29. Mr Millard must stand for re-election even though he intends to leave the Company later in the year.

**Directors (page 29)**

Biographical information for the current Directors of the Company is given on page 23.

Mr A G L Alexander, formerly Senior Independent Director, retired from the Board on 14 May 2004 at the Company's 2004 AGM. Mrs J F de Moller, non-executive Director and former Chair of the Remuneration Committee, retired from the Board on 1 October 2004. Mr S L Howard, formerly Group Chief Executive, resigned from the Board on 4 November 2004 and Mr R P Sharpe, former executive Director and Chief Executive of the Electronics division, resigned on 19 May 2004.

Mr G C Cozzani, Mr D H Millard and Mr B W Perry will retire at the AGM and will offer themselves for re-election. Mr J P Oosterveld, Mr N R Salmon and Mr J G Sussens will also retire at the AGM and will offer themselves for election. Further information on the service agreements of the executive Directors, including Messrs Cozzani, Millard and Salmon, is given on pages 33 and 34. The non-executive Directors, including Mr Perry who is standing for re-election and Messrs Oosterveld and Sussens who are standing for election, do not have such agreements.

The interests of Directors and their related parties in the ordinary shares of the Company, all of which are beneficial, as disclosed in accordance with the Companies Act 1985, are as set out on page 37 and details of the Directors' MTI awards, LTIP allocations and share options are set out on pages 37 to 39.

**DIRECTORS' REMUNERATION REPORT (extract pages 33 and 34)**

**Directors' service contracts**

It has been the Company's general practice for many years to employ executives on local terms while giving due consideration to global market practices. Where executive Directors are primarily employed outside the UK, their contracts reflect local law and employment practice for senior executives in the territory concerned. Mr Cozzani has an employment contract governed by Illinois, USA law and a secondment agreement governed by Belgian law. He is based in Belgium and mandatory Belgian employment law will continue to determine any severance payment, which will be offset against his Illinois contractual entitlement. His Illinois contract originates from his employment with Vesuvius Crucible Company.

The Board has determined that any new executive Director would be appointed with a notice period not exceeding one year, although in certain circumstances the Board would consider a longer initial term. All the current executive Directors have contractual notice periods not exceeding 12 months. Mr Millard has a pension provision which entitled him to pension accrual for two years should his contract have been terminated without cause. None of the Directors' contracts contain any change of control provisions. All the Directors' contracts contain a duty to mitigate should they find alternative employment during their notice period.

---

A summary of the main conditions of the contracts of the executive Directors is as follows:

**Executive Directors**

| Executive Director | Date and jurisdiction of contract(s) | Unexpired term | Notice period for employer | Basis of compensation on termination without cause |
|---|---|---|---|---|
| G C Cozzani | 23/02/04 (Illinois, USA) 05/05/97 (Belgium) | 12 months | 12 months from 31/12/04 to 06/10/05, thereafter no notice required under contract but six months required under Belgian law. | At all times subject to offset of any amounts mandatorily payable under Belgian law: salary and annual incentive compensation (based on percentage level paid in most recent prior payment year) for the applicable contractual notice period, payable half in a lump sum and the balance in equal monthly instalments commencing half way through the applicable contractual notice period, mitigated by any salary earned from new employment. |
| D H Millard | 19/02/04 (UK) | 12 months | 12 months | One times salary, benefits and average of last three years' annual and MTI Plan incentive payments, payable half in a lump sum and the balance in six separate monthly instalments commencing six months after leaving, mitigated by any salary earned from new employment. Pension accrual for two years. |
| N R Salmon | 14/06/04 (UK) | 12 months | 12 months | One times salary, pension allowance and benefits payable half in a lump sum and the balance in six separate monthly instalments commencing six months after leaving, mitigated by any salary earned from new employment. |

**3.136.1**  The Combined Code (2006) (and the Combined Code (2008)) states that notice or contract periods should be set at one year or less. If it is necessary to offer longer notice or contract periods to new directors recruited from outside, such periods should reduce to one year or less after the initial period. [CC B.1.6].

**3.137**   If a service contract does not specify a term, the term can be ascertained in one of the following ways:

- If the contract is determinable on the giving of notice, the expiration of the notice period will indicate the earliest date at which the contract could end.

- If no notice period is stated in the contract, there may be a custom or practice as to the length of the notice.

- In the absence of an express provision as to duration or expiry or a customary arrangement, there is a presumption at common law that (subject to the statutory minimum entitlements to notice) every contract of employment is terminable on reasonable notice by either party.

Where the length of the unexpired period of a director's service contract has been determined in one of the ways above, the details should be fully disclosed in the directors' report.

**Disclosure of directors' interests**

**3.137.1**   The UKLA's Listing Rules require a listed company's annual financial report to include a statement setting out all the interests of each person who is a director of the company as at the end of the period under review including:

- all changes in the interests of each director that have occurred between the end of the period under review and a date not more than one month prior to the date of the notice of the annual general meeting; or

- if there have been no changes in the interests of each director in the period described above, a statement that there have been no changes.

Interests of each director include the interests of 'connected persons' of which the listed company is, or ought upon reasonable enquiry to become, aware (see para 3.137.7 below).

[LR 9.8.6 R (1)].

**3.137.2**   The interests required to be disclosed are those in respect of transactions that are notifiable to the company under DTR 3.1.2 R. Under that rule, persons discharging managerial responsibilities (which includes, but is not restricted to, directors) and their connected persons, must notify the issuer in writing of the occurrence of all transactions conducted on their own account in the shares of the issuer, or derivatives or any other financial instruments relating to those shares within four business days of the day on which the transaction occurred. Connected persons are considered further from paragraph 3.137.7.

**3.137.3**   Persons who are directors during, but not at the end of, the period under review need not be included. [LR 9.8.6A G (1)].

**3.137.4** The UKLA's Listing Rules note that a listed company unable to compile the statement in LR 9.8.6 R (1) from information already available to it may need to seek the relevant information, or confirmation, from the director, including that in relation to connected persons, but would not be expected to obtain information directly from connected persons. [LR 9.8.6A G (2)].

**3.137.5** The Listing Rules also require a listed company's annual financial report to include a statement showing, as at a date not more than one month prior to the date of the notice of the AGM:

■ all information disclosed to the company in accordance with DTR 5 (in respect of notifiable shareholdings); or

■ that there have been no disclosures, if no disclosures have been made.

[LR 9.8.6 R (2)].

This requirement is considered from paragraph 3.130.

**3.137.6** Listed companies are required by Schedule 7A to the 1985 Act (and Schedule 8 to SI 2008/410, 'The Large and Medium-sized Companies and Groups (Accounts and Reports) Regulations 2008'), to make detailed disclosure in the directors' remuneration report about directors' share options. These are considered in detail in chapter 5. In practice, the disclosure of directors' interests in shares and options are sometimes combined and presented in a tabular manner, usually in the directors' remuneration report. A cross-reference should be given in the directors' report to the precise location of the information. Examples of how a company discloses its directors' interests in accordance with the Listing Rules are included in chapter 5.

### Connected persons

**3.137.7** The definition of 'connected persons' contained in the Listing Rules is wider than that contained in section 252 of the Companies Act 2006 (see para 3.137.10). (Although the Listing Rules in place at the time of writing refer, in the definition of 'connected persons', to section 346 of the 1985 Act, the transitional rules contained in the Listing Rules state that references to sections of the 1985 Act that are no longer in force should be should be read as references to the corresponding provision of the 2006 Act (or DTR rule), subject to any transitional arrangements.)

**3.137.8** The definition of 'connected persons' in the Companies Act 2006 includes:

■ Members of the director's family, including:

  ■ The director's spouse, civil partner or any other person with whom the director lives as a partner in an enduring family relationship.

  ■ The director's children or step-children.

- Any children or step-children (under the age of 18) of the director's enduring life partner.

- The director's parents.

- A body corporate with which the director is connected (see para 3.137.9).

- A trustee of a trust of which the beneficiary is (or can be, at the discretion of the Trustee) the director (or a family member or connected body corporate as defined above).

- A partnership in which the director (or any person connected with him) is a partner.

- A partnership with a partner that is, itself, either a company or a partnership, where the director (or a connected person of his) is either a director or partner.

[CA06 Secs 252, 253].

**3.137.9**  A body corporate is a connected person of a director if the director and his connected persons are interested in at least 20 per cent of the nominal value of the body corporate's equity share capital (excluding treasury shares), or are entitled to control at least 20 percent of the voting power at any general meeting (excluding votes attached to treasury shares). [CA06 Sec 254]. For this purpose, an 'interest' in shares is defined in Schedule 1 to the 2006 Act and is taken to mean any interest whatsoever and includes any right to acquire shares or control of the voting rights attached to the shares. The definition of 'equity share capital' is contained in section 548 of the 2006 Act and is considered further in chapter 23 of the Manual of Accounting – IFRS for the UK and chapter 23 of the Manual of Accounting – UK GAAP.

**3.137.10**  In addition to those that fall within the 2006 Act's definition of connected persons, the Listing Rules definition includes:

- Any relative of the director who, on the date of the transaction in question has shared the same household as the director for at least 12 months.

- A body corporate in which the director (or a person connected to him under the 2006 Act or the bullet point above) is a director or a senior executive who has the power to make management decisions affecting the future development and business prospects of that body corporate.

[LR Glossary].

### *Directors' interests in contracts of significance*

**3.137.11**  The Listing Rules require disclosure of particulars of any contract of significance (including substantial property transactions) subsisting during the period under review, to which the company, or one of its subsidiary undertakings, is a party and in which a director of the company is, or was, materially interested. [LR 9.8.4R(10)]. In this context, 'a contract of significance' is one which represents in value a sum equal to one per cent or more, calculated on a group basis where relevant, of:

- The aggregate of the group's share capital and reserves for a capital transaction or for a transaction of which the principal purpose is the granting of credit.

- The group's total purchases, sales, payments or receipts, as appropriate for other transactions.

[LR App 1.1].

**Waiver of dividends**

**3.138** Particulars of any arrangements under which any shareholder has waived or agreed to waive any dividends should be disclosed. This requirement applies to waivers of future dividends as well as to waivers of dividends payable during the past financial year. Waivers of dividend of less than one per cent of the total value of any dividend may be disregarded provided that some payment has been made on each share of the relevant class during the year. [LR 9.8.5G].

**Corporate governance**

**3.139** A corporate governance statement of compliance with the Combined Code should either be made in the directors' report or included in a separate statement in the annual report that deals with the more general aspects of corporate governance. See chapter 4 for further discussion of corporate governance matters.

**[The next paragraph is 3.142.]**

**Special business**

**3.142** Holders of listed securities who are sent a notice of a meeting that is to occur on the same day as an AGM, which includes business that is considered not to be routine business of an AGM must be provided with an explanation in the directors' report of such business, unless an explanatory circular accompanies the notice. [LR 13.8.8R(1)]. An example of matters that are regarded as special business in an AGM is given in Table 3.18 below.

*Directors' report*

Table 3.18 — Special business in an AGM

Dairy Crest Group plc — Annual report and accounts — 31 March 2005

**DIRECTORS' REPORT** (extract)

**Annual General Meeting**
The Annual General Meeting will be held at the Chartered Accountants' Hall, Moorgate Place, London EC2P 2BJ on Thursday 14 July 2005 at 11.00 am. Details of the resolutions to be proposed, including items of special business, are given in the Notice of Annual General Meeting and Explanatory Notes which appear on pages 58 to 60.

The directors believe that the resolutions are in the best interests of the Company and its shareholders as a whole and unanimously recommend that shareholders should vote in favour of all resolutions.

**Notice of Ninth Annual General Meeting (extract)**

**Special business**
To consider and, if thought fit, pass the following resolutions which will be proposed in the case of resolution 8, as an ordinary resolution and, in the case of resolutions 9, 10 and 11, as special resolutions:

**Ordinary resolution**
**8.** That the authority conferred on the directors by article 4(B) of the Company's articles of association to exercise all powers of the Company to allot relevant securities within the meaning of section 80 of the Companies Act 1985 (the 'Act') be renewed for the period from the date of the passing of this resolution until the conclusion of the next Annual General Meeting of the Company and for that period the 'section 80 amount' is £10,415,000.

**Special resolutions**
**9.** That, pursuant to article 41 of the Company's articles of association, the Company be generally and unconditionally authorised, in accordance with Section 166 of the Act to make market purchases (within the meaning of Section 163(3) of the Act) of ordinary shares of 25 pence each in the capital of the Company ('ordinary shares') provided that:

- the maximum number of ordinary shares hereby authorised to be acquired is 12,498,606;
- the minimum price which may be paid for any such ordinary share is 25 pence (exclusive of expenses and appropriate taxes);
- the maximum price (exclusive of expenses and appropriate taxes) which may be paid for any such ordinary share shall be not more than 5% above the average of the middle market values for an ordinary share as taken from the London Stock Exchange Daily Official List for the five business days immediately preceding the date of purchase; and
- the authority hereby conferred shall expire at the conclusion of the next Annual General Meeting of the Company (except in relation to a purchase of ordinary shares the contract for which was concluded before such time and which will or may be executed wholly or partly after such time).

**10.** That the Company's articles of association be amended by the deletion of article 147 and the insertion of a new article 147 so as to be in the form produced to the meeting and initialled by the Chairman for the purposes of identification.

**11.** That the power conferred on the directors by article 4(C) of the Company's articles of association to allot equity securities (within the meaning of section 94(2) of the Act) for cash be renewed for the period from the date of the passing of this resolution until the conclusion of the next Annual General Meeting of the Company and for that period the 'section 89 amount' is £1,562,275.

**Explanatory notes (extract)**
**Resolution 10**
Article 147 of the articles of association currently allows the Company to indemnify the directors and the company secretary against liability incurred in defending civil or criminal proceedings in which judgement is given in their favour or they are acquitted, and against the costs of successfully applying for relief under the Act. Section 19 of the Companies (Audit, Investigations and Community Enterprise) Act 2004 (the '2004 Act') amended the Act as of 6 April 2005 to permit companies to indemnify officers (other than auditors) in respect of liabilities (including legal costs) incurred by them in proceedings brought against them by third parties.

This form of indemnity was previously prohibited under section 310 of the Act. Amongst other things, the indemnity cannot cover: liability incurred by a director to the Company or any associated company; fines imposed in criminal proceedings and penalties imposed by regulatory authorities; costs incurred in criminal proceedings where the director is convicted; costs incurred in defending civil proceedings brought by the Company or an associated company where judgement is given against the director; or costs incurred in proceedings for relief where the court refuses to grant relief.

Companies are also permitted under the 2004 Act to provide their directors with funds to cover the costs incurred by them in defending legal proceedings brought against them. Previously, companies had only been able to fund their directors' defence costs once final judgment in their favour had been reached. Directors are increasingly being added as defendants in legal actions against companies, and litigation is often very lengthy and expensive; the risk of directors being placed under significant personal financial strain is increasing. The Board therefore believes that the provision of appropriate indemnities and the funding of directors' defence costs as they are incurred, as permitted by the new legislation, is both reasonable protection for the directors and an important means of ensuring that the Company continues to attract and retain the highest calibre of directors.

The Board therefore proposes that the articles of association be amended by adopting a new article 147 in place of the existing article 147. The new article 147 reflects the new provisions permitted under the 2004 Act and deletes provisions reflecting the old statutory provisions which are no longer relevant.

To ensure that the Board is able to exercise the discretionary power to fund defence costs, the new article 147 provides that each of the directors may vote and be counted in the quorum at any meeting considering a proposal which falls within the provisions of the new article 147(D), unless the director concerned is to receive a privilege or benefit not generally available to, or awarded to, any other director. (Individual directors of the Company would still be liable to repay their defence costs, to the extent funded by the Company, if their defence is unsuccessful.) The Company's auditors are excluded from the indemnity provisions of new article 147.

Further information about this resolution is provided under 'Directors' indemnities' on page 25.

**Corporate governance (extract from page 25)**
**Directors' indemnities**
An amendment to the Companies Act 1985 (the 'Act') came into force on 6 April 2005 under which companies may indemnify their directors and officers against liabilities (including against legal costs) to a greater extent than was previously possible. This amendment has been introduced by the Government following its consultation process in respect of director and auditor liability. The amendment addresses concerns raised in that process that exposure to liabilities arising from legal action brought against directors by third parties and the cost of lengthy court proceedings were affecting the recruitment and behaviour of directors. The Board wishes to continue to attract good quality directors and therefore believes it is in the interests of the Company to take advantage of this amendment. Accordingly resolution 10 at the AGM proposes the adoption of a new article 147 of the Company's articles of association to give the directors and the officers the benefit of the new indemnity provisions to the extent permitted by the Act.

## Additional disclosures for listed companies purchasing own share or selling treasury shares

**3.142.1**  The directors' report of a listed company must give the following additional information concerning purchases or proposed purchases of the company's own shares and sales of treasury shares:

- Particulars of any authority given by the shareholders in general meeting for the company to purchase its own shares that is still effective at the year end (that is, authority that has not yet been exercised and has not expired).

- In relation to purchases other than through the market or by tender or by partial offer to all shareholders, the names of the sellers of the shares that have been purchased, or are to be purchased, by the company.

- If the company has purchased any of its own shares since the year end, or has either been granted an option or entered into a contract to purchase its own shares since the year end, then the directors' report should disclose the equivalent information to that required under the Act as detailed in paragraph 3.76 above.

- In relation to sales of treasury shares made other than through the market, or in connection with an employees' share scheme, or other than pursuant to an opportunity available to all shareholders on the same terms, the names of the purchasers of such shares sold, or proposed to be sold, during the year.

[LR 9.8.6R(4)].

Examples of the relevant disclosures are given in chapter 7 dealing with the acquisition by a company of its own shares and chapter 23 of the PwC Manual of Accounting – UK GAAP and the Manual of Accounting – IFRS for the UK dealing with treasury shares.

## Directors' liability: safe harbour

**3.143**  A further amendment provided by the Companies Act 2006 arising from the consultation on narrative reporting is for directors to be given safe harbour from civil liability for statements or omissions in the directors' report and the directors' remuneration report (including any summary financial statements derived from those reports). These provisions are considered further in chapter 8.

**[The next paragraph is 3.147.]**

## Filing exemption for small companies

**3.147**  For financial years beginning on or after 6 April 2008, a company that is entitled to prepare its financial statements in accordance with the small companies regime (see further chapter 31 of the Manual of Accounting — UK GAAP), or would be if it were not a member of an ineligible group, is permitted, but not required, to exclude the directors' report from the financial statements filed with the Registrar of Companies. [CA06 Secs 444(1), 444A(1)]. These companies are described in the 2006 Act as being *"entitled to a small companies exemption in relation to the directors' report"*. [CA06 Sec 415A].

**3.148** An ineligible group is a group in which any of its members is (or was, at any time within the financial year) any one of the following:

■   A public company.

■   An authorised insurance company, a banking company, an e-money issuer, a MiFiD investment firm or a UCITS management company.

■   Carrying on insurance market activity.

■   A body corporate (other than a company, but including a foreign company) whose shares are admitted to trading on a regulated market in an EEA member State.

[CA06 Sec 384(2)].

**3.149** This does not affect the requirement for companies to *prepare* a directors' report: all companies are required to do so, although those entitled to the small companies exemption are permitted to exclude certain disclosures contained in the main body of the 2006 Act. The application of each of the requirements is considered throughout the chapter.

**[The next paragraph is 3.153.]**

## Approval and signing of directors' report

**3.153** The board of directors must formally approve the directors' report and it must be signed on behalf of the board by a director or the secretary of the company. [CA85 Sec 234A(1); CA06 Sec 419(1)].

**3.154** Every copy of the directors' report that is laid before the company in general meeting, or that is otherwise circulated, published or issued, must state the name of the person who signed it on behalf of the board. [CA85 Sec 234A(2); CA06 Sec 433(1) to (3)]. A copy of the directors' report that is to be delivered to the Registrar of Companies must also be signed on behalf of the board by a director or secretary of the company. [CA85 Sec 234A(3); CA06 Sec 433(1) to (3)]. The requirement for signature is expected to be repealed with effect from 1 October 2009 and Companies House will, in due course, issue rules for the authentication of documents after that date.

**Liability for contravention**

**3.155** Every person who was a director of the company at the end of the period within which the company's financial statements must be laid before the company in general meeting and be delivered to the Registrar of Companies may be guilty of an offence if the directors' report fails to comply with the Act's requirements (see further chapter 8). This offence is punishable by a fine. [CA85 Sec 234(5); CA06 Secs 415(4)(5), 419(3)(4)].

**3.156** It is a defence in such a situation for a director to prove that he took all reasonable steps to ensure that the directors' report complied with all the Act's requirements. [CA85 Sec 234(5); CA06 Secs 415(4), 419(3)].

**3.157** Furthermore, where the company does not comply with the requirements for the approval and signing of the directors' report as set out in paragraphs 3.153 and 3.154 above, the company and every officer of it who is in default will be guilty of an offence and liable to a fine. [CA85 Sec 234A(4); CA06 Secs 419(4), 433(5)].

## Position of the auditor

**3.158** The auditors are required to state in their report whether, in their opinion, *"the information given in the directors' report for the financial year for which the annual accounts are prepared is consistent with those accounts"*. [CA85 Sec 235(3); CA06 Sec 496]. There is no exemption from this requirement for auditors of small and medium-sized companies (other than those exempt from the audit requirement – see further chapter 8).

**3.159** Auditors have a statutory responsibility to review the directors' report for consistency with the financial statements. This approach is supported by the Auditing Practices Board's ISA (UK and Ireland) 720 (revised), 'Other information in documents containing audited financial statements' and by APB Bulletin 2006/06, 'Auditor's reports on financial statements in the United Kingdom'.

**3.159.1** Section B of ISA (UK and Ireland) 720 (revised) deals specifically with the auditor's statutory reporting responsibility in relation to directors' reports and requires the auditor to read the information in the directors' report and assess whether it is consistent with the financial statements.

**3.159.2** The auditor should seek to resolve any inconsistencies identified between the information in the directors' report and the financial statements. If a material inconsistency between the directors' report and the financial statements is not resolved, details should be provided in the audit report. In addition, a qualified or adverse opinion would be necessary where an amendment that is necessary to the financial statements has not been made.

**3.159.3** ISA (UK and Ireland) 720 (revised) confirms that the information given in the directors' report includes information that is included by way of a cross reference to other information presented separately from the directors' report. For example the auditor has a statutory responsibility to review a business review presented within a separate voluntary OFR for consistency with the financial statements. [ISA (UK & I) 720 (revised) para 3].

**[The next paragraph is 3.160.]**

## Enforcement

**3.160** The Financial Reporting Review Panel (FRRP), part of the Financial Reporting Council, is responsible for ensuring that both public and large private companies comply with relevant reporting requirements including the directors' report (and, thus, the business review). The Secretary of State (through Companies House) is responsible for enforcement in respect of other companies. [Companies (Audit, Investigation and Community Enterprise) Act 2004 Sec 14].

**3.161** Under the existing enforcement regime in respect of defective accounts, a company may be required to revise its directors' report where it is not compliant with the Act's requirements. In cases of non-compliance the FRRP will have the power, if necessary, to go to the court to compel a company to revise its report. Revision of defective accounts is considered in chapter 8.

**Chapter 4**

# Corporate governance

|  | Page |
|---|---|
| Introduction | 4001 |
| The development of corporate governance disclosures | 4002 |
| The Hampel Report | 4005 |
| Objectives | 4005 |
| 'Box ticking' | 4006 |
| Objectives of listed companies | 4006 |
| Shareholders/stakeholders | 4007 |
| Recommendations | 4007 |
| The development of the 1998, 2003, 2006 and 2008 Combined Codes | 4007 |
| Objective | 4007 |
| Combined Code (2006) | 4010 |
| Adoption of the Combined Code (2006) | 4010 |
| The FRC review of the Combined Code (2006) | 4010 |
| Adoption of the Combined Code (2008) and revised FSA rules | 4011 |
| Overview of the contents of the Combined Code (2006) | 4011 |
| Actions required by listed companies | 4012 |
| Combined Code (2006) | 4013 |
| Directors | 4013 |
| The board | 4013 |
| Chairman and chief executive officer | 4014 |
| Board balance and independence | 4015 |
| Appointments to the board | 4017 |
| Information and professional development | 4018 |
| Performance evaluation | 4019 |
| Re-election | 4020 |
| Remuneration | 4021 |
| Policy | 4021 |
| Service contracts and compensation | 4022 |
| Procedure | 4022 |
| Accountability and audit | 4023 |
| Financial reporting | 4023 |
| Internal control | 4024 |
| Audit committee and auditors | 4025 |
| Relations with shareholders | 4027 |
| Dialogue with institutional shareholders | 4027 |
| Constructive use of the annual general meeting (AGM) | 4027 |
| Institutional shareholders | 4028 |
| Schedules forming part of the Combined Code | 4029 |
| Additional guidance on the application of the Combined Code | 4030 |
| Revised FSA Rules on corporate governance | 4030 |

Requirement to have an audit committee. . . . . . . . . . . . . . . . . . . . 4030
Requirement to present a corporate governance statement . . . . . . 4031
Interaction between the FSA Rules and the Combined Code. . . . 4033
Combined Code (2008) . . . . . . . . . . . . . . . . . . . . . . . . . . . . . . . . . 4033
Details of modifications made to form the Combined Code (2008) 4033
Statement of compliance. . . . . . . . . . . . . . . . . . . . . . . . . . . . . . . . . . . 4034
Statements of non-compliance with the Combined Code provisions . . 4035
Statement of compliance and interaction with the Combined Code
(2008). . . . . . . . . . . . . . . . . . . . . . . . . . . . . . . . . . . . . . . . . . . . . . . . 4036
Reporting on going concern. . . . . . . . . . . . . . . . . . . . . . . . . . . . . . . . . 4037
Combined Code requirement . . . . . . . . . . . . . . . . . . . . . . . . . . . . . 4037
Form of disclosure. . . . . . . . . . . . . . . . . . . . . . . . . . . . . . . . . . . . . . 4038
Application to groups . . . . . . . . . . . . . . . . . . . . . . . . . . . . . . . . . . . 4040
Procedures. . . . . . . . . . . . . . . . . . . . . . . . . . . . . . . . . . . . . . . . . . . . . 4040
Foreseeable future . . . . . . . . . . . . . . . . . . . . . . . . . . . . . . . . . . . . . . 4041
Reporting on internal control . . . . . . . . . . . . . . . . . . . . . . . . . . . . . . 4041
Combined Code recommendation. . . . . . . . . . . . . . . . . . . . . . . . . 4041
Turnbull guidance (2005) for directors. . . . . . . . . . . . . . . . . . . . . 4042
The board's role. . . . . . . . . . . . . . . . . . . . . . . . . . . . . . . . . . . . . . . . 4043
Internal audit . . . . . . . . . . . . . . . . . . . . . . . . . . . . . . . . . . . . . . . . 4046
Application of Turnbull guidance to groups . . . . . . . . . . . . . . . . . 4047
Good practice reporting . . . . . . . . . . . . . . . . . . . . . . . . . . . . . . . . . . . 4047
Smaller listed companies. . . . . . . . . . . . . . . . . . . . . . . . . . . . . . . . . . . 4047
Non-listed organisations. . . . . . . . . . . . . . . . . . . . . . . . . . . . . . . . . . . 4047
Auditor review of compliance with the Combined Code . . . . . . . . . . . 4048
Listing Rule requirement . . . . . . . . . . . . . . . . . . . . . . . . . . . . . . . . 4048
Auditor's review. . . . . . . . . . . . . . . . . . . . . . . . . . . . . . . . . . . . . . . . 4050
International matters. . . . . . . . . . . . . . . . . . . . . . . . . . . . . . . . . . . . . . . . 4051
EU action plan. . . . . . . . . . . . . . . . . . . . . . . . . . . . . . . . . . . . . . . . . 4051
EU directives . . . . . . . . . . . . . . . . . . . . . . . . . . . . . . . . . . . . . . . . . . 4053
UK implementation of the EU 8th, 4th and 7th Directives. . . . . . . . . 4053
European Corporate Governance Forum. . . . . . . . . . . . . . . . . . . . . . 4054
Activities of FEE. . . . . . . . . . . . . . . . . . . . . . . . . . . . . . . . . . . . . . . . 4054
Other organisations. . . . . . . . . . . . . . . . . . . . . . . . . . . . . . . . . . . . . . . 4055
Changes impacting UK companies with a US listing. . . . . . . . . . . . . 4056

Chapter 4

# Corporate governance

## Introduction

**4.1** In December 1992 the Cadbury Committee defined corporate governance as *"the system by which companies are directed and controlled"* in its report 'The financial aspects of corporate governance'. [CR para 2.5]. Five years later, in January 1998, the Hampel Committee issued a report on corporate governance and, whilst noting that it was somewhat restrictive, endorsed the Cadbury Committee's definition. In addition, the Hampel report focussed on the processes by which enterprises are directed and controlled in response to the rights and aspirations of shareholders and other stakeholders.

**4.2** Most UK companies have a single 'unitary' board of directors. Corporate governance in the UK corporate sector is, therefore, primarily concerned with:

- The procedures adopted by the board and its committees to discharge its duties (for example, membership of the board; frequency of, and procedures at, board meetings; the role of non-executive directors; constitution and terms of reference of audit and remuneration committees; and the role of the company secretary).

- The board's accountability to shareholders and other stakeholders (for example, annual reporting; use of AGMs; and shareholder voting rights).

- The manner in which the board controls the company or group (for example, management structures; group legal structure; and internal control philosophy and practice).

**4.3** Corporate governance potentially covers a very wide range of issues and disciplines from company secretarial and legal, through to business strategy, executive and non-executive management and investor relations, to accounting and information systems.

**4.4** Governance went higher up the corporate agenda in the early 1990s partly in response to a series of scandals, fuelled by the recession. Business failures heightened concerns about effective governance and led amongst other things to the development of corporate governance disclosures.

**4.5** The importance of such disclosures is that, provided the information can be relied upon, it should help determine a company's value and be useful to stakeholders wishing to assess their risk exposure before deciding whether to commit resources to, or withdraw resources from, a company. Company failures have highlighted the need for stakeholders to obtain assurance on governance.

They have also heightened the need for directors to be able to give such assurance if they are to continue to attract funds.

**4.6** Some governance issues have attracted significant political and public interest, because they strike at the root of the objectives of companies – none more so than the accountability of boards to shareholders in relation to executive pay.

**4.7** Improvements in governance disclosures over the last few years have meant that UK public companies are among the most accountable of organisations. In addition to publishing their results and having their financial statements audited, public companies are required to disclose detailed information about their operations, relationships, remuneration and governance.

**4.8** There has been criticism from some sources that this emphasis on accountability has been at the expense of what should be considered as a board's primary responsibility, namely to enhance the prosperity of the business and the investment of their shareholders. Developments during past years in the field of corporate governance, in particular the Hampel Committee report in early 1998, have helped to refocus attention on these dual aims of accountability and prosperity.

## The development of corporate governance disclosures

**4.9** The response to the scandals and failures of the late 1980s was a series of committees, reports and recommendations. The first of these was the Committee on the Financial Aspects of Corporate Governance, generally referred to as the Cadbury Committee, after its chairman Sir Adrian Cadbury. Its report was issued in December 1992 as a result of which major changes occurred in the way in which governance was viewed by companies as well as in the disclosures that they give.

**4.10** Whilst board remuneration was one of a number of issues addressed by Cadbury, it was not the main focus. Nonetheless, the level of board remuneration continued to attract a high profile, particularly in relation to levels of pay in privatised utilities. In response to this a separate group was set up to study the matter and the result was 'Directors' remuneration: report of a study group chaired by Sir Richard Greenbury'. This is known as the Greenbury report and was published in July 1995. The Greenbury Report led to additional disclosure requirements being included in the Listing Rules. These are discussed in chapter 5.

**4.11** One of Cadbury's recommendations was that a successor body should be set up to review progress and it identified a number of issues which that body might consider. The successor body, 'The Committee on Corporate Governance' (the 'Hampel committee' – note: not the financial aspects of corporate governance) was set up in November 1995 under the chairmanship of Sir Ronald Hampel.

**4.12**  The final version of the Hampel report was published in January 1998. The recommendations aimed to ensure a balance between business prosperity and accountability.

**4.13**  Following the completion of its report, the Hampel Committee co-operated with the London Stock Exchange in producing 'The Combined Code – Principles of Good Corporate Governance and Code of Best Practice' in June 1998. The Combined Code (1998) embraced the Cadbury and Greenbury Reports taking into account the Hampel Committee's Report and changes made by the London Stock Exchange, with the committee's agreement, following consultation.

**4.14**  The original Combined Code, published in June 1998, contained both principles and detailed Combined Code provisions and was in two parts, part 1, 'Principles of good governance' and part 2, 'Code of best practice'. Each part of the Combined Code (1998) was split into two sections. Section 1 contained the corporate governance principles and Combined Code provisions applicable to companies incorporated in the UK. Section 2 contained the principles and Combined Code provisions applicable to institutional shareholders with regard to their voting, dialogue with the company and evaluation of governance arrangements.

**4.15**  The Combined Code (1998) was appended to the Listing Rules (although it did not form part of those rules) and a new listing rule required companies to include a two part disclosure statement in their annual report describing how they had applied the principles of the Combined Code (1998) and whether or not they had complied with its detailed provisions throughout the accounting period with details of any non-compliance. Although the changes to the Listing Rules in June 1998 only addressed the principles and Combined Code (1998) provisions in section 1 (that is for companies), the Hampel Committee regarded section 2 as an integral part of the recommendations and it encouraged institutions to make voluntary disclosure to their clients and the public based on these recommendations.

**4.16**  Also during 1998 the government announced a new initiative to modernise company law. In 2002 the government issued a White Paper outlining potential new legislation covering various matters including a statutory statement outlining directors' duties. The government did not advocate legislating for corporate governance requirements and disclosures, but has supported the best practice approach of having a code for companies and investors to follow.

**4.17**  In February 2002 the government announced that Sir Derek Higgs was to carry out a review of the role and effectiveness of non-executive directors. This review was in part building on the work of the company law review that noted a growing body of evidence from the USA suggesting that companies with a strong contingent of non-executives produced superior performance. Therefore, this review was focused on improving UK productivity performance by progressive strengthening of the quality and role of non-executive directors. The terms of reference of the review noted that in the decade following the introduction of the

Cadbury Code the role of non-executives had been seen to strengthen. The government sought recommendations from Higgs as to how to further strengthen the quality, independence and effectiveness of non-executive directors in the UK. It expressed a preference for an approach based on best practice, so the natural outcome was for Higgs, as part of his recommendations, to produce a revised draft Combined Code.

**4.18** Another strong influence on the review was the timing of its launch, since it took place when company accounting scandals and collapses, predominantly taking place in the USA were shocking investors and the public. Shortly after Higgs' review was announced, the government also formed a co-ordinating group to consider the implications for the arrangements for financial reporting and auditing in the UK in the light of the US scandals. This group requested the Financial Reporting Council ('FRC') to set up a working group to consider whether the remit of audit committees under the existing Combined Code (1998) needed to change. The working group was chaired by Sir Robert Smith. The group worked closely with Higgs and its output (suggested new provisions for the Combined Code (1998) around the role and responsibilities of audit committees and was known as the Smith Guidance) was incorporated into the revised draft Combined Code published as part of the Higgs Report in January 2003.

**4.18.1** In March 2008 the FRC announced the launch of a consultation on the Smith Guidance on Audit Committees following the release of recommendations by the FRC Market Participants Group ('MPG'). It is understood that a revised version of the Smith Guidance will be published later in 2008.

**4.19** The FRC approved the new Combined Code on Corporate Governance on 23 July 2003, hereafter referred to as the Combined Code (2003). The format of the Combined Code (2003) was slightly different to the original, containing both main and supporting principles with the provisions. The division into two sections, companies and institutional shareholders, remained the same.

**4.20** The Combined Code (2003) applied for reporting years beginning on or after 1 November 2003. Initially the Financial Services Authority ('FSA') replaced the Combined Code (1998) that was annexed to the Listing Rules with the Combined Code (2003). However, a change occurred on 1 July 2005. Since this date, the Combined Code (2003) has not been appended to the Listing Rules (although it remains linked to them), because it was recognised as being the responsibility of the FRC, rather than the UK Listing Authority.

**4.20.1** The FRC performed an informal review of the implementation of the Combined Code (2003) during 2004 and a formal review in 2005. Following these reviews the FRC proposed a few minor amendments to the Combined Code (2003) in early 2006, concluding that major change was unnecessary.

**4.20.2** Following a period of consultation, the FRC issued a revised Combined Code on Corporate Governance, hereafter referred to as the Combined Code

(2006), in June 2006. The development of the Combined Code (2006) is discussed further from paragraph 4.38.1 below.

**4.20.3**   In April 2007, the FRC announced a further review of the Combined Code on Corporate Governance. The review's main objective was to assess whether the Combined Code was *"appropriately enabling UK listed companies to be led in a way which facilitates entreprenurial success and the management of risk"*. To assist in this exercise, the FRC sought views from listed companies, directors, investors and other parties on their experience of implementing the Combined Code. The results of the consultation were published in November 2007 and concluded that the Combined Code continues to be broadly beneficial to the governance of UK listed companies, without undermining boards' entrepreneurial leadership. Separately, the BERR consulted on the implementation of the 4th and 8th Company Law Directives, which introduce mandatory requirements for corporate governance statements and credit commitments (see paras 4.183 to 4.186.4). These requirements overlap with some of the Code recommendations.

**4.20.4**   Following the 2007 review of the Combined Code, the FRC consulted on a further two possible changes and, on 27 June 2008, issued a revised Combined Code on Corporate Governance, hereafter referred to as the Combined Code (2008). The Combined Code (2008) is applicable for accounting periods beginning on or after 29 June 2008 and is discussed further from paragraph 4.100.13.

**4.20.5**   Also on 27 June 2008, the FSA released revisions to the Listing Rules and the Disclosure and Transparency Rules ('DTR') to implement the recent EU Company Law 4th and 8th Directives and make other minor changes. The FSA Rules on Corporate Governance, also applicable for accounting periods beginning on or after 29 June 2008, are discussed further from paragraph 4.100.1.

**4.21**   The commentary that follows concentrates on explaining the recommendations firstly of the Hampel Report, whose concepts led to the original Combined Code (1998) and then of the Combined Code (1998) itself and its successors, the Combined Code (2003), the Combined Code (2006) and the Combined Code (2008) and explains how companies should report on their compliance. The Listing Rules disclosure requirements relating to the requirements of the Combined Code concerning directors' remuneration are considered in detail in chapter 5.

# The Hampel Report

**Objectives**

**4.22**   The Committee on Corporate Governance, chaired by Sir Ronald Hampel (the Hampel Committee), was set up following the recommendations of the Cadbury and Greenbury Committees that a new committee should review the implementation of their findings. Following consultation, the final report of the committee, the Hampel Report, was issued in January 1998.

**4.23** The Hampel Committee's remit was to:

*"Seek to promote high standards of corporate governance in the interests of investor protection and in order to preserve and enhance the standing of companies listed on the Stock Exchange."*

This included reviewing the previous reports by the Cadbury Committee on the financial aspects of corporate governance and by the Greenbury Committee on boardroom pay.

**4.24** Hampel supported the contribution that Cadbury and Greenbury made to improvements in the accountability of public companies and endorsed the overwhelming majority of the findings of the two earlier committees.

**[The next paragraph is 4.26.]**

### 'Box ticking'

**4.26** Hampel argued for more flexibility when considering corporate governance standards and a proper regard for the individual circumstances of the companies concerned. Too often companies' experience of Cadbury and Greenbury was that the codes had been treated as sets of prescriptive rules with shareholders and their advisors following a 'box ticking' approach focussing only on whether a rule had been complied with rather than the particular circumstances involved.

**4.27** In Hampel's view this 'box ticking' approach did not take account of the diversity of circumstances and experience among different companies and within the same company. Although Hampel agreed with Cadbury that there are guidelines that are appropriate in most cases, Hampel considered that there will often be valid reasons for exceptions and companies should not be penalised for this. The focus by those considering corporate governance arrangements on 'box ticking' draws attention away from the diligent pursuit of corporate governance objectives and becomes an objective in itself. Compliance with every code recommendations does not guarantee that the business will not fail. It is possible for a company to arrange matters so that the letter of every governance rule is complied with, but not the substance.

### Objectives of listed companies

**4.28** These views led Hampel to broaden the Cadbury Committee's definition of corporate governance which was *"the system by which companies are directed and controlled"*. Hampel considered that this definition excluded many activities involved in the management of a company, which were also vital to the success of the business.

**4.29** The Hampel Committee considered that the single overriding objective shared by all listed companies is the preservation and enhancement of their shareholders' investment. Ultimately this is the responsibility of all boards and their policies and corporate governance arrangements should reflect this.

### Shareholders/stakeholders

**4.30** Hampel recognised that the board's relationship with the company's shareholders is different to that with other stakeholders. The board of directors is responsible for relations with stakeholders, but because the shareholders elect the directors the board is accountable to the shareholders. Although the directors' primary responsibility is to the shareholders, both present and future, different types of companies will have different relationships with stakeholders and the objective of enhancement of long-term shareholder value can only be met by directors developing and sustaining their relationship with stakeholders.

### Recommendations

**4.31** The Hampel Report identified a small number of broad principles directed largely at the process of corporate governance. It distinguished between principles of corporate governance and the more detailed guidelines in the Cadbury and Greenbury codes.

**4.32** The Hampel Report recommended that companies include a narrative statement, in their annual reports, of how they applied the broad principles of corporate governance to their particular circumstances. The Hampel Report did not prescribe the form or content of this statement, but recommended a number of principles that it felt could contribute to good governance expecting companies to explain their governance policies and any circumstances where departure from best practice was justified.

**4.33** The Hampel Committee recommended that those tasked with the evaluation of governance practices should apply the principles flexibly, with common sense and due regard to the company's individual circumstances. Hampel stated that *"box ticking is neither fair to companies nor likely to be efficient in preventing abuse"*.

## The development of the 1998, 2003, 2006 and 2008 Combined Codes

### Objective

**4.34** The Combined Code (1998) contained both principles and detailed provisions and was in two parts: part 1 dealt with 'Principles of good governance' and part 2 included the 'Code of best practice'. The Combined Code (2003), which, for companies with reporting periods beginning on or after 1 November 2003, superseded and replaced the Combined Code (1998), combined these two parts and also incorporated supporting principles. The Combined Code (2006) contains only a small number of amendments to the Combined Code (2003) and follows the same format. In a similar fashion, the Combined Code

(2008) contains only a small number of amendments to the Combined Code (2006) and also follows the same format. Thus, there are main principles, supporting principles and associated provisions. The principles in these four versions of the Combined Code are fairly general statements that expound the ideals of a company's corporate governance arrangements and promote transparency and openness in disclosure.

**4.35** The Hampel Committee considered that if companies do not let their investors know what they are doing and how, the investors will look elsewhere for information on whether or not the board is managing the company's affairs well. Inevitably investors will draw erroneous conclusions and as it is the investors who influence the market value of the company it is in the directors' interests to be open and transparent. The theme of the directors having a dialogue with investors based on mutual understanding of objectives appeared in the Higgs Report and was carried through into the Combined Code (2003).

**4.36** This underlying philosophy is responsible for the inclusion of a section in all four Combined Codes on institutional shareholders. Transparency and openness are less effective if the communication is a one-way process. Investors have duties and responsibilities too. Included in section 2 of each Combined Code are three principles relating to institutional shareholders. These cover dialogue with companies, evaluation of governance disclosures and shareholder voting. Although the Stock Exchange and the UK Listing Authority have little authority over institutional investors these issues are thought to be of sufficient note to include them in the Combined Code. The supporting principles in section 2 of each of the Combined Codes (2003), (2006) and (2008) expand upon the main principles (the latter have remained virtually identical to those of the Combined Code (1998)). However, unlike the Combined Code (1998), the 2003, 2006 and 2008 versions contain no provisions. This section of the Combined Code (2003), which was not changed in the Combined Code (2006) nor the Combined Code (2008), is discussed further from paragraph 4.93.

**4.37** Although the Hampel Committee's intention was to consolidate, this entailed review and some clarification of existing provisions. There were in fact a number of differences between the original Combined Code (1998) and its predecessor reports. The key change from the Cadbury-derived regime concerned internal control where the Combined Code (1998) said:

> *"The directors should, at least annually, conduct a review of the effectiveness of the group's system of internal controls and should report to shareholders that they have done so. The review should cover all controls, including financial, operational and compliance controls and risk management."*

The 2003 version is slightly different again, the final sentence reading as follows:

> *"The review should cover all **material** controls, including financial, operational and compliance controls and risk management **systems**."*

Note that neither version extends to making a statement about whether the board found the controls to be effective – it merely requires the board to say that they have reviewed them. But the significant extension in 1998 was that the review should cover the effectiveness of all internal controls each year and not just financial controls. It is unlikely that the Combined Code (1998) actually meant each and every control, no matter how minor; the intention was rather to expand the remit beyond financial controls, so the 2003 version clarifies that it is material controls that are to be covered in the annual effectiveness review. Again, this part of the Combined Code (2003) is unchanged in both the Combined Codes (2006) and (2008).

**[The next paragraph is 4.38.1.]**

**4.38.1**   In the autumn of 2004 the FRC carried out an informal assessment of the implementation of the Combined Code (2003) by analysing annual reports and holding discussions with businesses and investors.

**4.38.2**   The FRC performed a formal review on the implementation of the Combined Code (2003) during 2005, seeking views on a variety of issues such as: the overall quality and level of dialogue between boards and investors; whether 'comply or explain' was working successfully; and practical difficulties in relation to the new requirements.

**4.38.3**   As a result of the review, the FRC consulted on a number of proposed changes to the Combined Code (2003). The FRC confirmed that it would continue to monitor the impact of the Combined Code (2003) and the way that it is being implemented. It would also review the burden of new compliance requirements (on listed, and particularly smaller entities).

**[The next paragraph is 4.38.6]**

**4.38.6**   The 2005 review found no clear evidence that there is a generic problem in recruiting non-executive directors, but the FRC confirmed that it would keep the issue under review. In addition, the FRC encouraged companies to consider whether they could broaden the sources from which they seek to recruit new directors.

**4.38.7**   The FRC commented that due to the perception that identifying one individual as having recent and relevant financial experience may increase that individual's exposure to liability, some companies currently choose not to identify one individual, but rather explain that audit committee members collectively have recent and relevant financial experience. The FRC noted that the proposed 8th company law directive contains a requirement for audit committees to include an individual with 'competence in accounting or auditing' and has drawn this issue to the BERR's attention. The revised FSA Rules, which are discussed further in paragraph 4.100.1 below have adopted this proposal and now provide that at least one member of the audit committee (or the equivalent body) must have competence in accounting and/or auditing.

**4.38.8** The FRC further noted that changes to the Combined Code (2006) may be required as a result of forthcoming EU requirements under revised company law directives (relating to audit committees and corporate governance statements) or changes to UK law introduced in the Companies Act 2006. Following consultation the FRC issued a revised Combined Code (2008) on 27 June 2008. Also on this date the FSA released revisions to the Listing Rules and the DTR. Refer to paragraphs 4.20.4 and 4.20.5 above.

**Combined Code (2006)**

**4.38.9** On 27 June 2006, following its consultation on proposed changes to the Combined Code (2003), the FRC released an updated version of the Combined Code on Corporate Governance (Combined Code (2006)).

**4.38.10** In its review, the FRC found no appetite for major change to the Combined Code (2003). The Combined Code (2003) was reported to have bedded down well and had a positive impact on the quality of corporate governance among listed companies. Therefore, the Combined Code (2006) contained only a limited number of modifications.

**[The next paragraph is 4.38.12.]**

*Adoption of the Combined Code (2006)*

**4.38.12** The updated Combined Code on corporate governance published by the FRC in June 2006 ('Combined Code (2006)') takes effect for reporting periods commencing on or after 1 November 2006. This is the outcome of the adoption by the FSA of the Combined Code (2006) and the release of its amended Listing Rules in October 2006. No separate consultation was conducted for the adoption of the Combined Code (2006) by the FSA, due to the limited scope of the changes the new Code introduced.

*The FRC review of the Combined Code (2006)*

**4.38.13** In December 2007, the FRC consulted on two possible changes to the Combined Code (2006); one being the removal of the restriction on an individual chairing more than one FTSE 100 company; and the other, for listed companies outside the FTSE 350, to enable the company chairman to be a member of, but not chair, the audit committee.

**4.38.14** Simultaneously, the FSA consulted on revisions to its rules concerning corporate governance, which include requirements for listed companies to:

■ Have an audit committee.

■ Include a corporate governance statement in each annual report.

The FSA also proposed to delete the requirement for listed companies to state in their annual report how they have applied the principles of the Combined Code.

**Adoption of the Combined Code (2008) and revised FSA rules**

**4.38.15**  In June 2008, the FRC issued the Combined Code (2008), which is effective for accounting periods beginning on or after 29 June 2008. The revised Code incorporates the amendments that had been proposed in the 2007 consultation. In addition, the preamble to the Code was revised to provide guidance for companies on how to state how the main principles of the Code have been applied. Schedule C to the Code was also revised to acknowledge that certain recommended disclosures are required by the FSA's rules. The revisions to the Code are discussed further from paragraph 4.100.15.

**4.38.16**  Also in June 2008, the FSA issued revisions to the Listing Rules and the Disclosure and Transparency Rules that require all listed companies to:

- Have an audit committee.

- Present an annual statement of corporate governance containing a minimum level of information.

- State in the corporate governance statement how the company has applied the *main* principles of the Combined Code (as opposed to all the principles, as previously required).

The revised FSA rules are discussed further from paragraph 4.100.1.

**Overview of the contents of the Combined Code (2006)**

**4.39**  The Combined Code (2006) comprises main principles, supporting principles and provisions. The structure is as follows:

- Section 1 – Companies:

  - A – Directors.

  - B – Remuneration.

  - C – Accountability and audit.

  - D – Relations with shareholders.

- Section 2 – Institutional shareholders:

  - E – Institutional shareholders.

**4.39.1**  In the Combined Code (2006) three schedules provide further information:

- Schedule A – Provisions on the design of performance related remuneration.

- Schedule B – Guidance on liability of non-executive directors: care, skill and diligence.

- Schedule C – Disclosure of corporate governance arrangements.

**4.40** Section 1 of the Combined Code (2006) contains the corporate governance main and supporting principles and the provisions applicable to all listed companies. It is this section that is covered by the company's two-part statement required by the Listing Rules (discussed further in para 4.101). Section 2 of the Combined Code (2006) contains main and supporting principles applicable to institutional shareholders with regard to dialogue with companies, evaluation of a company's corporate governance arrangements and shareholder voting.

**Actions required by listed companies**

**4.41** Companies, on an ongoing basis, need to:

- Review the details of their compliance with the provisions of the Combined Code (2006).

- Ensure the Combined Code (2006)'s principles are embedded within their governance procedures.

- Identify any gaps that they need to address.

- Provide considered explanation where they choose to depart from Combined Code (2006) provisions.

**4.42** This review should not only deal with compliance, but also with how good corporate governance procedures can contribute to business success and shareholder value enhancement.

**4.43** Key actions that directors should take now, if they have not already done so, are summarised in the following table.

| **Action by directors of listed companies** |
|---|
| 1   Re-assess the existing process for reviewing the effectiveness of material internal controls. The Combined Code (2006) requires this review to cover financial, operational and compliance controls and risk management systems. In securing compliance, companies may wish to reappraise their approach and procedures, which may have become 'tired' or bureaucratic. |
| 2   Commission a point-by-point review of compliance with the 48 detailed provisions of the Combined Code (2006), report back to the board on any actions required to comply or provide a considered explanation for departure as appropriate. |
| 3   Commission preparation of a draft statement for the annual report explaining application of the 14 main principles and the 21 supporting principles in the Combined Code (2006) and justifying any departures from the provisions of the Combined Code (2006). |

4 Review board structure and balance of appointments between executive and non-executive directors. Review the contribution of individual directors to the board's overall objectives and effectiveness.

5 Consider who the 'senior independent non-executive director' is.

6 Reconsider or confirm the independent status of non-executive directors (independence considerations are listed under provision A.3.1 in the Combined Code (2006)).

7 For companies of all sizes, reconsider the need for an internal audit department.

8 Establish training arrangements for new directors on appointment and for all directors on an ongoing basis, to maintain and update their necessary skills and knowledge.

9 Review the relevance, quality and timeliness of information received by the board. The chairman has an explicit responsibility to ensure that all directors receive accurate, timely and clear information.

10 Consider the appropriate framework for a formal and rigorous evaluation of the board's performance and that of its committees and individual directors.

## Combined Code (2006)

### *Directors*

**4.44** The Combined Code (2006)'s principles cover the board and appointments and re-election to it, responsibilities of the chairman, the chief executive officer (CEO) and the senior independent director (SID), remuneration, the balance between executive and non-executive directors (NEDs) and their information and development needs.

### *The board*

**4.45** The references to the Combined Code's principles and provisions for the remainder of this chapter relate to the Combined Code (2006), unless stated otherwise. The first main principle is that every company should be headed by an effective board, which is collectively responsible for the success of the company. [CC A.1]. Supporting this are the following principles:

■ The board's role is to provide entrepreneurial leadership of the company within a framework of prudent and effective controls, which enables risk to be assessed and managed. It should set the company's strategic aims, ensure that necessary financial and human resources are in place for the company to meet its objectives and review management performance. It should set the company's values and standards and ensure that its obligations to its shareholders and others are met.

- All directors must take decisions objectively in the interests of the company.

- As members of a unitary board, non-executive directors should constructively challenge and help develop proposals on strategy. They should scrutinise management performance in meeting agreed goals and objectives and monitor the reporting of performance. They should satisfy themselves on the integrity of financial information and that financial controls and risk management systems are robust and defensible. Non-executives are responsible for determining the appropriate remuneration for executive directors and have a prime role in appointing, or removing, executives and in succession planning.

**4.46**   The best practice provisions relating to these principles recommend that:

- The board should meet sufficiently regularly to discharge its duties effectively and there should be a formal schedule of matters specifically reserved for its decision. The annual report should state how the board operates, explaining types of decisions to be taken by the board and those delegated to management.

- The annual report should identify the chairman, deputy chairman, chief executive and senior independent director, as well as the chairmen and members of the nomination, audit and remuneration committees. The number of board and committee meetings, and individual director attendance should be disclosed.

- The chairman should hold meetings with the non-executive directors without the executives present. The senior independent director should lead the non-executive directors in meetings without the chairman present when appropriate and at least annually to appraise the chairman's performance.

- Where directors have concerns that cannot be resolved about the running of the company or a proposed action, they should ensure that their concerns are recorded in the board minutes. On resignation, a non-executive director should provide a written statement to the chairman, for circulation to the board, with any such concerns.

- The company should arrange appropriate insurance cover in respect of legal action against its directors.

*Chairman and chief executive officer*

**4.47**   The second main principle explains that there are two key tasks at the top of every company – the running of the board (undertaken by the chairman) and the executive responsibility for the running of the company's business (undertaken by the chief executive officer (CEO)). There should be a clear division of responsibilities at the head of the company to ensure that no one individual has unfettered powers of decision. [CC A.2].

**4.48** Supporting this is the principle that the chairman is responsible for board's leadership, ensuring effectiveness on all aspects of its role and agenda. The chairman is also responsible for ensuring that directors receive accurate, timely and clear information. He/she should ensure effective communication with shareholders, facilitate the effective contribution of non-executive directors in particular and ensure constructive relations between executive and non-executive directors. [CC A.2].

**4.49** The best practice provisions underlying these principles require that the posts of chairman and CEO should not be exercised by one individual and the division of responsibilities between them should be clearly established, set out in writing and agreed by the board. On appointment, the chairman should meet independence criteria described in paragraph 4.51 (CC A.3.1) below. A CEO should not go on to be chairman of the same company, but where, exceptionally a board decides that he/she should, the board should consult major shareholders in advance and set out its reasons at the time of appointment and in the next annual report. [CC A.2.1-A.2.2].

*Board balance and independence*

**4.50** The third main principle is that the board should include a balance of executive and non-executive directors (and in particular independent non-executives) in order that no individual or small group of individuals can dominate the board's decision taking. [CC A.3]. The principles supporting this are as follows:

- The board should not be unwieldy, but of sufficient size that the balance of skills and experience is appropriate for the business' requirements and that changes to the board's composition can be managed without undue disruption.

- There should be a strong presence on the board of both executive and non-executive directors to ensure that power and information are not concentrated in one or two individuals.

- When deciding chairmanship and membership of committees there is value in ensuring that committee membership is refreshed and that undue reliance is not placed on particular individuals.

- No one other than the committee chairman and members is entitled to be present at a meeting of the nomination, audit or remuneration committee, but others may attend at the invitation of the committee.

**4.51** The best practice provisions underlying these principles recommend that:

- The board should identify each non-executive it considers to be independent in the annual report. It should determine whether each director is independent in character and judgement and whether there are relationships or circumstances which are likely to affect, or could appear to affect, the directors' judgement. The board should state its reasons if it determines that a director is independent notwithstanding the existence of relationships or circumstances that may appear relevant to its determination, including if the director:

- Has been an employee of the company or group within the last five years.

- Has, or has had, within the last three years, a material business relationship with the company either directly, or as a partner, shareholder, director or senior employee of a body that has such a relationship with the company.

- Has received or receives additional remuneration from the company apart from a director's fee, participates in the company's share option or a performance-related pay scheme, or is a member of the company's pension scheme.

- Has close family ties with any of the company's advisers, directors or senior employees.

- Holds cross-directorships or has significant links with other directors through involvement in other companies or bodies.

- Represents a significant shareholder.

- Has served on the board for more than nine years from the date of first election.

[CC A.3.1].

- At least half the board (excluding the chairman) should comprise independent non-executive directors. Thus a board that comprises a chairman, three executive directors and four independent non-executive directors would comply with this provision; at least half the board excluding the chairman (that is, four independent directors out of seven directors) are independent. This provision does not apply to smaller companies (defined as those companies categorised as falling outside of the FTSE 350 throughout the year immediately prior to the reporting year), which instead should have at least two independent non-executive directors.

- The board should appoint one of the independent non-executive directors to be the senior independent director. The senior independent director should be available to shareholders if they have concerns that contact through the normal channels of chairman, chief executive or finance director has failed to resolve, or for which such contact is inappropriate.

[CC A.3].

**4.52** As stated above, the Combined Code (2006) recommends that independent non-executives comprise at least half of the board, but in the case of smaller companies (see para 4.51 for definition) it states that they should have at least two independent non-executive directors. These recommendations can be difficult for smaller companies to comply with, given the practical difficulty of attracting and retaining high quality independent non-executives. This has been addressed by the Combined Code (2008), which amends provision C.3.1 to allow the company chairman of a smaller company (that is, outside the FTSE 350) to be a member of, but not chair, the audit committee, provided that he/she was considered independent on appointment as chairman. See paragraph 4.100.15 for further details of the amendments made by the Combined Code (2008). The chairman's membership of the audit committee is in addition to the two independent non-executive directors.

**4.53** The recommendation that a senior independent non-executive director should be identified in the annual report, provides an additional route for concerns to be conveyed to the board and/or an early warning system that may highlight poor management.

*Appointments to the board*

**4.54** The Combined Code principle relating to board appointments indicates that there should be a formal, rigorous and transparent procedure for the appointment of new directors to the board. [CC A.4]. The supporting principles state that:

- Appointments to the board should be made on merit and against objective criteria. Care should be taken to ensure that appointees have enough time available to devote to the job (particularly important for chairmen).

- The board should be satisfied that plans are in place for orderly succession for appointments to the board and senior management, to maintain an appropriate balance of skills and experience within the company and on the board.

**4.55** The best practice provisions recommend that there should be a nomination committee to lead the process for board appointments and make recommendations to the board.

**4.56** The majority of nomination committee members should be independent non-executive directors. The chairman or independent non-executive director should chair the committee, but the chairman should not chair the nomination committee when dealing with the appointment of his or her successor. The committee's terms of reference, explaining its role and the authority delegated to it by the board, should be made available on request or on the company's web site.

**4.57** The nomination committee should evaluate the balance of skills, knowledge and experience on the board and, in the light of this evaluation, prepare a description of the role and capabilities required for a particular appointment.

**4.58** For the appointment of a chairman, the nomination committee should prepare a job specification, including an assessment of the time commitment expected, recognising the need for availability in the event of crises. A chairman's other significant commitments should be disclosed to the board before appointment and included in the annual report. Changes to such commitments should be reported to the board as they arise and included in the next annual report. No individual should be appointed to a second chairmanship of a FTSE 100 company.

**4.58.1** This provision has been amended by the Combined Code (2008) by the removal of this restriction in provision A.4.3 on an individual chairing more than one FTSE 100 company. This amendment aims to remove any restriction for skilled non-executive directors who are able and willing to serve as chairman of FTSE 100 companies. See paragraph 4.100.15 for further details of the amendments made by the Combined Code (2008).

**4.59** The terms and conditions of appointment of non-executives should be made available for inspection. This means that they should be able to be inspected by any person at the company's registered office during normal business hours, and at the annual general meeting for fifteen minutes prior to the meeting and for the duration of the meeting. The letter of appointment for a non-executive director should set out the expected time commitment and non-executives should undertake that they have sufficient time available to meet what is expected of them. Their other significant commitments should be disclosed to the board before appointment, with a broad indication of the time involved and the board should be informed of subsequent changes.

**4.60** The board should not agree to a full time executive director taking on more than one non-executive directorship in a FTSE 100 company, nor the chairmanship of such a company. However, see paragraph 4.58.1 above, which sets out the changes made to this provision by the Combined Code (2008). The board should consider the impact of these other commitments and explain any such impact in the next annual report.

**4.61** The annual report should describe the nomination committee's work, including the process in relation to board appointments. A detailed description of the work of the committee during the year is considered to be best practice. An explanation should be given if neither an external search consultancy, nor open advertising, has been used in the appointment of a chairman or a non-executive director.

[CC A.4.1- A.4.6].

*Information and professional development*

**4.62** The Combined Code (2006) reinforces training and development of directors as an important part of good practice in governance and it is the board's responsibility to ensure that opportunities for training and development are available. The main principle is that the board should be supplied in a timely manner with information in a form and of a quality appropriate to enable it to discharge its duties. All directors should receive induction on joining the board and should regularly update and refresh their skills and knowledge. [CC A.5]. The supporting principles are that:

■ The chairman is responsible for ensuring that directors receive accurate, timely and clear information and management has an obligation to provide such information (but directors should seek clarification or amplification where necessary).

■ The chairman should ensure that the directors continually update their skills, knowledge and familiarity with the company required to fulfil their role both on the board and on board committees. The company should provide the necessary resources for developing and updating its directors' knowledge and capabilities.

■ Under the direction of the chairman, the company secretary's responsibilities include ensuring good information flows within the board and its committees and between senior management and non-executive directors, as well as facilitating induction and assisting with professional development as required.

■ The company secretary should be responsible for advising the board, through the chairman, on all governance matters.

**4.63** The Combined Code provisions are:

■ The chairman should ensure that new directors receive a full, formal and tailored induction on joining the board. As part of this, the company should offer major shareholders the opportunity to meet a new non-executive director.

■ The board should ensure that directors, especially non-executives, have access to independent professional advice at the company's expense where they judge it necessary to discharge their responsibilities as directors. Committees should be provided with sufficient resources to undertake their duties.

■ All directors should have access to the advice and services of the company secretary, who is responsible to the board for ensuring that board procedures are complied with. Both the appointment and removal of the company secretary should be a matter for the board as a whole.

[CC A.5.1-A.5.3].

*Performance evaluation*

**4.64** Another main principle is that the board should undertake a formal and rigorous annual evaluation of its own performance and that of its committees and individual directors. [CC A.6]. In support of this, individual evaluation should aim to show whether each director continues to contribute effectively and to demonstrate commitment to the role (including commitment of time for board and committee meetings and any other duties). The chairman should act on the results of the performance evaluation by recognising the strengths and addressing the weaknesses of the board and, where appropriate, proposing new members to be appointed to the board or seeking the resignation of directors.

**4.65** The related provision is that the board should state in the annual report how performance evaluation of the board, its committees and its individual directors has been conducted. The non-executive directors, led by the senior independent director, should be responsible for the chairman's performance evaluation, taking into account the executive directors' views. [CC A.6.1]. Disclosure of the results of the performance evaluation and actions arising is considered to be best practice.

*Re-election*

**4.66** The Combined Code principle on re-election of directors recommends that all directors should be submitted for re-election at regular intervals, subject to continued satisfactory performance and that the board should ensure planned and progressive refreshing of the board. [CC A.7]. The best practice provisions recommend:

- All directors to be subject to election by shareholders at the first annual general meeting after their appointment, and to re-election thereafter at intervals of no more than three years. The names of directors submitted for election or re-election should be accompanied by sufficient biographical details and any other relevant information to enable shareholders to take an informed decision on their election.

- Non-executive directors to be appointed for specified terms subject to re-election and to Companies Act provisions relating to the removal of a director. The board should set out to shareholders in the papers accompanying a resolution to elect a non-executive director why they believe an individual should be elected. The chairman should confirm to shareholders when proposing re-election that, following formal performance evaluation, the individual's performance continues to be effective and to demonstrate commitment to the role. Any term beyond six years (two three-year terms) for a non-executive director should be subject to particularly rigorous review, and should take into account the need for progressive refreshing of the board. Non-executive directors may serve longer than nine years (three three-year terms), subject to annual re-election. Serving more than nine years could be relevant to the determination of a non-executive director's independence (see para 4.51 (CC A.3.1) above).

[CC A.7.1-A.7.2].

**[The next paragraph is 4.68.]**

*Remuneration*

**4.68** The Combined Code principles concerning the level and make-up of remuneration, the procedure for developing policy on executive directors' remuneration and contract and notice periods, and the resulting disclosure in the financial statements is set out below.

*Policy*

**4.69** Levels of remuneration should be sufficient to attract, retain and motivate directors of the quality required to run the company successfully, but companies should avoid paying more than is necessary for this purpose. A significant proportion of executive directors' remuneration should be structured to link rewards to corporate and individual performance. [CC B.1].

**4.70** The supporting principle is that the remuneration committee should judge where to position their company relative to other companies, but should use comparisons with caution in view of the risk of an upward ratchet of remuneration levels with no corresponding improvement in performance. They should also be sensitive to pay and employment conditions elsewhere in the group, especially when determining annual salary increases.

**4.71** The following additional recommendations in relation to remuneration policy were made as part of the best practice provisions:

■ Performance-related elements of remuneration should form a significant proportion of the total remuneration package of executive directors and should be designed to align their interests with those of the shareholders and to give those directors keen incentives to perform at the highest levels. The remuneration committee should follow the provisions in Schedule A of the Combined Code, which offers additional guidance in designing performance-related remuneration schemes.

■ Executive share options should not be offered at a discount, unless permitted by the relevant provisions of the Listing Rules.

■ Levels of remuneration for non-executive directors should reflect the time commitment and responsibilities of the role. Remuneration for non-executive directors should not include share options but if, exceptionally, options are granted, shareholder approval should be sought in advance and any shares acquired by exercise of the options should be held until at least one year after the non-executive director leaves the board. Holding of share options could be relevant to the determination of a non-executive director's independence (see para 4.51 (CC A.3.1) above).

■ Where a company releases an executive director to serve as a non-executive director elsewhere, the remuneration report should include a statement as to whether or not the director will retain such earnings and, if so, what the remuneration is.

[CC B.1.1-B.1.4].

*Service contracts and compensation*

**4.72** In relation to service contracts and compensation:

■ Remuneration committees should carefully consider what compensation commitments (including pension contributions and all other elements) their directors' terms of appointment would entail in the event of early termination. The aim should be to avoid rewarding poor performance. They should take a robust line on reducing compensation to reflect departing directors' obligations to mitigate loss.

■ Notice or contract periods should be set at one year or less. If it is necessary to offer longer notice or contract periods to new directors recruited from outside, such periods should reduce to one year or less after the initial period.

[CC B.1.5-B.1.6].

*Procedure*

**4.73** The main principle in this area is that there should be a formal and transparent procedure for developing policy on executive remuneration and for fixing the remuneration packages of individual directors. No director should be involved in deciding his or her own remuneration. [CC B.2]. In support of this main principle are the following supporting principles:

■ The remuneration committee should consult the chairman and/or chief executive about their proposals relating to the remuneration of other executive directors. It should also be responsible for appointing any consultants in respect of executive director remuneration. Where executive directors or senior management are involved in advising or supporting the remuneration committee, care should be taken to recognise and avoid conflicts of interest.

■ The chairman of the board should ensure that the company maintains contact as required with its principal shareholders about remuneration, in the same way as for other matters.

**4.74** The Combined Code provisions recommend that:

■ The board should establish a remuneration committee of at least three, or in the case of smaller companies (see para 4.51 above) two, members, who should all be independent non-executive directors. In addition, the company chairman may also be a member of, but not chair, the committee if he or she was considered independent on appointment as chairman. The remuneration committee should make available its terms of reference on request and on the company website, explaining its role and the authority delegated to it by the board. Where remuneration consultants are appointed, a statement should be made available (in the same way as described for the terms of reference) of whether they have any other connection with the company.

■ The remuneration committee should have delegated responsibility for setting remuneration for all executive directors and the chairman, including pension rights and any compensation payments. The committee should also recommend and monitor the level and structure of remuneration for senior management. The definition of 'senior management' for this purpose should be determined by the board but should normally include the first layer of management below board level. Disclosure of the remuneration committee's activities throughout the year is considered to be good practice.

■ The board itself or, where required by the Articles of Association, the shareholders should determine the remuneration of the non-executive directors, within the limits set in the Articles of Association. Where permitted by the Articles, the board may delegate this responsibility to a committee, which might include the chief executive.

■ Shareholders should be invited specifically to approve all new long-term incentive schemes (as defined in the Listing Rules) and significant changes to existing schemes, save in the circumstances permitted by the Listing Rules.

[CC B.2.1-B.2.4].

**4.75** The Combined Code principles and best practice provisions concerning directors' remuneration are considered in more detail in chapter 5.

### Accountability and audit

### Financial reporting

**4.76** The Combined Code also covers how directors should present financial information to their shareholders and their responsibilities concerning internal control, as well as their relationship with external auditors. The principle concerning financial reporting requires that the board should present a balanced and understandable assessment of the company's position and prospects. [CC C.1].

**4.77** The supporting principle is that the board's responsibility to present a balanced and understandable assessment extends to interim and other price-sensitive public reports and reports to regulators, as well as to information required to be presented by statutory requirements.

**4.78**   The best practice provisions indicate that to achieve this:

- The directors should explain their responsibility for preparing the financial statements and there should be a statement by the auditors about their reporting responsibilities.

- The directors should report that the business is a going concern, with supporting assumptions or qualifications as necessary. Reporting on going concern is discussed further from paragraph 4.111.

[CC C.1.1-C.1.2].

*Internal control*

**4.79**   The Combined Code sets out the main principle that the board should maintain a sound system of internal control to safeguard shareholders' investment and the company's assets. [CC C.2]. There is no supporting principle, however the best practice provision provides that the board should, at least annually, conduct a review of the effectiveness of the group's system of internal controls and should report to shareholders that they have done so. The review should cover all material controls, including financial, operational and compliance controls and risk management systems. [CC C.2.1].

**4.80**   The importance of internal control to good governance is well recognised and, as explained in paragraph 4.87 (CC C.3.5) below, the Combined Code recommends that all companies, regardless of their size, consider the need for an internal audit function annually. Modern internal audit should be focussed on all aspects of internal control including business risk assessment and response, financial management, safeguarding assets and compliance with laws and regulations. In addition, internal audit can also add value to the organisation as well as providing assurance on the control environment.

**4.81**   The Combined Code recommends that the directors should at least annually review the effectiveness of all material controls, including operational, financial and compliance controls and risk management systems. Guidance was issued to directors in 1999 in order to assist them in complying with the internal control provision in the Combined Code (1998), known as the Turnbull guidance. In 2005, following a consultation process, the Turnbull guidance was updated. The Turnbull guidance (2005) supersedes and replaces the Turnbull guidance (1999).

**4.82**   The purpose of the review of controls effectiveness is to ensure that there is a strong control framework through which the organisation can both protect and increase shareholder value. For many companies this may be the most onerous aspect of the Combined Code and will require the active involvement of senior management. This, and the disclosure required by the Turnbull guidance, is discussed further from paragraph 4.131.

**4.83** The requirement for boards to review the effectiveness of all material controls also affects the company's auditors, who are currently required by the Listing Rules to review the directors' statement of compliance with that provision of the Combined Code. [LR 9.8.10R(2)(b)].

*Audit committee and auditors*

**4.84** The Combined Code includes the main principle that the board should establish formal and transparent arrangements for considering how they should apply the financial reporting and internal control principles and for maintaining an appropriate relationship with the company's auditors. [CC C.3].

**4.85** The best practice provisions underlying this principle provide that:

■ The board should establish an audit committee of at least three, or in the case of smaller companies (as defined in para 4.51 above) two, members, who should all be independent non-executive directors. The board should satisfy itself that at least one member of the audit committee has recent and relevant financial experience.

■ The main role and responsibilities of the audit committee should be set out in written terms of reference and made available (that is, on the web site). [CC C.3.3]. The role and responsibilities of the audit committee include:

　■ Monitoring the integrity of the financial statements of the company and any formal announcements relating to the company's financial performance, reviewing significant financial reporting judgments contained in them.

　■ Reviewing the company's internal financial controls and, unless expressly addressed by a separate board risk committee composed of independent directors or by the board itself, reviewing the company's internal control and risk management systems.

　■ Monitoring and reviewing the effectiveness of the company's internal audit function.

　■ Making recommendations to the board, for it to put to the shareholders for approval in general meeting, in relation to appointment, re-appointment and removal of the external auditor and to approve the remuneration and terms of engagement of the external auditor.

　■ Reviewing and monitoring the external auditor's independence and objectivity and the effectiveness of the audit process, taking into consideration relevant UK professional and regulatory requirements.

　■ Developing and implementing policy on the engagement of the external auditor to supply non-audit services, taking into account relevant ethical guidance regarding the provision of non-audit services by the external audit firm.

- Reporting to the board, identifying any matters in respect of which it considers that action or improvement is needed and making recommendations as to the steps to be taken.

[CC C.3.1-C.3.2].

- A separate section of the annual report should describe the work of the committee during the year in discharging those responsibilities.

**4.86** The Combined Code places considerable emphasis on the role of the audit committee. The provisions in relation to whistle-blowing and auditor objectivity and independence were introduced largely in response to corporate failures and scandals.

**4.87** The following provisions provide further clarification of the role of the audit committee:

- The audit committee should review arrangements by which staff of the company may, in confidence, raise concerns about possible improprieties in matters of financial reporting or other matters. The audit committee's objective should be to ensure that arrangements are in place for the proportionate and independent investigation of such matters and for appropriate follow-up action.

- The audit committee should monitor and review the effectiveness of the internal audit activities. Where there is no internal audit function, the audit committee should consider annually whether there is a need for an internal audit function and make a recommendation to the board, and the reasons for the absence of such a function should be explained in the relevant section of the annual report.

- A new provision in relation to appointment of external auditors was introduced. The audit committee should have primary responsibility for making a recommendation on the appointment, reappointment and removal of the external auditors. If the board does not accept the audit committee's recommendation, it should include in the annual report, and in any papers recommending appointment or re-appointment, a statement from the audit committee explaining the recommendation and should set out reasons why the board has taken a different position.

- To address concerns in relation to auditor independence, the Combined Code directs that the annual report should explain to shareholders how, if the auditor provides non-audit services, auditor objectivity and independence is safeguarded.

[CC C.3.3-C.3.7].

## Relations with shareholders

*Dialogue with institutional shareholders*

**4.88**   The Combined Code includes the principle that there should be a dialogue with institutional shareholders based on the mutual understanding of objectives. The board as a whole has responsibility for ensuring that a satisfactory dialogue takes place. [CC D.1].

**4.89**   The supporting principles are that whilst recognising that most shareholder contact is with the chief executive and finance director, the chairman (and the senior independent director and other directors as appropriate) should maintain sufficient contact with major shareholders to understand their issues and concerns. In addition, the board should keep in touch with shareholder opinion in whatever ways are most practical and efficient.

**4.90**   These principles are supplemented by the following best practice provisions:

- The chairman should ensure that the views of shareholders are communicated to the board as a whole and he/she should discuss governance and strategy with major shareholders. Non-executive directors should be offered the opportunity to attend meetings with major shareholders and should expect to attend if requested by the shareholders. The senior independent director should attend sufficient meetings with a range of major shareholders to listen to their views in order to help develop a balanced understanding of the issues and concerns of major shareholders.

- The board should state in the annual report the steps they have taken to ensure that the members of the board, and in particular the non-executive directors, develop an understanding of the views of major shareholders about their company, for example through direct face-to-face contact, analysts' or brokers' briefings and surveys of shareholder opinion.

[CC D.1.1-D.1.2].

*Constructive use of the annual general meeting (AGM)*

**4.91**   The main principle for the constructive use of the AGM is that the board should use the AGM to communicate with investors and encourage their participation. [CC D.2]. There are no supporting principles, but the following Combined Code provisions:

- At any general meeting, the company should propose a separate resolution on each substantially separate issue, and should in particular propose a resolution at the AGM relating to the report and accounts. For each resolution, proxy appointment forms should provide shareholders with the option to direct their proxy to vote either for or against the resolution or to withhold their vote. The proxy form and any announcement of the results of a vote should make it clear that a 'vote withheld' is not a vote in law and will not be counted in the calculation of the proportion of the votes for and against the resolution.

- The company should ensure that all valid proxy appointments received for general meetings are properly recorded and counted. For each resolution, after a vote has been taken, except where taken on a poll, the company should ensure that the following information is given at the meeting and made available as soon as reasonably practicable on a website that is maintained by or on behalf of the company:

  - The number of shares in respect of which proxy appointments have been validly made.

  - The number of votes for the resolution.

  - The number of votes against the resolution.

  - The number of shares in respect of which the vote was directed to be withheld.

- The chairman should arrange for the chairmen of the audit, remuneration and nomination committees to be available to answer questions at the AGM and for all directors to attend.

- The company should arrange for the notice of the AGM and related papers to be sent to shareholders at least 20 working days before the meeting.

[CC D.2.1-D.2.4].

**[The next paragraph is 4.93.]**

*Institutional shareholders*

**4.93**   The Combined Code includes three main principle recommendations for institutional shareholders concerning their relationship with listed companies. The areas covered are: dialogue with companies, evaluation of governance disclosures and shareholder voting. The first principle states that they should enter into a dialogue with companies based on the mutual understanding of objectives, which clearly aligns with the equivalent requirement for companies, set out in section 1 of the Combined Code. [CC E.1]. Supporting this is the principle that institutional shareholders should apply the principles set out in the Institutional Shareholder's Committee's 'The Responsibilities of Institutional Shareholders and Agents – Statement of Principles', which should be reflected in fund manager contracts.

**4.94**   The second main principle is that when evaluating companies' governance arrangements, particularly those relating to board structure and composition, institutional shareholders should give due weight to all relevant factors drawn to their attention. [CC E.2]. The supporting principle is that institutional shareholders should carefully consider explanations given for departure from the Combined Code and make reasoned judgments in each case. They should give an explanation to the company, in writing where appropriate, and be prepared to enter a dialogue if they do not accept the company's position. It is explicitly stated that they should avoid a box-ticking approach to assessing a company's corporate governance. They should bear in mind, in particular, the size and complexity of the company and the nature of the risks and challenges it faces.

**4.95** The last of the Combined Code three main principles relating to institutional investors states that they have a responsibility to make considered use of their votes. [CC E.3]. The supporting principles are that institutional shareholders should take steps to ensure their voting intentions are being translated into practice. They should also, on request, make available to their clients information on the proportion of resolutions on which votes were cast and non-discretionary proxies lodged. Finally, major shareholders should attend AGMs where appropriate and practicable. Companies and registrars should facilitate this.

**4.96** There are no best practice provisions in this section of the Combined Code.

**4.97** The principles and detailed provisions relating to institutional shareholders are not matters that are appropriate for the Listing Rules to include within the disclosure requirement for listed companies. The Hampel Committee did, however, regard section 2 of the Combined Code (1998), relating to institutional shareholders, as an integral part of the committee's recommendations and hoped that at least the major institutions would voluntarily disclose to their clients and to the public the extent to which they are able to give effect to these provisions. However this has not happened to any great extent.

### Schedules forming part of the Combined Code

**4.98** The Combined Code has three schedules offering further guidance:

- Schedule A: Provisions on the design of performance related remuneration.

- Schedule B: Guidance on liability of non-executive directors: care, skill and diligence.

- Schedule C: Disclosure of corporate governance arrangements.

**4.99** Schedule A was part of the Combined Code (1998). Schedules B and C were introduced as part of the Combined Code (2003). Schedule B provides a useful summary of the liability issues that impact non-executive directors. Schedule C focuses on disclosure and has been modified by the Combined Code (2008) and the FSA Rules on Corporate Governance. Further discussion of this can be found in paragraph 4.100.15 below. It summarises the information that should be included in a company's annual report and that which should be made available (that is, *via* the company's web site). In addition, it contains details of the information that the board should set out to shareholders in relation to election or re-election of directors and when recommending appointment or reappointment of an external auditor.

**4.99.1** The Listing Rules requirements in relation to the Combined Code have been included within Schedule C of the Combined Codes (2006) and (2008) for clarity and convenience.

*Additional guidance on the application of the Combined Code*

**4.100** The following sources of guidance on the practical application of the Combined Code are useful tools and remain relevant for the 2008 Code:

■ The Turnbull Guidance on Internal Control (2005).

■ The Smith Guidance on Audit Committees (2003). (At the time of writing, the FRC has consulted on revising the Smith Guidance, but no revised guidance has been issued).

■ The Higgs 'Suggestions for Good Practice' (July 2003).

**Revised FSA Rules on corporate governance**

**4.100.1** On 27 June 2008, the FSA released revisions to the Listing Rules and the DTR to implement the EU 4th and 8th Company Law Directives. These revised Rules are effective for accounting periods beginning on or after 29 June 2008 and are discussed further below.

*Requirement to have an audit committee*

**4.100.2** A new rule has been inserted into the DTR requiring certain companies (see para 4.100.3) to have an audit committee (or a body performing equivalent functions). At least one member must be independent and at least one member (who may, but need not be, the same person) must have competence in accounting and/or auditing. [DTR 7.1.1 R].

As a minimum the relevant body must:

■ Monitor the financial reporting process.

■ Monitor the effectiveness of the internal control, internal audit where applicable and risk management systems.

■ Monitor the statutory audit of the annual and consolidated financial statements.

■ Review and monitor the independence of the statutory auditor and, in particular, the provision of additional services provided by the auditors.

The FSA has indicated that compliance with the following provisions of the Combined Code (2008) regarding audit committees will result in compliance with DTR 7.1.1 R to DTR 7.1.5 R:

- A.1.2: The annual report should identify members of the board and board committees.

- C.3.1: The composition of the audit committee.

- C.3.2: The recommended minimum terms of reference for the audit committee.

- C.3.3: The annual report should describe the work of the audit committee.

**4.100.3** This rule applies to companies with transferable securities admitted to trading on either the London Stock Exchange or the PLUS-listed markets and that are required to appoint a statutory auditor. There are exemptions to this requirement for:

- A listed company whose parent is subject to this rule (or an equivalent rule of any EEA State).

- An issuer whose sole business is to act as the issuer of asset-backed securities, provided that the issuer makes a public statement explaining why it is not appropriate to have an audit committee.

- A credit institution whose shares are not admitted to trading if the total nominal value of its listed debt securities is less than €100 million and the company has not prepared a prospectus in accordance with section 85 of the Financial Services and Markets Act 2000.

*Requirement to present a corporate governance statement*

**4.100.4** For accounting periods beginning on or after 29 June 2008, certain companies (see para 4.100.5) will be required to present a separate corporate governance statement. It may be included: as part of the directors' report; or separately issued to accompany the annual report and financial statements; or may be made available on the company's web site, but with cross-references in the directors' report.

**4.100.5** This requirement applies to UK companies with shares admitted to trading on the London Stock Exchange or PLUS-listed markets or traded on a multi-lateral trading facility. [DTR 1B.1.5, 1B.1.6].

**4.100.6** The DTR contains a number of required disclosures in the corporate governance statement. Many of those requirements are also dealt with elsewhere in UK legislation or guidance. The requirements are listed below, together with any overlap with other legislation or guidance.

**4.100.7** The corporate governance statement must contain a reference to:

- Any corporate governance code to which the company is subject.

- Any corporate governance code which the company may have voluntarily decided to apply.

- All relevant information about the corporate governance practices applied beyond the requirements under national law.

- Where any corporate governance code that is applied (either mandatorily or voluntarily) is publicly available.

- An explanation of any departure from any corporate governance code applied. (This overlaps with the 'comply or explain' rule in LR 9.8.6R(5) – see further para 4.102).

[DTR 7.2.2R, 7.2.3 R].

**4.100.8** In addition, the corporate governance statement must contain:

- A description of the main features of the company's internal control and risk management systems in relation to the financial reporting process. [DTR 7.2.5 R]. (See para 4.100.10.)

- The information required to be included in the directors' report by paragraph 13(2), (c), (d), (f), (h) and (i) of Schedule 7 to the Large and Medium-sized Companies and Groups (Accounts and Reports) Regulations 2008, resulting from the EU Takeover Directive. [DTR 7.2.6 R]. (These requirements are discussed further in chapter 3.)

- A description of the composition and operation of the company's administrative, management and supervisory bodies and their committees. [DTR 7.2.7 R]. (See para 4.100.09.)

**4.100.9** The FSA has indicated that compliance with the following provisions of the Combined Code (2008) will ensure compliance with DTR 7.2.7 R (last bullet in para 4.100.8):

- A.1.1: The annual report should include a statement of how the board operates.

- A.1.2: The annual report should identify members of the board and board committees.

- A.4.6: The annual report should describe the work of the nomination committee.

- B.2.1: A description of the work of the remuneration committee should be made available.

- C.3.3: The annual report should describe the work of the audit committee.

**4.100.10** The only new requirement, over and above the recommendations of the Combined Code is a description of the main features of the company's internal control and risk management systems in relation to the financial reporting process. The FRC has indicated that while this requirement in DTR 7.2.5 R differs from the recommendation in the Combined Code provision C.2.1 below, the FRC envisages that both the Code and the DTR can be satisfied by a single internal control statement.

> *"The annual report should include a statement that a review of the effectiveness of the internal control system has been carried out." [C.2.1].*

**4.100.11**  For a parent company, this will include a description of the main features of the group's internal control and risk management systems in relation to the process for preparing consolidated financial statements.

*Interaction between the FSA Rules and the Combined Code*

**4.100.12**  Although many of the DTR requirements overlap with provisions of the Combined Code, the FRC has indicated that, where a company chooses to 'explain' rather than 'comply' with any of the overlapping provisions, it will need to ensure that it, nonetheless, meets the requirements in the FSA rules.

Combined Code (2008)

**4.100.13**  On 27 June 2008, the FRC released an updated Combined Code on Corporate Governance (Combined Code (2008)), which will take effect for reporting periods commencing on or after 29 June 2008. Therefore, for companies with December 2008 and March 2009 year ends, the Combined Code (2006) will continue to apply.

**4.100.14**  It is important to recognise that early compliance with the Combined Code (2008) provisions would trigger the need to explain a departure from the 2006 Code in the 2009 reporting season.

*Details of modifications made to form the Combined Code (2008)*

**4.100.15** The following changes were made to the Combined Code (2006) in order to produce the Combined Code (2008) (the references provided are to the Combined Code (2006)):

- **To remove the restriction in provision A.4.3 on an individual chairing more than one FTSE 100 company**

  This amendment aims to remove any restriction for skilled non-executive directors who are able and willing to serve as chairmen of FTSE 100 companies. Provision A4.3 already has safeguards in place regarding the time commitment of chairmen: before appointment, a chairman should disclose other significant commitments to the board and in the annual report. Any changes to these commitments should be reported to the board as they arise and their impact explained in the next annual report.

- **For listed companies outside the FTSE 350, to amend provision C.3.1 to allow the company chairman to be a member of, but not chair, the audit committee provided that he/she was considered independent on appointment as chairman**

*Corporate governance*

This amendment is intended to make it easier for smaller listed companies to comply with the Combined Code's recommendations on the composition of the audit committee. However, membership of the company chairman would be in addition to the minimum of two independent non-executive directors.

■ **Schedule C to the Combined Code (2006) has been amended to reflect that eight of its provisions now overlap with requirements in the new Corporate Governance Rules issued by the FSA**

Schedule C of the Combined Code (2006) has been amended to include a summary of the new Disclosure and Transparency Rules ('DTR') requirements in addition to the full text of Listing rule 9.8.6. An appendix has been added to give details of the overlaps between the mandatory DTR requirements and the expected Code provisions. In respect of disclosures relating to the audit committee and the composition and operation of the board and its committees, the FRC's view is that compliance with the relevant provisions of the Code will result in compliance with the relevant Rules.

■ **The preamble to the Combined Code is amended**

The preamble to the Combined Code (2008) reflects some of the findings of the FRC's 2007 review of the impact and implementation of the Combined Code (2006). It also includes new guidance to assist companies in complying with the Listing Rule requirement to explain how the codes' main principles have been applied.

**Statement of compliance**

**4.101**   A listed company has to include in its annual report and accounts a two-part statement on corporate governance. When reporting under the Combined Code (2006), in the first part the company is required to make a statement explaining how it has applied the principles including both main and supporting principles set out in section 1 of the Combined Code (that is, the part that applies to companies). This statement should provide sufficient information to enable the company's shareholders to evaluate how the principles have been applied. [LR 9.8.6R(5)].

**4.101.1**   For companies applying the Combined Code (2008), the compliance statement is restricted to compliance with the main principles only and not the supporting principles. [LR 9.8.6R(5)] This change to the compliance statement is for accounting years beginning on or after 29 June 2008.

**4.101.2**   The Combined Code (2008) includes guidance in its preamble to assist boards in applying this Listing Rule requirement.

**4.101.3**   The Listing Rules clarify that the Combined Code refers to:

- For reporting periods commencing on or after 29 June 2008, the Combined Code (2008).

- For reporting periods commencing before 29 June 2008, the Combined Code (2006).

**4.102**   In the second part, listed companies have to report whether or not the company has complied throughout the accounting period with the provisions set out in section 1 of the Combined Code. Where a company has not complied with the Combined Code's provisions, or has only complied with some of the Combined Code's provisions or (in the case of provisions whose requirements are of a continuing nature) has complied for only part of an accounting period, the compliance statement must specify the Combined Code provisions with which the company has not complied, for what part of the period such non-compliance continued (where relevant) and give reasons for any non-compliance. [LR 9.8.6R(6)].

**4.103**   There is no requirement in the Combined Code specifying where the statement of compliance should be located within the annual report. Such statements are commonly included within a separate section dealing with corporate governance just after the directors' report, or within the directors' report itself. Occasionally, the issue is dealt with or referred to within the chairman's statement. It is not appropriate to include the statement within the audited financial statements.

**4.103.1**   For a company that complies with the provisions of the Combined Code in their entirety, it is reasonable to assume that, in doing so, they have applied the main principles.

**4.103.2**   Where an explanation of non-compliance with one or more of the Code's provisions is given in respect of one particular main principle, it will be necessary to include an explanation of how the company has, nonetheless, applied that particular main principle.

**4.103.3**   At the extreme, where an explanation of non-compliance with a number of the Code's provisions is given and those provisions support the application of a number of main principles, it may be appropriate for the company to explain how it has applied the codes' main principles.

**4.104**   In support of the compliance statement, boards or audit committees would generally expect to see a paper that sets out how the company complies with each aspect of the Combined Code, supported by relevant documentation. It is helpful for the board or audit committee to minute its approval of such a paper.

**Statements of non-compliance with the Combined Code provisions**

**4.105**   Any element of non-compliance with the Combined Code provisions for any part of the period must be identified, giving reasons. The specific aspect of the Combined Code must be identified. This does not mean that the paragraph number in the Combined Code must be used, although some companies might do so. It would not be adequate simply to list the paragraph numbers of the Combined Code, because the reader would have to refer elsewhere to discover the significance of the statement.

**4.106** Statements of non-compliance might become quite lengthy where there are a significant number of departures from the Combined Code's recommendations. However, it would be very rare indeed for a company to fail to comply with all aspects. For example, few boards would wish to suggest that they do not *'meet sufficiently regularly',* do not include directors *'independent in character and judgement',* or that the aim of the remuneration committee is *'rewarding poor performance'.* [CC A.1.1, A.3.1, B.1.5].

**4.107** The shortest way to make a statement of non-compliance is to provide a list of areas of non-compliance with individual provisions or overall reasons for non-compliance. However, such a minimalist approach will be very negative, because it focuses on the areas of non-compliance. It is preferable to give a more balanced statement which gives information on compliance and/or on areas where the company is moving towards compliance or has decided that compliance will not best suit the circumstances of the company and, therefore, a departure from the Combined Code provisions is appropriate.

**4.108** There could be valid reasons why some of the provisions have not been followed or some alternative procedures may have been adopted. As long as the company explains and has reasonable justification for any non-compliance with specific aspects and governance is effective in practice, then in the spirit of transparency, it is hoped that the market will react in a positive way.

**4.108.1** However, as discussed in paragraph 4.100.12, it is necessary to bear in mind that, for accounting years beginning on or after 29 June 2008, where a company is explaining a departure from any of the Code's provisions that overlap with that disclosure requirement of the DTR, then this departure from the Code may result in a breach of the Listing Rules.

**4.109** It is recommended that shareholders and others monitoring compliance with the Combined Code should do so with flexibility, common sense and with regard to the individual company's circumstances, for example, in a newly listed company in its first year of reporting compliance with the Combined Code. The wording contained in section 2 of the Combined Code, in relation to institutional investors giving reasons to companies if they do not accept their explanations for departures, and the need to avoid a box-ticking approach, will hopefully result in improvements in this area.

### Statement of compliance and interaction with the Combined Code (2008)

**4.110** As mentioned in paragraph 4.101.3 above, the Listing Rules refer to the Combined Code (2008) for reporting periods commencing on or after 29 June 2008. Therefore, the Combined Code (2006) continues to apply for reporting periods beginning prior to 29 June 2008 and adoption of the new recommendations of the Combined Code (2008) for these periods would technically be a breach of the Combined Code (2006).

**4.110.1** For example, disclosure (reason for and nature and period of non-compliance) would be required for a company with a 31 December 2008 year end where the chairman had served as a member of the audit committee at any time during the year. However, a statement that includes reference to the reasons behind the revisions to the Combined Code (2006) would seem to be a reasonable approach when explaining the non-compliance.

**Reporting on going concern**

*Combined Code requirement*

**4.111** The Combined Code states that *"the directors should report that the business is a going concern, with supporting assumptions or qualifications as necessary"*. [CC C.1.2].

**4.112** This is unchanged from the situation under the Cadbury Code and the Combined Code (1998) and should be interpreted in the light of the guidance, 'Going concern and financial reporting' (GCFR), which was published by a joint working group in November 1994. The going concern statement became a separate requirement of the Listing Rules effective for accounting periods beginning on or after 31 December 1995 and this requirement remains in the Listing Rules. [LR 9.8.6R(3)]. Examples of this type of statement are shown in Tables 4.1 and 4.2.

---

**Table 4.1 – Going concern statement**

**GKN Plc – Annual report – 31 December 2006**

**Business review (extract)**

**Financial resources and going concern**
At 31 December 2006 the Group had net borrowings of £426 million. In addition it had available, but undrawn, committed borrowing facilities totalling £350 million.

Having assessed the future funding requirements of the Group and Company, the Directors are of the opinion that it is appropriate for the accounts to be prepared on a going concern basis.

---

---

**Table 4.2 – Going concern statement**

**The British Land Company Plc — 31 March 2006**

**Corporate governance extract**

**Going concern**

After making enquiries and examining major areas which could give rise to significant financial exposure the directors are satisfied that no material or significant exposures exist, other than as reflected in these financial statements, and that the Group has adequate resources to continue its operations for the foreseeable future. For this reason they continue to adopt the going concern basis in preparing the accounts.

---

**4.113** The GCFR guidance describes procedures that companies may undertake so that the directors are in a position to express a positive opinion on going concern and sets out what the disclosure should include.

*Form of disclosure*

**4.114** The form of disclosure depends on the directors' conclusions having undertaken procedures in relation to going concern. There are three basic conclusions:

■ they have a reasonable expectation that the company or group will continue in operational existence for the foreseeable future; or

■ they have identified factors that cast doubt on the ability of the company or group to continue in operational existence, but they consider it appropriate to use the going concern basis in preparing the financial statements; or

■ they consider that the going concern basis is not appropriate.

**4.115** Most companies fall into the first category. The guidance suggests the appropriate form of words in this case:

*"After making enquiries, the directors have a reasonable expectation that the company has adequate resources to continue in operational existence for the foreseeable future. For this reason, they continue to adopt the going concern basis in preparing the accounts."* [GCFR para 49].

**4.116** This form of disclosure has been adopted by most companies, although a significant number of blue chip companies, especially in the financial services sector, have chosen to be rather more positive, for example see Table 4.3.

> **Table 4.3 – Going concern statement**
>
> **Barclays PLC – Annual Report – 31 December 2006**
>
> **Corporate governance (extract)**
>
> **Going concern**
>
> The Directors confirm they are satisfied that the Company and the Group have adequate resources to continue in business for the foreseeable future. For this reason, they continue to adopt the 'going concern' basis for preparing the accounts.

**4.117**   The 'going concern' assumption, as explained in paragraph 24 of IAS 1 and paragraph 22 of FRS 18, is an hypothesis that the enterprise will continue in operational existence for the foreseeable future. The guidance requires directors to state that they believe it appropriate to continue to use the going concern basis, not to guarantee that the company will not fail.

**4.118**   The guidance recommends that the disclosure should be located in an operating and financial review (OFR) recognising that the OFR provides a context for a going concern statement. Despite this, it is quite common for the going concern statement to be included within the corporate governance statement with a separate sub-heading.

**4.119**   The guidance provides very limited indication of what might constitute *"factors which cast doubt"* on the company's or group's ability to continue in operational existence. An example is given of a company that is in breach of its loan covenants and where negotiations are continuing.

**4.120**   Where there are factors that cast doubt, directors are expected to perform more detailed work to determine the extent of the problem. The directors will then need to *"explain the circumstances so as to identify the factors which give rise to the problems"* and explain how they intend to deal with them.

**4.121**   The guidance gives an example of such a disclosure:

> *"The company is in breach of certain loan covenants at its balance sheet date and so the company's bankers could recall their loans at any time. The directors continue to be involved in negotiations with the company's bankers and as yet no demands for repayments have been received. The negotiations are at an early stage and, although the directors are optimistic about the outcome, it is as yet too early to make predictions with any certainty.*
>
> *In the light of the actions described elsewhere in the Operating and Financial Review, the directors consider it appropriate to adopt the going concern basis in preparing the accounts."* [GCFR para 51].

**4.122**   If the directors conclude that the company is unlikely to continue in operational existence for the foreseeable future, a non-going concern basis will be required in preparing the financial statements and this will require disclosure.

4039

Directors will generally wish to take legal advice before making such a disclosure, in particular in relation to whether the directors may be liable for wrongful trading.

**4.123** None of these disclosures obviate the need to make the disclosures relating to a non-going concern basis required by the Companies Act and accounting standards within the financial statements (see chapter 2 of the Manual of Accounting – UK GAAP and chapter 4 of the Manual of Accounting – IFRS for the UK).

### Application to groups

**4.124** The GCFR guidance recommends that directors of a parent company make disclosures in relation to both the parent and the group as a whole. This does not mean that each individual company in the group is a going concern, but it does mean that the directors' procedures will need to consider the impact of any difficulties in subsidiaries on the group as a whole.

### Procedures

**4.125** The guidance specifies a series of procedures that directors may wish to adopt in considering whether it is appropriate to adopt the going concern basis for the financial statements. It recognises that appropriate procedures will vary according to circumstances. The effect of the guidance is that the board should expect to see a paper that pulls together the evidence available from such procedures and any additional procedures that may be deemed necessary in the circumstances identified. The directors will need to consider this and other evidence available to them to determine whether it is appropriate to make the proposed statement on going concern.

**4.126** The procedures, which are explained more fully in an appendix to the guidance, cover the following areas:

- Forecasts and budgets.
- Borrowing requirements.
- Liability management.
- Contingent liabilities.
- Products and markets.
- Financial risk management.
- Other factors.
- Financial adaptability.

*Foreseeable future*

**4.127**   The guidance explains that directors should make their statement on the basis of information available to them at the date they approve the financial statements. In practice, the review procedures will be undertaken to an earlier date and then reviewed for any changes up to the date of approval.

**4.128**   During the drafting of the guidance there was significant discussion of how far forward the directors should look in considering whether the business is expected to remain a going concern. The guidance observes that any such consideration is inherently uncertain and can only represent a judgement at a point in time that may subsequently be overturned. The guidance recommends that directors consider all information of which they are aware at the time of approval. Events expected more than, say, a year beyond approval should not, therefore, be ignored.

**4.129**   The guidance seeks to avoid specifying a minimum period, but requires that *"where the period considered by the directors has been limited, for example, to a period of less than one year from the date of approval"*, the directors should consider whether additional disclosure should be made to explain this limitation. ISA (UK and Ireland) 570, 'Going concern', published by the APB and effective for audits of financial statements for periods beginning on or after 15 December 2004, states that:

> *"If the period to which those charged with governance have paid particular attention in assessing going concern is less than one year from the date of approval of the financial statements, and those charged with governance have not disclosed that fact, the auditor should do so within the section of the auditor's report setting out the basis of the audit opinion, unless the fact is clear from any other references in the auditor's report."* [ISA (UK&I) 570 para 31-4].

**4.130**   Most directors will find such a reference by auditors unattractive and, therefore, for practical purposes, companies will want to ensure that the period given active consideration is at least a year from the date of approval (or the directors themselves have to explain why this is inappropriate). For some companies this will mean extending budgets and cash flows, at least at group level, beyond the end of the following financial period to cover 12 months from the date of approval.

**Reporting on internal control**

*Combined Code recommendation*

**4.131**   The Combined Code states that:

> *"The board should, at least annually, conduct a review of the effectiveness of the group's system of internal controls and should report to shareholders*

*that they have done so. The review should cover all material controls, including financial, operational and compliance controls and risk management systems.''* [CC C.2.1].

**4.132** The recommendation for directors to review the effectiveness of all material controls goes further than the original Cadbury Code recommendation to review financial control and requires the active involvement of senior management.

**4.133** For many companies that had already accepted that in practice it is difficult to distinguish financial from other controls, this wider risk and control review may already have been well established. For others, when this provision was introduced, compliance with the Combined Code may have required a significant extension of the work previously done to review and report on internal financial control. Past experience shows that the review of internal financial control was one of the more onerous requirements of Cadbury. It was also one of the more fruitful where undertaken effectively.

**4.134** The remit for the review to cover risk management and operational, financial and compliance controls provides an ideal opportunity to review the effectiveness of the existing processes, taking into account developments in risk management thinking that have occurred in recent years. High level integrated risk management approaches that take account of strategy, organisation and people as well as business processes have, for some time, been seen by leading corporations as offering clear potential for enhancing shareholder value.

**4.134.1** Companies with a listing in the US are required to provide an internal control report containing an assessment by management of the effectiveness of controls and financial reporting procedures under section 404 of the Sarbanes-Oxley Act (see from para 4.194 below for further details).

**[The next paragraph is 4.138.]**

*Turnbull guidance (2005) for directors*

**4.138** The original Turnbull guidance, 'Internal Control: Guidance for directors on the Combined Code', was published in September 1999 (Turnbull guidance (1999)) and updated in October 2005 following a consultation process led by the Turnbull Review Group.

**4.139** The Turnbull guidance specifically outlines broad principles rather than boxes to be ticked, requiring directors to use their judgement to decide whether or not they have complied. Listed companies are expected to embrace the spirit of the guidance, rather than just follow the letter of it. The aim is to help companies to achieve their own business objectives. This challenges boards to develop an approach that fits the operating style of their organisation and builds upon any practices already in place. The Turnbull guidance deliberately does not attempt to set out prescriptive procedures that will fit all companies, as the 'right' procedures will be those that support the individual businesses.

**4.140** The framework of the Turnbull guidance is that companies adopt a risk-based approach to setting and managing their internal control processes. Throughout the guidance the importance of an embedded ongoing process of identifying and responding to risk is emphasised. This integrated approach will need to include procedures to:

- Establish business objectives.

- Identify the key risks associated with these.

- Agree on the risk profiles to be adopted and the control processes to address the accepted risks.

- Set up a system to implement the decisions, which will include regular feedback.

**4.141** The internal control system to be implemented should encompass all the policies and procedures that, taken together, facilitate the effectiveness and efficiency of a company's operations and enables it to respond to significant business, operational, financial, compliance and other risks. The internal control system is a crucial element in managing risks which if not operating effectively may adversely affect the fulfilment of business objectives.

**4.142** The main issues to address are that:

- The identification and management of risks needs to be linked to the achievement of business objectives and enhancing shareholder value.

- There should be a risk based approach to internal control including evaluation of the likelihood and impact of risks becoming a reality.

- Business, operational and compliance risks must be addressed as well as financial risks.

- Risk assessment must be embedded within ongoing operations.

- The board should receive regular reports during the year on internal control and risk (not just annually).

- The principal results of risk identification, evaluation and management review should be reported up to, and reviewed at, board level.

**4.143** The appendix to the Turnbull guidance includes questions to consider and related examples that will assist companies when implementing the guidance.

### The board's role

**4.144** The role of the board is crucial under the Turnbull guidance. There is onus on the board to sponsor and take ownership of internal control. Specifically, it is important that the board defines the process to be adopted for its ongoing review of the effectiveness of internal control. There needs to be regular reporting to the board during the year and the board must set out both the scope and frequency of the reports it wishes to receive during the year.

**4.144.1** The Turnbull guidance includes a preface highlighting to boards the importance of having a continuous process to review and update the system of internal controls. In addition, it encourages boards to take the opportunity to explain the specific risk and control issues facing the company, how the company maintains a framework of internal controls to address these issues and how the board has reviewed the effectiveness of that framework. The board should exercise the standard of care generally applicable to directors in the exercise of their duties when forming a view on the effectiveness of the internal control.

**4.145** These reports may cover particular business or risk areas rather than the whole system. They will, however, need to provide a balanced assessment of the significant risks relevant to the particular area and the effectiveness of the procedures put in place to manage those risks. Any significant control failings or weaknesses identified should be discussed in the reports, as the board will need to be aware of these and their implications, including the need for actions to rectify them. The board should confirm that necessary action has been (or is being) taken to remedy any significant failings or weaknesses identified from their review of the effectiveness of the internal control system. The board will also be interested in the financial or business impact that these failings have had or could have had, and the actions being taken.

**4.146** By setting out a requirement for full and open reporting, and defining the scope of such reports, the board should be able to build up a picture of the internal control system and its operation during the year. The board should be comfortable that it is aware of the significant risks and how these have been identified, evaluated and managed; it has been able to assess the effectiveness of the management of these risks, notably by considering how significant failings or weaknesses have occurred, been reported and rectified; and it has put in place any additional monitoring which may be required.

**4.147** Such regular reporting may be made to a board committee rather than the full board, but the board is still required to take responsibility and ownership of the overall issue. In addition to the regular reviews, the board also needs to undertake a separate assessment each year to enable it to make the public statements required by the Turnbull guidance. This annual assessment will cover the issues raised during the regular reporting process and any other issues necessary to ensure all significant aspects of the internal control process have been covered. In particular, the annual assessment should consider any changes in the risk profiles of the company; the company's ability and effectiveness in responding to such changes; the scope and results of the ongoing monitoring of the internal controls including the significance and response to any failings or weaknesses identified; and the extent and frequency of reports to the board and how comprehensive a picture has been obtained through this process.

**[The next paragraph is 4.147.5.]**

**4.147.5**  The Turnbull guidance proposes the inclusion in the annual report and financial statements of a statement by the board on internal control. The recommended content is simple disclosure with the intention of avoiding boilerplate descriptions of high level controls, which had become somewhat common previously.

**4.147.6**  The Turnbull guidance states that *"the annual report and accounts should include such meaningful, high-level information as the board considers necessary to assist shareholders' understanding of the main features of the company's risk management processes and system of internal control, and should not give a misleading impression"*.

**4.147.7**  Regarding the application of principle C.2 of the Combined Code, the board should disclose that there is an ongoing process for identifying, evaluating and managing the significant risks faced by the company, that this process has been in place for the year under review, and up to the date of approval of the annual report, that it is regularly reviewed by the board and accords with the Turnbull guidance (2005). This is the minimum disclosure acceptable, but additional information can be given, particularly if it would assist understanding of the company's risk management processes and system of internal control. Some companies, therefore, may take this as an opportunity to describe their significant risks (including opportunities) and how these are managed.

**4.147.8**  There should be a specific acknowledgement that the board is responsible for the company's system of internal control and for reviewing its effectiveness. The board should confirm that it has reviewed the effectiveness of controls during the year. It should also explain that such a system is designed to manage rather than eliminate the risk of failure to achieve business objectives and can only provide reasonable, and not absolute, assurance against material misstatement or loss.

**4.147.9**  In relation to provision C.2.1 of the Combined Code, the board needs to summarise the process undertaken to review the effectiveness of the internal control system. In addition, if any significant problems have been noted in the annual report and accounts (for example, in the chairman's statement) the process applied to deal with any material internal control aspects of these need to be identified. This is an area of disclosure which needs to be specifically addressed by boards prior to approving the annual report.

**4.147.10**  The board should confirm that necessary actions have been or are being taken to remedy any significant failings or weaknesses identified from that review. The Turnbull Review Group's published deliberations indicated that it considered requiring companies to provide details of material or significant changes made to the internal control system as a result of the board's annual review of effectiveness. However, the Review Group recognised that if this was imposed on companies, then in effect it would be asking them to disclose any material weaknesses, with consequences for market perceptions. It was precisely in order to avoid any such concerns, that the Review Group acknowledged that this may result in boilerplate disclosures, but at least it would provide investors with some additional assurance that the outcome of the annual review process was action-oriented. Table 4.4 provides an example of such disclosure.

---

**Table 4.4 – Disclosure**

**Cadbury Schweppes plc – Annual Report & Accounts 2006**

**Corporate governance (extract)**

On 20 February 2006, Cadbury Schweppes plc acquired a majority holding of Cadbury Nigeria, a listed entity in which the Group previously had been a minority investor and which it had treated as an associate for accounting purposes. Subsequently significant mis-statements of Cadbury Nigeria's balance sheet and profit and loss account were identified. Following an investigation, management ascertained that these irregularities dated back over a number of years and comprised inappropriate recognition of revenue, overvaluation of assets (including working capital balances and fixed assets) and the undervaluation of liabilities. These accounting mis-statements have been corrected in the consolidated financial statements of Cadbury Schweppes plc in 2006. The adjustment has been recorded within the associate line as the irregularities occurred in the period in which Cadbury Nigeria was treated as an associate. Consequently the Group has recognised a non-underlying charge of £23 million reflecting its share of the adjustments. Both the former CEO and CFO of Cadbury Nigeria have now left the business. The CEO has been replaced with a former Cadbury Schweppes General Manager who has extensive operational experience in Africa and the CFO with an experienced Cadbury Schweppes Finance Director.

The Group is performing a full review of the financial processes, systems and people capabilities in place at Cadbury Nigeria and anticipates further changes will be made in 2007. Our Group Internal Audit will also separately perform full audit reviews of the business in 2007.

Other than in relation to Nigeria, the Board's review of the system of internal control has not identified any failings or weaknesses which it has determined to be significant, and therefore no remedial actions are necessary.

---

**4.147.11**   Where a board cannot make one or more of the disclosures listed in the Turnbull guidance, it should state this fact and provide an explanation. The Listing Rules require the board to disclose if it has failed to conduct a review of the effectiveness of the company's system of internal control.

*Internal audit*

**4.147.12**   The Combined Code specifies the need for annual consideration of whether an internal audit function is required. When considering internal audit, resource implications are important. Whatever the role to be undertaken by the function, the autonomy, authority, access and responsibilities need to be clearly set out and communicated throughout the business.

**[The next paragraph is 4.154.]**

### Application of Turnbull guidance to groups

**4.154** The Turnbull guidance refers throughout to the 'company'. It states, however, that this should be taken to mean the group of which the reporting company is the parent company. The disclosures made and the reviews of internal control should be in relation to the group as a whole. This may not be possible for some joint ventures or associates. If those have not been dealt with as part of the group when undertaking internal control reviews, this fact should be disclosed by the board in the annual report.

### Good practice reporting

**4.155** Many UK listed companies have been able to report their considerable progress in light of the developments in corporate governance recommendations in recent years. A number have gone above and beyond the disclosure recommendations of the Combined Code (2006) in their corporate governance statement. PricewaterhouseCoopers' compendium, 'Best practice corporate governance reporting' issued in January 2008, features a wide range of good practice disclosures from the corporate governance statements published in annual reports. It provides examples of good practice disclosure in terms of both format and content and may be used as a practical guide to preparing corporate governance statements. Companies should, however, ensure that their statements reflect their own particular circumstances and are specific to the company and its activities during the year or period under review.

### Smaller listed companies

**4.156** The Combined Code provides a small number of concessions specific to smaller companies (those below the FTSE 350 for all of the preceding year). The board, the audit committee and the remuneration committee should have at least two independent non-executive directors. [CC A.3.2, CC B.2.1, CC C3.1]. The Combined Code (2008) introduced a relaxation and provided that in smaller companies the company chairman may be a member of, but not chair, the audit committee so long as he/she was considered independent on appointment as chairman. This appointment would be in addition to the existing independent non-executive members of the committee.

### Non-listed organisations

**4.157** Where non-listed organisations choose voluntarily to report on compliance with the Combined Code. We recommend that they report fully as though they were listed. We, therefore, advise against phrases such as:

*"We comply with all aspects of the Combined Code relevant to the organisation."*

This form of disclosure on its own provides the reader with no indication of what aspects of the Combined Code the organisation has considered relevant and, therefore, is of no real value. Some organisations, such as the National Health Service Management Executive, have issued their own code of governance. In these situations, reference will of course be made to such codes instead.

**4.158**   Although non-listed organisations are encouraged to aim at meeting the Combined Code's recommendations, this has been rare to date outside of public interest entities and financial services institutions.

**4.159**   Companies that are considering the possibility of a listing will need to consider establishing appropriate governance procedures well in advance of coming to the market. In particular, they should review and, if necessary, improve their systems of internal control. In seeking a listing, companies are expected to make a statement of 'support' for the principles of the Combined Code. It is also usual to describe the steps the company has taken to comply in the areas of non-executive directors, audit, remuneration and nomination committees (describing their composition and principal functions), even if they have only recently been appointed or established. The sponsors will also normally expect to see significant moves to compliance in other areas. In their first period following listing, the UK Listing Authority has generally permitted new registrants to make a statement of compliance for the period from the date of listing only, rather than for the full accounting period. Nevertheless, it will be important to be well prepared, because certain procedures can take some time to implement.

**[The next paragraph is 4.166.]**

**Auditor review of compliance with the Combined Code**

*Listing Rule requirement*

**4.166**   The Listing Rules include reference to the Combined Code and to explain auditor responsibilities in relation to it.

The Listing Rules clarify that the Combined Code refers to:

■   for reporting periods commencing on or after 29 June 2008, the Combined Code (2008); and

■   for reporting periods commencing before 29 June 2008 the Combined Code (2006).

**4.167**   The Listing Rule established auditors' review responsibilities for UK listed companies' corporate governance disclosures. It states that auditors should review companies' disclosures in relation to nine provisions of the Combined Code. This excludes provision C.1.2, relating to going concern, because this provision was already covered by Listing Rule 9.8.6R(3). The provisions covered by the review requirement are stated in Listing Rule 9.8.10R(2) and are as follows:

■ The directors should explain in the annual report their responsibility for preparing the financial statements and there should be a statement by the auditors about their reporting responsibilities. [CC C.1.1].

■ The board should, at least annually, conduct a review of the effectiveness of the group's system of internal controls and should report to shareholders that they have done so. The review should cover all material controls, including financial, operational and compliance controls and risk management systems. [CC C.2.1].

■ The board should establish an audit committee of at least three, or in the case of smaller companies two, members, who should all be independent non-executive directors. The board should satisfy itself that at least one member of the audit committee has recent and relevant financial experience. [CC C.3.1].

■ The main role and responsibilities of the audit committee should be set out in written terms of reference and should include:

   ■ To monitor the integrity of the company's financial statements and any formal announcements relating to the company's financial performance, reviewing significant financial reporting judgements contained in them.

   ■ To review the company's internal financial controls and, unless expressly addressed by a separate board risk committee composed of independent directors, or by the board itself, to review the company's internal control and risk management systems.

   ■ To monitor and review the effectiveness of the company's internal audit function.

   ■ To make recommendations to the board, for it to put to the shareholders for their approval in general meeting, in relation to the appointment, re-appointment and removal of the external auditor and to approve the remuneration and terms of engagement of the external auditor.

   ■ To review and monitor the external auditor's independence and objectivity and the effectiveness of the audit process, taking into consideration relevant UK professional and regulatory requirements.

   ■ To develop and implement policy on the engagement of the external auditor to supply non-audit services, taking into account relevant ethical guidance regarding the provision of non-audit services by the external audit firm.

   ■ To report to the board, identifying any matters in respect of which it considers that action or improvement is needed and making recommendations as to the steps to be taken.

[CC C.3.2].

- The terms of reference of the audit committee, including its role and the authority delegated to it by the board, should be made available. A separate section of the annual report should describe the work of the committee in discharging those responsibilities. [CC C.3.3].

- The audit committee should review arrangements by which the company's staff may, in confidence, raise concerns about possible improprieties in matters of financial reporting or other matters. The audit committee's objective should be to ensure that arrangements are in place for the proportionate and independent investigation of such matters and for appropriate follow-up action. [CC C.3.4].

- The audit committee should monitor and review the effectiveness of the internal audit activities. Where there is no internal audit function, the audit committee should consider annually whether there is a need for an internal audit function and make a recommendation to the board, and the reasons for the absence of such a function should be explained in the relevant section of the annual report. [CC C.3.5].

- The audit committee should have primary responsibility for making a recommendation on the appointment, reappointment and removal of the external auditors. If the board does not accept the audit committee's recommendation, it should include in the annual report, and in any papers recommending appointment or re-appointment, a statement from the audit committee explaining the recommendation and should set out reasons why the board has taken a different position. [CC C.3.6].

- The annual report should explain to shareholders how, if the auditor provides non-audit services, auditor objectivity and independence is safeguarded. [CC C.3.7].

**4.168**   In addition to the review requirement under the Listing Rule, the scope of the auditor's report on the financial statements must cover certain disclosure requirements concerning directors' remuneration. These include the disclosures required by Listing Rules 9.8.11R(1), (2), (3) and (4) (see further chapter 5). The auditor must state in the audit report if in his or her opinion the company has not complied with the disclosures specified above and, where this information has not been given, must include in the report, so far as he/she is reasonably able to do so, a statement giving the required information. [LR 9.8.12R].

**[The next paragraph is 4.171.]**

*Auditor's review*

**4.171**   Detailed guidance on how to perform the auditor's review in relation to companies' reporting under the Combined Code was issued by the APB in September 2006: 'Bulletin 2006/05: The Combined Code on corporate governance: requirements of auditors under the Listing Rules of the Financial Services Authority and the Irish Stock Exchange'. It set out specific procedures to be followed in relation to each relevant provision.

**4.171.1** The guidance covers the auditor's review responsibilities in relation to the directors' statement on internal control, which includes the confirmation referred to in paragraph 4.147.8 above.

**4.172** There is no requirement, in either the Combined Code or the Listing Rules for publication of an auditors' report on corporate governance. In 1999 the APB concluded that such a report could be seriously misleading for readers. They were of the view that the narrow scope of the auditors' review and the introduction of a statement of auditors' responsibilities meant that it was no longer appropriate for auditors' reports on the directors' compliance statement to be published in the annual report. For listed companies this position resulted in the discontinuance of published auditors' reports on corporate governance matters in annual reports of listed companies.

**4.173** The APB recommends that prior to the release of the annual report, the auditor communicates, and discusses, with the directors the scope and factual findings of their review.

**[The next paragraph is 4.176.]**

# International matters

### EU action plan

**4.176** In May 2003 the EC issued a paper, 'Modernising company law and enhancing corporate governance in the European Union (EU) – a plan to move forward', outlining its action plan on corporate governance throughout the EU. The paper was presented as a response to the Winter Report published in November 2002. The objectives of the reforms were:

- To strengthen shareholders' rights and protection for employees, creditors and other parties with which companies deal, while adapting company law and corporate governance rules appropriately for different categories of company.

- To foster efficiency and competitiveness of business, with special attention to some specific cross-border issues and harmonisation of defined national issues.

**4.177** The intention was not to create a European corporate governance code, but rather to encourage a common approach with a few essential rules and co-ordination of national codes. A forum would be created to achieve this latter aim. In addition, the EC wished to reduce cross-border barriers (particularly given the enlargement of the EU through the addition of ten new Member States). The belief was that it would be in a company's interests to ensure that its corporate governance framework is worthy of investor confidence. Investors were paying more attention to governance issues, demanding more transparency and better information.

**4.178** The EU and the US have identified broadly similar problems and share broadly the same goals (as demonstrated in the US through the Sarbanes-Oxley Act). A dynamic and flexible company law and corporate governance framework is essential to protect investors from fraud and malpractice and to ensure that they have appropriate information to make investment decisions.

**4.179** The measures in the action plan covered a range of issues relating to corporate governance, capital maintenance, corporate restructuring, legal forms of enterprises and groups of companies. The measures were prioritised over time. In the short-term, there was more need for change in continental Europe than here in the UK, where many of the elements of the proposals were already features of the Combined Code. Below are listed a number of short-term out comes from the action plan:

■  The European Corporate Governance Forum was set up by the EC in October 2004 (see from para 4.187 below).

■  In December 2004, a recommendation encouraging Member States to adopt a number of measures in relation to directors' remuneration, including the disclosure of remuneration policy in the financial statements.

■  In February 2005, a recommendation encouraging Member States to ensure that independent directors have a key role in relation to the audit of financial statements, determining board appointments and board remuneration.

**4.180** Governance areas for consideration under the action plan in the medium-term (between 2006 and 2009) originally included:

■  Enhanced disclosure by institutional investors of their investment and voting policies.

■  Allowing listed companies to choose between a one or two tier board structure.

■  Enhanced responsibilities of board members.

■  Shareholder democracy for listed companies – one share, one vote.

**4.181** In early 2006, the EC consulted on future priorities for the action plan and issued a report summarising the results. Respondents encouraged a systematic consultation process and systematic regulatory impact assessments. In addition, they called for 'light touch regulation' and for legislation only to be adopted as necessary. There was continued support for the one share, one vote issue, however, the issue of board structure was not viewed as a high priority. The adoption of EU legislation regarding wrongful trading was opposed as it was not considered to raise substantial cross-border problems and legislation regarding directors' disqualification was also opposed due to the significant differences that currently exist between national systems. The European Corporate Governance forum is currently reviewing a study on shareholders rights across EU countries. It will provide its recommendations to the EC in Autumn 2007.

**4.182**   The EC published two reports in July 2007 on Member States' application of EU recommendations on company director's pay and independence. Both reports include that the application of corporate governance standards has improved, but some weaknesses remain. The report on director's remuneration shows that transparency standards are widely followed, but in some Member States it is still not recommended that shareholders vote on this issue. The report on the rule of independent non-executive directors finds that there is real progress in improving governance standards in this field, but some of the recommended standards have not been followed in all Member States. For instance, some Member States do not recommend a sufficient number of independent board members in renumeration and audit committees.

**EU directives**

**4.183**   Following a consultation in 2004 on amendments to the 4th and 7th company law directives on financial statements and consolidated financial statements, the EC announced proposals to:

■   Establish that board members collectively are responsible for the financial statements and key non-financial information that they publish.

■   Increase the disclosure requirements for off-balance sheet arrangements and transactions with related parties.

■   Require listed companies to issue an annual corporate governance statement.

**4.184**   The amendments, including the introduction of a requirement for a mandatory corporate governance statement for listed companies in law with specified contents, such as the provision of information on internal controls, were adopted in May 2006 and published in the Official Journal in August 2006.

**[The next paragraph is 4.186.]**

**4.186**   In addition to the above, in April 2006 the EC mandated the creation of audit committees by EU public interest entities (including listed companies and banks and other financial institutions) through the 8th directive on statutory audit. Member States will be able to take advantage of an exemption if such entities have a body that carries out equivalent functions.

**UK implementation of the EU 8th, 4th and 7th Directives**

**4.186.1**   The EU 4th, 8th and 7th Directives have been implemented in the UK in the Combined Code (2008) and revised FSA Rules on Corporate Governance. Further discussion can be found from paragraph 4.100.1.

## European Corporate Governance Forum

**4.187** The European Corporate Governance Forum initially had three items on its agenda:

- The role of shareholders (focusing on shareholder rights).

- The 'comply or explain' principle.

- The functioning of companies (focusing on internal control and the independence of directors).

**4.188** The Forum has since issued a statement on the 'comply or explain' principle. In March 2006 it expressed strong support for the 'comply or explain' principle, acknowledging that its success is driven by an obligation to report and through transparent, coherent and focused disclosures. The Forum also encouraged Member States that have not already done so, to adopt a corporate governance code and encouraged those that have adopted such a code to monitor its application.

**4.189** In June 2006 the European Corporate Governance Forum adopted a statement on risk management and internal control. The Forum was of the view that in the EU there is no need to introduce a legal obligation, as required in the US by the Sarbanes-Oxley Act, for boards to certify the effectiveness of internal controls.

### Activities of FEE

**4.190** FEE (Fédération des Experts Comptables Europeéans – the representative body of the European accountancy profession) published a discussion paper on the financial reporting and auditing aspects of corporate governance in July 2003. The paper concluded that while there is no need for a separate European corporate governance code, some principles and benchmarks should be set at European level to ensure a co-ordinated approach. It recommended:

- A balance of power at board level.

- An audit committee function for all listed companies (including defined responsibilities).

- A principles based approach for independence.

- Comprehensive disclosure on corporate governance.

- Extended reporting by auditors to boards.

- Audit committees to establish policy for non-audit services.

- Risk-based approach in establishing a sound system of internal controls.

Details on the roles of both internal and external audit were also discussed.

**4.191** On 31 March 2005, FEE published a review of current best practice amongst companies in risk management and internal control. The paper's proposals were shared informally with a wide range of EU stakeholders and brought together four main pieces of work:

■ Details of current best practice amongst companies in risk management and internal control.

■ A review of recent regulatory developments (in response to financial scandals in the US and Europe).

■ Recent European Commission proposals on corporate governance.

■ A survey of regulatory requirements on risk management and internal control in certain Member States applicable outside regulated financial services.

**4.192** FEE's key findings were:

■ There is a need for (a) increased use of mechanisms to give more transparency to risk management, including dialogue with shareholders; and (b) voluntary or required 'comply or explain' reporting against corporate governance requirements.

■ FEE is currently not convinced about the usefulness of requiring EU companies to publish conclusions on the effectiveness of their internal controls over financial reporting as required by section 404 of the Sarbanes-Oxley Act (see from paragraph 4.194 below). However, FEE acknowledges that as section 404 is implemented in the US, it will be important to consider the views of investors, companies and others, as well as forthcoming evidence about the usefulness, costs and benefits of such conclusions to investors.

■ External auditors' provision of assurance services in respect of risk management and internal control cannot exceed the responsibilities of those charged with governance to form their own conclusions.

**Other organisations**

**4.193** The IASB does not produce guidance on corporate governance matters. Guidance has been developed at international level by other bodies, such as the Organisation for Economic Co-operation and Development (OECD), which published its 'Principles of corporate governance' in 1999 and revised them in 2004. However, these high level international principles do not carry any enforcement authority. Corporate governance rules have instead tended to develop on a national basis, reflecting local business culture and a number of countries have adopted their own governance codes. Some of these codes were inspired by the UK's ground-breaking Cadbury and Hampel reforms and contain similar recommendations. Compliance with these national codes is often voluntary except where, as in the UK, the requirements have been incorporated in local listing rules.

## Changes impacting UK companies with a US listing

**4.194**   The Sarbanes-Oxley Act, issued in July 2002, set out many changes to corporate governance requirements and disclosures for US registrants and introduced new oversight procedures for auditors of US registrants. The Act was finalised by the US Congress in some haste and the provisions of the Act were subject to further interpretation and supplementary rulemaking by the Securities and Exchange Commission. The Act does not make a distinction between domestic and foreign issuers (for example, UK companies), although in subsequent rule-making, recognition of the effect of the rules on foreign registrants is covered in some areas.

**4.195**   The Act includes sections on the Public Company Accounting Oversight Board (PCAOB), auditor independence, corporate responsibility (with reference to both non-executive and executive directors), enhanced financial disclosures, corporate and criminal fraud accountability and white-collar crime penalty enhancements.

**4.196**   In practical terms, the most significant provision for UK SEC registrants arising from the Act has been section 404 on internal control over financail reporting. The annual US filing should include separate assessments by management and the external auditor of the effectiveness of internal controls over financial reporting. Most foreign private issuers (including UK registrants) began complying with the requirements for the first fiscal year ending on or after 15 July 2006. Those affected by the Sarbanes-Oxley Act and subsequent rule making will need to consider the requirements in a depth.

# Chapter 5

# Disclosure of directors' remuneration

|  | Page |
|---|---|
| Introduction | 5001 |
| Scope of the requirements | 5002 |
| Section I – All companies | 5006 |
| General rules – all companies | 5006 |
| Directors' and auditors' duties | 5006 |
| Payment for directors' services | 5006 |
| Disclosure in which year | 5009 |
| Other matters | 5010 |
| Aggregate emoluments and other benefits – all companies | 5012 |
| Aggregate emoluments and other benefits | 5012 |
| Aggregate emoluments | 5013 |
| Benefits in kind | 5015 |
| Gains on share options and amounts receivable under long-term incentive schemes | 5016 |
| Pension contributions | 5019 |
| General – readily ascertainable from other information | 5022 |
| Section II – Unquoted companies (including AIM companies) | 5023 |
| Highest paid director's emoluments and other benefits | 5023 |
| Excess retirement benefits of directors and past directors | 5029 |
| Compensation for loss of office | 5030 |
| Sums paid to third parties in respect of directors' services | 5035 |
| Examples of disclosure | 5037 |
| Section III – AIM companies | 5037 |
| Section IV – Quoted companies (excluding companies listed on AIM) | 5038 |
| Remuneration report | 5038 |
| Information not subject to audit | 5040 |
| Consideration by the directors of matters relating to directors' remuneration | 5040 |
| Statement of policy on directors' remuneration | 5042 |
| Statement of consideration of conditions elsewhere in the company and group | 5046 |
| Performance graph | 5047 |
| Service contracts | 5053 |
| Compensation for past directors | 5056 |
| Interaction between the Combined Code and the remuneration report | 5057 |
| Information subject to audit | 5057 |
| Individual directors' emoluments and compensation | 5057 |
| Share options | 5064 |
| Long-term incentive schemes | 5073 |

Long-term incentive scheme for an individual. . . . . . . . . . . . . . . . .   5084
Pensions . . . . . . . . . . . . . . . . . . . . . . . . . . . . . . . . . . . . . . . . . . . . . .   5086
  Practical application of pensions disclosures. . . . . . . . . . . . . . . .   5091
Excess retirement benefits of directors and past directors . . . . . . . .   5097
Compensation for past directors. . . . . . . . . . . . . . . . . . . . . . . . . . . .   5098
Sums paid to third parties in respect of directors' services . . . . . . .   5101
Approval of remuneration report . . . . . . . . . . . . . . . . . . . . . . . . . . .   5102
Section V – Audit requirements. . . . . . . . . . . . . . . . . . . . . . . . . . . . . .   5102
Section VI – Group situations. . . . . . . . . . . . . . . . . . . . . . . . . . . . . . .   5104
Annex 1 – Combined Code . . . . . . . . . . . . . . . . . . . . . . . . . . . . . . . . .   5111
Annex 2 – Directors' remuneration disclosure – decision tree. . . . . . . .   5115

# Chapter 5

# Disclosure of directors' remuneration

## Introduction

**5.1** Directors' remuneration is one of the most sensitive and closely regulated aspects of financial reporting. Generally, directors are well rewarded and it is inevitable, given their stewardship role, that comparisons will be made by investors and others between the company's performance and the level of the directors' remuneration. One facet of this subject is the extent of the disclosure of remuneration in financial statements.

**5.2** The rules relating to disclosure of directors' remuneration for all companies are contained in the Companies Act 1985. Under the Companies Act 2006, these rules are replaced by 'The Large and Medium-sized Companies and Groups (Accounts and Reports) Regulations 2008' (SI 2008/410) for accounting periods beginning on or after 6 April 2008. Under both Act's, the rules fall broadly into three main sections; those that apply to all companies; those that apply only to unquoted companies and those that apply to quoted companies. AIM companies, whilst largely treated as unquoted companies, have to give more information than other unquoted companies in relation to share option gains and long-term incentives received in shares. The scope of the requirements is dealt with from paragraph 5.6 onwards.

**5.3** Under UK company law, remuneration should be disclosed when it is paid to or receivable by a director in respect of qualifying services to the company and its subsidiaries. Generally, disclosure is required in respect of:

- The aggregate amount of emoluments (including salary, fees, bonuses and benefits in kind).

- Share options.

- Long-term incentive schemes.

- Pension schemes.

- Compensation for loss of office.

- Sums paid to or receivable by third parties for making available directors' services.

These disclosure requirements are covered in detail in this chapter.

**5.4** Directors' remuneration disclosures made by quoted companies are extensive. They include information on policy and details of remuneration given by individual director. The legal requirements for quoted companies substantially reproduce the requirements in the Listing Rules relating to disclosure of directors' remuneration, but they also contain additional disclosures over and above those in the Listing Rules. Also, there are some differences between the legal requirements and those of the Listing Rules, which are discussed later in the chapter.

**5.5** In addition, for companies that are preparing their financial statements under IFRS, IAS 24, 'Related party disclosures', requires disclosure of 'key management compensation' in the notes to the financial statements.

## Scope of the requirements

**5.6** Disclosure of directors remuneration is governed by:

■ The Companies Act 1985 (replaced by SI 2008/410 – see para 5.7).

■ The Listing Rules of the Financial Services Authority ('FSA').

■ The Combined Code published by the Financial Reporting Council ('FRC').

**5.6.1** In addition, as noted in paragraph 5.5 above, for companies that are preparing their financial statements in accordance with IFRS, IAS 24 requires disclosure of 'key management compensation' in the notes to the financial statements. The requirements of IAS 24 differ from those contained in both the Act and the Listing Rules. The requirements are considered in chapter 29 of the Manual of Accounting – IFRS for the UK.

**5.6.2** The legal rules relating to disclosure of directors' remuneration are contained in Schedule 6 and Schedule 7A to the Companies Act 1985 (and under the Companies 2006, in Schedule 5 and Schedule 8 to SI 2008/410). The rules in the 1985 and 2006 Acts fall broadly into three main sections; those that apply to all companies; those that apply only to unquoted companies and those that apply to quoted (as defined in section 262(1) of the 1985 Act (section 385(2) of the 2006 Act)) companies. AIM companies, whilst largely treated as unquoted companies, have to give more information than other unquoted companies in relation to share option gains and long-term incentives received in shares.

**5.6.3** The definition of quoted company for the purposes of disclosure is:

*"...a company whose equity share capital –*

*(a)  has been included in the official list in accordance with the provisions of Part VI of the Financial Services and Markets Act 2000; or*

*(b)  is officially listed in an EEA State; or*

*(c)  is admitted to dealing on either the New York Stock Exchange or the exchange known as Nasdaq;*

*and in paragraph (a) 'the official list' shall have the meaning given it by section 103(1) of the Financial Services and Markets Act 2000."*

[CA85 Sec 262(1); CA06 Sec 385(2)].

**5.6.3.1** The 2006 Act clarifies that *"a company is a quoted company in relation to a financial year if it is a quoted company immediately before the end of the accounting reference period by reference to which that financial year was determined".* [CA06 Sec 385(1)]. This is consistent with the interpretation under the 1985 Act where our view is that if a company is quoted at the year end then any disclosures required by that Act (or accounting standards) that are applicable to quoted companies must be complied with. In this respect a delisting is regarded as a non-adjusting post balance sheet event.

**5.6.4** 'Company' means a company formed and registered under the Companies Act 1985 or a company formed and registered under the Companies Acts 1948 to 1983 or the Companies Act 1929. The definition of quoted company applies only to UK companies. [CA85 Sec 735(1); CA06 Sec 1(1)]. Quoted, as defined above, effectively means listed on the London Stock Exchange or officially listed in the European Economic Area (which includes EU Member States plus Iceland, Norway and Liechtenstein) or admitted to dealing on the New York Stock Exchange or on Nasdaq. For the purpose of this definition, therefore, companies dealt in on AIM are not included.

**5.6.5** The requirements of Schedule 7A to the Companies Act 1985 (Schedule 8 to SI 2008/410) substantially reproduce the requirements of Listing Rule 9.8.8R relating to disclosure of directors' remuneration, although there are some differences. The requirements of LR 9.8.8R are set out in Section IV below, but as its requirements are generally similar to Schedule 7A to the 1985 Act (Schedule 8 to SI 2008/410), these are not discussed in detail in this chapter. However, it should be noted that there are some differences between the requirements of the Listing Rules and those of the 1985 and 2006 Acts and so the disclosures can be complicated. An illustrative example is given in the directors' remuneration report for IFRS GAAP plc (see separate publication containing illustrative financial statements). Other Listing Rules relating to directors' remuneration that are not covered by Schedule 7A to the 1985 Act (Schedule 8 to SI 2008/410) are also dealt with in section IV below. Annex 1 sets out the principles and provisions of the Combined Code that relate to directors' remuneration.

**5.6.6** Where a company is not quoted, but has debt or fixed income shares listed in the UK, it does not have to comply with the requirements of Schedule 7A to the Companies Act 1985 (Schedule 8 to SI 2008/410). Such an entity has to comply with the disclosures relating to directors' remuneration contained in Schedule 6 to the Companies Act 1985 (Schedule 5 to SI 2008/410). Although such a company has to comply with the Listing Rules, it is not required to comply with the requirements concerning directors' remuneration in LR 9.8.8R (See annex 2).

**5.6.7**  Where a company is quoted on an overseas exchange, but has debt or fixed income shares listed in the UK, it has to comply with the directors' remuneration requirements contained in chapter 1 of Schedule 6 and in Schedule 7A to the Companies Act 1985 (Schedule 5 and Schedule 8 to SI 2008/410). In addition, such an entity is exempt from the Listing Rule requirement concerning the disclosure of directors' remuneration in LR 9.8.8R (see annex 2). [LR 9.8.6R].

**5.6.8**  As noted in paragraph 5.6.2 above, AIM companies are not treated as quoted companies for the purpose of disclosure of directors' remuneration.

**Example – AIM companies and directors' remuneration**

Are AIM companies required to present a directors' remuneration report in accordance with Schedule 7A to the Companies Act 1985 (Schedule 8 to SI 2008/410)?

No. The requirement in section 234B of the Companies Act 1985 (Section 420(1) of the Companies Act 2006) is that quoted companies should prepare a directors' remuneration report compliant with Schedule 7A to the 1985 Act (Schedule 8 to SI 2008/410). The definition of a quoted company is given in paragraph 5.6.3 above.

A company with equity shares listed on AIM does not fall within the definition of a quoted company, so is not required to prepare a directors' remuneration report compliant with Schedule 7A to the Companies Act 1985 (Schedule 8 to SI 2008/410).

However, AIM companies, whilst largely treated as unquoted companies, have to give more information than other unquoted companies in relation to share option gains and long-term incentives received in shares. The requirements for AIM listed companies are dealt with from paragraph 5.118.

**5.7**  The Companies Act 2006 (the 2006 Act) replaces all the provisions of the 1985 Act covered by this chapter. Implementation of the 2006 Act has been staggered and different parts have different commencement dates. This chapter covers both the requirements under the 1985 and 2006 Acts. The requirements under the 2006 Act (including those in SI 2008/410) relating to disclosure of directors' remuneration are generally applicable for accounting periods commencing on or after 6 April 2008. Attention has been drawn in the text below where the requirements have been changed by the 2006 Act or SI 2008/410.

**5.8**  The disclosure of directors' remuneration can be considered under a number of headings and sub-headings:

- Section I – All companies.
  - General Rules.
    - Directors' and auditors' duties.
    - Payment for directors' services.
    - Disclosure in which year.
    - Other matters.

- Aggregate emoluments and other benefits.
    - Aggregate emoluments.
    - Benefits in kind.
    - Gains made on exercise of share options and amounts received or receivable under long-term incentive schemes.
    - Pension contributions.
- Section II – Unquoted companies (including AIM companies).
- Highest paid director's emoluments and other benefits.
- Excess retirement benefits of directors and past directors.
- Compensation for loss of office.
- Sums paid to third parties in respect of directors' services.
- Section III – AIM companies.
- Section IV – Quoted companies (excluding companies listed on AIM).
    - Remuneration report.
    - Information not subject to audit.
        - Composition of remuneration committee and advisors.
        - Statement of policy on directors' remuneration.
        - Performance graph.
        - Service contracts.
        - Compensation for past directors.
        - Appendix – Combined Code.
    - Information subject to audit.
        - Individual directors' emoluments and compensation.
        - Share options.
        - Long-term incentive schemes.
        - Pensions.
        - Excess retirement benefits of directors and past directors.
        - Compensation for past directors.
        - Sums paid to third parties in respect of directors' services.
        - Approval of remuneration report.
    - Section V – Audit requirements.
    - Section VI – Group situations.

*Disclosure of directors' remuneration*

Each of these is considered in turn below and annex 2 to the chapter includes a directors' remuneration decision tree, which shows for different companies the parts of the 1985 and 2006 Acts that apply and whether the Listing Rules need to be followed.

# Section I — All companies

## General rules — all companies

### *Directors' and auditors' duties*

**5.9** A company's directors have a duty to give information about their remuneration (including pensions, compensation for loss of office and sums paid to third parties) to the company so that the information discussed below can be disclosed in the financial statements. This requirement applies also to a person who has been a director of the company within the preceding five years. Any director failing to give notice of the required information to the company is liable to a fine. [CA85 Sec 232(3)(4); CA06 Sec 412(5)(6)].

**5.10** If the required information is not disclosed in the financial statements or if information subject to audit that is required to be included in the directors' remuneration report of a quoted company is not disclosed in that report, the auditors have a duty to include the information (so far as they are reasonably able to do so) in their audit report. [CA85 Sec 237(4); CA06 Sec 498(4)].

### *Payment for directors' services*

**5.11** The remuneration to be disclosed should include all amounts paid to a director for his services as a director of the company and any subsidiary, or for managing the company and its subsidiaries. [CA85 6 Sch 1(5); CA85 7A Sch 16(1); SI 2008/410 5 Sch 15(1); SI 2008/410 8 Sch 17(1)]. All payments should be included, whether those payments are made by the company, or by a subsidiary undertaking of the company or by any other person, unless the director has to account in turn to another group company, or to members under sections 314 and 315 of the 1985 Act (section 219 of the 2006 Act) (directors' duty to make disclosure on company takeover and consequences of non-compliance), for the receipt of the remuneration. [CA85 6 Sch 10(2); CA85 7A Sch 18; SI 2008/410 5 Sch 8(1); SI 2008/410 8 Sch 19(2)]. This also applies to payments by way of compensation for loss of office.

#### Example – Director paid by non-group company

Mr Smith spends part of his time as an executive director of company A and part of his time as an employee of company B, which is controlled by him. Company B pays Mr Smith's salary and it invoices company A for an amount to cover that part of the time that Mr Smith spends working for company A. Although Mr Smith is paid by company B (and not by company A of which he is a director), the amount that he receives from company B is partially in respect of his services as a director of company A.

Consequently, Mr Smith should disclose to company A, and company A should disclose in its financial statements as remuneration, the proportion of his salary that relates to his services as a director of company A. This figure may or may not be the same as the amount that company B has invoiced company A. This will depend on whether the invoiced amount is intended to cover an amount that is either more or less than the actual cost of the director's services to company A.

**5.12** Overlooking this point can have serious consequences as illustrated by the findings of the Financial Reporting Review Panel (FRRP) on the financial statements of Foreign & Colonial Investment Trust plc (FCIT) for the year ended 31 December 1991. The FRRP found that the financial statements of FCIT reflected the emoluments receivable by the directors from the company and its subsidiaries. However, remuneration receivable by five directors from the company's investment manager, an associate of one of its subsidiaries, relating to services provided to FCIT and its subsidiaries had not been disclosed in FCIT's financial statements. Following discussions with the Panel, the directors agreed to provide, in the 1992 financial statements, additional information concerning that proportion of remuneration receivable by the directors from the company's investment manager, which related to services to FCIT and its subsidiary undertakings. Appropriate comparative figures for 1991 were also presented in the 1992 financial statements.

**5.13** The disclosure in the 1992 financial statements is shown in Table 5.1.

---

**Table 5.1 — Payment for directors' services**

**Foreign & Colonial Investment Trust PLC — Report and Accounts— 31 December 1992**

**Directors' emoluments (extract)**

Mr A.C. Barker, Mr O.N. Dawson, Mr E.C. Elstob, Mr M.J. Hart and The Hon. James Ogilvy receive emoluments from Foreign & Colonial Management Limited for their services to that company. The proportion of their emoluments which relates to the management of the affairs of the Company or any of its subsidiary undertakings amounts to approximately £227,000 (1991—£195,000). This amount has been taken into account, together with the £106,000 (1991—£100,000) paid directly by the Company to the non-executive directors, in providing the following disclosure:

Directors' emoluments (including payments by all subsidiary undertakings but excluding pensions contributions).

Comparatives for 1991 have been restated.

|  | 1992 | 1991 |
|---|---|---|
| Chairman | **£29,000** | £25,000 |
| Highest paid director | **£138,000** | £114,000 |
| £1-£5,000 | **1** | — |
| £10,001-£15,000 | **6** | 7 |
| £15,001-£20,000 | **1** | 1 |
| £25,001-£30,000 | **2** | 2 |

---

**5.14** There is also nothing in the Companies Act 1985 (or 2006 Act) to suggest that the director must receive payments personally in order that they should be subject to disclosure as remuneration. Amounts paid to or receivable by a director, including amounts paid in respect of compensation for loss of office, will include amounts paid to or receivable by a person connected with, or a body corporate controlled by that director (but such amounts should not be counted twice). [CA85 6 Sch 10(4); CA85 7A Sch 18(3); SI 2008/410 5 Sch 7(3); SI 2008/410 8 Sch 19(3)]. The definitions of connected persons and body corporate controlled by a director are in sections 252 to 255 of the 2006 Act. [CA85 6 Sch 13(4); CA85 7A Sch 16(4); SI 2008/410 5 Sch 15(2); SI 2008/410 8 Sch 17(4)]. Consequently, even where a director sets up another company specifically to receive remuneration, that remuneration will be deemed to be remuneration received by him if that company is controlled by him.

**5.15** Furthermore, if the company has nominated (either directly or indirectly) the director to be a director of another company, that other company is treated as if it were a subsidiary undertaking for the purposes of determining the amounts to be disclosed for directors' remuneration, compensation for loss of office and payments to third parties for directors' services. Accordingly, the director's remuneration and compensation for loss of office should include any amount he receives as a director of that other company (whether or not that other company is a subsidiary of the company). [CA85 6 Sch 13(2)(a); CA85 7A Sch 15(1),16(1); SI 2008/410 5 Sch 14; SI 2008/410 8 Sch 16(1), 17(1)]. Any sums that the other company pays to third parties in respect of his services should be disclosed as sums paid to third parties.

**Example — Nominated director of an associate**

Company A has nominated one of its directors to the board of its associate, company B. Company B pays £20,000 per year to the director in respect of his services to that company. Does this £20,000 have to be disclosed as directors' remuneration in company A's financial statements?

The Companies Act requires disclosure of emoluments received by a director of a company for qualifying services, which includes services as a director of the company or its subsidiaries. This might appear to exclude services to associates, but paragraph 13(2) of Schedule 6 to the 1985 Act (para 14 of Schedule 5 to SI 2008/410) and for quoted companies paragraph 16(1) of Schedule 7A to the 1985 Act (para 17(1) of Schedule 5 to SI 2008/410) state that reference to a subsidiary undertaking, in relation to a person who whilst a director of the company is also a director of any other undertaking by virtue of the company's nomination, includes that other undertaking whether or not it is in fact a subsidiary undertaking.

This means that because the director has been nominated by company A as a director of the associate, the associate is deemed for the purposes of directors' emoluments disclosure to be a subsidiary. The director is performing qualifying services for company A by being its representative on company B's board. Therefore, in this situation, the director must disclose to company A, as remuneration, the amount of £20,000 that he receives from company B. Company A will need to disclose, as directors' remuneration, the aggregate of the amount paid to the director in respect of his services as director of company A and the amount of £20,000 he receives from company B.

If, on the other hand, the amount of £20,000 is paid to company A (that is, as a sum to be accounted for to the company, see para 5.11) and not to the director personally, then this amount need not be included as directors' emoluments in company A's financial statements. However, company B will need to disclose the payment of £20,000 in its own financial statements as a sum paid to a third party in respect of the director's services.

Note that the answer would be the same if company B was not related to company A, but company A had nominated one of its directors to company B's board (for example, if it was able to do this because of a significant trading relationship).

### Disclosure in which year

**5.16** A director's remuneration that should be disclosed in the financial statements for a particular year is the remuneration receivable by the director in respect of that year, regardless of when it is paid to the director. [CA85 6 Sch 11(1); CA85 7A Sch 19(1); SI 2008/410 5 Sch 7(4); SI 2008/410 8 Sch 20(1)]. For example, if a bonus is receivable by a director in respect of services performed in year one, but is not paid to the director until year two, it is disclosable as that director's emoluments in year one.

**5.17** In the case of remuneration that is receivable by a director in respect of a period that extends beyond the financial year, for example, a long-term incentive scheme covering a period of three years, with no further conditions to be satisfied, disclosure should be made in the year it is paid. [CA85 6 Sch 11(1); CA85 7A Sch 19(1); SI 2008/410 5 Sch 7(4); SI 2008/410 8 Sch 20(1)]. Whilst not explicitly stated, the implication of this is that where remuneration is receivable in respect of a period, be that a period of one year or more than one year, it should be disclosed when due, that is in the year in which it becomes receivable.

**[The next paragraph is 5.19.]**

**5.19** Where remuneration is not receivable in respect of a period, whether of a single financial year or a period of over one financial year, it should be disclosed in the financial statements of the period in which it is paid. This might apply, for instance, when a single *ex gratia* payment is made to a director that is unrelated to a financial year or other period. An example might be a payment made as compensation for a reduction in the length of a director's service contract.

**5.20** One problem that sometimes arises in respect of long-term incentive schemes is where the performance period lasts three years, but a director must then remain with the company for a further period, say six months, before he becomes entitled to receive any amounts under the scheme. The question that arises in such a case is whether the amounts due under the scheme are receivable in respect of the three-year performance period and are, therefore, disclosable in the third year of the scheme, or whether they are receivable only after a further six months, when the additional service period has been completed, in which case they would be disclosable in the fourth year.

**5.21** The answer to the question may depend on the particular terms of the scheme and on when the remuneration becomes a firm entitlement. If, for instance, the additional service period has no real effect in practice, and the director would receive the remuneration whether or not he stayed for the extra six months, this would imply that the substance was that the remuneration was effectively a firm entitlement in respect of the three-year performance period and should be disclosed in the third year. If, however, the additional service period was of real significance, for instance if the director would get nothing if he were to leave the company within that additional period, then it is probable that the remuneration should be disclosed in the fourth year.

**5.22** In practice, there is some variation on the way that companies apply the rules to the situation described in paragraphs 5.20 and 5.21 above, with some companies preferring to disclose when all performance conditions have been satisfied, even when there is a further service period. For quoted companies, where the problem mainly arises, Schedule 7A to the 1985 Act (Schedule 8 to SI 2008/410) requires disclosure of full details of long-term incentive schemes, which means that, whichever approach is taken, there is still full disclosure of the benefits arising, or the benefits that have arisen, under such schemes during the period for which they operate. This is discussed further in paragraph 5.185.

**5.23** The above rules apply to emoluments generally and also extend to compensation for loss of office.

### *Other matters*

**5.24** Under the 1985 and 2006 Acts, a company is permitted to end its financial year on the same day in the week rather than on the same date, if it wishes to (see further chapter 8). Therefore a financial year (and, consequently, the financial statements) may cover a period slightly longer than one year. In this situation, the amounts disclosed for directors' remuneration are those in respect of the longer period, as explained in the following example.

**Example – Emoluments for a 53-week period**

A company has a 53 week financial year this year. Can the disclosure of directors' emoluments be given for a 52 week (365 day) period, rather than for 53 weeks?

Paragraph 11(1) of Schedule 6 to the Companies Act 1985 (para 7(4) of Schedule 5 to SI 2008/410) (unquoted companies) and paragraph 19(1) of Schedule 7A (para 20(1) of Schedule 8 to SI 2008/410) (quoted companies) require that the amounts of emoluments to be shown for any financial year are the sums receivable in respect of that year (whenever paid).

Section 223(3) of the Companies Act 1985 (section 390(3) of the Companies Act 2006) states that *"subsequent financial years begin with the day immediately following the end of the company's previous financial year and end with the last day of its next accounting reference period or such other date, not more than seven days before or after the end of that period, as the directors may determine".* Therefore, the company's financial year is 53 weeks and so the amounts to be disclosed must be for the 53 weeks of the financial year.

As an analogy, if the company prepares statutory accounts for a short period (for example, nine months), the amounts to be disclosed under the Act are the emoluments for that period (that is, nine months).

**5.24.1**  Where a director is appointed during the year, only the remuneration while he is a director of the company is disclosable as director's remuneration, as explained in the example in paragraph 5.167.

**5.24.2**  If it is necessary to apportion remuneration and compensation for loss of office paid to a director between the matters in respect of which it has been paid or is receivable, the directors may apportion it in any way that they consider appropriate. [CA85 6 Sch 12; CA85 7A Sch 20; SI 2008/410 5 Sch 7(6); SI 2008/410 8 Sch 21].

**5.25**  In certain situations, directors' remuneration might not be included in the notes to the financial statements (or in the directors' remuneration report, in the case of a quoted company) for a period because either the director is liable to account for it to the company or to another group company, or because it is considered to be an expense allowance not chargeable to UK income tax. Where this is so, and these reasons are subsequently found not to be justified, the remuneration must be disclosed in a note to the first financial statements (or in the first directors' remuneration report, in the case of a quoted company) in which it is practicable for this to be done, and the remuneration must be identified separately. This also applies to compensation for loss of office. [CA85 6 Sch 11(2); CA85 7A Sch 19(2); SI 2008/410 5 Sch 7(5); SI 2008/410 8 Sch 20(2)].

**5.26**  An example of disclosure is given in Table 5.2.

---

**Table 5.2 – Corrections to emoluments disclosed in previous years**

**The Plessey Company plc – Report and Accounts – 1 April 1988**

**Directors and senior employees (extract)**

The emoluments of the Chairman, who in 1988 was the highest paid director, amounted to £391,956. The emoluments of the highest paid director in 1987 amounted to £237,347.

The above amount of £391,956 includes an adjustment of £93,750 resulting from the reclassification of expenses in respect of the financial years 1979/80 to 1986/87 following a settlement agreed with the Inland Revenue.

---

*Disclosure of directors' remuneration*

## Aggregate emoluments and other benefits — all companies

*Aggregate emoluments and other benefits*

**5.27** The Act requires the following information to be disclosed in the notes to the annual financial statements:

- The aggregate amount of emoluments paid to or receivable by directors in respect of qualifying services. [CA85 6 Sch 1(1)(a); SI 2008/410 5 Sch 1(1)(a)].

- The aggregate of the amount of gains made by directors on the exercise of share options (but see para 5.28 below). [CA85 6 Sch 1(1)(b); SI 2008/410 5 Sch 1(1)(b)].

- The aggregate of the following:

  - the amount of money paid to or receivable by directors under long-term incentive schemes in respect of qualifying services; and

  - the net value of assets (other than money and share options) received or receivable by directors under such schemes in respect of such services (but see para 5.28 below).

  [CA85 6 Sch 1(1)(c); SI 2008/410 5 Sch 1(1)(c)].

- The aggregate value of any company contributions paid, or treated as paid, to a pension scheme in respect of directors' qualifying services, being contributions by reference to which the rate or amount of any money purchase benefits that may become payable will be calculated. [CA85 6 Sch 1(1)(d); SI 2008/410 5 Sch 1(1)(d)].

- In the case of each of the following:

  - money purchase schemes; and

  - defined benefit schemes.

  The number of directors (if any) to whom retirement benefits are accruing under such schemes in respect of qualifying services. [CA85 6 Sch 1(1)(e); SI 2008/410 5 Sch 1(2)].

**5.28** The above requirements relate to *all* companies with the following exception. Companies which are not quoted (see para 5.6.3) and are not dealt in on the Alternative Investment Market (AIM) do not have to disclose either the aggregate of the amount of gains made by the directors on the exercise of share options or the net value of shares received or receivable under long-term incentive schemes in respect of qualifying services. Instead, such companies must disclose:

- the number of directors who exercised share options; and

- the number of directors in respect of whose qualifying services shares were received or receivable under long-term incentive schemes.

[CA85 6 Sch 1(2)(a)(b); SI 2008/410 5 Sch 1(3)].

5012

**[The next paragraph is 5.31.]**

**5.31** Each of the elements of the disclosure described above is discussed in turn in the following paragraphs.

*Aggregate emoluments*

*All companies*

**5.32** All companies (that is, quoted, and unquoted, including AIM) have to disclose aggregate emoluments paid to or receivable by directors in respect of qualifying services.

**5.33** Qualifying services means:

■ Services as a director of the company.

■ Services as a director of any subsidiary undertaking of the company, during the time in which a person is a director of the company.

■ Services in connection with the management of the affairs of either the company or any subsidiary undertaking of the company, during the time in which a person is a director of the company.

[CA85 6 Sch 1(5); SI 2008/410 5 Sch 15(1)].

**5.34** In addition, qualifying services includes services, while a director of the company, as a director of any other undertaking of which he is a director by virtue of the company's nomination (direct or indirect). [CA85 6 Sch 13(2)(a); SI 2008/410 5 Sch 14(1)]. See further paragraph 5.15 above.

**5.35** If an undertaking is a subsidiary undertaking at the time the service is rendered by the directors, it should be included even where the undertaking is no longer a subsidiary at the reporting date. [CA85 6 Sch 13(2)(b); SI 2008/410 5 Sch 14(2)].

**5.36** For this purpose, 'emoluments' paid to or receivable by a director include not only his salary, but also the following:

■ Fees and bonuses.

■ Any expense allowances (to the extent that they are chargeable to UK income tax).

■ The estimated money value of any other benefits received otherwise than in cash (but see para 5.37 below).

■ Emoluments in respect of a person accepting office as director.

[CA85 6 Sch 1(3), (6)(b); SI 2008/410 5 Sch 9(1), 15(3)].

**5.37** The term emoluments does not include the value of share options granted to or exercised by directors. It does not include any company pension contributions paid on behalf of directors (although it does include contributions that directors themselves pay by way of a compulsory deduction from salary) nor any benefits to which directors are entitled under any pension scheme. Also excluded from the definition are money or other assets paid to or receivable by directors under long-term incentive schemes. [CA85 6 Sch 1(3)(b); SI 2008/410 5 Sch 9(2)].

**5.38** The reason for excluding those elements from the disclosure of emoluments is, quite simply, that they are picked up by separate disclosure requirements that are discussed below.

**5.39** The term 'paid to or receivable by' is discussed from paragraph 5.16 above.

**5.40** Whether the director receives emoluments for services as a director of the company or in connection with the management of its affairs is a question of fact. It should be presumed that all payments made to a director, except for reimbursement of expenses, will generally fall within one of these categories, unless it can clearly be demonstrated otherwise. However, an exception could be where payments have been made to a director in a self-employed or professional capacity. Consider the following example:

**Example – Director paid on a self-employed basis**

A director of a company is paid for technical services supplied on a 'self-employed persons' basis. How should this be disclosed?

Provided that it can be clearly established that the fees are genuinely for technical services and that they are not connected with management services (which they might be if the director were a technical director), then the amounts paid need not be disclosed as emoluments. However, the transaction may need to be disclosed as a related party transaction (see chapter 29 of the Manual of Accounting – UK GAAP or chapter 29 of the Manual of Accounting – IFRS for the UK). In practice, however, it is often difficult to make such a precise distinction and the remuneration for other services is often included with directors' remuneration.

**5.41** When considering directors' emoluments, there is no need to distinguish between a director's service contract and a contract for services that a director has with the company. Remuneration received in either capacity will fall to be disclosed in the company's financial statements as directors' emoluments. However, a director's service contract makes him essentially an employee of the company and, therefore, such emoluments will have to be included in staff costs. On the other hand, a contract for services puts the director in essentially the same position as a third party hired to do a particular job. Amounts invoiced to the company should be recognised as an expense, but should not be classified as 'staff costs'.

## Benefits in kind

**5.42**  The estimated money value of a benefit in kind that must be included in directors' emoluments should be taken as the market value of the facility that is provided for the director's private benefit, less any contribution the director pays. The amount used to assess the taxable benefit should be used *only* where it is an approximation of the market value of the benefit. However, in practice the value of the taxable benefit is often a good starting point for considering the value that should be placed on the amounts for accounting disclosure purposes.

**5.43**  Where there is a tax concession such that part of a benefit is not taxable even though it is a benefit for the director (as opposed to a valid business expense), the value of the taxable benefit will not be an appropriate starting point. If there is a benefit to the director, the total amount receivable by a director is disclosable as a benefit in kind. The fact that the tax rules allow some of this benefit to be tax-free (for instance, certain relocation allowances) does not change the position.

**5.44**  Benefits in kind may include: provision of accommodation at below market rates; provision of a car or health benefits; and share options. Gains on exercise of share options are dealt with separately (see para 5.47 below).

### Example — Premium paid for director's life assurance cover

A company pays a premium to an insurance company to purchase life assurance cover for a director. This life cover is in addition to the life cover provided by the pension scheme and is an entirely separate arrangement. The beneficiary would be the next of kin of the director. How should this be disclosed for the purpose of directors' remuneration?

The premium should be included as a benefit in kind in arriving at the aggregate directors' emoluments and will be included in the aggregate of emoluments to be disclosed (for all companies) under paragraphs 1(1), 1(3) of Schedule 6 to the Companies Act 1985 (paras 1(1), 9(1) of Schedule 5 to SI 2008/410). If the company is quoted the benefit would also be disclosed in the total of benefits received by the director, which is required to be shown separately in the table of individual directors' remuneration in the directors' remuneration report, together with the nature of the benefit (see further para 5.164). [CA85 7A Sch 6(1), 6(3); SI 2008/410 8 Sch 7(1), 7(3)].

**5.44.1**  Where a company pays a director's tax liability on benefits, the amount disclosed in respect of benefits should be grossed up for the tax paid, that is, the amount disclosed should reflect the gross amount payable in cash to leave the director in the same position had the company not paid the tax on his behalf. For example, if the benefit received is £100,000 and the director is taxed at 40% (that is, the director would expect to receive a net amount of £60,000, even though this would be disclosed as £100,000 in the remuneration disclosure). However, where the company pays the tax, such that the benefit received is actually a net amount of £100,000, then the gross amount the director would receive is $100,000/(1-0.4) =$ £167,000 and hence it is the £167,000 that should be disclosed as part of the director's emoluments.

*Disclosure of directors' remuneration*

**5.45** Whilst separate disclosure of expenses or benefits in kind is not required by the Companies Act 1985 (or SI 2008/410), some companies do so. An example is in Table 5.4. As noted in the example in paragraph 5.44 above, for quoted companies separate disclosure of benefits by individual director is required (see para 5.164 onwards).

---

**Table 5.4 – Benefits in kind**

**National Westminster Bank Plc – Annual Report and Accounts – 31 December 1993**

**Emoluments of directors (extract)**
The total remuneration and benefits of the highest paid director in the UK, Mr R K Goeltz, were £554,238 (1992 £383,900), which comprised £230,564 basic salary and other emoluments (inclusive of director's fee), a performance related bonus of £72,739, expenses and disbursements amounting to £242,170 incurred by the Bank and Mr Goeltz in connection with his relocation from New York to London and £8,765 of benefits in kind. Mr Goeltz participates in the Bank's pension fund.

---

**5.46** Emoluments in respect of a person accepting office as director (see the last point in para 5.36) requires disclosure of incentive payments (so-called 'golden hellos') that are made by companies to attract people to join the board of directors.

### Gains on share options and amounts receivable under long-term incentive schemes

*Quoted and AIM companies*

**5.47** For quoted (see para 5.6.3) and AIM companies, separate totals for the aggregate of gains made by directors on exercising share options and for the aggregate of amounts of money and the net value of other assets received or receivable under long-term incentive schemes must be disclosed. [CA85 6 Sch 1(1)(b), (c); SI 2008/410 5 Sch 1(1)(b), (c)]. This disclosure has to be given in the notes to the financial statements even if it is readily ascertainable from information shown elsewhere (see para 5.72). An example of disclosure of gains made on the exercise of share options is given in Table 5.5.

---

**Table 5.5 – Disclosure of gains made on the exercise of share options**

**Fine Art Developments p.l.c. – Annual Report & Accounts – 31 March 1997**

**Report of the Remuneration Committee (extract)**

No share options were exercised by the directors in the year to 31 March 1997. In the previous year the seven executive directors on the board in that year exercised options granted under the savings related share option scheme. The aggregate of the gains made on these exercises, calculated on the difference between the option price and the mid-market price on the date of the option maturity, was £92,949, of which £14,676 related to the gain attributable to the highest paid director.

---

**5.48** The amount of the gain on exercising share options (quoted and AIM companies only) is the difference between market price of the shares on the day of exercise and the price actually paid for the shares. [CA85 6 Sch 1(5); SI 2008/410 8 Sch 17(1)].

**Example – Market price of shares**

A quoted company (see para 5.6.3 for definition) is disclosing gains on exercise of directors' share options in accordance with the Companies Act disclosure rules. In the rules the gain is defined as the difference between the market price of the shares on the day the option was exercised and the exercise price. A company wishes to know what price it should take as market price, as there was considerable price movement on the day in question, for instance can the definition in taxes legislation be used?

We consider that the mid-market price is the price that should be used. By way of support for this the FSA Listing Rules define market value as the middle-market quotation for a share as derived from the Daily Official List of the London Stock Exchange. [LR 9.5.10R (2)]. It seems to us this is a straight forward and sensible interpretation of the term 'market value' in the absence of a more precise definition in the Companies Act. The definition of market value in taxes legislation is not relevant to this disclosure issue.

**5.49** Share options granted in respect of a person's accepting office as a director are to be treated as share options granted in respect of that person's services as a director. [CA85 6 Sch 1(6)(b); SI 2008/410 5 Sch 15(3)]. Accordingly, the exercise of such options requires disclosure by quoted and AIM companies of the amount of the gain made in accordance with the requirement in paragraph 5.47 above.

*Unquoted companies excluding companies listed on AIM*

**5.50** Unquoted companies, excluding companies listed on AIM, are not required to include the amount of gains made by directors on the exercise of share options. Nor do they have to include the value of any shares received or receivable under long-term incentive schemes. Instead they should give the aggregate amount of money and net value of other assets (excluding shares) received and receivable under long-term incentive schemes and disclose separately:

- The number of directors who exercised share options.

- The number of directors in respect of whose qualifying services shares were received or receivable under long-term incentive schemes.

[CA85 6 Sch 1(2); SI 2008/410 5 Sch 1(3)].

**Example — Exercise of share options by director of unquoted company**

A director of an unquoted subsidiary of a quoted company (see para 5.6.3 for definition) has share options convertible into shares of the parent company. The director has exercised some of these options in the year. Do the gains on the exercise (which can be measured because the parent is quoted) need to be disclosed in the subsidiary's financial statements in the directors' remuneration note under the disclosure rules set out in Schedule 6 to the Companies Act 1985 (Schedule 5 to SI 2008/410)?

No. The Act's disclosure rules for unquoted companies (unless they are AIM companies) specifically exclude gains on the exercise of share options, even if they can be measured. Instead, the subsidiary should disclose the number of directors who exercised share options. [CA85 6 Sch 1(2)(b); SI 2008/410 5 Sch 1(3)].

Similarly, for an unquoted company (unless it is an AIM company), disclosure of the highest-paid director's remuneration does not include an amount for gains on exercise of share options, but the fact that the highest-paid director exercised options must be disclosed. [CA85 6 Sch 2(3)(a); SI 2008/410 5 Sch 2(3)(a)].

The accounting implications under IFRS 2 (and FRS 20) of share options in a group situation are dealt with in chapter 12 of the Manual of Accounting – IFRS for the UK and chapter 12 of the Manual of Accounting – UK GAAP.

In addition, for companies reporting under IFRS, IAS 24, requires disclosure of remuneration (in total and split into five categories) for key management personnel in respect of services provided to the entity. One of the categories is share-based payment and would include the share options, because the remuneration includes *"all forms of consideration paid, payable or provided by the entity, or on behalf of the entity in exchange for services rendered to the entity"*. The options are provided by the quoted parent to the director of the subsidiary in return for his services to the subsidiary. Therefore, insofar as it relates to directors and key managers, amounts charged in the subsidiary's financial statements under IFRS 2 would be disclosed as part of key management personnel compensation under the category 'share-based payment'.

*Definitions*

**5.51**   Share options are defined as the right to acquire shares. [CA85 6 Sch 1(5); SI 2008/410 5 Sch 12(b)]. We interpret this to include the right to acquire shares through subscription, by way of gift, by purchasing shares from an ESOP or indeed any other form of acquisition. It should be noted that there is a difference between the definition in Schedule 6 to the 1985 Act (Schedule 5 to SI 2008/410) of share options for the purpose of disclosure of aggregate gains and the definition in Schedule 7A to the 1985 Act (Schedule 8 to SI 2008/410) for the purpose of disclosure of individual directors' share options in the directors' remuneration report. See further paragraph 5.178.

**5.52**   A long-term incentive scheme is defined as *"an agreement or arrangement (a) under which money or other assets may become receivable by a director, and (b) which includes one or more qualifying conditions with respect to service or performance which cannot be fulfilled within a single financial year"*. [CA85 6 Sch 1(4); SI 2008/410 5 Sch 11(1)]. The definition specifically excludes:

■   Bonuses the amount of which is determined by reference to service or performance within a single financial year.

■   Compensation for loss of office, payments for breach of contract and other termination payments.

■ Retirement benefits.

[CA85 6 Sch 1(4); SI 2008/410 5 Sch 11(2)].

**5.53** Amounts received or receivable means amounts that become due to directors during the financial year. For example, if a long-term incentive scheme runs for three years and amounts or other assets become due to the directors at the end of the third year, they are disclosable in that year, even if they are not actually paid over to or received by the directors until the following year (see from para 5.16 above).

**5.54** Other assets received or receivable under long-term incentive schemes may include all sorts of non-cash items, for example, diamonds, gold, wine or works of art. Most commonly, however, such assets will be in the form of shares. Shares are defined as shares (whether allotted or not) in the company, or any undertaking which is a group undertaking in relation to the company and it includes share warrants. [CA85 6 Sch 1(5); SI 2008/410 5 Sch 12(a)]. A share warrant is a warrant that states that the bearer of the warrant is entitled to the shares specified in it. The phrase *"any undertaking which is a group undertaking in relation to the company"* would, we believe, include the parent undertaking and fellow subsidiary undertakings as well as subsidiary undertakings of the company. The 'value' of the shares received or receivable is the market price of the shares on the day the shares are received or receivable. [CA85 6 Sch 1(5)].

**5.55** The net value of other assets received or receivable by a director under a long-term incentive scheme means the value after deducting any money paid or other value given by the director. [CA85 6 Sch 1(5); SI 2008/410 5 Sch 15(1)].

**[The next paragraph is 5.58.]**

*Pension contributions*

**5.58** Company pension contributions do not form part of aggregate emoluments. Instead, the Act requires separate disclosure of the aggregate value of company contributions paid, or treated as paid, to a money purchase pension scheme in respect of directors' qualifying services by a person other than the director. Contributions mean those according to which the rate or amount of any money purchase benefits that may become payable will be calculated. [CA85 6 Sch 1(1)(d); SI 2008/410 5 Sch 1(1)(d)].

**5.59** In addition, a company must separately disclose the number of directors to whom retirement benefits are accruing under money purchase schemes and under defined benefit schemes in respect of qualifying services. [CA85 6 Sch 1(1)(e); SI 2008/410 5 Sch 1(2)].

**5.60** Although disclosure of contributions to money purchase schemes gives a reasonable indication of the benefit to a director, disclosure of contributions to defined benefit schemes may often not do so, as the level of funding will depend upon whether the scheme is in surplus or deficit. Schedule 7A to the 1985

Act (Schedule 8 to SI 2008/410) requires quoted companies (see para 5.6.3) to make detailed disclosures about directors' pension entitlements under defined benefit schemes (see section IV below). Because of the cost of obtaining information to satisfy the requirements of Schedule 7A to the 1985 Act (Schedule 8 to SI 2008/410), which would be considered unduly onerous for unquoted companies, disclosure of the number of directors to whom benefits are accruing must be disclosed to, at least, put members on notice that such schemes exist.

**5.61** Pension schemes are defined as meaning the same as a retirement benefits scheme under section 611 of ICTA 1988. [CA85 6 Sch 13(3); SI 2008/410 5 Sch 13(1)]. Section 611 defines a retirement benefits scheme as a scheme for the provision of benefits consisting of or including relevant benefits, but not including any national scheme providing such benefits. References to a scheme include references to a deed, agreement, series of agreements or other arrangements providing for relevant benefits notwithstanding that it relates or they relate only to:

- A small number of employees, or to a single employee (including company payments to personal pension plans – see example below).

- The payments of a pension starting immediately on the making of the arrangements.

**Example – Payments to director's personal pension plan**

A company makes a payment to a personal pension plan for one if its directors. The pension plan was arranged by the director some time before joining the company. Should these payments be disclosed under the Companies Act 1985 (2006 Act) requirement to disclose company contributions to money purchase schemes?

Yes, if the company makes the payments to the pension scheme, the payments should be disclosed in the aggregate of company contributions to money purchase schemes in respect of directors' qualifying services. [CA85 6 Sch 1(d); SI 2008/410 5 Sch 1(d)]. (If the company is quoted there should also be disclosure of the contributions in respect of each individual director – see further para 5.194.)

**5.62** The definition of pension schemes above is generally interpreted as extending to unfunded pension arrangements. Accordingly, where a company makes provisions in respect of unfunded pensions of a money purchase type, it should disclose the amounts provided as contributions to money purchase schemes. Where it makes provisions in respect of unfunded pensions of a defined benefit type, it should take the related benefits provided to directors into account when determining the amounts to be disclosed in respect of directors' pension entitlements under defined benefit schemes.

**5.63** Retirement benefits has the meaning given by section 612 of ICTA 1988. [CA85 6 Sch 13(3)(b); SI 2008/410 5 Sch 13(1)]. That is, any pension, lump sum, gratuity or other like benefit given or to be given:

- on retirement; or

- on death; or

- in anticipation of retirement; or

- in connection with past service, after retirement or death; or

- to be given on or in anticipation of or in connection with any change in the nature of the service of the employee in question;

except that it does not include any benefit which is to be afforded solely by reason of the disablement by accident of a person occurring during his service or of his death by accident so occurring and for no other reason.

**5.64** 'Money purchase benefits' for the purpose of the requirement set out in paragraph 5.58 above means retirement benefits payable under a pension scheme the rate or amount of which is calculated by reference to payments made, or treated as made, by the director or by any other person in respect of the director and which are not average salary benefits. [CA85 6 Sch 1(5); SI 2008/410 5 Sch 13(4)].

**5.65** 'Company contributions' do not have to be paid by the company itself as the definition states that the term means any payments (including insurance premiums) made, or treated as made to the scheme in respect of the director by a person other than the director. [CA85 6 Sch 1(5); SI 2008/410 5 Sch 13(3)]. Thus, for instance, contributions paid by the company's parent undertaking would qualify for disclosure as company contributions.

**5.66** A 'money purchase scheme' for the purpose of the requirement set out in paragraph 5.59 above means a pension scheme under which all of the benefits that may become payable to or in respect of the director are money purchase benefits. A 'defined benefit scheme' is a pension scheme that is not a money purchase scheme. [CA85 6 Sch 1(5); SI 2008/410 5 Sch 13(4)].

**5.66.1** The disclosure for the purpose of directors' remuneration is based on the legal form of the pension scheme. This is particularly relevant where a company does not account for a pension scheme as defined benefit (where it is entitled to an exemption in the relevant accounting standard for pensions), as illustrated in the following example.

**Example – Industry-wide pension scheme**

Company F, a private company, participates in an industry-wide defined benefit pension scheme. Company F is unable to identify its share of the scheme's underlying assets and liabilities and has taken the exemption available to it to account for the scheme as a defined contribution scheme, with the appropriate disclosure.

In the disclosure of directors' emoluments required by the Companies Act 1985 (2006 Act), should the scheme be treated as a defined contribution scheme so that the disclosures are consistent?

*Disclosure of directors' remuneration*

The disclosure of the directors' emoluments required for a private company by Schedule 6 to the Companies Act 1985 (Schedule 5 to SI 2008/410) is determined by the pension scheme's legal form and not by the accounting treatment. Company F should not make disclosure of the contributions paid to the industry-wide scheme as 'company contributions to money purchase schemes'.

Disclosure should be made of the number of directors to whom benefits are accruing under the defined benefit scheme and, if the aggregate emoluments of the directors exceeds £200,000, the accrued benefit and accrued lump sum at the end of the year for the highest paid director. [CA85 6 Sch 1(1 )(e), 2(2); SI 2008/410 5 Sch 1(2)(b), 2(2)].

It may be useful to include some disclosure in the directors' emoluments note to the financial statements to explain the apparent inconsistency.

**5.67** Where a pension scheme is a hybrid scheme and provides that any benefits that become payable will be the greater of money purchase benefits as determined under the scheme and defined benefits as determined, then the company may elect to treat the scheme as a money purchase scheme or as a defined benefit scheme, whichever seems more likely at the end of the financial year. [CA85 6 Sch 1(7); SI 2008/410 5 Sch 13(6)].

**5.68** The effect of the provision in the preceding paragraph is that where a pension scheme has both money purchase and defined benefit elements the company has an option as to how directors' remuneration disclosure is made. It can either take advantage of the provision and classify the scheme as money purchase or defined benefit in its entirety according to the type of benefits which appear to be higher in respect of the director at the end of the year. If the scheme is classified as a money purchase arrangement, the relevant disclosures as described in paragraph 5.58 above are made. If the scheme is classified as a defined benefit arrangement, the disclosure required by paragraph 5.59 is made.

**5.69** Alternatively, the company can elect not to take advantage of the option and make separate disclosure of information relating to the money purchase element of the scheme following the requirement in paragraph 5.58 above. If this is done then the scheme is counted as a defined benefit scheme for the purpose of the requirement in paragraph 5.59.

**5.70** The choice between the two alternatives may also be influenced by the requirement (discussed below from para 5.84) to disclose the pension entitlement of the highest paid director under any defined benefit scheme.

**5.71** For the purpose of determining whether a pension scheme is a money purchase or defined benefit scheme any death in service benefits provided by the scheme are disregarded. [CA85 6 Sch 1(8); SI 2008/410 5 Sch 13(7)].

*General — readily ascertainable from other information*

**5.72** Where the information discussed in the above sections is readily ascertainable from the other information that is shown, this satisfies the disclosure requirements. [CA85 6 Sch 1(6)(a); SI 2008/410 5 Sch 6(2)]. For example, a quoted company that gives detailed information by individual director in its directors' remuneration report (as required by Schedule 7A to the 1985 Act (Schedule 8 to SI 2008/410)) could satisfy the Schedule 6 to the 1985 Act (Schedule 5 to SI 2008/410) requirement for disclosure of the aggregate emoluments (described above) if the total is readily ascertainable, provided that there is a cross-reference from the notes to the financial statements (where the Schedule 6 to the 1985 Act (Schedule 5 to SI 2008/410) disclosure is required to be given) to the relevant part of the directors' remuneration report.

**5.73**  However, under the Companies Act 1985, this concession does not apply to the aggregate of gains made by directors on the exercise of share options.

## Section II — Unquoted companies (including AIM companies)

**5.74**  In addition to the requirements described in section I, unquoted companies (including companies listed on AIM) must comply with the following requirements. Quoted companies (for definition see para 5.6.3) must comply instead with the requirements described in section IV.

### Highest paid director's emoluments and other benefits

**5.75**  The Companies Act 1985 (SI 2008/410) requires details of the highest paid director's emoluments and other benefits to be disclosed.

**5.76**  Quoted companies have to give details of individual directors' emoluments and other benefits (see section IV below) and so for them there is no requirement to give details of the highest paid director's emoluments separately, as such a requirement would be superfluous.

**5.77**  For unquoted (and AIM) companies the requirement to disclose additional information on the highest paid director enables the reader of the financial statements at least to determine the maximum amounts received or receivable by any director and thus to assess and evaluate this against company performance or whichever other criteria the reader chooses.

### *Ascertaining the highest paid director*

**5.78**  There is a *de minimis* level below which the highest paid director's emoluments and other benefits need not be disclosed. If the total of the following items shown for all directors exceeds or is equal to £200,000, the information on the highest paid director must be given. These items are:

- Aggregate emoluments paid to or receivable by directors in respect of qualifying services.
- Aggregate amount of gains made by directors on exercise of share options (but see para 5.82).

■ Aggregate amount of (a) money paid to or receivable by directors under long-term incentive schemes in respect of qualifying services and (b) net value of assets (other than money and share options) received or receivable by directors under such schemes in respect of such services (but see para 5.82).

[CA85 6 Sch 2(1); SI 2008/410 5 Sch 2(1)].

**5.79** The highest paid director is the director to whom is attributable the greatest part of the total calculated in paragraph 5.78 above. [CA85 6 Sch 2(5); SI 2008/410 5 Sch 10]. Note that only the elements listed above are included in the calculation. Other items, for example compensation for loss of office and company pension contributions, are not included in determining the highest paid director.

**5.80** The total of the amounts listed in paragraph 5.78 is the figure to be taken into account in determining whether the £200,000 level is reached or exceeded.

**5.81** The threshold figure of £200,000 is not increased or decreased when the financial year for which financial statements are prepared exceeds or is less than 12 months. This is because it is determined by reference to the actual figures disclosed (see para 5.78 above) which are those for the financial period, whether that period is 12 months or not.

**5.82** For unquoted companies other than companies listed on AIM the items described do not include the amounts of gains made on exercise of share options or the value of shares received under long-term incentive schemes, because these amounts do not have to be calculated or disclosed by such unquoted companies (see para 5.28 above).

### Disclosure

**5.83** If the limit of £200,000 is reached or exceeded, the following two amounts must be disclosed in respect of the highest paid director:

■ The total of the aggregate amounts described in paragraph 5.78 above that is attributable to the director.

■ The amount of any company contributions paid, or treated as paid to a money purchase pension scheme in respect of the director's qualifying services.

[CA85 6 Sch 2(1); SI 2008/410 5 Sch 2(1)].

**5.84** If the highest paid director has also participated in a defined benefit pension scheme, in respect of his qualifying services during the year, then the following information must also be disclosed:

■ The amount at the end of the year of his accrued pension.

■ Where applicable, the amount at the end of the year of his accrued lump sum.

[CA85 6 Sch 2(2); SI 2008/410 5 Sch 2(2)].

**5.85** Where a company is unquoted and not listed on AIM and, therefore, does not include details of gains on options exercised or the value of shares awarded under long-term incentive schemes, it must disclose:

■ Whether the highest paid director exercised any share options.

■ Whether any shares were received or receivable by that director in respect of qualifying services under a long-term incentive scheme.

[CA85 6 Sch 2(3); SI 2008/410 5 Sch 2(3)].

**5.86** However, if the director has not been involved in any such transactions there is no need to state that fact. [CA85 6 Sch 2(4); SI 2008/410 5 Sch 2(4)].

**5.86.1** Comparative figures are required for the director's emoluments information in the normal way – see paragraph 5.92 onwards below.

*'Accrued pension' and 'accrued lump sum'*

**5.87** The terms 'accrued pension' and 'accrued lump sum' mean the amount of the annual pension and the amount of the lump sum that would be payable to the director when he reaches normal pension age if:

■ He had left the company's service at the end of the financial year.

■ There were no increase in the general level of prices during the period from the end of the year to the director's pension age.

■ There was no question of there being any commutation of the pension or inverse commutation of the lump sum.

■ Any amounts attributable to voluntary contributions (AVCs) paid by the director to the scheme, and any money purchase benefits payable under the scheme were disregarded.

[CA85 6 Sch 2(5); SI 2008/410 5 Sch 13(2)].

**5.88** 'Normal pension age' is the earliest date at which the director is entitled to receive a full pension on retirement of an amount determined without reduction to take account of its payment before a later age (but disregarding any entitlement to pension upon retirement in the event of illness, incapacity or redundancy). [CA85 6 Sch 2(5); SI 2008/410 5 Sch 13(5)]. This means that a pension is not a 'full pension' if the benefits are reduced to take account of early payment and that any entitlement in the event of illness, incapacity or redundancy is disregarded for these purposes.

**5.89** The third bullet point in paragraph 5.87, which refers to commutation of the pension or inverse commutation of the lump sum, should be interpreted as follows. Disclosure of the amount of accrued lump sum should only be made where, under the pension scheme rules, the director will automatically receive a lump sum on retirement. No disclosure should be made of a lump sum when a lump sum may be payable by way of commutation (that is, reduction) of rights to an annual pension. In the same way, disclosure of the amount of accrued pension should not include any reverse commutation of a lump sum entitlement. In practice, schemes that have both lump sums and pensions are extremely rare outside the public sector.

**5.90** If, for example, a director was entitled at the end of the year to an accrued pension of £30,000, but could commute that into a pension of £20,000 per annum and a lump sum of £100,000, the only disclosure to be made would be the accrued pension of £30,000. If he was entitled to a pension of £30,000 and a lump sum of £50,000 (without any reduction in the pension), both figures would be disclosed. If he was entitled to a pension of £30,000 and a lump sum of £50,000, but could commute the lump sum such that he could instead take a pension of £35,000 and no lump sum, then the figures to be disclosed would be £30,000 and £50,000, that is ignoring the right to the reverse commutation of the lump sum.

**Example 1 – Accrued pension (no entitlement to lump sum)**

The highest paid director is 50 at the beginning of the year. He joined the company when he was 40 and is entitled to retire at 60. His salary in the previous year was £120,000 per annum. In the current year his salary is also £120,000. His maximum pension is 20/30 of his final salary after 20 years, but he has no entitlement to a lump sum (although he may commute part of his pension and take a lump sum in place of the amount commuted).

| | |
|---|---|
| The pension accrual would be calculated as follows: | |
| Accrued pension at the end of the previous year | $10/30 \times £120,000 = £40,000$ |
| Accrued pension at the end of the current year | $11/30 \times £120,000 = £44,000$ |
| The disclosure would, therefore, be: | |
| Accrued pension of the highest paid director | £44,000 (previous year £40,000) |

**Example 2 – Accrued pension and lump sum**

The highest paid director is 50 at the beginning of the year. He joined the company at 20 and is entitled to retire at 60. His salary in the previous year was £150,000 and is £160,000 in the current year. His maximum pension is 40/80 of his final salary after 40 years and he is also entitled to a maximum lump sum of 120/80 of his final salary after 40 years. (He may commute the lump sum by taking an increased pension instead of all or part of the lump sum.)

| | |
|---|---|
| The pension accrued and accrual of the lump sum entitlement would be as follows: | |
| Accrued pension at the end of the previous year | $30/80 \times £150,000 = £56,250$ |
| Accrued pension at the end of the current year | $31/80 \times £160,000 = £62,000$ |
| Accrued lump sum at the end of the previous year | $90/80 \times £150,000 = £168,750$ |
| Accrued lump sum at the end of the current year | $93/80 \times £160,000 = £186,000$ |

| | |
|---|---|
| The disclosure would, therefore, be: | |
| Accrued pension of highest paid director | £62,000 (previous year £56,250) |
| Accrued lump sum of highest paid director | £186,000 (previous year £168,750) |

**5.90.1** The examples below consider the implications for disclosure in respect of the highest paid director's pension entitlements when the director is appointed or retires in the year.

**Example 1 – director appointed in the year**

A director was appointed during the year. He had previously been an employee of the (unquoted) company for many years. He is the highest paid director. In disclosing his accrued pension entitlement (in accordance with the requirements of Schedule 6 to the Companies Act 1985 (Schedule 5 to SI 2008/410) for unquoted companies) should it be calculated on the basis of the period for which he has been a director or on the basis of the whole period for which he has been both an employee and a director?

The accrued pension entitlement disclosed under Schedule 6 to the 1985 Act (Schedule 5 to SI 2008/410) should be calculated and disclosed, based on the whole period of his service as an employee and a director. However, the company could add a note to explain how much of the entitlement was earned prior to his becoming a director.

This is further explained in the similar example for a quoted company – see further paragraph 5.203

**Example 2 – director retires in the year**

The highest paid director of an unquoted company retired during the year and started drawing his pension. What should be disclosed as the pension entitlement of the highest paid director at the year end under Schedule 6 to the Companies Act 1985 (Schedule 5 to SI 2008/410)?

For the purposes of the Schedule 6 to the 1985 Act (Schedule 5 to SI 2008/410) disclosure, the amount of the annual pension payable to the director should be disclosed, because up until his retirement he performed qualifying services by reference to which the final pension was calculated. A note could be given to explain that the figure disclosed was the pension entitlement at the date of retirement.

*Examples of disclosure*

**5.90.2** The examples below illustrate disclosures in respect of the highest paid director.

**Example 1 – Disclosure for highest-paid director (AIM company)**

An example of disclosure in respect of the highest paid director that incorporates all of the above elements would be as follows for an AIM company:

*Disclosure of directors' remuneration*

| Highest paid director | 20X2 | 20X1 |
|---|---|---|
| | £ | £ |
| Aggregate emoluments, gains on share options exercised and benefits under long-term incentive schemes | 200,000 | 180,000 |
| Company pension contributions to money purchase scheme | 2,000 | 2,000 |
| Defined benefit scheme: | | |
|    Accrued pension at end of year | 30,000 | 25,000 |
|    Accrued lump sum at end of year | 60,000 | 50,000 |

**Example 2 – Disclosure for highest-paid director (unquoted company)**

For an unquoted company that is not listed on AIM disclosure that incorporates all the above elements would be:

| Highest paid director | 20X2 | 20X1 |
|---|---|---|
| | £ | £ |
| Aggregate emoluments and benefits (excluding gains on exercise of share options and value of shares received) under long-term incentive schemes | 250,000 | 240,000 |
| Company pension contributions to money purchase scheme | 2,000 | 2,000 |
| Defined benefit scheme: | | |
|    Accrued pension at end of year | 60,000 | 53,000 |
|    Accrued lump sum at end of year | 100,000 | 90,000 |

The highest paid director exercised share options during the year and received shares under the executive long-term incentive scheme.

### General – readily ascertainable from other information

**5.91**  Where information on the highest paid director's emoluments is readily ascertainable from the other information that is shown, this satisfies the disclosure requirements. [CA85 6 Sch 2(6); SI 2008/410 5 Sch 6(2)].

### Comparative figures

**5.92**  Comparative figures are required for the director's emoluments information in the normal way.

**5.92.1**  Where the highest paid director in the current year was not the highest paid in the previous year, we consider that the comparative figure disclosed should be the emoluments of the actual highest paid director last year. Therefore, the comparative figures may relate to a different person from the highest paid director this year. Where this is the case, the company may wish to indicate this in the disclosure.

**5.92.2**  Where a company reaches the £200,000 threshold (see para 5.78) in the current year and so is required to disclose the highest paid director's emoluments, the requirement to disclose comparatives applies even where the company did not reach the £200,000 threshold in the previous year and the information has not previously been disclosed.

**5.92.3**  Where a company is below the £200,000 threshold in the current year, it is not required to disclose the highest paid director's emoluments in the current year. However, if the company reached the £200,000 threshold in the prior year, our view is that it will not be exempt from disclosure for that year and so the comparative should be disclosed, together with an explanation that the company is exempt from disclosure in the current year. Furthermore, if the company is likely to reach the £200,000 threshold in the next year, it will be required to disclose information for that year with comparatives (see para 5.92.1). Therefore, the company should consider giving the disclosure for the current year, so that this is then available for the comparatives in next year's financial statements.

**5.92.4**  The above requirements for disclosure of comparatives in respect of the highest paid director's emoluments are summarised in the table below.

| Current year | Prior year | Disclosure |
| --- | --- | --- |
| £200,000 or more | £200,000 or more | Disclose highest paid director's emoluments for both years. |
| £200,000 or more | Less than £200,000 | Disclose highest paid director's emoluments for both years (para 5.92.2). |
| Less than £200,000 | £200,000 or more | No disclosure of highest paid director's emoluments for current year, but comparative disclosure required for prior year (para 5.92.3). |
| Less than £200,000 | Less than £200,000 | No disclosure of highest paid director's emoluments for both years. |

**Excess retirement benefits of directors and past directors**

**5.93**  If retirement benefits paid to or receivable by directors or past directors are in excess of the retirement benefits to which they were entitled at the time when the benefits first became payable or 31 March 1997 (whichever is the later) the notes must disclose the aggregate amount of:

■  The amount of the excess benefits paid to or receivable by directors under pension schemes.

■  The amount of the excess benefits paid to or receivable by past directors, again under pension schemes.

[CA85 6 Sch 7(1); SI 2008/410 5 Sch 3(1)].

**5.94** The excess amounts referred to above do not include amounts paid or receivable if:

■ The scheme's funding was such that the amounts were or could have been paid without recourse to additional contributions; and

■ The amounts were paid to or receivable by all pensioner members of the scheme on the same basis ('pensioner members' being persons entitled to the present payment of retirement benefits under the scheme).

[CA85 6 Sch 7(2); SI 2008/410 5 Sch 3(2), 3(3)].

**5.95** The exception described above means that the excess retirement benefits disclosed do not include retirement benefits paid to all pensioners on the same basis out of an adequately funded pension scheme.

**5.96** 'Retirement benefits' for the purpose of the above includes benefits otherwise than in cash, and where benefits other than in cash are given the amount should be calculated as their estimated money value. The nature of any such benefit should also be disclosed. [CA85 6 Sch 7(3); SI 2008/410 5 Sch 3(4)].

**Compensation for loss of office**

**5.97** Disclosure must be made of the aggregate amount of any compensation received or receivable by directors or past directors in respect of loss of office. [CA85 6 Sch 8(1); SI 2008/410 5 Sch 4(1)]. This disclosure should include amounts received or receivable in respect of the loss of office by the director of the reporting company. It should also include amounts received or receivable in respect of loss, while a director of the reporting company or in connection with ceasing to be a director of that company, of office as a director of any subsidiary undertaking or of any office that involved management of the affairs of the company or of any subsidiary undertaking. [CA85 6 Sch 8(2); SI 2008/410 5 Sch 4(2)]. 'Subsidiary undertaking' includes an undertaking at the time the services were rendered and a subsidiary undertaking immediately before the loss of office as a director. It also includes an undertaking where the director was a director, whilst being a director of the company, by virtue of the company's nomination (direct or indirect), whether or not it was in fact a subsidiary undertaking. [CA85 6 Sch 13(2); SI 2008/410 5 Sch 14].

**5.98** Compensation for loss of office includes compensation for or in connection with a person's retirement from office. Where such retirement is caused by a breach of the person's contract with the company or with a subsidiary undertaking compensation includes payments made by way of damages for the breach or payments made in settlement or compromise of any claim in respect of the breach. [CA85 6 Sch 8(4); SI 2008/410 5 Sch 4(3)].

*General – readily ascertainable from other information*

**5.99** Where information on compensation for loss of office is readily ascertainable from the other information that is shown this satisfies the disclosure requirements. [CA85 6 Sch 8(5); SI 2008/410 5 Sch 6(2)]. For example, if compensation had been paid to two people and each person's compensation is shown separately, but the aggregate can be readily ascertained this would satisfy the requirement to disclose the aggregate.

### Pension scheme top ups

**5.100**   We consider that a payment made to top up a pension scheme for the benefit of a director on his retirement is disclosable as it is effectively a benefit in kind (see para 5.102 below). This would be so even if the top up were funded out of an existing scheme surplus [CA85 6 Sch 10(2)(c); SI 2008/410 5 Sch 7(2)], because the reduction in the surplus would involve the company paying increased contributions to the scheme and the top up is, therefore, even in that case, indirectly a cost to the company.

**Example – Enhanced pension on retirement**

A director retired in the year and as part of his leaving package the company enhanced his pension by giving him extra years of pensionable service. The enhancement was funded out of a surplus in the company's pension scheme and the capital value of the added pension entitlement was £250,000. How should this be disclosed in the financial statements? Would the answer be different if the company had paid £250,000 into the pension scheme?

Since the pension enhancement was given in connection with the director's retirement, it should be included as part of the director's compensation for loss of office for disclosure under the Companies Act 1985 (SI 2008/410). The amount to be disclosed would be £250,000, the capital value of the increase, because this is the value of the benefit to the retiring director. The disclosure would be the same, irrespective of whether the director's enhanced pension was funded out of a surplus in the scheme or by a special company contribution to the scheme.

**5.101**   An example of disclosure of a top up payment made by the company is given in Table 5.6.

---

**Table 5.6 – Disclosure of a top up payment**

**XYZ Group Limited – Annual Report – 31 March 2XXX**

**Directors' emoluments (extract)**

During the year, Mr X, the previous chief executive, left the company. Mr X had a service contract with the company terminable by the company on one years' notice. The company has agreed to pay Mr X as compensation for loss of office an amount approximately equivalent to one year's salary and other benefits. This amount was £398,400, which is subject to deduction of tax, and includes a sum of £60,000 in respect of Mr X's pension arrangements.

(Note: This example is made up, but includes features from a real example of disclosure)

---

### Benefits in kind

**5.102**   In addition to any monetary payment, the term compensation for loss of office includes benefits received or receivable otherwise than in cash. The value of the benefit should be determined according to its estimated money value. [CA85 6

Sch 8(3); SI 2008/410 5 Sch 4(4)]. Where compensation is given in kind, the company's financial statements should disclose its nature. [CA85 6 Sch 8(3); SI 2008/410 5 Sch 4(4)]. For example, the compensation might be the gift to the director of a car that he had previously used, but that was owned by the company. In this situation, the money value of the car and the fact that the compensation is in the form of a car will have to be disclosed. Normally, the market value of the car at the time of transfer should be used for this purpose. If, however, compensation includes both cash and a car, only the nature and not the amount of the benefit relating to the car needs to be separately disclosed. The cash and the amount of the benefit may be shown as one figure.

### Ex gratia payments

**5.103** The statutory description of 'compensation to directors for loss of office' is widely drawn. In deciding whether compensation to a director or a former director is required to be disclosed, regard should be had to both the nature of the compensation and the circumstances in which it was made, rather than just to the description the company gives to it. For example, *'ex gratia'* payments made on either a director's retirement or his removal from office can be regarded not as gratuitous payments, but as payments in compensation for loss of office and they should be disclosed as such.

### Payments made on retirement

**5.104** In some cases, directors may have terms in their service contracts which entitle them to continue to receive remuneration for a period after they cease to be directors, perhaps in their capacity as employees. In other cases, they may have more than one service contract with different companies in a group. In such cases, the company may be obliged to make payments for periods after the directors cease to act as directors of the parent company. Where such arrangements exist or where they are terminated by payment of an additional lump sum on retirement as director we consider that the amounts should be disclosed as part of the compensation for loss of office disclosure.

**5.105** Additionally, on retirement a director might enter into a consultancy agreement with a company whereby he is paid an annual retainer for one or more years. Again we consider that such arrangements should be disclosed. In some cases, where genuine services are to be provided disclosure may be as a transaction in which a director is interested (caught by related party disclosures). In others where no genuine services will be provided or the services to be provided have a fair value that is less than the compensation payable by the company, we consider that the amounts payable under the arrangement are, in substance, compensation for loss of office. For quoted companies, see also paragraph 5.214.

**5.106** A further benefit sometimes allowed to directors on retirement is that they may retain share options previously granted to them where such options would normally lapse on their leaving the company. Alternatively, they may be entitled to keep the options as a result of the terms in their service contract. Again, where there is a benefit to the retiring director to which he is not entitled under the scheme rules, the value of this benefit should be included in 'compensation' for loss of office and its nature disclosed in accordance with paragraph 5.102, disclosure should be made (see Table 5.7).

**5.107**   Further examples of disclosure of compensation which include the above features are Tables 5.7 to 5.10 below.

---

**Table 5.7 – Disclosure of compensation for loss of office**

**XYZ plc (AIM company) – Annual Report and Accounts – 30 June 2XX1**

**Remuneration of directors (extract)**

Mr X resigned as a Director on 16th February 2XX1 and his contracts of employment with the Company and a Group subsidiary undertaking in the USA were terminated with effect from 31st March 2XX1. Under the terms of his contract with the Company, he has been paid £105,000 upon termination of that contract. Under the terms of his contract with the US subsidiary undertaking he is entitled, subject to certain conditions, to continue to receive his annual salary of US$635,000 and certain other incidental benefits for a period of up to three years from 31st March 2XX1; these salary payments have been fully provided for in these accounts and are disclosed as payments for termination of executive office when paid. He will retain his participation in the cycle of the long-term performance-related incentive plan ending on 30th June 2XX1, pro rata to the period during which he was an employee of the Group. Payments to him under this plan will be disclosed as payments to a former Director when paid. He retains his right to share options, numbering 93,217 at 31st March 2XX1, which lapse on dates up to 20th March 2XX4.

*(Note: This example is made up but includes features from a real example of disclosure)*

---

**Table 5.8 – Disclosure of compensation for loss of office**

**XYZ Limited – Report and Accounts – 31 December 2XX1**

**7. EMOLUMENTS OF THE DIRECTORS OF THE HOLDING COMPANY (extract)**

Mr. X, a former Director of the Company and of Subsidiary Y, resigned on 12 October 2XX1. He will continue to receive cash and non-cash benefits under the terms of his contract of employment dated 19 March 199x for the two year period to 31 October 2XX3. As compensation for his loss of office as Managing Director of Subsidiary Y, this contract was changed so that over the two year period he is free to undertake other employment, subject to certain non-compete conditions, and is to be available for consultation by the Company. The estimated money value of the benefit to Mr. X, being the estimated total cash and non-cash benefits, is £670,000.

*(Note: This example is made up but contains features from a real example of disclosure)*

---

**Table 5.9 – Disclosure of compensation for loss of office**

**XYZ Limited – Annual Report and Accounts – 31 December 2XX1**

**Directors and employees (extract)**

Following Mr X's resignation as director on 6 July 2XX1, Mr X and Associates, of which Mr X is a partner, entered into a consultancy agreement with the company. The agreement has a term of two years from 1 August 2XX1. Under the provisions of the agreement, Mr X and Associates will provide consultancy services as required by the company and receive remuneration comprising a day rate and payments at specified intervals. The agreement also provides for the partnership to receive a start-up loan of £50,000 free of interest but repayable by three instalments at specified dates in 2XX2 and 2XX3. The amount paid to the partnership for the services rendered in 2XX1 was £95,750. The amount payable in 2XX2 and 2XX3, provided the agreement is not terminated, will depend on the work undertaken but will include specified payments which may total a maximum of £145,000.

*(Note: This example is made up but contains features from a real example of disclosure)*

---

**Table 5.10 – Disclosure of compensation for loss of office**

**X plc (AIM company) – Annual Report and Accounts – 2 April 2XX3**

**SUPPLEMENTARY PROFIT AND LOSS INFORMATION (extract)**
The value of the compensation received by a former director for loss of office amounted to £100,000 (2XX2-£1,162,536 relating to five directors). He also retained and has exercised options over 113,732 shares (granted under the executive share option scheme in May 2XX1), and 144,975 shares (granted in May 2XX3).

*(Note: This example is made up but contains features from a real example of disclosure)*

---

### Requirement for member approval

**5.108** The Companies Act 2006 requires companies to obtain member approval for payments made to a director (or former director) or to persons connected with them relating to loss of office. This includes payments by way of compensation for loss of office and those in connection with the directors' retirement and includes payments relating to the loss of office of a subsidiary undertaking or any other office in connection with the company's management. The provisions are set out in sections 215 to 222 of the Companies Act 2006 (including some exceptions) and are effective for retirements occurring on or after 1 October 2007.

**[The next paragraph is 5.110.]**

### Disclosure in the financial statements

**5.110** Amounts to be disclosed include all relevant sums paid by or receivable from the company, the company's subsidiary undertakings and any other person, unless the director has to account for the sums to the company, its subsidiaries or to members. [CA85 6 Sch 10(2); SI 2008/410 5 Sch 7(2)].

**5.111** For this purpose, a subsidiary undertaking includes a company that was a subsidiary undertaking immediately before the date on which the director lost office. It also includes an undertaking of which the director, while a director of the company, was a director by virtue of the company's nomination (direct or indirect), whether or not it is or was in fact a subsidiary undertaking of the company. [CA85 6 Sch 13(2)(a)(b); SI 2008/410 5 Sch 14(1)].

**5.112** Compensation paid to a director for loss of office is a category of payment different from an 'emolument'. Consequently, it should not be included in the disclosure of that person's aggregate emoluments.

**Sums paid to third parties in respect of directors' services**

**5.113** Paragraph 9 of Schedule 6 to the Companies Act 1985 (para 5 of Schedule 5 to SI 2008/410) requires companies to disclose in their financial statements any consideration paid to or receivable by third parties for making available the services of any person:

■ As a director of the company.

■ While a director of the company, as director of any of its subsidiary undertakings, or otherwise in connection with the management of the affairs of the company or any of its subsidiary undertakings.

[CA85 6 Sch 9(1); SI 2008/410 5 Sch 5(1)].

**5.114** In this context, third parties do not include:

■ The director himself or a person connected with him or a body corporate controlled by him.

■ The company or any of its subsidiary undertakings.

[CA85 6 Sch 9(3); SI 2008/410 5 Sch 5(3)].

**5.115** For the purpose of this disclosure 'subsidiary undertaking' includes an undertaking which is a subsidiary undertaking at the time the services were rendered and an undertaking where the director, while a director of the company, was a director by virtue of the company's nomination (direct or indirect), whether or not it is or was in fact a subsidiary undertaking. [CA85 6 Sch 13(2)(a)(b); SI 2008/410 5 Sch 14(1)]. See further paragraph 5.15.

**5.116** For the purposes of this disclosure, the definition of consideration includes non-cash benefits. Where a benefit is given, its amount should be determined by reference to its estimated money value. The nature of the non-cash benefit must also be disclosed. [CA85 6 Sch 9(2); SI 2008/410 5 Sch 5(2)].

**5.117** The requirement to disclose amounts paid to third parties for making available the services of a director is illustrated in the following example.

**Example – Amounts paid to third party**

Company A borrows money from a venture capital company. As part of the financing arrangement, a director of the venture capital company has been appointed to the board of directors of company A. Company A pays £10,000 per year to the venture capital company in respect of the director's services. The director is remunerated by the venture capital company and does not receive the money paid in respect of his services by company A personally. In this situation, the amount of £10,000 would be disclosed in the financial statements of the company as sums paid to third parties in respect of directors' services in accordance with paragraph 9 of Schedule 6 to the 1985 Act (para 5 of Schedule 5 to SI 2008/410).

**5.117.1**   A further example is given in Table 5.11.

---

**Table 5.11 – Sums paid to third parties in respect of directors' services**

**XYZ Limited – Report and Accounts – 2 May 2XX2**

**EMOLUMENTS OF DIRECTORS (extract)**
ABC Bank plc, of which Mr X was a director, were paid fees of £23,000 during the period for the release of Mr X's services during the illness of the then Chairman.
*(Note: This example is made up but contains features from a real disclosure example)*

---

**5.117.2**   The disclosure applies where third parties make available the services of a director. It does not apply to other services, as illustrated in the following example.

**Example – Payments to a headhunter**

Would payments to a third party for making available the services of any person as a director include payments to a headhunter in respect of the appointment of a new director?

Paragraph 9 of Schedule 6 to the Companies Act 1985 (para 5 of Schedule 5 to SI 2008/410) (for unquoted companies) states that there shall be shown the aggregate amount of any consideration paid to or receivable by third parties for making available the services of any person as a director of the company. (Note that paragraph 15 of Schedule 7A to the 1985 Act (para 16 of Schedule 8 to SI 2008/410) (for quoted companies) requires the information to be disclosed by individual director.)

Where the fees paid by a company to a headhunter relate solely to services to the company for finding and introducing the person, we consider that a head-hunter is not making available the services of a person as director in the sense envisaged in the 1985 Act (SI 2008/410). The headhunter receives a fee for finding the person who the company appoints to perform the services, but is not being paid in respect of the services. Our interpretation is that the 1985 Act (SI 2008/410) only applies to third parties who make the services of the director available (for instance, where another company lends a director part-time).

## Examples of disclosure

**5.117.3** An example of disclosure of directors' remuneration under the 1985 Act (or 2006 Act) by an unquoted company not listed on AIM is given below.

**Example – Disclosure of directors' remuneration (unquoted company)**

The following is an example of disclosure under the Act by an unquoted company not listed on AIM.

|  | 2XX2 | 2XX1 |
|---|---|---|
| Directors | £ | £ |
| Aggregate emoluments | 350,000 | 320,000 |
| Amounts (excluding shares) receivable under long-term incentive schemes | 50,000 | 40,000 |
| Company pension contributions to money purchase schemes | 5,000 | 5,000 |
| Compensation for loss of office | 100,000 | — |
| Sums paid to third parties for directors' services | — | 20,000 |
| Excess retirement benefits – current directors | 5,000 | 5,000 |
| – past directors | 10,000 | 10,000 |

Two directors exercised share options in the year (2XX1: two) and one director became entitled to receive shares under the long-term incentive scheme (2XX1:three). Retirement benefits are accruing to two directors under the company's money purchase pension scheme (2XX1: two) and to one director under a defined benefit scheme (2XX1: one).

(Note: details of the highest paid director's emoluments must also be disclosed. An example of disclosure is given in para 5.90.)

An example of disclosure under the Act by an AIM company is given in the next section in paragraph 5.11.

## Section III — AIM companies

**5.118** AIM companies are effectively treated as unquoted companies by the Companies Act 1985 and the Companies Act 2006. Therefore, unlike quoted companies (see para 5.6.3) they do not have to produce a directors' remuneration report in the form set out in Schedule 7A to the 1985 Act (Schedule 8 to SI 2008/410).

**5.119** However, AIM companies do have to give certain information, that other unquoted companies not listed on AIM do not have to give. This information relates principally to disclosures of aggregate gains on exercise of share options and the aggregate net value of shares received or receivable under long-term incentive schemes. In addition, in their disclosure of highest paid director's emoluments, AIM companies have also to include amounts in respect of gains on the exercise of share options and net value of shares received or receivable under long term incentive schemes.

**5.120** These points are dealt with in section I and section II above, which distinguish, where applicable, the provisions relating to AIM companies from those relating to unquoted companies not listed on AIM. In general, however, the requirements for AIM companies are, with the above exceptions, the same as those for other unquoted companies. An example of disclosure under the 1985 Act (or 2006 Act) by an AIM company is given below.

**Example – Disclosure of directors' remuneration (AIM company)**

The following is an example of disclosure under the Act by an AIM company.

|  | 2XX2 | 2XX1 |
|---|---|---|
| Directors | £ | £ |
| Aggregate emoluments | 650,000 | 580,000 |
| Gains made on exercise of share options | 50,000 | — |
| Amounts receivable under long-term incentive schemes | 400,000 | 350,000 |
| Company pension contributions to money purchase schemes | 50,000 | 50,000 |
| Compensation for loss of office | — | 100,000 |
| Sums paid to third parties for director's services | 20,000 | 20,000 |
| Excess retirement benefits     – current directors | 5,000 | 5,000 |
|                                 – past directors | 10,000 | 10,000 |

Retirement benefits are accruing to two directors under the company's money purchase pension scheme and to one director under a defined benefit scheme.

(Note: details of highest paid director's emoluments must also be disclosed. An example of the disclosure is given in para 5.90.)

# Section IV — Quoted companies (excluding companies listed on AIM)

**Remuneration report**

**5.121**   The Companies Act 1985 (SI 2008/410) contains requirements for quoted companies (for definition see para 5.6.3), which substantially duplicates the requirements contained in the FSA Listing Rules. The 1985 Act (SI 2008/410) requirements also contain additional disclosures over and above those contained in the Listing Rules. As explained in paragraph 5.6.5, it should be noted that there are some differences between the requirements of the Listing Rules and those of the 1985 Act (SI 2008/410) and so the disclosures could be complicated. An illustrative example is given in the directors' remuneration report for IFRS GAAP plc (see separate publication containing illustrative financial statements). The requirements of the Listing Rules are covered in this section in addition to those in the 1985 Act and SI 2008/410.

**5.122**   Quoted companies must comply with the disclosure requirements that are applicable to all companies, and these are described above in section I of this chapter. In addition, section 234B of the 1985 Act requires that the directors of a quoted company prepare a directors' remuneration report that contains the information specified in Schedule 7A and complies with any requirement of that Schedule as to how the information is to be set out in the report. [CA85 Sec 234B(1)]. Sections 420 to 422 of the Companies Act 2006 replace sections 234B and 234C of the 1985 Act. Section 421 of the Companies Act 2006 gives the

Secretary of State power to make provision by regulations as to the information that must be contained in a directors' remuneration report and how it should be set out. These matters are currently set out in Schedule 7A to the 1985 Act and are replaced by regulations in Schedule 8 to SI 2008/410 effective for accounting periods beginning on or after 6 April 2008.

**5.123** The directors' remuneration report must be approved by the board and signed on its behalf by a director or the secretary of the company. [CA85 Sec 234C(1); CA06 Sec 422(1)].

**5.124** Schedule 7A to the 1985 Act (Schedule 8 to SI 2008/410) contains four parts:

■ Introductory.

■ Information not subject to audit — information about remuneration committees, performance related remuneration and liabilities in respect of directors' contracts.

■ Information subject to audit — detailed information about directors' remuneration.

■ Interpretation and supplementary.

**5.125** This section considers the provisions of Schedule 7A to the Companies Act 1985 (Schedule 8 to SI 2008/410) in two parts: first the information that is not subject to audit and second the information that is subject to audit, which was mainly derived from the requirements of the Listing Rules, but with some changes – notably on pensions disclosure.

**5.126** The introductory part of Schedule 7A of the Companies Act 1985 (Schedule 8 to SI 2008/410) merely states that the directors' remuneration report shall show the information specified in the Schedule and that information required to be shown in the report for, or in respect of, a particular person shall be shown in the report in a manner that links the information to that person identified by name. [CA85 7A Sch 1; SI 2008/410 8 Sch 1].

**5.127** The information not subject to audit covers:

■ Consideration by the directors of matters relating to directors' remuneration.

■ A statement of policy on directors' remuneration.

■ Statement of consideration of conditions elsewhere in the company and group.

■ Performance graph.

■ Service contracts.

■ Compensation for past directors (explanation for awards).

There is also some discussion on the interaction between the Combined Code and the remuneration report at the end of this section.

**5.128**   The information that is subject to audit covers:

■   Individual directors' emoluments and compensation.

■   Share options.

■   Long-term incentive schemes.

■   Pensions.

■   Excess retirement benefits of directors and past directors.

■   Compensation for past directors (details of awards).

■   Sums paid to third parties in respect of directors' services.

**5.129**   Each of these above requirements is considered below and finally the approval and audit requirements are described.

**Information not subject to audit**

*Consideration by the directors of matters relating to directors' remuneration*

**5.130**   The Companies Act 1985 (SI 2008/410) requires that if a committee of a company's directors has considered matters relating to directors' remuneration for the year, the names of each of the directors on the committee must be given in the remuneration report. [CA85 7A Sch 2(1)(a); SI 2008/410 8 Sch 2(1)(a)].

**5.131**   An example of such disclosure is Table 5.12.

---

Table 5.12 – Disclosure of remuneration committee composition

National Grid plc – Annual report – 31 March 2008

**Remuneration Committee**

The Remuneration Committee members are John Allan, Ken Harvey, Stephen Pettit and George Rose. Each of these Non-executive Directors is regarded by the Board as independent and served throughout the year.

---

**5.132**   The name must be given of anyone (which may include a director who was not a member of the committee) who provided advice or services that materially assisted the committee in considering any matter relating to directors' remuneration. For anyone so named, who is not a director of the company, further information must be given as follows:

■ The nature of any other services that the person provided to the company during the year.

■ Whether the person was appointed by the committee.

[CA85 7A Sch 2(1)(b),(c); SI 2008/410 8 Sch 2(1)(b), (c)].

**5.132.1** This requirement is illustrated in the following examples.

**Example 1 – Report benchmarking remuneration**

The remuneration committee of a quoted company engaged an HR consultant to prepare a report benchmarking the remuneration of the company's directors against the remuneration of directors of comparable companies. Does this constitute material assistance for the purpose of disclosure under Schedule 7A of the Companies Act 1985 (Schedule 8 of SI 2008/410)?

This would be material assistance. The HR consultant prepared a report with the purpose of assisting the remuneration committee in their consideration of directors' remuneration by benchmarking against similar companies.

**Example 2 – Independent benchmarking survey**

A different HR consultant has prepared and published widely an independent benchmarking survey that the remuneration committee has used when considering whether the relative importance of performance-related and non-performance-related remuneration is appropriate. Would this constitute material assistance?

This would not be material assistance. The HR consultant prepared a report for the purposes of general publication, which the remuneration committee used to assist itself in its consideration of directors' remuneration. No assistance was given by the HR consultant to this remuneration committee.

**Example 3 – Preparation of performance graph**

A third HR consultant was engaged by the same remuneration committee to prepare the total shareholder return graph for inclusion in the directors' remuneration report. Would this constitute material assistance?

This would not be material assistance. The HR consultant is putting together a graph of factual information, all of which is publicly available, for the purposes of disclosure and not to assist the remuneration committee in its consideration of directors' remuneration.

**Example 4 – Auditors' review of remuneration report**

During the course of an audit, the auditors reviewed the directors' remuneration report and made some comments to the directors on the presentation and content of the remuneration report. Would this constitute material assistance?

This would not be material assistance. The review of the directors' remuneration report is undertaken by the auditor as part of the audit and does not assist the remuneration committee in its consideration of directors' remuneration.

**5.133** An example of disclosure that complies with this requirement is given in Table 5.13.

---

**Table 5.13 – Disclosure of advisors to the remuneration committee**

**BP plc – Annual Report – 31 December 2007**

**Advice**

Advice is provided to the committee by the company secretary's office, which is independent of executive management and reports to the chairman of the board. Mr Aronson, an independent consultant, is the committee's secretary and special adviser. Advice was also received from Mr Jackson, the company secretary.

The committee also appoints external advisers to provide specialist advice and services on particular remuneration matters. The independence of the advice is subject to annual review.

In 2007, the committee continued to engage Towers Perrin as its principal external adviser. Towers Perrin also provided limited ad-hoc remuneration and benefits advice to parts of the group, principally changes in employee share plans and some market information on pay structures.

Freshfields Bruckhaus Deringer provided legal advice on specific matters to the committee, as well as providing some legal advice to the group.

Ernst & Young reviewed the calculations on the financial-based targets that form the basis of the performance-related pay for executive directors, that is, the annual bonus and share element awards described on page 66, to ensure they met an independent, objective standard. They also provided audit, audit-related and taxation services for the group.

---

### *Statement of policy on directors' remuneration*

**5.134** The directors' remuneration report should contain a statement of the company's policy on directors' remuneration for the following year and for subsequent financial years. [CA85 7A Sch 3(1); SI 2008/410 8 Sch 3(1)]. For companies listed in the UK, the Listing Rules also require a statement of the company's policy on executive directors' remuneration. [LR 9.8.8R (1)]. The policy statement required under the Act should include:

■ For each director, a detailed summary of any performance conditions to which the director's entitlement to share options or long-term incentive awards is subject, together with an explanation as to why those performance conditions were chosen.

■ A summary of the methods to be used to assess whether the performance conditions are met and an explanation of why those methods have been chosen.

■ If any of the performance conditions involves comparison with factors external to the company, a summary of the factors to be used in the comparison. If any of the factors relates to the performance of another company, or of two or more companies, or of an index on which a company or companies are listed, the identity of the company or companies or of the index must be given.

- A description of, and explanation for, any significant amendment that is proposed to the terms and conditions of any entitlement of a director to share options or under a long-term incentive scheme.

- If there are no performance conditions attached to the entitlement of a director to share options or under a long-term incentive scheme, an explanation as to why that is the case.

[CA85 7A Sch 3(2); SI 2008/410 8 Sch 3(2)].

**5.135** The policy statement must, in respect of each director's terms and conditions relating to remuneration, explain the relative importance of the elements that are related to performance and those that are not. [CA85 7A Sch 3(3); SI 2008/410 8 Sch 3(3)].

**5.136** The Listing Rules also require an explanation and justification of any element of remuneration, other than basic salary, which is pensionable. [LR 9.8.8R (7)].

**5.136.1** In addition to the above disclosure required by the Act in respect of performance conditions and of any significant amendments to the terms of share options or long-term incentive schemes, the Listing Rules also require a statement of the company's policy on the granting of options or awards under its employees' share schemes and other long-term incentive schemes, explaining and justifying any departure from that policy in the period under review and any change in the policy from the preceding year. [LR 9.8.8R (10)].

**5.137** As detailed in paragraph 5.134, the 1985 Act (SI 2008/410) requires certain disclosures in respect of performance conditions to which the director's entitlement to share options or long-term incentive awards is subject. The Companies Act 1985 (SI 2008/410) does not distinguish between performance conditions and additional service conditions that have to be met before an award vests. This is considered in the example below.

**Example – Service conditions outstanding**

A quoted company is preparing a directors' remuneration report. A director has been awarded share options that vest if the company meets certain targets for the first three years of the scheme and he remains employed by the company for a further two years. Is the requirement for him to stay for the further two years a performance condition?

The Companies Act 1985 (SI 2008/410) does not distinguish between performance conditions and service conditions that must be met before an award under a share option scheme is exercisable or under an LTIP is receivable. Although it is possible to interpret the Acts to have a narrow definition of 'performance conditions', we believe that the intention of the Acts is that service conditions should be included within the umbrella of 'performance conditions'. This is consistent with both the company's perspective that during the period in which the director is fulfilling his service conditions, the company is receiving qualifying services. It is also consistent with IFRS 2 (FRS 20), 'Share-based payment', which recognises the charge to the profit and loss account for employee services received over the 'vesting period' which includes the performance and service periods.

Hence, given that the director is not entitled to exercise his share options unless he remains employed by the company for a period of five years, this would be a performance condition requiring disclosure under paragraph 3 of Schedule 7A to the Companies Act 1985 (para 3 of Schedule 8 to SI 2008/410).

**5.137.1** Further disclosure requirements in respect of share options are given in paragraph 5.170 onwards and in respect of long-term incentive schemes are given in paragraph 5.180 onwards.

**5.138** The policy statement must summarise and explain the company's policy on:

■ The duration of contracts with directors.

■ Notice periods and termination payments under such contracts.

[CA85 7A Sch 3(4); SI 2008/410 8 Sch 3(4)].

Further disclosure requirements in respect of service contracts are given in paragraph 5.149 onwards.

**5.139** The directors who are covered by the detailed requirements in paragraphs 5.134 to 5.135 above are those who are serving as directors at any time in the period from the end of the financial year to the date on which the directors' remuneration report is laid before the company in general meeting. [CA85 7A Sch 3(5); SI 2008/410 8 Sch 3(5)].

**5.140** An example of disclosure of long-term incentive awards, which have no performance conditions and the reasons for that is given in Table 5.15. An example of a note that deals with policy for service contracts and termination payments is given in Table 5.16.

---

**Table 5.15 – Explanation of reason for no performance conditions**

**EMI Group plc – Annual Report – 31 March 2003**

**Remuneration Report (extract)**

*Long-term incentive arrangements (extract)*

Mr Bandier was also granted a restricted share award under the SEIP of 662,500 shares. These shares will vest no earlier than 31 March 2006. The award was in lieu of additional base salary and is not, therefore, subject to performance requirements. The aim of the award was to bring Mr Bandier's basic annual remuneration into line with competitive practice in the US, where he is based, whilst aligning his interests more closely with those of the shareholders and providing him with a strong incentive to remain with the Group. No further awards of this nature are envisaged.

---

**Table 5.16 – Statement of policy for service contracts and termination payments**

**EMI Group plc – Annual Report – 31 March 2007**

**Directors' service contracts**

The Code recommends that notice or contract periods should be set at one year or less. It is the Group's policy to achieve that, where possible.

The Committee endorses the principle of mitigation of loss on early termination of a service contract and recognises the advantage of service contracts including an explicit calculation, subject to mitigation, of compensation payable upon early termination, other than for misconduct or in other circumstances justifying summary termination. The Committee's policy is that such compensation should generally be calculated by reference to base salary, annual bonus at target level and other benefits, including pension contributions, for the notice period or unexpired term of the service contract. The contract should also include an explicit obligation to mitigate and to offset earnings from alternative employment undertaken during the notice period or unexpired term of the contract against all or part of the compensation payment.

However, the Committee is conscious that fixed-term contracts of three or more years are common for senior executives in the global entertainment industry and such agreements often include no (or only a limited) obligation to mitigate. The Committee, therefore, considers that it is in the best interests of EMI and its shareholders to retain the flexibility to compete for top executive talent, where necessary, through the ability to offer contract terms in excess of one year. However, as an alternative, the Committee may agree compensation payments calculated without mitigation in order to limit contract terms or notice periods to one year.

*Group CEO and Group CFO — Eric Nicoli and Martin Stewart*
The service contracts of Mr Nicoli and Mr Stewart, dated 11 April 2003 and 5 January 2005, respectively, are terminable by the Company on one year's notice.

In the case of gross misconduct or other circumstances justifying summary dismissal, the Company may terminate their service contracts without payment of compensation. Termination by the Company in other circumstances, without the required notice being given, entitles the departing executive to compensation, calculated on:

- his then base annual salary (currently £788,000 pa for Mr Nicoli and £551,250 pa for Mr Stewart) for one year; plus,
- the value of retirement benefits and either the continued enjoyment of, or the value of, benefits in kind provided to him for one year (the accrued value of such retirement contributions and the benefits in kind would have been £471,695 for Mr Nicoli and £229,405 for Mr Stewart had either one of them been dismissed on 31 March 2007); plus,
- a sum in respect of lost annual bonus opportunity, being 50% of his maximum bonus for the period from the date of his departure to the end of the contractual notice period.

Their entitlement to such compensation is subject to both a duty to mitigate and, also, offset for any earnings which they derive from other employment during the unworked part of the notice period for which they have been compensated.

*Chairman and CEO EMI Music Publishing — Roger Faxon*
Mr Faxon was reappointed as a Director on 1 April 2006 and became Chairman and sole CEO of EMI Music Publishing on 6 March 2007. His employment agreement, which is effective as of 1 February 2005, allows EMI to terminate the contract at any time on 30 days' notice. If termination is for cause (as defined in the contract), no compensation is payable. If termination is without cause or Mr Faxon terminates the agreement for good reason (for example, breach by EMI), he is entitled to compensation based on one year's pay, as follows:

- continued payment of his base annual salary (currently US$1,7,00,000 pa) for one year; plus,
- continued provision of retirement benefits and the continued enjoyment of benefits in kind provided to him for one year (the annual value of such retirement contributions and the benefits in kind would have been US$914,884 had he been dismissed on 31 March 2007); plus,
- a lump sum equal to his target annual bonus opportunity for the next following financial year, being not less than 50% of his base salary in effect immediately prior to termination.

In the light of competitive music industry practice, and in recognition of Mr Faxon's agreement, when he was promoted to Group CFO on 2 February 2002, to reduce his basic contract term from two years to one year, there is no obligation on him to mitigate, or to offset against the compensation payment any earnings from alternative employment during the year following termination. However, the Company's obligation to continue to provide insurance benefits will cease to the extent that similar benefits are provided by another employer during the 12 months following termination.

**5.141**  To a large extent, the above requirements are drawn from the Combined Code 2006. The principles of the Combined Code that relate to directors' remuneration are described in an appendix to this chapter. Whilst the legal requirements above set out what must be disclosed, the Combined Code also contains best practice provisions for a range of issues including setting remuneration levels, awarding options and service contracts.

### Statement of consideration of conditions elsewhere in the company and group

**5.142**  Under the Companies Act 2006, there is a new requirement for quoted companies to report in their directors' remuneration report on how they have taken pay and employment conditions elsewhere in the group into account when determining directors' remuneration for the relevant financial year. [SI 2008/410 8 Sch 4]. This new requirement will only have to be included in reports for financial years beginning on or after 6th April 2009. An example of disclosure of consideration of conditions elsewhere in the group is given in Table 5.16.1.

---

**Table 5.16.1 Mitchells and Butlers — Annual report — 29th Spetember 2007**

**Remuneration report (extract)**

**Remuneration policy for Executive Directors (extract)**

In fixing remuneration, note will be taken of reward levels in the wider community and of the remuneration structure throughout the organisation.

**Basic salary (extract)**

Salary levels in the Group and in the wider employment market are also taken into account.

The proportion of the Group's basic salary bill attributable to the Executive Directors and other members of the Executive Committee was 0.8% (2006 0.8%).

The average basic salary of the Executive Directors, on the basis that no short-term bonus was paid during the year, was £419,250 (2006 £710,250) and the average per non-board employee was £13,686 (2006 £13,387); the ratio is therefore 1:31 (2006 1:53). The Board and the Remuneration

---

Committee do not have a policy on this ratio, but aim to reward all employees fairly according to the nature of their role, their performance and market forces.

In the year under review, the average base salary increase for members of the Executive Committee, which includes the Executive Directors was 3.4%, whereas the average increase for other employees, including retail staff and management, was 2.3%

*Performance graph*

**5.143** The directors' remuneration report is required to include a performance graph showing the total shareholder return for the company against an index.

**5.144** The detailed requirement is for a line graph to be presented that shows the total shareholder return for each of:

- A holding of shares of the company's equity share capital whose listing or admission to dealing has led to the company being defined as a quoted company (for definition see para 5.6.3 above).

- A hypothetical holding of shares made up of shares of the same kind and number as those by reference to which a broad based equity market index is calculated.

[CA85 7A Sch 4(1)(a); SI 2008/410 8 Sch 5(1)(a)].

**5.145** The name of the index selected for the purpose of the graph and the reason for selecting that index should be disclosed. [CA85 7A Sch 4(1)(b); SI 2008/410 8 Sch 5(1)(b)].

**5.146** The line graph should cover five financial years of which the last is the current financial year (that is, the year for which financial statements are being presented). However, if the company has been in existence for less than five years, a shorter period may be given comprising only the number of financial years completed since the company came into existence. For example, if the current financial year is the company's third, the graph would cover three financial years. [CA85 7A Sch 4(2), (3); SI 2008/410 8 Sch 5(2), (3)]. The situation where the company has been listed for less than five years, despite existing for longer is dealt with in paragraph 5.148.2 below. The situation where the index itself has existed for less than five years is considered in paragraph 5.148.4 below.

**5.147** Total shareholder return is calculated using a fair method that:

- Starts with the percentage change in the market price of the holding over the period.

- Makes the following assumptions as to reinvestment of income:

  (a) That any benefit in the form of shares of the same kind as those in the holding is added to the holding when that benefit becomes receivable.

    (b)    That any benefit in cash, and the value of any benefit not in cash and not falling into (a) above, is used when the benefit becomes receivable to purchase shares of the same kind as the existing holding at market price and that the notional shares so purchased are added to the existing holding at that time.

    (c)    'Benefit' in paragraphs (a) and (b) means any benefit (including dividends) receivable in respect of the holding from the company of whose share capital the holding forms part.

■ Makes the following assumptions as to the funding of liabilities:

    (a)    Where the holder has a liability to the company of whose share capital the holding forms part, shares are sold from the holding:

        (i)    immediately before the time by which the liability is due to be settled; and

        (ii)    they are sold in such numbers that, at the time of sale, the market price of the shares sold equals the amount of the liability in respect of the shares in the holding that are not sold.

    (b)    in paragraph (a) 'liability' means a liability in respect of any shares in the holding or from the exercise of a right attached to any of those shares.

[CA85 7A Sch 4 (4)-(8); SI 2008/410 8 Sch 5(4)-(8)].

■ Makes provision for any replacement of shares in the holding by shares of a different description.

The same method must be used for each of the holdings mentioned in paragraph 5.144.

[CA85 7A Sch 4 (4)-(8); SI 2008/410 8 Sch 5(4)-(8)].

**5.148**  In general there are a number of indices that are widely available and which show total returns. For example the UK Series of the FTSE Actuaries Share indices include Total Return indices. As noted in paragraph 5.145, the Companies Act 1985 (SI 2008/410) requires disclosure of the name of the index, therefore, it is not acceptable to use an index created by the company alone, although it may be possible to give some disclosure as additional information. This is considered in the example below.

**Example – Selection of index for total shareholder return graph**

A quoted company is preparing its directors' remuneration report and is selecting the index to use in the total shareholder return graph. Can the company 'create' an index of companies of a similar size and nature? If not, which index should it use?

Given the Companies Act's requirement for disclosure of the name of the index (see para 5.145 above), using an index created by the company alone is not acceptable.

   

There are a number of published indices for total shareholder return that are publicly available. These include indices that are industry-based, such as the TechMark index, as well as indices that are size-based, such as the FTSE 100.

We consider that when selecting an index, the directors should generally use an index of which the company is a constituent and that they use internally to measure the company's performance against its peers. The remuneration committee should consider a range of appropriate indices and, based on the relative merits of each, select the index that is, in their opinion, most appropriate.

However, we also consider that, if a company has also devised a more specific index for a peer group of companies, that it actually uses for the purpose of setting performance targets, a total return graph, plotting the company's performance against the performance of the peer group, could be given as additional information. The composition of the peer group, the basis of preparation of the graph and reasons for producing it, should be given.

**5.148.1**   A straightforward example of disclosure is given in Table 5.17 below. See also the example in Table 5.18, which gives the information required by the legislation, but compares the company's performance with three indices, each of which is relevant because each gives a different perspective on the group's performance

---

**Table 5.17 – Performance graph**

**Reuters Group Plc – Annual Report – 31 December 2007**

**Performance graph**

Reuters TSR for the five years to 31 December 2007 compared with the return achieved by the FTSE100 index of companies is shown below. As Reuters is a member of the FTSE100, the Committee believes it is the most appropriate market index for comparison.

The calculations assume the reinvestment of dividends.

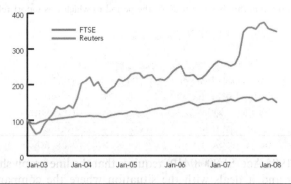

---

**Table 5.18 – Performance graph**

**Pearson Plc – Annual Report – 31 December 2007**

**Total shareholder return performance**

Below we set out Pearson's total shareholder return on three bases. Pearson is a constituent of all the indices shown.

First, we set out Pearson's total shareholder return performance relative to the FTSE All-Share index on an annual basis over the five-year period 2002 to 2007. We have chosen this index, and used it consistently in each report on directors' remuneration since 2002, on the basis that it is a recognisable reference point and an appropriate comparator for the majority of our investors.

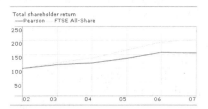

Secondly, to illustrate performance against our sector, we show Pearson's total shareholder return relative to the FTSE Media index over the same five-year period.

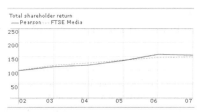

And thirdly, we show Pearson's total shareholder return relative to the FTSE All-Share and Media indices on a monthly basis over 2007, the period to which this report relates.

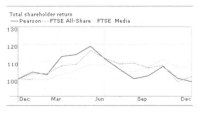

**5.148.2** The 1985 Act (SI 2008/410) requires that the line graph should cover five financial years and it deals with the situation where the company has been in existence for less than five years (see para 5.146 above). The situation where the company has existed for more than five years, but been listed for less than five years in considered in the example below.

**Example – Performance graph for company listed less than five years**

A quoted company is preparing its directors' remuneration report for the year ended 31 December 20X2. Paragraph 4 of Schedule 7A to the Companies Act 1985 (para 5 of Schedule 8 to SI 2008/410) requires the company to present, in the remuneration report, a line graph showing, for the previous five years and for each of the securities that results in the company being a quoted company, the Total Shareholder Return (TSR) for a holding of those shares and the TSR for a hypothetical holding of shares on a broad equity market index. The company listed in April 20X0 and, consequently, the TSR for the company cannot be calculated prior to that date. Is it acceptable to present the TSR graph only from the date of listing?

Within paragraph 4 of Schedule 7A to the Companies Act 1985 (para 5 of Schedule 8 to SI 2008/410), there is an exemption from presenting the full five year history when the company has been in existence for less than five years, but there is no similar exemption where the company has been listed for less than five years.

However, paragraph 4(4) of Schedule 7A to the Companies Act 1985 (para 5(4) of Schedule 8 to SI 2008/410) states that TSR is calculated taking as the starting point the percentage change in the market price over the period. As the shares have only been listed since April 2000 and, therefore, only have a listed market price since that date, we consider that the Act would require the company's TSR to be calculated taking the change in the period from April 20X0 to 31 December 20X0 as the starting point.

**5.148.3** Another situation where a company's total shareholder return may not be available for the five year period is where there has been a demerger. In Table 5.19. reference is made to how the company has chosen to overcome the complication caused by a demerger in the five year period.

---

**Table 5.19 – Performance graph**

**Peninsular and Oriental Steam Navigation Company – Annual Report and Accounts – 31 December 2002**

PERFORMANCE GRAPH

In line with the Regulations, the following graph compares the performance of the Company's deferred stock on a TSR basis for the past five years against the FTSE 350 Index. This index has been selected as P&O is a constituent of the FTSE 350 and uses this index for their comparator group for the Matching Plan. However, the line representing the FTSE 350 on the graph is based on the market index weighted by market capitalisation whereas the Matching Plan is based on the performance of the companies comprising the FTSE 350 at the commencement of the relevant performance period. TSR is shown as the value of £100 invested in P&O and in the FTSE 350 index over the five year period.

The demerger of P&O Princess Cruises occurred on 23 October 2000. There are a number of different accepted methodologies that are used to take account of such a demerger in assessing how much £100 invested in P&O at the beginning of 1998 would be worth at the end of 2002. Therefore two methods are shown on the performance graph:

- P&O's TSR including the TSR performance of P&O Princess Cruises; and
- P&O's TSR using data which has been adjusted to exclude the value attributable to P&O Princess Cruises by reference to the proportionate value of the two businesses at the demerger date.

---

TSR is calculated for each year relative to the base date of 1 January 1998 and taking the percentage change of the market price over the relevant period, reinvesting any dividends at the ex dividend date.

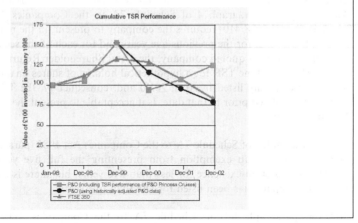

**5.148.4** The situation can also arise where the index being used has existed for less than five years. This is considered in the following example.

**Example – New index used for total shareholder return graph**

A quoted company is preparing its directors' remuneration report for the year ended 31 December 20X2 and is selecting the index to use in the total shareholder return graph. The remuneration committee consider that the most appropriate index to use would be a new index, but this has only existed since 20X1. The remuneration committee consider that the second most appropriate index would be the FTSE All Share index. The remuneration committee do not want to have to use the FTSE All Share index until 20X6 and then change to the new index and explain the change. What should they do?

As the information for the new index is not available for the full five year period, then to select this index would not comply with the Act's requirements.

The Companies Act 1985 (SI 2008/410) does not prohibit the presentation of two performance graphs: one showing a five year comparison against the FTSE All Share index and one showing a two year comparison with the new index. The remuneration committee can disclose both graphs and explain the reasoning, then in 20X6 when a five-year history for the new index is available, they can drop the disclosure of the FTSE index.

**5.148.5** In other examples, not reproduced here, several companies have given explanations of how their long-term incentive scheme criteria differ from the measure of performance provided by comparison with stock exchange indices and this provides useful additional information. Others, as in Table 5.19 above have given explanations of how significant changes in the composition of the group, such as mergers or demergers, have been dealt with. Where companies have been listed for only part of the five year period required, and thus a market price has not been available, the shorter period since listing has generally been used as explained in paragraph 5.148.2 above.

## Service contracts

**5.149** The remuneration report is required to contain details of the service contract or contract for services of each person who has served as a director at any time during the financial year. The details required to be disclosed are:

■ The date of the contract, the unexpired term and details of any notice periods.

■ Any provision for compensation payable on early termination of the contract.

■ Such details of other provisions in the contract as are necessary to enable shareholders to estimate the liability of the company in the event of early termination of the contract.

[CA85 7A Sch 5(1); SI 2008/410 8 Sch 6(1)].

**5.149.1** The requirement to disclose any provision for compensation payable on early termination of the contract refers to the contract's terms and includes 'golden parachute' provisions in service contracts, that is, where the directors receive a payment if they leave, for example, following a hostile take-over bid (see also para 5.149.2 below).

**5.149.2** In addition, a UK company that has securities carrying voting rights admitted to trading on a regulated market at the end of its financial year is required to disclose, in its directors' report, details of any agreement with employees (including directors) of the company providing for compensation for loss of office on the takeover of the company. [CA85 7 Sch 13(2)(k); SI 2008/410 7 Sch 13(2)(k)]. Disclosures in respect of contracts relating to takeovers are dealt with in chapter 3 of the Manual of Accounting — Management reports and governance.

**5.149.3** The above disclosure requirements in the Acts apply equally to executive and non-executive directors, because the Acts do not differentiate between the two roles that directors take within a quoted company. This is illustrated in the following example.

**Example – Details of contracts with non-executive directors**

A quoted company is preparing its directors' remuneration report. Paragraph 5 of Schedule 7A to the Companies Act 1985 (para 6 of Schedule 8 to SI 2008/410) requires the company to present, in the remuneration report, details of directors' service contracts. Is this just for the executive directors or should details of contracts with non-executive directors be disclosed as well?

As noted above, the disclosure requirements contained in Schedule 7A to the Companies Act 1985 (Schedule 8 to SI 2008/410) apply equally to executive and non-executive directors, because the Act does not differentiate between the two roles that directors take within a quoted company.

*Disclosure of directors' remuneration*

The requirement in paragraph 5 of Schedule 7A to the Companies Act 1985 (para 6 of Schedule 8 to SI 2008/410) surrounds the disclosure of certain, specified, details of each "*... contract of service or contract for services of each person who has served as a director of the company at any time during the relevant financial year ...*". [CA85 7A Sch 5(1); SI 2008/410 8 Sch 6(1)]. We consider that the term 'contract for services' encompasses all written agreements between a director and the company under which the director agrees to perform services for the company, regardless of the legal form that those agreements may take.

**5.150**  In addition, for companies listed in the UK, the Listing Rules require disclosure of:

- Details of any directors' service contract with a notice period in excess of one year or with provisions for pre-determined compensation on termination which exceeds one year's salary and benefits in kind, giving the reasons for such notice period.

- The unexpired term of any directors' service contract of a director proposed for election or re-election at the forthcoming annual general meeting and, if any director proposed for election or re-election does not have a directors' service contract, a statement to that effect.

[LR 9.8.8R (8), (9)].

**5.151**  An example of disclosure in respect of all the matters in the bullet points in paragraph 5.149 is given in Table 5.20 below.

---

**Table 5.20 – Details of service contracts**

**BG Group plc – Annual Report – 31 December 2007**

**Service contracts**

The Executive Directors' service contracts, including arranements for early termination, are carefully considered by the Committee and are designed to recruit, retain and motivate Directors of the quality required to manage the Company. The Committee considers that a rolling contract with a notice period of one year is appropriate.

In line with the Company's policy, the Executive Directors' service contracts contain change of control provisions. Should the Directors' employment be terminated within 12 months of a change of control, they are entitled to liquidated damages. The amount of liquidated damages is equal to one year's gross salary and a credit of one year's pensionable service (less any deductions the employer is required to make), which the Committee considers to be a genuine pre-estimate of loss. The Committee considers that these provisions assist with recruitment and retention and that their inclusion is therefore in the best interests of shareholders.

Other than change of control, the Executive Directors' service contracts do not contain provisions for compensation in the event of early termination. When calculating termination payments, the Committee takes into account a variety of factors, including individual and Company performance, the obligation for the Director to mitigate his or her own loss (for example, by gaining new employment) and the Directors' length of service. Further details of the Executive Directors' service contracts can be found on page 67.

---

**Non-Executive Directors (extract)**

The Board aims to recruit non-executive Directors of a high calibre, with broad commercial, international or other relevant experience. Non-executive Directors are appointed by the Board on the recommendation of the Nominations Committee. Their appointment is for an initial term of three years, subject to election by shareholders at the first AGM following their appointment. Upon the recommendation of the Nominations Committee, they are generally re-appointed for a second term of three years, subject to re-election by shareholders. There is no notice period and no provision for termination payments.

The terms of engagement of the non-executive Directors are set out in a letter of appointment.

**Directors' service contracts**

**Executive Directors**

Details of the service contracts of the Executive Directors who served during the year are set out below:

| | Contract date | Unexpired term | Notice period | Compensation payable upon early termination [a] |
|---|---|---|---|---|
| Ashley Almanza | 01 Aug 02 | rolling 1yr | 1yr | n/a |
| Frank Chapman | 14 Sep 00 | rolling 1yr | 1yr | n/a |
| William Friedrich [b] | 14 Sep 00 | rolling 1yr | 1yr | n/a |

[a] Other than the change of control provisions, the Executive Directors' service contracts do not contain provisions for compensation payable upon early termination.

[b] William Friedrich retired as a Director on 13 December 2007.

**Change of control**

As described on page 65, the Executive Directors' service contracts contain change of control provisions.

For the purposes of these provisions, a change of control is deemed to occur if the Company becomes a subsidiary of another company; or if 50% or more of the voting rights of the Company or the right to appoint or remove the majority of the Board of the Company become vested in any individual or body or group of individuals or bodies acting in concert; or if all or substantially all of the business, assets and undertakings of the Company become owned by any person, firm or company (other than a subsidiary or associated company). A change of control is also deemed to occur if the whole of the issued capital of BG Energy Holdings Limited or a substantial part of the undertaking of that company (including its subsidiaries) is transferred to another company, unless that transferee company is a subsidiary of the Company, or a company ultimately owned by substantially the same shareholders as are the ultimate owners of the Company.

However, a change of control does not occur if (and only if) through a process of reconstruction the Company becomes a subsidiary of another company owned by substantially the same shareholders as are the shareholders of the Company. The Executive Directors' service contracts provide that any payments made pursuant to these provisions will be made, less any deductions the employer is required to make. Any such payments shall be in full and final settlement of any claims the Executive Director may have against the employer or any associated company arising out of the termination of employment, except for any personal injury claim, any claim in respect of accrued pension rights, or statutory employment protection claims.

**Chairman and non-executive directors**

| | Date of letter of appointment or re-appointment | Unexpired term |
|---|---|---|
| Sir Robert Wilson [a] | 14 Dec 06 | 1yr 9mths |
| Peter Backhouse | 3 Jan 07 | 2yrs 2mths |
| Sir John Coles | 24 Jan 07 | 1yr 2mths |
| Paul Collins | 5 Feb 07 | 2yrs 2mths |
| Jürgen Dormann | 23 May 05 | 1yr 2mths |
| Baroness Hogg | 9 Feb 05 | 2mths |
| Dr John Hood [b] | 28 Apr 07 | 3yrs 2mths |
| Lord Sharman | 8 Jan 07 | 2yrs 2mths |
| Philippe Varin | 2 May 06 | 1yr 2mths |

The non-executive Directors' letters of appointment do not contain any notice period or provision for compensation in the event of early termination of their appointment.

[a] Sir Robert Wilson was re-appointed as Chairman with effect from 1 January 2007. This is subject to his re-election by shareholders at the 2009 AGM.
[b] The unexpired term is subject to election by shareholders at the 2008 AGM.

*Compensation for past directors*

**5.152**   The remuneration report must contain an explanation for any significant award made in the circumstances described in paragraph 14 of Schedule 7A to the 1985 Act (para 15 of Schedule 8 to SI 2008/410) to a past director, including, in particular, compensation for loss of office and pensions but excluding any sums shown separately in the table of individual directors' emoluments and compensation in accordance with the requirement of paragraph 6(1)(d) of Schedule 7A to the 1985 Act (para 7(1)(d) of Schedule 8 to SI 2008/410). [CA85 7A Sch 5(2); SI 2008/410 8 Sch 6(2)].

**5.153**   Paragraph 14 of Schedule 7A to the Companies Act 1985 (para 15 of Schedule 8 to SI 2008/410) contains a 'sweep-up' requirement to disclose any significant award to a past director that has not already been disclosed in the table of individual directors' emoluments and compensation (see below from para 5.209). This is disclosed in the 'auditable part' of the remuneration report. The requirement of paragraph 5(2) of Schedule 7A to the Companies Act 1985 (para 6(2) of Schedule 8 to SI 2008/410), which is outside the auditable part, is to give an explanation for any such payment.

**5.154**   The example in Table 5.21 below gives details of such a payment and the explanation (outcome of dispute in relation to employment which ceased in a previous year).

> **Table 5.21 – Outcome of dispute in relation to employment which ceased in a previous year**
>
> **United Utilities PLC – Report and Accounts – 31 March 1999**
>
> **Remuneration report (extract)**
>
> **Directors emoluments (extract)**
> During the year the company settled its dispute with Brian Staples, the previous Chief Executive, whose employment with the company terminated on 31 July 1997. The company paid £60,000 (plus VAT) towards Mr Staples' legal fees. Mr Staples was allowed to exercise options granted on 18 September 1995 to subscribe for 124,435 ordinary shares at an exercise price of 530.12p per ordinary share. All other options to subscribe for ordinary shares granted to him subsequently under the executive share option scheme and options granted to him under the employee sharesave scheme, lapsed. The mid market price of a share on the day of exercise was 895 pence. Mr Staples was reimbursed for previously incurred relocation expenses of £34,142 (inclusive of VAT) in accordance with the company's relocation policy. Pursuant to that policy, that amount was grossed up to take account of higher rate income tax payable by Mr Staples on receipt of that payment.

## Interaction between the Combined Code and the remuneration report

**5.155**  The Listing Rules require a listed company to comply with the Combined Code, or to explain any departures from it (see chapter 4). The Code recommends that where a company releases an executive director to serve as a non-executive director elsewhere, the remuneration report should include a statement as to whether or not the director will retain such earnings and, if so, what the remuneration is. [CC B.1.4].  Further details on the principles and provisions of the Combined Code that relate to directors' remuneration are set out in annex 1.

## [The next paragraph is 5.163.]

**Information subject to audit**

*Individual directors' emoluments and compensation*

**5.163**  Schedule 7A to the Companies Act 1985 (Schedule 8 to SI 2008/410) requirements for disclosure of individual directors' emoluments and compensation are similar to those contained in the Listing Rules. This section of the chapter deals mainly with the legal requirements for quoted companies, but also refers to the requirements of the Listing Rules where appropriate.

**5.164**  For quoted companies, the remuneration report is required to show, in tabular form, for each director of the company who served as such at any time in the financial year, each of the following:

- The total amount of salary and fees paid to or receivable by the director in respect of qualifying services (see para 5.33).

- The total amount of bonuses paid or receivable the amount of which is determined by reference to service or performance within a single year (see para 5.181).

- The total amounts paid by way of expenses allowance that are:

    (a)  chargeable to UK income tax, or would be if the person was an individual; and

    (b)  paid to or receivable by the director in respect of qualifying services.

- The total amount of:

    (a)  any compensation for loss of office paid to or receivable by the director (see para 5.168 below); and

    (b)  any other payments paid to or receivable by the director in connection with the termination of qualifying services.

- The total estimated value of any benefits received by the director otherwise than in cash (see para 5.166 below) that:

    (a)  do not fall within any of the bullet points above or which are not included in the other information required to be disclosed in the auditable part of the remuneration report in respect of share options and long-term incentive schemes;

    (b)  are emoluments of the director; and

    (c)  are received by the director in respect of qualifying services.

- The total of the sums mentioned in the bullet points above.

[CA85 7A Sch 6(1), 6(4); SI 2008/410 8 Sch 7(1), 7(4)].

**5.164.1**  In respect of comparative amounts, the Act states that *"the directors' remuneration report shall show, for each person who has served as a director of the company at any time during the relevant financial year, the amount that for the financial year preceding the relevant financial year is the total of the sums mentioned in paragraphs (a) to (e) of sub-paragraph (1)"*. Therefore, comparative amounts for the total referred to in the last bullet point above must be given for each director. [CA85 7A Sch 6(2); SI 2008/410 8 Sch 7(2)]. Comparatives for each component of the total are not required.

**5.164.2**  Comparatives are required in respect of each person who has served as a director of the company at any time during the *relevant financial year*. The relevant financial year means the financial year in respect of which the report is prepared. [CA85 7A Sch 1(1); SI 2008/410 8 Sch 1(1)]. Therefore, strictly the 1985 Act (SI 2008/410) does not require disclosure of the comparatives in respect of individual directors who retired last year. However, it is common practice for such disclosure to be made. It provides useful additional information for readers and it means that the figures in the directors' remuneration report can be reconciled to the aggregate figures disclosed in the notes to the financial statements under Schedule 6 to the Companies Act 1985 (Schedule 5 to SI 2008/410).

**5.165** For companies listed in the UK, the Listing Rules require disclosure of:

■ The amount of each element in the remuneration package for the period under review of each director by name, including, but not restricted to, basic salary and fees, the estimated money value of benefits in kind, annual bonuses, deferred bonuses, compensation for loss of office and payments for breach of contract or other termination payments.

■ The total remuneration for each director for the period under review and for the corresponding prior period.

■ Any significant payments made to former directors during the period under review.

[LR 9.8.8R (2)(a)-(c)].

**5.165.1** In addition, the Listing Rules require listed companies to disclose particulars of any arrangement under which a director has either waived or agreed to waive any future or current emoluments and details of such waivers. This applies in respect of emoluments from either the company or any of its subsidiaries. [LR 9.8.4R(5)]. An example of disclosure of waivers is given in Table 5.22 below.

---

**Table 5.22 – Disclosure of waivers**

**Saatchi & Saatchi Company PLC – Report and Accounts – 31 December 1993**

**Directors' and senior executives' emoluments (extract)**

In addition to the emoluments shown above, certain Directors were entitled to the following amounts which were waived. These waivers were without prejudice to any existing entitlements to pension contributions and to entitlements of those Directors to emoluments in the future.

| **WAIVERS BY EXECUTIVE DIRECTORS** | Year ended 31 Dec 1993 £ | Year ended 31 Dec 1992 £ |
|---|---|---|
| M. Saatchi (Chairman) | 312,500 | 312,500 |
| C. Saatchi | 290,064 | 312,500 |
| C.T. Scott | - | 83,355 |
| J.T. Sinclair | 70,000 | 70,000 |
| R.L.M. Louis-Dreyfus | 53,420 | 230,473 |
| | 725,984 | 1,008,828 |

In addition, M. Saatchi and J.T. Sinclair have agreed to waive a portion of their emoluments, £312,500 and £70,000 respectively, for the year to 31st December 1994.

---

**5.166** For quoted companies, separate disclosure of benefits by individual director is required. The nature of any element of each director's remuneration package that is not cash must also be stated. [CA85 7A Sch 6(3); SI 2008/410 8 Sch 7(3)]. However, the amount attributed to each non-cash element of a director's remuneration does not need to be disclosed. Further guidance on benefits is kind (applicable to all companies) is given in paragraph 5.42 onwards and in the example below.

**Example – Flexible benefits scheme**

A quoted company has a flexible benefits scheme, whereby a director may apply part of his/her salary in purchasing additional benefits, such as increased holiday or health cover. Assuming the director takes advantage of this and purchases, say, two weeks additional holiday, should the value of this be disclosed in the individual directors' remuneration table required by Schedule 7A to the Companies Act 1985 (Schedule 8 to SI 2008/410) as salary/fees or as benefits in kind?

We consider that in a case such as this the basic salary figures should not be adjusted (reduced). This is because the director is entitled to the basic salary and it is his/her option to apply it in purchasing whatever he/she wants. The fact that holiday/other benefits are purchased from the company rather than from some third party is not relevant. If, however, the additional benefits and reduction in base salary were imposed on the director (that is, it was not at his/her option) the amounts would be adjusted and the benefit included in the total of his/her benefits disclosed in the individual directors' remuneration table with the nature of the benefit also being disclosed. [CA85 7A Sch 6(1), 6(3); SI 2008/410 8 Sch 7(1), (3)].

**5.167** Where a director is appointed during the year, only the remuneration while he is a director of the company is disclosable as director's remuneration, as explained in the following example.

**Example – Employee appointed as director during year**

As noted above, quoted companies are required to disclose details of each element of the remuneration of each director by name and the total for each director. If a person has been an employee for part of the year and is then appointed a director during the year, should the figures disclosed for him include remuneration paid to him whilst he was an employee or should it just include remuneration paid to or receivable by him whilst a director?

Schedule 7A to the Companies Act 1985 (Schedule 8 to SI 2008/410) requires only the amounts paid to or receivable by the person in respect of 'qualifying services' to be disclosed. Qualifying services means services as a director of the company or whilst a director of the company, as a director of a subsidiary undertaking or as director of any other company of which he is a director as a result of the company's nomination (direct or indirect) or otherwise in connection with the management of the affairs of the company or any such subsidiary or other undertaking. Therefore, only the remuneration while he is a director of the company is disclosable as director's remuneration.

Note that for companies reporting under IFRS, additional disclosure for the whole period may be necessary. IAS 24 requires disclosure of remuneration (in total and split into five categories) for key management personnel in respect of services provided to the entity. In this context we consider that the services provided to the entity means services while the person is a member of key management personnel. Where a director fell into the key management classification prior to appointment as a director, remuneration for the whole period under review should be given in the aggregate IAS 24 disclosure.

**5.167.1**  In some situations, directors are remunerated in a currency that differs from the company's presentation currency. This is considered in the following example.

**Example – Director paid in foreign currency**

A quoted company is preparing its remuneration report. Although most of the directors are UK resident and are paid by the company in pounds sterling (which is both the company's functional and presentation currency), one of its directors is resident in the United States and is paid by the UK company in US dollars. Should his emoluments be disclosed in US dollars or pounds?

Paragraph 6 of Schedule 7A to the Companies Act 1985 (para 7 of Schedule 8 to SI 2008/410) requires disclosure of a table disclosing the emoluments paid to or receivable by each director in respect of qualifying services. The legislation is silent as to the currency in which the directors' remuneration should be denominated.

We consider, however, that it would be misleading and confusing to users of the remuneration report to denominate different directors' emoluments in different currencies, as it hinders the comparability of the information. We consider, therefore, that the directors' remuneration should all be disclosed in the company's presentation currency and that, where this results in translation of directors' remuneration, the exchange rate used for that translation should be disclosed.

This enables users of the remuneration report to make meaningful comparisons of the directors' remuneration packages whilst fully understanding their nature.

**5.168**  As noted in paragraph 5.164 above, quoted companies are required to disclose for each director the total amount of compensation for loss of office paid to or receivable by the director and any other amounts paid or receivable in connection with the termination of qualifying services. This disclosure is required to be given in the table of directors' emoluments. The amount that should be disclosed when the compensation is conditional on uncertain future events is considered in the example below. Further guidance on compensation for loss of office (applicable to all companies) is given in paragraph 5.97 onwards. There is a further 'sweep-up' requirement for quoted companies, which is discussed in paragraph 5.209 onwards.

**Example – Compensation contingent on uncertain future events**

A director of a quoted company resigned during the year. Contractually, he is entitled to receive compensation for loss of office of one year's annual salary in twelve equal monthly instalments during the year post-resignation. If at any point during the twelve months immediately following his resignation he secures alternative employment on the same (or higher) salary, payments to the director will cease, but there are no provisions for the company to claw-back any payments already made to him pursuant to this arrangement.

The company's year end is 31 December, the director resigned on 31 August and the directors' remuneration report is signed on 28 February. The monthly instalment is £10,000. The company has recognised the full £120,000 as an expense in the profit and loss account for the period, as it considers it probable that the full amount will become payable.

What should be included as the director's compensation for loss of office in the annual report in the year in which he resigns?

Paragraph 6 of Schedule 7A to the Companies Act 1985 (para 7 of Schedule 8 to SI 2008/ 410) requires disclosure of compensation for loss of office, which is defined in terms of amount paid to or receivable by a director in connection with loss of office.

Of the full £120,000 that the director may be entitled to, £40,000 has been paid at the year end. Consequently, £40,000 meets the definition of compensation for loss of office and must be disclosed as compensation for loss of office.

Although the remaining £80,000 is not technically receivable by the director at the year end, our view is that it is to be paid to him in the future as part of his compensation for leaving office and should also be included in the remuneration table as compensation for loss of office, taking the total to £120,000. This is consistent with the accounting treatment. Disclosure should be made in a footnote to the table (that the amount in the table should be cross-referred to) of full details of the contingency, to draw readers' attention to the fact that an element of the amount disclosed may not become payable. The 'full details' in the footnote should include the nature of the contingency, the amount that was paid during the year (£40,000) and the amount that was paid between the year end and the date of signing of the remuneration report (£20,000).

An alternative view, which is also acceptable and compliant with the Companies Act 1985 (SI 2008/410), is to include only the £40,000 that technically meets the definition of compensation for loss of office in the emoluments table prepared in accordance with paragraph 6 of Schedule 7A to the Companies Act 1985 (para 7 of Schedule 8 to SI 2008/ 410). Full disclosure must be made in a footnote to the table (that the amount in the table should be cross-referred to) of full details of the arrangements to draw readers' attention to the fact that the total compensation payable may be higher. The 'full details' in the footnote should note that the amount included in the table is only that which was paid during the year, disclose the maximum that could become payable (an additional £80,000) and the amount that was paid between the end of the year and the date of signing of the remuneration report (£20,000). In the following year, the director may be omitted from the tabular disclosures required by paragraph 6 (see para 5.164.2), but all amounts paid to or receivable by him will meet the definition of an 'award to a former director' and will be required to be disclosed in the remuneration report (albeit outside the table) by paragraph 14 of Schedule 7A to the Companies Act 1985 (para 15 of Schedule 8 to SI 2008/410).

Under either option, there will be a 'payment to a former director' in the subsequent year, which must be disclosed in accordance with the Listing Rules (see para 5.165). [LR 9.8.8 R (2)(c)].

**5.169**   An example is given below of the sort of presentation that may be given to comply with the legislation. In Table 5.23 details are given by individual director of salaries/fees, bonuses, compensation for loss of office, expense allowances, benefits and totals.

**Table 5.23 – Table showing directors' emoluments**

**Reuters Group PLC – Annual Report – 31 December 2007**

**Directors' remuneration for 2007 (audited)**

The disclosures required by Part 3 of schedule 7A to the Companies Act 1985 ('the auditable part') are contained within the following sections of the Remuneration report.

| | Salary/Fees £000 | Bonus £000 | Benefits[1] £000 | Allowance[2&5] £000 | Compensation for Loss of Office £000 | 2007 Total £000 | 2006 Total £000 |
|---|---|---|---|---|---|---|---|
| Niall FitzGerald, KBE[3&4] | 525 | – | 3 | – | – | **528** | 503 |
| Lawton Fitt[6] | 69 | – | – | 30 | – | **99** | 88 |
| Penny Hughes[7] | 54 | – | – | 10 | – | **64** | 50 |
| Ed Kozel[16] | 17 | – | – | 10 | – | **27** | 85 |
| Sir Deryck Maughan[7] | 54 | – | – | 25 | – | **79** | 70 |
| Nandan Nilekani[8] | 55 | – | – | 25 | – | **80** | – |
| Ken Olisa[8] | 55 | – | – | 10 | – | **65** | 50 |
| Dick Olver[9] | 67 | – | – | 10 | – | **77** | 68 |
| Ian Strachan[10] | 64 | – | – | 10 | – | **74** | 60 |
| Tom Glocer[11&15] | 888 | 1,267 | 451 | – | – | **2,606** | 2,265 |
| David Grigson[12] | 482 | 579 | 13 | 80 | – | **1,154** | 1,087 |
| Devin Wenig[13] | 448 | 532 | 43 | 10 | – | **1,033** | 1,001 |
| Total emoluments of directors[14] | 2,778 | 2,378 | 510 | 220 | – | **5,886** | 5,327 |

Notes:

All amounts have been rounded up to the nearest thousand.

The following conversion rates were used: US$2: £1, Swiss Franc 2.4: £1, Hong Kong $15.59: £1. These were the average rates in effect during 2007.

[1] Items included under Benefits are those provided as goods and services received during the year.

[2] Items included under Allowances are contractual benefits, which are paid in cash rather than as goods and services during the year.

[3] Non-cash benefits received by Niall FitzGerald consist of chauffeur benefits of £2,661.

[4] Niall FitzGerald has waived his £10,000 Nominations Committee chairman fee.

[5] Allowances paid to Lawton Fitt, Penny Hughes, Ed Kozel, Deryck Maughan, Nandan Nilekani, Ken Olisa, Dick Olver and Ian Strachan represent travel allowances to attend overseas board meetings.

[6] Fees paid to Lawton Fitt include £18,333 in respect of her position as Chairman of the Audit Committee.

[7] Fees paid to Penny Hughes and Deryck Maughan include £3,333 each as members of the Remuneration Committee.

[8] Fees paid to Nandan Nilekani and Ken Olisa include £5,000 each as members of the Audit Committee.

[9] Fees paid to Dick Olver include £5,000 in respect of his position as member of the Audit Committee, and £11,667 in respect of his position as the Senior Independent Director. Dick Olver was over-paid in error by the company in 2007 by £8,351 and the amount was repaid after year end.

[10] Fees paid to Ian Strachan include £13,333 in respect of his position as Chairman of the Remuneration Committee.

[11] Non-cash benefits received by Tom Glocer included accommodation costs of £268,143, tax services of £109,681 (including those related to the Thomson transaction), company car and

healthcare benefits totalling £36,210, long-term disability insurance of £2,100, and family travel of £34,473.

[12] Non-cash benefits received by David Grigson included healthcare benefits of £1,311 and long-term disability insurance of £1,300, tax services of £3,231 and a car benefit of £6,425. Cash allowances consisted of an annual car allowance of £7,420, of which £3,188 was repaid after year end in lieu of his car benefit and a retirement allowance of £74,930.

[13] Non-cash benefits received by Devin Wenig consisted of healthcare benefits of £36,323 and tax services of £6,081. Cash allowances consisted of a car allowance of £9,600. Devin Wenig's salary is paid in US dollars and the total amount reflected in the table is contractually split between his role as executive director and Chief Operating Officer.

[14] The total aggregate emoluments for the directors for the period 1 January 2007 to 31 December 2007 were £5.9m. The total emoluments for 2006 were £5.3m.

[15] During the year a group company paid certain personal expenses on behalf of Tom Glocer. The amount due from Tom Glocer at 31 December 2007, which was the maximum outstanding during the year, was £1,435. No interest was charged. Tom Glocer repaid the amount as soon as he was informed that any personal expenses had been borne by the company.

[16] Ed Kozel resigned as a director on 27 April 2007.

## Share options

**5.170**  The remuneration report must contain details, by individual director, of share options granted in respect of qualifying services. The information in (a) to (d) below should be in tabular form, but may be aggregated to avoid excessively lengthy reports (see para 5.174). [CA85 7A Sch 7(1)-(3); SI 2008/410 8 Sch 8(1)-(3)]. The Listing Rules require disclosure of information on share options, including SAYE options, for each director by name in accordance with the requirements of Schedule 7A to the Companies Act 1985 (Schedule 8 to SI 2008/410). [LR 9.8.8R (2)(d)].

**5.170.1**  The information to be given (in tabular form for (a) to (d) below) for each director who served as such at any time in the financial year is:

(a)  Number of shares subject to a share option at the beginning of the financial year or, if later, at the date of appointment as a director (differentiating between options having different terms and conditions).

(b)  Number of shares at the end of the financial year or, if earlier, at the date of ceasing to be a director (differentiating between options having different terms and conditions).

(c)  Details of options awarded, options exercised, options expiring unexercised and options whose terms and conditions have been varied in the financial year.

(d)  For each share option that is unexpired at any time in the financial year:

(i)  The price paid, if any, for its award.

(ii)  The exercise price.

(iii)  The date from which the option may be exercised.

(iv)  The date on which the option expires.

(e)    A description of any variation made in the year to the terms and conditions of a share option.

(f)    A summary of any performance criteria on which the award or exercise of an option is conditional and a description of any variation in such performance criteria made in the year.

(g)    For each option that has been exercised in the financial year, the market price of the shares in relation to which the option was exercised, at the date of exercise (see also para 5.48 above).

(h)    For each option that is unexpired at the end of the financial year:

(i)    The market price of the related shares at the end of that year.

(ii)   The highest and lowest market prices of the related shares in that year.

[CA85 7A Sch 7, 8; SI 2008/410 8 Sch 8, 9].

**5.171**    The following examples illustrate some of the disclosure requirements above. The examples are extracts only and, therefore, may not meet all of the above requirements, as information on, for example, performance conditions may have been included elsewhere in the remuneration report. In Table 5.24 options are disclosed at the beginning and end of the year together with options granted and exercised.

---

**Table 5.24 – Share options**

**Galliford Try plc – Annual Report & Accounts – 30 June 2001**

**6 Directors' remuneration and interests in share schemes continued**

The directors' holdings of options over ordinary shares were as follows

| | Date of grant | At 1.7.00 | Granted in year | Exercised in year | At 30.6.01 | Exercisable from | Exercisable to | Exercise price |
|---|---|---|---|---|---|---|---|---|
| **D M Calverley** | | | | | | | | |
| Executive | 31.3.94* | 567,214 | - | - | 567,214 | 01.04.97 | 31.03.04 | 17.63p |
| Executive | 3.4.95* | 450,000 | - | - | 450,000 | 04.04.98 | 03.04.05 | 12.0p |
| Executive | 24.10.95* | 1,442,250 | - | - | 1,442,250 | 25.10.98 | 24.10.05 | 6.67p |
| SAYE | 1.6.1 | - | 47,393 | - | 47,393 | 01.06.06 | 30.11.06 | 23.5p |
| **Total** | | **2,459,464** | **47,393** | **-** | **2,506,857** | | | |
| **G R Marsh** | | | | | | | | |
| Executive | 7.11.91 | 200,000 | - | - | 200,000 | 07.11.94 | 06.11.01 | 89.5p |
| Executive | 13.4.93 | 50,000 | - | - | 50,000 | 13.04.96 | 12.04.03 | 38.5p |
| SAYE | 1.6.96 | 8,842 | - | - | 8,842 | 01.06.01 | 30.11.01 | 19.0p |
| SAYE | 1.6.97 | 36,000 | - | 36,000 | - | 01.06.00 | 30.11.00 | 19.5p |
| SAYE | 1.6.99 | 6,988 | - | - | 6,988 | 01.06.02 | 30.11.02 | 17.0p |
| SAYE | 1.6.01 | - | 20,446 | - | 20,446 | 01.06.04 | 30.11.04 | 23.5p |
| **Total** | | **301,830** | **20,446** | **36,000** | **286,276** | | | |

---

*Disclosure of directors' remuneration*

| | | | | | | | | |
|---|---|---|---|---|---|---|---|---|
| **F E Nelson** | | | | | | | | |
| Executive | 3.9.91* | 158,820 | - | - | 158,820 | 04.09.94 | 03.09.01 | 28.33p |
| Executive | 27.4.93* | 158,820 | - | - | 158,820 | 28.04.96 | 27.04.03 | 20.77p |
| Executive | 18.10.94* | 150,000 | - | - | 150,000 | 19.10.97 | 18.10.04 | 16.0p |
| Executive | 24.10.95* | 375,000 | - | - | 375,000 | 25.10.98 | 24.10.05 | 6.67p |
| SAYE | 1.6.01 | - | 47,393 | - | 47,393 | 01.06.06 | 30.11.06 | 23.5p |
| | **Total** | **842,640** | **47,393** | **-** | **890,033** | | | |
| **C King** | | | | | | | | |
| SAYE | 1.6.98 | 80,232 | - | - | 80,232 | 01.06.03 | 30.11.03 | 21.5p |
| | **Total** | **80,232** | **-** | **-** | **80,232** | | | |
| **B K Luckett** | | | | | | | | |
| Executive | 2.9.91* | 27,793 | - | - | 27,793 | 03.09.94 | 02.09.01 | 28.33p |
| Executive | 27.4.93* | 15,882 | - | - | 15,882 | 28.04.96 | 27.04.03 | 20.77p |
| Executive | 18.10.94* | 15,000 | - | - | 15,000 | 19.10.97 | 18.10.04 | 16.0p |
| | **Total** | **58,675** | **-** | **-** | **58,675** | | | |
| **M A Noble** | | | | | | | | |
| SAYE | 1.6.97 | 53,076 | - | - | 53,076 | 01.06.02 | 30.11.02 | 19.5p |
| SAYE | 1.6.01 | - | 10.882 | - | 10.882 | 01.06.04 | 30.11.04 | 23.5p |
| | **Total** | **53,076** | **10,882** | **-** | **63,958** | | | |

\* Denotes option originally held over Try Group shares.

Following the merger of the Company with Try Group, outstanding options over shares in Try were replaced by an equivalent value option over shares in Galliford Try calculated on the merger basis of 1.5 Galliford Try shares for every 1 Try Group share. The market price of the Company's shares at 30 June 2001 was 34p and the range of market prices during the year was between 19.75p and 39.75p. G R Marsh exercised 36,000 SAYE options on 17 July 2000 when the market price was 23.75p. This resulted in a gain of £1,530. The options granted in September 1991 have lapsed.

Further details of the above schemes are given in the remuneration report on pages 27 and 28.

**5.172** In Table 5.25 details of performance conditions on which the exercise of options is conditional are given.

---

**Table 5.25 – Performance conditions**

**Manchester United PLC – Annual Report – 31 July 2001**

**Report on Directors' Remuneration (extract)**

Under the Executive Share Option Plan options over the Company 's shares may be granted each year to executive directors and senior managers, on a discretionary basis, at not less than the prevailing market price and subject to an overall maximum holding of four times remuneration. All options granted under the Plan are subject to performance conditions on exercise as determined annually by the Remuneration Committee. Options granted prior to 25 September 1998 may not be exercised unless the percentage growth in adjusted earnings per share over a period of not less than three consecutive years exceeds the percentage growth in the retail price index over such period by an average of at least 3 per cent per annum. In addition to the percentage growth in adjusted earnings per share condition, options granted after 25 September 1998 may not be exercised unless the Company 's Total Shareholder Return (defined as share price growth and net dividends paid) over a period of three consecutive years exceeds

# Disclosure of directors' remuneration

the Total Shareholder Return of a company placed in the median position of those companies in the FTSE Mid-250 at the start and still remaining in the FTSE Mid-250 at the end of the measurement period. Options must be held for three years before they are exercisable and lapse if not exercised within ten years from grant.

Under the Savings Related Share Option Scheme all Group employees are given an opportunity to acquire shares in the Company.

The details of each executive director 's interests in share options arising from the Executive Share Option Plan and the Savings Related Share Option Scheme are set out below:

| | | Number at 1 August 2000 | Granted | Exercised | Number at 31 July 2001 | Exercise Price £ | Date from which exercisable | Expiry date |
|---|---|---|---|---|---|---|---|---|
| P F Kenyon | (a) | 500,000 | - | – | **500,000** | 1.59 | 20.11.2000 | 20.11.2007 |
| P F Kenyon | (a) | – | 137,711 | – | **137,711** | 2.36 | 17.11.2003 | 17.11.2010 |
| D A Gill | (a) | 400,000 | – | – | **400,000** | 1.59 | 20.11.2000 | 20.11.2007 |
| D A Gill | (a) | – | 95,338 | – | **95,338** | 2.36 | 17.11.2003 | 17.11.2010 |
| D A Gill | (b) | 11,101 | – | – | **11,101** | 1.52 | 01.02.2005 | 01.08.2005 |

(a) Executive Share Option Plan

(b) Savings Related Share Option Scheme

The Remuneration Committee have confirmed that the performance condition in respect of the options exercisable from 20 November 2000 has been met.

No options lapsed during the Year. The market price of the shares at 31 July 2001 was £1.75 (2000 – £3.21) and the range during the year was £1.46 to £3.30.

**5.173** In Table 5.26 details are given of rebasing of share options as to volume and price terms. 324,000 options were rebased, which can be identified in the table as those with an exercise price (rebased) of 849p. Details of performance conditions are given elsewhere in the remuneration report.

**Table 5.26 – Rebasing of share options**

**SurfControl plc – Annual Report – 30 June 2001**

**Remuneration Report (extract)**

**Share options** The Group operated two share option schemes over the year that are referred to in note 18 to the financial statements. The Remuneration Committee determines the allocation of share options to both directors and employees subject to predetermined individual, product group, or corporate performance criteria that are usually based upon revenue targets. Share options are regarded as vital both to retain and motivate staff, and to more closely align their interests with those of shareholders. During the year options were granted under the Unapproved Schedule to the Company's 1998 Inland Revenue Approved Executive Share Option Scheme.

The following table shows the movement in interests in share options held by directors.

## Disclosure of directors' remuneration

| | Exercise price | Exercise period | 1 June 2000 (after rebasing) | Granted in the period (after rebasing) | Lapsed in period | Exercised in the period | 30 June 2001 |
|---|---|---|---|---|---|---|---|
| Rob Barrow | 434p | 30/11/00-29/11/09 | 150,000 | - | - | - | 150,000 |
| Rob Barrow | 849p | 14/6/01-13/6/10 | – | 80,000 | – | – | 80,000 |
| Rob Barrow – non-beneficial | 321p | 5/10/00-4/10/09 | – | 3,000 | (3,000) | – | – |
| Steve Purdham | 29.4p | 5/7/97-5/7/03 | 153,237 | – | | –(153,237)* | – |
| Steve Purdham | 331p | 15/7/00-15/7/09 | 150,000 | – | – | – | 150,000 |
| Steve Purdham | 434p | 30/11/00-29/11/09 | 150,000 | – | – | – | 150,000 |
| Steve Purdham | 849p | 14/6/01-13/6/10 | 160,000 | – | – | – | 160,000 |
| Steve Purdham – non-beneficial | 321p | 5/10/00-4/10/09 | 3,000 | – | – | – | 3,000 |
| Steve Purdham – non-beneficial | 849p | 14/6/01-13/6/10 | 3,200 | – | – | – | 3,200 |
| Shelagh Rogan | 238p | 30/4/00-29/4/09 | 102,000 | – | – | (85,000)* | 17,000 |
| Shelagh Rogan | 331p | 15/7/00-15/7/09 | 150,000 | – | – | – | 150,000 |
| Shelagh Rogan | 434p | 30/11/00-29/11/09 | 150,000 | – | – | – | 150,000 |
| Shelagh Rogan | 849p | 14/6/01-13/6/10 | 80,000 | – | – | – | 80,000 |
| George Hayter | 186p | 11/9/99-7/10/08 | 10,200 | – | – | (5,000)* | 5,200 |
| George Hayter | 849p | 9/2/01-8/2/01 | 800 | – | – | – | 800 |

*Exercised on 31 October 2000 when the market price was £17.75.

Gains made on exercise of options totalled £2,674,905 for Steve Purdham; £1,306,450 for Shelagh Rogan and £79,450 for George Hayter.

Included in the above table were 324,000 share options with exercise periods in the range of 9 February 2001 to 26 February 2011 that were rebased in volume and price terms on 4 May 2001. The number of options held by the then option holders was decreased by 20% and the original exercise price reset at £8.49 per ordinary share, being 20% above the closing middle market price on 4 May 2001. The market price of the Company's shares at the end of the financial period was £3.65 and the range was between £26.625 and £3.225.

**5.174** If disclosure of the details set out in paragraph 5.170.1 above would result in disclosure of excessive length, the disclosure may be summarised as follows:

- Information disclosed in relation to an individual director need not differentiate between options having different terms and conditions (para 5.170.1 (a) and (b) above).

- In respect of the disclosure of the price paid for the award and the exercise price of options that are unexpired at any time in the year (para 5.170.1 (d)(i) and (ii) above) and in respect of disclosure of the market price at the end of the year and the highest and lowest prices in the year for shares related to options unexpired at the end of the year (para 5.170.1 (h) above), share options may be aggregated and, instead of disclosing prices for each option, disclosure may be made of weighted average prices of aggregated share options.

- In respect of disclosure of dates from which options may be exercised or of dates of expiry of options that are unexpired at any time in the year (para 5.170.1 (d)(iii) and (iv) above) options may be aggregated and, instead of disclosing dates for each option, disclosure may be made of ranges of dates for aggregations of share options.

[CA85 7A Sch 9(1); SI 2008/410 8 Sch 10(1)].

**5.175** The relaxations in the last two bullet points above are, however, subject to the condition that options in relation to shares whose market price at the end of the year is below the option exercise price (out of the money options) may not be aggregated with options relating to shares whose market price at the end of the year is equal to or above the option exercise price (in the money options). [CA85 7A Sch 9(2); SI 2008/410 8 Sch 10(2)].

**5.176** The relaxations in the bullet points above do not apply in respect of options that have been awarded or exercised or had their terms and conditions varied in the year. [CA85 7A Sch 9(3); SI 2008/410 8 Sch 10(3)].

**5.177** The following examples illustrate aggregated disclosures as permitted by these provisions. In Table 5.27 aggregated disclosures are given for options, but the table shows separately options that are out of the money from those that are in the money.

*Disclosure of directors' remuneration*

---

**Table 5.27 – Separate disclosure for out of the money options**

**Marconi plc – Annual Report and Accounts – 31 March 2001**

**Remuneration Report (extract)**
(b) Options

The following table shows the interests of Directors in options over ordinary shares of 5 pence each in the Company:

| | At April 2000 | | Granted in year | | At 31 March 2001 | | Exercisable | |
|---|---|---|---|---|---|---|---|---|
| | No. | Average exercise price pence | No. | Exercise price pence | No. | Average exercise price pence | From | To |
| Lord Simpson | 1,407,159 | 311 | - | - | 1,407,159 | 311 | Dec 2000 | Sep 2003 |
| Lord Simpson | 1,543,408 | 801.5* | - | - | 1,543,408 | 801.5* | Nov 2002 | Nov 2009 |
| Mr J Donovan | 266,271 | 338 | - | - | 266,271 | 338 | Nov 1999 | Oct 2008 |
| Mr J Donovan | 335,681 | 844* | 198,084 | 787* | 533,729 | 823* | Nov 2002 | Nov 2010 |
| J C Mayo | 1,146,303 | 331.5 | - | - | 1,146,303 | 331.5 | Dec 2000 | Oct 2007 |
| J C Mayo | 1,739,279 | 730* | 104,828 | 787* | 1,844,107 | 733* | Jul 2001 | Nov 2010 |
| R I Meakin | 252,185 | 331.5 | - | - | 252,185 | 331.5 | Dec 2000 | Oct 2007 |
| R I Meakin | 599,110 | 801* | 57,274 | 787* | 656,384 | 800* | Jul 2001 | Nov 2010 |
| M W J Parton | 340,321 | 328 | - | - | 340,321 | 328 | Nov 1999 | Oct 2007 |
| M W J Parton | 1,036,896 | 680* | 79,374 | 777* | 1,116,270 | 687* | Jul 2001 | Nov 2010 |

* Exercise price exceeds market price as at 31 March 2001.

**Notes**

1. No options were exercised during the year to 31 March 2001.

2. The mid-market price of a Marconi share as at 31 March 2001 was 340 pence with a range during the year of 340 pence to 1250 pence.

3. The options set out above relate to those granted under the 1997 Executive Share Option Scheme, the Marconi 1999 Stock Option Plan, the Phantom Option Schemes, the Employee 1992 Savings-Related Share Option Scheme and the Marconi UK Sharesave Plan.

4. On 30 November 1999, each of the executive Directors was granted the right to receive 1,000 Marconi shares at nil cost under the Marconi Launch Share Plan.

5. The information provided above is a summary and full details of Directors' shareholdings and options are contained in the Company's Register of Directors' Interests.

**5.178**  It should be noted that there is a difference between the definition of share options required to be disclosed by quoted companies in the directors' remuneration report under Schedule 7A to the 1985 Act (Schedule 8 to SI 2008/410) and the definition of share options for the purposes of the requirement in Schedule 6 to the 1985 Act (Schedule 5 to SI 2008/410) for the disclosure of aggregate gains made on the exercise of share options. In Schedule 7A to the 1985 Act (Schedule 8 to SI 2008/410), share options are defined as options granted in respect of qualifying services of the person. [CA85 7A Sch 7(4); SI 2008/410 8 Sch 8(4)]. However, share options in Schedule 6 to the 1985 Act (Schedule 5 to SI 2008/410) are defined merely as rights to acquire shares (that is, it includes share options that are not in respect of qualifying services). [CA85 6 Sch 1(5); SI 2008/410 5 Sch 12(b)]. This is illustrated in the following example:

**Example – Definition of share options**

Three years ago, company A acquired 100 per cent of the share capital of company B from Mr C, a director of both companies. As part of the consideration, Mr C was granted options to subscribe for shares in company A at 25p per share. These options have recently been exercised at a time when the market price of company A's shares was 75p. Will the gain on exercising these options be disclosable as part of directors' emoluments in company A's financial statements?

Under paragraph 1(1)(b) of Schedule 6 to the Companies Act 1985 (para 1(1)(b) of Schedule 5 to SI 2008/410) disclosure is required of the aggregate amount of gains – being the difference between the market price of the shares on the day on which the options were exercised and the price actually paid – on the exercise of any right to acquire shares. However, in the case of a company that is not quoted (as defined in section 262(1) of the 1985 Act (section 385(2) of the 2006 Act)) or dealt in on AIM, only the number of directors who exercised options should be shown.

If company A is quoted, it seems that disclosure of the gains made by Mr C would be required. Under the provisions of Schedule 6 to the Companies Act 1985 (Schedule 5 to SI 2008/410), only aggregate disclosure would be required, so Mr C's gains could be combined with those of the other directors and a single figure disclosed. It is arguable that such disclosure does not belong in a note concerning directors' emoluments, as Mr C was granted the options only as consideration for the acquisition of company B. Indeed, each of the other requirements of paragraph 1 of Schedule 6 to the Companies Act 1985 (para 1 of Schedule 5 to SI 2008/410) (that is, other than the gains on the exercise of share options) refers specifically to 'qualifying services' and these options were not a reward for qualifying services. However, the fact that reference to qualifying services is not included in the requirement must be relevant. Hence, we consider that disclosure of Mr C's gains in the aggregate figure required by Schedule 6 to the Companies Act 1985 (Schedule 5 to SI 2008/410) would be appropriate.

There is a further disclosure requirement in Schedule 7A to the Companies Act 1985 (Schedule 8 to SI 2008/410) for quoted companies to disclose, in tabular form, by individual director, details of share options. In this case, however, paragraph 7(4) of Schedule 7A to the Companies Act 1985 (para 8(4) of Schedule 8 to SI 2008/410) specifically states that 'share option' (for the purpose of the Schedule 7A to the Companies Act 1985 (Schedule 8 to SI 2008/410) disclosures) means a share option granted in respect of qualifying services of a person. Therefore, as the options were not granted in respect of

Mr C's services to company A, the options do not require to be disclosed in the table of individual directors' share options.

**5.179** The examples below consider the disclosure requirements when share options are exercised by a director after retirement.

**Example 1 – Options exercised immediately after retirement**

A director of a quoted company (for definition see para 5.6.3) resigned during the year. He was allowed to retain and exercise his share options early and did so one day after resignation (but still during the year). He is the only director who has exercised options. At present the company has not included the director in the disclosure table of directors' individual interests in options required by Schedule 7A to the Companies Act 1985 (Schedule 8 to SI 2008/410), but has included a footnote with some but not all the information. For example, it has not disclosed the gain on exercise of the options. Should this be disclosed?

If the director had exercised his option whilst still a director then disclosure of the gain would be required by the 1985 Act (SI 2008/410) requirements for disclosure of aggregate gains made by directors on exercise of options. However, as he exercised them a day after resigning it is not caught by this requirement.

If the options were retained not as an entitlement of employment, but as part of compensation for leaving, they form part of the director's compensation for loss of office. The question arises generally as to whether if a director retains options on leaving the company, but exercises them in the following year, the gain needs to be disclosed. In that situation our view is that no disclosure is required, but there should have been full disclosure at the time of leaving (see example 2 below).

In this case, however, the early exercise of options is connected with the resignation and took place immediately afterwards. Therefore, we consider there should be disclosure of the exercise of the options in the compensation for loss of office note. This can be done by including the director in the individual directors' share options table which should cover directors during the year and not just those at the year end. Schedule 7A to the Companies Act 1985 (Schedule 8 to SI 2008/410) requires disclosure (in tabular form) in the directors' remuneration report of interests in options of each person who has served as a director at any time in the financial year. It requires, therefore, that the director is included in the table and the director's interest should be disclosed as at the date of his resignation. [CA85 7A Sch 7, 8; SI 2008/410 8 Sch 8, 9]. A note should then be added to say that the director was permitted to retain the options on resigning and that they have subsequently been exercised. In addition, we consider that the gain on exercise should be disclosed by way of a note. Schedule 7A to the 1985 Act (Schedule 8 to SI 2008/410) requires disclosure of compensation for loss of office not otherwise disclosed in the table of individual directors' emoluments. [CA85 7A Sch 14; SI 2008/410 8 Sch 15].

**Example 2 – Options exercised by former directors**

Two directors of a quoted company (for definition see para 5.6.3) retired in the previous financial year and, at the end of that year, the financial statements disclosed that they had retired and had been permitted to retain their share options, giving details as part of the disclosure on compensation for loss of office. In the course of this year, those former directors exercised their options. Does any disclosure have to be given under the Companies Act relating to directors' remuneration?

There is no Companies Act requirement to disclose the gains as the directors left before the end of the previous year. Schedule 7A to the 1985 Act (Schedule 8 to SI 2008/410) requires significant awards of compensation to former directors to be disclosed, but the exercise of share options after retirement is not the same as a payment or award made to the former director by the company. [CA85 7 Sch 14; SI 2008/410 8 Sch 15]. Therefore, there does not appear to be any requirement in the Acts to disclose anything this year (given full disclosure of the retained options in last year's financial statements), but the company could disclose, if it wished, in the spirit of 'full disclosure'.

## Long-term incentive schemes

**5.180**  A long-term incentive scheme is defined under the Companies Act 1985 (SI 2008/410) as *"…any agreement or arrangement under which money or other assets may become receivable by a person and which includes one or more qualifying conditions with respect to service or performance that cannot be fulfilled within a single financial year".* [CA85 7A Sch 10(5); SI 2008/410 8 Sch 11(5)].

**5.181**  A long-term incentive scheme does not include bonuses the amount of which fall to be determined by reference to service or performance within a single financial year. [CA85 7A Sch 10(5); SI 2008/410 8 Sch 11(5)]. A feature of many bonus arrangements is that a bonus is payable after the end of the financial year and only if the director is in office at the payment date. In such circumstances we consider that under the 1985 Act (SI 2008/410) the bonus may fall within the definition of a long-term incentive scheme.

### Example – Bonuses paid after the end of the period

A company calculates its directors' bonuses by reference to the company's results for the year ended 31 December 20X5. However, under the terms of the bonus scheme, the bonuses are paid on 28 February 20X6. If the director is not in office at 28 February 20X6, entitlement to the bonus is forfeited.

We consider that the amount of the bonus is not calculated by reference to service or performance conditions that can be fulfilled within a single financial year. Instead it is calculated by reference to the company's performance for the financial year ended 31 December 20X5 and the directors' service for the fourteen month period to 28 February 20X6. Thus, we consider that the most appropriate disclosure of these bonuses is as long-term incentive schemes.

However, the definitions under the Listing Rules differ from those in the Act, which can impact on disclosure – see further the example in paragraph 5.188.1.

**5.182**  A long-term incentive scheme also does not include compensation for loss of office, payments for breach of contract and other termination payments. Nor does it include retirement benefits. [CA85 7A Sch 10(5); SI 2008/410 8 Sch 11(5)].

**5.183**   Bonuses and deferred bonuses and compensation for loss of office would instead be disclosed in the table of each director's emoluments and compensation (see para 5.164 above). Pensions and other retirement benefits would be separately disclosed (see para 5.193 onwards below).

**5.184**   The difference between a long-term incentive scheme and a deferred bonus may sometimes be difficult to determine. For example, if a three-year performance scheme is introduced whereby a director is entitled to an award if the performance of the company over the three years satisfies certain conditions, this is a long-term incentive scheme. This is because the award relates to a three year period and the conditions cannot be fulfilled within a single financial year.

**5.184.1**   The example below considers the disclosure requirements for a long-term incentive scheme where the performance conditions have been met, but the final award of shares is still subject to approval.

**Example – Share awards subject to approval**

A quoted company (for definition see para 5.6.3) operates a long-term incentive plan (LTIP) for directors based on performance conditions over a three year period. At the end of the current reporting period, the performance conditions have been met, but the final award of shares will not be approved until after the date of approval of the financial statements. What should be disclosed for directors' remuneration?

Paragraph 1(1)(c) of Schedule 6 to the Companies Act 1985 (para 1(1)(c) of Schedule 5 to SI 2008/410) requires separate disclosure of the aggregate of (i) the amount of money paid to or receivable by directors under long term incentive schemes in respect of qualifying services and (ii) the net value of assets (other than money and share options) received or receivable by directors under such schemes in respect of such services.

Therefore, the Schedule 6 to the Companies Act 1985 (Schedule 5 to SI 2008/410) disclosure will depend upon when the amounts were receivable (and can be quantified). The relevant amount would be measured as at the date the shares were receivable by the directors, that is, no longer contingent. If the award is subject to approval after the date of approval of the financial statements, the amounts would be contingent at that date and would, therefore, not be disclosed as finally awarded until the following year.

The LTIP awards are not included in the table showing directors' individual emoluments, as Schedule 7A to the Companies Act 1985 (Schedule 8 to SI 2008/410) requires separate disclosure (in tabular form) of details of any long-term incentive schemes (see para 5.189 below for the information to be disclosed).

This disclosure, required by Schedule 7A to the Companies Act 1985 (Schedule 8 to SI 2008/410), is similar to that in Listing Rule 9.8.8 R (3) (see para 5.189.2 below) and so compliance with the 1985 Act (SI 2008/410) will also cover the requirements of the Listing Rules. If the awards were not receivable at the year end (because they are still awaiting formal approval), then the shares will be included in the scheme interests at the end of the year. A note should, however, be included to indicate that the performance conditions have been met, but that the award is still subject to formal approval after the date of approval of the financial statements and, therefore, further details of the final determination of the award will be included in the following year.

**5.185** If, however, there is a scheme that lasts three years, but a director receives an award in each of those three years dependent on the performance of that year, this is a bonus. If the three years of bonus is only payable after the end of the three years it is a deferred bonus, but not a long-term incentive, because the conditions were satisfied by reference to performance in each of the three years, considered separately. However, if the three years of bonus, although earned by reference to each of the individual years is only payable if the director stays for the three years, this may fall within the definition of a long-term incentive scheme as there is then a service condition added that cannot be satisfied within one year (see also para 5.188.1 below).

**5.186** Sometimes a scheme may provide for a bonus payable in respect of the year, but where part of the bonus may be taken in shares, which have to be held for a further three years and are then supplemented by a further award of shares, dependent on cumulative performance over the three years. In this case, the whole of the initial bonus, whether reinvested in shares or not, is emoluments in year one because it is receivable in respect of that year, but the additional potential award may be treated as a long-term incentive.

**5.187** The remuneration report is required to disclose details of long–term incentives by individual director in tabular form (see para 5.189). [CA85 7A Sch 10(1)(3); SI 2008/410 8 Sch 11(1), (3)].

**5.188** Details of share options are not required to be included. This is because they are separately disclosed (see from para 5.149 above). [CA85 7A Sch 10(2); SI 2008/410 8 Sch 11(2)]. Sometimes in practice, awards of long-term incentives are received in the form of options with a nil exercise price. Thus, there may sometimes be a cross over between the disclosure of long-term incentives and the disclosure of share options. In such cases full details and a clear cross reference between information contained in each of the tables should be given.

**Example – Gain on exercise of nil cost options awarded under LTIP**

A quoted company (for definition see para 5.6.3) has had a long-term incentive scheme in operation for three years, whereby three years ago directors were awarded the right to receive a number of shares that would vary depending on the company's performance over three years. The scheme has always, to date, been disclosed and described as a long-term incentive scheme. This year the final awards were made and the shares vest with the directors. Normally the disclosures required would be the value of the shares awarded on the date they vested. However, it transpires that the form of the award is the grant of nil cost options exercisable from that date. As these are options, is the requirement of the Act to give the total gain on the exercise of options, calculated as at the date of exercise and not, as with long-term incentive schemes, as at the date of vesting?

In this case we consider that the substance of the scheme is a long-term incentive scheme and that there is no difference in reality between vesting the shares in the directors at a particular date and awarding them nil cost options exercisable from that date. For this reason we consider that the disclosures should be made as if the scheme were a long-term incentive scheme and not an option scheme. Thus the disclosures should be made, by individual director, of the value of the shares received on the vesting date. This is because the options are exercisable immediately so that it is the same as if an outright award of shares had been made on the same day. Details of the awards should be given in the table of individuals' interests in long-term incentive schemes required by paragraphs 10 and 11 of Schedule 7A to the Companies Act 1985 (paras 11 and 12 of Schedule 8 to SI 2008/410) and the resulting options should then also be disclosed in the table of share options required by paragraphs 7 and 8 of Schedule 7A to the Companies Act 1985 (paras 8 and 9 of Schedule 8 to SI 2008/410). There will need to be a note and cross reference to describe the situation so that it is clear to a reader of the remuneration report.

**5.188.1**   A further complication can arise as a result of different definitions in the 1985 Act (SI 2008/410) and in the Listing Rules. This is explained in the example below.

**Example – Deferred bonuses**

The directors of a quoted company (for definition see para 5.6.3) have met performance targets for this financial year and have been allocated shares as a bonus. The shares will vest with the directors unconditionally in three years' time if the directors are still with the company. How should such bonuses be disclosed in the annual report?

Under the 1985 Act (SI 2008/410) an arrangement conditional on fulfilment of one or more qualifying conditions with respect to service or performance that cannot be fulfilled in a single financial year is classed as a 'long-term incentive scheme'. Bonuses whose amount can be determined by reference to service or performance within a single financial year are disregarded for this purpose. [CA85 7A Sch 10(5); SI 2008/410 8 Sch 11(5)].

Although the amount is initially determined by reference to performance within a single year, this amount is only provisional. The final amount receivable (all or nothing in this case) depends on a further service condition. Therefore, the final amount of the bonus cannot be determined by performance or service within one year and so qualifies as a long-term incentive scheme under the 1985 Act (SI 2008/410). Therefore, the award should be treated as a long-term incentive and disclosed by individual director in tabular form in the directors' remuneration report required by the 1985 Act (SI 2008/410).

If, in practice, the service conditions were not observed such that a director would receive the shares whether or not he stayed with the company for three years, this would not be a long-term incentive scheme. If the service condition either does not exist or is not observed, the bonus would be treated as an amount to be disclosed in the table of individual directors' emoluments as a bonus under paragraph 6(1)(b) of Schedule 7A to the Companies Act 1985 (para 7(1)(b) of Schedule 8 to SI 2008/410).

Under the Listing Rules deferred bonuses are defined as *"any arrangement pursuant to the terms of which an employee or director may receive a bonus (including cash or any security) in respect of service and/or performance in a period not exceeding the length of the relevant financial year notwithstanding that the bonus may, subject only to the person remaining a director or employee of the group, be receivable by the person after the end of the period to which the award relates"*. This definition effectively requires the service period to be ignored and thus the bonus would be disclosed in the year as remuneration for the purpose of the Listing Rules.

There is, therefore, a difference between the disclosure under the legal requirements (as a long-term incentive) and the disclosure under the Listing Rules (as directors' emoluments for the year). We suggest that this is dealt with by excluding the amount from the detailed directors' remuneration table given under the Listing Rules, but including a note to that table to say that the amount is included in the long-term incentive scheme table given in accordance with the 1985 Act (SI 2008/410). The note to the detailed directors' remuneration table should also give the amount of the bonus by individual director and the total emoluments that would be disclosed under the Listing Rules, if the bonus were to be included in the table of emoluments required by the Listing Rules. The bonus should then be included in accordance with the 1985 Act (SI 2008/410) in the disclosure of directors' long-term incentive scheme interests.

In addition, for companies reporting under IFRS, there could be a further difference. Under IAS 24, long-term benefits include long-service, profit-sharing, bonuses and deferred compensation not payable wholly within 12 months of the end of the period. The 1985 Act (SI 2008/410) does not rigidly divide bonuses between amounts *payable* within a year of the period end and amounts payable thereafter as the IAS 24 definitions do, but rather divides them by reference to the *period of service to which they relate*. That is, the 1985 Act (SI 2008/410) divides them between the amounts payable in respect of the year and amounts not payable specifically in respect of the year.

**5.189**  For quoted companies, the information to be disclosed by individual director in tabular form is as follows:

■  Details of the scheme interests of each director at the beginning of the financial year or date of appointment as director, if later. For this purpose and for the purpose of the remaining disclosure requirements 'scheme interest' means an interest under a long-term incentive scheme whereby assets may become receivable in respect of the director's qualifying services. [CA85 7A Sch 10(4)(a), 11(1)(a); SI 2008/410 8 Sch 11(4)(a), 12(1)(a)].

■  Details of scheme interests awarded to each director during the financial year, including (if shares may become receivable) the number of shares, the market price of those shares at the date of award and details of performance conditions. [CA85 7A Sch 11(2),11(1)(b); SI 2008/410 8 Sch 12(2); 12(1)(b)].

■  Details of scheme interests of each director at the end of the financial year or on ceasing to be a director, if earlier. [CA85 7A Sch 11(1)(c); SI 2008/410 8 Sch 12(1)(c)].

■  For each scheme interest referred to above:

(i)  The end of the period over which the qualifying conditions for that interest have to be met (or the end of the last such period where there are different periods for different conditions).

(ii)  A description of any variation in the terms and conditions of the scheme interests in the year.

[CA85 7A Sch 11(1)(d); SI 2008/410 8 Sch 12(1)(d)].

■  For each scheme interest that has vested in the year:

(i)  the relevant details of any shares, that is the number of shares, the date on which the scheme interest was awarded, the market price of each of those shares when the scheme interest was awarded, the market price when the scheme interest vested and details of performance conditions;

(ii)   the amount of any money; and

(iii)  the value of any other assets;

that have become receivable in respect of the interest. [CA85 7A Sch 11(1)(e), 11(3); SI 2008/410 8 Sch 12(1)(e), 12(3)].

■  For the purpose of the disclosure in the last bullet point above a scheme interest vests at the earliest date when:

(i)   It has been ascertained that the qualifying conditions have been met.

(ii)  The nature and quantity of the assets receivable under the scheme in respect of the interest have been ascertained.

[CA85 7A Sch 10(4)(b); SI 2008/410 8 Sch 11(4)(b)]

**5.189.1**  It should be noted that there is a distinction between the disclosures required to be made by quoted companies and those by unquoted companies. Quoted companies have to disclose the amounts that *may* become receivable (the 'scheme interests') and also give information regarding performance conditions, so that the reader of the remuneration report can understand what will have to occur for the director to earn that amount. If the director earns the right to the award in the period (that is, it vests), this must also be disclosed. Unquoted companies only have to disclose the amount that is received or receivable by the director in the period (see para 5.27) — that is, the amount that the director has earned the right to (in other words, the amount that has vested).

**5.189.2**  For companies listed in the UK, the Listing Rules require disclosure of details of any long-term incentive schemes, other than share options (details of which are disclosed separately), including:

■  The interests of each director by name in the long-term incentive schemes at the start of the period under review.

■  Entitlements or awards granted and commitments made to each director under such schemes during the period, showing which crystallise either in the same year or subsequent years.

■  The money value and number of shares, cash payments or other benefits received by each director under such schemes during the period.

■  The interests of each director in the long-term incentive schemes at the end of the period.

[LR 9.8.8R (3) to (6)].

**5.190**  The example below considers the disclosure implications for long-term incentives where the incentive was awarded before appointment as a director.

**Example – LTIP awarded before appointment as a director**

A director of a quoted company (for definition see para 5.6.3) is appointed during the year. Immediately prior to being appointed a director, he had been awarded benefits under a long-term incentive plan (LTIP) and at the date of appointment and the year end date, the performance conditions remain unfulfilled.

(a) Does the director's interest in the LTIP need to be disclosed in the directors' remuneration report?

(b) If the award had been made a number of years ago and he had completed his performance criteria, but is required to remain in the company's employment for a further period, does this make any difference?

Paragraphs 10 and 11 of Schedule 7A to the Companies Act 1985 (paras 11 and 12 of Schedule 8 to SI 2008/410) require disclosure of each director's interests in LTIPs that are receivable *"in respect of qualifying services"*.

(a) Where a director is appointed during the period and has outstanding performance conditions in respect of an award made under an LTIP prior to his appointment, we consider that the award is receivable in respect of qualifying services, because he must perform those qualifying services in order to be entitled to receive that award. Consequently, disclosure of the interest in the LTIP is required in the directors' remuneration report.

(b) The 1985 Act (SI 2008/410) does not distinguish between performance conditions and service conditions (see para 5.137). Where a director is required to remain in the company's employment in order for an entitlement under an LTIP to vest, the company is receiving performance from that director over that extended period, so it would be included as a performance condition under the 1985 Act (SI 2008/410). Consequently, if the director is required to remain in employment after his date of appointment in order to become entitled to receive the award, then we would consider that the award is in respect of qualifying services and disclosure of the interest in the LTIP is required in the directors' remuneration report. However, an explanation could be given in a note of the circumstances, that is, that the performance conditions were satisfied before becoming a director and only the service condition remains to be satisfied.

**5.190.1** The example below summarises the disclosures required under the 1985 Act (SI 2008/410) in respect of performance conditions relating to awards that have not vested at the year end.

**Example – Disclosure of performance conditions**

A quoted company is preparing a directors' remuneration report. Several of the directors have awards that have been granted to them under the company's share option scheme and Long-Term Incentive Plan (LTIP), but which are yet to vest. Do the performance criteria upon which vesting depends need to be disclosed in the remuneration report?

Paragraph 3 of Schedule 7A to the Companies Act 1985 (para 3 of Schedule 8 to SI 2008/410) requires disclosure of a policy statement that explains the company's policy on directors' remuneration for the following financial year and for financial years subsequent to that. The policy statement should include a summary of performance criteria to which any entitlement under a share option scheme or LTIP is subject and an explanation as to why those performance criteria were chosen (see para 5.134).

Paragraph 8(e) of Schedule 7A to the Companies Act 1985 (para 9(e) of Schedule 8 to SI 2008/410) also requires a summary of performance criteria on which the award or exercise of a share option is conditional, including a description of any variation in the year, to be given (see para 5.170.1).

Paragraph 11(2) and 11(3) of Schedule 7A to the Companies Act 1985 (paras 12(2) and 12(3) of Schedule 8 to SI 2008/410) require disclosure of performance conditions in respect of scheme interests awarded in the year and scheme interests that been received or become receivable in the year respectively (see para 5.189).

An award under a share option scheme or an LTIP forms part of the director's remuneration in the year in which the share options are exercised or when the awards under the LTIP are received or receivable.

Consequently, if an award under either a share option scheme or an LTIP is outstanding at the year end, it will form part of the director's remuneration in the following or subsequent periods and the performance criteria on which vesting depends should be disclosed, together with an explanation as to why those performance criteria were chosen.

**5.191** Table 5.29 is an example of disclosure of performance conditions attaching to a scheme. In this case the performance condition is related to total shareholder return.

---

**Table 5.29 – Disclosure of performance conditions**

**WPP – Annual Report – 31 December 2007**

**Share plans (extract)**

Following the policy review in 2005, the committee continues to believe that share plans approved by share owners later that year remain appropriate in terms of grant levels, performance criteria and vesting schedules. None of WPP's share awards are pensionable and, other than the stock option awards, all will be satisfied out of one of the Company's ESOPs or WPP shares held in treasury.

**Renewed Leadership Equity Acquisition Plan (Renewed LEAP)**

2007 was the fourth year of operation for Renewed LEAP and awards were once again granted to the Group's key executives.

Under Renewed LEAP, which was approved by share owners in 2004, participants have to commit to acquire and retain WPP shares (investment shares) in order to have the opportunity to earn additional WPP shares (matching shares). The number of matching shares that a participant can receive at the end of the investment and performance period depends on the Company's TSR performance measured over five years (four years in the case of awards made in 2004).

Because relative TSR may not always reflect the true performance of the Company, the Compensation Committee is required to perform a 'fairness review' on the basis of which it may, in exceptional circumstances, decide to vary the number of matching shares that will vest. Factors the committee considers in its fairness review of any awards include, amongst others, various measures of the Group's financial performance (such as growth in revenues and in

---

earnings per share) and any evidence of distortions in the share price of either WPP or the peer group (such as bid price premia).

For awards made in respect of LEAP programs commencing in 2005, 2006 and 2007 the vesting schedule is as follows:

| Rank compared to peer group* | Number of matching shares |
| --- | --- |
| 1 | 5 |
| 2 | 5 |
| 3 | 4.5 |
| 4 | 3.5 |
| 5 | 2.5 |
| Median | 1.5 |
| Below median | 0 |

Notes
* For actual performance between these positions the match is calculated on a pro rata basis.

The comparator companies for the awards made in 2007 were: Aegis, Arbitron, Dentsu, Gfk, Havas, Interpublic, Ipsos, Omnicom, Publicis and Taylor Nelson Sofres.

**Vesting of the 2004-2007 LEAP Award**

For awards made in respect of the LEAP program commencing in 2004 the vesting schedule was as follows:

| Rank compared to peer group* | Number of matching shares |
| --- | --- |
| 1 | 4 |
| 2 | 4 |
| 3 | 3.6 |
| 4 | 2.8 |
| 5 | 2 |
| 6 | 1.6 |
| Median | 1.2 |
| Below median | 0 |

Notes
* For actual performance between these positions the match is calculated on a pro rata basis.

TSR results indicated a vesting level of 3.27 matching shares reflecting a ranking between third and fourth place against the peer group of 13 companies. The committee then undertook its fairness review, the purpose of which was to ensure that the TSR ranking accurately reflected the true underlying performance of the Company and took into account any exceptional circumstances deemed relevant by the committee.

The committee compared WPP's financial performance to that of the peer group. It was noted that over the investment and performance period, WPP ranked first on margin improvement, and between third and fifth on other key measures such as growth in EBITDA, EBITA, EPS and Revenue. The committee was therefore comfortable that the TSR ranking was consistent with WPP's relative competitive performance over the period.

However, the committee noted two exceptional circumstances that materially affected the TSR performance of WPP relative to that of its peers.

First, based on the advice of WPP's broker, the committee concluded that the ending share prices of two of WPP's comparator companies (Aegis and Ipsos) contained an element of 'bid premium'. The committee concluded that including these premia did not reflect the underlying performance of these companies and therefore adjusted the TSR data accordingly. Removing the

# Disclosure of directors' remuneration

bid premia had no effect on WPP's ranking, but increased the vesting percentage by moving its TSR closer to that of the company ranked above it.

Second, it was also noted that there had been relatively large currency swings over the performance period that dampened the TSR performance of comparator stocks denominated in US dollars or Japanese yen. The committee determined that this currency factor, which was outside management control, had materially affected WPP's relative TSR ranking and vesting percentage.

The fairness review took both of these factors into account, each of which had a different impact on the results. The committee's judgement was to make an overall net reduction of 0.67 in the number of matching shares vesting from 3.27 to 2.60. This implies a ranking between fourth and fifth place against the peer group of 13 companies; the committee felt this was a fair reflection of WPP's true relative underlying performance over the period in question. As a result the number of ordinary matching shares that actually vested (including additional shares from reinvested dividends) along with the number at median and maximum, are shown in the following table.

|  | Median** | Maximum** | Actual |
|---|---|---|---|
| Sir Martin Sorrell* | 1,238,899 | 4,129,664 | 2,823,786 |
| Paul Richardson | 37,168 | 123,892 | 84,715 |

Notes

* Sir Martin deferred receipt of the shares until November 2011.
** Not including additional shares from reinvested dividends.

## Renewed Leadership Equity Acquisition Plan[1]

| Name | Grant/award date | Share price on grant date | Performance period | Share units | At median level of performance | | | At maximum level of performance | | |
|---|---|---|---|---|---|---|---|---|---|---|
| | | | | | Number of matching units at 01.01.07 | Granted/(lapsed) units | Number of matching units at 31.12.07 | Number of matching units at 01.01.07 | Granted/(lapsed) units | Number of matching units at 31.12.07 |
| M Read | 15.12.05 | £6.175 | 01.01.05 — 31.12.09 | Ords | 15,255 | | 15,255 | 50,850 | | 50,850 |
| | 15.11.06 | £6.84 | 01.01.06 — 31.12.10 | Ords | 24,788 | | 24,788 | 82,625 | | 82,625 |
| | 11.12.07 | £6.23 | 01.01.07 — 31.12.11 | Ords | | 22,311 | 22,311 | | 74,370 | 74,370 |
| P W G Richardson | 28.10.04 | £5.535 | 01.01.04 — 31.12.07 | Ords | 37,168 | | 37,168 | 123,892 | | 123,892 |
| | 15.12.05 | £6.175 | 01.01.05 — 31.12.09 | Ords | 122,037 | | 122,037 | 406,790 | | 406,790 |
| | 15.11.06 | £6.84 | 01.01.06 — 31.12.10 | Ords | 99,153 | | 99,153 | 330,510 | | 330,510 |
| | 11.12.07 | £6.23 | 01.01.07 — 31.12.11 | Ords | | 89,246 | 89,246 | | 297,485 | 297,485 |
| Sir Martin Sorrell | 28.10.04 | £5.535 | 01.01.04 — 31.12.07 | Ords | 1,238,899 | | 1,238,899 | 4,129,664 | | 4,129,664 |
| | 15.12.05 | £6.175 | 01.01.05 — 31.12.09 | Ords | 305,091 | | 305,091 | 1,016,970 | | 1,016,970 |
| | 15.11.06 | £6.84 | 01.01.06 — 31.12.10 | Ords | 234,804 | | 234,804 | 782,680 | | 782,680 |
| | 11.12.07 | £6.23 | 01.01.07 — 31.12.11 | Ords | | 223,113 | 223,113 | | 743,710 | 743,710 |

Notes

[1] All awards shown in the above table, are dependent on WPP's TSR performance against a comparator group over the relevant performance period and maintenance of a participant's holding of Investment Shares and continued employment throughout the Investment Period. The comparator group for the awards made in 2004 comprises of Aegis, Arbitron, Dentsu, Digitas, Gfk, Grey Advertising, Havas Advertising, Interpublic, Ipsos, Omnicom Group, Publicis, Taylor Nelson Sofres, and VNU. The comparator group for the awards made in 2005 remained the same with the exception of the removal of Digitas and Grey Advertising. The comparator group for the awards made in 2006 and 2007 was the same as for the awards made in 2005 with the exception of the removal of VNU. Where a company delists during the performance period, the committee deems this to be a disposal and the proceeds are treated as being reinvested in an index that tracks the TSR of the remaining companies.

*Long-term incentive scheme for an individual*

**5.192**   Where the only participant of a long-term incentive scheme is a director (or a prospective director) and the arrangement is established specifically to facilitate, in unusual circumstances, the recruitment or retention of the relevant individual, disclosure of the following details are required to be given in the first annual report and accounts published by the company following the date on which the individual becomes eligible to participate in the arrangement:

■   The full text of the scheme or a description of its principal terms.

■   Details of trusteeship in the scheme or interest in the trustees, if any, of directors of the company.

■   A statement that the principal provisions of the scheme (set out in detail in rule 13.8.11R(3) of the Listing Rules) cannot be altered to the advantage of the participant without shareholders' approval.

■   A statement as to whether benefits under the scheme will be pensionable and if so the reasons for this.

■   The name of the sole participant.

■   The date on which he or she first became eligible to participate in the arrangement.

■   An explanation as to why the circumstances in which the arrangement was established were unusual.

■   The conditions to be satisfied under the arrangement's terms.

■   The maximum award(s) under the arrangement's terms, or, if there is no maximum, the basis on which the awards will be determined.

[LR 9.4.3R, 13.8.11R].

An example of disclosure is given in Table 5.31 below.

---

**Table 5.31 – Long-term incentive scheme for a single director**

**First Leisure Corporation PLC – Annual report and financial statements – 31 October 1997**

**Report of the Remuneration Committee (extract)**

(iv)   Senior executive long term incentive scheme

The Remuneration Committee approved the introduction of the senior executive long term incentive scheme as from 1st November 1994. The total potential bonus for each executive was fixed at the beginning of the scheme which covers the four financial years up to and including 1997/98. The maximum bonus payable in respect of each of the four years covered by the scheme increases evenly from 22% to 28% of the total potential bonus payable.

The scheme provides executives with the opportunity of earning significant cash bonuses if sustained real earnings per share growth and share price appreciation are achieved. In order to qualify for the maximum bonus in any year, the real growth in the Group's earnings per share and share price must exceed 6% over a maximum three year rolling period. Where

---

real growth is below 6% the maximum potential bonus is reduced on a sliding scale. Where real growth is below 1.2% no bonus is payable.

Each annual bonus is deferred for a minimum of two years, except for the final award which is deferred for a minimum of one year. Payment of the annual bonus is subject to the following further conditions:

- 25% of the annual bonus is contingent solely on the executive being in the Group's employment at the end of the minimum deferral period. This element of the bonus is accrued for in the year in which it is conditionally earned;

- the remaining 75% of the annual bonus is dependent upon an additional condition that there is a further increase in earnings per share over the deferral period. The maximum deferral period is unlimited. This element of the bonus is accrued for evenly over the minimum deferral period.

Currently, Mr Coles is the only scheme member. However, Mr Payne's service contract with the Company entitles him to receive bonuses equivalent to Mr Coles under the scheme, as though he was a scheme member.

For the annual awards in respect of the 1994/95 and 1995/96 financial years, the growth in earnings per share and share price were such that the maximum bonus in respect of these years will become payable if the further conditions relating to employment and further earnings per share growth are met. No annual award has been made in respect of the 1996/97 financial year since the required level of real growth in earnings per share and share price was not achieved. Accordingly, the total conditional interests of Mr Payne and Mr Coles, which relate to the 1994/95 and 1995/96 annual awards, are the same at the beginning and end of the year and amounted to £230,000 each.

The maximum average annual award payable to Mr Payne and Mr Coles over the life of the scheme is £125,000 each.

To date no amounts have been paid under the scheme to either Mr Coles or Mr Payne although the conditions attaching to the payment of the first 25% of 1994/95 have been satisfied and this amount is now payable. However, as regards the remaining 75% of the 1994/95 award, the required further increase in earnings per share was not achieved in 1996/97 and therefore this payment remains deferred.

Senior executive long term incentive scheme (1997)

The Remuneration Committee approved the introduction of the senior executive long term incentive scheme (1997) from 1st November 1997. Mr Grade is the sole participant. The terms and conditions to apply will reflect the advice received by the Remuneration Committee from independent remuneration consultants, and will be broadly the same as those described above except that the scheme will cover the four financial years from 1997/98 up to 2000/01 and the minimum real growth that must be achieved before an award can be made has been increased from 1.2% to 2%. The average maximum annual award payable under the scheme is £625,000.

As permitted by paragraph 13.13A of the Listing Rules, the scheme was not approved by shareholders in advance, since in establishing the scheme the Remuneration Committee considered that exceptional circumstances existed in that these arrangements needed to be put in place at the earliest opportunity to attract, motivate and retain the services of a senior executive of Mr Grade's calibre. For similar reasons the Remuneration Committee approved the grant of options to Mr Grade under the 1994 executive share option scheme set out on page 28.

*Pensions*

**5.193** The definitions of pension scheme, money purchase scheme, money purchase benefits and retirement benefits are the same under Schedule 7A to the 1985 Act (Schedule 8 to SI 2008/410) as they are for the purpose of the requirement to disclose total emoluments under Schedule 6 to the Companies Act 1985 (Schedule 5 to SI 2008/410). The definitions are described from paragraph 5.61 above.

**5.194** The disclosure requirements for money purchase schemes are to show, by individual director, the details of company contributions paid or payable in respect of the director for the year or paid by the company in the year in respect of another financial year. [CA85 7A Sch 12(3); SI 2008/410 8 Sch 13(3)]. This is similar to the requirement in the Listing Rules for disclosure of details of the contribution or allowance payable or made by the company in respect of each director during the period under review. [LR 9.8.8R (11)].

**5.195** 'Company contributions' means any payments (including insurance premiums) made, or treated as made, to the scheme in respect of the director by anyone other than the director, that is the term would include payments by parties other than the company in respect of the director. [CA85 7A Sch 16; SI 2008/410 8 Sch 17]. This definition is consistent with that given for the purpose of disclosure of aggregate contributions by all companies (see para 5.65 above). See further paragraph 5.202 for practical application of the rules.

**5.195.1** An example of disclosure of company contributions to money purchase schemes is given in Table 5.32.

---

**Table 5.32 – Money purchase pension schemes**

**Aggreko PLC – Annual Report – 31 December 2007**

**Pension Entitlements**

Executive Directors participate in defined contribution plans that are designed to be in line with the median practice in the relevant country. Executive Directors who reside in the United Kingdom and who joined the Board after 1 April 2002 also participate in a defined contribution plan.

| | Company contributions during 2007 £ | Company contributions during 2006 £ |
|---|---|---|
| R C Soames | 103,750 | 65,835 |
| G P Walker | 81,482 | 73,276 |
| K Pandya | 15,840 | 15,840 |

Mr R C Soames and Mr K Pandya are members of the Aggreko plc Group Personal Pension Plan. Mr Soames is entitled to a pension contribution from the Company of 25% of his basic salary and Mr Pandya is entitled to a Company contribution of 20%. Until 5 April 2006, any contributions in excess of the maximum set by the plan or HM Revenue & Customs were paid by cash compensation and are disclosed under the section headed 'Emoluments'; after this date

---

Directors were allowed to voluntarily opt to take part of their pension entitlement as cash compensation, any compensation taken being disclosed under Other Pay.

Mr G P Walker is entitled to participate in the Employees' Savings Investment Retirement plan and the Supplemental Executive Retirement plan of Aggreko LLC, which are governed by the laws of the United States. These plans allow contributions by the employee and the Group to be deferred for tax.

**5.196** The Schedule 7A to the Companies Act 1985 (Schedule 8 to SI 2008/410) disclosure requirements in respect of directors' rights under defined benefit schemes are to show, for each director of the company who has served as such at any time during the financial year, the following information:

- Changes in the director's accrued benefits during the year.

- Details of the director's accrued benefits at the end of the year.

- Transfer value of the director's accrued benefits at the end of the year, calculated in accordance with 'Retirement Benefit Schemes – Transfer Values (GN11)' published by the Institute of Actuaries and the Faculty of Actuaries and dated 6 April 2001.

- Transfer value of the director's accrued benefits, either at the end of the previous year as shown in the previous period's remuneration report or, if none was produced, as at the beginning of the financial year.

- The amount of the difference between the two transfer values disclosed in the previous two bullet points, less the amount of any contributions made to the scheme by the director during the year.

[CA85 7A Sch 12(1),(2); SI 2008/410 8 Sch 13(1), (2)].

**5.196.1** An example of disclosures required under Schedule 7A to the Companies Act 1985 (Schedule 8 to SI 2008/410) might be as follows:

| Director | Increase in accrued benefits | Accrued benefits at 31 December 2002 | Transfer value 31 December 2002 | Transfer value 31 December 2001 | Increase in transfer value less director's contributions |
|---|---|---|---|---|---|
| | £ | £ | £ | £ | £ |
| A Smith | 2,000 | 30,000 | 216,000 | 190,000 | 21,000 |
| B Jones | 10,000 | 150,000 | 1,500,000 | 1,360,000 | 137,000 |

See further paragraph 5.203 for practical application of the rules.

**5.197** For companies listed in the UK, the Listing Rule disclosure requirements in respect of directors' rights under defined benefit schemes are to show the following information:

- Details of the amount of the increase during the period under review (excluding inflation) and of the accumulated total amount at the end of the period in respect of the accrued benefit to which each director would be entitled on leaving service or is entitled having left service during the period under review;

- And either:

  - The transfer value (less director's contributions) of the relevant increase in accrued benefit (to be calculated in accordance with Actuarial Guidance Note GN11, but making no deduction for any underfunding) as at the end of the period; or

  - So much of the following information as is necessary to make a reasonable assessment of the transfer value in respect of each director:

    - Current age;

    - Normal retirement age;

    - The amount of any contributions paid or payable by the director under the scheme's terms during the period under review;

    - Details of spouse's and dependants' benefits;

    - Early retirement rights and options, expectations of pension increases after retirement (whether guaranteed or discretionary); and

    - Discretionary benefits for which allowance is made in transfer values on leaving and any other relevant information which will significantly affect the value of the benefits.

  Voluntary contributions and benefits should not be disclosed.

  [LR 9.8.8R (12)].

**5.198**   There is some overlap between the disclosure requirements in respect of defined benefit pensions in the Listing Rules and the legal requirements in the 1985 Act (SI 2008/410), but there are differences. The legal disclosure requirements go much further than the requirements of the Listing Rules. This is principally because the 1985 Act (SI 2008/410) specifically requires the transfer value of a director's accrued pension at the beginning and end of the year to be given, which is not a requirement of the Listing Rules. The difference between these two values less the director's contributions also has to be disclosed. Under the Listing Rules either the transfer value of the increase in accrued pension or sufficient information to enable it to be ascertained only has to be given. The main disclosures, which are considered further below, are as follows:

- The 1985 Act (SI 2008/410) requires disclosure of any changes during the year in a director's accrued benefits under a pension scheme, which includes inflation, whereas the Listing Rule requirement excludes inflation (see para 5.199 below).

■ The 1985 Act (SI 2008/410) requires disclosure of the change in the transfer value of accrued benefits (based on the opening and closing values of the transfer value), whilst the Listing Rules require the transfer value of the increase in the accrued benefit to be disclosed (or sufficient information about the Director's pension entitlements from which that value can be derived) (see para 5.200 below).

**5.199** The Listing Rules require disclosure of the increase excluding inflation of the director's accrued benefit during the period under review, whereas the 1985 Act (SI 2008/410) requires disclosure of any changes during the relevant financial year in the person's accrued benefits under the scheme, which would include inflation. [LR 9.8.8 R(12)(a); CA85 7A Sch 12(2)(a)(i); SI 2008/410 8 Sch 13(2)(a)(i)]. Although the only difference between the disclosures is the inflationary element, they are aimed at telling different stories: the 1985 Act (SI 2008/410) disclosure is aimed at telling the reader the difference between the annual pension that each director would have received if they had retired at the end of the year and the annual pension that they would have received if they had retired at the end of the previous year. However, the Listing Rules disclosure is designed to disclose the element of the director's increase in their accrued benefit that is earned during the year. If the director's annual pension entitlement increased only because of inflation, they would have earned no additional pension benefit by reason of employment, as their pension would have been increased by an inflationary element even if they had left. An example of an adjustment for inflation is given below.

**Example – Adjustment for inflation**

This example shows how the entitlement should be calculated for a director given the relevant facts as follows:

A director has ten years service at the beginning of the year and earns £120,000 per annum. He is entitled to a pension of one-sixtieth of final pensionable salary for each year of pensionable service. At the end of the year his salary was £130,000. The increase for the year and the accumulated total at the year end are calculated as follows:

| | |
|---|---|
| *Accumulated totals* | |
| At the beginning of the year: | $10/60 \times £120,000 = £20,000$ |
| At the end of the year: | $11/60 \times £130,000 = £23,833$ |
| Calculation of increase in the year (excluding inflation) | |
| Increase: | £23,833 less £20,000 = £3,833 |
| Inflation is assumed to be 5%. | |
| The increase due to inflation is: | $£20,000 \times 5\% = £1,000$ |
| The increase excluding inflation is, therefore, £2,833. | |

Note: The inflation rate used should be that published by the Secretary of State for Social Security each year (Schedule 3 of the Pension Schemes Act 1993).

**5.200** A further difference between the Listing Rules and the legal requirements is that the Listing Rules require disclosure of the transfer value (less director's contributions) of the relevant increase in accrued benefit as at the end of the period or sufficient information about the director's pension entitlements from which that value can be derived. [LR 9.8.8 R(12)(b)]. The 1985 Act (SI 2008/410), however, requires disclosure of the amount obtained by subtracting the transfer value of the person's accrued benefits at the end of the previous period from the transfer value of his accrued benefits at the end of the current period, then subtracting the director's personal contributions from that total. [CA85 7A Sch 12(2)(d); SI 2008/410 8 Sch 13(2)(d)]. The transfer value of the increase in accrued benefits, required by the Listing Rules, discloses the current value of the increase in accrued benefits that the director has earned in the period, whereas the change in the transfer value, required by the 1985 Act (SI 2008/410) discloses the absolute increase or decrease in the director's transfer value and includes the change in value of the accrued benefits that results from applying a different actuarial factor to the accrued benefits at the beginning of the period, as well as the additional value earned in the year.

**5.201**   The above differences between the 1985 Act (SI 2008/410) requirements and those of the Listing Rules are illustrated in the following example.

**Example – Transfer values under the 1985 Act (SI 2008/410) and the Listing Rules**

A UK listed company is preparing its directors' remuneration report in compliance with the disclosure requirements in the Listing Rules and Schedule 7A to the Companies Act 1985 (Schedule 8 to SI 2008/410). The company's executive directors are members of the company's defined benefit pension scheme. The Listing Rules require disclosure of the transfer value of the increase in each director's accrued benefits under the scheme, excluding inflation, while the 1985 Act (SI 2008/410) requires disclosure of the increase in the transfer value of their accrued benefits less the director's personal pension contributions.

What is the difference between these disclosures and does the company need to disclose both figures?

A transfer value is an actuarially calculated value that measures the fair value of a pension scheme's liability in respect of a director's accrued benefit. The Listing Rules require disclosure of the transfer value of the increase in the director's accrued benefit excluding inflation. So, using an example, if a director's accrued benefit at the end of 20X2 was £100,000 and his accrued benefit at the end of 20X3 was £110,000, inflation was steady at 3% and the actuarially calculated 'factor' for this director to be applied is 9.27, the transfer value of the increase in accrued benefit excluding inflation is £64,890, being 9.27 × (£110,000 − (103% × £100,000)).

The 1985 Act (SI 2008/410) requires disclosure of the difference between the transfer value at the year-end and the transfer value at the beginning of the year, less any personal contributions paid by the director. Using the same facts as in the example above and assuming that the 'factor' at the end of 20X2 was 8.5 and the director contributed £500 per month (gross), the figure disclosed will be £163,700 (the difference between the transfer value at the end of 20X3 (£110,000 × 9.27 = £1,019,700) and the transfer value at the end of 20X2 (£100,000 × 8.5 = £850,000), less the director's personal contributions of £6,000).

So, although the requirements of the Listing Rules and the 1985 Act (SI 2008/410) may appear similar, the resulting disclosures can be significantly different. The company will need to comply with both requirements.

**5.201.1** An example of disclosure that gives the information required by both the 1985 Act (SI 2008/410) and the Listing Rules is Table 5.33.

---

**Table 5.33 – Disclosure of directors' pension benefits**

**BT Group plc – Annual Report and Form 20-F 2005**

The table below shows the increase in the accrued benefits, including those referred to above, to which each director has become entitled during the year and the transfer value of the increase in accrued benefits:

| | Accrued pension | | Transfer value of accrued benefits | | Change in transfer value c-d less directors' contributions | Additional accrued benefits earned in the year | Transfer value of increase in accrued benefits less directors' contributions |
|---|---|---|---|---|---|---|---|
| | 2005 £000a | 2004 £000b | 2005 £000c | 2004 £000d | 2005 £000 | 2005 £000e | 2005 £000f |
| P Danonh | 66 | 52 | 696 | 519 | 163 | 12 | 113 |
| A Green | 131 | 117 | 1,848 | 1,553 | 268 | 10 | 115 |
| H Lalanii | 73 | 57 | 668 | 494 | 158 | 14 | 109 |
| P Reynolds | 123 | 116 | 1,578 | 1,405 | 149 | 3 | 12 |

a-d As required by the Companies Act 1985 Schedule 7A.

a-b These amounts represent the deferred pension to which the directors would have been entitled had they left the company on 31 March 2004 and 2005, respectively.

c Transfer value of the deferred pension in column (a) as at 31 March 2005 calculated on the basis of actuarial advice in accordance with Actuarial Guidance Note GN11. The transfer value represents a liability of the company rather than any remuneration due to the individual and cannot be meaningfully aggregated with annual remuneration, as it is not money the individual is entitled to receive.

d The equivalent transfer value but calculated as at 31 March 2004 on the assumption that the director left service at that date.

e The increase in pension built up during the year, net of inflation.

f The transfer value of the pension in column (e), less directors' contributions.

g Directors' contributions in the financial year 2004/05 were as follows: Pierre Danon, £14,025 (2004 – £14,580); Andy Green, £26,625 (2004 – £25,500); Hanif Lalani £16,300 (2004 – £13,350) and Paul Reynolds, £24,000 (2004 – £24,000).

h Pierre Danon resigned as a director on 28 February 2005.

i Hanif Lalani joined the Board on 7 February 2005.

---

*Practical application of pensions disclosures*

**5.202** As noted in paragraph 5.194, quoted companies are required to show, by individual director, the details of company contributions paid or payable in respect of the director to money purchase pension schemes. This requirement applies both to company pension schemes and to company payments to personal pension schemes (see further para 5.61 above).

**5.202.1** However, contributions that directors themselves pay by way of a compulsory deduction from salary are disclosed as part of directors' emoluments, rather than pension contributions (see para 5.37 above). Similarly, payments made directly to a director, which the director then elects to pay into a pension scheme should be disclosed as emoluments, rather than pension contributions, as illustrated in the examples below.

#### Example 1 – Cash in lieu of pension contributions

A quoted company is preparing its directors' remuneration report in accordance with Schedule 7A to the Companies Act 1985 (Schedule 8 to SI 2008/410). All but one of the directors have contributions paid by the company into its defined contribution scheme. One director elected instead to receive a direct payment through payroll, in lieu of the contributions that would have been made by the company to the defined contribution scheme. Although it is expected that he will use the cash in a personal pension scheme, he is under no obligation to do so. How should the payments be presented in the remuneration report?

Because the cash in lieu of pension contributions is paid directly to the director through the payroll system it cannot be classified as a company contribution to a pension scheme.

The cash received in lieu of pension contributions is remuneration and should be included appropriately in the tabular disclosure given under Schedule 7A to the Companies Act 1985 (Schedule 8 to SI 2008/410). Although it is not a company pension contribution, in our view it is equally not salary, bonus, expense allowance or benefit in kind (which are required to be disclosed separately – see para 5.164). In the interests of transparency we believe that the company should disclose the amounts in the emoluments table in a separate column, explaining the nature of the payment.

#### Example 2 – Waiver of bonus in favour of pension contributions

A director of a quoted company is entitled to an annual salary and other benefits, including an annual bonus. After the end of the year, the value of his bonus is determined and he is given three options:

(a)   He receives the bonus in cash.

(b)   He waives the bonus and the company pays the same amount into his defined contribution pension arrangement

(c)   He waives the bonus and the company pays the same amount into his final salary-based pension to buy additional years' service in the scheme.

What would be disclosed in the remuneration report under each of these options?

Would the answer be any different if he waived part of his salary, rather than his bonus?

Paragraph 6 of Schedule 7A to the Companies Act 1985 (para 7 of Schedule 8 to SI 2008/410) requires disclosure, in a table, of the emoluments (including bonus) paid to or receivable by each director in respect of qualifying services for the financial year.

The bonus was receivable by the director in respect of qualifying services and it was his choice to convert the bonus into a pension contribution, so the amount should continue to be disclosed as emoluments.

If emoluments are waived, then they are excluded from the emoluments table, but disclosed in the remuneration report, as required by the Listing Rules. [LR 9.8.4 R (5)]. However, the bonus has not, in substance, been waived: as the director has received consideration (additional pension contributions) for the waiver – therefore, the amount should continue to be disclosed as emoluments.

**5.203**   The examples below consider the implications for disclosure in respect of pension entitlements in various situations, including when the director is appointed or retires in the year. The examples cover the following situations:

- A director (who was previously an employee) is appointed during the year (example 1). (For unquoted companies see para 5.90.1.)

- Serving director receives pension (example 2).

- Retired director becomes non-executive director (example 3).

- Director retires during the year, but remains as an employee (example 4).

- Director retires and commutes pension (example 5).

**Example 1 – Director (previously an employee) appointed during the year**

A quoted company is preparing its directors' remuneration report. One of the directors has been an employee of the company and a member of its defined benefits pension scheme, for a number of years, but was appointed as a director of the company during this year.

(a) Under Schedule 7A to the Companies Act 1985 (Schedule 8 to SI 2008/410), should the disclosures in respect of the benefits accruing to that director under the defined benefits scheme include all benefits accruing or just those that have accrued to him in respect of qualifying services?

Paragraph 12 of Schedule 7A to the Companies Act 1985 (para 13 of Schedule 8 to SI 2008/410) requires disclosure of specified information (see para 5.196) in respect of a director, where *"...the person has rights under a ... defined benefit scheme ... and any of those rights are rights to which he has become entitled in respect of qualifying services..."*. This means that the disclosures apply where any of the rights are earned in respect of qualifying services. As the director was appointed in the year and some of the benefits accrued at the year-end are in respect of the qualifying services performed since the appointment date, this means that the disclosures apply. These disclosure requirements do not state that they should be made only in respect of the period since appointment and they should, therefore, be calculated based on the director's total accrued benefit under the scheme and not just on the portion that has been earned in respect of qualifying services.

(b) Should the change in the director's accrued benefit disclosed under Schedule 7A to the Companies Act 1985 (Schedule 8 to SI 2008/410) be the difference between his accrued benefit at the end of the year and at the beginning of the year or the date of appointment?

*Disclosure of directors' remuneration*

Paragraph 12 of Schedule 7A to the Companies Act 1985 (para 13 of Schedule 8 to SI 2008/410) requires disclosure of the change in the director's accrued benefit during the year and does not contain a *proviso* that where the director was appointed during the year the change should be given only since the date of appointment. Therefore, the change in the director's accrued benefit disclosed should be the total difference between the director's accrued benefit at the end of the year and at the beginning of the year. However, whilst disclosing the full year's increase an explanation could be added to the effect that the increase for the year of £x arose after the director became a director.

**Example 2 – Serving director receives pension**

The chairman of a quoted company is past retirement age and has been receiving a pension from the company for the whole of the current year, in addition to his emoluments (which are not pensionable). Does the table of accrued pension benefits, required by paragraph 12 of Schedule 7A to the Companies Act 1985 (para 13 of Schedule 8 to SI 2008/410) have to disclose, in respect of the chairman, details of the change (if any) in his accrued benefit, the accrued benefits at the end of the year and the transfer values?

The disclosure requirements for the chairman's defined benefit pension entitlement are the same as the requirements in respect of each of the other directors and are as set out in paragraph 12(2) of Schedule 7A to the Companies Act 1985 (para 13(2) of Schedule 8 to SI 2008/410). The Act requires disclosure of the information specified in paragraph 12 of Schedule 7A to the Companies Act 1985 (para 13 of Schedule 8 to SI 2008/410) in respect of each person's defined benefit pension entitlements where that person has performed qualifying services at any point during the year (which the chairman has) and has benefits accruing to him/her under a defined benefits scheme (which the chairman has), any of which were accrued in respect of qualifying services. So even though the chairman received no pensionable emoluments during the year (so no further benefits accrued to him during the year), full disclosure is required.

The requirement in Schedule 7A to the Companies Act 1985 (Schedule 8 to SI 2008/410) differs from the requirement in Schedule 6 to the Companies Act 1985 (Schedule 5 to SI 2008/410) (for unquoted companies) and from the Listing Rules (for UK listed companies).

Schedule 6 to the Companies Act 1985 (Schedule 5 to SI 2008/410) requires disclosure (by unquoted companies) of the highest paid director's accrued benefits (and accrued lump sum where applicable) only if the director has performed qualifying services in the year that earn pension entitlements, which a director who is drawing his pension will normally not do. This requirement applies only to the highest paid director.

The Listing Rules require disclosure (by UK listed companies) of the increase in the accrued benefit (excluding inflation) and the transfer value of that increase (which can be substituted by specified details as outlined in the Listing Rules) for each director (or person who resigned as a director during the year). As the Chairman is receiving a pension, there will be no increase in the accrued benefit and, consequently, no disclosure is required by the Listing Rules.

However, Schedule 7A to the Companies Act 1985 (Schedule 8 to SI 2008/410) requires disclosure (by quoted companies) of pension entitlements where a director has rights under a scheme and any of those rights are rights to which he has become entitled in respect of qualifying services. However, it does not make disclosure conditional on his having performed qualifying services in the year that accrue pension entitlements.

Therefore, the Schedule 7A to the Companies Act 1985 (Schedule 8 to SI 2008/410) requirements differ from those of the Listing Rules and under Schedule 7A to the Companies Act 1985 (Schedule 8 to SI 2008/410), even if a person has retired and is performing non-qualifying services as a director of the company, perhaps in a non-executive capacity, such that the accrued benefit does not increase, all the pensions entitlement disclosures of Schedule 7A to the Companies Act 1985 (Schedule 8 to SI 2008/410) are still required to be given in the directors' remuneration report, as he has rights under the pension scheme that were earned in respect of qualifying services in the past (before he retired).

**Example 3 – Retired director becomes non-executive director**

A director of a quoted company is a member of the company's defined benefit pension scheme. During the prior year, he reached retirement age, stood down as an executive director and was appointed a non-executive director. He is receiving his pension from the pension scheme in addition to fees in respect of his services as a non-executive director.

(a) Does the director's annual pension received need to be included in his emoluments?

Paragraph 6 of Schedule 7A to the Companies Act 1985 (para 7 of Schedule 8 to SI 2008/410) requires disclosure, in a table, of the emoluments paid to or receivable by each director in respect of qualifying services for the financial year. The pension payment is receivable by the director, but it was accrued in respect of qualifying services in years prior to his retirement, so is not receivable in respect of qualifying services for the period and should be excluded from the disclosure of his emoluments.

(b) Should the director be included in the defined benefit pension disclosures?

Paragraph 12 of Schedule 7A to the Companies Act 1985 (para 13 of Schedule 8 to SI 2008/410) requires disclosure of specified information (see para 5.196) in respect of a director, where *"...the person has rights under a ... defined benefit scheme ... and any of those rights are rights to which he has become entitled in respect of qualifying services..."*. This means that the disclosures apply where the director (the Act does not differentiate between executive and non-executive directors) has any entitlement under a defined benefit scheme and any of those rights are earned in respect of qualifying services.

As the director served as a director during the year and has an entitlement under a defined benefit scheme, some of which was accrued in respect of qualifying services (albeit in years prior to his retirement), the above disclosures are required in respect of him, even though pension entitlements were not accruing in respect of services during the period.

**Example 4 – Director retires during the year, but remains as an employee**

A quoted company is preparing its directors' remuneration report. One of the directors, who is a member of its defined benefits pension scheme, resigned as a director of the company during this year, but will remain an employee of the company, accruing further pensionable service.

(a) Should the disclosures in respect of the benefits accruing to that director under the defined benefits scheme include all benefits accruing or just those that have accrued to him in respect of qualifying services?

## Disclosure of directors' remuneration

Schedule 7A to the Companies Act 1985 (Schedule 8 to SI 2008/410) requires disclosure of specified information (see para 5.196) in respect of any person who has served as a director at any time during the year and has defined benefit pension entitlements, any of which were accrued in respect of qualifying services. This means that the disclosures apply where any of the rights are earned in respect of qualifying services. As the director resigned in the year and some of the benefits accrued at the year end are in respect of qualifying services, this means that the disclosures are required in respect of all benefits accrued (that is, determined as at the year end, rather than at the date of retirement).

(b) Should the change in the director's accrued benefit disclosed be the difference between his accrued benefit at the beginning of the year and at the end of the year or at the date of resignation?

Paragraph 12 of Schedule 7A to the Companies Act 1985 (para 13 of Schedule 8 to SI 2008/410) requires disclosure of the change in the director's accrued benefit during the year and does not contain a *proviso* that where the director resigned during the year the change should be given only until the date of resignation. Therefore, the change in the director's accrued benefit disclosed should be the total difference between the director's accrued benefit at the end of the year and at the beginning of the year.

### Example 5 – Director retires and commutes pension

A quoted company is preparing its directors' remuneration report for the year ended 31 December 20X4. One of its directors retired during the year and, as permitted by the rules of the defined benefit pension scheme, commuted part of her pension entitlement into a tax-free lump sum. In the 20X3 remuneration report, her disclosed accrued benefit was £100,000 and the transfer value of her accrued benefit at that date was £950,000. When she retired, she elected to forfeit £25,000 of her annual pension entitlement in consideration for a cash receipt of £235,000. At 31 December 20X4, her accrued pension is £76,000 (the £1,000 increase being inflationary) and the transfer value is £724,000. She made no personal contributions during the year.

What should be disclosed in this year's remuneration report under the Companies Act?

Schedule 7A to the Companies Act 1985 (Schedule 8 to SI 2008/410) requires disclosure of specified information (see para 5.196) in respect of any person who has served as a director at any time during the year and has defined benefit pension entitlements, any of which were accrued in respect of qualifying services. So full disclosure in accordance with paragraph 12 of Schedule 7A to the Companies Act 1985 (para 13 of Schedule 8 to SI 2008/410) is required of information about the director's pension entitlement.

A literal reading of the 1985 Act (SI 2008/410) requirements would lead to disclosure of her accrued benefits of £76,000, the reduction in accrued benefit of £24,000, the transfer values at 1 January 20X4 and 31 December 20X4 of £950,000 and £724,000 respectively and the reduction in transfer value (excluding personal contributions) of £226,000. However, disclosure of this information without disclosure of the cash lump sum of £235,000 would be misleading to the user of the remuneration report so disclosure of this must be given.

An alternative view is that a more representative disclosure would be based on her entitlement had she not commuted her benefit into cash. That is, disclosure of her accrued benefit of £101,000 and a transfer value at the end of the year calculated by reference to that amount. However, as this is not the benefit that she will actually receive, in order that the readers of the remuneration report are not misled, a footnote must be given, explaining that she has commuted 25% of her benefit and received a cash lump sum.

In our view, either disclosure is acceptable, but either disclosure must be clear to the users of the remuneration report.

### Excess retirement benefits of directors and past directors

**5.204** The remuneration report must disclose, for each director who served during the year and for each past director, the amount of excess retirement benefits paid to or receivable by that director or past director under pension schemes. [CA85 7A Sch 13; SI 2008/410 8 Sch 14].

**5.205** The requirement for disclosure by individual director or past director in the remuneration report prepared by quoted companies is subject to similar criteria and definitions as the aggregate disclosure requirement that applies only to unquoted companies (see para 5.93). Thus, for example, the excess amounts referred to above do not include amounts paid or receivable if:

- the scheme's funding was such that the amounts were or could have been paid without recourse to additional contributions; and

- the amounts were paid to or receivable by all pensioner members of the scheme on the same basis ('pensioner members' being persons entitled to the present payment of retirement benefits under the scheme).

[CA85 7A Sch 13(3); SI 2008/410 8 Sch 14(3)].

**5.206** Retirement benefits, for the purpose of the above, includes benefits otherwise than in cash and where benefits otherwise than in cash are given the amount is their estimated money value. The nature of any such benefit should also be disclosed. [CA85 7A Sch 13(4); SI 2008/410 8 Sch 14(4)].

**5.207** Retirement benefits means retirement benefits to which the director or past director became entitled in respect of his qualifying services. [CA85 7A Sch 13(2); SI 2008/410 8 Sch 14(2)].

**5.208** An example of disclosure of excess retirement benefits by individual director or past director is given in Table 5.35. The example also includes other payments to former directors.

---

**Table 5.35 – Excess retirement benefits paid to past director**

**Marks and Spencer Group p.l.c. – Annual report & financial statement – 29 March 2003**

Remuneration report (extract)

**4 Payments to former directors**
Details of payments made under the Early Retirement Plan and other payments made to former directors during the year are:

| | Paid in 2003 £000 | Paid in 2002 £000 |
|---|---|---|
| Early retirement pensions1 (payable until) | | |
| James Benfield (22 April 2009) | 71 | 70 |
| Lord Stone of Blackheath (7 September 2002) | 47 | 93 |
| Derek Hayes (19 November 2008) | 66 | 65 |
| Chris Littmoden (28 September 2003) | 89 | 88 |
| Keith Oates (3 July 2002) | 59 | 174 |
| Unfunded pensions | | |
| Clinton Silver2 | 89 | 88 |
| Other | | |
| Robert Colvill3 | 19 | 177 |
| Chris Littmoden | – | 87 |
| Sir David Sieff | – | 13 |

1 Under the Early Retirement Plan the Remuneration Committee could, at its discretion, offer an unfunded Early Retirement Pension, separate from the Company pension, which was payable from the date of retirement to age 60. With effect from 31 March 2000, the Early Retirement Plan was withdrawn but payments continue for awards made before this date.

2 The pension scheme entitlement for Clinton Silver is supplemented by an additional, unfunded pension paid by the Company.

3 Robert Colvill continued to receive a fee as non-executive chairman of Marks & Spencer Financial Services until 31 August 2002.

---

## Compensation for past directors

**5.209** The general rules for disclosure of compensation for loss of office, applicable for all companies, are dealt with in paragraph 5.97 onwards. In addition, for quoted companies, the remuneration report is required to disclose details of compensation for loss of office for individual directors (see para 5.163). However, there may be other payments or benefits given to past directors that may not legally qualify as compensation for loss of office and so the 1985 Act (SI 2008/410) contains a 'sweep-up' requirement for such awards to be disclosed.

**5.210** The requirement is to disclose details of any significant award made in the financial year to any director who was not a director at the time when the award was made, but was previously a director. This requirement covers, in particular, compensation for loss of office and pensions, but excludes any sums already disclosed in the table of individual directors' emoluments and compensation for loss of office. [CA85 7A Sch 14; SI 2008/410 8 Sch 15].

**Example – Awards to former directors**

(i) Paragraph 14 of Schedule 7A to the Companies Act 1985 (para 15 of Schedule 8 to SI 2008/410) requires disclosure of the details of any significant award made in the financial year to any director who was not a director at the time when the award was made, but was previously a director. How should this be interpreted for awards in the current period to:

(a) A director who retires in the period?

Paragraph 6(1) of Schedule 7A to the Companies Act 1985 (para 7(1) of Schedule 8 to SI 2008/410) requires disclosure in respect of each person who has served as a director of the company at any time during the year. Therefore, if a director retires in the period then his emoluments (for qualifying services) should be included in the analysis by individual director as normal. This analysis would also include any compensation for loss of office. Any further awards made after the person ceased to be a director that are not included in compensation would fall to be disclosed separately under paragraph 14 of Schedule 7A to the Companies Act 1985 (para 15 of Schedule 8 to SI 2008/410).

(b) A director who retired in the previous period?

We interpret significant awards to former directors during the year to include awards (cash or non-cash) to former directors who had ceased to be directors by the beginning of the current accounting period. These awards would be picked up by the paragraph 14 of Schedule 7A to the Companies Act 1985 (para 15 of Schedule 8 to SI 2008/410) requirement detailed above.

(ii) Do significant awards to former directors have to be disclosed by individual director, naming them, or can they just be disclosed in aggregate, without names?

If the awards are not already disclosed in the table by individual director as compensation under paragraph 6 of Schedule 7A to the Companies Act 1985 (para 7 of Schedule 8 to SI 2008/410), they would be separately disclosed by director under paragraph 14 of Schedule 7A to the Companies Act 1985 (para 15 of Schedule 8 to SI 2008/410). Disclosure by individual director is clearly required by the wording of paragraph 14 of Schedule 7A to the Companies Act 1985 (para 15 of Schedule 8 to SI 2008/410).

**5.211** Of particular note is that the requirement also relates to pensions and so will lead to disclosure of any pension top-ups (see para 5.100 onwards) or benefits in respect of early retirement not disclosed elsewhere.

**5.211.1** In addition, for companies listed in the UK, the Listing Rules require disclosure of any significant payments made to former directors during the period under review. [LR 9.8.8R (2)(c)].

**5.212** Examples of items that may fall to be disclosed under these requirements are contained in Table 5.35. This example has been used above to illustrate disclosure of excess retirement benefits required to be disclosed separately (see from para 5.203), but also includes disclosure that may fall under this section of other significant awards to former directors that are not compensation for loss of office or excess retirement benefits.

**5.213**   Another example might be one such as that shown in Table 5.21 in paragraph 5.154 of a payment made in respect of a dispute with a former director, which is resolved several years after the director ceased to act as such.

**5.214**   Another example might be a consultancy contract entered into with a former director. This is considered in the example below.

**Example – Consultancy contract with former director**

A quoted company is preparing its directors' remuneration report. During the year it entered into a contract for services with a person who was previously a director of the company, but who had resigned as a director three years previously. The rate being paid to the former director is in excess of the market rate for the services he is contracted to provide.

(a) Is there any disclosure requirement in the directors' remuneration report?

(b) Would it make any difference if the payment for services was an arm's length rate?

As noted in paragraph 5.210 above, paragraph 14 of Schedule 7A to the Companies Act 1985 (para 15 of Schedule 8 to SI 2008/410) requires disclosure in the directors' remuneration report of *"...any significant award made in the relevant financial year to any person who was not a director of the company at the time the award was made but had previously been a director of the company, ..."*.

Paragraph 5(2) of Schedule 7A to the Companies Act 1985 (para 6(2) of Schedule 8 to SI 2008/410) requires disclosure of an explanation for any significant award made in the circumstances described in paragraph 14 of Schedule 7A to the Companies Act 1985 (para 15 of Schedule 8 to SI 2008/410).

(a) Where the director receives reward for the services he provides to the company at a value in excess of arm's length, this would be an award under the terms of paragraph 14 of Schedule 7A to the Companies Act 1985 (para 15 of Schedule 8 to SI 2008/410) and disclosure would be required of amounts received by him, together with an explanation.

(b) Where the director receives payment at a value that is arm's length, the award of the contract to the former director would require disclosure under paragraph 14 of Schedule 7A to the Companies Act 1985 (para 15 of Schedule 8 to SI 2008/410), together with an explanation, in the year in which it is awarded. In subsequent accounting periods, there will be no 1985 Act (SI 2008/410) disclosure requirements in respect of the ongoing arm's length contract because there will be no award in those years.

In either case, the Listing Rules require disclosure of significant payments to former directors and would require disclosure of this payment in the directors' remuneration report (see para 5.165). [LR 9.8.8R 2(c)].

**[The next paragraph is 5.216.]**

*Sums paid to third parties in respect of directors' services*

**5.216** The Companies Act 1985 (SI 2008/410) contains a requirement for quoted companies to disclose, by individual director, the aggregate amount of any consideration paid to or receivable by third parties for making available the services of the director.

■ As a director of the company.

■ While a director of the company:

 (i) as director of any of its subsidiary undertakings;

 (ii) as director of any other undertaking of which he was a director by virtue of the company's nomination (direct or indirect); or

 (iii) otherwise in connection with the management of the affairs of the company or any such other undertaking.

[CA85 7A Sch 15(1); SI 2008/410 8 Sch 16(1)].

**5.217** In this context, third parties do not include:

■ The director himself or a person connected with him or a body corporate controlled by him.

■ The company or any other undertaking of which he is a director (while director of the company) by virtue of the company's nomination (direct or indirect).

[CA85 7A Sch 15(3); SI 2008/410 8 sch 16(3)].

**5.218** This part of the 1985 Act (SI 2008/410) does not specifically exclude from the definition of third party the company's subsidiary undertakings, whilst the rule relating to disclosure of aggregate amounts by unquoted companies in paragraph 9(3) of Schedule 6 to the Companies Act 1985 (para 5(3) of Schedule 5 to SI 2008/410) does do so (see para 5.114 above). This may be an oversight and common sense would suggest that subsidiary undertakings should also be excluded.

**5.219** The reference to consideration includes benefits otherwise than in cash and where such benefits are given the amount to be disclosed is the estimated money value of the benefit. [CA85 7A Sch 15(2); SI 2008/410 8 Sch 16(2)]. An example of disclosure of sums paid to third parties is given in Table 5.11 in paragraph 5.117.1 above.

**5.220** The disclosure applies where third parties make available the services of a director. It does not apply to other services, for example, payments to a headhunter that relate solely to services to the company for finding and introducing a director. This is illustrated in the example in paragraph 5.117.2 above.

**[The next paragraph is 5.222.]**

*Approval of remuneration report*

**5.222**  Section 234C of the 1985 Act (section 447 of the 2006 Act) requires that the remuneration report (quoted companies only) has to be approved by the board of directors and signed on behalf of the board by a director or the secretary of the company. [CA85 Sec 234C(1); CA06 Sec 447(3)].

**5.223**  Quoted companies are required by section 241A of the 1985 Act (section 439 of the 2006 Act) to give notice to members, prior to the general meeting at which accounts are laid, of an ordinary resolution to approve the directors' remuneration report for the year. However, no entitlement of a director to remuneration is made conditional on the resolution being passed by reason only of the requirements in section 241A of the 1985 Act (section 439 of the 2006 Act). [CA85 Sec 241A(4); CA06 Sec 439(2)]. In other words, the success or failure of the resolution does not affect the entitlement of the directors to the remuneration disclosed in the report. This is because remuneration will already be the subject of contracts that cannot be overturned. However, any 'no vote' or significant opposition is likely to spell trouble for the company in terms of investor relations.

# Section V — Audit requirements

**5.224**  As indicated in the previous sections, the Companies Act 1985 (SI 2008/410) requires part of the remuneration report ('the auditable part') to be audited. This requirement and the general provisions of the Act in relation to auditors' duties in respect of directors' remuneration information given in financial statements or accompanying them, are discussed below.

**5.225**  Section 232 of the Companies Act 1985 (section 412 of the Companies Act 2006) requires that the information in Schedule 6 to the 1985 Act (Schedule 5 to SI 2008/410) must be given in the notes to a company's annual accounts. [CA85 Sec 232(1); CA06 Sec 412]. Section 234B of the Companies Act 1985 (section 420 of the Companies Act 2006) requires that, in the case of quoted companies, a remuneration report must be prepared, which must contain the information required by Schedule 7A to the Companies Act 1985 (Schedule 8 to SI 2008/410) and comply with any requirement of that Schedule as to how the information is to be set out in the report. [CA85 Sec 234B(1); CA06 Secs 420(1); 412(1),(2)].

**5.226**  Section 237(1) and section 237(2) of the Companies Act 1985 (sections 498(1) and 498(2) of the Companies Act 2006) require the auditors to determine whether the accounts (including the notes) and the auditable part of the company's directors' remuneration report (in the case of quoted companies) are in accordance with the accounting records and returns and are required to include a statement in their report if they are not in agreement. [CA85 Sec 237(1),(2); CA06 Sec 498(1),(2)].

**5.227** Section 237(4) of the 1985 Act (section 498(4) of the 2006 Act) requires that if the requirements of Schedule 6 to the Companies Act 1985 (Schedule 5 to SI 2008/410) and, where a remuneration report is required to be prepared (that is, for quoted companies), the requirements of Schedule 7A to the Companies Act 1985 (Schedule 8 to SI 2008/410) in respect of the auditable part of that report, are not complied with, the auditors must, so far as they are reasonably able to do so, include in their report the required information. [CA85 Sec 237(4); CA06 Sec 498(4)].

**5.228** Section 235 of the 1985 Act (section 497 of the 2006 Act) requires that if a directors' remuneration report is prepared (that is, for quoted companies only) the auditors shall report on the auditable part and state in their report whether in their opinion that part (the auditable part) of the directors' remuneration report has been properly prepared in accordance with the Companies Act 1985. [CA85 Sec 235(4); CA06 Sec 497(1)].

**5.229** The auditable part of the directors' remuneration report is the part containing the information required by Part 3 of Schedule 7A to the 1985 Act (Part 3 of Schedule 8 to SI 2008/410). This has been discussed above under the heading 'Information subject to audit' from paragraph 5.163.

**5.230** In October 2002, the APB issued Bulletin 2002/2, 'The United Kingdom Directors' Remuneration Report Regulations 2002'. The Bulletin discusses the auditors' responsibilities with respect to the unaudited part of the directors' remuneration report.

**Example – Identification of auditable and non-auditable information**

A quoted company is preparing its directors' remuneration report. The company is proposing to mix the auditable information and the non-auditable information within the remuneration report, rather than keeping them as separate parts. Is this acceptable under Schedule 7A to the Companies Act 1985 (Schedule 8 to SI 2008/410)?

There is no requirement in the 1985 Act (SI 2008/410) to separate the auditable and the non-auditable information within the remuneration report, or even to state in that report which information has been audited and which has not. However, APB Bulletin 2002/2, 'The United Kingdom Directors' Remuneration Report Regulations 2002', considers the practical difficulties in describing, in the audit opinion, the scope of the audit when part but not all of a section in the annual report has been audited. It is insufficient for the directors and auditors of a company to assume that the user of the financial statements has existing knowledge to be able to determine which information has and which has not been audited.

The bulletin suggests that the auditors should discuss the format of the directors' remuneration report with management before the year end and should agree, possibly by including terms in the letter of engagement, that the auditable and the non-auditable parts of the remuneration report will be clearly distinguished. Where this is the case, a cross-reference in the audit opinion to the identifiable audited part will satisfy the need to make clear the scope of the opinion.

However, where the remuneration report does not clearly distinguish the auditable and non-auditable information, the audit report should identify specifically by page and paragraph number or heading if necessary each section of the directors' remuneration report that has been audited. This will need to be sufficient to enable the user to identify the information that has and has not been audited.

**5.231**   Also, under the Listing Rules, the scope of the auditors' report on the financial statements must cover the disclosures specified below. The auditors must state in their report if, in their opinion, the company has not complied with any of these requirements and, in such a case, must include in their report, so far as they are reasonably able to do so, a statement giving details of the non-compliance. [LR 9.8.12]. The relevant disclosures are as follows:

■   Detail of elements in the remuneration package (see para 5.165).

■   Information on share options (see para 5.170).

■   Details of other long-term incentive schemes (see para 5.189.2).

■   Details of defined benefit schemes (see para 5.197).

■   Details of contributions to money purchase schemes (see para 5.194).

**[The next paragraph is 5.233.]**

# Section VI — Group situations

**5.233**   Common problems arise with the disclosure of directors' emoluments in a group context. Consider the following examples where a director of a parent company has also been nominated to the board of one of its subsidiaries. In all the situations it is assumed that the director is remunerated by the parent company in connection with his services as director of the parent company, but also receives payment for services to the subsidiary (as set out in the examples below). It is also assumed that all the relevant information concerning emoluments is available to the reporting company and that both companies are private companies (that is, the relevant disclosures are governed by Schedule 6 to the Companies Act 1985 (Schedule 5 to SI 2008/410)).

**Example 1 – Director paid by subsidiary**

Where the subsidiary pays the director directly in respect of his services as a director of the subsidiary.

In this situation the parent company will need to disclose, as directors' emoluments, the aggregate of the amount paid to the director in respect of his services as a director of the parent company and the amount he receives in respect of his services as a director of the subsidiary. [CA85 6 Sch 10(2); SI 2008/410 5 Sch 7(2)]. This will be the case even if the parent is not preparing consolidated financial statements.

The subsidiary will also need to disclose the amount paid to the director by the subsidiary in respect of the director's services to that subsidiary, as directors' emoluments, in its own financial statements.

## Example 2 – Payment passed back to parent

Where the subsidiary pays the director, but the director is liable to account to the parent company for the remuneration he receives in respect of his services as director of the subsidiary.

In this situation, the notes to the financial statements of the parent company need only disclose, as directors' emoluments, the amounts paid to the director in respect of his services as director of the parent company.

The amount paid by the subsidiary in respect of the director's services to that subsidiary, needs to be disclosed, as directors' emoluments, in the subsidiary's financial statements. Where, however, the director is subsequently released from the obligation to account for the remuneration, the remuneration must be disclosed in a note to the first financial statements of the parent company in which it is practicable to show it, and the remuneration must be distinguished from other remuneration. [CA85 6 Sch 11(2); SI 2008/410 5 Sch 8(2)].

## Example 3 – Parent recharges subsidiary

Where the parent company pays the director directly and recharges the subsidiary for his services as a director of the subsidiary.

The aggregate amount that needs to be disclosed, as directors' emoluments, in the parent company's financial statements is the same as in example 1.

The notes to the subsidiary's financial statements must disclose, as directors' emoluments, the amount receivable by the director for services to the subsidiary, that is, in this situation, the amount recharged by the parent company in respect of the director's services.

## Example 4 – Parent does not recharge subsidiary

Where the parent company pays the director directly, but no recharge is made to the subsidiary.

Again, the aggregate amount that needs to be disclosed, as directors' emoluments, in the parent company's financial statements is the same as in example 1.

The notes to the subsidiary's financial statements, however, must include details of the remuneration paid by the parent company in respect of the director's services to the subsidiary. An explanation to the effect that the charge for director's remuneration has been borne by the parent company may be useful, although there is no requirement in the Act to do so. If it is necessary for the parent company to apportion the director's remuneration, the directors may apportion it in any way they consider appropriate. [CA85 6 Sch 12; SI 2008/410 5 Sch 7(6)].

**5.234** Practical difficulties may arise in connection with disclosure of remuneration in a subsidiary's financial statements where a director of the subsidiary is also:

*Disclosure of directors' remuneration*

- a director or employee of the parent and is paid by the parent; or

- a director of another subsidiary and is paid by that other subsidiary.

**5.235**  In such cases, it is often difficult to ascertain the emoluments of the director that are paid to or receivable by him in respect of his services to the subsidiary in question. This difficulty may be aggravated if there is no charge made to the subsidiary by the payer of the emoluments. It may also sometimes be aggravated by a desire on the part of either the parent or the subsidiary to limit the amount of disclosure in the subsidiary's financial statements, if, for instance, the parent-appointed director is more highly rewarded than other directors.

**5.236**  Paragraph 14 of Schedule 6 to the 1985 Act (para 6 of Schedule 5 to SI 2008/410) states that the schedule requires information to be given regarding emoluments, pensions and compensation for loss of office only so far as it is contained in the company's books and papers or the company has the right to obtain it from the persons concerned.

**5.237**  As noted in paragraph 5.9 above, section 412(5) of the Companies Act 2006 (section 232 of the Companies Act 1985) states that *"...it is the duty of any director of a company, and any person who is or has at any time in the preceding five years been a director of the company, to give notice to the company of such matters relating to himself as may be necessary for the purposes of regulations under this section"*.

**5.238**  Where, despite the requirements of section 232 of the 1985 Act (section 412 of the 2006 Act), there are difficulties in obtaining information one or more of the steps described below might be taken.

**5.239**  If the subsidiary is a party to the directors' service agreement, and that agreement stipulates what the director is paid in respect of his services to the subsidiary, then the information is contained in the subsidiary's books and papers and the subsidiary should disclose it.

**5.240**  If the subsidiary is not a party to the service agreement (possibly because the agreement is with the parent or a fellow subsidiary) the subsidiary or its directors should *"make reasonable efforts"* to obtain the information, for instance by asking the parent or fellow subsidiary for details of the terms of the service agreement, or by obtaining a detailed breakdown of any management charge.

**5.241**  If any fellow director of the subsidiary has obtained the necessary information in his capacity as a director of the subsidiary, he should disclose it to the board of the subsidiary. The information will then be under the subsidiary's control and it should disclose it.

**5.242**  If the information needed is not obtainable by any of the above means, companies often make an apportionment. This is relatively simple where a director is a director of both the subsidiary and the parent, but spends the vast majority of his time in an executive capacity on the subsidiary's affairs. It is less easy if the director is also a director of a large number of different subsidiaries. Schedule 6 to the Companies Act 1985 (Schedule 5 to SI 2008/410) permits apportionment (see para 5.24 above). We suggest that where apportionment is relatively straightforward it may be the best way of determining the emoluments to be disclosed in the subsidiary.

**5.243** The above steps may be summarised as follows:

- Inspect the subsidiary's relevant books and papers including service contracts to which it is party.

- Analyse any management charges for details of emoluments charged.

- Request information from other group companies that have service contracts with directors to which the company is not a party or from the director himself.

- Apportion where total emoluments are known and the apportionment can be made with a high degree of confidence and accuracy.

These steps should result in disclosure in the majority of cases.

**5.244** If, in rare circumstances, the necessary information is not contained in the company's books and papers and the company does not have the right to obtain it from the director, the company is not required to disclose it, (see para 5.236 above). In addition, the auditors would not be able to give the information required in their report (see para 5.10 above).

**5.245** Where this situation occurs it might be that the financial statements would not give a true and fair view if no disclosure were made of the facts. Hence in these circumstances, if the financial statements are to give a true and fair view, some narrative needs to be given. Table 5.38 is an example of such a note.

**5.246** We suggest that appropriate notes for three situations that may arise where no information is available would be as follows:

**Example 1 – Recharge cannot be separately identified**

A recharge is made to the subsidiary by a parent company or fellow subsidiary, but the management charge includes other costs and the emoluments cannot be separately identified.

> *"The above details of directors' emoluments do not include the emoluments of Mr X, which are paid by the parent company (fellow subsidiary) and recharged to the company as part of a management charge. This management charge, which in 20XX amounted to £95,000 also includes a recharge of administration costs borne by the parent company (fellow subsidiary) on behalf of the company and it is not possible to identify separately the amount of Mr X's emoluments."*

**5.247** It is envisaged that this situation would be very rare as normally a full breakdown of management charges should be possible.

---

**Table 5.38 – Directors' emoluments in a group situation**

The Telegraph plc   Annual Report and Accounts – 31 December 1994

**Directors (extract)**

During the year a charge of £871,192 was made by Hollinger Inc. under the services agreement referred to in note 26(c). It is not possible to identify whether any portion of the charge relates to services provided by any director of the company.

**26(c)    Services agreement**

Under the terms of a services agreement with Hollinger Inc., for so long as Mr Black remains chairman of the board, the Telegraph will bear 66.7% of the cost of the office of the chairman incurred by Hollinger or such other proportion as may be agreed from time to time by the Audit Committee. Other services will be provided at cost and may include the arrangement of insurance, assistance in the arrangement of finance and assistance and advice on acquisitions, disposal and joint venture arrangements. Charges to the company in respect of Mr Black's office and these other services amounted to £871,192 in 1994 *(1993: £1,044,000)*.

**32.    Ultimate parent company**

Hollinger Inc., incorporated in Canada and listed on the Toronto, Montreal and Vancouver stock exchanges, is regarded by the directors of the company as the company's ultimate parent company.

The largest group in which the results of the company are consolidated is that of which Hollinger Inc. is the parent company. The consolidated accounts of Hollinger Inc. may be obtained from Montreal Trust Company of Canada, 151 Front Street West, 8th Floor, Toronto, Ontario, Canada M5J 2N1.

The smallest such group is that of which DT Holdings Limited is the parent company, whose consolidated accounts may be obtained from 21 Wilson Street, London EC2M 2TQ. DT Holdings Limited is registered in England and Wales.

---

**Example 2 – Non-executive role in subsidiaries**

The director is an executive of the parent and also a director of a large number of other subsidiaries for which he carries on work. He is paid by the parent company which makes no recharge to the subsidiaries. His role is chiefly that of non-executive director of the subsidiaries overseeing the subsidiaries' affairs on behalf of the parent.

*"The emoluments of Mr X are paid by the parent company. Mr X's services to this company and to a number of fellow subsidiaries are of a non-executive nature and his emoluments are deemed to be wholly attributable to his services to the parent company. Accordingly, the above details include no emoluments in respect of Mr X."*

**Example 3 – Executive role in subsidiaries**

The director is also a director of a number of other subsidiaries for which he carries on work. He is paid by the parent company that makes no recharge to the subsidiaries. His role is that of an executive director of each of the subsidiaries.

*"The emoluments of Mr X are paid by the parent company which makes no recharge to the company. Mr X is a director of the parent company and a number of fellow subsidiaries and it is not possible to make an accurate apportionment of his*

*emoluments in respect of each of the subsidiaries. Accordingly, the above details include no emoluments in respect of Mr X. His total emoluments are included in the aggregate of directors' emoluments disclosed in the financial statements of the parent company."*

**5.248**  It is suggested that where a similar situation applies, but the emoluments are paid by a fellow subsidiary, there should normally be a recharge. This is because the situation of a subsidiary paying emoluments of group directors normally only arises with a group services company and such a company would usually recharge for the services it performs. In such a case, the note would not be needed, because the appropriate amount to be disclosed should be ascertainable.

# Annex 1 — Combined Code

The Combined Code (2006) is dealt with in detail in chapter 4. Section 1 of the Combined Code contains two main principles relating to directors' remuneration. The main principles, supporting principles and related best practice provisions are described below.

## *The level and make-up of remuneration*

The first main principle concerning directors' remuneration states that levels of remuneration should be sufficient to attract, retain and motivate directors of the quality required to run the company successfully, but companies should avoid paying more than is necessary for this purpose. A significant proportion of executive directors' remuneration should be structured to link rewards to corporate and individual performance. [CC B.1].

This is supplemented by the supporting principle, which states that the remuneration committee should judge where to position their company relative to other companies, but should use comparisons with caution in view of the risk of an upward ratchet of remuneration levels with no corresponding improvement in performance. They should also be sensitive to pay and employment conditions elsewhere in the group, especially when determining annual salary increases. [CC B.1].

The following additional recommendations in relation to remuneration policy were made as part of the best practice provisions:

- Performance-related elements of remuneration should form a significant proportion of the total remuneration package of executive directors and should be designed to align their interests with those of the shareholders and to give those directors keen incentives to perform at the highest levels. The remuneration committee should follow the provisions in Schedule A of the Combined Code, which offers additional guidance in designing performance-related remuneration schemes,

- Executive share options should not be offered at a discount, unless permitted by the relevant provisions of the Listing Rules.

- Levels of remuneration for non-executive directors should reflect the time commitment and responsibilities of the role. Remuneration for non-executive directors should not include share options but if, exceptionally, options are granted, shareholder approval should be sought in advance and any shares acquired by exercise of the options should be held until at least one year after the non-executive director leaves the board. Holding share options could be relevant to determining a non-executive director's independence.

- Where a company releases an executive director to serve as a non-executive director elsewhere, the remuneration report should include a statement as to whether or not the director will retain such earnings and, if so, what the remuneration is.

[CC B.1.1 to B.1.4].

The best practice provisions also include the following relating to service contracts and compensation:

- Remuneration committees should carefully consider what compensation commitments (including pension contributions and all other elements) their directors' terms of appointment would entail in the event of early termination. The aim should be to avoid rewarding poor performance. They should take a robust line on reducing compensation to reflect departing directors' obligations to mitigate loss.

- Notice or contract periods should be set at one year or less. If it is necessary to offer longer notice or contract periods to new directors recruited from outside, such periods should reduce to one year or less after the initial period.

[CC B.1.5 to B.1.6].

### Procedure

The main principle in this area is that there should be a formal and transparent procedure for developing policy on executive remuneration and for fixing the remuneration packages of individual directors. No director should be involved in deciding his or her own remuneration. [CC B.2].

In support of this main principle are the following supporting principles:

- The remuneration committee should consult the chairman and/or chief executive about their proposals relating to the remuneration of other executive directors. It should also be responsible for appointing any consultants in respect of executive director remuneration. Where executive directors or senior management are involved in advising or supporting the remuneration committee, care should be taken to recognise and avoid conflicts of interest.

- The chairman of the board should ensure that the company maintains contact as required with its principal shareholders about remuneration in the same way as for other matters.

[CC B.2].

These principles are further supplemented by the following best practice provisions:

- The board should establish a remuneration committee of at least three, or in the case of smaller companies (that is, those falling outside the FTSE 350 throughout the year immediately prior to the reporting year) two independent non-executive directors. In addition the company chairman may also be a member of, but not chair, the committee if he or she was considered independent on appointment as chairman. The remuneration committee should make available its terms of reference on request and on the company website, explaining its role and the authority delegated to it by the board. Where remuneration consultants are appointed, a statement should be made available (in the same way as described for the terms of reference) of whether they have any other connection with the company.

- The remuneration committee should have delegated responsibility for setting remuneration for all executive directors and the chairman, including pension rights and any compensation payments. The committee should also recommend and monitor the level and structure of senior managements' remuneration. The definition of 'senior management' for this purpose should be determined by the board, but should normally include the first layer of management below board level. Disclosure of the remuneration committee's activities throughout the year is considered to be good practice.

- The board itself or, where required by the articles of association, the shareholders should determine the non-executive directors' remuneration within the limits set in the articles of association. Where permitted by the articles, the board may, however, delegate this responsibility to a committee, which might include the chief executive.

- Shareholders should be invited specifically to approve all new long-term incentive schemes (as defined in the Listing Rules) and significant changes to existing schemes, save in the circumstances permitted by the Listing Rules.

[CC B.2.1 to B.2.4].

*Schedule A*

Schedule A of the Combined Code, which is referred to above, deals with the design of performance related remuneration and includes the following:

- The remuneration committee needs to consider whether the directors should be eligible for annual bonuses. If so, performance conditions should be relevant, stretching and designed to enhance shareholder value. Upper limits should be set and disclosed. There may be a case for part of the bonuses to be paid in shares to be held for a significant period.

- The remuneration committee needs to consider whether the directors should be eligible for benefits under long-term incentive schemes. Traditional share option schemes should be compared to other kinds of long-term incentive scheme. Generally, shares granted or other forms of deferred remuneration should not vest, and options should not be exercisable, in less than three years. Directors should be encouraged to hold their shares for a further period after vesting or exercise, subject to the need to finance any costs of acquisition and associated tax liabilities.

■ Any new long-term incentive schemes that are proposed should be approved by shareholders and should preferably replace any existing schemes or at least form part of a well considered overall plan, which should incorporate existing schemes. Furthermore, the total rewards potentially available should not be excessive.

■ Payouts or grants under all incentive schemes, including new grants under existing share option schemes, need to be subject to challenging performance criteria reflecting the company's objectives. Consideration needs to be given to criteria that reflect the company's performance relative to a group of comparator companies in some key variables, for example total shareholder return.

■ Normally, grants under executive share option and other long-term incentive schemes should be phased rather than awarded in one large block.

■ Generally, only basic salary should be pensionable.

■ The remuneration committee needs to consider the pension consequences and associated costs to the company of basic salary increases and any other changes in pensionable remuneration, especially for directors close to retirement.

[CC Sch A].

# Annex 2 — Directors' remuneration disclosure — decision tree

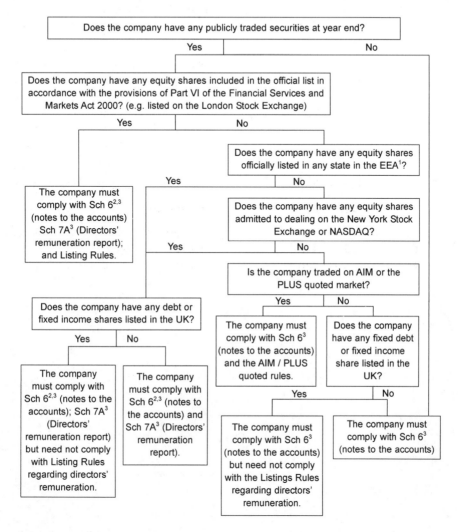

[1] At the time of writing, the EEA comprises the members states of the European Union plus Norway, Iceland and Liechtenstein.

[2] Companies required to prepare a Directors' Remuneration report under Schedule 7A[3] are exempt from paragraphs 2-14 of Schedule 6[3].

[3] For accounting periods beginning on or after 6 April 2008, references to Schedule 6 and Schedule 7A to the Companies Act 1985 above are replaced by Schedule 5 and Schedule 8 respectively to 'The Large and Medium-Sized Companies and Groups (Accounts and Reports) Regulations' (SI 2008/410).

# Chapter 6

# Loans and other transactions involving directors

|                                                                         | Page |
| ----------------------------------------------------------------------- | ---- |
| Introduction                                                            | 6001 |
| Definitions                                                             | 6003 |
| Director                                                                | 6003 |
| Shadow director                                                         | 6003 |
| *De facto* director                                                     | 6004 |
| Alternate director                                                      | 6005 |
| Connected persons                                                       | 6006 |
| Members of a director's family                                          | 6007 |
| Body corporate with which a director is connected                       | 6007 |
| Control of shares or votes                                              | 6008 |
| Interests in shares                                                     | 6008 |
| Limits on aggregation                                                   | 6009 |
| Relevant company                                                        | 6011 |
| Associated company                                                      | 6011 |
| Body corporate                                                          | 6011 |
| Company                                                                 | 6012 |
| Holding company and subsidiary                                          | 6012 |
| Transactions with directors entered into prior to 1 October 2007        | 6012 |
| Transactions with directors entered into after 1 October 2007           | 6013 |
| Loans                                                                   | 6013 |
| Definition                                                              | 6013 |
| Value of loans                                                          | 6013 |
| Member approval                                                         | 6013 |
| Eligible member                                                         | 6014 |
| Exceptions                                                              | 6014 |
| Small loans                                                             | 6014 |
| Groups                                                                  | 6015 |
| Quasi-loans                                                             | 6016 |
| Definition                                                              | 6016 |
| Value of quasi-loans                                                    | 6016 |
| Conditions for quasi-loans                                              | 6017 |
| Exceptions                                                              | 6017 |
| Small quasi-loans                                                       | 6017 |
| Credit transactions                                                     | 6017 |
| Definition                                                              | 6017 |
| Value of credit transactions                                            | 6018 |
| Conditions for credit transactions                                      | 6018 |
| Exceptions                                                              | 6019 |
| Minor transactions                                                      | 6019 |
| Business transactions                                                   | 6019 |

Assignment or assumption of rights, obligations or liabilities. . . . . . . .  6019
  Value of assignment or assumption. . . . . . . . . . . . . . . . . . . . . . . . . .  6020
Indirect arrangements . . . . . . . . . . . . . . . . . . . . . . . . . . . . . . . . . . . . . . .  6021
  Value of indirect arrangements . . . . . . . . . . . . . . . . . . . . . . . . . . . . . .  6021
General exceptions from the requirement for member approval for
loans and similar transactions . . . . . . . . . . . . . . . . . . . . . . . . . . . . . . . . .  6021
  Intra-group transactions. . . . . . . . . . . . . . . . . . . . . . . . . . . . . . . . . . . .  6022
  Directors' business expenditure . . . . . . . . . . . . . . . . . . . . . . . . . . . . .  6022
  Funding of director's expenditure on defending proceedings . . . . . .  6023
  Funding of director's expenditure in connection with regulatory
  action or investigation. . . . . . . . . . . . . . . . . . . . . . . . . . . . . . . . . . . . . .  6023
Civil consequences of contravention . . . . . . . . . . . . . . . . . . . . . . . . . . .  6024
Disclosure requirements for loans, quasi-loans, credit arrangements and
guarantees. . . . . . . . . . . . . . . . . . . . . . . . . . . . . . . . . . . . . . . . . . . . . . . . .  6024
  Introduction . . . . . . . . . . . . . . . . . . . . . . . . . . . . . . . . . . . . . . . . . . . . . .  6024
  Disclosure in financial statements for financial years beginning and
  ending before 6 April 2008 . . . . . . . . . . . . . . . . . . . . . . . . . . . . . . . . .  6025
  Information to be disclosed for all transactions . . . . . . . . . . . . . . . .  6026
  Additional disclosure for loans . . . . . . . . . . . . . . . . . . . . . . . . . . . . .  6026
  Additional disclosure for guarantees or securities. . . . . . . . . . . . . . .  6027
  Additional disclosure for quasi-loans and credit transactions. . . . . .  6028
  Exemptions for certain intra-group loans. . . . . . . . . . . . . . . . . . . . . .  6028
  Transactions excluded from disclosure . . . . . . . . . . . . . . . . . . . . . . .  6029
  Penalties for failure to disclose transactions with directors . . . . . . .  6030
  Disclosure in financial statements - financial years beginning before 6
  April 2008 and ending after 6 April 2008. . . . . . . . . . . . . . . . . . . . . .  6030
  Disclosure in financial statements – financial years beginning on or
  after 6 April 2008 . . . . . . . . . . . . . . . . . . . . . . . . . . . . . . . . . . . . . . . .  6030
Transactions in which directors have material interests – financial years
beginning before 6 April 2008 . . . . . . . . . . . . . . . . . . . . . . . . . . . . . . . .  6031
  Introduction . . . . . . . . . . . . . . . . . . . . . . . . . . . . . . . . . . . . . . . . . . . . . .  6031
  Interpretation of 'material interest'. . . . . . . . . . . . . . . . . . . . . . . . . . . .  6032
  Disclosure requirements – financial years beginning before 6 April 2008  6033
  Exemptions from disclosure under the Companies Act 1985. . . . . . . .  6036
  Penalties for failure to disclose transactions with directors . . . . . . . .  6037
Transactions in which directors have material interests – financial years
beginning on or after 6 April 2008 . . . . . . . . . . . . . . . . . . . . . . . . . . . .  6038
Substantial property transactions . . . . . . . . . . . . . . . . . . . . . . . . . . . . . .  6038
  Introduction . . . . . . . . . . . . . . . . . . . . . . . . . . . . . . . . . . . . . . . . . . . . . .  6038
  Shareholders' approval of substantial property transactions. . . . . . . .  6038
  Substantial property transaction value . . . . . . . . . . . . . . . . . . . . . . . . .  6039
  Exemptions from obtaining approval . . . . . . . . . . . . . . . . . . . . . . . . . .  6040
  Liabilities for contravention of section 190 . . . . . . . . . . . . . . . . . . . . .  6041
  Disclosure requirements for substantial property transactions for
  financial beginning before 6 April 2008 . . . . . . . . . . . . . . . . . . . . . . .  6042
  Disclosure requirements for substantial property transactions for
  financial years beginning on or after 6 April 2008 . . . . . . . . . . . . . . .  6042

Disclosure requirements of the Listing Rules and AIM and PLUS-quoted rules . . . . . . . . . . . . . . . . . . . . . . . . . . . . . . . . . . . . . . . . . . . . . 6043
Invalidity of certain transactions involving directors . . . . . . . . . . . . . . . . 6044
    General rule . . . . . . . . . . . . . . . . . . . . . . . . . . . . . . . . . . . . . . . . . . . . . . . 6044
    Effects of contravention . . . . . . . . . . . . . . . . . . . . . . . . . . . . . . . . . . . . . . 6044
Transactions with directors who are sole members. . . . . . . . . . . . . . . . . . 6045
Transactions with officers. . . . . . . . . . . . . . . . . . . . . . . . . . . . . . . . . . . . . . 6046
    Transactions to be disclosed – for financial years beginning before 6
    April 2008. . . . . . . . . . . . . . . . . . . . . . . . . . . . . . . . . . . . . . . . . . . . . . . . . . . 6046
        Information to be disclosed . . . . . . . . . . . . . . . . . . . . . . . . . . . . . . . . 6047
        Exemptions from disclosure. . . . . . . . . . . . . . . . . . . . . . . . . . . . . . . . 6047
        Penalty for failure to disclose transactions with officers. . . . . . . . . . 6047
    Transactions to be disclosed – for financial years beginning on or after
    6 April 2008 . . . . . . . . . . . . . . . . . . . . . . . . . . . . . . . . . . . . . . . . . . . . . . . . 6047
Money-lending and banking companies. . . . . . . . . . . . . . . . . . . . . . . . . . . 6048
    Introduction and definition of a money-lending company. . . . . . . . . . . 6048
    Exception for money lending companies . . . . . . . . . . . . . . . . . . . . . . . . 6049
        Loans on commercial terms. . . . . . . . . . . . . . . . . . . . . . . . . . . . . . . . 6049
            Transactions to which the exception from approval is not
            applicable . . . . . . . . . . . . . . . . . . . . . . . . . . . . . . . . . . . . . . . . . . . . 6049
        Relaxation for loans on beneficial terms for house purchase . . . . . . 6050
    Disclosure requirements – money lending companies. . . . . . . . . . . . . . 6050
    Disclosure requirements – banking company or group for financial
    years beginning before 6 April 2008 . . . . . . . . . . . . . . . . . . . . . . . . . . . 6051
        Disclosure in financial statements . . . . . . . . . . . . . . . . . . . . . . . . . . 6051
        Statement of transactions. . . . . . . . . . . . . . . . . . . . . . . . . . . . . . . . . 6051
        Register of transactions . . . . . . . . . . . . . . . . . . . . . . . . . . . . . . . . . . 6053
        Special statement for members . . . . . . . . . . . . . . . . . . . . . . . . . . . . . 6053
    Disclosure requirements – banking company or group for financial
    years beginning on or after 6 April 2008 . . . . . . . . . . . . . . . . . . . . . . . . 6054
Other matters. . . . . . . . . . . . . . . . . . . . . . . . . . . . . . . . . . . . . . . . . . . . . . . . 6054
    Notification to the board . . . . . . . . . . . . . . . . . . . . . . . . . . . . . . . . . . . . . 6054
        Declaration of interest under section 317 of the 1985 Act (sections
        177 and 182 of the 2006 Act). . . . . . . . . . . . . . . . . . . . . . . . . . . . . . . 6054
    Disclosure required by the articles of association. . . . . . . . . . . . . . . . . . 6055
    Penalties for failure to disclose certain transactions. . . . . . . . . . . . . . . 6056
    Criminal sanctions under the 1985 Act . . . . . . . . . . . . . . . . . . . . . . . . . 6057
    Civil consequences of contravention of the 2006 Act. . . . . . . . . . . . . . 6058
    Annex – Directors loan decision tables. . . . . . . . . . . . . . . . . . . . . . . . . 6059

Chapter 6

# Loans and other transactions involving directors

## Introduction

**6.1** Transactions between a company and its directors are governed by Company law to ensure that directors do not put themselves in a position where their personal interest and the interest of their company conflict.

**6.2** The 2006 Act has replaced all the provisions of the 1985 Act. Implementation of the 2006 Act has been staggered and different parts have different commencement dates. The table below summarises the key items covered within this chapter and the relevant sections under the 2006 Act and the 1985 Act as well as any transitional provisions that apply.

| | 2006 Companies Act requirements | 1985 Companies Act requirements | Effective date and transitional provisions |
|---|---|---|---|
| Definition of a connected person (para 6.18) | Sections 252-255 | Section 346 | 1 October 2007 |
| Transactions with directors (loans, quasi-loans, credits and guarantees) (para 6.29) | Sections 197-214 | Sections 330-338 | 1 October 2007 |
| Disclosure of transactions with directors (loans, quasi-loans, credits and guarantees) (para 6.69) | Section 413 and paragraph 72 of Schedule 1 to SI 2008/410 (related party transactions, see para 6.112.1) | Parts II and III of Schedule 6 | For financial years beginning on or after 6 April 2008. Refer to additional transitional provisions in paragraph 6.83.1 |
| Disclosure of transactions with connected persons | No specific requirement | Parts II and III of Schedule 6 | For financial years beginning on or after 6 April 2008. Refer to additional transitional provisions in paragraph 6.83.1 |
| Disclosure of transactions in which directors have material interests (para 6.84) | No specific requirement, but paragraph 72 of Schedule 1 to SI 2008/410 (related party transactions, see para 6.112.1) | Part II of Schedule 6 | For financial years beginning on or after 6 April 2008 |

| | | | |
|---|---|---|---|
| Substantial property transactions (para 6.100) | Sections 190-196 | Sections 320-322 | 1 October 2007 |
| Transactions with directors who are sole members (para 6.126) | Section 231 | Section 322B | 1 October 2007 |
| Transactions with officers (para 6.129) | No specific requirement, but paragraph 72 of Schedule 1 to SI 2008/410 (related party transactions, see para 6.112.1) | Part III of Schedule 6 | For financial years beginning on or after 6 April 2008 |
| Money-lending and banking companies – disclosure exceptions (para 6.133) | Section 209 Section 413(8) and paragraph 72 of Schedule 1 to SI 2008/410 (related party transactions, see para 6.112.1) | Section 338 Part IV of Schedule 9 | 1 October 2007 For financial years beginning on or after 6 April 2008, with some amendments from 6 April 2007. |
| Penalties for failure to disclose transactions<br><br>- Civil remedy<br>- Criminal sanctions | Section 412(5), (6)<br><br>Section 213<br>Not applicable | Section 232(3), (4)<br><br>Section 341<br>Section 342 | For financial years beginning on or after 6 April 2008 1985 Act provisions continue to apply for contraventions occurring before 1 October 2007. For transactions entered into after 1 October 2007 the 2006 Act is applicable. |

**6.3** Listed companies and those traded on AIM or the PLUS-quoted market are required to make additional disclosures of transactions between a company and its directors or their related parties to comply with the UKLA Listing and Disclosure and Transparency Rules, the AIM rules or the PLUS-quoted market rules (see from para 6.113). In addition, the transactions with directors and key management caught by the related party provisions of Schedule 1 to SI 2008/410 (refer to para 6.112.1) will require disclosure. For IFRS reporters complying with IAS 24, 'Related party disclosures' (see chapter 29 of Manual of Accounting – IFRS for the UK) will meet the related party disclosure requirements under the 2006 Act. This was clarified by the European Commission's Accounting Regulatory Committee (ARC) at their November 2007 meeting. For UK GAAP reporters, the 2006 Act may introduce additional disclosures over those contained within FRS 8, 'Related party disclosures' (see chapter 29 of Manual of Accounting – UK GAAP).

**[The next paragraph is 6.7.]**

**6.7** This chapter deals, first, with loans, quasi-loans and credit transactions as they apply to public and private companies. It explains their legality, the disclosure requirements for transactions with directors and officers and the sanctions imposed if the rules are breached. It deals, secondly, with the procedural and disclosure requirements of other types of transactions or arrangements involving a company and a director, including transactions in which the director has a material interest. Thirdly, it deals with the special provisions for such transactions that apply exclusively to money lending companies and banking companies. Lastly, it mentions sanctions for non-disclosure. In each case the requirements set out by the Companies Act 2006 are stated with any transitional provisions from the 1985 Act that still apply.

# Definitions

**6.8** The definitions that follow are essential to an understanding of the types of transaction that the Act regulates.

## Director

**6.9** The word 'director' as used in the Act includes any person who occupies the position of director by whatever name called. [CA06 Sec 250; CA 85 Sec 741(1)]. This means that it is the person's responsibilities and duties and not their title that determines whether or not somebody is a director. A director is a person who actively takes part in board meetings and votes at them. 'Directors' may be called governors, managers or trustees.

**6.10** Directors can be of three kinds: *de jure* directors (that is, directors who have been validly appointed as such); *de facto* directors (that is, directors who assume to act as directors without having been appointed validly or at all); and shadow directors. Shadow directors and *de facto* directors are considered below.

## Shadow director

**6.11** A 'shadow director' is defined in both the 2006 and 1985 Companies Act as *"...a person in accordance with whose directions or instructions the directors of the company are accustomed to act. A person is not to be regarded as a shadow director by reason only that the directors act on advice given by him in a professional capacity"*. [CA06 Sec 251(1),(2); CA85 Sec 741(2)]. There is a similar definition in section 22(5) of the Company Directors Disqualification Act 1986 (CDDA 1986). Important guidelines on the meaning of the definition in the CDDA 1986 were set out in *Secretary of State v Deverell [2000] 2BCLC 133*, which reviewed the earlier cases. The facts of this case were as follows. D and H had declared themselves consultants, but they were much more closely connected with the management of the company than that would suggest. The Court found that D bossed everyone around including the directors (who habitually followed what he said) and that H took the lead in important matters relating to the company's affairs, although not so directly as D. Both were held to be shadow directors. The guidelines are outlined briefly below.

**6.12** "Directions and instructions" – For the purposes of the definition in section 22(5) of the CDDA 1986, the question whether a particular communication constituted a direction or instruction had to be answered in the light of the evidence. Non-professional advice could come within the definition. The proviso excepting advice given *"...in a professional capacity"* appears to assume that advice given generally is, or may come, within that statutory description. Moreover, the concepts of direction and instruction do not exclude the concept of advice since all three share the common feature of 'guidance'. The directions or instructions do not have to extend over all or most of the company's corporate governance activities, but must cover at least those matters essential to the company's corporate governance, including its financial affairs. Frequent non-professional advice usually acted upon by the board would be sufficient.

**6.13** "Accustomed to act" – It will not always be necessary (although it would be sufficient) to show that, in the face of the 'directions or instructions', the properly appointed directors (that is, the whole board of directors) cast themselves in a subservient role or surrendered their respective discretions. It is not necessary to demonstrate a degree of compulsion beyond the fact that the whole board was accustomed to act in accordance with the directions or instructions. Further, it is not necessary for the shadow director to lurk in the shadows although he/she might frequently do so. An example was given where a foreign resident owns all the shares in a company operating openly through a local board of directors. From time to time the owner gives directions to the local board what to do but takes no part in management himself/herself. The judge considered that the owner may be a shadow director although he or she takes no steps to hide the part played in the company's affairs.

**6.14** The consequences of being found to be a shadow director have particular relevance if the company goes into insolvent liquidation. For instance, in an insolvent liquidation a shadow director may be liable with the directors and *de facto* directors (a) to be disqualified if their conduct makes them unfit to be concerned in the management of company; and (b) to contribute to the company's assets under the wrongful trading provisions.

**[The next paragraph is 6.15.1.]**

### *De facto* director

**6.15.1** The distinction between a *de facto* director and a shadow director has been further clarified in the *Deverell* case mentioned above by subdividing *de facto* directors into two types: *de facto* directors type 1 (that is, directors who assume to act, claim to be and are held out by the company as being directors); and *de facto* directors type 2 (that is, directors who directly assume the functions of the directors and act on an equal footing with those who are but without having any sort of label). However, the judge expressed no view on whether the categories of shadow directors or *de facto* directors are mutually exclusive. The following cases indicate the factors that the courts will take into account in ascertaining whether a person is a *de facto* director.

**6.15.2**   It was held in *Secretary of State v Tjolle* [1998] IBCLC 333 that there is no one decisive test of whether a person is a *de facto* director. The Court had to take account of all the relevant factors, including whether or not the company considered the individual a director, whether the individual used the title, whether the individual had proper information (for example, access to management accounts) on which to base decisions, whether the individual had to make major decisions and so on. The question was then, whether the individual was part of the corporate governing structure. It followed that someone who had no, or only peripheral, knowledge of matters of vital company concern (for example, financial state) and had no right, legal or *de facto*, to access such matters was not be regarded by the law as in substance a director.

**6.15.3**   In the *Tjolle* case, K used the title director principally in the form 'sales and marketing director'. She did not have real access to, or responsibility for, the financial records. The Court held that the use of the title 'director' did not make her a *de facto* director, because she was not in fact directing the company. K was a manager, but she did not form part of the real corporate governance of the company. There was no function she performed that could only properly be discharged by a director. She was not, therefore, a *de facto* director.

**6.15.4**   In *Re Kaytech International plc* [1999] 2 BCLC 351 the Court had to decide whether P was a *de facto* or shadow director. P had been deeply and openly involved in the company's affairs. Although he had done his best to avoid being seen as a director, using his office as company secretary as a camouflage, on some very important occasions he acted as a director. For all practical purposes the company was run by K (who was a director) and P. Between them they were its owners. It was essentially a quasi-partnership although P, owning only 20 per cent, might be called the junior partner. K assumed the task of making the final decisions and had the casting vote. Even so, P was held to be a *de facto* director as he was openly acting as a director and was held out as such.

**Alternate director**

**6.16**   The position of an 'alternate director' is determined by the articles of association of a company. If the articles adopted are those of Table A, the alternate director has the following position:

- He/she is appointed and can be removed by the same director of the company.
- If the potential alternate director is not already a director, his/her appointment must be approved by a resolution of the board.

- If the director who appointed the alternate director ceases to be a director, the appointment of the alternate ceases immediately.

- The alternate director is, unless the articles provide otherwise, a director of the company, and can, at meetings of the board, fulfil all the functions of the director appointing him/her, in the absence of that director. Attendance and voting at board meetings is only permitted when the appointing director is absent.

**6.17** Where the term 'director' is used in this chapter, it includes references to directors (both *de facto* and *de jure*), shadow directors, and alternate directors.

## Connected persons

**6.18** A 'connected person' is a person who is connected with a director of a company and is either an individual or a legal person (for example, a company). A connected person is defined by section 252 of the 2006 Act and comes into effect from 1 October 2007. For financial years including that date, the connected person definition under the 1985 Act should be used up until 30 September 2007. A connected person as defined by the 2006 Act includes any of the following:

(a)   A member of the director's family (see further para 6.18.1). [CA06 Secs 252(2)(a), 253].

(b)   A body corporate with which the director is connected (see further para 6.19). [CA06 Secs 252(2)(b), 254].

(c)   A person acting in his capacity as a trustee of any trust in either of the following situations:

- The trust includes as a beneficiary the director, a member of the director's family or a body corporate with which the director is connected (see further paras 6.18.1-6.19).

- The trust confers a power on the trustees that may be used to benefit the director, a member of the director's family or a body corporate with which the director is connected.[CA06 Secs 252(2)(c)].

However, a person acting as trustee of either an employee share scheme or a pension scheme is not connected with a director merely by virtue of that trusteeship. [CA06 Secs 252(2)(c)].

(d)   A partner of the director or of a person who is connected with him under (a), (b) or (c) above. [CA06 Secs 252(2)(d)].

(e)   A firm that is a legal person in which one of the following applies:

- The director is a partner, or persons connected with him/her under (a), (b) or (c) above, are partners.

- Another firm is a partner, and the director or persons connected with him/her under (a), (b) or (c) above are partners of that other firm. [CA06 Secs 252(2)(e)].

This is particularly relevant in Scotland, as in accordance with Scottish law, a firm is a legal person distinct from the partners of whom it is composed, but each partner can still be compelled to pay the firm's debts.

However, none of the above persons are connected if they themselves are also directors of the company. [CA06 Secs 252(3)].

### Members of a director's family

**6.18.1** The members of a director's family are defined as:

- The director's spouse, civil partner or any other person with whom the director lives as a partner in an enduring family relationship.

- The director's adult children or adult step-children.

- The children or step children of the directors' partner, who live with the director and are under 18 (but are not themselves the director's children or step-children).

- The director's parents.

[CA06 Sec 253].

### Body corporate with which a director is connected

**6.19**  A director is 'connected' with a body corporate if, the director, together with the persons connected with him satisfy either of the following two conditions:

- They are *interested* (according to the rules set out in schedule 1 of the 2006 Act) in at least 20 per cent of its equity share capital (excluding any shares held as treasury shares).

- They are entitled to *exercise or control the exercise* of more than 20 per cent of the voting power at any general meeting (excluding any voting rights attached to any shares held as treasury shares).

[CA06 Sec 254(2)-(5)].

For simplicity, a body corporate (that is, an entity incorporated in Great Britain or elsewhere, but excluding a Scottish firm) is referred to below as a company. A person connected with a director can be a foreign-registered company.

**6.20**  For the purposes of establishing whether a director is 'connected' with a company, a director's *interest* in at least 20 per cent of the equity share capital, or his ability to *exercise or control the exercise* of 20 per cent of the voting power, may be either *direct* (that is, he or his connected parties own the shares or control the votes) or *indirect* (that is, a company that he or his connected parties 'control' owns the shares or controls the votes). [CA06 Sec 254(4)]. These rules are set out below.

### Control of shares or votes

**6.21** In determining whether the director and those connected with him can *control the exercise* of more than 20 per cent of the voting power of a company in general meeting, any votes held *indirectly* by a director through another company are to be included in the calculation, but only if the director 'controls' that second company. [CA06 Sec 254(4), 255(4)]. A director of a company is deemed to 'control' that second company if, but only if, both the following two conditions in section 255(2) of the 2006 Act are satisfied:

■ The director, or any person connected with him/her is *interested* in any part of the equity share capital of that second company, or is entitled to *exercise or control the exercise* of any part of the voting power at any general meeting of that company.

■ The director, the persons connected with him/her and the other directors of that company, together, are *interested* in more than 50 per cent of the second company's share capital (excluding any shares in the company held as treasury shares) or are entitled to *exercise or control the exercise* of more 50 per cent of that voting power (excluding any voting rights attached to any shares in the company held as treasury shares).

[CA06 Sec 255(2), (5)].

Sections 254 and 255 of the 2006 Act (sections 346(4) and (5) of the 1985 Act) are illustrated in example 4 in paragraph 6.24 below.

### Interests in shares

**6.22** Under the above provisions, a director's *interests* in shares must be aggregated with those of his connected persons. Schedule 1 to the 2006 Act lays down rules for determining whether a person is interested in shares. These state that a person, is interested in shares if a company is interested in them and either of the following two conditions are met:

■ The person is entitled to exercise or control the exercise of more than 50 per cent of that company's voting power at general meetings.

■ That company or its directors are accustomed to act in accordance with his directions or instructions.

[CA06 1 Sch 5].

See also examples 2 and 3 in paragraph 6.24 below.

## Limits on aggregation

**6.23** For the purpose *only* of determining whether a company is connected with a director, another company with which the director is connected is not regarded as a connected person (see para 6.18 above), except where that company is:

■ a partner of the director or of a person who is connected with the director under (a), (b) or (c) in paragraph 6.18 above [CA85 Sec 346(6)(a); CA06 Secs 254(6), 255(6)]; or

■ a trustee of a trust the beneficiaries of which include, or may include the persons mentioned in (c) of paragraph 6.18. [CA85 Sec 346(6)(b); CA06 Secs 254(6), 255(6)].

Further, a trustee of a trust the beneficiaries of which include (or may include) a company with which a director is associated is not to be treated as connected with a director by reason only of that fact [CA85 Sec 346(6)(b); CA06 Secs 254(6), 255(6)].

**6.24** The following examples illustrate the operation of the rules mentioned in the above paragraphs to establish whether a director is connected with a company – firstly, connected through an interest in shares and, secondly, connected through control of voting power:

### Example 1 – Not connected through an interest in shares

Mr Jones owns 18% of company A's equity share capital, and he also owns 25% of company B's equity share capital. Company B owns 19% of company A's equity share capital.

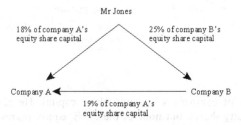

Mr Jones is connected with company B, because he has an *interest* in more than 20% of the equity share capital of that company. [CA85 Sec 346(4); CA06 Sec 254(2)].

In the situation of company A, despite Mr Jones having an effective holding of 22.75% (that is, 18% + 25% × 19% = 22.75%), company A is *not connected* with him. This is because in deciding whether company A is connected with Mr Jones, company B's interest in company A's shares should be ignored. The reason for this is that, although company B is connected with Mr Jones, its interest in company A cannot be aggregated with Mr Jones' own interest for the purposes of section 254(2) of the 2006 Act (section 346(4) of the 1985 Act). Company B is *not connected with* him for these purposes, because company B is not a partner or trustee of Mr Jones. [CA85 Sec 346(6); CA06 Secs 254(6), 255(6)].

**Example 2 – Connected through an interest in shares**

The facts are the same as in example 1 except that Mr Jones owns 5% of company A and he also owns 51% of company B.

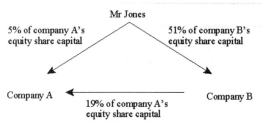

In this situation, although Mr Jones has an effective holding of 14.69% (that is, 5% + 51% × 19% = 14.69%), company A is *connected* with him. This is because, although company B's interest in company A's shares should be ignored by virtue of section 255(6) of the 2006 Act (section 346(6) of the 1985 Act), nevertheless, Mr Jones is taken to be *interested* in the shares of company A held by company B, because he is entitled to exercise, or control the exercise of, more than 50% of the voting power of company B. [CA85 Sec 346(5); CA06 Sec 255(2)]. Consequently, company A is *connected with* Mr Jones via the operation of section 254(2), because he has an interest in 24% (all of the 19% and not a proportion of it, together with a direct holding of 5%) that is greater than 20% of company A's equity share capital.

**Example 3 – Not connected through control of voting power**

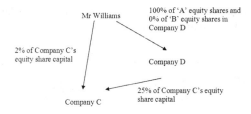

Mr Williams owns 2% of company C's equity share capital. He also owns 100% of company D's £1 'A' equity shares, but none of the £1 'B' equity shares. The issued share capital of company D consists of 5,000 £1 'A' equity shares and 45,000 £1 'B' equity shares. Each 'A' share carries 3 votes and each 'B' share carries 1 vote. Company D owns 25% of company C's equity share capital (which represents 25% of company C's votes).

Although Mr Williams holds only 10% of the total equity share capital of company D, he is able to exercise 15,000 votes out of a maximum of 60,000 votes, which represent in total 25% of the voting power. Therefore, Mr Williams is connected with company D, because he is able to control more than 20% of the voting power of that company. [CA85 Sec 346(4); CA06 Sec 254(2)(b)].

In determining whether company C is connected with Mr Williams, the interest of company D in the shares of company C should be disregarded. [CA85 Sec 346(6); CA06 Secs 254(6), 255(6)]. However, unlike in the second example above, Mr. Williams is also not taken to have an interest in the shares in company C held by company D for the purposes of the operation of section 255 of the 2006 Act (section 346 of the 2006 Act), because he is only *entitled to exercise, or control the exercise of, 25% of the voting power* of company D. Because Mr Williams neither controls nor is presumed to control company D, company C is *not connected* with Mr Williams by the operation of section 255(2)(b) of the 2006 Act (section 346(5) of the 1985 Act).

**Example 4 – Connected through control of voting power**

The facts are the same as in example 3, except that Mr Williams has acquired a further 18,000 £1 'B' equity shares in company D from some of the existing 'B' equity shareholders.

Mr Williams is now able to exercise 33,000 votes out of a maximum of 60,000 votes, which represent in total 55% of the voting power of company D. Therefore, Mr Williams is not only connected with company D, but because he is also interested in part of its equity share capital and is able to exercise more than 50% of its voting power the conditions in section 255(2) of the 2006 Act (section 346(5) of the 1985 Act) for determining whether he 'controls' are met. Because Mr Williams controls company D, he is regarded as controlling company D's exercise of its voting power in company C. [CA85 Sec 346(8); CA06 Secs 254(4)]. Because company D's *voting power exceeds 20%* of the potential voting power at company C's general meeting, company C is regarded as being connected with Mr Williams by the operation of section 254(2)(b) of the 2006 Act (section 346(4) of the 1985 Act).

**Relevant company**

**6.25**   The 1985 Act classified companies for the purpose of the provisions of the Act that relate to directors' transactions  as being either a 'relevant' or 'non-relevant' company. The 2006 Act abolished this terminology and the related provisions of the 1985 Act were repealed from 1 October 2007. A 'relevant company', was defined as being either a public company or a company that belongs to a group in which either the parent company or any subsidiary is a public company.  A non-relevant company was any company other than a relevant company.

**Associated company**

**6.25.1**   The 2006 Act introduces a new term 'associated company' with effect from 1 October 2007. Two companies or two bodies corporate are associated if one is a subsidiary of the other or both are subsidiaries of the same body corporate.  [CA06 Sec 256].

**Body corporate**

**6.25.2**   This term includes a company incorporated outside the UK and limited liability partnerships, but does not include a corporation sole or a partnership that is not regarded as a company under local laws (eg a Scottish partnership is considered a legal person under Scottish law) (see para 6.18(e)). [CA06 sec 1173(1)].

**Company**

**6.26** A 'company' is a company formed and registered under the Companies Act 2006 or any of the former Companies Acts. [CA85 Sec 735(1); CA06 Sec 1(1)].

**Holding company and subsidiary**

**6.27** These terms are defined in section 736 of the 1985 Act (section 1159 of the 2006 Act). A company is a 'subsidiary' of another company, its 'holding company', if that other:

- holds a majority of the voting rights in it, or

- is a member of it and controls the board or a majority of voting rights in it.

It will also be a subsidiary if it is a subsidiary of a company which is itself a subsidiary of that other company. This is different from the definition of 'parent company' used for accounting purposes.

**[The next paragraph is 6.29.]**

# Transactions with directors entered into prior to 1 October 2007

**6.29** Section 330 of the 1985 Act prohibited a company from entering into certain types of transactions (listed below) for the benefit of its directors or persons connected with those directors, unless they fell within specific exemptions set out in sections 332 to 338 of the 1985 Act. The 2006 Act abolished this prohibition for transactions entered into on or after 1 October 2007. However, loans, quasi-loans, credit transactions and related arrangements between a company and its directors or persons connected with the director now require approval by the company's members. The transactions that were prohibited by the 1985 Act were:

- Loans.

- Quasi-loans.

- Credit transactions.

- Guarantees or securities in connection with any of the above transactions made by another person.

- Assignments or assumptions of rights, obligations or liabilities under the above types of transactions.

- Indirect arrangements for the above.

The transactions requiring member approval under the 2006 Act and the exemptions to them for public and private companies, and money-lending and banking companies are considered in detail in this chapter from paragraph 6.30.

# Transactions with directors entered into after 1 October 2007

## Loans

### Definition

**6.30**   Although the expression 'loan' is not defined in the 2006 Act, it was interpreted in a case brought under the Companies Act 1948. In that case it was held that the dictionary definition should be applied. The dictionary definition of a loan is *"a sum of money lent for a time to be returned in money or money's worth"*. [*Champagne Perrier-Jouet S.A. v H.H. Finch Ltd.* [1982] 1 WLR 1359]. Therefore, a loan arises when monies are advanced on the understanding that they will be repaid.

### Value of loans

**6.31**   The value of a loan is the principal amount of the loan. [CA06 Sec 211(2)]. For these purposes, the interest due on the loans may be ignored. If the value cannot be ascertained as a specific sum, it is deemed to exceed £50,000 [CA06 Sec 211(7)]. The value is relevant for ascertaining the 'relevant amounts' to be aggregated for the purpose of establishing whether a proposed transaction is within the exceptions from requiring member approval. [CA06 Secs 204(2), 207(1)(2), 210(1)-(5)].

### Member approval

**6.32.1**   Under the 2006 Act a company may not make a loan to a director of the company or its holding company, or provide a guarantee or security in connection with a loan by any person to such a director, unless the transaction has been approved by a resolution of the company's members. [CA06 Sec 197(1)]. If the director is also a director of the company's holding company, the transaction must be approved by a resolution of the holding company's members. [CA06 Sec 197(2)]. This is a change from the 1985 Act that prohibited all loans to directors, with only a few specific exceptions being provided. These provisions of the 2006 Act are effective for transactions or agreements entered into on or after 1 October 2007.

**6.32.2**   Prior to a resolution being passed to approve a loan to a director, a memorandum containing details of the nature of the transaction, the amount of the loan, its purpose and the extent of the company's liability must be made available to all members. In the case of a written resolution this memorandum must be sent to every eligible member (see para 6.32.3) at the time the proposed resolution is sent out, or in the case of a resolution to be passed at a meeting, it must be made available at the company's registered office for at least 15 days prior to the meeting and at the meeting itself. [CA06 Sec 197(3), (4)].

*Loans and other transactions involving directors*

*Eligible member*

**6.32.3** The eligible members are the members who would have been entitled to vote on the resolution on the circulation date of the resolution. [CA06 Sec 289(1)]. This may also include persons who have been nominated by members to vote on their behalf as set out in section 145 of the 2006 Act.

**6.32.4** Where a person has been nominated by a member of a company whose shares are admitted on a regulated market to enjoy information rights under section 146 of the 2006 Act, that person is not entitled to vote unless an agreement exists between the person and the member who nominated him. [CA06 Sec 149].

## *Exceptions*

### *Small loans*

**6.33** There is a general exception from the need to obtain member approval for small loans. A company does not need to obtain member approval under sections 197, 198 or 200 of the 2006 Act for a company to make a loan or to give a guarantee or security in connection with a loan provided that the aggregate of the value of the transaction and any other relevant transactions does not exceed £10,000. [CA06 Sec 207(1)].

**6.34** The relevant amounts to be aggregated are:

(a) The value of the *proposed transaction.*

(b) The amount outstanding under *any existing transaction or arrangement* (described in para 6.54). Where the proposed transaction or arrangement is to be made for a director of the company or director of the holding company or a person connected with the director, the conditions are that the transaction or arrangement is entered into for that director (or a person connected with him). [CA06 Sec 210(2)-(4)].

The amount outstanding is the value less any amount by which the value has been reduced. [CA06 Sec 211(1)].

**Example – Small loan exception**

A subsidiary is asked to lend £8,000 to the director of its parent company. The director already has a loan of £2,500 from the parent company. The directors of the subsidiary are unsure whether this proposed loan requires member approval of either the parent or the subsidiary.

Section 210 of the 2006 Act requires that amounts lent by the parent company or any subsidiary should be added to any proposed additional loan to the director of the parent company in order to determine whether the new loan falls within any available exception. In this situation, the small loans exception from member approval is £10,000, which is less than the total of the two loans combined (£8,000 plus £2,500). Assuming that the amount outstanding on the parent company's loan is still £2,500, the subsidiary should restrict its

6014     © 2008 PricewaterhouseCoopers LLP. All rights reserved.

proposed loan by £500 to £7,500 to fall within the small loans exception from member approval. If the loan was not restricted, member approval would be required from both the members of the parent and the subsidiary company. [CA06 Sec 197(2)].

**6.35**   There is a further limitation for the purposes of calculating the relevant amounts. Transactions entered into by a company that, at the time of entering into the transactions, was a subsidiary or fellow-subsidiary, but that at the time when the calculation under section 210 of the 2006 Act has to be done, is no longer a subsidiary or fellow subsidiary, need not be taken account into such calculation. [CA06 Sec 210(5)].

**[The next paragraph is 6.38.]**

**6.38**   A foreign subsidiary (that is, one incorporated outside the UK) of a company formed and registered under the 2006 Act or its predecessor is not required under sections 197, 198, 200 and 201 of the 2006 Act to obtain member approval for a loan to a director of its UK parent, provided that the parent or any UK subsidiary does not compensate the foreign subsidiary for making the loan or guarantee it. This is because a foreign subsidiary does not fall within the definition of a 'company' (see para 6.26). Such a foreign subsidiary may, however, be subject to restrictions under the laws of its home state.

*Groups*

**6.39**   The second exception relates to loans to an associated body corporate (inter-company loans). An associated body corporate is defined in paragraphs 6.25.1 and 6.25.2. A company is not required to obtain member approval for a loan or quasi-loan to another company within the same group by reason only that a director of one of the group companies is associated with another group company. This also applies where the company enters into a guarantee, or provides any security in connection with a loan or quasi-loan made by any person to another group company. [CA06 Sec 208(1)].

**6.40**   A holding company is not prohibited from making loans to a director of its subsidiary. Similarly, a subsidiary may be able to lend to a director of a fellow subsidiary. However, in these instances the subsidiary or the fellow subsidiary must not be a party to any indirect arrangement under which they provide any benefit or compensation to the lending company. Indirect arrangements are described in paragraph 6.58. The transaction might also be a related party transaction under the Listing Rules (see para 6.113 below).

**6.41**   In addition, although the 2006 Act requires member approval for loans to directors, a loan made before a person becomes a director does not automatically require approval. However, it would become disclosable as a loan to a director when he becomes a director.

**6.41.1**   More general exceptions which may also be available are set out from paragraph 6.62 below.

## Quasi-loans

### *Definition*

**6.42**  A quasi-loan is a transaction where one party (the creditor) either:

(a)  agrees to pay, or pays, a sum *for another* (the borrower); or

(b)  agrees to reimburse, or reimburses, expenditure another party incurs for another (the borrower); and either of the following two conditions apply:

- the transaction's terms are such that the borrower (or a person on his behalf) will reimburse the creditor; or

- the circumstances surrounding the transaction give rise to a liability on the borrower to reimburse the creditor.

[CA06 Sec 199(1)].

The liabilities of a borrower under a quasi-loan include the liabilities of any person who has agreed to reimburse the creditor on the borrower's behalf. [CA06 Sec 199(3)].

The following are common examples of a quasi-loan:

**Example 1 – Company credit card**

A director uses a company credit card to buy goods for personal use and he does so on the understanding that the company will settle the liability and will be reimbursed by the director at a later date. The quasi-loan is the amount that the company has paid the credit card provider for the directors' personal expenditure.

**Example 2 – Company buys goods directly**

Companies in a group pay for goods and services for the personal use of a director of the parent company, on the basis that the director will reimburse those companies at a later date. The quasi-loan is the amount that is paid for the directors' personal expenditure.

### *Value of quasi-loans*

**6.43**  The value of a quasi-loan is the amount, or maximum amount, that the person to whom it is made is liable to reimburse the creditor. [CA06 Sec 211(3)]. If the value is not ascertainable as a specific sum it is deemed to exceed £50,000. [CA06 Sec 211(7)]. The value is relevant in connection with the disclosure of quasi-loans to be made in the company's financial statements (see from para 6.79) as well as for ascertaining the 'relevant amounts' to be aggregated for the purpose of establishing whether a proposed transaction is within the exceptions from requiring member approval (see para 6.34).

### Conditions for quasi-loans

**6.44** A private company not associated with a public company is permitted to make a quasi-loan of any amount to a director of the company, or its holding company without shareholder approval.

**6.45** A public company, or a private company associated with a public company, may only make a quasi-loan, or provide a guarantee or security in connection with a quasi-loan made by any person to a director of the company, or its holding company if the transaction is approved by a resolution of the members of the company. [CA06 Sec 198(1)(2)]. If the director is a director of the company's holding company the transaction must also be approved by a resolution of the holding company's members. [CA06 Sec 198(3)].

**6.45.1** Prior to a resolution being passed to approve a quasi-loan to a director, a memorandum containing details of the nature of the transaction, the amount of the quasi-loan, its purpose and the extent of the company's liability must be made available to all members. In the case of a written resolution this must be sent to every eligible member at or before the time the proposed resolution is sent out. In the case of a resolution to be passed at a meeting, it must be made available at the company's registered office for at least 15 days prior to the meeting and at the meeting itself. [CA06 Sec 198(4), (5)].

### Exceptions

### Small quasi-loans

**6.46** Approval is not required under section 200 of the 2006 Act for a company entering into a quasi-loan, or to give a guarantee or security in connection with a quasi-loan, if the aggregate of the value of the proposed transaction and the value of any other relevant transactions or arrangements does not exceed £10,000. [CA06 Sec 207(1)].

**6.46.1** A quasi-loan is relevant for these purposes if it meets the criteria set out in paragraph 6.34 above.

**6.47** More general exceptions that may also be available are set out from paragraph 6.62 below.

### Credit transactions

### Definition

**6.48** A credit transaction is any transaction where one party (the creditor):

- supplies any goods or sells any land under a hire purchase agreement or a conditional sale agreement;
- leases or hires any land or goods in return for periodic payments; or

- otherwise disposes of land, or supplies goods or services, on the understanding that payment (whatever form it takes) is to be deferred.

[CA06 Sec 202(1)].

'Services' means anything other than goods or land. [CA06 Sec 202(3)].

### Value of credit transactions

**6.49**   The value of a credit transaction is the price that it would be reasonable to expect could be obtained for the goods, land or services to which the transaction relates if they had been supplied in the ordinary course of the company's business and on the same terms (apart from price). [CA06 Sec 211(4)]. If the value of the transaction cannot be ascertained, it is deemed to exceed £50,000. [CA06 Sec 211(7)]. The value is relevant in connection with the exception for business transactions (see para 6.53), for ascertaining the 'relevant amounts' in connection with the exception for minor transactions (see para 6.52), and in connection with the information relating to credit agreements to be disclosed in the company's financial statements (see para 6.79).

### Conditions for credit transactions

**6.49.1**   A private company not associated with a public company is permitted to enter into a credit transaction or give a guarantee or provide security in connection with a credit transaction entered into by another third party with a director of the company, or its holding company without shareholder approval.

**6.50**   A public company, or a private company associated with a public company, may only enter into a credit transaction or give a guarantee or provide security in connection with a credit transaction entered into by another third party with a director of the company, or its holding company or a person connected with such a director, if the transaction is approved by a resolution of the company's members. [CA06 Sec 201(1)(2)]. If the director, or connected person is a director of the company's holding company or person connected with such a director, the transaction must also be approved by a resolution of the holding company's members. [CA06 Sec 201(3)].

**6.51**   Prior to a resolution being passed to approve a credit transaction to a director, a memorandum containing details of the nature of the transaction, the value of the credit transaction, its purpose and the extent of the company's liability must be made available to all members. In the case of a written resolution this must be sent to every eligible member at the time the proposed resolution is sent out, or in the case of a resolution to be passed at a meeting, it must be made available at the company's registered office for at least 15 days prior to the meeting and at the meeting itself. [CA06 Sec 201(4), (5)].

## Exceptions

### Minor transactions

**6.52** Approval is not required under section 201 of the 2006 Act for a public company or a private company associated with a public company entering into a credit transaction, or to give a guarantee or security in connection with a credit transaction for a person if the aggregate of the value of the proposed transaction and the relevant amounts under other credit transactions, guarantees and securities and arrangements relating to such transactions and made for any one director or his connected persons, does not exceed £15,000. [CA06 Sec 207(2)]. (Arrangements are discussed in para 6.54.)

**6.52.1** The 'relevant amounts' to be aggregated are set out in paragraph 6.34. In the context of this exception, the reference in that paragraph to the small loans exception should be read as a reference to the exception for minor transactions.

### Business transactions

**6.53** Approval is not required under section 201 of the 2006 Act for a public company or a private company associated with a public company entering into a credit transaction, or to give a guarantee or security in connection with a credit transaction for a person if:

■ the transaction in question was entered into in the ordinary course of its business; and

■ the value and the terms on which the company enters into the transaction are no more favourable, for the person for whom it is made, than those the company would have normally offered to a person who was of similar financial standing, but was unconnected with the company.

[CA06 Sec 207(3)].

The value of a credit transaction is considered in paragraph 6.49 above.

**6.53.1** More general exceptions that may also be available are set out from paragraph 6.62 below.

### Assignment or assumption of rights, obligations or liabilities

**6.54** Both *public and private companies associated with public companies* are prohibited by section 203(1)(b) of the 2006 Act from arranging for the assignment to them, or the assumption by them, of any rights, obligations or liabilities under transactions which, had they, themselves, *entered into* them, would have required member approval under sections 197, 198, 200 or 201 of the 2006 Act, unless the arrangement is approved by special resolution of the company's members. The transactions mentioned in these sub-sections are loans, quasi-loans and credit transactions (and guarantees, indemnities and the provision of security in respect of such loans, quasi-loans or credit transactions).

**6.54.1**  In addition, private companies not associated with public companies are prohibited by section 203(1)(b) of the 2006 Act from arranging for the assignment to them, or the assumption by them, of any rights, obligations or liabilities under loans which, had they, themselves, *entered into* them, would have required member approval under section 197 of the 2006 Act, unless the loan is approved by special resolution of the company's members.

**6.55**  For the purposes of section 203 and the other provisions relating to loans, quasi-loans and credit transactions in sections 197, 198, 200 and 201 of the 2006 Act, the transaction will be treated as having been *entered into* on the date of the arrangement for the assignment or assumption of rights, obligations or liabilities mentioned above. [CA06 Sec 203(6)].

**6.56**  An illustration of an 'assignment' is given in example 1 below and an illustration of an 'assumption of liabilities' in example 2 below:

**Example 1 – Loan assignment**

A third party makes a loan to a director of a company and, subsequently, the director's company purchases the third party's rights to the loan. In this situation, the company has paid out resources to acquire an asset and the company purports to become a creditor of the director just as if it had advanced the loan itself.

**Example 2 – Assumption of liabilities**

A third party guarantees a loan that a fourth party makes to a director of a company and, subsequently, the director's company enters into an arrangement with the third and the fourth parties, whereby the third party is released from his guarantee, and the company purports to assume the liability under the guarantee. Again, in this situation, the company's resources are tied up by a contingent liability when the company purports to assume the guarantee on behalf of the director.

*Value of assignment or assumption*

**6.57**  The value of this type of arrangement is the value of the transaction to which the arrangement relates less any amount by which the liabilities of the person for whom the transaction or arrangement was made have been reduced. [CA06 Sec 211(6)]. If the value of the transaction cannot be ascertained as a specific sum, it is deemed to exceed £50,000. [CA06 Sec 211(7)]. The value is relevant in connection with the information regarding the arrangement to be disclosed in the company's financial statements and in the calculation of 'relevant amounts' (see para 6.34).

**Indirect arrangements**

**6.58**  Indirect arrangements are regulated by section 203 of the 2006 Act. Thus, a company cannot take part in an arrangement whereby another person:

■  enters into a transaction that would have required member approval under sections 197, 198, 200 or 201 had the company itself entered into it; and

■  that other person has obtained, or is to obtain, under the arrangement a benefit of any kind from the company, or a body corporate associated with it, unless the arrangement in question has been approved by a resolution of the company's members. [CA06 Sec 203(1)].

**6.59**  This provision expressly prevents a company's resources from being used to procure another person to provide one of the various forms of credit that require member approval without the company itself either entering into, or subsequently becoming a party to, the transaction.

**6.60**  As a consequence, the provision is very widely drafted and is intended to cover the wide variety of forms that these types of arrangement can take. For example, it covers the situation where a company agrees to make a loan to another company's director in return for that other company making a loan to one of the first company's directors. It also covers the situation where a director persuades a bank to make a loan on favourable terms to him/her in return for his company placing business with the bank. Furthermore, by the use of the term 'body' corporate it captures indirect arrangements using the company's foreign subsidiaries.

*Value of indirect arrangements*

**6.61**  The value of an indirect arrangement is ascertained in the same way as the value of an assignment or an assumption of rights considered in paragraph 6.57 above. The value is relevant for the same purposes.

**General exceptions from the requirement for member approval for loans and similar transactions**

**6.62**  In addition to the exceptions that apply only to particular types of transactions (for example, the *de minimis* exception for loans and quasi-loans totalling not more than £10,000, the Companies Act 2006 includes more general exceptions in respect of:

■  Intra-group transactions.

■  Directors' business expenditure.

■  Director's expenditure on defending proceedings.

■  Director's expenditure in connection with regulatory action or investigation.

*Loans and other transactions involving directors*

### Intra-group transactions

**6.63**   The following transactions between associated companies are not covered by the requirement for member approval that sections 197, 198, 200 and 201 of the 2006 Act imposes on loans, quasi-loans and credit transactions:

- A loan or a quasi-loan a company makes to an associated company, or a company's guarantee or provision of security to a third person who has made a loan or quasi-loan to an associated company.

- A credit transaction a company enters into as creditor for an associated company, or a guarantee or security that a company provides in connection with a credit transaction a third party makes for an associated company.

[CA06 Sec 208].

This exception would apply, for instance, where the holding company is a director of the subsidiary. Transactions that fall within the above provisions do not, therefore, require member approval.

### Directors' business expenditure

**6.64**   Section 204 of the 2006 Act provides an exception from the requirement to obtain member approval for any action by a company to provide a director with funds to meet expenditure incurred or to be incurred by him/her for the purposes of the company, or to enable him/her to perform his duties properly as an officer of the company. [CA06 Sec 204(1)]. Furthermore, the company is not prohibited from doing anything to enable a director to avoid incurring expenditure of the kind described in section 204(1). [CA06 Sec 204(1)(b)]. The company may provide these funds by way of a loan, or a quasi-loan or a credit transaction, or by any other similar arrangement. This exception applies only if the aggregate of the transaction in question and the value of any other relevant transactions or arrangements does not exceed £50,000. [CA06 Sec 204(2)]. The relevant amounts to be aggregated are those referred to in paragraph 6.34.

### [The next paragraph is 6.66.]

**6.66**   The most common form of transaction of this nature relates to travelling expenses between different places of business. Another form of transaction of this nature is a bridging loan a company gives to a director, who changes location within the company and so is required to move house.

**6.67**   Section 204 of the 2006 Act does not restrict advances to an amount appropriate to the specific business expenditure it is anticipated the director will incur. However, where the amount is clearly excessive or remains unspent for an unduly long time, then the recipient is likely to have derived some personal benefit and the transaction takes on the nature of a loan. In such a case the amount may require member approval.

### Funding of director's expenditure on defending proceedings

**6.67.1** Member approval is not required for a company to provide a director of the company or its holding company with funds to meet expenses incurred or to be incurred in connection with:

■ Defending any civil or criminal proceedings in connection with any alleged negligence, default, breach of duty, or breach of trust in relation to the company or an associated company

■ Any application to the courts for relief from a liability or claim under section 661(3) and (4) of the 2006 Act (acquisition of shares by innocent nominee) or section 1157 (general power to grant relief in case of honest and reasonable conduct).

[CA06 Sec 205(1)(5)].

**6.67.2** Furthermore, approval is not needed for a company acting to enable a director to avoid incurring such expenditure. [CA06 Sec 205(1)(b)].

**6.67.3** This exception is contingent as the terms of the arrangment requiring that the loan to the director or (if the transaction is a quasi-loan or credit transaction) the liability of the company is repaid or discharged no later than:

■ The date on which the directors conviction becomes final (if he is convicted).

■ The date on which judgement against the director becomes final (if judgement is found against him/her).

■ The date on which the court's refusal of relief becomes final (if an application for relief is refused).

[CA06 Sec 205(2)].

**6.67.4** For the purpose of section 205(2) of the 2006 Act, a conviction, judgement or refusal becomes final when the period for bringing an appeal expires (if no appeal has been made) or when the appeal has been disposed of (that is, it is determined that the period for bringing any further appeal has ended or the appeal is abandoned or otherwise ceases to have effect). [CA06 Sec 205(3), (4)].

### Funding of director's expenditure in connection with regulatory action or investigation

**6.67.5** The Companies Act 2006 introduced a further exception to the requirement for member approval in relation to regulatory investigations. A company may, without member approval, provide a director of the company or its holding company with funds to meet expenditure incurred or to be incurred in defending himself in an investigation by a regulatory authority or against action proposed to be taken by a regulatory authority. [CA06 Sec 206(a)].

**6.67.6**   Furthermore, approval is not needed for a company acting to enable a director to avoid incurring such expenditure. [CA06 Sec 206(b)].

### Civil consequences of contravention

**6.68**   The consequences of failing to comply with sections 197, 198, 200, 201 or 203 of the 2006 Act are set out in detail in paragraph 6.175.

## Disclosure requirements for loans, quasi-loans, credit arrangements and guarantees

### Introduction

**6.69**   The 1985 Act requires considerable detail to be disclosed regarding loans, quasi-loans and credit transactions with directors. It also requires a director to declare any interest in any proposed contract with the company to the board of directors. [CA85 Sec 317; CA06 Sec 177]. These requirements in respect of directors' interests in proposed contracts are discussed from paragraph 6.163 onwards. The 1985 Act requires particulars of the transactions to be disclosed in the notes to a company's financial statements whether they are lawful under the 1985 Act or not. The circumstances in which disclosure is required in the financial statements and the particulars regarding disclosure are set out in Part II of Schedule 6 to the 1985 Act. The disclosure requirements relating to transactions with officers are set out in Part III of Schedule 6. [CA85 Sec 232(1)(2);]. Banking companies may, however, take advantage of a relaxation in the disclosure requirements set out by Part II of Schedule 6 by virtue of paragraph 2 of Part IV of Schedule 9 of the 1985 Act.

**6.69.1**   Section 413 of the 2006 Act (contained in Part 15: Accounts and reports) replaces Part II of Schedule 6 and Part IV of Schedule 9 of the 1985 Act as regards to the disclosure of loans, quasi-loans, credit arrangements and guarantees granted to a company's directors or those of its holding company. Somewhat confusingly, section 413 of the 2006 Act uses different terminology for the disclosure requirements from that used in sections 197, 198, 200 and 203 of that Act dealing with the legality of such transactions. Section 413 refers to the transactions as advances, credits and guarantees. It requires disclosure of (a) advances and credits granted by the company to its directors and (b) guarantees of any kind entered into by the company on behalf of its directors. It also covers the disclosure of such transactions with the directors of a company's holding company. There are no corresponding provisions under the 2006 Act for Part III of Schedule 6 or the remaining disclosures in Part II of Schedule 6 or Part IV of Schedule 9 to the 1985 Act. Part 15 of the 2006 Act is effective for financial years beginning on or after 6 April 2008.

**6.69.2**   The following three sections describe the disclosure requirements for advances, credits and guarantees for particular financial years; the first section is for financial years beginning and ending before 6 April 2008 and includes details of the disclosure requirements under the 1985 Act. The second section is for financial years beginning before 6 April 2008 and ending after 6 April 2008 and includes details of the disclosure requirements under the 1985 Act, amended by the 2006 Act and the third section is for financial years beginning on or after 6 April 2008 and sets out the disclosure requirements under the 2006 Act.

**Disclosure in financial statements for financial years beginning and ending before 6 April 2008**

**6.70** Details of the transactions that are required to be disclosed must be given in the notes to the consolidated financial statements of a holding company (or if it is not required to prepare consolidated financial statements, its individual financial statements), or in the financial statements of any company other than a holding company. Such transactions are required to be disclosed for shadow directors as well as for directors. [CA85 6 Sch 27(2)]. Disclosure is required regardless of whether the company prepares its financial statements in accordance with EU-adopted IFRS or UK GAAP.

**6.70.1** The disclosure requirements are governed by the 1985 Act for financial years beginning before 6 April 2008. However, it should be noted that some parts of the 1985 Act have been repealed and replaced by the 2006 Act. These amendments are summarised in paragraph 6.2 and are effective for transactions with directors entered into on or after 1 October 2007. Where this has happened the 2006 Act references have also been given.

**6.71** Any transaction or arrangement of a type described in section 330 of the 1985 Act (sections 197, 198, 200, 201 or 203 of the 2006 Act) (that is, loans, quasi-loans, credit transactions and related arrangements) and agreements to enter into such transactions must, unless they are specifically exempted (see para 6.81) be disclosed in the notes to the financial statements. [CA85 6 Sch 15(a)(b), 16(a)(b)].

**6.72** The transactions, arrangements and agreements that are required to be disclosed in their financial statements by all reporting companies are those entered into by the reporting company and (if it is a holding company) by its subsidiaries:

- For a person who was a director at any time during the financial year of either the company or its holding company.

- For a person who was connected with such a director.

[CA85 6 Sch 15(a)(b), 16(a)(b)].

**6.73** The disclosure provisions apply irrespective of whether or not:

- The transaction was either prohibited by section 330 of the 1985 Act or if entered into after 1 October 2007, was one in respect of which approval was required under sections 197, 198, 200, 201 or 203 of the 2006 Act.

*Loans and other transactions involving directors*

- The person for whom the transaction was made was a director, or was a person connected with a director, at the time the transaction was made. What is relevant is that the person should have been a director at some time during the financial year.

- The company that entered into the transaction was a subsidiary of the company of which the person was a director at the time the transaction was made.

[CA85 6 Sch 19].

### Information to be disclosed for all transactions

**6.74** The following information must be given in the notes to the financial statements for each disclosable transaction, arrangement or agreement:

- Particulars of its principal terms. [CA85 6 Sch 22(1)]. The 'principal terms' will include those terms that relate to the provision of either the cash or the non-cash asset and also the arrangements for repaying the value of that asset (including any interest component, together with any related security or guarantees).

- A statement that the transaction either was made during the financial year or existed during that period. [CA85 6 Sch 22(2)(a)].

- The name of the director concerned in the transaction and where applicable, the name of the connected person. [CA85 6 Sch 22(2)(b)].

- The additional disclosures, as appropriate, set out below.

Corresponding amounts for the immediately preceding financial period must also be given, even where no amount is disclosed in respect of the current period. [FRS 28 paras 8,10].

### Additional disclosure for loans

**6.75** For any loan, any agreement for a loan, or any arrangement relating to a loan under section 330(6) or (7) of the 1985 Act (section 203 of the 2006 Act if entered into after 1 October 2007) (related arrangements), the following information has to be disclosed:

- The amount of the liability (in respect of both principal and interest), both at the beginning and the end of the financial year.

- The maximum amount of the liability during that period.

- The amount of any interest due but unpaid.

■ The amount of any provision that the company has made against the failure or the anticipated failure of the borrower to repay the whole, or any part, of the principal or interest.

[CA85 6 Sch 22(2)(d)].

**[The next paragraph is 6.77.]**

*Additional disclosure for guarantees or securities*

**6.77** For any guarantee or security, or any arrangement under section 330(6) of the 1985 Act (section 203(1)(b) of the 2006 Act if entered into after 1 October 2007) relating to any guarantee or security, the following information has to be disclosed:

■ The amount of the liability of the company or its subsidiary, both at the beginning and the end of the financial year.

■ The maximum amount for which the company or its subsidiary may become liable.

■ Any amount the company or its subsidiary has paid, and any liability it has incurred, either in fulfilling the guarantee or in discharging the security.

[CA85 6 Sch 22(2)(e)].

The 'value' of such a guarantee or security is the amount guaranteed or secured [CA06 Sec 211(5); CA85 Sec 340(4)].

**6.78** The above disclosure requirements are illustrated in Table 6.2.

---

**Table 6.2 – Disclosure of securities**

**British Aerospace Public Limited Company – Annual Report – 31 December 1994**

**Notes to the accounts (extract)**

**Transactions**

Under a housing loan scheme operated by the Company, Mr M J Turner has a bank loan, bearing interest at 5% per annum, incurred in buying his house and entered into prior to him becoming a Director of the Company, as a result of relocating at the Company's request. At 31st December, 1994 the amount of principal outstanding under this loan was £23,883 (1993 £25,208) and the accrued interest outstanding was £43 (1993 £66). Mr Turner's loan is secured on his house and certain insurance policies and is repayable not later than September 2010. For the duration of the loan the Company maintains with the bank a deposit equal to the amount outstanding under the loan, such deposit bears interest at 3.75% per annum and is available as additional security for the loan.

---

### Additional disclosure for quasi-loans and credit transactions

**6.79** For quasi-loans, credit transactions and related arrangements for assignment and indirect arrangements under sections 330(6) and (7) of the 1985 Act (section 203 of the 2006 Act for transactions entered into after 1 October 2007) or agreements for such transactions, disclosure has to be made of the 'value' of the transaction or arrangement, or the 'value' of the transaction or arrangement to which the agreement relates. [CA85 6 Sch 22(f)]. The effect of this provision is to require, for example, the disclosure of:

■ The amount, or the maximum amount, to be reimbursed in respect of a quasi-loan. [CA85 Sec 340(3)].

■ The value, that is, the arm's length price of any goods and services purchased, of a credit transaction. [CA85 Sec 340(6)].

■ For an arrangement for assignment or an indirect arrangement, the value of the transaction to which that arrangement relates, less any amount by which the liabilities under the arrangement have been reduced. [CA85 Sec 340(5)].

If the value is not capable of being ascertained as a specific sum, it is deemed to exceed £100,000 (under the 2006 Act this value is reduced to £50,000). The meaning of 'value' is discussed in greater detail in connection with the specific type of transaction or arrangement concerned.

### Exemptions for certain intra-group loans

**6.80** Some of the additional information outlined in the above paragraphs need not be disclosed for loans and quasi-loans where:

■ A company ('lender') makes or agrees to make them to or for a body corporate ('borrower') of which the lender is a wholly-owned subsidiary, or to or for a fellow wholly-owned subsidiary or the lender's wholly-owned subsidiary; and

■ The information would not have been disclosable in the lender's financial statements if the borrower had not been *associated with* a director of the lender. For the meaning of a company being associated with a director see paragraph 6.18(b).

[CA85 6 Sch 23].

But where this type of transaction does exist, the financial statements still have to give particulars of the transaction's principal terms, a statement that the transaction was made or existed during the year, and the name of the body corporate concerned (see para 6.74 above). This exception means that, where certain intra-group loans are made by the company, only those details are required to be disclosed.

**Transactions excluded from disclosure**

**6.81**   The disclosure requirements in Schedule 6 Part II to the 1985 Act do not apply to the transactions, arrangements and agreements ('transactions') referred to below.

- A transaction between two companies, where a director of one of the companies (or of its subsidiary or its holding company) is interested *only* by virtue of the fact that he is also a director of that other company [CA85 6 Sch 18(a)]. This exemption means that, among other things, details of many general *intra-group trading* transactions between companies are not required to be disclosed.

- A transaction that was not entered into during the period to which the financial statements relate and that did not exist at any time during that period. [CA85 6 Sch 18(c)]. (Although note the requirement to disclose comparative information described in paragraph 6.74.)

- A transaction of the kind mentioned below made by a company or its subsidiary for a person who, at any time during the financial year, was a director of the company or its holding company, or was connected with any such director, provided that the aggregate of the amounts outstanding (see below) under each such transaction did not exceed £5,000 (under the 2006 Act this value has increased to £10,000) at any time during the period. These transactions are:

  - Credit transactions.

  - Guarantees or securities relating to credit transactions.

  - Assignments, or assumptions or indirect arrangements of the type referred to in section 330(6) and (7) of the 1985 Act (section 203 of the 2006 Act for transactions entered into after 1 October 2007) relating to credit transactions.

  - Agreements to enter into credit transactions.

The 'aggregate amount outstanding' mentioned above means the following in relation to the limit of £5,000 (under the 2006 Act this value has increased to £10,000) for a particular director. The aggregate of the values of all such transactions made for him/her or for any person connected with him/her, less any amount by which the liability of the person for whom the transaction was made has been reduced. [CA85 6 Sch 24(1)]. The value of a transaction is discussed above in connection with that kind of transaction.
[CA85 6 Sch 24(1)(2)].

**6.82**   Without this threshold limit, a company's financial statements would sometimes contain an excessive amount of information about directors' transactions. Petty credit transactions involving deferred payment by directors are very common and it is not the intention of the 1985 Act to require disclosure of these. The Act intends that disclosure should prevent abuse where the transactions involve larger sums. It should be noted however, that this exclusion does not extend to loans or quasi-loans. Even small loans must be disclosed.

**Penalties for failure to disclose transactions with directors**

**6.83**   The penalties which apply when directors do not disclose the information required by Schedule 6 Part II of the 1985 Act are set out from paragraph 6.171 onwards.

**Disclosure in financial statements — financial years beginning before 6 April 2008 and ending after 6 April 2008**

**6.83.1**   One of the main changes in the 2006 Act is to remove the requirement to disclose transactions between the company and persons connected with the director. From 1 October 2007 the definition of connected persons for use in respect of the disclosure requirements under the 1985 Act changed to that contained in the 2006 Act (refer to para 6.18). This broadened the definition to include the directors' parents, life-partner and adult children. As a result, this imposes additional requirements on companies, particularly money lending companies, to make additional disclosures during the transitional period. For financial years including 1 October 2007, the old definition of connected persons is used up to 30 September 2007 and the new one thereafter. For financial years ending on or after 6 April 2008, the disclosures required under the 1985 Act are amended by SI 2008/948, 'The Companies Act 2006 (Consequential Amendments etc) Order 2008', to remove the requirement to disclose the transactions and arrangements of a person who is connected with a director.

**6.83.2**   For financial years beginning before 6 April 2008 and ending on or after 6 April 2008 the disclosure requirements are the same as those set out from paragraph 6.70 above, except the requirement to disclose the transactions with a person who is connected to a director has been removed as detailed in paragraph 6.83.1.

**Disclosure in financial statements — financial years beginning on or after 6 April 2008**

**6.83.3**   The main change under the 2006 Act is to remove the requirement to disclose transactions between the company and persons connected with the director. However, such transactions may fall to be disclosed under the related party disclosure requirements. For IFRS reporters, complying with IAS 24 (refer to chapter 29 of the Manual of Accounting – IFRS for the UK) will meet the related party disclosure requirements. For UK GAAP reporters, additional related party disclosure requirements have been introduced by the 2006 Act over and above those within FRS 8 (refer to chapter 29 of the Manual of Accounting – UK GAAP).

**6.83.4**   The disclosure requirements in respect of advances (which include loans and quasi-loans), credit and guarantees entered into with directors are contained in section 413 of the 2006 Act. Where a company does not prepare consolidated financial statements, it is required to disclose details of advances and credits granted by the company to its directors and guarantees entered into by the company on behalf of its directors. Where a parent company prepares consolidated financial statements, it is required to disclose details of advances and credit granted to the directors of the parent company, by that company or by any of its subsidiaries and guarantees entered into on behalf of the directors of the parent company, by that company or by any of its subsidiaries. [CA06 Sec 413(1), (2)].

**6.83.5** The details required to be disclosed in respect of an advance or credit are:

- Its amount.
- An indication of the interest rate.
- Its main conditions.
- Any amounts repaid.

[CA06 Sec 413(3)].

**6.83.6** The 2006 Act also requires disclosure of the totals of the amounts of advances and credits and the total of the amounts repaid. [CA06 Sec 413(5)(a),(b)].

**6.83.7** The disclosures required in respect of a guarantee are:

- Its main terms.
- The amount of the maximum liability that may be incurred by the company (or its subsidiary).
- Any amount paid and any liability incurred by the company (or its subsidiary) for the purpose of fulfilling the guarantee (including any loss incurred by reason of enforcement of the guarantee).

[CA06 Sec 413(4)].

**6.83.8** In respect of guarantees entered into with the directors, the 2006 Act also requires disclosure of the total amounts of the maximum liability that may be incurred and of the total amounts paid and any liability incurred for the purpose of fulfilling the guarantee. [CA06 Sec 413(5)(c), (d)].

## Transactions in which directors have material interests — financial years beginning before 6 April 2008

### Introduction

**6.84** Section 232 of the 1985 Act requires the information specified in Schedule 6 Part II regarding certain dealings in favour of directors to be disclosed in a company's financial statements for financial years beginning before 6 April 2008. The following paragraphs describe the disclosure requirements under Part II of Schedule 6 of the 1985 Act for financial years beginning before 6 April 2008 for other dealings in favour of directors. These are transactions and arrangements with the company (or a subsidiary of it) in which a director of the company or its holding company had, directly or indirectly, a *material interest*. A director of a company or its holding company is also treated as having a material interest where the transaction is between the company and a person connected with the director.

**6.85** A holding company must disclose in its consolidated financial statements or, if it is not required to prepare consolidated financial statements, in its individual financial statements, such transactions or arrangements with it or with a subsidiary of it. A company that is not a holding company must disclose such transactions or arrangements in its financial statements.

**6.86** Paragraphs 15(c) and 16(c) of Schedule 6 to the 1985 Act require disclosure where the director has, directly or indirectly, a *material* interest. For these purposes, paragraph 17(2) of Schedule 6 of the 1985 Act says that an interest in a transaction or arrangement is not 'material' if in the board's opinion it is not material; but this is without prejudice to the question whether or not such an interest is material in a situation where the board has not considered the matter. 'The board' means the directors of the company who prepare the financial statements, but it excludes the particular director who has the interest in the transaction.

**6.87** Although paragraph 17(2) of Schedule 6 does not say so explicitly, it is, of course, implicit that the directors' opinion on the materiality of a director's interest in a transaction must have been formed reasonably and in good faith. Where the directors have not considered the question of materiality, the materiality will be a matter of fact. This does not mean that the director's interest in a transaction will be regarded as material. It simply means that, in the absence of an opinion from the directors, it cannot be presumed not to be material.

**Interpretation of 'material interest'**

**6.88** In practice, the interpretation of the words 'material interest' has caused considerable debate. Although the test of materiality is not clear, two tests, the 'relevant' test and the 'substantial' test, are regarded as having some authority. The 'relevant' test considers a director's interest to be material if the transaction is likely to be of interest or relevance either to the shareholders or to the other users of the financial statements. The 'substantial' test considers a director's interest to be material if the director's interest in the transaction is substantial whether or not it is of significance to shareholders or creditors.

The 'substantial' test can be illustrated by the following example:

**Example**

Where a director buys a bar of chocolate in the company's shop, he is the other party to the contract, and accordingly his interest in the transaction (his purchase of the bar of chocolate from the company) is material.

**6.89** Counsel has advised that the 'relevant' test of the two tests referred to above is to be preferred. Counsel has said that the correct approach should be to find out whether the existence of the arrangement would be significant to a shareholder. It could be significant either because it is one of importance to the company or because it is one of importance to the individual director. Where the transaction is of importance either to the company or to the individual director, then a material interest does exist, and it should be disclosed. On the other hand, it should be borne in mind that other Counsel have advised that the substantial test is preferred. However, there is also a view that both tests may serve a complementary function. Some of the extreme implications of the 'substantiality' test are removed by the exemptions from disclosure – see bullet points 6 and 7 in paragraph 6.98.

### [The next paragraph is 6.91.]

**6.91** There is still considerable uncertainty about the meaning of this term. Therefore, if a director has an interest in a transaction that may or may not be material, legal advice should be taken.

**6.92** Certain other types of transaction involving a director (or the persons connected with him/her) and the company may not be regarded as material, and if so, they do not have to be disclosed in the financial statements. These are considered in paragraph 6.98 below.

### [The next paragraph is 6.94.]

**Disclosure requirements — financial years beginning before 6 April 2008**

**6.94** For financial years beginning before 6 April 2008, disclosure of transactions in which a director has a material interest is governed by the Companies Act 1985. This requires disclosure of any transaction or arrangement with the company or (if it is a holding company) its subsidiary in which a person who at any time during the financial year was a director of the company or its holding company had, either directly or indirectly, a material interest. [CA85 6 Sch 15(c), 16(c)]. This requirement also applies if the transaction or arrangement is with a person who is connected with a director: it is then treated as one in which the director is interested. [CA85 6 Sch 17(1)].

**6.95** A company must disclose the necessary particulars in its individual financial statements, unless it is a holding company preparing consolidated financial statements, when it must disclose them in its consolidated financial statements. [CA85 Sec 232(1)(2); 6 Sch 15, 16]. Where a company with subsidiaries has not prepared consolidated financial statements (either because it is a wholly-owned subsidiary or because its subsidiaries are excluded from consolidation), the notes to its individual financial statements must give the equivalent information that would have been given if it had prepared consolidated financial statements. [CA85 6 Sch 15]. Such transactions are required to be disclosed for shadow directors as well as for other directors. [CA85 6 Sch 27(2)]. Where a company has entered into a transaction or arrangement of the type described in paragraph 6.94 above that is required to be disclosed in the financial statements, the financial statements must contain the following information:

- Particulars of the principal terms of the transaction or arrangement. [CA85 6 Sch 22(1)]. The 'principal terms' will include those terms that relate to the provision of either the cash or the non-cash asset and also the arrangements for repaying the value of that asset (including any interest component, together with any related security or guarantees).

- A statement that the transaction or arrangement either was made during the financial year or existed during that period. [CA85 6 Sch 22(2)(a)].

- The name of the director concerned in the transaction. Where a transaction is made for a director's connected person, the name of the connected person and the director concerned have to be given. [CA85 6 Sch 22(2)(b)].

- The name of the director who has the material interest in the transaction, and the nature of the interest. [CA85 6 Sch 22(2)(c)].

- The 'value' of the transaction or arrangement or, where applicable, the value of the transaction or arrangement to which the agreement relates. This is the arms' length price of the goods, land or services to which the transaction or arrangement relates. [CA85 Sec 340(6)].

Corresponding amounts for the immediately preceding financial period must also be given, even where no amount is disclosed in respect of the current period. [FRS 28 paras 8,10].

**6.96** The above disclosure requirements for transactions in which a director has a material interest are illustrated in Tables 6.3 and 6.4.

---

**Table 6.3 – Transactions in which a director has a material interest**

**The Royal Bank of Scotland Group plc – Report and Accounts – 30 September 1999**

**Notes to the accounts (extract)**

**51 Transactions with directors, officers and others**

Sir George Mathewson, a director and chief executive of the company and the Bank has a right to repurchase from the Bank his former dwellinghouse which the Bank purchased from him and his wife in May 1988 at a price of £125,000. The right will become exercisable (1) in the event that Sir George ceases to be an executive director of the company or its subsidiaries; or (2) on 31 May 2008 in the event that he remains an executive director at that date; or (3) on such earlier date as the directors of the company may allow. Any repurchase is to be at the higher of the purchase

---

price paid by the Bank or a price determined by independent professional valuation at the time of repurchase.

The dwellinghouse is at present let by the Bank on a commercial basis, with any rental payments being received wholly by the Bank.

---

**Table 6.4 – Transactions in which directors have material interest**

**Abingworth plc – Annual Report – 30 June 1989**

**Directors' report (extract)**

**Board of directors (extract)**

Certain Directors of the Company were the principal promoters of and are shareholders in Interven Capital S.A., Interven II S.A., Tetraven Fund S.A. and Biotechnology Venture Fund S.A. ("the Luxembourg companies") to each of which Abingworth Management Limited provides investment advice, under the terms of separate investment advisory contracts, for which it is remunerated on the basis of cost plus ten per cent thereof. Each such contract subsisted throughout the course of the year. Details of the Directors' approximate percentage interests in the equity capital of each of the Luxembourg companies at 30 June 1989 are shown below:

| | Interven Capital S.A. | Interven II S.A. | Tetraven Fund S.A. | Biotechnology Venture Fund S.A.* |
|---|---|---|---|---|
| Hon A.T.S. Montagu | 7.63 | 5.90 | 5.69 | 3.61 |
| P.F. Dicks | 7.50 | 5.30 | 5.17 | 3.33 |
| S.M. Gray | 2.56 | 2.05 | 0.63 | 0.36 |
| Dr N.W. Horne | - | 0.13 | 0.13 | 0.08 |
| D.F.J. Leathers | - | - | - | 5.00 |
| D.J. Morrison | - | 0.13 | 1.75 | 1.13 |
| D.W. Quysner | 0.54 | 3.65 | 4.10 | 2.38 |
| Sir James Spooner | 1.50 | 1.30 | 0.31 | 0.15 |

*Fully diluted for committed subscriptions outstanding

On 17 August 1989, the Company entered into a conditional contract for the sale of Abingworth Management Limited to a company owned by Messrs. Montagu, Bunting, Dicks, Leathers, Morrison and Qusyner. The sale was approved by shareholders at an Extraordinary General meeting held on 13 September 1989, at which time the Company also entered into a revised Investment Advisory Agreement with Abingworth Management Limited.

Save as disclosed, there was no contract of significance subsisting during the year ended 30 June 1989 in which a Director of the Company had no material interest.

---

**6.97** In addition to the statutory disclosure requirements outlined above, the Listing Rules require listed companies to give particulars in their statutory financial statements of any contract of significance in which a director was materially interested and which existed during the financial year. [LR 9.8.4R(10)]. The UKLA's Listing Rules' requirements are dealt with in paragraph 6.113.

**Exemptions from disclosure under the Companies Act 1985**

**6.98** The disclosure requirements set out in paragraph 6.95 above do not apply to the following transactions and arrangements:

- A transaction between two companies, where a director of one of the companies (or of its subsidiary or its holding company) is interested only by virtue of the fact that he is also a director of that other company [CA85 6 Sch 18(a)]. This exemption means that, among other things, details of many general intra-group trading transactions between companies are not required to be disclosed.

- A contract of service between a company and one of its directors, or a director of its holding company, or between a director of the company and any of its subsidiaries. [CA85 6 Sch 18(b)]. The inspection of such contracts by the company's members is regulated by section 318 of the 1985 Act. A listed company must also disclose details of certain service contracts under the requirements of the UKLA Listing Rules. [LR 9.8.4 R(10),(11)]. This requirement is considered in chapter 3. There is a distinction between a *contract of service,* where a director is employed by the company, and a *contract for services,* where a director is an independent contractor. There is *no exemption* from disclosure for the latter type of contract.

- A transaction that was not entered into during the period to which the financial statements relate and that did not exist at any time during that period. [CA85 6 Sch 18(c)].

- There is a *de minimis* exception for any transactions with a company or any of its subsidiaries in which a director of the company or its holding company had, directly or indirectly, a material interest if the aggregate value did not exceed £1,000 at any time during the relevant period. The aggregate value is the aggregate of the following:

  - The value of each such transaction which was made after the commencement of the financial year.

  - The value of each such transaction that was made before the commencement of the financial year, less the amount (if any) by which the liability of the person for whom the transaction was made has subsequently been reduced.

Alternatively, if that value did exceed £1,000, no disclosure is required if the aggregate value did not exceed the lower of £5,000 and one per cent of the value of the company's net assets as at the end of the financial year [CA85 6 Sch 25]. For this purpose, 'net assets' are the aggregate of the company's assets less the aggregate of its liabilities (including provisions for liabilities). This minimum figure is flexible in order that it should take account of the needs of different sizes of company. The Secretary of State has power to increase by Statutory Instrument the financial limits mentioned above.

- Transactions that, in the opinion of the board, are not material (see paras 6.86 and 6.87 above).

- Transactions involving other members of the same group that are entered into by those group companies in the ordinary course of their business and at arm's length and that would otherwise be disclosable under paragraphs 15(c) or 16(c) of Schedule 6 to the 1985 Act (that is, those transactions outlined in para 6.94 above). [CA85 6 Sch 20(a)(b)]. There is some confusion on the interpretation of paragraph 20 of Schedule 6 to the 1985 Act and it has been suggested that the exemption can be read as applying even where there is no group. If this interpretation is correct (it is in line with the interpretation of the paragraph as stated in the Explanatory Note published with SI1984/1860, 'The Companies (Accounts) Regulations 1984'), the exemption will apply whether or not the company entering into the transaction is a member of a group. This would mean that any transaction in which a director has a material interest is exempted from disclosure under paragraph 15(c) or 16(c) of Schedule 6 to the 1985 Act if the transaction is entered into by the reporting company or by a company in the same group at arms' length and in the ordinary course of its business.

- A transaction or arrangement that would otherwise be disclosable under paragraph 15(c) or 16(c) of Schedule 6 to the 1985 Act because the director had a material interest, but only on account of the fact that he was associated with the company. ('Associated' is defined in para 6.19.) This exemption applies only if the company is a member of a group of companies and if one of the following situations exists:

    - The company is a wholly-owned subsidiary.

    - No company within the same group, other than the company itself or one of its subsidiaries, was a party to the transaction or arrangement.

  [CA85 6 Sch 21].

  These conditions mean that the exemption from disclosure is available only if minority interests in the company are not affected. The effect of this provision is that, provided the conditions are satisfied, a director who is associated with the company and who would, therefore, have an interest in every contract that the company is party to that may be disclosable, does not have to disclose that interest in the financial statements.

### Penalties for failure to disclose transactions with directors

**6.99** The penalties for failure to disclose in the financial statements a transaction in which a director has a material interest are dealt with from paragraph 6.171.

## Transactions in which directors have material interests — financial years beginning on or after 6 April 2008

**6.99.1** For financial years beginning on or after 6 April 2008, the disclosure requirements of the 1985 Act for transactions in which directors have material interests no longer apply. However, the 2006 Act does not contain a specific replacement for Schedule 6 Part II of the 1985 Act for such transactions. Disclosure may be required as a related party transaction in accordance with IAS 24 (chapter 29 of the Manual of Accounting – IFRS for the UK) or FRS 8 (chapter 29 of the Manual of Accounting – UK GAAP).

## Substantial property transactions

### Introduction

**6.100** In addition to the requirement for member approval for loans, quasi-loans and credit transactions between a company and its directors as set out above, a company's ability to contract with a director is similarly restricted where it wishes to enter into certain substantial property transactions. The provisions in the 2006 Act are unchanged from those in the 1985 Act other than a change in the definition of connected person (see para 6.18), an increase in the financial thresholds, provisions relating to the aggregation of transactions and enabling a company to enter into a substantial property transaction that is conditional upon shareholder approval. The 2006 Act provisions are effective from 1 October 2007; the information below is, therefore, based on the requirements of the 2006 Act.

### Shareholders' approval of substantial property transactions

**6.100.1** A company (whether a public or private company) is prohibited from entering into an arrangement whereby:

- a director of the company or its holding company, or a person connected with the director, acquires one or more substantial non-cash assets from the company; or

- the company acquires one or more substantial non-cash assets from such a director or connected person,

unless the prior approval by resolution of the company and (if the director is a director of the holding company) its holding company in general meeting is given, or is conditional on such approval being given. [CA06 Sec 190(1)(2)]. Consequently, unless such prior approval is given or the arrangement is affirmed by resolution of the company in general meeting within a reasonable period the transaction is voidable by the company. [CA06 Sec 195(2)].

**6.101** Stricter rules apply to companies that are charities. In this case, the approval or affirmation by the company in general meeting of a substantial property transaction under section 190 of the 2006 Act, is ineffective unless the prior written consent of the Charity Commissioners is obtained. [Charities Act 1993 Sec 66].

**Substantial property transaction value**

**6.102**  A substantial non-cash asset occurs if at the time the arrangement is entered into its value exceeds 10 per cent of the company's asset value and is more than £5,000 or the asset value exceeds £100,000. [CA06 Sec 191(2)]. The 2006 Act does not define the criteria by which the non-cash asset's value is to be determined for the purpose of calculating the £5,000 or £100,000 threshold. However, it has been held that the aim of section 191 of the 2006 Act is the protection of shareholders in arrangements that would or might benefit directors to the detriment of the company. The company and its advisers valuing the asset should, therefore, have regard to its value to the director (or connected person) proposing to acquire it. For instance, any special value that the asset would have to such person would need to be taken into account. *Micro Leisure Ltd v County Properties & Developments Ltd & Anor.* [2000] BCC 872. However, the 2006 Act defines the 'company's asset value' for the purposes of the 10 per cent threshold as meaning the value of the company's net assets as disclosed in its latest financial statements laid before shareholders. Where there are no such financial statements, the 'company's asset value' means the amount of the company's called-up share capital. [CA06 Sec 191(3)].

**6.103**  In the context of section 190 of the 2006 Act, 'non-cash asset' means any type or form of property, or any interest in property other than cash. (For this purpose, 'cash' includes foreign currency.) 'Property' means any type of asset of a company and is not only buildings or land. The acquisition or transfer of a non-cash asset also includes the creation or extinction of an interest in property (for example, a lease) and the discharge of any person's liability other than a liability for a liquidated sum. [CA85 Sec 739; CA06 Sec 1163]. For illustrations of 'non-cash assets' see Table 6.5 below and the example in paragraph 6.111.

**[The next paragraph is 6.106.]**

**6.106**  The same rules apply to substantial property transactions of this nature that involve a shadow director or a person connected with the shadow director. [CA06 Sec 223(1)].

**6.107**  Section 190 of the 2006 Act also affects certain intra-group transactions. Where, for example, a director of a company owns or controls a certain percentage of the shares in another group company, that other group company may fall within the definition of a connected person (see para 6.18). In these circumstances, all dealings between the company and any company that falls within the definition of a person connected with a director will require prior approval of the company in general meeting (see para 6.109 for the exemptions).

**6.108**  An example of a substantial property transaction is given in Table 6.5.

---

**Table 6.5 – Substantial property transaction**

**Fine Art Developments p.l.c. – Annual Report & Accounts – 31 March 1993**

**Directors' Report (extract)**
**Proposed transaction with an associated party**

In accordance with their policy to dispose of businesses which are not considered core to the group, the directors have decided there should be a sale of Herbert Walker & Son (Printers) Limited. This company is engaged in commercial printing and, if it was retained, would require considerable investment in plant and equipment in the near future.

The profit before tax of Herbert Walker in the year to 31 March 1993 amounted to £66,450 and its net assets on completion of a sale are estimated to be £664,000. The independent directors have concluded that a fair value of the company would be £764,000. In reaching this conclusion it has been assumed that the group will continue to purchase printed products from Herbert Walker on normal commercial terms of no less than an annual total purchase price of £1.5m in each of the three years following completion of a sale. The independent directors have sought advice from BDO Binder Hamlyn who consider that the terms of the proposed disposal, taking into account all relevant factors, are fair and reasonable so far as concern the shareholders of Fine Art Development p.l.c.

Mr K Chapman, a director, has agreed to purchase and Britannia Products Limited, a subsidiary of Fine Art Developments p.l.c. and the holder of the whole of the issued share capital of Herbert Walker, has agreed to sell the whole of such capital for a cash consideration of £764,000 payable on completion, subject to approval of the transaction by shareholders in general meetings as required under Section 320 of the Companies Act 1985. The contract for sale will contain a provision that Fine Art Developments p.l.c. shall procure that the group place orders for printed products with Herbert Walker on the terms referred to above.

An ordinary resolution to approve the sale is set out in the notice of annual general meeting on page 11.

---

## Exemptions from obtaining approval

**6.109** Although a company must comply with the disclosure requirements set out in paragraph 6.112, the shareholders' approval is not required for a substantial property transaction of the type described in paragraph 6.100 where one of the exceptions set out below applies:

■ The value of the non-cash asset at the time of the arrangement is less than £5,000 and is less than 10 per cent of the company's asset value. Asset value is defined in paragraph 6.102 above. [CA06 Sec 191(1)(2)].

■ The body corporate in question is not a company formed and registered under the Companies Act 2006. [CA06 Sec 190(4)].

■ The company in question is a wholly-owned subsidiary of any company, wherever incorporated. [CA06 Sec 190(4)(b)]. In these circumstances, in practice, the holding company's directors have control over the subsidiary's directors.

■ The non-cash asset is to be acquired:

- By a holding company from any of its wholly-owned subsidiaries.

- By a wholly-owned subsidiary from its holding company.

- By a wholly-owned subsidiary from a fellow wholly-owned subsidiary.

[CA06 Sec 192].

In effect, this exemption relieves companies that would otherwise be required by section 190 of the 2006 Act to obtain approval at a general meeting for intra-group transactions that take place in a wholly-owned group.

- The arrangement is entered into by a company that is being wound up, and the winding-up is not a members' voluntary winding-up. [CA06 Sec 193].

- The following two conditions are satisfied:

  - A member of the company acquires an asset from the company.

  - The arrangement was made with that person (for example, a director of the company or the holding company or a person connected with such a director) in his capacity as a member of the company.

  [CA06 Sec 192(a)].

- The transaction is effected on a recognised investment exchange by a director, or a person connected with him/her, through an independent broker. [CA06 Sec 194].

**Liabilities for contravention of section 190**

**6.110**  An arrangement for which the shareholder approval required by section 190 of the 2006 Act has not been obtained (and any transaction pursuant thereto) may be treated as voidable by the company unless one of the following three conditions is satisfied:

- It is no longer possible to obtain the return of the subject matter of the transaction, or the company has been indemnified for any loss or damage it has suffered. [CA06 Sec 195(2)].

- A third party has acquired rights, in good faith and for value, and without having notice of the contravention, which would be affected. [CA06 Sec 195(2)].

**6.111**  A director who contravenes section 190 of the 2006 Act may incur civil penalties. The director and any connected person who entered into the arrangement, and any director who authorised it may all be liable to account to the company for any gain they have received. They may also be liable to indemnify the company from any resultant loss or damage it has incurred. [CA06 Sec 195(3)(4)]. However, a director will not be liable if the arrangement was made with a connected person, and if they took all reasonable steps to ensure that the company obtained the required approval or if they can show that they did not know the relevant circumstances that formed the contravention. [CA06 Sec 195(6)(7)].

**Example — Transaction that would contravene section 190 of the 2006 Act**

Although the transaction was determined to be in contravention of section 320 of the 1985 Act, it nevertheless remains as relevant case law for the purposes of section 190 of the 2006 Act.

C and his wife owned company O. Company O agreed to buy a property for £495,000 and paid a deposit of £49,500. On completion the property was conveyed to another company, D, of which C was also a director on the basis that company O would take 50% of any profit but not bear any loss. D borrowed £350,000 to fund the purchase. Company D paid the balance of the purchase price and reimbursed company O the deposit. Company D then sought to avoid the transaction, as the value of the property had subsequently fallen, on the grounds that it had not been approved by the members of company D. It was held that company D was connected to C and that the transaction contravened section 320 (of the 1985 Act). There was an inquiry as to what damage D had suffered, as the property was subsequently sold for £177,970.

It was held that the indemnity D was entitled to under section 322(3)(b) (of the 1985 Act) was the loss caused by the depreciation of the property. A further hearing established that this loss was limited to the difference between the cost of the property and the proceeds of sale plus interest on that sum. [*Re Duckwari plc (No.3) Duckwari v Offerventure (No.3)* [1999] 1BCLC 168].

**Disclosure requirements for substantial property transactions for financial beginning before 6 April 2008**

**6.112** A substantial property transaction is likely to require disclosure as a transaction in which a director has a material interest. Consequently, the disclosure requirements outlined in paragraph 6.93 onwards for transactions in which a director has a material interest, that is, disclosure by way of notification to the board of directors and disclosure in financial statements, apply equally to substantial property transactions and arrangements of a kind described in paragraph 6.100 above. The requirements apply irrespective of whether the transactions and arrangements have been approved by the company in general meeting.

**Disclosure requirements for substantial property transactions for financial years beginning on or after 6 April 2008**

**6.112.1** There are no specific disclosure requirements relating to substantial property transactions under the 2006 Act. However, paragraph 72 of Schedule 1 to 'The Large and Medium-sized Companies and Groups (Accounts and Reports) Regulations 2008' (SI 2008/410) sets out disclosure requirements for related party transactions that may include substantial property transactions. Details may be given of transactions that the company has entered into with related parties, and must be given if such transactions are material and have not been concluded under normal market conditions. The details that are required to be disclosed are:

■ The amount of the transaction.

■ The nature of the related party relationship.

■ Other information about the transactions necessary to understand the company's financial position.

**6.112.2** The disclosure requirements do not apply to medium-sized companies. [SI 2008/410 reg 4(2)(b)]. In addition, there is an exemption for transactions entered into between two or more members of a group, provided that any subsidiary undertaking which is a party to the transaction is wholly-owned. [SI 2008/410 1 Sch 72(4)].

**6.112.3** For the purpose of this disclosure, 'related parties' has the same meaning as under IAS. Therefore, compliance with IAS 24 ensures compliance with this Companies Act requirement as confirmed by the ARC in its meeting in November 2007. The requirements of IAS 24 are dealt with in chapter 29 of the Manual of Accounting – IFRS for the UK.

**6.112.4** UK GAAP reporters will need to consider the wider IAS definition to determine who their related parties are. The Act required disclosure of related party transactions that *"have not been concluded under normal market conditions"*. This subjective wording is less than helpful, but it will require disclosure of fewer transactions than IAS 24. Therefore, UK GAAP reporters will need to identify those transactions that were carried out other than under normal market conditions. The requirements of FRS 8 are dealt with in chapter 29 of the Manual of Accounting – UK GAAP.

**Disclosure requirements of the Listing Rules and AIM and PLUS-quoted rules**

**6.113** The Listing Rules, for listed companies, the AIM Rules, for those traded on AIM and the PLUS trading rules for those traded on the PLUS-quoted market contain further rules and disclosure requirements for substantial property transactions and other transactions with directors that come within following categories:

■ Transactions with related parties (which include directors).

■ Contracts of significance with directors (not AIM or PLUS-quoted companies).

**6.114** The UKLA's Listing Rules provide certain safeguards to prevent directors and other related parties from taking advantage of their position. These are based on disclosure, primarily to shareholders, and are set out in chapters 9 and 11 of the Listing Rules – Continuing obligations. They apply to listed companies unless they do not have any equity securities listed. Added to these requirements, disclosure of information regarding contracts of significance with directors must be made in the financial statements. Related party transactions and contracts of significance under the Listing Rules, the AIM and PLUS-quoted rules are discussed in chapter 29 of the Manual of Accounting – IFRS for the UK, whilst only the AIM Rules are discussed in chapter 29 of the Manual of Accounting – UK GAAP in the context of related party disclosures in general.

[The next paragraph is 6.121.]

# Invalidity of certain transactions involving directors

### General rule

**6.121** Where a company proposes to enter into a transaction with a director of the company or its holding company, the board of directors will need to ensure that, in doing so, they are not exceeding any limitation on their powers under the company's constitution, that is, its articles of association, any resolution of the company or any agreement between members. If they exceed their powers the transaction is voidable at the option of the company unless it is ratified by the shareholders. [CA85 Sec 322A; CA06 Sec 41]. This also applies where the party to the transaction includes a person connected with a director (including a company with which he is associated). The provisions of Part 4 of the 2006 Act commence on 1 October 2009. Until that time the similar provisions of the 1985 Act prevail.

### Effects of contravention

**6.122** Whether or not the transaction is avoided, the director or connected person concerned, and any director who authorised the transaction, is liable to account to the company for any gain and indemnify the company against any loss or damage it suffers as a consequence. Nothing in the rules referred to in this paragraph and in the paragraph above, however, affects any other rule of law under which the transaction may be called into question or under which liability to the company may arise (for instance, if it is an illegal loan). [CA85 Sec 322A (3)(4); CA06 Sec 41(3)]. A person other than a director of the company is not liable to account or to indemnify the company if he can show that, at the time the transaction was entered into, he did not know that the directors were exceeding their powers. [CA85 Sec 322A(6); CA06 Sec 41(5)].

**6.123** The company may treat the transaction as voidable unless one of the following conditions is satisfied:

■ Restitution of the money or other asset which was the subject of the transaction is no longer possible.

■ The company is indemnified for any loss or damage resulting from the transaction.

- Rights acquired *bona fide* for value and without actual notice of the directors' exceeding their powers by a person who is not a party to the transaction would be affected by the avoidance.

- The transaction is ratified by the company in general meeting by ordinary or special resolution or otherwise as the case may require.

[CA85 Sec 322A (5); CA06 Sec 41(4)].

**6.124** However, section 322A of the 1985 Act (section 41 of the 2006 Act) provides for the situation where the transaction is voidable, but is valid under section 35A of the 1985 Act (section 40 of the 2006 Act) (power of directors to bind the company free of any limitation under the company's constitution). Where the person dealing with the company (not being a director of the company or its holding company or a person connected with him/her) has acted in good faith, the court may (on the application of that person or the company) make an order either confirming, severing, or setting aside the transaction, on such terms as appears to the court to be just.

[CA85 Sec 322A(7); CA06 Sec 41(6)].

**6.125** Where the company enters into a transaction which is outside the directors' powers and thus voidable under section 322A of the 1985 Act (section 41 of the 2006 Act), it will be disclosable under Schedule 6 Part II of the 1985 Act as a contract in which a director has, directly or indirectly, a material interest (see para 6.93 onwards) for financial years beginning before 6 April 2008. For financial years beginning on or after 6 April 2008, such disclosure is not required by the Companies Act 2006. However, it may require disclosure under Schedule 1 to SI 2008/410 (refer to para 6.112.1) as a related party transaction if the transaction has not been concluded under normal market conditions. IFRS reporters complying with IAS 24, 'Related party disclosures' (see chapter 29 of Manual of Accounting – IFRS for the UK) will meet equivalent related party disclosures. This was clarified by the ARC in their November 2007 meeting. For UK GAAP reporters, the 2006 Act may introduce additional disclosures over those contained within FRS 8, 'Related party disclosures' (see chapter 29 of Manual of Accounting – UK GAAP).

## Transactions with directors who are sole members

**6.126** There are special requirements for a single member company to document transactions with a director who is also its sole member. Where a private company with a sole member who is also a director (or shadow director) contracts with that director, it must ensure that the terms of the contract are set out in a written memorandum or are recorded in the minutes of the first meeting of directors of the company following the making of the contract. This requirement does not apply where the contract is in writing or is entered into in the company's ordinary course of business. [CA85 Sec 322B; CA06 Sec 231].

**6.127** Failure to comply with this requirement does not affect the validity of the contract. However, it is a criminal offence and the company and every officer in default is liable to a fine. [CA85 Sec 322B(4)(6); CA06 Sec 231(3)(4)(6)].

**6.128** A sole director also has a duty to comply with the statutory provisions of section 317 of the 1985 Act (section 182 of the 2006 Act) which requires him/her to declare at a meeting of the directors the nature of his/her interest in any contract or proposed contract with the company. This was established by *Neptune Vehicle Washing Equipment Ltd v Fitzgerald* [1995] 1 BCLC 352, where the judge said that he was satisfied that for the purpose of section 317 of the 1985 Act there can be a directors meeting in the case of a sole directorship. This case law is still applicable as the requirements of section 317 of the 1985 Act have been replaced without change by section 182 of the 2006 Act (as described in para 6.163).

## Transactions with officers

**Transactions to be disclosed — for financial years beginning before 6 April 2008**

**6.129** In contrast to the substantial number of provisions in the 1985 Act relating to directors' transactions with their company, section 232 of the 1985 Act requires less disclosure of similar transactions with officers who are not directors.

**6.129.1** The requirements set out in Part III of Schedule 6 to the 1985 Act (described in para 6.130) are effective for financial years beginning before 6 April 2008. While the disclosure requirements are still governed by the 1985 Act, some of the definitions within the 2006 Act are now relevant and have been inserted as appropriate. The provisions apply to the following types of transactions, arrangements and agreements made by the company or any of its subsidiaries for persons who at any time during the financial year were officers of the company (but not directors or shadow directors):

■ Loans (including any guarantees and securities for loans), arrangements of the types described in section 330(6) or (7) of the 1985 Act (section 203 of the 2006 Act) relating to loans, and agreements to enter into any such transactions.

■ Quasi-loans (including any guarantees and securities for quasi-loans), arrangements of the types described in section 330(6) or (7) of the 1985 Act (section 203 of the 2006 Act) relating to quasi-loans, and agreements to enter into any such transactions.

■ Credit transactions (including any guarantees and securities for credit transactions), arrangements of the types described in section 330(6) or (7) of the 1985 Act (section 203 of the 2006 Act) relating to credit transactions, and agreements to enter into any such transactions. [CA 85 6 Sch 28].

For this purpose, the term 'officer' includes the company secretary and the company's senior managers. [CA85 Sec 744; CA06 Sec 1121(2)]. There is also little doubt that a person appointed to hold the office of auditor of a company is an officer of the company. [*R v Shacter* [1960] 2 QB 252].

## Information to be disclosed

**6.130**   A statement containing the following information relating to transactions with officers of the kind mentioned in the paragraph above must be made in (a) the individual accounts of the company that has the transaction and (b) the consolidated accounts by a holding company for all transactions made with officers of the group:

■ The aggregate amounts outstanding at the end of the financial year under such transactions, made by either the company or (if it is a holding company) its subsidiaries. The aggregate amounts must relate to each category of transaction described above.

In this respect, 'amount outstanding' means the amount of the outstanding liabilities of the person for whom the transaction was made. With a guarantee or a security, it means the amount guaranteed or secured. [CA85 6 Sch 30].

■ The number of officers for whom transactions in each category were made. [CA85 6 Sch 29(1)].

Corresponding amounts for the immediately preceding financial period must also be given, even where no amount is disclosed in respect of the current period. [FRS 28 paras 8,10; IAS 1 para 36].

## Exemptions from disclosure

**6.131**   No statement need be given in respect of the transactions outlined in paragraph 6.129 made by the company for an officer of the company where the aggregate amount outstanding at the end of the financial year for that officer does not exceed £2,500. [CA85 6 Sch 29(2)]. The Secretary of State has power to increase this limit by statutory instrument. [CA85 6 Sch 29(3)].

## Penalty for failure to disclose transactions with officers

**6.132**   If the directors approve accounts in which they have failed to make the disclosure the 1985 Act requires in respect of transactions with a company's officers in the company's financial statements, they will be guilty of an offence and liable to a fine. [CA85 Sec 233(5)]. In addition, the auditors must include a statement in their audit report giving the required particulars, so far as they are reasonably able to do so [CA85 Sec 237(4)]. (See para 6.171 onwards.)

**Transactions to be disclosed — for financial years beginning on or after 6 April 2008**

**6.132.1**   For financial years beginning on or after 6 April 2008, companies are no longer required to disclose transactions made between the company and officers who are not directors. However, if the officers meet the definition of 'key management' disclosure of transactions with such officers is required by paragraph 72 of Schedule 1 to SI 2008/410 for companies preparing Companies Act accounts. For companies preparing IAS accounts such disclosure is governed by IAS 24.

## Money-lending and banking companies

### Introduction and definition of a money-lending company

**6.133**  The 2006 Act defines a 'money-lending company' as *"a company whose ordinary business includes the making of loans or quasi-loans, or the giving of guarantees or provision of security in connection with loans or quasi-loans"*. [CA06 Sec 209(2); CA85 Sec 338(2)]. This has been altered slightly from the 1985 Act by the addition of the wording *"or provision of security"*. Money-lending companies are not necessarily banking companies under the 2006 Act, but banking companies fall within the definition of 'money-lending companies' for this purpose.

**6.134**  A banking company is defined as a company *"who has permission under Part 4 of the Financial Services and Markets Act 2000 (c8) to accept deposits, other than (a) a person who is not a company, and (b) a person who has such permission only for the purpose of carrying on another regulated activity in accordance with permission under that Part"*. [CA85 Sec 742B; CA06 Sec 1164(2)]. A deposit-taking business is one where money received in the course of business by way of deposit is lent to others or used to finance any other activity of the business. Unless otherwise indicated, the term 'money-lending company' where used below will include a company which is a banking company.

**6.134.1**  'Credit institution' is defined in section 1173 of the 2006 Act. This section refers to the definition in Article 4.1(a) of Directive 2006/48/EC of the European Parliament and of the Council relating to the taking up and pursuit of the business of credit institutions. That is to say, an undertaking whose business is to receive deposits or other repayable funds from the public and to grant credits for its own account. A credit institution would, therefore, include an institution, wherever incorporated, carrying on banking-type business.

**6.134.2**  A 'banking company' is defined in section 742B of the 1985 Act (section 1164 of the 2006 Act) (see para 6.134) and, refers to the subset of credit institutions incorporated in the UK, which are authorised under Part 4 of the Financial Services and Markets Act 2000 to conduct a deposit-taking business in the UK.

**6.134.3**  In addition, a company that is a credit institution is within the definition of a money-lending company as defined in section 209 of the 2006 Act (see para 6.133), because a credit institution makes loans in the ordinary course of its business. However, a money-lending company will not be a credit institution, unless the money-lending company, in addition to making loans, receives deposits or other repayable funds from the general public in the ordinary course of its business.

**6.135** The transactions requiring member approval under section 197, 198, 200, 201 and 203 of the 2006 Act and the relevant exceptions to this requirement (see para 6.29 onwards) that apply to companies also apply to money-lending companies.

**6.136** Money-lending companies may, however, take advantage of a further exception from the requirement to obtain member approval relating to loans, quasi-loans, guarantees and provision of security of loans and quasi-loans. This exception and the disclosure requirements for money-lending companies (including banking companies) and those specifically for banking companies are considered in the paragraphs that follow.

### Exception for money lending companies

*Loans on commercial terms*

**6.137** For transactions entered into on or after 1 October 2007, section 209 of the 2006 Act contains exceptions (subject to certain conditions) for money-lending companies. Consequently, a money-lending company does not require approval for:

■ Making a loan or quasi-loan to any person (for instance, to a director of the company or its holding company or a person connected with the director); or

■ Entering into a guarantee or providing security for a loan or quasi-loan.

The exception is only available if the following two conditions are satisfied:

■ The money-lending company makes the loan or quasi-loan or enters into the guarantee in the ordinary course of its business. [CA06 Sec 209(1)(a)].

■ The amount of the loan or quasi-loan or the amount guaranteed is not greater than, and the terms of that transaction are not more favourable, in the case of the person for whom the transaction is made, than those that the company might reasonably be expected to have offered to, or in respect of, a person of the same financial standing who was unconnected with the company. (In other words, the facility is offered on the money-lending company's normal commercial terms.) [CA06 Sec 209(1)(b)].

**[The next paragraph is 6.140.]**

*Transactions to which the exception from approval is not applicable*

**6.140** It should be noted, however, the exception from member approval for money-lending companies in section 209 of the 2006 Act that relates to loans, quasi-loans, guarantees and the provision of security for them (see para 6.137), does not extend to the following types of transaction:

■ Credit transactions, or the provision of a guarantee or security in connection with them.

■ The assignment of rights or obligations or assumption of liabilities under the above types of transaction.

■ Indirect arrangements under the above types of transaction.

These transactions require member approval. Consequently, in these situations, money-lending companies are subject to the same rules as any other company and the provisions set out in sections 201 to 203 of the 2006 Act (as outlined in paras 6.29 and 6.68) apply to them.

### Relaxation for loans on beneficial terms for house purchase

**6.141** The second condition that the exception applies only where the loan is made on normal commercial terms (sec 209(1)(b) to the Companies Act 2006) is relaxed where a money-lending company makes a loan to one of its directors or a director of its holding company for the purpose of house purchase or improvement (housing loan). [CA06 Sec 209(3)(4)]. Consequently, a money-lending company (whether a public or private company) is not prevented by that condition from making a loan (but not a quasi-loan or a guarantee) to such a director on *beneficial* terms provided that all the following conditions are satisfied:

■ The loan is to assist the director either to purchase or to improve his only or main residence, or land enjoyed with it. This type of loan will also include a loan made by the company in substitution for a loan that another person has made to the director.

■ The company ordinarily makes similar loans of that type available to its employees on no less favourable terms.

[CA06 Sec 209(3)(4)].

**[The next paragraph is 6.143.]**

### Disclosure requirements — money lending companies

**6.143** For financial years beginning before 6 April 2008, a money-lending company (unless it is a banking company or the holding company of a credit institution – see definition below) is required to disclose the particulars required by Parts II and III of Schedule 6 of the 1985 Act in connection with loans, quasi-loans and other dealing with directors and other officers in the same way as any other company.

**6.144** As previously noted, for financial years beginning on or after 6 April 2008, there are no equivalent disclosure provisions under the 2006 Act. However, such transactions may be caught by the related party disclosure provisions of Schedule 1 to SI 2008/410 (refer to para 6.112.1). For IFRS reporters complying with IAS 24, 'Related party disclosures' (see chapter 29 of Manual of Accounting – IFRS for the UK) will meet the related party disclosure requirements under the 2006 Act. This was clarified by the ARC in their November 2007 meeting. For UK GAAP reporters, the 2006 Act may introduce additional disclosures over those contained within FRS 8, 'Related party disclosures' (see chapter 29 of Manual of Accounting – UK GAAP). The guidance in this section is, therefore, based on the requirements of the 1985 Act. These requirements are in force until repealed for financial years beginning on or after 6 April 2008.

**[The next paragraph is 6.147.]**

**Disclosure requirements — banking company or group for financial years beginning before 6 April 2008**

*Disclosure in financial statements*

**6.147** A banking company, or a company that is the holding company of a credit institution, may exempt itself from some of the disclosure requirements that apply to other companies. Section 255B(2) of the 1985 Act provides that the provisions in Schedule 6 to the 1985 Act relating to the disclosure of information in the financial statements concerning loans, quasi-loans and other dealings with directors have effect subject to Part IV of Schedule 9 to the 1985 Act.

**6.148** Part IV of Schedule 9 to the 1985 Act provides that a banking company or a company that is the holding company of a credit institution does not have to comply with Part II of Schedule 6 in the following respects. It need not disclose the detailed information outlined in paragraphs 6.74 to 6.79 (for loans, quasi-loans credit transactions and related dealings) in relation to a transaction or arrangement of a kind mentioned in sections 197, 198, 200, 201 and 203 of the 2006 Act or an agreement to enter into such a transaction or arrangement to which that banking company or credit institution is a party. [CA85 9 Sch Part IV, 2]. A banking company or company which is the holding company of a credit institution is still required to disclose transactions in which a director has a material interest (see Table 6.3).

**6.149** Where, however, a company takes advantage of these exemptions it must include a statement in relation to the specified transactions in its financial statements. The requirements to keep a register of the specified transactions and to make a special statement including particulars of those transactions available to members has been abolished with effect from 7 April 2007, refer to paragraph 6.155 for further details.

*Statement of transactions*

**6.150** Where a banking company or company that is the holding company of a credit institution takes advantage of the above provisions, it must instead comply with the provisions of Part III of Schedule 6 to the 1985 Act. This means that it must include in its financial statements a statement of the information outlined below in respect of certain transactions, arrangements and agreements. These relate to quasi-loans, credit transactions and related guarantees, securities, arrangements of the kind described in section 203(1) of the 2006 Act (section 330(6) and (7) of the 1985 Act) and agreements to enter into such transactions and arrangements made by that banking company or credit institution for:

■ A director or a shadow director of the company preparing the financial statements, or a person connected with such a director.

■ A person who was a chief executive or manager (within the meaning of the Banking Act 1987) of that company or its holding company.

[CA85 9 Sch Part IV 3]

**6.151** The Banking Act 1987 defines a chief executive as *"a person who, either alone or jointly with one or more persons, is responsible under the immediate authority of the directors for the conduct of the business of the institution"*. If the principal place of business is outside the UK, the chief executive also includes a person who alone or jointly with other persons, is responsible for the conduct of its business in the UK. [BA 1987 Sec 105(7)(8)].

**6.152** A manager is defined by the Banking Act as a person (other than a chief executive) who, under the immediate authority of a director or chief executive of the institution, undertakes one of the following tasks:

■ Exercises managerial functions.

■ Is responsible for maintaining accounts or other records of the institution.

[BA 1987 Sec 105(6)].

**6.153** The statement in the financial statements must contain the following details:

■ The aggregate amounts outstanding at the end of the financial year, analysed under loans, quasi-loans and credit transactions.

■ The number of persons (that is, of the directors and shadow directors of the company and persons connected with them and chief executive of the company or its holding company) for whom transactions in each of the above categories were made by the banking company.

[CA85 6 Sch 28, 29; CA85 9 Sch Part IV 3].

An illustration of this disclosure is given in Table 6.6.

Table 6.6 – Statement of transactions

TSB Group plc – Annual Report and Accounts – 31 October 1994

Notes to the accounts (extract)

7 Directors' and officers' loans

At 31 October 1994 the aggregate amounts outstanding under transactions, agreements and agreements entered into by the Group's banking subsidiaries with directors, persons connected with directors, and officers were

| | Directors and connected persons | | | | Officers |
| | Loans | Quasi loans | Guarantees | Loans | Quasi loans |
|---|---|---|---|---|---|
| Number of persons | 4 | 5 | 1 | 3 | 2 |
| Amounts £000 | 568 | 7 | 30 | 433 | 2 |

**6.154**   For the purpose of these provisions:

■   In so far as they relate to loans, quasi-loans and credit transactions, a body corporate that a person does not control should not be treated as being connected with him/her. [CA85 9 Sch Part IV 3(4)]. For the meaning of a director 'controlling' a company, see section 255(2) of the 2006 Act and paragraph 6.21.

■   The interpretation of a person connected with a director or controlling a body corporate is given in section 346 (see also para 6.35). [CA85 9 Sch Part IV, 3(5)].

■   References to officers in Part III are to be construed as including the persons mentioned in paragraph 6.150. [CA85 9 Sch Part IV 3(2)].

### Register of transactions

**6.155**   With effect from 6 April 2007, the requirement has been abolished for a banking company or holding company of a credit institution to keep a register of transactions where it took advantage of the relaxation in paragraph 2 of Part IV of Schedule 9 to the 1985 Act relating to the disclosure requirements.

### Special statement for members

**6.156**   With effect from 6 April 2007, the requirement has been abolished for a company which took advantage of paragraph 2 of Part IV of Schedule 9 to the 1985 Act to make a special statement for members. This statement was required to have been available at its registered office and included particulars of the transactions, arrangements and agreements which it would have had to disclose in its financial statements or consolidated financial statements for that financial year.

**[The next paragraph is 6.161.]**

**Disclosure requirements — banking company or group for financial years beginning on or after 6 April 2008**

**6.161** Section 413 of the 2006 Act sets out the new disclosure requirements in respect of advances and credits granted by the company to its directors and guarantees of any kind entered into by the company on behalf of its directors. Under section 413(8) of the 2006 Act banks and the holding companies of credit institutions need only disclose two items in the financial statements:

- The amount of an advance or credit.

- For a guarantee, the amount of the maximum liability that may be incurred by the company (or its subsidiary).

[CA06 Sec 413(8)].

**6.162** It should be noted, however, that transactions with directors (and officers that are 'key management') may be caught by the related party disclosure provisions of Schedule 1 to SI 2008/410 (refer to para 6.112.1). For IFRS reporters complying with IAS 24, 'Related party disclosures' (see chapter 29 of Manual of Accounting – IFRS for the UK) compliance with that standard will meet the related party disclosure requirements under the 2006 Act. This was clarified by the ARC in their November 2007 meeting. For UK GAAP reporters, the 2006 Act may introduce additional disclosures over those contained within FRS 8, 'Related party disclosures' (see chapter 29 of Manual of Accounting – UK GAAP).

# Other matters

**Notification to the board**

*Declaration of interest under section 317 of the 1985 Act (sections 177 and 182 of the 2006 Act)*

**6.163** Section 317 of the 1985 Act and sections 177 and 182 of the 2006 Act are an indication of the importance in company law of the principle that a company should be protected against a director who has a conflict in interest and duty. It applies to a shadow director and to a sole director (*Neptune Vehicle Washwax Equipment Limited v Fitzgerald [1995]* 1BCLC 352). [CA85 Sec 317(8); CA06 Sec 187]. Where a director is in any way interested in a contract that involves the company, section 317 of the 1985 Act imposes a specific duty on the director to declare the precise nature of his/her interest in the contract at a meeting of the company's directors. A contract for this purpose includes any transaction or arrangement. This applies whether the director is either directly or indirectly interested in the contract, or the proposed contract, with the company. Section 182 of the 2006 Act restates and also amends the provisions of section 317 of the 1985 Act. This section is effective from 1 October 2008, for transactions prior to this date the provisions of the 1985 Act are still in force. The basic rule is that a director must disclose any interest in a proposed contract at one of the following:

- At the directors' meeting at which the contract is first considered.

- If, however, the director acquires an interest in the contract at a later date, he/she must disclose his interest at the first meeting held after he/she became interested.

[CA85 Sec 317(2)].

**6.163.1**   Under the 2006 Act notice may be given at a meeting of the directors or by written notice or by general notice.[CA06 Secs 177(2), 182(2)]. If notice is given by writing then it must be sent to the other directors by either hard copy or in electronic form. [CA06 Sec 184(3)].

**6.164**   In certain circumstances a general notice will be sufficient. When a director is, for example, a member of another company that might enter into transactions with the company, he/she can give a general notice to the directors that he/she is to be regarded as interested in any future contract with that other company. [CA85 Sec 317(3); CA06 Sec 185].

**6.165**   These notification requirements apply to all transactions and arrangements in which a director (or a person connected with him/her) has a direct or indirect interest, including loans, quasi-loans and credit transactions covered by section 203 of the 2006 Act (see para 6.29). [CA85 Sec 317(6)].

**6.166**   If a director fails to disclose an interest in a contract in accordance with section 317 of the 1985 Act (section 182 of the 2006 Act), this will be a criminal offence and he/she will be liable to a fine. [CA85 Sec 317(7); CA06 Sec 183].

**6.167**   Compliance with section 317 of the Companies Act 1985 (section 182 of the 2006 Act), on the other hand, does not, of itself make a contract with a director valid. The basic rule is that a director should not contract with his/her company without the company's approval or ratification in general meeting, unless it is permitted by the articles. Generally articles relax these requirements permitting directors to contract with their companies, but subject to appropriate disclosure to the board of directors.

**6.168**   The 2006 Act introduces a new provision for companies with only one director. In these circumstances, the director must record in writing the nature and extent of his interest and this declaration is deemed to form part of the proceedings at the next directors meeting. [CA06 Sec 186(1)].

**[The next paragraph is 6.170.]**

### Disclosure required by the articles of association

**6.170**   To overcome the general rule restricting contracts between directors and their companies, a company's articles of association will generally contain specific requirements for the disclosure to the board by a director of his interest in a contract with the company. If these requirements are not followed, the director risks being accountable to the company for any benefit he derives from the contract. For example, Table A of SI 1985/805, 'Companies (Tables A to F) Regulations 1985', deals, in articles 85 and 86, with directors' material interests in contracts. The requirements of these articles are as follows:

*"Subject to the provisions of the Act, and provided that he has disclosed to the directors the nature and extent of any material interest of his, a director notwithstanding his office –*

*(a) may be a party to, or otherwise interested in, any transaction or arrangement with the company or in which the company is otherwise interested;*

*(b) may be a director or other officer of, or employed by, or a party to any transaction or arrangement with, or otherwise interested in, any body corporate promoted by the company or in which the company is otherwise interested; and*

*(c) shall not, by reason of his office, be accountable to the company for any benefit which he derives from any such office or employment or from any such transaction or arrangement or from any interest in any such body corporate and no such transaction or arrangement shall be liable to be avoided on the ground of any such interest or benefit.*

*For the purposes of [the above] regulation 85*

*(a) a general notice given to the directors that a director is to be regarded as having an interest of the nature and extent specified in the notice in any transaction or arrangement in which a specified person or class of persons is interested shall be deemed to be a disclosure that the director has an interest in any such transaction of the nature and extent so specified; and*

*(b) an interest of which a director has no knowledge and of which it is unreasonable to expect him to have knowledge shall not be treated as an interest of his."* [Table A articles 85, 86].

**Penalties for failure to disclose certain transactions**

**6.171**   Section 232 of the 1985 Act (section 412 of the 2006 Act) requires companies to give the information specified in Schedule 6 Part II and III to the 1985 Act regarding transactions with directors and officers in the notes to their financial statements. These are described in the paragraphs above. The provisions of the 2006 Act that replace Schedule 6 part II to the 1985 Act are set out in Section 413 and significantly reduce the disclosures required. There is no equivalent to Schedule 6 Part III to the 1985 Act, however, Schedule 1 to SI 2008/410 requires disclosure of certain related party transactions (refer to para 6.112.1).

Schedule 6 to the 1985 Act will apply until repealed by the 2006 Act for financial years beginning on or after 6 April 2008.

**6.171.1** It is the duty of any director and any person who has been a director of the company within the preceding five years to give the company any of the information necessary for it to comply with the regulations. Failure to do so is an offence. [CA85 Sec 232(3)(4); CA06 Sec 412(5)(6)].

**6.172** The 1985 Act (2006 Act) also imposes a penalty on the company's directors for failure to disclose the information about directors' and officers' transactions referred to above in the company's financial statements. If the financial statements that are approved by the directors do not comply with the 1985 Act (2006 Act) by not disclosing the required information (required either by the Act or Article 4 of the IAS regulation), then every director of the company who is party to their approval and who knows that they do not comply or is reckless as to whether they comply is guilty of an offence. [CA85 Sec 233(5); CA06 Sec 414(4)].

**6.173** Moreover, where the financial statements do not disclose the information required by the 1985 Act (2006 Act), the auditors must include, in their report (so far as they are reasonably able to do so), a statement giving the details that have been omitted. [CA85 Sec 237(4); CA06 498(4)]. In addition, the auditors have certain responsibilities for considering any transactions to which the company was a party which may have been illegal or in breach of applicable regulations. [ISA (UK & I) 250]. Non-compliance refers to acts of omission or commission by the company being audited (either intentional or unintentional) that are contrary to law (comprising common law or statute) or regulations.

**6.174** Auditors may, during their audit, become aware of information indicating that there may be non-compliance with law or regulations that they may need to refer to in their report. They may, therefore, need to include an explanatory paragraph in their report if they conclude that the view given by the financial statements could, as a result of the non-compliance, be affected by a level of uncertainty which is fundamental. If, however, they conclude that the non-compliance has a material affect on the financial statements and they disagree, for instance, with the accounting treatment or the disclosure, they may have to issue an adverse or qualified opinion. If they are unable to determine whether non-compliance has occurred because of a limitation in the scope of their work, they may have to issue a disclaimer or a qualified opinion. [ISA (UK & Ire) 250 paras 35-37].

**Criminal sanctions under the 1985 Act**

**6.175** The 1985 Act imposed criminal sanctions for failure to comply with section 330 of the 1985 Act relating to directors' loans. To be guilty of the offence, the director (or other person) must have known, or have had reasonable cause to believe, that the transaction contravened section 330 of the 1985 Act.

[CA85 Sec 342]. A company could, as a civil remedy, seek to treat an unlawful transaction as voidable under section 341 of the 1985 Act.

**6.175.1** These criminal penalties continue to apply under the 2006 Act for contraventions occurring before 1 October 2007. For transactions entered into after 1 October 2007 sections 330 to 342 of the 1985 Act have been repealed.

**Civil consequences of contravention of the 2006 Act**

**6.176** If a company enters into a transaction or an arrangement that contravenes sections 197, 198, 200, 201 or 203 of the 2006 Act (members' approval for loans, quasi loans, credit transactions and related arrangements), the company may seek to treat the transaction as voidable.

**6.177** A company may, as a civil remedy under section 213 of the 2006 Act, seek to treat an unlawful transaction as voidable. This means that a company does not need to regard itself as bound by any agreement that it has entered into with the director or any other person. However, because a transaction is not actually void, a company may wish to elect to affirm the agreement instead. [CA06 Sec 214]. Also, the company will not be entitled to treat the transaction as voidable if the subject matter of the transaction cannot be restored (for example, where the sum a company has lent to a borrower who is unable to repay has been used to buy goods which have been consumed), or if the person who benefited under the transaction has indemnified the company.

**6.178** Similarly, a transaction will not be voidable if a third party has, *bona fide* for value and without actual notice of the contravention, acquired rights under the agreement and these rights would be affected if the company avoided the liability. [CA06 Sec 213(2)].

**6.179** Moreover, whether or not an unlawful transaction has been avoided, the person who benefited from the unlawful transaction and any other director who authorised the transaction have a statutory duty to reimburse the company. They are, consequently, liable to account to the company for any gain they have made (whether directly or indirectly) and also to indemnify the company for any loss or damage resulting from the transaction. [CA06 Sec 213(3)]. Their liability may, however, be limited if either of the following applies.

■ Where the transaction in question was made for a person connected with a director of the company or its holding company, that director is not liable to account to the company or to indemnify it if he shows that he/she took all reasonable steps to ensure that the transaction did not contravene section 203 of the 2006 Act. [CA06 Sec 213(6)].

■ A connected person (and a director who authorised the transaction) will avoid civil liability if he can show that, at the time the company entered into the transaction, he did not know of the circumstances that amounted to a contravention. [CA06 Sec 213(7)].

# Annex – Directors loan decision tables

**Loans to directors – requirement for members approval**

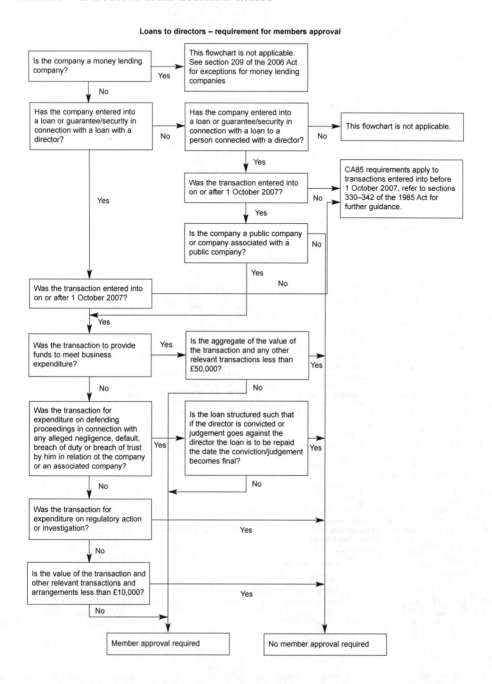

# *Loans and other transactions involving directors*

**Quasi-loans to directors – requirement for members approval**

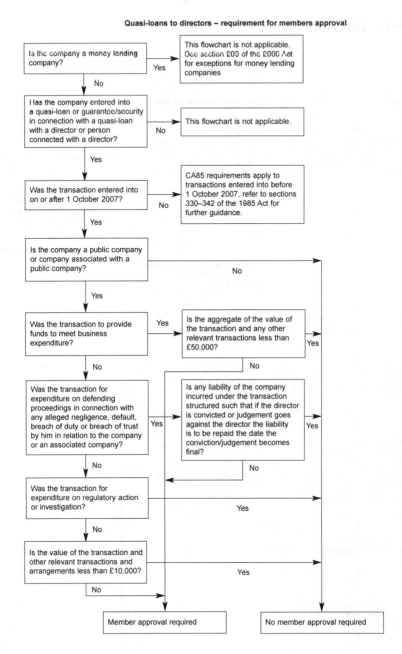

Is the company a money lending company?
→ **Yes** → This flowchart is not applicable. See section 209 of the 2006 Act for exceptions for money lending companies

↓ **No**

Has the company entered into a quasi-loan or guarantee/security in connection with a quasi-loan with a director or person connected with a director?
→ **No** → This flowchart is not applicable.

↓ **Yes**

Was the transaction entered into on or after 1 October 2007?
→ **No** → CA85 requirements apply to transactions entered into before 1 October 2007, refer to sections 330–342 of the 1985 Act for further guidance.

↓ **Yes**

Is the company a public company or company associated with a public company?
→ **No**

↓ **Yes**

Was the transaction to provide funds to meet business expenditure?
→ **Yes** → Is the aggregate of the value of the transaction and any other relevant transactions less than £50,000?
→ **Yes**

↓ **No** ... ↓ **No**

Was the transaction for expenditure on defending proceedings in connection with any alleged negligence, default, breach of duty or breach of trust by him in relation to the company or an associated company?
→ **Yes** → Is any liability of the company incurred under the transaction structured such that if the director is convicted or judgement goes against the director the liability is to be repaid the date the conviction/judgement becomes final?
→ **Yes**

↓ **No** ... ↓ **No**

Was the transaction for expenditure on regulatory action or investigation?
→ **Yes**

↓ **No**

Is the value of the transaction and other relevant transactions and arrangements less than £10,000?
→ **Yes**

↓ **No**

**Member approval required**    **No member approval required**

**Credit transactions with directors – requirement for members approval**

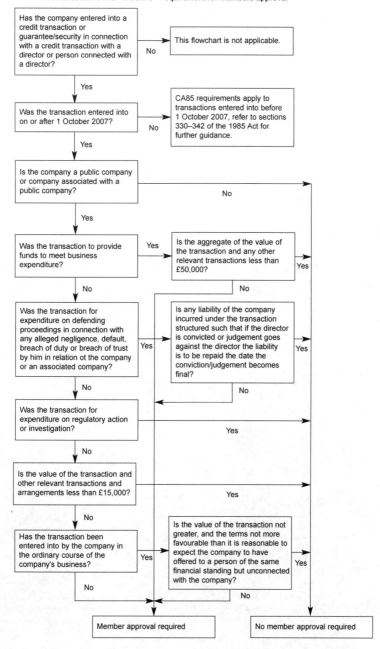

Chapter 7

# Acquisition of own shares

|  | Page |
|---|---|
| Introduction | 7001 |
| Summary of requirements | 7002 |
| Redeemable shares | 7003 |
| Initial matters to consider | 7005 |
| Conditions for acquisition | 7005 |
| Consideration for the acquisition | 7006 |
| Accounting and funding requirements | 7006 |
| Acquisition out of distributable profits or proceeds of fresh issue | 7007 |
| Payment out of capital | 7007 |
| Summary of basic funding rules | 7008 |
| Capital maintenance | 7008 |
| Cancellation of shares | 7009 |
| Issue of further shares | 7009 |
| Consent from shareholders having priority rights | 7009 |
| Effect of acquisition | 7009 |
| Accounting for acquisitions of shares | 7010 |
| Acquisition out of distributable profits | 7010 |
| Where to charge the purchase cost | 7012 |
| Expenses relating to the acquisition | 7013 |
| Acquisition at a premium out of fresh share issue | 7014 |
| Capital maintenance | 7018 |
| Acquisition at a discount out of fresh share issue | 7022 |
| Disclosure requirements | 7023 |
| Directors' report | 7023 |
| Notes to the financial statements – UK GAAP | 7024 |
| Notes to the financial statements – IFRS | 7024 |
| Acquisitions out of capital | 7024 |
| Permissible capital payment | 7025 |
| Available profits | 7025 |
| No available profits due to losses | 7028 |
| Capital maintenance | 7028 |
| Transfer to capital redemption reserve | 7029 |
| Nominal value less than PCP and proceeds of fresh issue | 7032 |
| Shares to be purchased at a premium in excess of the original premium on issue | 7034 |
| Legal procedures for purchase | 7035 |
| Definition of 'off-market' and 'market' | 7035 |
| Purchases by public companies | 7036 |
| Authority for market purchase | 7036 |
| Authority for an off-market purchase | 7037 |

Variation of existing contract. . . . . . . . . . . . . . . . . . . . . . . . . . . . . . 7038
Purchases by private companies. . . . . . . . . . . . . . . . . . . . . . . . . . . . . 7038
Insider dealing and market abuse . . . . . . . . . . . . . . . . . . . . . . . . . . . . 7039
Returns and contracts. . . . . . . . . . . . . . . . . . . . . . . . . . . . . . . . . . . . 7039
Prohibition on assignment of rights . . . . . . . . . . . . . . . . . . . . . . . . . 7040
Contingent purchase contracts. . . . . . . . . . . . . . . . . . . . . . . . . . . . . . 7041
Acquisitions out of capital. . . . . . . . . . . . . . . . . . . . . . . . . . . . . . . . . 7042
    Statutory declaration. . . . . . . . . . . . . . . . . . . . . . . . . . . . . . . . . . 7042
    Auditors' report to the directors . . . . . . . . . . . . . . . . . . . . . . . . . 7044
    Procedure for acquisition . . . . . . . . . . . . . . . . . . . . . . . . . . . . . . 7044
    Publication of notice of acquisition. . . . . . . . . . . . . . . . . . . . . . . 7045
    Liability on winding up. . . . . . . . . . . . . . . . . . . . . . . . . . . . . . . . 7046
Failure to acquire shares. . . . . . . . . . . . . . . . . . . . . . . . . . . . . . . . . 7047
Treasury shares . . . . . . . . . . . . . . . . . . . . . . . . . . . . . . . . . . . . . . . 7047
    Conditions applying to treasury shares. . . . . . . . . . . . . . . . . . . . 7048
    Sale or cancellation of treasury shares . . . . . . . . . . . . . . . . . . . . 7049
    Delivery of returns. . . . . . . . . . . . . . . . . . . . . . . . . . . . . . . . . . . 7050
    Accounting treatment . . . . . . . . . . . . . . . . . . . . . . . . . . . . . . . . 7051
Requirements of regulators and other bodies . . . . . . . . . . . . . . . . . . 7051
Listing Rules. . . . . . . . . . . . . . . . . . . . . . . . . . . . . . . . . . . . . . . . . . 7051
    Buying back shares during prohibited (close) periods . . . . . . . . . . 7052
    Insider trading and market abuse . . . . . . . . . . . . . . . . . . . . . . . . 7053
    Accounting requirements . . . . . . . . . . . . . . . . . . . . . . . . . . . . . 7053
    Purchases from related parties. . . . . . . . . . . . . . . . . . . . . . . . . . 7054
    Purchase of own equity shares. . . . . . . . . . . . . . . . . . . . . . . . . . 7054
    Purchase of own securities other than equity shares. . . . . . . . . . . 7056
    Treasury shares . . . . . . . . . . . . . . . . . . . . . . . . . . . . . . . . . . . . 7057
    Redemption of redeemable shares. . . . . . . . . . . . . . . . . . . . . . . 7058
    Major Shareholding Notification Rules . . . . . . . . . . . . . . . . . . . 7059
Institutional shareholders . . . . . . . . . . . . . . . . . . . . . . . . . . . . . . . . 7059
Financial assistance for acquisition of shares . . . . . . . . . . . . . . . . . . 7059
Private companies . . . . . . . . . . . . . . . . . . . . . . . . . . . . . . . . . . . . . 7059
Public companies. . . . . . . . . . . . . . . . . . . . . . . . . . . . . . . . . . . . . . 7060
Effect of contravention . . . . . . . . . . . . . . . . . . . . . . . . . . . . . . . . . . 7062
    Authorised reduction of share capital. . . . . . . . . . . . . . . . . . . . . 7063
    Court confirmation procedure . . . . . . . . . . . . . . . . . . . . . . . . . . 7063
    Solvency statement procedure . . . . . . . . . . . . . . . . . . . . . . . . . . 7065

Chapter 7

# Acquisition of own shares

## Introduction

**7.1** The general rule that prevented a company acquiring its own shares was established in 1887 by the case of *Trevor v Whitworth* on the grounds that such action might amount to 'trafficking' in its own shares or operate as a reduction of capital. The general prohibition, now set out in section 143 of the 1985 Act (section 658 of the 2006 Act), is that a company cannot acquire its own shares whether by purchase, subscription or otherwise, unless it falls within one of the exceptions specified in section 143(3) of the 1985 Act (sections 658 and 659(2) of the 2006 Act). However, unlimited companies can reduce their capital or purchase their own shares without restriction if the company is authorised to do so by its articles. For other companies, an acquisition that does not come within the specified exceptions is void and, therefore, has no effect. In addition, there are criminal sanctions available against the company and its officers in such a circumstance. The rules apply also to companies limited by guarantee that have a share capital.

**7.2** The only situations where a company can acquire its own shares are as follows:

- The shares are purchased under section 162 of the 1985 Act (section 690 of the 2006 Act). This includes the purchase of qualifying shares that are held in treasury.

- Redeemable shares are redeemed under section 159 of the 1985 Act (section 684 of the 2006 Act).

- The acquisition of shares is an authorised reduction of capital under section 135 of the 1985 Act (section 641 of the 2006 Act).

- The purchase of shares is made under a court order (for example, in a reconstruction).

- The shares are forfeited or surrendered as a result of calls on the shares not having been paid.

- The shares are acquired without the payment of any consideration (for example, a bequest or a gift).

[CA85 Sec 143(3); CA06 Sec 659].

**7.3** This chapter deals with the first three exceptions and is a practical guide to the company law requirements concerning the purchase and redemption by a limited company of its own shares. In setting out the requirements of the law, this guide is not a substitute for taking professional legal advice in light of the specific facts and circumstances of the company wishing to acquire its own shares. This chapter does not deal with the tax implications, which are complex and need to be considered thoroughly before a company embarks on acquiring its own shares.

**7.3.1** Most of the requirements in this chapter regarding acquisition of own shares are legal and, consequently, not covered by accounting standards. The accounting implications of the transactions considered in this chapter are dealt with in of the Manual of Accounting – IFRS for the UK and the Manual of Accounting – UK GAAP. In particular, it should be noted that any contract that contains an obligation (including contingent obligations) for a company to repurchase or redeem its own shares are subject to the special accounting treatment set out in paragraph 23 of IAS 32 and FRS 25.

**7.3.2** Since December 2003, companies with 'qualifying shares' have been permitted to purchase them out of distributable profits and hold them in treasury. See further paragraph 7.111.1.

**7.4** If a company follows the statutory procedure when it purchases or redeems its own shares, the prohibition in section 143 of the 1985 Act will not apply (section 658 of the 2006 Act). Non-compliance with that procedure results in a purchase or redemption being illegal and the purported acquisition having no effect. The law in this area is, however, complicated and this chapter gives general guidance by referring to the legal provisions to be considered; it primarily considers the accounting implications of such transactions. It is not, therefore, intended to be a substitute for taking legal advice on specific transactions.

**7.4.1** The provisions of the 2006 Act relating to acquisition of own shares come into effect from 1 October 2009, with the provisions of the 1985 Act remaining applicable until that date. At the time of writing, the 8th Commencement Order has been published in draft form by BERR, but has not been laid before parliament. This chapter has been drafted on the basis of that draft Commencement Order. The guidance in this chapter is based on the requirements of the Companies Act 2006. The provisions of the 2006 Act are similar to those of the 1985 Act but, where there are differences, these are highlighted in this chapter.

## Summary of requirements

**7.5** A company's ability to purchase its own shares can have advantages, particularly for private companies who can for example, remove a dissident shareholder or enable an outside investor to realise an investment.

**7.6** The advantages of being able to purchase own shares are, perhaps, less significant for public companies than for private ones, but they can nonetheless be of real benefit. In particular, public companies are able to return surplus funds to shareholders by purchasing and cancelling some of their shares. Some companies have purchased their own shares to boost their net asset value per share or earnings per share. Also, this ability provides public companies with flexibility both in ordering their capital structure and in matching that structure to their needs at any stage of their development. (see for example Table 7.1).

---

**Table 7.1 – Market purchase of own shares**

**AstraZeneca PLC – Annual Report – 31 December 2005**

**DIRECTORS' REPORT (extract)**

**Shareholders' return strategy and purchase of own shares**
The Company's stated distribution policy contains both a regular dividend cash flow and a share re-purchase component to give the Company more flexibility in managing its capital structure over time. The Board continually reviews its shareholders' return strategy and recently restated its intention to grow dividends in line with earnings while maintaining dividend cover in the two to three times range. The Board firmly believes that the first call on free cash flow is business need and, having fulfilled that, will return surplus cash to shareholders. Accordingly, in 2006, the Board intends to re-purchase shares at around the same level as 2005.

As previously reported, between August 1999 and December 2003 the Company re-purchased $4 billion of its own shares under two share re-purchase programmes. In January 2004 the Board approved a further $4 billion re-purchase programme to be completed by the end of 2005, of which $2.2 billion was completed in 2004.

In 2005 the Board approved an increase of the programme by a further $1.2 billion (making a total of $3 billion for 2005).

During 2005, the Company purchased 67.65 million of its own Ordinary Shares with a nominal value of $0.25 each for an aggregate cost of $3 billion. Following the purchase of these shares, they were all cancelled. This number of shares represents 4.28% of the Company's total issued share capital at 31 December 2005.

Since the beginning of the original re-purchase programme in 1999, the Company has purchased for cancellation in total 210.55 million of its Ordinary Shares with a nominal value of $0.25 each for an aggregate cost of $9.2 billion. This number of shares represents approximately 11.75% of the Company's total issued share capital at the time the re-purchase programme commenced in 1999.

The Company continues to maintain robust controls in respect of all aspects of the share re-purchase programme to ensure compliance with English law and the FSA's Listing Rules, Disclosure Rules and Prospectus Rules. In particular, the Company's Disclosure Committee meets to ensure that the Company does not purchase its own shares during prohibited periods. At the AGM on 27 April 2006, the Company will seek a renewal of its current permission from shareholders to purchase its own shares.

---

**[The next paragraph is 7.8.]**

## Redeemable shares

**7.8** Many of the requirements in sections 159 to 181 of the 1985 Act (sections 648 to 737 of the 2006 Act) apply to the redemption of redeemable shares as well as to purchases by a company of shares which are not issued as redeemable. In fact sections 159 to 161 of the 1985 Act (sections 684 to 689 of the

2006 Act) specifically set out the rules that apply to the redemption of redeemable shares and then section 162(2) of the 1985 Act (section 690 of the 2006 Act) applies those same rules to the purchase by a company of its own shares. One rule, however, differs under the 1985 Act: the terms and manner of purchase need not be determined by the company's articles of association, although there must be a general power to purchase its own shares. A company may acquire any of its own shares either by initial agreement, as in the issue of redeemable shares, or by subsequent agreement to purchase, as with a purchase from an existing shareholder.

**7.8.1**   Even though redeemable shares will often meet the definition of debt in IAS 32 and FRS 25 and be accounted for as such (see further chapter 6 of the Manual of Accounting – IFRS for the UK and the Manual of Accounting – UK GAAP) they are legally shares and the provisions of the 1985 and 2006 Acts apply to their redemption.

**7.9**   In order to issue redeemable shares, a public company must be authorised to do so by its articles of association. Redeemable shares are those shares that are specifically redeemable under the terms of their issue at the option of the company or the shareholder. [CA06 Sec 684(1)]. In this respect, Table A of SI 1995/805, 'The Companies (Tables A to F) Regulations 1985', includes regulation 3 which states that *"subject to the provisions of the Act, shares may be issued which are redeemable or are to be liable to be redeemed at the option of the company or the holder on such terms and in such manner as may be provided by the articles"*. At the time of writing, BERR has issued draft Model Articles that are due to come into force from 1 October 2009 and replace SI 1995/805. Redeemable shares include shares that are to be redeemed on a particular date, as well as shares that are merely redeemable at the option of either the company or the shareholder. A private company requires no such authorisation in its articles but the members may restrict the company's ability to issue redeemable shares by inserting a provision to this effect into the company's articles. However, if a private company was registered under the 1985 Act, it must either:

- be authorised by its articles to issue redeemable shares; or

- not be prevented by its articles from issuing redeemable shares and have passed a special resolution that the company has the power to issue redeemable shares.

[Draft 8th CO 2 Sch 69].

This represents a change from the 1985 Act (due to come into effect on 1 October 2009) under which authorisation in the articles was required for any company, both private and public. [CA85 Sec 159].

**7.10**   The directors of both public and private companies are able to specify the terms, conditions and manner of redemption (including the amount payable on redemption and the redemption date) if authorised to do so by either the articles or a company resolution. The resolution required in these circumstances is only an ordinary resolution. [CA06 Sec 685(1),(2)]. If the directors are not so authorised then the terms of redemption must be set out in the articles. This represents a change from the 1985 Act, which specified that the terms and manner of redemption must be set out in the company's articles. [CA85 Sec 160(3)].

**7.10.1** Directors exercising these rights must do so before the shares are allotted and include the terms, conditions and manner of redemption on the statement of capital. This statement of capital must accompany the return of the allotment made to the registrar. [CA06 Sec 685(3)].

**7.11** As mentioned above, the provisions that apply to the acquisition of redeemable shares are in the main the same as those that apply to the acquisition of other shares. However, the legal procedures relating to both market and off-market purchases (defined in para 7.64) do not apply to redeemable shares. There are, however, a few additional provisions that apply to redeemable shares and where these apply they are mentioned in the text.

**Initial matters to consider**

**7.12** A public or private company may purchase any of its own shares (including redeemable shares before their date for redemption), provided the company:

- It is not prohibited from doing so by its articles of association, by a shareholders' agreement or by any similar restrictions on the transfer of its shares by members. [CA06 Sec 690(1)]. This will apply particularly to a private company. Prior to 1 October 2009, the company must be authorised to do so by its articles of association. [CA85 Sec 162(1)]. Where a company was registered under the 1985 Act it must either have authorisation in its articles (as was the case under the 1985 Act) or must not be prohibited by its articles from doing so and must pass a special resolution giving it the power to do so. [CA85 Sec 162(1) Draft 8th CO 2 Sch 72].

- Complies with certain conditions (see para 7.13).

- Follows the appropriate procedure, which depends on whether it is a *market* (listed companies only) or an *off-market* purchase (see from para 7.63) or the purchase of a right to purchase (a contingent purchase contract – see from para 7.89). [CA85 Secs 163-166; CA06 Secs 693-708].

**Conditions for acquisition**

**7.13** A company must, after the purchase or redemption of its own shares, have other non-redeemable shares in issue. Shares held in treasury do not count for this purpose. [CA85 Sec 162(3); CA06 Sec 690(1)(b)]. At least two shares must remain for a public company, or if the company is private or limited by guarantee only one share need remain in issue. The company cannot purchase or redeem any of its own shares that are not fully paid. For example, it would not be possible to purchase a £1 redeemable preference share issued at a premium of £11, where only £5 has been paid on the share. There appears to be no requirement for a public company to re-register as a private one where, as a result of the repurchase or redemption of its own shares, the nominal value of its allotted share capital has fallen below the authorised minimum of £50,000. This is likely to be because on cancellation of the repurchased shares an equivalent amount is replaced either by a fresh issue of shares or by a transfer to the capital redemption reserve under the capital maintenance provisions.

**Consideration for the acquisition**

**7.14**   Under the 2006 Act, the terms of redemption of redeemable shares may provide for the company and the holder of the shares to agree that payment may be made on a later date than the redemption date (for example, by way of a loan), provided that the terms of redemption are fixed on or after 1 October 2009. [CA06 Sec 686(2); Draft 8th CO 2 Sch 70]. This is a change from the 1985 Act. A matter still under discussion with BERR is whether the amount should be undiscounted or should be discounted for the time value of money. This is an important point as the value has to be covered by distributable profits at the point of redemption. If the amount is the net present value of the future payment, less distributable profits are required for the redemption to be lawful.

**7.14.1**   Shares being purchased, as opposed to redeemed, by the company must be paid for in cash in full on the date of purchase. They cannot, for example, be paid for by instalments. [CA85 Sec 159; CA06 Sec 691(1)]. It s also thought unacceptable for, say, the seller of the shares to loan the company a sum of money equivalent to a deferred instalment on the shares being purchased or for the company to exchange a debenture for shares, because the seller has not effectively received payment in cash for the shares. Under the 1985 Act, these provisions apply for both a purchase and a redemption of shares. [CA85 Sec 162(2)].

**7.15**   It is generally accepted that the term 'purchase' in the context of a company purchasing its own shares, means a purchase of shares for cash. An exchange of shares for other forms of property, such as land, would not be a 'purchase' falling within sections 159 to 181 of the 1985 Act (sections 684-737 of the 2006 Act). Such a transaction might be possible, however, in the form of a reduction of capital, which would require the approval of the court under section 135 of the 1985 Act (section 645 of the 2006 Act) (see further from para 7.145).

**Accounting and funding requirements**

**7.16**   The accounting and funding requirements of purchases and redemptions of shares can be complex. A purchase or redemption can only be made out of:

■   Distributable profits.

■   Proceeds of a fresh issue of shares.

■   Share premium (where there is a fresh issue at a premium and the shares being purchased were similarly issued at a premium).

■   Capital (where the company is a private company and the above have been exhausted).

These rules are summarised in the paragraphs that follow and dealt with in detail in the body of the chapter.

### *Acquisition out of distributable profits or proceeds of fresh issue*

**7.17**  Where a company redeems or purchases its own shares, the shares can only be redeemed or purchased out of distributable profits or out of the proceeds of a new issue of shares (called a 'fresh issue' in sections 687(2)(b) and 692(2)(b) of the 2006 Act) made for the purposes of the purchase or redemption. In addition, any premium payable on the purchase or redemption must be paid out of the company's distributable profits. However, if a premium arose on the original issue of the shares being acquired, the premium payable on their acquisition may be funded out of a fresh issue of shares made for that purpose (see further para 7.32). [CA85 Sec 160(1); CA06 Sec 692(2)]. 'Distributable profits' are defined in section 181(a) of the 1985 Act (section 736 of the 2006 Act) as those profits out of which a company could lawfully make a distribution equal in value to the payment. A private company can additionally fund a purchase out of its capital (having first depleted its distributable profits) (see para 7.19).

**7.18**  Certain other payments relating to a purchase of shares can only be made out of distributable profits. For example, payments in consideration for varying a contract for an off-market purchase of a company's own shares (see para 7.70) or for the release of any obligations under a contract to purchase a company's own shares. [CA85 Sec 168(1); CA06 Sec 705(1)].

### *Payment out of capital*

**7.19**  If the total distributable profits and the proceeds of a new issue of shares (if any) are not sufficient to meet the purchase or redemption price, a private company may make up the shortfall by a payment from 'capital' (that is, otherwise than out of its distributable profits or the proceeds of a fresh issue of shares). [CA85 Sec 171; CA06 Sec 709]. The conditions considered from paragraph 7.47 must be met before a payment out of capital can be made, including first using all its distributable profits and proceeds of any new issue made for the purpose.

**7.20**  If a company redeems or purchases its shares out of 'capital' without having sufficient distributable profits or, as a private company, without following the statutory procedure, the acquisition will be void as it would be an unlawful reduction of capital. In such a situation, the shares will remain in issue and are deemed to be held by the shareholders who held them at the time of the attempted purchase or redemption was made. If a purchase is made in this way, the company is liable to a fine and, in addition, the directors are liable to a fine and/or imprisonment. [CA85 Sec 143(2); CA06 Sec 658(2)(3)]. Such a payment out of capital may be an illegal distribution and the directors risk being in breach of their fiduciary duty to the company to act in its best interests and, since 1 October 2007, their legal duties to exercised reasonable care, skill and diligence and to promote the success of the company. [CA06 Secs 172, 174].

## Summary of basic funding rules

**7.21**  The basic rules mentioned above are represented in the following diagram. This shows how the purchase or redemption can be funded and is the basis of tables used in each of the examples in this chapter.

| PLC | | Private company | |
|---|---|---|---|
| Funding of purchase: | | Funding of purchase: | |
| | | | |
| Out of the proceeds of a fresh issue of shares: | | Out of the proceeds of a fresh issue of shares: | |
| 1  Nominal value of shares purchased restricted to proceeds of fresh issue | X | 1  Nominal value of shares purchased restricted to proceeds of fresh issue | Y |
| 2  Where there is a premium on the shares being purchased and on their initial issue – the premium on purchase restricted to the lower of: | | 2  Where there is a premium on the shares being purchased and on their initial issue – the premium on purchase restricted to the lower of: | |
| (a)  initial premium on issue of shares being purchased | | (a)  initial premium on issue of shares being purchased | |
| (b)  balance on share premium account including any premium on fresh issue of shares | X | (b)  balance on share premium account including any premium on fresh issue of shares | Y |
| Total not to exceed the proceeds of the fresh issue | X | Total not to exceed the proceeds of the fresh issue | Y |
| Balance out of distributable profits | X | Out of distributable profits | Y |
| | | | Y |
| Total cost of purchase | X | | |
| | | Balance out of capital | Y |
| | | Total cost of purchase | Y |

## *Capital maintenance*

**7.22**  Unless it is a private company making an acquisition of its own shares out of capital (see para 7.19), any other company is required to maintain its capital before and after the acquisition of shares. This generally means that a company has to make a transfer to a capital redemption reserve of an amount equal to the nominal value of the shares that it acquires, or on cancellation of shares held as treasury shares. [CA85 Sec 170(1); CA06 Sec 733(1)(2)(4)]. But where the acquisition is funded wholly or partly by an issue of new shares (a 'fresh issue' of shares), which must be made specifically for the purpose of the redemption/ repurchase, the amount that is required to be transferred to the capital redemption reserve is the difference between the proceeds of the fresh issue and the nominal value of the shares being purchased. [CA85 Sec 170(2); CA06

Sec 733(3)]. In this situation, where the acquisition is funded by a fresh issue, the company's capital is still maintained, although some of the capital may now be represented partly by share premium and partly by an amount transferred to the capital redemption reserve.

**Cancellation of shares**

**7.23** Unless the purchase is a permitted acquisition of 'treasury shares' (see paras 7.111.1 to 7.111.7 below), the company must treat any shares that it purchases or redeems as being cancelled immediately on acquisition and so the acquisition will reduce the issued (but not the authorised) share capital by the nominal amount of the shares purchased. [CA85 Sec 160(4); CA06 Sec 688, 706]. An acquisition will generally be complete when the executed stock transfer form and relevant share certificate are delivered to the company. The shares acquired must then be cancelled and cannot, therefore, be reissued.

**Issue of further shares**

**7.24** Under the 1985 Act, where a company is about to purchase (other than to hold as 'treasury shares') or redeem its own shares, it has the power to issue shares up to the nominal value of the shares to be purchased or redeemed. [CA85 Sec 160(5)]. This is because the shares the company acquires have to be cancelled and, as a consequence after the acquisition, the company's shares in issue will remain within its authorised share capital limit (albeit that this limit could have been exceeded for a short period between the issue of the new shares and the cancellation of the shares acquired, but this is allowed under section 160). This permission has not been carried into the Companies Act 2006 and was repealed on 1 October 2008.

**Consent from shareholders having priority rights**

**7.25** Where the capital of the company includes shares that have priority on a return of capital over the shares that the company proposes to purchase, the company will need to obtain consent to a variation of their rights from the holders of the shares that have the priority right.

**Effect of acquisition**

**7.26** Whenever any company wishes to purchase its own shares and this is not done in proportion to existing shareholdings, the effect of that purchase on the remaining shareholders needs to be considered carefully. For example, the cancellation of the shares purchased will, if no new issue is made, proportionately increase the holdings of the remaining shareholders. This may result in one shareholder or group of shareholders obtaining the power to pass ordinary or special resolutions.

## Accounting for acquisitions of shares

### Acquisition out of distributable profits

**7.27** As explained above, section 160(1) of the 1985 Act (sections 687(2) and 692(2) of the 2006 Act) requires that the acquisition of own shares (including any premium paid on the acquisition) must be made out of the company's distributable profits (or out of the proceeds of a fresh issue). An illustration of the legal position of a company purchasing its own shares out of distributable profits and showing the effect on its balance sheet is given in the example below. The example also illustrates some of the steps a company needs to consider before making such a purchase. The legal procedures for purchasing or redeeming a company's shares are considered from paragraph 7.63 and the disclosure requirements that have to be made in the company's financial statements are dealt with in paragraph 7.41.

**7.27.1** For simplicity, the added complexity of the accounting requirements for a contract to purchase own shares under the requirements of paragraph 23 of IAS 32 and FRS 25, 'Financial instruments: Presentation', have been excluded from this illustration.

### Example — Purchase made out of distributable profits

Company Z (a private company) is a long established family manufacturing company. Mr Brown (a director of company Z) purchased for £10,000, many years ago, 10,000 of company Z's 100,000 issued ordinary £1 shares. He has now had a major disagreement with his fellow directors about the way in which company Z is run. The directors and the shareholders have agreed that it is in everyone's best interests for Mr Brown to sever his links with the company. He will resign as a director and the company will purchase his shares from him for £24,000 (which is the agreed market value). The company will make the payment out of distributable profits.

At present, company Z's articles of association do not permit it to purchase its own shares. Company Z cannot proceed with the purchase until it alters its articles of association and this will require a special resolution.

In addition, company Z can purchase Mr Brown's shares only under a contract with him. The terms of this contract will need to be authorised by a special resolution of the company before the contract is entered into. (Mr Brown cannot vote on this special resolution.) The company must send a copy of the special resolution to the Registrar of Companies within 15 days of its being passed. The terms of the contract will need to include, amongst other things, a description of, and the number of, the shares to be purchased, the amount of the payment, the date of the purchase and a statement that payment will be made at the time of the purchase. (The company can then purchase Mr Brown's shares at any time after the date of the special resolution to authorise the contract.)

If the special resolution is to be effective, company Z will need to make the contract available for inspection both at its registered office during the 15 days immediately preceding the meeting that will consider the special resolution and at the meeting itself. Within 28 days of the date on which Mr Brown's shares are delivered to company Z, the company will need to make a return to the Registrar of Companies together with any stamp duty payable. The return must be on the prescribed form and it must state the following:

- Class of shares.

- The number and the nominal value of the shares purchased.

- Aggregate amount paid for the shares.

- The date on which the shares were delivered to the company.

- The stamp duty payable.

Furthermore, company Z will need to keep the contract for the purchase at its registered office for ten years from the date of purchase. Throughout this time, the contract must be available during business hours for members to inspect.

In their report attached to the financial statements that relate to the year in which the purchase took place, the directors will have to state the following details in respect of the purchase:

- The number and the nominal value of the shares the company purchased and the percentage of the called-up capital of that description that these shares represent.

- The aggregate consideration the company paid and the reasons for the purchase.

Company Z must treat Mr Brown's shares as being cancelled on purchase and make the necessary entry in the Register of Members. Because the company made the payment out of distributable profits, company Z will need to transfer £10,000 (that is, the nominal value of the shares purchased) to the capital redemption reserve.

Using the table from paragraph 7.21 above, the purchase is made in the following way:

| Funding of purchase: | £'000 |
|---|---|
| Out of the proceeds of a fresh issue of shares | – |
| Balance out of distributable profits | 24 |
| Total cost of purchase | 24 |

The effect on the balance sheet of company Z would be as follows, showing the position both before and after the purchase:

| Balance sheet | Before purchase £'000 | Purchase of shares £'000 | Maintain capital £'000 | After purchase £'000 |
|---|---|---|---|---|
| Share capital | 100 | (10) | | 90 |
| Capital redemption reserve | – | | 10 | 10 |
| Capital | 100 | (10) | 10 | 100 |
| Distributable reserves | 50 | (14) | (10) | 26 |
| | 150 | (24) | – | 126 |
| Net assets other than cash | 125 | | | 125 |
| Cash | 25 | (24) | | 1 |
| | 150 | (24) | – | 126 |

## Acquisition of own shares

The double entry for this transaction is as follows:

|  | £'000 | £'000 |
|---|---|---|
| Dr Share capital | 10 | |
| Dr Distributable profits | 14 | |
| Cr Cash | | 24 |
| | | |
| To reflect the purchase of 10,000 £1 shares at a premium of £14,000 | | |
| | | |
| Dr Distributable profits | 10 | |
| Cr Capital redemption reserve | | 10 |
| | | |
| To maintain the capital of the company | | |

**7.28** It can be seen from the above example that the company's capital has been maintained at £100,000. The company is making the purchase out of distributable profits, as the total debited to distributable profits is £24,000 which equals the consideration for the purchase. Some might argue that the double entry should be to credit cash £24,000 and to debit distributable profits £24,000 and to debit share capital with £10,000 and credit the capital redemption reserve with £10,000, which is the way the 1985 Act expresses the purchase in sections 160 and 170 (section 733 of the 2006 Act). However, for clarity, the double entry throughout this chapter shows each step in the process separately: namely the entries for any issue of fresh capital (there are none in the example above); then the entries for the acquisition of the old capital; followed by the entries needed to maintain the company's capital.

### Where to charge the purchase cost

**7.29** The requirement in IAS 32 and FRS 25 to account for shares according to the substance of their contractual terms results in some shares (or parts of shares) being presented as liabilities. When such shares are redeemed or repurchased the resulting accounting entries have to reflect both the requirements of the relevant accounting standards and the law regarding the preservation of capital. Where a company purchases out of distributable profits some of its shares that had been presented as liabilities, the final result has to show that an amount equal to the redemption/repurchase price has been charged against distributable profits, any share premium previously classified within liabilities is added to the share premium account in equity and the nominal value of the shares redeemed/repurchased is added to the capital redemption reserve in equity. However, the accounting will also show the elimination of the shares as liabilities, the outflow of cash and the recognition of any gain or loss on elimination of the liabilities.

**7.29.1** If the shares meet the definition in IAS 32 and FRS 25 of debt and they are repurchased for an amount in excess of their amortised cost carrying amount, the loss on the repurchase of the shares should be recognised in the profit or loss for the period. For companies preparing their financial statements in accordance with EU-adopted IFRS (or in accordance with UK GAAP and applying FRS 26), this is required by paragraph 41 of IAS 39 (or FRS 26). For companies preparing their financial statements in accordance with UK GAAP and not applying FRS 26 (see further chapter 6 of the Manual of Accounting – UK GAAP), this is required by paragraph 32 of FRS 4. Additional accounting entries must be made to ensure that the nominal value of the repurchased shares is credited to the capital redemption reserve in equity, that the full repurchase price has been charged against distributable profits and any share premium associated with the repurchased shares is credited to the share premium account in equity.

**7.29.2**  If the shares meet the definition of equity in IAS 32 and FRS 25 and are repurchased at a premium, the loss on the repurchase of the shares should be recognised directly in equity in the profit and loss reserve and shown in the reconciliation of movements in shareholders' funds (required by FRS 3) or the statement of changes in equity (required by IAS 1). It should not be recognised in the statement of total recognised gains and losses (for companies applying UK GAAP) or the statement of recognised income and expense (or statement of comprehensive income), where one is presented, (for companies applying EU-adopted IFRS), because the charge represents the capital repaid to shareholders and, therefore, it is not a recognised loss. Additional accounting entries must be made to ensure that the nominal value of the repurchased shares is credited to the capital redemption reserve in equity, that the full repurchase price has been charged against distributable profits and that any share premium associated with the repurchased shares is credited to share premium account in equity.

*Expenses relating to the acquisition*

**7.30**  The expenses directly relating to the acquisition should be treated as part of the overall cost of acquisition and should be treated in the same way as the purchase cost itself (see Table 7.2).

---

**Table 7.2 – Disclosure of expenses relating to an acquisition of own shares**

**British Sky Broadcasting Group – Annual Report – 30 June 2005**

**23 Reconciliation of movement in shareholders' funds (extract)**

**(b) Company**

| | Share capital £m | Share premium £m | Shares to be issued £m | Capital reserve £m | Special reserve £m | Capital redemption reserve £m | Profit and loss account £m | Total equity shareholders' funds £m |
|---|---|---|---|---|---|---|---|---|
| AT 1 JULY 2003 | 969 | 2,536 | 3 | 844 | – | – | (1,121) | 3,231 |
| Issue of share capital | 2 | 21 | (3) | – | – | – | – | 20 |
| Share premium reduction | – | (1,120) | – | – | 14 | – | 1,106 | – |
| Profit for the financial year | – | – | – | – | – | – | 456 | 456 |
| Dividends | – | – | – | – | – | – | (116) | (116) |
| AT 1 JULY 2004 | 971 | 1,437 | – | 844 | 14 | – | 325 | 3,591 |
| Profit for the financial year | – | – | – | – | – | – | 576 | 576 |
| Dividends | – | – | – | – | – | – | (170) | (170) |
| Share buy-back | (37) | – | – | – | – | 37 | (416) | (416) |
| AT 30 JUNE 2005 | 934 | 1,437 | – | 844 | 14 | 37 | 315 | 3,581 |

**Share buy-back**

On 12 November 2004, the Company's shareholders approved a resolution at the AGM for the Company to purchase up to 97 million Ordinary Shares. During the financial year, the Company purchased, and subsequently cancelled, 74 million Ordinary Shares at an average price of £5.60 per share, with a nominal value of £37 million, for a consideration of £416 million. Consideration included stamp duty and commission of £3 million. This represents 4% of called-up share capital at the beginning of the financial year.

---

**[The next paragraph is 7.32.]**

**Acquisition at a premium out of fresh share issue**

**7.32** The nominal value of the shares being acquired can, instead of being made out of distributable profits, be funded out of the proceeds of a fresh issue of shares made for the purpose of the acquisition. [CA85 Sec 160(1)(a); CA06 Sec 692(2)(a)]. Generally, any premium paid on the shares that the company acquires has to be made out of distributable profits, but where the shares were initially issued at a premium, the company may fund the premium payable on their acquisition (or part of that premium) from the proceeds of a new issue of shares. The amount of premium that can be funded in this way is equal to the lower of the following two amounts:

■ The aggregate of the premiums the company received when it issued the shares it is now purchasing.

■ The amount of the company's share premium account after crediting the premium, if any, on the new issue of shares it makes to fund the purchase or redemption.

[CA85 Sec 160(2); CA06 Sec 692(3)].

**7.32.1** A company should be able to identify the amount of premiums it had received on the original issue of the shares it repurchases or redeems by using the unique numbers on the share certificates and tracing them back through its register of members that are required to be kept and maintained under section 352 of the 1985 Act (section 113 of the 2006 Act). For many companies, and particularly listed companies that have many shareholders and millions of shares in issue, identification of the premiums associated with the repurchased shares can be a tedious and time consuming task.

**7.33** The example below illustrates a private company that uses the proceeds of a new issue as well as distributable profits to fund the purchase of its own shares and the resulting effect on its balance sheet.

**Example — Purchase out of a fresh issue of capital**

In January 20X0, company Y issued 1,000,000 ordinary shares of £1 each, including 100,000 to Mrs Green, at a premium of 10p per share. After the issue, the balance on company Y's share premium account was £100,000. In January 20X2, company Y utilised the balance of £100,000 on its share premium account to make a bonus issue of shares to its shareholders.

In July 20X4, company Y made an issue of 75,000 ordinary shares of £1 each at a premium of £1 per share for the purposes of purchasing, at a premium of £1.40 per share, Mrs Green's 100,000 ordinary shares issued in January 20X0. The balance of £90,000 of the purchase price of £240,000 was paid out of the cash resources of company Y.

Using the table in paragraph 7.21 company Y would make the purchase in the way shown below:

|  | £'000 | £'000 |
|---|---|---|
| Out of the proceeds of a fresh issue of shares: | | |
| Nominal value shares purchased | | 100 |
| Premium on purchase – the lower of: | | |
| (a) Initial premium on issue of the shares being purchased (100,000 at 10p) | 10 | |
| (b) Balance on share premium account including premium on fresh issue of shares (see below) | 75 | |
|  | | 10 |
| Total not to exceed proceeds of fresh issue | | 110 |
| Balance out of distributable profits | | 130 |
| Total cost of purchase (nominal value plus premium = £2.40 × 100,000) | | 240 |

*Acquisition of own shares*

The effect on the balance sheet of company Y is as follows:

| Balance sheet | Before purchase £'000 | Issue of shares £'000 | Purchase of shares £'000 | Maintain capital £'000 | After purchase £'000 |
|---|---|---|---|---|---|
| Ordinary shares | 1,100 | | (100) | | 1,000 |
| New ordinary shares | – | 75 | | | 75 |
| Share premium | – | 75 | (10) | | 65 |
| Capital redemption reserve* | – | – | – | – | – |
| Capital | 1,100 | 150 | (110) | – | 1,140 |
| Distributable profits | 500 | | (130) | – | 370 |
| | 1,600 | 150 | (240) | – | 1,510 |
| Net assets other than cash | 1,350 | | | | 1,350 |
| Cash | 250 | 150 | (240) | | 160 |
| | 1,600 | 150 | (240) | – | 1,510 |

The double entry for this purchase is as follows:

| | £'000 | £'000 |
|---|---|---|
| Dr Cash | 150 | |
| Cr Share capital | | 75 |
| Cr Share premium | | 75 |
| To show the issue of 75,000 £1 shares at a premium of £1 per share. | | |
| Dr Share capital | 100 | |
| Dr Share premium account | 10 | |
| Dr Distributable profits | 130 | |
| Cr Cash | | 240 |
| To recognise the purchase of £100,000 £1 shares at a premium of £1.40 per share. | | |

*There is no transfer to capital redemption reserve because the nominal value of the shares purchased (that is, £100,000) is less than the aggregate proceeds of the new issue (that is £150,000 – see para 7.38) and, as a consequence, the company's capital has been maintained without the need to make such a transfer. The increase in capital is made up of the £50,000 additional capital arising from the fresh issue of shares and a reduction in capital of £10,000 which represents the amount by which the share premium account has been reduced. This is because of the effect of section 160(2) of the 1985 Act (section 692(4) of the 2006 Act) that allows the share premium account to be reduced, in the example by £10,000. This is the part of the premium payable on repurchase/redemption that is allowed to be funded out of the proceeds of the fresh issue of shares as opposed to being made out of distributable profits.

**7.34** Table 7.3 below shows the redemption by English China Clays plc of 500 preference shares having a nominal value of $0.5million (£0.3million). The purchase is made out of the proceeds of a rights issue and it can be seen from the reserves note that the payment has been made out of the share premium account and distributable reserves. There is no transfer to the capital redemption reserve, because the proceeds of the fresh issue of shares exceeds the nominal value of the shares redeemed. Note that under both EU-adopted IFRS and UK GAAP, many preference shares (and any related share premiums) are presented as debt in the balance sheet. This extract demonstrates the accounting for shares that are recognised as equity.

---

**Table 7.3 – Redemption of preference shares**

**English China Clays plc – Annual Report & Account – 31 December 1993**

**Notes to the Accounts (extract)**

| **15 SHARE CAPITAL** | **£M** |
|---|---|
| **(a) Ordinary shares** | |
| **(i) Authorised and issued** | |
| Authorised: 360,000,000 ordinary shares of 25p each | **90.0** |
| Allotted, called up and fully paid: | |
| At 31st December 1992 267,646,174 ordinary shares | **66.9** |
| Allotment of 35,243,638 ordinary shares | **8.8** |
| At 31st December 1993 302,889,812 ordinary shares | **75.5** |

| | 1993 | 1992 |
|---|---|---|
| Ordinary shares were issued as follows: | | |
| Rights Issue | **33,497,162** | 51,612,153 |
| Scrip dividend elections | **457,457** | 425,623 |
| Exercise of share options | **417,055** | 323,469 |
| Conversion of 6½% Convertible Bonds Due 2003 | **871,964** | 241,991 |
| | **35,243,638** | 52,603,236 |

The shares issued under the Rights Issue, announced on 11th June 1993, were issued at 350p per share and raised approximately **£113.8M** net of expenses. Over 93% of the ordinary shares were taken up and those not taken up were sold on the market. The proceeds of the issue were used to repay US dollar bank borrowings and to redeem the remaining $50M of the US dollar preference shares.

**(b) US dollar preference shares**

| | Authorised, allotted, called up and fully paid | |
|---|---|---|
| | $M | £M |
| At 31st December 1992 | | |
| 500 preference shares | | |
| of US$ 1,000 each | 0.5 | 0.3 |
| Redemption of 500 preference shares | (0.5) | (0.3) |
| At 31st December 1993 | – | – |

The Company completed the redemption of the 500 preference shares on 30th July 1993.

**16 RESERVES (Extract)**

| | Group and Company | Group | | Company |
|---|---|---|---|---|
| | Share Premium Account | Revaluation Reserve | Profit and Loss Account | Profit and Loss Account |
| | £M | £M | £M | £M |
| At 31st December 1992 | | | | |
| as previously reported | 355.1 | 98 | 298.1 | 180.8 |
| Prior year adjustment | – | – | (2.2) | – |

---

| | | | |
|---|---|---|---|
| At 31st December 1992 as restated | **355.1** | **98.2** | **295.9** | **180.8** |
| Issue of ordinary shares | 113.9 | – | – | – |
| Costs in respect of the Rights Issue | (3.5) | – | – | – |
| Redemption of preference shares | (32.4) | – | (1.1) | (1.1) |
| Retained profit/(loss) for the year | – | – | 0.5 | (66.3) |
| Goodwill arising on acquisition | – | – | (155.5) | – |
| Transfer | – | (0.3) | 0.3 | – |
| Exchange rate movements | 0.1 | (0.1) | (3.4) | 0.3 |
| At 31st December 1993 | **433.2** | **97.8** | **136.7** | **113.7** |

**[The next paragraph is 7.36.]**

**Capital maintenance**

**7.36** The 2006 Act (like the 1985 Act) requires both public and private companies to transfer certain amounts to the capital redemption reserve when they purchase for cancellation any of their own shares, whether these shares are classified as debt or equity. This is to safeguard creditors by ensuring that the company's legal capital is maintained (except to the extent that a private company purchases its own shares out of capital or where the shares are qualifying shares that are held in treasury). The capital redemption reserve carries the same restrictions on its use as share capital (so that the ordinary rules regarding the reduction of capital apply to it). One use to which the capital redemption reserve can be put is to pay up unissued shares allotted as fully paid bonus shares (see chapter 23 of the Manual of Accounting – IFRS for the UK and chapter 23 of the Manual of Accounting – UK GAAP). The Act also contains provisions that enable a private company to use its capital redemption reserve or share premium account or fully paid share capital to fund the purchase or redemption of shares in certain circumstances.

**7.37** The provisions explained below relate to the maintenance of capital where a public or a private company purchases or redeems its own shares. These rules are, however extended further for private companies and these additional rules are explained from paragraph 7.55 onwards.

**7.38** A transfer to the capital redemption reserve must be made by a company, whether public or private, in the following circumstances:

- Where the company has purchased or redeemed its shares wholly out of distributable profits (that is, where no fresh issue of shares is made or no payment is made out of capital or the shares are not held in treasury), it must transfer to the capital redemption reserve an amount equivalent to the nominal value of the shares it purchased. [CA85 Sec 170(1); CA06 Sec 733(2)]. It also has to reduce the issued share capital by the nominal value of the shares purchased (see example in para 7.27).

- Where the company cancels shares held as treasury shares, it must transfer to the capital redemption reserve an amount equivalent to the nominal value of the shares cancelled. [CA85 Sec 170(1), CA06 Sec 733(4)]. The company must reduce the amount of its issued share capital by the nominal value of the cancelled shares. [CA85 Sec 162D(4); CA06 Sec 729(4)].

■ Where a company has purchased or redeemed its own shares wholly or partly out of the proceeds of a fresh issue (that is, where no payment out of capital is made) and the nominal value of the shares purchased (or redeemed) exceeds the amount of the proceeds, the company must transfer the difference to the capital redemption reserve. [CA85 Sec 170(2); CA06 Sec 733(3)]. This treatment is illustrated in the example that follows:

**Example — Nominal value of shares purchased exceeds proceeds of fresh share issue**

Company H decides to redeem 100,000 £1 ordinary shares at a premium of £1 (the initial premium on the shares when they were issued was 10p). It also has a further 50,000 ordinary shares in issue which were issued for no premium. Company H makes the purchase partly out of the proceeds of a fresh issue of shares and partly out of its distributable profits. Company H issues 30,000 50p 'A' ordinary shares (a different class of share that meets the definition of equity) at a premium of £1.50 (that is, proceeds of £60,000).

The amount that will need to be transferred to the capital redemption reserve is calculated as follows:

|  | £'000 |
|---|---|
| Nominal value of shares redeemed | 100 |
| Proceeds of fresh issue | 60 |
| Amount to be transferred to the capital redemption reserve | 40 |

Following the table in paragraph 7.21, company H makes the purchase in the way shown below:

|  | £'000 | £'000 |
|---|---|---|
| Out of the proceeds of the fresh issue: | | |
| (a) Nominal value of shares purchased restricted to proceeds of fresh issue | 60 | |
| (b) Share premium account* | – | 60 |
| Balance out of distributable profits | | 140 |
| Total cost of purchase (nominal value plus premium = £2 × 100,000) | | 200 |

*Some might argue that part of the purchase can be made out of the share premium account (£10,000 in the example, being the premium on the issue of the shares being purchased). However, if this argument is pursued, the effect is that the company's capital is reduced by £10,000 and, as a consequence, is not maintained, which is the intention of the 2006 Act (like the 1985 Act). This approach can also be said to be wrong on the grounds that the proceeds of the fresh issue are £60,000 and this has all been used funding the purchase of the nominal value of the shares being purchased and as a consequence there is nothing else that can come out of the share premium account.

7019

## Acquisition of own shares

The effect on the balance sheet of company H is as follows:

| Balance sheet | Before purchase £'000 | Issue of shares £'000 | Purchase of shares £'000 | Maintain capital £'000 | After purchase £'000 |
|---|---|---|---|---|---|
| Ordinary shares | 150 | | (100) | | 50 |
| 'A' ordinary shares | – | 15 | – | – | 15 |
| Share premium | 10 | 45 | – | – | 55 |
| Capital redemption reserve | – | – | – | 40 | 40 |
| Capital | 160 | 60 | (100) | 40 | 160 |
| Reserves – Distributable profits | 150 | – | (100) | (40) | 10 |
| | 310 | 60 | (200) | – | 170 |
| Net assets other than cash | 150 | – | – | – | 150 |
| Cash | 160 | 60 | (200) | – | 20 |
| | 310 | 60 | (200) | – | 170 |

The double entry for the purchase would be as follows:

| | £'000 | £'000 |
|---|---|---|
| Dr Cash | 60 | |
| Cr Share capital | | 15 |
| Cr Share premium | | 45 |
| To show the issue of 30,000 50p shares at a premium of £1.50 per share. | | |
| Dr Share capital | 100 | |
| Dr Distributable profits | 100 | |
| Cr Cash | | 200 |
| To recognise the purchase of £100,000 £1 shares at a premium of £1 per share. | | |
| Dr Distributable profits | 40 | |
| Cr Capital redemption reserve | | 40 |
| To maintain the capital of the company. | | |

In total, distributable profits have been reduced by £140,000 being the cost of the repurchase (£200,000) less the amount funded out of the proceeds (£60,000) of the fresh issue for the purpose of the repurchase.

**7.39** Table 7.5 below illustrates a simple purchase out of distributable profits and maintenance of capital by the transfer of an amount equal to the nominal value of the shares redeemed to the capital redemption reserve.

---

**Table 7.5 – Maintenance of capital**

**Next plc – Annual Report & Accounts – 29 January 2005**

**Directors' Report (extract)**

**Share Capital**
The Company was authorised by its shareholders to purchase the Company's own shares for cancellation. During the year the Company purchased a total of 3,967,421 ordinary shares of 10p each for cancellation at a cost of £57.3m, representing 1.5% of its issued share capital. The authority to purchase shares is renewable annually and approval will be sought from shareholders at the Annual General Meeting in 2005 to renew the authority.

---

On 29 January 2005 the Company had 261,103,082 shares in issue. Since that date the Company has continued to purchase shares off-market under contingent purchase contracts. As at 21 March 2005, the Company had purchased and cancelled a further 750,000 shares at a cost of £11.9m, representing 0.3% of its issued share capital.

## 21 Called up share capital (extract)
The share capital of the Company is shown below:

|  | 2005 '000 | 2004 '000 | 2005 £m | 2004 £m |
|---|---|---|---|---|
| **Authorised** |  |  |  |  |
| Ordinary shares of 10p each | 400,500 | 400,500 | 40.1 | 40.1 |
| **Allotted, called up and fully paid** |  |  |  |  |
| Ordinary shares of 10p each | 261,103 | 265,071 | 26.1 | 26.5 |

The Company purchased 3,517,421 of its own ordinary shares of 10p each in the open market for cancellation between 17 May 2004 and 11 January 2005 at a cost of £50.2m. The Company also purchased for cancellation 450,000 of its own ordinary shares of 10p each under off-market contingent purchase contracts between 8 December 2004 and 26 January 2005 at a cost of £7.1m. At the year end date, the Company was party to two off-market contingent purchase contracts under which a maximum of 2,300,000 shares might be purchased for cancellation at a maximum potential cost of £36.2m. The purchase of these shares is dependent upon the Company's share price not reaching a pre-determined level during the remainder of each contract period.

## 22 Share capital and reserves (extract)

|  | Ordinary shares £m | Share premium £m | Revaluation reserve £m | Capital redemption £m | ESOP reserve £m | Other reserves £m | Profit and loss account £m |
|---|---|---|---|---|---|---|---|
| **The group** |  |  |  |  |  |  |  |
| At January 2004 as previously stated | 26.5 | 0.6 | 14.0 | 3.4 | – | (1,448.9) | 1,625.4 |
| Prior period adjustment | – | – | – | – | (72.8) | – | 6.9 |
| At January 2004 as restated | 26.5 | 0.6 | 14.0 | 3.4 | (72.8) | (1,448.9) | 1,632.3 |
| Shares purchased for cancellation | (0.4) | – | – | 0.4 | – | – | (57.3) |
| Shares purchased by ESOP | – | – | – | – | (41.1) | – | – |
| Shares issued by ESOP | – | – | – | – | 16.0 | – | – |
| ESOP adjustment | – | – | – | – | 4.6 | – | (3.2) |
| Transfer of depreciation on revalued property | – | – | (0.2) | – | – | – | 0.2 |
| Transfer of realised property profits | – | – | (4.4) | – | – | – | 4.4 |
| Exchange movement | – | – | – | – | – | – | 0.6 |
| Profit transferred for the year | – | – | – | – | – | – | 198.0 |
| **At January 2005** | **26.1** | **0.6** | **9.4** | **3.8** | **(93.3)** | **(1,448.9)** | **1,775.0** |

7021

## Acquisition at a discount out of fresh share issue

**7.40** In certain circumstances, it is possible to make acquisitions of shares at a discount. Where a fresh issue of shares has been made for the purpose of the acquisition, it will still be necessary to maintain the company's capital in accordance with the rules discussed above from paragraph 7.36, by transferring the difference between the amount raised on the fresh issue of shares and the nominal value of the shares being redeemed (if greater) to the capital redemption reserve. [CA85 Sec 170(2); CA06 Sec 733(3)].

### Example — Acquisition at a discount out of the fresh share issue

Company A decides to purchase 100,000 of its £1 shares for £90,000, a discount of 10% (the shares were initially issued at a premium of 10p per share). In addition, there are another 100,000 shares in issue which were issued at par. The purchase is made out of the proceeds of a fresh issue of 45,000 £1 redeemable preference shares issued at a premium of £1 (that is, proceeds of £90,000). Under IAS 32 and FRS 25 such redeemable shares and their related premiums will be accounted for as liabilities in the balance sheet. The company has no distributable profits.

Following the table in paragraph 7.21, the company makes the purchase in the following way:

|  | £'000 |
|---|---|
| Out of proceeds of fresh share issue: |  |
| (a)  Nominal value of shares purchased | 90 |
| (b)  Share premium | – |
|  | 90 |
| Out of distributable profits | – |
| Total cost of purchase | 90 |

The amount to be transferred to the capital redemption reserve is then calculated as follows:

|  | £'000 |
|---|---|
| Nominal value of shares purchased | 100 |
| Less: Proceeds of fresh issue (restricted) | 90 |
| Amount transferred to the capital redemption reserve | 10 |

The balance sheets before and after are shown below:

| Balance sheet | Before purchase £'000 | Issue of shares £'000 | Purchase of shares £'000 | Maintain capital £'000 | After purchase £'000 |
|---|---|---|---|---|---|
| Ordinary shares | 200 | – | (100) | – | 100 |
| Share premium | 10 | – | – | – | 10 |
| Capital redemption reserve | – | – | – | 10 | 10 |

| | | | | | |
|---|---|---|---|---|---|
| Capital | 210 | – | (100) | 10 | 210 |
| Reserves – Distributable profits | – | – | 10 | (10) | – |
| | 210 | 90 | (90) | – | 210 |
| Net assets other than cash and preference shares | 210 | – | – | – | 210 |
| Liabilities (preference shares related including share premium) | – | (90) | – | – | (90) |
| Cash | – | 90 | (90) | – | – |
| | 210 | – | (90) | – | 120 |

The double entry for the purchase would be as follows:

| | £'000 | £'000 |
|---|---|---|
| Dr Cash | 90 | |
| Cr Liabilities (preference shares and related share premium) | | 90 |
| To show the issue of 45,000 £1 redeemable preference shares at a premium of £1 per share. | | |
| Dr Share capital | 100 | |
| Cr Distributable reserves | | 10 |
| Cr Cash | | 90 |
| To recognise the purchase of £100,000 £1 shares at a discount of 10 per cent. | | |
| Dr Distributable reserves | 10 | |
| Cr Capital redemption reserve | | 10 |
| To maintain the capital of the company. | | |

It should be noted that no profit arises on this transaction, although it might appear at first sight that a profit of £10,000 arises on the purchase. This is because no profit is regarded as arising on a transaction with shareholders.

**Disclosure requirements**

**7.41** A company's directors' report and financial statements have to give various information concerning the shares it purchases during the year, the rights of redemption of any redeemable shares and the authority the company has to acquire any of its shares.

*Directors' report*

**7.42** In the year in which a company purchases or redeems its own shares, certain information is required to be included in the directors' report by the Companies Acts 1985 and 2006 and, in the case of listed companies, the FSA's Listing Rules. These requirements are considered in detail in chapter 3.

**7.43** In addition, certain disclosures relating to shares are required in the directors' report of a company with any of its securities that carry voting rights admitted to trading on a regulated market (see paras 7.112.2 and 7.112.3 below for regulated securities markets in the UK) at the end of its financial year. These are discussed in detail in chapter 3.

**[The next paragraph is 7.46.]**

*Notes to the financial statements — UK GAAP*

**7.46** Where any part of a company's allotted share capital consists of redeemable shares the following information is required, by paragraph 38(2) of Schedule 4 to the 1985 Act (and, for financial statements for periods beginning on or after 6 April 2008, paragraph 47(2) of Schedule 1 to SI 2008/410, 'The Large and Medium-sized Companies and Groups (Accounts and Reports) Regulations 2008', and paragraph 46(2) of Schedule 1 to SI 2008/409, 'The Small Companies and Groups (Accounts and Reports) Regulations 2008'), to be given in the notes to financial statements of a company preparing 'UK GAAP financial statements':

■ The earliest and latest dates on which the company has power to redeem the shares.

■ Whether the shares must be redeemed or are redeemable at the option of the company or the shareholder.

■ The premium (if any) payable on redemption.

*Notes to the financial statements — IFRS*

**7.46.1** IAS 1, 'Presentation of financial statements', requires certain disclosures in respect of capital, to enable users of a company's financial statements to evaluate its objectives, policies and processes for managing capital. These are considered in chapter 23 of the Manual of Accounting — IFRS for the UK.

## Acquisitions out of capital

**7.47** The power to purchase or redeem shares out of 'capital' is available only to private companies as an exception to the rules safeguarding the maintenance of capital designed to protect creditors. Even then the company must comply with the stringent provisions of sections 171 to 177 of the 1985 Act (sections 709 to 723 of the 2006 Act) (referred to in paras 7.93 to 7.106) before a payment out of 'capital' is made. These provisions apply equally to the redemption of redeemable shares. There are certain penalties that apply where the Act's provisions are not followed. Paragraphs 7.107 and 7.108 consider the situation where a liability can arise for directors and shareholders where a payment out of capital has been made and the company goes into liquidation within one year of the payment. Under the 1985 Act, the company needed authority in its articles of association before making an acquisition out of capital. [CA85 Sec 171]. The provisions of the 2006 Act largely re-enact the existing law, but the requirement for pre-authorisation in the articles is removed (but see para 7.47.2) and the legislation has been made consistent in certain respects with the new solvency statement procedure for reduction of capital.

**7.47.1** The members may restrict or prohibit redemptions or purchases of capital by including a provision to this effect in the articles. (See para 1018 of the Explanatory Notes of the 2006 Act).

**7.47.2** The relaxation in the 2006 Act only applies to a company that was incorporated under the 1985 or earlier Acts if either:

■ the company's articles of association contain authority for a purchase of shares out of capital; or

■ the articles of association do not prohibit a purchase of shares out of capital and the members have passed a special resolution giving it the company the authority to do so.

[Draft 8th CO 2 Sch 76].

**7.48** For the purposes of payments made out of capital, 'capital' is any payment by a company from a fund other than its distributable profits and the proceeds of a fresh issue. [CA85 Sec 171; CA06 Sec 709(1)]. Therefore, a company makes a payment out of capital if it purchases or redeems its shares otherwise than out of distributable profits or the proceeds of a fresh issue of shares. Unrealised profits would be capital for this purpose. Before a payment can be made out of capital, a company must first exhaust its distributable profits and proceeds of any fresh issue.

**Permissible capital payment**

**7.49** The payment that a company may make out of capital when purchasing its own shares is restricted to the permissible capital payment. The 'permissible capital payment' (PCP) is equal to the price of the shares being purchased or redeemed less the aggregate of any available profits and the proceeds of a fresh issue made to fund the purchase. [CA85 Sec 171(3); CA06 Sec 710(1)]. The effect of this rule is to require a private company to utilise its available profits and any proceeds arising from a new issue before it makes a payment out of capital. The calculation of the permissible capital payment is represented by the following formula:

PCP = acquisition price – (available profits + proceeds of fresh issue)

*Available profits*

**7.50** The reference to available profits in the calculation of the permissible capital payment is to the company's profits that are available for distribution within the meaning of section 263 of the 1985 Act (section 830 of the 2006 Act). Under section 263 of the 1985 Act (section 830 of the 2006 Act), a private company's profits available for distribution are its accumulated realised profits, so far as not previously utilised by distribution or capitalisation, less its accumulated realised losses, so far as not previously written off in a reduction or re-organisation of capital. However, whether the company has any profits to use for the purchase or redemption and for the purposes of calculating the permissible capital payment is affected further by the provisions in section 172(2) to (6) of the Act 1985 (section 712 of the 2006 Act).

**7.51** Under those provisions the amount of the available profits is determined by reference to the items listed in paragraph 7.52 as they are stated in the relevant accounts. The relevant accounts for determining the permissible capital payment are those accounts drawn up as at any date within the period of three months ending on the date of the statutory declaration (under the Company Act 2006 and with effect from 1 October 2009, that is the directors' statement made in accordance with section 714 of the 2006 Act) that the directors are required to make regarding the purchase out of capital (see further para 7.95).

**7.52** The items that must be considered in determining whether the company has any distributable profits are as follows:

■ Profits, losses, assets and liabilities.

■ Where the company is preparing IAS individual financial statements, provisions of any kind.

■ Where the company is preparing Companies Act individual financial statements (that is, UK GAAP individual financial statements), provisions for depreciation, diminution in value of assets and retentions to meet liabilities (that is, provisions of the kind mentioned in paragraphs 88 and 89 of Schedule 4 to 1985 Act (or, for financial statements for periods beginning on or after 6 April 2008, paragraphs 1 and 2 of Schedule 9 to SI 2008/410, 'The Large and Medium-sized Companies and Groups (Accounts and Reports) Regulations 2008', and paragraphs 1 and 2 of Schedule 7 to SI 2008/409, 'The Small Companies and Groups (Accounts and Reports) Regulations 2008').

■ Share capital and reserves (including undistributable reserves).

[CA85 Sec 172(2); CA06 Sec 712(2)].

**7.53** The relevant accounts, which need not be audited, must enable a reasonable judgment to be made of the amount of any of the items mentioned above. In order to arrive at the permissible capital payment, any of the 'distributions' mentioned below where lawfully made after the date of the relevant financial statements and before the date of the directors' declaration must be deducted from the amount of the company's available profits:

■ Financial assistance made out of distributable profits for the purpose of acquiring the company's own shares or its parent company's shares where the assistance comes within sections 154 or 155 of the 1985 Act (sections 677 to 683 of the 2006 Act) (see para 7.133).

■ Any payment made out of distributable profits in respect of the purchase of any of the company's own shares.

■ Any payment made out of distributable profits in respect of the company's acquisition of rights to purchase its own shares under a contingent purchase contract or the variation of an existing contract of purchase or the release from any obligation relating to such a purchase.

[CA85 Sec 172 (4)(5); CA06 Sec 712(4)].

**7.54**    The example below illustrates the calculation of the permissible payment.

**Example — Calculation of permissible capital payment**

Company X purchases Mr Smith's shares partly out of the proceeds of a new issue of shares, partly out of distributable profits and partly out of capital. The rules can be illustrated as follows:

In January 20X0, company X issued 100,000 ordinary shares of £1 each to Mr Smith at their nominal value. It had previously issued 100,000 at a premium of 50p per share. In July 20X5, company X has distributable profits of £60,000 and it issues 50,000 ordinary shares of £1 each at a premium of £1 per share for the purposes of purchasing at a premium of £1 per share Mr Smith's 100,000 ordinary shares issued in January 20X0.

In these circumstances, the permissible capital payment is calculated as follows:

|  | £'000 | £'000 |
|---|---|---|
| Price of purchase: | | |
| 100,000 £1 shares at a premium of £1 per share | | 200 |
| Less:    Proceeds of issue of 50,000 £1 shares at a premium of £1 per share | 100 | |
| Distributable profits | 60 | 160 |
| Permissible capital payment | | 40 |

Following the table in paragraph 7.21, the purchase would be made in the following way:

|  | £'000 | £'000 |
|---|---|---|
| Out of the proceeds of the fresh issue: | | |
| (a) Nominal value of shares purchased | 100 | |
| (b) Share premium account* | – | 100 |
| Out of distributable profits | | 60 |
| Balance out of capital | | 40 |
| Total cost of purchase (nominal value plus premium = £2 × 100,000) | | 200 |

*No share premium arose on the issue of the shares being purchased.

The balance sheets would be as follows:

| Balance sheet | Before purchase £'000 | Issue of shares £'000 | Purchase of shares £'000 | After purchase £'000 |
|---|---|---|---|---|
| Share capital | 200 | 50 | (100) | 150 |
| Share premium | 50 | 50 | (40)* | 60 |
| Capital | 250 | 100 | (140) | 210 |
| Reserves – Distributable profits | 60 | – | (60) | – |
|  | 310 | 100 | (200) | 210 |
| Net assets other than cash | 210 | – | – | 210 |
| Cash | 100 | 100 | (200) | – |
|  | 310 | 100 | (200) | 210 |

The double entry for the purchase would be as follows:

*Acquisition of own shares*

|  | £'000 | £'000 |
|---|---|---|
| Dr Cash | 100 | |
| Cr Share capital | | 50 |
| Cr Share premium | | 50 |
| To show the issue of 50,000 £1 shares at a premium of £1 per share. | | |
| Dr Share capital | 100 | |
| Dr Distributable profits | 60 | |
| Dr Capital reduction* | 40 | |
| Cr Cash | | 200 |
| To recognise the purchase of £100,000 £1 shares at a premium of £1 per share. | | |

* The capital reduction should be deducted from a capital redemption reserve or a share premium account or the fully paid share capital or any unrealised profits of the company (see further para 7.59). In the example it has been deducted from the share premium account.

*No available profits due to losses*

**7.54.1** A company that has cumulative losses will not have any available profits to take into account in determining a permissible capital payment. The law is seemingly silent on whether in such circumstances a purchase out of capital is possible.

**7.54.2** Arguably, as the law is silent it might be that such a company could purchase its shares out of its unrealised profits and share capital, ignoring its cumulative losses. However, the directors have to make a statutory declaration of solvency (a 'solvency statement' under the Companies Act 2006). In doing so, it will be necessary to take into account the company's loss making status and the impact this has on its solvency. Although, the directors may conclude that the company is solvent in the terms demanded by the Act, the auditors when providing their report are required to consider whether they are aware of anything to indicate that the opinion expressed by the directors is not unreasonable in all the circumstances; they may consider the loss making status precludes them from giving such a report. [CA85 Sec 173(5)(c); CA06 Sec 714(6)(c)]. If the required directors' statutory declaration and/or the auditors' report cannot be given, then the conditions for the payment out of capital are not met. Before commencing the process for a permissible capital payment, legal advice should be sought to establish the robustness of the legal position. See also paras 7.62.1 to 7.62.2.

**Capital maintenance**

**7.55** The general provisions concerning capital maintenance are explained from paragraph 7.36, but the rules differ for private companies purchasing or redeeming out of capital as explained in the paragraphs that follow.

*Transfer to capital redemption reserve*

**7.56**  Where a private company purchases or redeems its shares with a payment that includes a payment out of capital, the following transfers must be made to the company's capital redemption reserve (CRR):

■  If the nominal value of the shares purchased or redeemed *exceeds* the permissible capital payment (where no fresh issue of shares is made), the company must transfer the difference to the capital redemption reserve.

   [CA85 Sec 171(4); CA06 Sec 734(2)].

■  If the nominal value of the shares purchased or redeemed *exceeds* the aggregate of the permissible capital payment *and* the proceeds of a fresh issue, the difference must be transferred to the capital redemption reserve.

   [CA85 Sec 171(6); CA06 Sec 734(4)].

**7.57**  This rule can be represented in the following way:

$$\text{Transfer to CRR} =$$
$$\text{nominal value of shares purchased} - (\text{PCP} + \text{proceeds of fresh issue})$$

The position where the permissible capital payment plus the proceeds of a fresh issue of shares exceeds the nominal value of the shares purchased or redeemed is considered in paragraph 7.59.

**7.58**  The example below illustrates the transfer that is required to be made to the capital redemption reserve.

**Example — Transfer to the capital redemption reserve**

Companies A, B, C and D (all private companies) each purchase 10,000 of their own shares that were originally issued at their nominal value of £1 per share. In each case, a premium of £1.40 per share is payable on purchase. Company B is issuing 7,000 redeemable preference shares at par and company D is issuing 4,000 redeemable preference shares at par. The preference shares issued by both companies B and D are redeemable at par and are presented as liabilities in the balance sheets of companies B and D respectively in accordance with IAS 32 and FRS 25. The retained profits (all distributable) are company A £50,000, company B £30,000, company C £16,000 and company D £15,000. Following the table in paragraph 7.21, the purchases are thus to be made as follows:

*Acquisition of own shares*

| | A £'000 | B £'000 | C £'000 | D £'000 |
|---|---|---|---|---|
| Out of proceeds of new issue: | | | | |
| (a) Nominal value of shares purchased restricted to proceeds of fresh issue | – | 7 | – | 4 |
| (b) Share premium | – | – | – | – |
| | – | 7 | – | 4 |
| Out of distributable profits | 24 | 17 | 16 | 15 |
| | 24 | 24 | 16 | 19 |
| Balance out of capital | – | – | 8 | 5 |
| | 24 | 24 | 24 | 24 |

In these circumstances, the amount that each company must transfer to its capital redemption reserve is as follows:

| | A £'000 | B £'000 | C £'000 | D £'000 |
|---|---|---|---|---|
| Nominal value of shares purchased | 10 | 10 | 10 | 10 |
| Less: | | | | |
| Proceeds of fresh issue | – | 7 | – | 4 |
| Permissible capital payment | – | – | 8 | 5 |
| | – | 7 | 8 | 9 |
| Transfer to the capital redemption reserve | 10 | 3 | 2 | 1 |

The effect on the summarised balance sheets can be illustrated as follows:

| Balance sheets | A £'000 | B £'000 | C £'000 | D £'000 |
|---|---|---|---|---|
| *Before purchase* | | | | |
| Share capital | 100 | 100 | 100 | 100 |
| Distributable profits | 50 | 30 | 16 | 15 |
| | 150 | 130 | 116 | 115 |
| Net assets other than cash | 125 | 105 | 90 | 80 |
| Cash | 25 | 25 | 26 | 35 |
| | 150 | 130 | 116 | 115 |
| *After purchase* | | | | |
| Ordinary shares | 90 | 90 | 90 | 90 |
| Capital redemption reserve | 10 | 3 | 2 | 1 |
| | 100 | 93 | 92 | 91 |
| Distributable profits | 26 | 13 | – | – |
| | 126 | 106 | 92 | 91 |
| Cash | 1 | 8 | 2 | 15 |
| Net assets other than cash and preference shares | 125 | 105 | 90 | 80 |
| Liabilities (preference shares) | – | (7) | – | (4) |
| | 126 | 106 | 92 | 91 |

The double entry for the purchases is as follows:

| | £'000 | £'000 |
|---|---|---|
| *Company A* | | |
| Dr Share capital | 10 | |
| Dr Distributable profits | 14 | |
| Cr Cash | | 24 |

To recognise the purchase of £10,000 £1 shares at a premium of £1.40 per share.

| | | |
|---|---|---|
| Dr Distributable profits | 10 | |
| Cr Capital redemption reserve | | 10 |

To maintain the capital of the company

| | | |
|---|---|---|
| *Company B* | | |
| Dr Cash | 7 | |
| Cr Liabilities (preference shares) | | 7 |

To recognise 7,000 £1 redeemable preference shares issued at par.

| | | |
|---|---|---|
| Dr Share capital | 10 | |
| Dr Distributable profits | 14 | |
| Cr Cash | | 24 |

To recognise the purchase of £10,000 £1 shares at a premium of £1.40 per share.

| | | |
|---|---|---|
| Dr Distributable profits | 3 | |
| Cr Capital redemption reserve | | 3 |

To maintain the capital of the company

| | | |
|---|---|---|
| *Company C* | | |
| Dr Share capital | 10 | |
| Dr Distributable profits | 14 | |
| Cr Cash | | 24 |

To recognise the purchase of £10,000 £1 shares at a premium of £1.40 per share.

| | | |
|---|---|---|
| Dr Distributable profits | 2 | |
| Cr Capital redemption reserve | | 2 |

To maintain the capital of the company (£10,000 less the permissible capital payment of £8,000).

| | | |
|---|---|---|
| *Company D* | | |
| Dr Cash | 4 | |
| Cr Liabilities (preference shares) | | 4 |

To recognise 4,000 £1 redeemable preference shares issued at par.

| | | |
|---|---|---|
| Dr Share capital | 10 | |
| Dr Distributable profits | 14 | |
| Cr Cash | | 24 |

*Acquisition of own shares*

> To recognise the purchase of £10,000 £1 shares at a premium of £1.40 per share.
>
> Dr Distributable profits                                                    1
>   Cr Capital redemption reserve                                                      1
>
> To maintain the capital of the company (£10,000 less the permissible capital payment of £9,000).

### Nominal value less than PCP and proceeds of fresh issue

**7.59** Where shares are purchased or redeemed with a payment that includes a payment out of capital (but not the proceeds of a new issue of shares) and the permissible capital payment exceeds the nominal value of the shares purchased or redeemed, the company may use the excess to reduce one of the following:

■   The capital redemption reserve.

■   The share premium account.

■   Fully paid share capital.

■   The revaluation reserve.

[CA85 Sec 171(5); CA06 Sec 734(3)].

**7.60** Furthermore, even where shares are purchased or redeemed out of the proceeds of a new issue, if the nominal value of the shares being purchased or redeemed is *less* than the permissible capital payment *plus* the proceeds of the new issue, the company may use the excess to reduce the items listed in paragraph 7.59. [CA85 Sec 171(6); CA06 Sec 734(4)]

**7.61** This rule is represented in the following way:

$$\text{Dr to reduce capital} =$$
$$\text{PCP} + \text{proceeds of fresh issue} - \text{nominal value of shares purchased}$$

The position where the permissible capital payment plus the proceeds of a fresh issue of shares is less than the nominal value of the shares purchased is considered in paragraph 7.56.

**7.62** The following example illustrates the reduction of the capital redemption reserve and the share premium account to fund the excess.

#### Example — Nominal value less than permissible capital repayment

Companies E and F (both private companies) purchase 10,000 of their own shares that were originally issued at a premium of 10p per share. The nominal value of the shares in question is £1 per share and, in each case, a premium of £1.40 per share is payable. Company F issues 4,000 £1 preference shares at par (which are reedemable at par) to make the purchase. Company F's new shares will be classified as liabilities in accordance with IAS 32 and FRS 25. Before the purchase both companies have 100,000 £1 ordinary shares in issue and companies E and F have £11,000 and £9,000 distributable profits respectively. Following the table in paragraph 7.21, the purchases are to be made as follows:

|  | E £'000 | F £'000 |
|---|---|---|
| Out of proceeds of fresh issue of shares: | | |
| (a)  Nominal value of shares purchased restricted to proceeds of fresh issue | – | 4 |
| (b)  Share premium account | – | – |
|  | – | 4 |
| Out of distributable profits | 11 | 9 |
|  | 11 | 13 |
| Balance out of capital | 13 | 11 |
| Total cost of purchase (nominal value plus premium = £2.40 × 10,000) | 24 | 24 |

In the above circumstances, the aggregate amount by which company E and company F may reduce their capital redemption reserve, the share premium account or the fully-paid share capital is as follows:

|  | E £'000 | F £'000 |
|---|---|---|
| Permissible capital payment | 13 | 11 |
| Proceeds of new issue | – | 4 |
|  | 13 | 15 |
| Nominal value of shares purchased | 10 | 10 |
| Excess available | 3 | 5 |

If companies E and F use the available excess solely to reduce the share premium account, the effect on the summarised balance sheets can be illustrated as follows:

| Balance sheet Company E | Before purchase £'000 | Issue of shares £'000 | Purchase of shares £'000 | After purchase £'000 |
|---|---|---|---|---|
| Ordinary shares | 100 | – | (10) | 90 |
| Share premium | 10 | – | (3) | 7 |
| Capital | 110 | – | (13) | 97 |
| Distributable profits | 11 | – | (11) | – |
|  | 121 | – | (24) | 97 |
| Net assets other than cash | 96 | – | – | 96 |
| Cash | 25 | – | (24) | 1 |
|  | 121 | – | (24) | 97 |

| **Balance sheet** Company F | Before purchase £'000 | Issue of shares £'000 | Purchase of shares £'000 | After purchase £'000 |
|---|---|---|---|---|
| Ordinary shares | 100 | – | (10) | 90 |
| Share premium | 10 | – | (5) | 5 |
| Capital | 110 | – | (15) | 95 |
| Distributable profits | 9 | – | (9) | – |
|  | 119 | – | (24) | 95 |
| Net assets other than cash and preference shares | 83 | – | – | 83 |
| Liabilities (preference shares) | – | (4) | – | (4) |
| Cash | 36 | 4 | (24 | 16 |
|  | 119 | – | (24) | 95 |

The double entry for the purchases is as follows:

| *Company E* | £'000 | £'000 |
|---|---|---|
| Dr Share capital | 10 | |
| Dr Distributable profits | 11 | |
| Dr Capital (share premium account) | 3 | |
| Cr Cash | | 24 |

To recognise the purchase of £10,000 £1 shares at a premium of £1.40 per share.

| *Company F* | | |
|---|---|---|
| Dr Cash | 4 | |
| Cr Liabilities (preference shares) | | 4 |

To show the issue of 4,000 £1 redeemable preference shares at par.

| | | |
|---|---|---|
| Dr Share capital | 10 | |
| Dr Distributable profits | 9 | |
| Dr Capital (share premium account) | 5 | |
| Cr Cash | | 24 |

To recognise the purchase of £10,000 £1 shares at a premium of £1.40 per share.

### Shares to be purchased at a premium in excess of the original premium on issue

**7.62.1** In its 1998 technical release Tech 7/98, 'Improvements in company law', the ICAEW identified a particular problem with the way in which the permissible capital payment is defined, which meant that in some fairly common circumstances a private company was able to redeem shares out of capital. Furthermore, the company was able to make a purchase or redemption using its share premium account under section 160 of the 1985 Act. The same problem is present with sections 710 and 692 of the 2006 Act.

**7.62.2** The permissible capital payment is defined as the amount, if any, by which the aggregate of the company's available (distributable) profits and proceeds of a fresh issue of shares made for the purpose of the purchase is less than the purchase price of the shares. The normal rules in section 160 of the 1985

Act (section 692 of the 2006 Act) apply in relation to the balance of the purchase price. The problem arises where the proceeds of the fresh issue of shares (that is, nominal value and share premium) exceeds the nominal value of the shares to be purchased. For example, if shares having a nominal value of 100 that were issued for 100 are to be purchased at a premium of 50 (that is for 150) using the proceeds of a fresh issue of 120 (and there are no available profits) the transaction would be unlawful even though the company's overall capital would be reduced only by the amount of the permissible capital payment. This is because, although the permissible capital payment would be 30 (that is, 150 less 120) the remaining premium on purchase of 20 (that is, 120 less 100) would be unlawful under section 160 of the 1985 Act (section 692 of the 2006 Act) as there are no available (distributable) profits.

## Legal procedures for purchase

**7.63** The procedures that a company must follow if it wishes to purchase its own shares will depend on whether the purchase is to be an 'off-market' purchase or a 'market' purchase. Certain initial matters to consider are mentioned in paragraph 7.12.

**7.63.1** Irrespective of whether a contract for a repurchase of own shares is an 'off-market' or a 'market' purchase or is a contingent contract, if it contains an obligation on the company then the accounting treatment specified in paragraph 23 of IAS 32 and FRS 25 must be followed (see chapter 23 of the Manual of Accounting – IFRS for the UK and the Manual of Accounting – UK GAAP).

### Definition of 'off-market' and 'market'

**7.64** A company's purchase of its own shares is an *off-market* purchase if either of the following apply:

- The shares are not purchased on a recognised investment exchange.

- The shares are purchased on a recognised investment exchange, but are not subject to a marketing arrangement on that investment exchange.

[CA85 Sec 163(1); CA06 Sec 693(2)].

Any other purchase is a market purchase.

**7.65** Shares are subject to a marketing arrangement where either they are listed on a recognised investment exchange or they can be dealt with on that exchange without prior permission for individual transactions from the authority governing the exchange and without time limit as to when those dealings can take place.

**7.66** An off-market purchase will, therefore, *exclude* a purchase of shares listed on the London Stock Exchange, the PLUS-listed market, AIM and the PLUS-quoted market.

**7.67** A company can make an off-market purchase only where the terms of the proposed contract of purchase have received prior authorisation by the shareholders (see para 7.73) or as a contingent purchase contract under section 165 (section 694(2),(3) of the 2006 Act) (see para 7.89). The purchase by a private or an unquoted public company of its own shares will normally be an off-market purchase (see paras 7.79 and 7.73). A listed company will purchase its own shares either as an off-market purchase or a market purchase depending on the circumstances (see para 7.69).

## Purchases by public companies

**7.68** As discussed above, the statutory procedure that a public company should follow will depend on whether the purchase will be a market purchase or an off-market purchase.

### Authority for market purchase

**7.69** A market purchase by a listed public company of its own shares must first be authorised by ordinary resolution of the company in general meeting. The authority may be general or specific to a class or description of shares and unconditional or subject to conditions. The authority, however, must:

- Specify the maximum number of shares authorised to be acquired.

- Determine both the maximum and the minimum prices that may be paid for the shares. It may do this by specifying a particular sum or providing a basis or formula for calculating the amount of the price as long as the amount can be calculated without reference to any person's discretion or opinion.

- Specify a date not more than 18 months from the date of the resolution on which the authority is to expire. The terms of the authority may permit a purchase to be made after its expiry if the contract of purchase was concluded before the authority expired.

[CA85 Sec 166; CA06 Sec 701].

**7.70** The authority may be varied, revoked or renewed at a company's general meeting by an ordinary resolution, but the company must comply with the conditions in paragraph 7.69 above. [CA85 Sec 166(4); CA06 Sec 701(4)]. A copy of any resolution giving, varying, revoking or renewing an authority to make a market purchase of a company's own shares must be sent to the Registrar of Companies within 15 days of the resolution being passed. [CA85 Secs 380, 166(7); CA06 Sec 701(8)].

**7.71** Two important differences exist between the authority for a market purchase and the authority for an off-market purchase. With a market purchase, it is the purchase of the shares that requires approval in the form of the authority of the company in general meeting. With an off-market purchase, a specific purchase contract (rather than the shares to be purchased) must be approved and it must be approved by special resolution. The authority for a market purchase need not relate to any particular shares and it need be approved only by an ordinary resolution. However, this less stringent statutory requirement is supplemented for listed companies, first by the Listing Rules and secondly by the insider dealing provisions referred to in paragraph 7.81. Furthermore, the Investments Committee of the Association of British Insurers has also made recommendations regarding market purchases (see further para 7.131).

*Authority for an off-market purchase*

**7.72**   In the case of a public company, the special resolution giving the necessary authority mentioned in para 7.73 must specify a date not later than 18 months from the date of the resolution, on which the authority is to expire. [CA85 Sec 164; CA06 Sec 694].

**7.73**   A company may make an off-market purchase of its own shares only if it does so under a contract the terms of which have received prior authorisation by a special resolution at a general meeting of the company. Under the 2006 Act, the directors may enter into a contract conditional on approval being received from shareholders, but shares cannot be purchased until approval is obtained. If approval is not obtained the contract will lapse (but see para 7.73.1). [CA06 Sec 694(2)]. This contrasts with the 1985 Act, under which prior authorisation was required prior to the directors entering into such a contract, with any variations requiring authorisation by special resolution. [CA85 Sec 164].

**7.73.1** The provisions in section 694(2) of the 2006 Act permitting directors to enter into a contract for the off-market purchase of own shares that is conditional on shareholder approval apply to contracts that:

■   are entered into after 1 October 2009; or

■   are entered into before 1 October 2009 but provide that no shares may be repurchased until after that date and are authorised by special resolution passed on or after that date.

[Draft 8th CO Sch 74].

For other contracts, the provisions of the 1985 Act will continue to apply.

**7.74**   The special resolution that confers the authority on the company to enter into a contract to purchase its own shares (or to authorise a contingent purchase contract) or to vary or to revoke or renew such authority will not be effective in the two situations described below.

**7.75**   First, the special resolution will not be effective where a shareholder to whom the resolution relates exercises his voting rights on the shares that are subject to the acquisition in voting on the resolution and the resolution would not have been passed if he had not voted. For this purpose the following will apply:

- a member who holds shares to which the resolution relates is regarded as exercising the voting rights carried by those shares not only if he votes in respect of them on a poll on the question whether the resolution shall be passed, but also if he votes on the resolution otherwise than on a poll;

- notwithstanding anything in the company's articles, any member of the company may demand a poll on that question; and

- a vote and a demand for a poll by a person or a proxy for a member are the same respectively on a vote and a demand by the member.

[CA85 Sec 164(5); CA06 Sec 698(1)(3)(4)].

**7.76** Secondly, the resolution will not be effective unless a copy of the contract or, if it is not in writing, a written memorandum of its terms giving the names of the members whose shares are to be purchased, is available for inspection. The contract or memorandum must be available for inspection by members at the company's registered office for not less than 15 days ending on the day of the meeting of the company at which the resolution is to be passed and at the meeting itself. The memorandum must include the names of the members to which the contract relates and the contract must also have annexed to it a memorandum specifying any such names that do not appear on the contract itself. [CA85 Sec 164(6); CA06 Sec 699(1)-(6)]. In addition, the same procedure must be followed where there is a variation of any existing contract including a contingent purchase contract.

**7.77** A copy of each special resolution passed by the company, including one passed as a written resolution, must be sent to the Registrar of Companies in the usual manner within 15 days of its being passed. [CA85 Sec 380; CA06 Sec 30(1)].

### Variation of existing contract

**7.78** Where a company wishes to vary any of the terms of an existing contract to purchase its own shares, or the terms of a contingent purchase contract, there is a similar requirement for a special resolution and for the provisions described in paragraphs 7.73 to 7.77 to be complied with. [CA85 Sec 164(7); CA06 Sec 697(1)-(4)]. A payment in consideration of the variation of a contract approved under section 164 or section 165 of the 1985 Act (section 694(2)(3) of the 2006 Act) must be made out of distributable profits. If this is not done, the purchase itself will be unlawful. [CA85 Sec 168(1)(b), (2)(b); CA06 Sec 705].

### Purchases by private companies

**7.79** Unlike for public companies, a private company's special resolution giving the necessary authority does not have to specify a date on which the authority expires. In addition, where a private company makes a payment out of capital it must comply with the provisions referred to from paragraph 7.93.

**7.80** Where a company uses a written resolution to authorise the purchase, or to vary such a contract or contingent purchase contract, a shareholder whose shares are the subject of the written resolution is not allowed to sign it and each relevant member must be supplied with a copy of the contract and the names of the vendors before signature. [CA06 Secs 695, 696]. (Written resolutions are dealt with fully in chapter 8.)

## Insider dealing and market abuse

**7.81** The provisions relating to the criminal offence of insider dealing are contained in Part V of the Criminal Justice Act 1993. Since 2001, the FSA is a prosecuting authority for the criminal offence of insider dealing (as defined in the Criminal Justice Act 1993). The provisions prohibit certain dealings in the shares and other securities (such as debt securities) of listed companies. Directors (and others who discharge managerial responsibilities) of such companies should be aware of the provisions of this Act that might affect a company's acquisition of its own shares.

**7.81.1** In addition, the FSA's DTR govern the prompt and fair disclosure of relevant information to the markets; set out specific circumstances when an issuer can delay public disclosure of inside information; and contain requirements to ensure that such information is kept confidential in order to protect investors and prevent insider dealing. [DTR para 2]. Persons discharging managerial responsibilities (including directors) and their connected persons must notify their company in writing of all transactions conducted on their own account in their company's shares or derivatives or any other financial instruments relating to those shares within four business days of the day on which the transaction occurred. [DTR para 3.1].

**7.81.2** The Financial Services and Markets Act 2000 (FSMA) creates civil penalties for market abuse, which includes insider dealing as one of seven behaviours that can constitute a civil offence. As the level of evidence is lower than in criminal prosecutions, the government hoped that it would be easier to obtain prosecutions for insider dealing. Directors of listed companies are also subject to the Code of Market Conduct issued by the FSA, criminal offences under the Code of Market Conduct and the FSMA include making a misleading statement and engaging in a misleading course of conduct for the purpose of inducing another person to exercise or refrain from exercising rights in relation to investments. In 2005, two directors of AIT Group Plc received custodial sentences for releasing a misleading trading update statement to the market. This was the first time that the FSA had used its powers to take criminal proceedings under the FSMA.

## Returns and contracts

**7.82** Following the completion of the purchase of its own shares (including redeemable shares) a company must make certain returns under the Act. No later than 28 days after the delivery of shares to it, the company, whether public or private, must deliver a return in the prescribed form to the Registrar of Companies stating with respect to each class the number and nominal value of the shares purchased, the date they were delivered to the company. The form also requires the amount of stamp duty payable to be specified. Additionally, a public company must state the aggregate amount paid for the shares and the maximum and minimum prices paid in respect of shares of each class purchased. [CA85 Sec 169(2)]. Failure to file the form is a criminal offence and the directors in default are liable to a fine. Under the 2006 Act, for shares delivered to the company on or after 1 October 2009, a similar return is required, but it must also state the number of shares that are of a type that could have been held in treasury and or whether these shares are treated as cancelled or are being held in treasury. [CA06 Sec 707(2); Draft 8th CO 2 Sch 75].

**7.83**  Both private and public companies must keep a copy of each contract for an off-market purchase or contingent purchase contract they enter into, together with any variations to any such contracts. These documents must be kept at the company's registered office from the date the contracts are concluded until the end of a period of ten years from the date of the purchase to which they relate. Section 1136 of the 2006 Act allows the Secretary of State to specify places other than a company's registered office where company records can be kept available for inspection but, at the time of writing, no such legislation is in place. A private company must make a copy of such a contract available for inspection by any member without charge. A public company making an off-market purchase must similarly keep a copy of the contract available for inspection not only by any member, but also by any other person. [CA85 Sec 169(5); CA06 Sec 702(6)].

**7.84**  A public company that makes a market purchase must keep a copy of each contract for a purchase authorised by the company in general meeting, together with any variations to it. Again these must be kept at the company's registered office from the date the contract is concluded until the end of a period of ten years from the date of the purchase to which it relates. Similarly, a public company must make any such contract available for inspection not only by members, but also by any other person.

**7.85**  If any contract is not in writing, the company must keep a memorandum of its terms at its registered office and make that available instead of a copy of the contract. A company's obligations in relation to making the contracts and memoranda available for inspection by members and non-members are set out in the Companies (Inspection and Copying of Registered Indices and Documents) Regulations 1991 (SI 1991/1998).

**7.86**  For redeemable shares, within one month of redemption the company must give notice on the appropriate form, to the Registrar of Companies specifying the shares redeemed. [CA85 Sec 122(1)(e); CA06 Sec 689(1)].

**Prohibition on assignment of rights**

**7.87**  The rights of a public or private company under a contract to make a market or an off-market purchase of its own shares or a contingent purchase contract cannot be assigned. This prohibition is designed to prevent a company from speculating against its own share price by buying or selling its rights to purchase its own shares. [CA85 Sec 167(1); CA06 Sec 704].

**7.88** An agreement by a company to release all or any of its rights under a contract to make an off-market purchase of its own shares or a contingent purchase contract is void unless the terms of the release are approved in advance by a special resolution of the company before the contract is entered into. The procedures referred to in paragraphs 7.72 to 7.77 and 7.79 apply to a company when seeking approval for the release as they apply to a proposed variation. [CA85 Sec 167(2); CA06 Sec 700(1)-(5)]. A payment made in consideration for the release of the company's obligations must be paid out of distributable profits or the release will be void. [CA85 Sec 168; CA06 Sec 705].

**Contingent purchase contracts**

**7.89** A contingent purchase contract is defined in section 165 of the 1985 Act (section 694 of the 2006 Act) and is, briefly, a contract under which a company may (subject to any conditions) become either entitled or obliged to purchase its own shares. A contingent contract may give the company an option to purchase them or the shareholder the option to require their purchase by the company. Such a purchase contract might arise, for example, where a shareholder is prepared to maintain an investment in a company only if there are arrangements that ensure that he will be able to sell his shares back to the company at any time in the future. In this circumstance, the company may not wish to issue a new class of redeemable shares in order to satisfy the shareholder's wishes. Instead, it may prefer to make a contractual arrangement with the shareholder under which the company may purchase the shares at a later date at the shareholder's option. Similarly, a contingent purchase contract would include, for example, a contract under which a company may be obliged to purchase an employee's shares on his retirement.

**7.89.1** Contracts for the repurchase of a company's own shares of the nature discussed in paragraph 7.89 will fall to be accounted for in accordance with paragraph 23 of IAS 32 and FRS 25 (see chapter 23 of the Manual of Accounting – IFRS for the UK and the Manual of Accounting – UK GAAP).

**7.90** The use of contingent purchase contracts to buy a company's own shares may be open to abuse unless they are accompanied by certain safeguards for other shareholders. The approach of the Act is to treat contingent purchase contracts as if they were off-market contracts of purchase, that is, to require the same full range of safeguards for shareholders that apply to off-market contracts (see para 7.72).

**7.91** A company may only purchase its own shares under a contingent purchase contract if the terms of the contract have been approved in advance by a special resolution of the company before the contract is entered into. Such approval may be varied or revoked or renewed by a subsequent special resolution.

7041

**7.92**   The prohibition on assignment by a company of its rights under a purchase contract referred to in paragraph 7.87 or the release of its rights under a purchase contract set out in paragraph 7.88, apply also to a contingent purchase contract. [CA85 Sec 167; CA06 Sec 700, 704]. A payment in consideration of acquiring any right under a contingent purchase contract must be made out of distributable profits, or the purchase will be unlawful. [CA85 Sec 168; CA06 Sec 705].

### Acquisitions out of capital

**7.93**   To make a payment out of capital, the company must be a private company and must be authorised to do so by its articles of association. (See SI 1985/805, 'The Companies (Tables A to F) Regulations 1985', Table A Regulation 35.) Pre-authorisation in a company's articles will not be required when the provisions in the Companies Act 2006 are implemented from October 2009 (the circumstances under which a company may make an acquisition of own shares out of capital are considered from para 7.47).

**7.93.1**   Although similar to the 1985 Act, the provisions of the 2006 Act (contained in sections 709 to 723) do alter slightly the procedures required when a company makes an acquisition out of capital. These sections of the 2006 Act apply to acquisitions where the 'directors' statement' (see para 7.95) is made on or after 1 October 2009. [Draft 8th CO 2 Sch 77].

**7.94**   The payment out of capital must be approved by a special resolution of the company in general meeting (see para 7.103). [CA85 Sec 173(2), CA06 Sec 716(2)]. Alternatively, the company may by written resolution obtain the unanimous agreement of all shareholders. However, in that situation, a member holding shares to which the resolution relates is not entitled to sign the resolution. [CA85 15A Sch 6; CA06 Sec 717].

#### *Statutory declaration*

**7.95**   The directors of a company proposing to make a payment out of capital must make a statutory declaration in the prescribed form. [CA85 Sec 173]. From 1 October 2009, the provisions of the 2006 Act will require a statement in a similar prescribed form from the directors rather than a statutory declaration. The main effect is that the statement will not have to be sworn under oath as is the case for a statutory declaration. The prescribed form requires the directors to declare:

■   Whether the company's business is that of an authorised institution, an authorised insurance company or some other business.

■   That the company is proposing to make a payment out of capital.

■   What the amount of the permissible capital payment for the shares in question will be.

The statement and its content and the procedures required of the directors are consistent with those for the new solvency statement procedure for a reduction of capital by a private company. [CA06 Secs 641, 642]. (See paras 1019 to 1022 of the Explanatory Notes to the 2006 Act.)

**7.96** The form also requires the directors to declare that they have made full enquiry into the affairs and prospects of the company and formed the opinion that both the following apply:

■ As regards its initial situation immediately following the date the payment out of capital is proposed to be made, that there will be no grounds on which the company could then be found unable to pay its debts.

■ As regards its prospects for the year immediately following that date, that, having regard to the directors' intentions for the management of the company's business during that year and to the amount and character of the financial resources that will in their view be available during that year, the company will be able to continue to carry on business as a going concern (and will accordingly be able to pay its debts as they fall due) throughout that year.

[CA85 Sec 173(3); CA06 Sec 714(1)-(3)].

**7.97** In forming their opinion on the first point in the paragraph above, the Act states that directors must take into account the same liabilities (including prospective and contingent liabilities) that would be relevant under section 122 of the Insolvency Act 1986 to the question of whether a company is unable to pay its debts. A company will be deemed unable to pay its debts, for the purposes of section 122, if the value of the company's assets is less than the amount of its liabilities (taking into account its contingent and prospective liabilities). However, there is some doubt as to whether 'taking into account' means that the full value of all such liabilities should be included or only the amount of those liabilities that are likely to crystallise immediately and in the following 12 months. This is an area where a company's directors should take legal advice.

**7.98** The overall policy of the legislation may be summarised as being to produce a situation where creditors are not going to be prejudiced by the company continuing in business after making a payment out of capital. Consequently, if directors are in doubt as to whether their company would be able to pay all its debts if all the company's prospective and contingent liabilities were included in assessing its solvency, they should take legal advice before making the statutory declaration or directors' statement. If the company becomes insolvent the directors may incur certain penalties. For instance, under section 76 of the Insolvency Act 1986 a director has a liability to contribute to the company's assets if it is wound up within a year of the payment out of capital, unless he can show that he had reasonable grounds for forming the opinion set out in the declaration. See further paragraph 7.107.

**7.99** It is a criminal offence (punishable by a fine and/or imprisonment) for a director to make a declaration without having reasonable grounds for the opinion expressed in the declaration. The directors should, therefore, arrange for financial statements to be prepared to enable the calculation of the permissible capital payment and arrange for properly worked out cash flow projections to support the opinion required to be expressed in the statutory declaration.

### Auditors' report to the directors

**7.100** The directors' statutory declaration must have attached to it a report by the company's auditors addressed to the directors stating that:

- The auditors have enquired into the company's state of affairs.

- The amount specified in the declaration as the permissible capital payment for the shares in question is, in the auditors' view, properly determined in accordance with sections 171 and 172 of the 1985 Act (sections 710 to 712 of the 2006 Act).

- The auditors are not aware of anything to indicate that the opinion expressed by the directors in the declaration as to any of the matters mentioned in paragraph 45.96 is unreasonable in the circumstances.

[CA85 Sec 173(5); CA05 Sec 714(6)].

### Procedure for acquisition

**7.101** The special resolution for the payment out of capital mentioned in paragraph 7.94 must be passed by the company either on the same day as, or within one week after, the date on which the directors make the statutory declaration. The resolution will be ineffective in the following circumstances:

- If any member holding shares to which the resolution relates exercises the voting rights carried by any of those shares in voting on the resolution and the resolution would not have been passed if he had not done so.

  In considering whether a sufficient number of votes have been cast on a show of hands or a poll, sections 174(3) and 174(5) of the 1985 Act (CA06 Sec 717(4)) contain similar provisions to those described in paragraph 7.75 in relation to section 164(5) of the 1985 Act (CA06 Secs 698(1)(3)(4)).

- If the statutory declaration of solvency and the auditors' report attached to it are not available for inspection by members at the meeting at which the resolution is passed. This means that the directors must liaise with the company's auditors at an early stage, to ensure that they can obtain the auditors' report by the date on which the special resolution is to be passed.

[CA85 Sec 174; CA06 Sec 717(4)].

**7.102** The company must make the payment out of capital between five and seven weeks after the date of the resolution. This ensures that members and creditors who wish to object have time to apply to the court under section 176 of the 1985 Act (section 721 of the 2006 Act) (see para 7.103). This period cannot be shortened even if all members agree. The accounts required which are mentioned in the following diagram are discussed in paragraph 7.51.

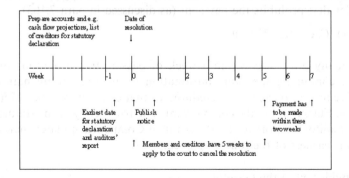

**7.103** Where a resolution is passed approving a payment out of capital, any member (other than one who voted in favour of the resolution) and any creditor may within five weeks of the date on which the resolution is passed apply to the court to cancel the resolution. [CA85 Sec 176; CA06 Sec 721(1)(2)]. The court's powers are set out in section 177 of the 1985 Act. (CA06 Sec 721). The company is obliged to give notice to the Registrar of Companies if an application is made. [CA85 Sec 176(3); CA06 Sec 722(3)].

**7.103.1** The government announced in June 2007 that it intends to bring into UK domestic law, at the same time as implementing the provisions of the 2006 Act, an amendment to the EU 2nd Company Law Directive. The effect will be to restrict applications by creditors for court protection to those creditors that demonstrate that their position will be prejudiced by the company's proposed reduction of capital.

*Publication of notice of acquisition*

**7.104** Within a week of passing the resolution for payment out of capital referred to in paragraph 7.94 the company must publish a notice in the London Gazette (for companies registered in England and Wales) or in the Edinburgh Gazette (for companies registered in Scotland) giving the following details:

- A statement that the company has approved a payment out of capital for the purpose of purchasing or redeeming its own shares.

- The amount of the permissible capital payment.

- The date of the resolution.

- A statement that the statutory declaration or directors' statement and the auditors' report are available for inspection at the company's registered office.

7045

■ A statement that any creditor (but see para 7.103.1) of the company may, at any time within five weeks after the date of the resolution, apply to the court for an order that prohibits the payment (as discussed in para 7.103).

[CA85 Sec 175(1); CA06 Sec 719(1)].

**7.105** The company must also within a week of passing the resolution either publish a notice containing the same information in an appropriate national newspaper or give notice to each of its creditors to that effect. [CA85 Sec 175(2); CA06 Sec 719(2)]. Furthermore, the company must deliver a copy of the statutory declaration and auditors' report to the Registrar of Companies no later than the date on which the earliest of the following occurs:

■ Notice is published in the Gazette.

■ Notice is published in the national newspaper.

■ Notice is given to creditors.

[CA85 Sec 175(4)(5); CA06 Sec 719(4)].

The special resolution must also be filed with the Registrar of Companies within 15 days of it being passed.

**7.106** The statutory declaration or directors' statement and auditors' report must be available for inspection by members and creditors without charge during business hours at the company's registered office for five weeks beginning with the date of the resolution for the payment out of capital. Failure to do so renders the company and every officer in default liable to a fine and the court can compel an immediate inspection. [CA85 Sec 175(6)-(8)]. (See also SI 2007/2612, 'Companies (Fees for Inspection and Copying of Company Records) Regulations 2007', for the obligations of companies in relation to inspection). The 2006 Act allows these documents to be held at a place specified by the Secretary of State as an alternative to the company's registered office. [CA06 Sec 1136]. If the documents are not held at the company's registered office, the company is required to give notice to the Registrar of the place where they are held.

### Liability on winding up

**7.107** Under section 76 of the Insolvency Act 1986, if a company is wound up within a year of making a payment out of capital in respect of a purchase or redemption of its shares and it proves to be insolvent, any shareholder whose shares were purchased or redeemed and the directors who signed the statutory declaration are liable to contribute to the assets of the company. However, a director will be exempt from such a liability if he can show that he had reasonable grounds for forming the opinion stated in the statutory declaration or directors' statement.

**7.108** The liability of a person whose shares were redeemed or purchased to contribute to the assets of the company is limited to the amount of the payment out of capital he received when the company purchased his shares. Where this applies, the company's directors are jointly and severally liable with the past shareholder for that amount. A shareholder or director who has contributed to the assets of the company under section 76 of the Insolvency Act 1986 has certain rights to claim against any other person who is jointly and severally liable. A shareholder whose shares have been redeemed or purchased with a payment out of capital and who is, therefore, potentially liable to contribute to the assets under section 76, has the right, in order to limit his liability and prevent further loss to the assets, to petition for winding up. The grounds of the petition would be either that the company is unable to pay its debts or that it is just and equitable for the company to be wound up. [Sec 124(3) Insolvency Act 1986].

**Failure to acquire shares**

**7.109**   Where a company has agreed to purchase or redeem any of its shares and then fails to do so, the affected shareholder cannot sue the company for damages. However, this does not affect any other right that the shareholder has, except that a court will not order specific performance of the contract if the company shows that it cannot meet the costs of purchasing the shares in question out of distributable profits. [CA85 Sec 178(2)(3); CA06 Sec 735(3)].

**7.110**   If a company is liable to purchase or redeem shares, but has failed to do so at a time when it goes into liquidation, the terms of the purchase or redemption can be enforced against it. However, this will only apply if:

■   Under their terms, the purchase or redemption was to take place before the winding up commenced.

■   The company would have had distributable profits equal to the purchase or redemption price.

[CA85 Sec 178(5); CA06 Sec 735(4)(5)].

**7.111**   Payments to creditors and to members who have preferred rights, however, will have priority in the winding up. [CA85 Sec 178(6); CA06 Sec 735(6)]. The shares purchased or redeemed must then be cancelled.

**Treasury shares**

**7.111.1**   The Act permits companies with *'qualifying shares'* to purchase such shares out of distributable profits and hold them in treasury for resale, transfer or cancellation at a later date. As can be seen from the definition of qualifying shares, private companies are effectively prohibited from holding treasury shares.

**7.111.2**   'Qualifying shares' are defined as shares that:

■   are included in the Official List maintained by the FSA (that is, listed on the main market of the London Stock Exchange or Plus Market's PLUS-listed market);

- are traded on AIM;

- are officially listed in another EEA State; or

- are traded on a market established in an EEA State, which is a regulated securities market.

[CA85 Sec 162(4); CA06 Sec 724(2)].

Shares traded on Plus Market's PLUS-quoted market are excluded from this definition.

**7.111.3**   In the UK, the regulated securities markets referred to in the last bullet point in paragraph 7.111.2 above, include:

- LIFFE.

- OM London.

- Virt-X.

- Coredeal MTS.

- Jiway.

**7.111.4**   Where qualifying shares are purchased by a company out of distributable profits (see from para 7.17) in accordance with section 162 of the 1985 Act (section 724 of the 2006 Act), the company may:

- hold the shares (or any of them) in treasury; or

- deal with any of them, at any time, as follows:

    - sell the shares (or any of them) for cash (see para 7.111.10);

    - transfer the shares (or any of them) for the purposes of, or pursuant to, an employees' share scheme; or

    - cancel the shares (or any of them) (see para 7.111.12).

[CA85 Secs 162A(1), 162D(1); CA06 Secs 724(3), 727(1), 729(1)].

*Conditions applying to treasury shares*

**7.111.5**   References to a company holding shares as treasury shares are references to the company holding shares that were (or are treated as having been) purchased by it in circumstances in which section 162A of the 1985 Act (section 724 of the 2006 Act) applies and have been held by the company continuously since they were so purchased. [CA85 Sec 162A(3); CA06 Sec 724(5)].

**7.111.6**   Where a company has only one class of shares, the aggregate nominal value of shares held as treasury shares must not at any time exceed 10 per cent of the nominal value of the company's issued share capital at that time. Similarly, where the company has more than one class of shares, the aggregate nominal value of the shares of any class held as treasury shares must not at any time exceed 10 per cent of the nominal value of the issued share capital of the shares in that class at that time. If the limit is exceeded, the excess shares must be disposed of or cancelled within 12 months. [CA85 Sec 162B; CA06 Sec 725(1)-(3)].

**7.111.7** The company may not exercise any rights over the treasury shares, including voting rights. Furthermore, no dividend can be paid, and no other distribution of the company's assets (including any distribution of assets to members on a winding up) can be made, to the company in respect of the treasury shares. However, rights over bonus issues or redemption rights (if the shares are redeemable) do still remain. [CA85 Sec 162C; CA06 Sec 726].

**7.111.8** A company may not purchase its shares if as a result of the purchase there would no longer be any issued shares of the company other than redeemable shares or shares held as treasury shares. [CA85 Sec 162(3); CA06 Sec 690(2)].

**7.111.9** Where shares are held in treasury, the company must be entered in the register of members as the member holding those shares. [CA85 Sec 162A(2); CA06 Sec 724(4)].

*Sale or cancellation of treasury shares*

**7.111.10** As stated in paragraph 7.111.4 above, one of the ways in which a company can deal with its treasury shares is to sell the shares for 'cash consideration', a defined term in the Act. The definition of 'cash consideration' in the 2006 Act, states that 'cash' means one of the following:

■ Cash (including foreign currency) received by the company.

■ A cheque received by the company in good faith that the directors have no reason for suspecting will not be paid.

■ A release of a liability of the company for a liquidated sum.

■ An undertaking to pay cash to the company within 90 days of the date on which the company agrees to sell the shares.

■ Payment by any other means giving rise to a present or future entitlement (of the company or a person acting on the company's behalf) to a payment, or credit equivalent to payments, in cash.

[CA85 Sec 162D(2); CA06 Sec 727(2)].

The 2006 Act also includes a provision enabling the Secretary of State to determine that other means of payments are also included within the definition of 'cash consideration'.

**7.111.10.1** Under the 1985 Act, the last bullet in the list above was excluded from the definition. Paragraphs 1027 to 1029 of the Explanatory Notes of the 2006 Act state that the extension of 'cash consideration' and the power conferred on the Secretary of State are intended to remove uncertainties surrounding other methods of settlement (than those already specified in section 727(2) of the 2006 Act), for example, the CREST settlement system and to provide a future proof mechanism in the event new methods of settlement are developed or identified. See also paragraphs 879 to 880 of the Explanatory Notes of the 2006 Act.

**7.111.11** Where treasury shares are sold, if the proceeds are equal to or less than the purchase price paid by the company for the shares, the proceeds are treated as a realised profit. As the original purchase price was treated as a realised loss (that is charged against distributable profits) this treatment of the proceeds results in a full or partial restoration of that loss. If the proceeds exceed the purchase price, the excess over the purchase price has to be transferred to the share premium account. The balance is transferred to the profit and loss reserve where it offsets the original loss caused by the purchase price. The purchase price paid by the company for the shares is determined by the use of a weighted average price method. If the shares were allotted to the company as fully paid bonus shares, the purchase price is deemed to be nil. [CA85 Sec 162F; CA06 Sec 731].

**7.111.12** If the company cancels shares held as treasury shares, the company must reduce the amount of its issued share capital by the nominal value of the cancelled shares. However, the cancellation does not reduce the amount of the company's authorised share capital. [CA85 Sec 162D(4); CA06 Sec 729(4)]. The amount by which the company's issued share capital is diminished on cancellation of shares held as treasury shares is required to be transferred to a capital redemption reserve. [CA85 Sec 170(1); CA06 Sec 733(4)].

**7.111.13** If shares held as treasury shares cease to be 'qualifying shares', other than when shares are suspended from listing, the company is required to cancel them immediately. [CA85 Sec 162E; CA06 Sec 729(2)].

*Delivery of returns*

**7.111.14** Where a company purchases its own shares under the rules for treasury shares set out above, it is required to deliver a return to the Registrar of Companies no later than 28 days after the delivery of shares to it (except where all of the shares have been cancelled immediately), stating with respect to each class of shares purchased (other than any cancelled shares) the number and nominal value of each of those shares that are held as treasury shares and the date on which they were delivered to the company. [CA85 Sec 169(1B); CA06 Sec 707(1)-(3)]. The return should also state the aggregate amount paid by the company for the shares and the maximum and minimum prices paid in respect of each class of shares purchased. [CA85 Sec 169(2); CA06 Sec 707(4)].

**7.111.15** Where a company purchases its own shares under the rules for treasury shares set out above and immediately cancels some or all of these, it is required to deliver a return to the Registrar of Companies with respect to the cancelled shares under the general requirements for a purchase of own shares (see para 7.82). [CA85 Sec 169(1A)]. Where the cancellation occurs on or after 1 October 2009, the provisions of the 2006 Act apply: consistent with other areas of that Act, when a company cancels shares it has held in treasury it will be required to give notice to the Registrar, accompanied by a statement of capital. [CA06 Sec 730(4)]. That statement must include:

- The total number of shares of the company.

- The aggregate nominal value of those shares.

- For each class of shares:

  - Prescribed particulars of the rights attached to the shares.

  - The total number of shares of that class.

  - The aggregate nominal value of the shares of that class.

- The amount to be paid up and the amount (if any) to be unpaid on each share (whether on account of the share's nominal value or its premium).

[CA06 Sec 708(1)].

**7.111.16**   Where a company is or was required to make a return as set out in paragraph 7.111.14 above and the shares have subsequently been cancelled, sold or transferred for the purposes of, or pursuant to, an employees' share scheme, the company is required to deliver another return to the Registrar of Companies no later than 28 days after the date on which the shares are cancelled or disposed of. This return is required to state with respect to each class of shares, the number and nominal value of those shares cancelled or disposed of and the date on which they were cancelled or disposed of. [CA85 Sec 169A; CA06 Sec 728, 730].

*Accounting treatment*

**7.111.17**   The accounting treatment for and disclosure of treasury shares is considered in chapter 23 for the Manual of Accounting – IFRS for the UK and the Manual of Accounting – UK GAAP.

# Requirements of regulators and other bodies

### Listing Rules

**7.112**   A listed company proposing to purchase its own shares must comply with the relevant conditions set out in rule 12 of the UKLA's Listing Rules, 'Dealing in own securities and treasury shares'. The rule distinguishes between 'equity shares' (which are defined in a similar manner to the Companies Acts and are thus a broader category of shares than 'equity' in IAS 32 and FRS 25) including warrants or options to subscribe or purchase equity shares and 'own securities other than equity shares' including securities convertible into or exchangeable for equity shares.

**7.113**   The provisions described in paragraphs 7.116 to 7.126 do not apply, however, to transactions entered into in the ordinary course of business by securities dealing businesses or transactions entered into by the company or other group member on behalf of third parties if the company has effective 'Chinese walls' between those responsible for the decision-making relating to the transaction and those in possession of inside information. [LR 12.1.3 R, LR 9.2.7 R].

### Buying back shares during prohibited (close) periods

**7.114**   A listed company (or any member of its group on its behalf) must not purchase or redeem (or make early redemptions of) its own securities during a prohibited period (that is, when a company is in a close period or any period when there exists any matter that constitutes inside information), unless:

■   The company has in place a buy back programme where the dates and quantities of securities to be purchased are fixed and have been disclosed in a notification to a Regulatory Information Service (see para 7.113).

■   The company has in place a buy back programme managed by an independent third party which makes its trading decisions in relation to the company's securities independently of, and uninfluenced by, the company.

■   The company is purchasing or redeeming securities other than shares or securities whose price or value would be likely to be significantly affected by the publication of the information giving rise to the prohibited period.

■   The company is redeeming securities (other than equity shares) which, at the time of issue, set out the date of redemption, the number of securities to be redeemed and the redemption price.

[LR 12.2.1 R]

**7.114.1**   The exemption in LR 12.2.1 R (second bullet point in para 7.114) is very useful for those companies that need a full twelve month period in order to complete an announced buy-back programme, although shorter periods are also common, or to gain maximum pricing flexibility while doing so. Listed companies can utilise this permission to buy back shares in their close period by giving the company's broker an authority, prior to the start of a close period, to continue buying shares during the close periods. The purchases should be effected pursuant to the annual buy back authority passed at most companies' AGMs in the usual way and, therefore, no new authority should generally be needed. As companies cannot have control over these independent programmes, directors must be satisfied with the authority they invest in their broker before entering into one of these programmes.

**7.114.2**   The documents required are relatively straightforward, the main one being an agreement between the company and its broker confirming the broker's authority. The key issues are the parameters around the broker's discretion in the agreement that do not amount to the broker acting as the company's agent. For example, the following may be included:

- Prices to comply with the annual authority (that is, by reference to the trading price five business days preceding the purchase).

- A maximum cap (that is, an absolute number) on the price to be paid per share.

- Limits on the number of shares to be bought back. Practically, as well as to comply with the shareholder authority, these may operate as restrictions on a daily and/or monthly volume basis as well as an aggregate basis.

- Operation of the buy-back programme and in particular whether it should be conducted within the market abuse 'safe harbour' (introduced on 1 July 2005). In essence, this imposes limits by reference to trading volumes and prices and requires additional disclosure.

- Termination rights. Ideally the company may want to provide that the agreement terminates at its absolute discretion or if a material event occurs, such as a profit forecast or major corporate transaction is announced. However, care needs to be exercised, since such termination rights may, in effect, make the broker no more than an agent of the company or even raise market abuse concerns.

### *Insider trading and market abuse*

**7.114.3**   Companies need to consider insider trading and market abuse legislation (see para 7.81) before entering into independent purchase programmes, as such programmes will be potentially caught by such legislation. Purchase programmes can only be carried out if the relevant individuals at the company are not in possession of inside information. For example, if the agreement is entered into too close to the beginning of the close period, the directors or others who discharge managerial responsibilities (Model Code appended to Listing Rule 9) may be in possession of inside information, thus prohibiting dealing. However, once the contract is entered into any future inside information on the part of the company should not prevent dealing. The broker will need to ensure that its 'Chinese walls' are effective so that its advisory side is not contaminated with inside information from its trading side. Generally, it is not an insider trading offence to take a decision not to trade, so it should be possible to terminate an agreement at any time even if the company is then in possession of inside information. However, there are market abuse issues and legal advice should, therefore, be taken.

### *Accounting requirements*

**7.114.4**   These agreements with a company's broker are contracts to repurchase own shares. They, therefore, fall to be accounted for as prescribed by paragraph 23 of IAS 32 and FRS 25 (see chapter 23 of the Manual of Accounting – IFRS in the UK and the Manual of Accounting – UK GAAP).

### Purchases from related parties

**7.115** Where the purchase of own equity securities or preference shares is from a related party (for example, a director, substantial shareholder or person exercising significant influence or associates of these) the requirements of chapter 11 of the UKLA's Listing Rules (as amended from 6 August 2007 by FSA 2007/40 – Listing, Prospectus and Disclosure Rules (Miscellaneous Amendments) Instrument 2007) must be complied with (see further chapter 29 of the Manual of Accounting – IFRS for the UK and the Manual of Accounting – UK GAAP). This is unless a purchase is made by way of a tender offer to all holders of the class of securities or, in the case of a market purchase pursuant to a general authority granted by shareholders, it is made without prior understanding, arrangement or agreement between the company and any related party. [LR 12.3.1 R].

### Purchase of own equity shares

**7.116** Where a company purchases less than 15 per cent of its equity shares (excluding treasury shares) it may make the purchase through the market in the ordinary way, provided the price paid is not more than the higher of five per cent above the average of the market value of the shares for the five business days before the purchase is made and that stipulated by Article 5(1) of EC Regulations 2273/2003, 'The buy-back and stabilisation regulation'. Otherwise a tender offer has to be made to all shareholders of the class of equity shares to be purchased. [LR 12.4.1 R].

**7.117** Where the company proposes to purchase 15 per cent or more of its equity shares (excluding treasury shares), it must make these purchases by way of a tender offer to all shareholders. [LR 12.4.2 R]. Where a series of purchases are made (and shareholders have granted a general authority) that, in aggregate, amount to 15 per cent or more of any class of its equity shares in issue immediately following the grant of that authority, a tender offer need only be made in respect of any purchase that takes the aggregate to, or above, the 15 per cent level. Purchases that have been specifically approved by shareholders should not be taken into account in determining whether the 15 per cent level has been reached. [LR 12.4.3 G].

**7.118** The company must notify a Regulatory Information Service immediately when the board decides to submit to the company's shareholders a proposal that the company should be authorised to purchase its own equity shares. The notification should indicate whether the proposal relates either to specific purchases (giving the names of the persons from whom the purchases are to be made) or to a general authorisation to make purchases [LR 12.4.4 R]. The company should immediately notify a Regulatory Information Service of the outcome of the shareholders' meeting. [LR 12.4.5 R]. However, see paragraph 7.119 as to the timing of the notification of purchase.

**7.119** The company should notify to a Regulatory Information Service all of its purchases of its equity shares as soon as possible and in any event by 07:30 am on the business day following the day of the purchase. The notification should include:

- The date of purchase.

- The number of shares purchased.

- The purchase price per share for each of the highest and the lowest prices paid were relevant.

- The number of equity shares purchased for cancellation and the number purchased to be held as treasury shares.

- Where equity shares are purchased to be held as treasury shares, a statement of:

  - The total number of treasury shares of each class held by the company following the purchase and non-cancellation of the shares.

  - The number of shares of each class that the company has in issue less the total number of treasury shares of each class held by the company following the purchase and non-cancellation of the shares.

[LR 12.4.6 R].

**7.120** Where there are in issue convertible securities or warrants or options to subscribe for equity shares of the class proposed to be purchased, the company must hold a separate class meeting of the holders. The purpose of the meeting is to obtain the shareholders' approval by extraordinary resolution before the company either enters into any contract to purchase its equity shares of any class or first exercises a general authority to make purchases in the market. However, the company does not require such approval where there are provisions in the relevant trust deed or terms of issue permitting the company to purchase its own equity shares. [LR 12.4.7 R, LR 12.4.8 R].

**7.121** The circular containing the notice of meeting required by the preceding paragraph must comply with the requirements for all circulars. In addition, it must set out clearly the apparent effect, in terms of attributable assets and earnings, on the expectations of the holders on conversion or subscription if the company were to exercise fully the authorisation that it seeks to purchase its own shares at the maximum price allowed. In addition, any adjustments that the company may propose should be set out and the information concerning the effect should be restated on the revised basis. [LR 12.4.9 R].

**7.122** Where, within a period of 12 months, a company purchases warrants or options over its own equity shares which would, on exercise, comprise 15 per cent or more of the company's existing issued shares (excluding treasury shares), the company must send its shareholders a circular containing the following information:

*Acquisition of own shares*

- A statement of the directors' intentions regarding future purchases of the company's warrants and options.

- The number and terms of the warrants or options acquired and to be acquired and the method of acquisition.

- Where warrants or options have been, or are to be, acquired from specific parties, a statement of the names of those parties and all material terms of the acquisition.

- The prices to be paid.

[LR 12.5.7 R].

### Purchase of own securities other than equity shares

**7.123** Except where the purchases will consist of individual transactions made in accordance with the terms of the issue of the securities, a listed company that intends to purchase, any of its equity securities (other than equity shares) for example securities convertible into equity shares, or preference shares, it must:

- Ensure that no dealings in the relevant securities are carried out by or on behalf of the company or any member of the group, until the proposal has either been notified to a Regulatory Information Service or abandoned.

- Notify a Regulatory Information Service of its decision to purchase.

[LR 12.5.1 R].

**7.124** Purchases, early redemptions or cancellations of the company's own listed equity securities (other than equity shares) or preference shares by or on behalf of the company or any other member of its group must be notified to a Regulatory Information Service when an aggregate of ten per cent of the initial amount of the relevant class of securities has been purchased, redeemed or cancelled and for each five per cent in aggregate of the initial amount of that class acquired thereafter. [LR 12.5.2 R]. Such notifications must be made as soon as possible and, in any event, no later than 07:30 am on the business day following the calendar day on which the dealing occurred to reach or exceed the relevant threshold. The notification must state the amount of the securities acquired, redeemed or cancelled since the last such notification, the number of that class of the securities remaining outstanding and whether or not the securities acquired are to be cancelled. [LR 12.5.3 R]. In addition, for early redemptions and purchases of shares other than equity shares the notification must also include a statement indicating the number of the shares purchased to be held as treasury shares and the number of shares purchased or redeemed early for cancellation. [LR 12.5.4 R].

**7.125** In circumstances where the purchase of own securities is not being made pursuant to a tender offer and the purchase causes a relevant threshold to be reached or exceeded, no further purchases may be undertaken until after a notification to a Regulatory Information Service has been made as per the preceding paragraph. [LR 12.5.5 R].

**7.126** In the case of securities which are convertible into, exchangeable for or carrying a right to subscribe for equity shares, unless a tender offer is made to all holders of the class of securities, purchases must not be made at a price more than five per cent above the average of the market values for the securities for the five business days immediately preceding the date of purchase. [LR 12.5.6 R].

*Treasury shares*

**7.126.1** Sales for cash, or transfers for the purposes of, or pursuant to, an employees' share scheme, of treasury shares can not be made during a prohibited period; that is, when a company is in a close period or any period when there exists any matter that constitutes inside information. [LR 12.6.1 R]. However, this prohibition does not apply to:

- Transfers of treasury shares in connection with the operation of an employees' share scheme, where the transfer facilitates dealings that do not fall within the provisions of the Model Code (section 2(h) to (k)) appended to LR9. These include:

  - Transfers to a savings scheme investing only in the company's securities following either the exercise of an option under a savings related share option scheme or the release of shares from a HM Revenue and Customs approved share incentive plan.

  - With the exception of a recipient of the shares who is a restricted person (that is one discharging managerial responsibilities), dealings in connection with a HM Revenue and Customs approved SAYE option scheme or share incentive plan (or a scheme on similar terms and conditions) under which participation is extended on similar terms to all or most employees of the participating companies in that scheme.

  - The transfers of securities by the company to an independent trustee of an employees' share scheme to a beneficiary who is not a restricted person.

- Sales or transfers by the company of treasury shares (other than equity shares) of a class whose price or value would not be likely to be significantly affected by the publication of the information giving rise to the prohibited period.

[LR 12.6.2 R].

**7.126.2** If, by virtue of it holding treasury shares, a company is allotted shares as part of a capitalisation issue, the company must notify a Regulatory Information Service as soon as possible (no later than 07:30 am on the following business day). The notification must include:

- The date of the allotment.

- The number of shares allotted.

*Acquisition of own shares*

- A statement as to what number of shares allotted have been cancelled and what number is being held as treasury shares.

- Where shares allotted are being held as treasury shares, a statement of:
  - The total number of treasury shares of each class held by the company following the allotment.
  - The number of shares of each class that the company has in issue less the total number of treasury shares of each class held by the company following the allotment.

[LR 12.6.3 R].

**7.126.3** Any sale for cash, transfer for the purposes of or pursuant to an employees' share scheme or cancellation of treasury shares by a listed company must be notified to a Regulatory Information Service as soon as possible and in any event by no later than 07:30 am on the business day following the calendar day on which the sale, transfer or cancellation occurred. The notification must include:

- The date of the sale, transfer or cancellation.

- The number of shares sold, transferred or cancelled.

- The sale or transfer price for each of the highest and lowest prices paid, where relevant.

- A statement of:
  - The total number of treasury shares of each class held by the company following the sale, transfer or cancellation.
  - The number of shares of each class that the company has in issue less the total number of treasury shares of each class held by the company following the sale, transfer or cancellation.

[LR 12.6.4 R].

**[The next paragraph is 7.128.]**

*Redemption of redeemable shares*

**7.128** Listed companies must notify a Regulatory Information Service as soon as possible of details of a redemption of listed shares. The particulars to be notified are the number of shares redeemed and the number of shares of that class that remain outstanding following the redemption. [LR 9.6.4 R (3)].

**[The next paragraph is 7.130.]**

### Major Shareholding Notification Rules

**7.130**  It is possible to acquire up to 29.9 per cent of a listed company in one go. The only disclosure rules that apply to acquirers of shares in listed companies are those now contained in the Major Shareholding Notification Rules in the UKLA's DTR. [DTR para 5]. The Major Shareholding Notification Rules cover the acquisition of shares and also an 'interest in shares', which may be represented by qualifying financial instruments, such as options, that are held directly or indirectly.

### Institutional shareholders

**7.131**  The interests of large institutional shareholders are represented by investor protection committees that issue guidelines on matters of concern to shareholders. The Investments Committee of the Association of British Insurers has made certain recommendations on the subject of a purchase by a company of its own shares, but no formal guidelines have been published. They request that a special resolution is given for a market purchase, that the authority to purchase shares is renewed annually and that the effect on earnings per share, capital and dividend cover should be considered. They also request that companies undertake in the document that the authority to purchase its own shares will only be exercised if to do so would result in an increase in earnings per share and is in the best interests of shareholders generally.

**7.132**  The institutions are unlikely to object to small purchases (up to five per cent of the issued equity share capital in any one year). Hence, it is common for such approval to be sought at each annual general meeting. Between five and ten per cent, enquiries may be raised as to any special features which might make the proposal undesirable. Above ten per cent, prior consultation should take place or support for the resolution will depend on the circumstance.

## Financial assistance for acquisition of shares

### Private companies

**7.132.1**  Under the 1985 Act, no company was permitted to give financial assistance for the acquisition of its shares (although there were procedures, known as 'whitewash procedures', under which private companies were often able to do so. This prohibition on financial assistance by private companies has been abolished under the 2006 Act from 1 October 2007.

**7.132.2**  Despite this relaxation, directors will still need to ensure that:

■  The transaction is in the best interests of the company, such that they are not in breach of their duty under section 172 of the 2006 Act to promote its success.

■  The transaction does not breach the rules on distributions or otherwise constitute an illegal reduction in capital (see further the Manual of

Accounting — IFRS for the UK and the Manual of Accounting — UK GAAP).

**7.132.3** In practice directors may wish to take steps to demonstrate that they are not in breach of their duties, for example, ensuring that board minutes confirm that the directors have considered the matter carefully and/or are obtaining shareholder approval for the transaction.

**7.132.4** It should be noted that, subsidiaries of public companies are prohibited from giving financial assistance for the acquisition of the public companies' own shares. [CA06 Sec 678(1)]. (See para 7.133.1.)

**Public companies**

**7.133** A public company is not permitted by section 678(1) of the 2006 Act to give financial assistance for the acquisition of its shares. This general prohibition on giving financial assistance by a public company is required by the EU 2nd Company Law Directive (77/91/EEC).

**7.133.1** The prohibition extends to a public company subsidiary giving financial assistance for the acquisition of shares in its private holding company. A change introduced by section 678 of the 2006 Act gives statutory effect to the decision in *Arab Bank plc vs Mercantile Holdings Ltd* [1994] 2 All ER 74, that the statutory prohibition on a company giving financial assistance for the purpose of acquiring its own shares or shares in its holding company does not apply to the giving of assistance by a subsidiary incorporated in an overseas jurisdiction. The prohibition on post acquisition assistance is retained only for companies that are public companies at the time the assistance is given. [CA06 Sec 678(3)].

**7.134** Subject to the exemptions set out below the general rule is that companies cannot give, either directly or indirectly, financial assistance for the purpose of acquiring their own shares or the shares of their holding company. This applies to financial assistance given:

- Both before or at the same time as the acquisition.

- After the acquisition for the purpose of reducing or discharging a liability incurred by any person for the purpose of the acquisition.

[CA06 Secs 678(1), 679(1), 678(3), 679(3), 680(1)(2)].

**7.135** The above provisions do not prohibit the following transactions for a public company provided that it has net assets that are not thereby reduced or the reduction is provided out of distributable profits:

- Lending of money by a company in the ordinary course of its business.

- Provision of financial assistance for an employees' share scheme.

- Provision of financial assistance to enable or facilitate transactions in the company's shares by employees, former employees or their families.

- Loans to employees (who are not directors) to enable them to acquire beneficial ownership of fully paid shares in the company.

[CA 06 Secs 678(2)(4), 679(2)(4), 681(1)(2), 682(1)(2)(5)].

Giving financial assistance by these means would result in a reduction in the company's net assets if provision had to be made in the financial statements for the resultant debt. However, provided this reduction was made out of distributable profits, the financial assistance would be allowed.

**7.136** The prohibition in section 678 of the 2006 Act does not apply if the company's principal purpose in giving financial assistance is not to give it for the purpose of acquiring shares, or the assistance given is an incidental part of some larger purpose of the company and the assistance is given in good faith and in the interests of the company. [CA06 Sec 678(2)(4)]. In the case of *Brady v Brady* [1989] AC 755 the House of Lords drew a distinction between the purpose of a transaction and the reason for which it was undertaken. It decided that a larger purpose was not the same as a more important reason and, therefore, even though the financial or commercial advantages of the transaction were possibly the most important reason for providing the assistance, they could not constitute part of the larger purpose. It is thought that the effect of this judgement is to severely reduce the usefulness of these exemptions. Although this case was tried under the 1985 Act, the relevant provisions have been carried forward into the 2006 Act without amendment, so the ruling remains relevant.

**7.137** The above provisions do not prohibit the following transactions, even though they may effectively represent financial assistance:

- Distributions made as a lawfully paid dividend or made in the course of winding up.

- Allotment of bonus shares.

- Reduction of capital confirmed by court order.

- Redemption or purchase of own shares made in accordance with sections 159-181 of the 1985 Act (see above) (CA06 Secs 684 to 708).

- A scheme of arrangement between the company and its members or its creditors under section 425 of the 1985 Act or an arrangement under section 110 or Part I of the Insolvency Act 1986.

[CA06 Sec 681(1)(2)].

**7.138** However, in spite of this exemption, it is thought that the source of the money out of which the purchase or redemption is made is important. Thus, if the company makes the payment with borrowed money, there is a risk that it will not be covered by the exemption and the company may be giving financial assistance for the acquisition of its own shares. As a result, where a company is borrowing to fund the purchase and grants security for the borrowing, the giving of security or payment of interest may amount to financial assistance by the company. As there are criminal penalties for giving illegal financial assistance, it is, therefore, advisable for a company to consider the financial assistance provisions and to take legal advice.

**[The next paragraph is 7.141.]**

**Effect of contravention**

**7.141**  Where a company gives financial assistance in contravention of section 678(1),(3) or 679(1),(3), it is liable to a fine and every officer of it who is in default is liable to imprisonment and a fine. In addition, the transaction is void so that any property transferred is irrecoverable. The effect of a loan made in contravention of the prohibition from giving financial assistance was considered in *Coulthard v Neville Russell* (a firm) [[1998] 1 BCLC 143]. Although the case was tried under the 1985 Act, the law (insofar as it relates to public companies) is unchanged in this area.

**7.142**  The facts in the case were that the subsidiary had made a loan to its parent to enable the parent to repay loans which financed the purchase of the subsidiary's shares. The subsidiary subsequently went into insolvent liquidation and the Secretary of State brought proceedings seeking disqualification orders against the directors of the subsidiary. The directors in the meantime brought an action against the subsidiary's auditors alleging that the auditors owed them a duty of care to warn them that the loans were or might be in breach of the 1985 Act, and that, as a consequence of the loans' illegality, the financial statements would not give a true and fair view if they were included as assets. The auditors appealed that the proceedings disclosed no cause of action.

**7.143**  In the case the Court of Appeal considered the effect of a loan made in breach of the prohibition in the 1985 Act. A loan made for the purpose of giving financial assistance contrary to this prohibition is illegal and unenforceable against the borrower. It follows that the loans made in contravention of the section cannot, properly, be treated as assets of the lending company and that a balance sheet in which such a loan is shown as the company's asset will fail to give a true and fair view of its financial affairs.

**7.144**  The Court of Appeal dismissed the appeal, without wishing to express any view that the directors' claim would succeed, on the basis that the directors had at least an arguable case against the auditors. The case highlights the importance of identifying potential financial assistance at an early stage by obtaining legal advice.

### Authorised reduction of share capital

**7.145**  A limited company, whether public or private, may reduce its share capital by special resolution confirmed by the court (but see para 7.146). [CA85 Sec 135; CA06 Sec 641(1)(b)]. The 1985 Act required that the articles contain specific authorisation for such capital reductions; the 2006 Act relaxes this rule by requiring only that the articles do not restrict or prohibit the capital reduction. [CA85 Sec 135(1); CA06 Sec 641(6)]. For private companies, the 2006 Act introduces a new procedure for capital reductions that requires a special resolution, does not require court confirmation but instead requires the directors to make a 'solvency statement'. [CA06 Sec 641(1)(a)]. Both public and private companies may continue to use the court confirmation procedure.

### Court confirmation procedure

**7.146**  Under this procedure, having passed the special resolution, the company must apply to the court for an order confirming the reduction. Every creditor to whom the company owes a debt or claim on a date specified by the court is entitled to object to the reduction of capital. For this purpose, the court must draw up a list of those creditors and may publish notices fixing a day (or days) from which any other creditors will be excluded from the right to object. [CA85 Sec 136(3); CA06 Sec 646]. Any officer of the company who intentionally or recklessly conceals the name of a creditor, or who misrepresents a creditor's debt or claim, commits an offence and is liable to a fine.

**7.147**  The court may then make an order confirming the reduction of capital on such terms and conditions as it thinks fit. In doing so, the court must be satisfied that every creditor who has raised an objection has either consented subsequently or that his debt or claim has been discharged or has determined, or has been secured. [CA85 Sec 137; CA06 Sec 648].

**7.148**  The court order must be delivered to the Registrar of Companies. For capital reductions performed under the 1985 Act (that is, prior to 1 October 2009), the order must be accompanied by a court approved minute showing in respect of the altered share capital, the amount of the share capital, the number of shares into which it is to be divided (and the amount of each share), and the amount (if any) at the date of registration deemed to be paid up on each share. [CA85 Sec 138(1)]. For those capital reductions performed under the 2006 Act (that is, on or after 1 October 2009), instead of a court approved minute, a court approved statement of capital must be delivered to the Registrar of Companies. This statement of capital must contain the information set out in paragraph 7.111.15 in respect of the altered share capital only.

**7.149**  A court approved capital reduction takes effect when the court order and court approved minute (or statement of capital) is *registered* by the Registrar, with one exception for capital reductions made under the 2006 Act (on or after 1 October 2009). A capital reduction that forms part of a compromise or arrangement under Part 26 of the 2006 Act will take effect at the same time as the other aspects of that compromise or arrangement; that is, on *delivery* of the court order and statement of capital to the Registrar. [CA06 Sec 649(3)]. Once registered, the Registrar's certificate under section 138 of the 1985 Act (section 649 of the 2006 Act) is conclusive evidence that the company's share capital is as stated in the minute or statement of capital.

**7.150** One of the grounds mentioned in section 135 of the 1985 Act (section 641 of the 2006 Act) on which a company may reduce its capital is where capital is lost or is unrepresented by available assets. An example would be where the financial statements show a deficit on the profit and loss account. The company must, in these circumstances, prove to the court that the loss of capital is permanent and not temporary. If the loss is permanent, the court will generally sanction the application without opposition. This is on the basis that the reduction would not affect creditors and no members or class of members would be disadvantaged.

**7.151** However, to prevent a company reducing its capital more than is necessary the court will generally require it to credit to a special reserve any excess over the amount required to write off the deficit. This reserve will be subject to certain conditions, for instance, that it will be undistributable other than for the specific purposes mentioned.

**7.152** Where, however, the loss of capital cannot be shown to be permanent, a cancellation of paid-up share capital will prejudice creditors. An example might be where a company writes off an investment in a loss-making subsidiary, but the loss is not proved to be permanent. The court will in these circumstances consider the extent to which the interests of creditors must be fully safeguarded. An undertaking offered by the company may enable the court to dispense with the need to obtain creditors' consent and sanction the reduction.

**7.153** In addition to the creation of a special reserve as mentioned above, the undertaking may specify that any amounts received in respect of its investment or release of a provision on a subsequent revaluation of assets would need to be credited to the special reserve. This special reserve would generally be made undistributable for so long as there remain outstanding any liabilities of the company that would be admissible in a winding up beginning on the date of the reduction of capital.

**Table 7.6 – Transfer of special reserve**

**Trafalgar House Public Limited Company – Report & Accounts – 30 September 1994**

**26 Reserves Company**

|  | Special Reserve £m | Profit and loss account £m | Total £m |
|---|---|---|---|
| As at 1 October 1993 | 95.0 | 102.0 | 197.0 |
| Special Reserve transfer | (95.0) | 95.0 | – |
| Transfer to profit and loss account | – | (20.2) | (20.2) |
| Arising on scrip dividends |  | 7.3 | 7.3 |
| As at 30 September 1994 | – | 184.1 | 184.1 |

Following the rights issue and placing on 7 January 1994, the balance of the Special Reserve in the accounts of the company became distributable and has accordingly been transferred to the profit and loss account. This is in accordance with the undertaking given to the Court during the year ended 30 September 1991 whereby the amount standing to the credit of the Special Reserve may be reduced by the amount of any increase in its share capital or share premium as a result of any issue of shares paid up by receipt of new consideration

## Solvency statement procedure

**7.154** The solvency statement procedure is only available to private companies and applies to capital reductions occurring on or after 1 October 2008; public companies must use the court confirmation procedure.

**7.155** Companies electing to use the solvency statement procedure must pass a special resolution supported by a solvency statement made not more than 15 days before the date on which the resolution is passed. A copy of the solvency statement must be made available to all members either at the meeting at which the resolution is to be proposed or, in the case of a written resolution, by being sent to the members at or before the time at which he is sent the proposed resolution. [CA06 Sec 642(2),(3)]. Once the resolution has been passed, the company must deliver a copy of the solvency statement and a statement of capital (as in para 7.111.15) to the Registrar of Companies who must register the documents on receipt at which time the resolution takes effect.

**7.156** The solvency statement is made by all the company's directors. In the event that a director is unwilling to make the statement, the company will not be able to use the solvency statement procedure, unless the dissenting director resigns as a director of the company in which case the remaining directors may make the statement. A solvency statement is a statement that each of the directors:

- Has formed the opinion, as regards the company's situation at the date of the statement, that there is no ground on which the company could then be found to be unable to pay (or otherwise discharge) its debts.

- Has also formed the opinion:

- if it is intended to commence the company's winding within twelve months of that date, that the company will be able to pay (or otherwise discharge) its debts in full within twelve months of commencing the winding up; or

- in any other case, that the company will be able to pay (or otherwise discharge) its debts as they fall due during the year immediately following that date.

[CA06 Sec 643(1)].

**7.157** In forming their opinions, the directors must take into account all the company's liabilities, including contingent and prospective liabilities. A proposed redemption of preference shares treated as liabilities for accounting purposes should be regarded as a contingent or prospective liability. [CA06 Explanatory Notes para 961]. A director who makes a solvency statement without having reasonable grounds for the opinions expressed in it commits an offence punishable by imprisonment or a fine, or both.

**7.158** The solvency statement must be in writing, be signed by the directors and state:

- The date on which it is made.

- The name of each director of the company.

- That it is a solvency statement for the purposes of section 642 of the Companies Act 2006.

[CA06 Sec 643(3); SI 2008/1915 para 2].

**7.159** If a company's directors make a solvency statement without reasonable grounds for the opinions expressed in it and that solvency statement is delivered to the registrar, each director who is in default is guilty of an offence, punishable by a fine and/or imprisonment. [CA06 Sec 643(4),(5)]

Chapter 8

# Secretarial matters

|  | Page |
|---|---|
| Introduction | 8001 |
| Accounting records and statutory books | 8003 |
| General requirements – accounting records | 8003 |
| Adequate accounting records | 8004 |
| Counsel's opinion on section 221 of the 1985 Act | 8005 |
| Duty to keep accounting records | 8005 |
| Disclosure of the financial position at any time | 8006 |
| Sums of money | 8007 |
| A record of the assets and liabilities | 8007 |
| Statements of stock | 8008 |
| Statements of all goods sold and purchased | 8008 |
| Penalties and disqualification orders | 8008 |
| Requirements to prepare financial statements | 8008 |
| Directors' duty regarding accounting records | 8011 |
| Auditors' duties and rights | 8012 |
| Senior statutory auditor | 8015 |
| Criminal offence for auditors | 8015 |
| Auditors' limitation of liability agreements | 8016 |
| Form of records | 8016 |
| Statutory books and records and their location | 8017 |
| Accounting records | 8017 |
| Statutory books and other records | 8017 |
| Company identification | 8020 |
| Company name | 8020 |
| Memorandum and articles of association | 8022 |
| Annual return | 8023 |
| Members' lists | 8024 |
| Penalties | 8024 |
| Information annexed to annual return | 8025 |
| Document quality | 8025 |
| Retention of accounting and other records | 8026 |
| Penalties | 8030 |
| Electronic communications with members, others and the Registrar of Companies | 8032 |
| Introduction | 8032 |
| Meaning of electronic communication | 8033 |
| Delivery of documents generally to the Registrar of Companies using electronic communications | 8034 |
| Accounting reference periods | 8034 |
| Accounting reference date | 8034 |

Financial year. . . . . . . . . . . . . . . . . . . . . . . . . . . . . . . . . . . . . . . . . . . 8035
First and subsequent accounting reference periods. . . . . . . . . . . . . . . . 8035
    Change of accounting reference date by a listed company . . . . . . . . 8036
    Change of accounting reference date by an AIM or PLUS-quoted
    company . . . . . . . . . . . . . . . . . . . . . . . . . . . . . . . . . . . . . . . . . . . . . . . 8037
Current and previous periods. . . . . . . . . . . . . . . . . . . . . . . . . . . . . . . . . 8037
Previous periods. . . . . . . . . . . . . . . . . . . . . . . . . . . . . . . . . . . . . . . . . . . 8038
Preparing and approving financial statements. . . . . . . . . . . . . . . . . . . . 8039
    Directors' duty. . . . . . . . . . . . . . . . . . . . . . . . . . . . . . . . . . . . . . . . . . . . 8039
    Company individual financial statements. . . . . . . . . . . . . . . . . . . . . . 8040
    Company consolidated financial statements. . . . . . . . . . . . . . . . . . . . 8041
    Approval, signing, publishing and filing. . . . . . . . . . . . . . . . . . . . . . 8042
    Liability for approving defective financial statements. . . . . . . . . . . . 8044
    Liability if balance sheet is unsigned. . . . . . . . . . . . . . . . . . . . . . . . . 8044
    Directors' duties regarding their directors' report. . . . . . . . . . . . . . . 8045
    Preparation. . . . . . . . . . . . . . . . . . . . . . . . . . . . . . . . . . . . . . . . . . . . . . 8045
    Approval and signing . . . . . . . . . . . . . . . . . . . . . . . . . . . . . . . . . . . . . 8045
    Directors' duties regarding directors' remuneration report . . . . . . . . . 8046
    Preparation. . . . . . . . . . . . . . . . . . . . . . . . . . . . . . . . . . . . . . . . . . . . . . 8046
    Approval and signing . . . . . . . . . . . . . . . . . . . . . . . . . . . . . . . . . . . . . 8046
Directors' 'safe harbour' provision for directors' reports and remu-
neration reports . . . . . . . . . . . . . . . . . . . . . . . . . . . . . . . . . . . . . . . . . . . 8047
Persons entitled to receive financial statements. . . . . . . . . . . . . . . . . . . 8047
    Financial statements transmitted electronically. . . . . . . . . . . . . . . . . 8048
Listing, Disclosure and Transparency Rules and electronic commu-
nications . . . . . . . . . . . . . . . . . . . . . . . . . . . . . . . . . . . . . . . . . . . . . . . . . 8050
Public companies – presentation of financial statements at general
meetings . . . . . . . . . . . . . . . . . . . . . . . . . . . . . . . . . . . . . . . . . . . . . . . . . 8051
    Private companies – dispensation from AGMs and laying financial
    statements. . . . . . . . . . . . . . . . . . . . . . . . . . . . . . . . . . . . . . . . . . . . . . . 8051
    Private companies – 1985 Act elective regime for AGMs transitional
    provisions . . . . . . . . . . . . . . . . . . . . . . . . . . . . . . . . . . . . . . . . . . . . . . . 8052
    Liability for public companies for not laying financial statements. . 8053
Quoted companies – members' approval of directors' remuneration
report. . . . . . . . . . . . . . . . . . . . . . . . . . . . . . . . . . . . . . . . . . . . . . . . . . . . 8053
Delivery to the Registrar of Companies. . . . . . . . . . . . . . . . . . . . . . . . . 8054
    Filing obligations for quoted and unquoted companies. . . . . . . . . . . 8054
    Filing obligations of companies subject to the small companies
    regime . . . . . . . . . . . . . . . . . . . . . . . . . . . . . . . . . . . . . . . . . . . . . . . . . . 8055
    Filing obligations for companies subject to the small companies
    regime . . . . . . . . . . . . . . . . . . . . . . . . . . . . . . . . . . . . . . . . . . . . . . . . . . 8057
    Filing obligations of medium-sized companies . . . . . . . . . . . . . . . . . 8057
    Consolidated financial statements not prepared . . . . . . . . . . . . . . . . 8058
    Period allowed for sending out, laying and filing . . . . . . . . . . . . . . . 8058
    Filing exemption for unlimited companies. . . . . . . . . . . . . . . . . . . . . 8060
    Exemption for qualifying undertakings . . . . . . . . . . . . . . . . . . . . . . . 8061
    Rejection of documents by the Registrar. . . . . . . . . . . . . . . . . . . . . . 8061
    Company's liability for late filing . . . . . . . . . . . . . . . . . . . . . . . . . . . 8062

Directors' liability for late delivery . . . . . . . . . . . . . . . . . . . . . . . . . . 8063
Exemptions from audit of financial statements . . . . . . . . . . . . . . . . . . . . . . 8064
Small companies and groups . . . . . . . . . . . . . . . . . . . . . . . . . . . . . . . . . 8064
Small companies ineligible for audit exemption . . . . . . . . . . . . . . . . . . 8065
Dormant companies . . . . . . . . . . . . . . . . . . . . . . . . . . . . . . . . . . . . . . . 8069
Effect on financial statements . . . . . . . . . . . . . . . . . . . . . . . . . . . . . . 8070
Definition of 'dormant company' . . . . . . . . . . . . . . . . . . . . . . . . . . . 8071
Examples of significant accounting transactions . . . . . . . . . . . . . . . . 8071
Additional disclosure to be made by dormant agency company . . . . 8072
Publication of financial statements . . . . . . . . . . . . . . . . . . . . . . . . . . . . . 8072
Definition of publication . . . . . . . . . . . . . . . . . . . . . . . . . . . . . . . . . . . 8072
Statutory accounts . . . . . . . . . . . . . . . . . . . . . . . . . . . . . . . . . . . . . . . . 8073
Full financial statements . . . . . . . . . . . . . . . . . . . . . . . . . . . . . . . . . . 8073
Abbreviated Companies Act accounts . . . . . . . . . . . . . . . . . . . . . . . 8074
Shorter-form Companies Act accounts for small companies . . . . . . . 8075
Balance sheet and notes . . . . . . . . . . . . . . . . . . . . . . . . . . . . . . . . . . 8076
Summary financial statements . . . . . . . . . . . . . . . . . . . . . . . . . . . . . . . 8076
Background . . . . . . . . . . . . . . . . . . . . . . . . . . . . . . . . . . . . . . . . . . . . 8076
General conditions . . . . . . . . . . . . . . . . . . . . . . . . . . . . . . . . . . . . . . . 8077
Ascertaining wishes of members . . . . . . . . . . . . . . . . . . . . . . . . . . . 8078
Consultation by notice . . . . . . . . . . . . . . . . . . . . . . . . . . . . . . . . . . . 8079
Relevant consultation . . . . . . . . . . . . . . . . . . . . . . . . . . . . . . . . . . . . 8080
Statements to be included in all summary financial statements . . . . . 8081
Form and content of summary financial statement . . . . . . . . . . . . . . 8083
Summary directors' emoluments and remuneration report
information . . . . . . . . . . . . . . . . . . . . . . . . . . . . . . . . . . . . . . . . . . . 8084
Summary profit and loss account . . . . . . . . . . . . . . . . . . . . . . . . . . . 8084
Summary balance sheet . . . . . . . . . . . . . . . . . . . . . . . . . . . . . . . . . . . 8086
Dividends . . . . . . . . . . . . . . . . . . . . . . . . . . . . . . . . . . . . . . . . . . . . . 8086
Comparative information . . . . . . . . . . . . . . . . . . . . . . . . . . . . . . . . . 8087
Penalties . . . . . . . . . . . . . . . . . . . . . . . . . . . . . . . . . . . . . . . . . . . . . . 8087
Non-statutory accounts . . . . . . . . . . . . . . . . . . . . . . . . . . . . . . . . . . . . 8087
Additional rules for listed companies . . . . . . . . . . . . . . . . . . . . . . . . . . . 8089
Preliminary announcements . . . . . . . . . . . . . . . . . . . . . . . . . . . . . . . . . 8089
Half-yearly reports . . . . . . . . . . . . . . . . . . . . . . . . . . . . . . . . . . . . . . . . 8090
Interim management statements . . . . . . . . . . . . . . . . . . . . . . . . . . . . . . 8090
AIM Companies . . . . . . . . . . . . . . . . . . . . . . . . . . . . . . . . . . . . . . . . . . 8090
PLUS-quoted Companies . . . . . . . . . . . . . . . . . . . . . . . . . . . . . . . . . . . 8090
Status of half yearly reports, preliminary announcements and other
statements . . . . . . . . . . . . . . . . . . . . . . . . . . . . . . . . . . . . . . . . . . . . . 8091
Compensation for false statements in reports and financial statements 8092
Revision of defective financial statements . . . . . . . . . . . . . . . . . . . . . . . 8092
Voluntary revision . . . . . . . . . . . . . . . . . . . . . . . . . . . . . . . . . . . . . . . . 8093
Approving and signing revised financial statements . . . . . . . . . . . . . 8094
Approving and signing revised directors' report or directors'
remuneration report . . . . . . . . . . . . . . . . . . . . . . . . . . . . . . . . . . . . 8095
Auditors' report . . . . . . . . . . . . . . . . . . . . . . . . . . . . . . . . . . . . . . . . 8096
Reporting accountant's report . . . . . . . . . . . . . . . . . . . . . . . . . . . . . . 8097

Effects of revision . . . . . . . . . . . . . . . . . . . . . . . . . . . . . . . . . . . . . . . 8097
Abbreviated financial statements. . . . . . . . . . . . . . . . . . . . . . . . . . . 8099
Companies exempted from audit. . . . . . . . . . . . . . . . . . . . . . . . . . 8099
Summary financial statements . . . . . . . . . . . . . . . . . . . . . . . . . . . . 8100
Compulsory revision . . . . . . . . . . . . . . . . . . . . . . . . . . . . . . . . . . . . . . . 8100
Meetings and resolutions . . . . . . . . . . . . . . . . . . . . . . . . . . . . . . . . . . . 8101
Directors' meetings . . . . . . . . . . . . . . . . . . . . . . . . . . . . . . . . . . . . . . 8101
General meetings. . . . . . . . . . . . . . . . . . . . . . . . . . . . . . . . . . . . . . . . 8102
Annual general meetings. . . . . . . . . . . . . . . . . . . . . . . . . . . . . . 8103
Notice . . . . . . . . . . . . . . . . . . . . . . . . . . . . . . . . . . . . . . . . . . . . . . 8103
Single member companies. . . . . . . . . . . . . . . . . . . . . . . . . . . . 8105
Class meetings . . . . . . . . . . . . . . . . . . . . . . . . . . . . . . . . . . . . . . 8105
Resolutions. . . . . . . . . . . . . . . . . . . . . . . . . . . . . . . . . . . . . . . . . . . . . 8105
Ordinary resolutions . . . . . . . . . . . . . . . . . . . . . . . . . . . . . . . . . 8106
Special resolutions. . . . . . . . . . . . . . . . . . . . . . . . . . . . . . . . . . . 8106
Written resolutions . . . . . . . . . . . . . . . . . . . . . . . . . . . . . . . . . . 8107
Records of meetings . . . . . . . . . . . . . . . . . . . . . . . . . . . . . . . . . 8108

Chapter 8

# Secretarial matters

## Introduction

**8.1** Company law imposes certain duties and obligations regarding a company's financial management and administration on both the company and its directors. Many of these duties and obligations are of a company secretarial nature and these are considered in this chapter.

**8.1.1** In recent years, legislation in this area for GB companies has been contained in the Companies Act 1985 (the 1985 Act). In a similar way, the Northern Ireland Order 1986 applies to NI companies. Although the requirements of the 1985 Act include requirements that are similar to those of the Northern Ireland Order, references to the NI Order are not given in this chapter. The Companies Act 2006 (the 2006 Act) and its supporting regulations replaces all the provisions of the 1985 Act and the Northern Ireland Order and their supporting regulations are covered by this chapter. Implementation of the 2006 Act has been staggered and different parts have different commencement dates. Each section of this chapter sets out the principal changes to be introduced by the 2006 Act and states the date of commencement of the relevant section. Most of the provisions in Parts 15 and 16 (covering financial statements, reports and audit) of the 2006 Act are in force for financial years commencing on or after 6 April 2008. The provisions of the 1985 Act and the Northern Ireland Order are repealed in line with the commencement dates of the 2006 Act, but remain effective until then. One consequence of the 2006 Act applying to Northern Ireland will be that it will in future be correct to refer to UK company law and UK companies. References to 'the Act' cover both the Companies Acts 1985 and 2006.

**8.1.2** The main supporting regulations to the 2006 Act that impact on the subject matter of this chapter (in the order they appear in the text) are:

- SI 2008/409, 'The Small Companies and Groups (Accounts and Directors' Report) Regulations 2008'.

- SI 2008/410, 'The Large and Medium-sized Companies and Groups (Accounts and Reports) Regulations 2008'.

- SI 2008/489, 'The Companies (Disclosure of Auditor Remuneration and Liability Limitation Agreements) Regulations 2008'.

- SI 2007/2612, 'Companies (Fees for Inspection and Copying of Company Records) Regulations 2007'.

- SI 2008/495, 'The Companies (Trading Disclosures) Regulations 2008'.

- SI 2008/373, 'The Companies (Revision of Defective Accounts and Reports) Regulations 2008'.

- SI 2008/374, 'The Companies (Summary Financial Statement) Regulations 2008'.

**8.2**  A company's business letters, other documents and web sites must show the correct information regarding the company's name and other details. Furthermore, a company is under an obligation to keep proper (1985 Act)/ adequate (2006 Act) accounting records and statutory books and to retain them for the appropriate period. From such records, the directors have to prepare financial statements for the company for each financial year. When a company's annual financial statements have been prepared in accordance with the Act's provisions, the company's directors are required to approve, sign and lay the financial statements and reports before the company in general meeting (for financial years beginning on or after 6 April 2008, private companies have no statutory requirement to lay their financial statements before the company in general meeting). The company's directors are required to deliver the financial statements to the company's members and other persons entitled to receive them and the Registrar of Companies.

**8.3**  This chapter considers the responsibilities of a company's directors for the company's financial statements and the role of its auditors. It discusses the accounting period that a company's financial statements must cover and the rules with which companies have to comply when they publish their financial statements. In addition, the rules for preparing summary financial statements and for revising defective financial statements (including defective directors' reports and, for public companies, defective directors' remuneration reports) are dealt with. These aspects of company law, together with the formalities regarding meetings and resolutions, including the right of private companies to elect to dispense (the 1985 Act)/automatically dispense (the 2006 Act) with laying their financial statements before the company at a general meeting, are considered in detail in this chapter.

**8.4**  In many cases where the company or its directors fail to comply with the Act's provisions, they will be liable to a fine and in certain situations, the directors can be imprisoned. These types of penalties apply to criminal offences. Breach of other sections of the Act may involve directors or companies in civil penalties, for instance, section 242A (section 453 of the 2006 Act) imposes such a penalty on companies who breach the rules on the period allowed for filing their financial statements with the Registrar of Companies.

**8.5**  Penalties for breaching the 1985 Act's provisions are set out in full in Schedule 24 to the 1985 Act. In that Schedule the maximum fine for the offences on summary conviction is calculated by reference to the statutory maximum that may be imposed by a magistrate's court. On conviction on indictment there is no limit placed on the fine than can be imposed. The possible period of imprisonment on conviction, where such a penalty can be imposed, is set out in Schedule 24 to the 1985 Act. In the 2006 Act there is no equivalent schedule to schedule 24 to the

1985 Act. Instead, penalties have been embedded in the body of that Act in proximity to the description of the relevant offence.

## Accounting records and statutory books

### General requirements — accounting records

**8.6** A company must ensure that it keeps accounting records sufficient to show the items set out in the Act (see para 8.9). [CA85 Sec 221 (1); CA06 Sec 386(1),(2)]. Part 15 of the 2006 Act replaces the provisions of the 1985 Act concerning accounting records and company financial statements. The majority of this Part of the 2006 Act applies for years commencing on or after 6 April 2008. A company's directors are under an obligation to present to the company's members, once a year, the following:

■ The company's annual financial statements.

■ The directors' report, including the business review (unless the company is entitled to the small companies' exemption).

■ In the case of a quoted company, the expanded business review and the directors' remuneration report.

■ The auditors' report on those financial statements and directors' report and, in the case of a quoted company, on the auditable part of the directors' remuneration report.

[CA85 Sec 241(1); CA06 Secs 437, 438].

For years commencing on or after 6 April 2008, private companies have no statutory requirement to present the annual accounts and reports to members in general meeting, but they are still required to circulate them to members and others entitled to receive them.

**8.7** The company's directors have a duty to prepare annual 'individual accounts' (financial statements) in accordance with the general requirements of the Act and either in accordance with International Accounting Standards (IAS individual accounts) or in accordance with section 226A of the 1985 Act (section 395 of the 2006 Act) (Companies Act individual accounts). [CA85 Sec 226; CA06 Sec 394]. Directors also have a duty to prepare annual 'group accounts' (consolidated financial statements), unless the company falls within the small companies regime or is exempt, in accordance with the general requirements of the Act and in accordance with either International Accounting Standards (IAS group accounts) or in accordance with section 227A of the 1985 Act (section 404 of the 2006 Act) (Companies Act group accounts) [CA85 Sec 227(1),(2); CA06 Secs 399, 403]. Directors must not approve financial statements unless they are satisfied that they give a true and fair view. [CA06 Sec 393]. International Accounting Standards means those as adopted by the European Union. See further from paragraph 8.25.2.

**8.8** There may be other legislation or regulation that specifies the way in which particular companies should keep their accounting records. For example, specific legislation governs charities, registered social landlords, friendly societies, building societies, banks and insurance companies. In addition, a company whose securities are admitted to trading on a regulated market (for example, one listed on the Main Market of the London Stock Exchange (LSE) or on Plus Market's PLUS-listed market) or traded on AIM or on Plus Market's PLUS-quoted market must comply with the UKLA's Listing Rules (LR) and Disclosure and Transparency Rules (DTR) or the AIM or PLUS-quoted Rules respectively.

### Adequate accounting records

**8.9** The Act's requirement that every company must keep accounting records in accordance with section 221(1) of the 1985 Act (sections 386(1),(2) of the 2006 Act). Section 221 of the 1985 Act is summarised below and Counsel had advised on the meaning of certain words and phrases used in section 221 of the 1985 Act, which are shown below in italics. Section 221 of the 1985 Act states that the accounting records must be sufficient to show and explain the company's transactions and, consequently, to:

- Disclose with reasonable accuracy the company's financial position at any time.

- Enable the directors to ensure that any financial statements required to be prepared from the accounting records comply with the Act's requirements (and, where applicable, of Article 4 of the IAS Regulation).

[CA85 Sec 221(1); CA06 Sec 386(2)].

**8.10** A company's accounting records should detail the following:

- The sums of money the company received and expended on a day-to-day basis, together with explanations of the amounts it received and expended. [CA85 Sec 221(2)(a); CA06 Sec 386(3)(a)].

- A record of the assets and liabilities of the company. [CA85 Sec 221(2)(b); CA06 Sec 386(3)(b)].

- If the company deals in goods:

    - Statements of stocks the company held at the financial year end, together with supporting statements of stocktakes.

    - Statements of all goods sold and purchased by the company, in sufficient detail to enable the goods and the buyers and sellers to be identified. (This requirement, however, does not apply to companies carrying on retailing).

[CA85 Sec 221(3); CA06 Sec 386(4)].

**8.10.1** The 2006 Act restates the requirement to keep accounting records and obliges the company to keep 'adequate accounting records'. The 1985 Act requires a company to keep 'proper' accounting records. 'Adequate accounting records' are defined as those that are sufficient to give the information listed in paragraphs 8.9 and 8.10 above. While it appears that the government did not intend the change in wording to represent a substantive change to the requirements for keeping accounting records, it has sparked a degree of controversy and debate. To obtain clarity on this, the Financial Reporting Council (FRC) has adopted a project to assess the implications of the change in wording. The wording of the requirement will, under the 2006 Act, be consistent with the wording of the auditor's obligation to form an opinion as to the adequacy of the company's accounting records (see para 8.31).

*Counsel's opinion on section 221 of the 1985 Act*

**8.11** In March 1992 the Council of the ICAEW issued a guidance statement for members (published in Accountancy April 1992) on the obligation of companies to keep proper accounting records under the Act. This statement was settled in consultation with Counsel. The interpretation of section 221 of the 1985 Act set out below is based on that statement.

**8.11.1** The requirements of Part 15 of the 2006 Act are virtually identical and until or unless the project currently underway by the FRC issues new guidance on the obligation under the 2006 Act, it is reasonable to continue to apply the ICAEW guidance issued in 1992. Hence, directors should continue to keep accounting records as they have for the purposes of the 1985 Act so as to meet their obligation under section 386 of the 2006 Act. [CA06 Sec 386(5)].

**8.11.2** Equivalent references from the 2006 Act have been inserted into the 1992 guidance for the sake of ease, but this does not imply that Counsel's opinion extends to the 2006 Act.

**8.12** Section 221(1) of the 1985 Act (section 386(1),(2) of the 2006 Act) obliges companies to keep accounting records. In addition, a parent company must also take reasonable steps to ensure that its subsidiary undertakings (which are not themselves companies) keep such accounting records to enable the parent company's directors to ensure that any financial statements required to be prepared under Part VII of the Act (Part 15 of the 2006 Act) comply with the requirements of the Act and, where applicable, or Article 4 to the IAS Regulation. [CA85 Sec 221(4); CA06 Sec 386(5)].

*Duty to keep accounting records*

**8.13** To fulfil the directors' duty to keep accounting records, they should be made up of an orderly, classified collection of information capable of prompt retrieval, containing details of the company's transactions, assets and liabilities. An unorganised collection of vouchers and documents is not sufficient. The records must enable a trial balance to be constructed from them whatever their physical form. For example, where information is held in a computer database, the software should be capable of retrieving the appropriate data.

**8.14**   Whether a company is keeping the right kind of accounting records to meet the Act's requirements is a question of fact, which can only be decided on the facts of any particular case. In addition, the prevailing practice of the time in businesses of the type in question would be taken into account in determining whether proper accounting records have been kept. The records must also be sufficient to enable the directors to prepare annual financial statements that satisfy the Act's requirements. [CA85 Sec 221(1) and (4); CA06 Sec 386(2)].

**8.15**   The company's accounting records must be kept in a form that will enable it to comply with the retention period set in the Act. Accounting records must be preserved for six years for public companies or three years for private companies. [CA85 Sec 222(5); CA06 Sec 388(4)]. Furthermore, programmed instructions and supporting documentation in usable form, for example, from a computer database, and any necessary hardware, must be available for the same period.

*Disclosure of the financial position at any time*

**8.16**   In the requirement in section 221(1)(a) (section 386(2)(b) of the 2006 Act), the words 'at any time' emphasise the obligation to keep accounting records up to date. This does not mean that transactions and events must be recorded instantaneously. It is sufficient if they are recorded within a reasonable time, which will depend upon the nature of the business and other circumstances. What is urgent for, say, a bank, may be less so for another business. In addition, records made to disclose the current financial position (including any stock records or memoranda, such as are referred to in paras 8.19 and 8.20) must be retained for the statutory period.

**8.17**   The Act requires the accounting records to be sufficient to disclose with reasonable accuracy, at any time, the company's financial position at that time. In doing so the legislation recognises that it is not practicable to keep accounting records in such a way so that financial statements can be prepared, giving a true and fair view, at every moment during the year. In other words, the Act does not expect a company to be able to reconstruct the financial statements as at any past date at random.

**8.18**   The directors should, at any time, be able to prepare a reasonably accurate statement of the company's financial position from the accounting records. The records should, therefore, contain the primary material on which a set of financial statements would be based. These records need not contain whatever additional items of information it would be necessary to know in order to make those financial statements true and fair. This is because the concept of 'true and fair' is extremely wide and embraces information not necessarily contained within the accounting records themselves. Furthermore, the financial position is not restricted to the cash position, it comprises the assets and liabilities including items such as those referred to in paragraph 8.20 below.

**8.19** What constitutes a sufficient record of stocks will depend on the circumstances, for instance, the materiality of stock and stock movements. Continuous stock records can provide adequate information when they are supported by systematic physical checks. Furthermore, the information gathered from those physical checks would generally also be supplemented by accounting entries recording judgements of the stocks' realisable value and times of possible realisation. These entries may need to be in the form of memorandum as indicated in paragraph 8.20 below. Continuous records are not essential if the stock position can be assessed with sufficient reliability from other accounting records, for instance, interim stocktakings.

**8.20** Provisions for depreciation, bad debts and other losses are often only made at the end of an accounting year, but section 221(1)(a) (section 386(2)(b) of the 2006 Act) requires the records to disclose the financial position of the company with reasonable accuracy at any time during the financial year. This requirement can normally be satisfied if the company has a procedure to ensure that an adequate record is made and retained (for example, by way of memorandum), of any expected loss, liability or contingency material to the assessment of the stocks' current position. This type of memorandum would form part of the accounting records.

*Sums of money*

**8.21** Section 221(2)(a) (section 386(3)(a) of the 2006 Act) states that the accounting records must contain entries from day to day of all sums of money received and expended. The accounting records must, therefore, contain:

- The transaction date.

- The sums received and expended.

- The matters in respect of which the receipt and expenditure took place.

Such entries do not have to be made instantaneously, but must be made within a reasonable time (see para 8.16 above). Where a record of individual receipts is not necessary to explain the transactions (for example, in the daily cash takings of a shop), groups of transactions may be recorded rather than individual ones.

*A record of the assets and liabilities*

**8.22** The accounting records must include details of all the company's assets and liabilities such as debtors, creditors, properties and plant. The records must show the dates of the transactions. Counsel's opinion in 1992 could not have covered 'IAS individual accounts' or 'Companies Act individual accounts', as these were not introduced until 2004 by SI 2004/2947. The following is for information only. For companies preparing 'IAS individual accounts', the IASB's Framework contains definitions of assets and liabilities and rules for their recognition (see chapter 2 of the Manual of Accounting – IFRS for the UK). For companies preparing 'Companies Act individual accounts', the ASB's Statement of principles and FRS 5 contain equivalent definitions and rules (see chapters 2 and 3 of the Manual of Accounting – UK GAAP).

*Statements of stock*

**8.23**   Where companies deal in goods, the statements of stock held at the end of each financial year are part of the accounting records. These statements and any statements of stocktakes supporting the year-end stock summary form part of the accounting records. Any continuous stock records or original stock sheets from a physical stocktake also have to be treated as part of the accounting records.

*Statements of all goods sold and purchased*

**8.24**   Where the company deals in goods, details of goods sold and purchased and of individual buyers and sellers must be recorded. However, this requirement does not apply to sales made by retailers.

*Penalties and disqualification orders*

**8.25**   Failure to comply with the provisions of section 221 of the 1985 Act (section 386 of the 2006 Act) is an offence. [CA85 Sec 221(5)(6); CA06 Sec 387]. Furthermore, under section 9 of the Company Directors Disqualification Act 1986, the extent of a director's responsibility for the company's failure to comply with section 221 of the 1985 Act (section 386 of the 2006 Act) is one of the matters the courts must take into account on an application to disqualify the director (see para 8.76).

**8.25.1**   In an unreported case in March 2000, *R v Anthony Stevens*, the Court of Appeal sentenced a director to three months imprisonment and disqualified him for two years for failing to take all reasonable steps to preserve accounting records of a company under section 222(5) and (6) of the 1985 Act, even though there was no allegation of fraud or dishonesty. The company had gone into liquidation with a deficiency of £376,000. It was accepted that during its trading life accounts had been maintained on a computer system and audited accounts had been prepared for two periods. However, the director had failed to preserve the accounting records and could not hand them over to the liquidator for him to ascertain the full scale of the company's deficiency. Some records were found, but they comprised mainly copies of sales and purchase records and nothing else. Key documents were missing, the sales and purchase ledgers, the cash book, the petty cash book, bank statements, cheque books, paying-in books, VAT returns, correspondence files and records as to assets and liabilities.

*Requirements to prepare financial statements*

**8.25.2**   As noted in paragraph 8.6, the directors of every company are required to prepare (and present to members) annual 'individual accounts' (financial statements) and, where applicable, annual 'group accounts' (consolidated financial statements). [CA85 Secs 266, 227(1); CA06 Secs 394, 399].

**8.25.3** The Act requires the annual individual accounts (financial statements) to be prepared in accordance with the general requirements of the Act and either international accounting standards ('IAS individual accounts') or section 226A of the 1985 Act (section 396 of the 2006 Act) ('Companies Act individual accounts'). [CA85 Sec 226(2); CA06 Sec 395]. International accounting standards are those accounting standards published by the International Accounting Standards Board as adopted by the EU. These standards are also referred to as International Financial Reporting Standards (IFRS). Section 226A of the 1985 Act requires the form and content of Companies Act individual accounts to follow Schedule 4 to the 1985 Act. For companies in the small companies regime, they may use Schedules 8 or 8A to the 1985 Act. For accounting periods beginning on or after 6 April 2008, section 395 of the 2006 Act requires the Companies Act individual accounts to comply with SI 2008/409, 'The Small Companies and Groups (Accounts and Reports) Regulations (2008)', for companies subject to the small companies regime and SI 2008/410, 'The Large and Medium-sized Companies and Groups (Accounts and Reports) Regulations (2008)', for all other companies.

**8.25.3.1** The annual consolidated financial statements must also be prepared in accordance with the general requirements of the Act and either international accounting standards ('IAS group accounts') or section 227A of the 1985 Act (section 404 of the 2006 Act) ('Companies Act group accounts'). Section 227A of the 1985 Act requires the form and content of Companies Act group accounts to follow Schedule 4A to the 1985 Act. For accounting periods beginning on or after 6 April 2008, section 404 of the 2006 Act requires Companies Act group accounts to comply with SI 2008/409 for companies subject to the small companies regime (where the directors choose to prepare group accounts) and SI 2008/410 for all other companies.

**8.25.3.2** Under the 1985 Act, Companies Act accounts are required to give a true and fair view whereas for IAS accounts the requirement under international accounting standards is to achieve a fair presentation. Section 262(2A) of the 1985 Act attempted to give equal meaning to 'true and fair view' and 'fair presentation'.

**8.25.3.3** However, many investor groups were unconvinced and believed 'fair presentation' to be inferior to the 'true and fair' 'gold' standard. To alleviate demands from these investor groups about this and audit quality, the 2006 Act introduces an overarching obligation on directors not to approve financial statements for financial periods starting on or after 6 April 2008, irrespective of whether they are IAS or Companies Act 'accounts', unless they are satisfied that they give a true and fair view of the assets, liabilities, financial position and profit or loss:

■   in the case of the company's individual accounts, of the company;

■   in the case of the company's group accounts, of the undertakings included in the consolidation as a whole, so far as concerns members of the company.

[CA06 Sec 393(1)].

This provision reflects the underlying legal duty already expressed in EU law.

**8.25.3.4** For companies subject to the UKLA's DTR chapter 4, the directors must also make a statement that the financial statements do, in fact, give a true and fair view.

**8.25.3.5** Section 393 of the 2006 Act and the UKLA's DTR reflect the underlying legal duty already expressed in EU law. In 2008 the FRC obtained an opinion from Martin Moore QC on the 'true and fair' concept under the 2006 Act. This, among other things, found that the central conclusions of earlier opinions of Lord Hoffman and Lady Justice Arden on the relationship of accounting standards and the 'true and fair' requirement (see the ASB's 'Foreword to accounting standards') have been endorsed by the courts, which will approach the true and fair requirement in the manner described in those opinions. The 2008 Moore opinion also confirms that the IAS 1 requirement 'to present fairly' is not a different requirement to that of showing a true and fair view, but is a different articulation of the same concept. Furthermore, in June 2005 the FRRP published a legal opinion on the effect of the IAS Regulation on the requirement for financial statements to give a true and fair view in the context of the 1985 Act. The findings in this opinion are still valid under the 2006 Act.

**8.25.3.6** The 2006 Act places a requirement on auditors to take this overarching duty to give a true and fair view into consideration when giving an opinion on the financial statements. [CA06 Sec 393(2)].

**8.25.4** After the first financial year in which the individual and/or group financial statements are prepared in accordance with IFRS as adopted by the EU (the 'first IAS year'), the individual and/or group financial statements for all subsequent years must also be prepared in accordance with IFRS as adopted by the EU, unless there is a 'relevant change of circumstances'. A relevant change of circumstances occurs if, at any time during or after the first IFRS year:

- The company becomes a subsidiary undertaking of another undertaking that does not prepare IAS individual financial statements.
- The company ceases to be a subsidiary undertaking.
- The company ceases to have securities admitted to trading on a regulated market (that is, it de-lists).
- A parent undertaking of the company ceases to have securities admitted to trading on a regulated market.

[CA85 Sec 226(5); CA06 Sec 395(3)(4)].

**8.25.5** The detailed requirements for the format of financial statements prepared in accordance with EU-adopted IFRS are considered in chapter 4 of the Manual of Accounting – IFRS for the UK, whilst the detailed requirements for the format of financial statements prepared in accordance with section 226A of the Act (section 396 of the 2006 Act) are considered in chapter 4 of the Manual of Accounting – UK GAAP.

**8.25.6** The requirements for preparing consolidated financial statements is considered in chapter 24 of the Manual of Accounting – IFRS for the UK and the Manual of Accounting – UK GAAP for consolidated financial statements prepared in accordance with IFRS and UK GAAP respectively.

**8.25.7** Details about which companies are required or permitted to apply IFRS or UK GAAP in their individual and consolidated financial statements are considered in chapter 2 of the Manual of Accounting – IFRS for the UK and the Manual of Accounting – UK GAAP.

*Directors' duty regarding accounting records*

**8.26** Section 8.1 of the ICAEW 2008 Members Handbook contains a statement concerning the main duties and responsibilities of a financial or accounting nature under the 1985 Act that directors owe to their company and its shareholders and others. The statement is prepared principally for the guidance of ICAEW members in business but may also be useful to other members and to directors who are not members of the ICAEW. The 2006 Act codifies the general duties of directors, but does not make any specific reference to their financial and accounting responsibilities. [CA06 Sec 170]. The ICAEW Members Handbook statement has been updated to reflect the 2006 Act and the revised statement is included in the 2009 Members Handbook and can be obtained from the ICAEW's website.

**8.27** The ICAEW's revised statement sets out what, under the 2006 Act, is considered to be best practice rather than what may be acceptable as the legal minimum. It has a section that deals with books of account and other accounting records. The statement gives the following guidance:

> *"69. In addition to the statutory requirement to keep adequate accounting records, the directors have an overriding responsibility to ensure that they have adequate information to enable them to discharge their duty to promote the success of the company."*
>
> *70. The duty to promote the success of the company will involve ensuring that adequate control is kept over its records and transactions, for example:*
>
> *(a) cash;*
>
> *(b) debtors and creditors;*
>
> *(c) stock and work in progress;*
>
> *(d) capital expenditure; and*
>
> *(e) major contracts.*

*The nature and extent of the accounting and management information needed to exercise this control will depend upon the nature and extent of the company's business.*

*71. To restrict the possibility of actions for wrongful trading, directors will need constantly to be aware of the company's financial position and progress, and the accounting records should be sufficient to enable them to be provided with the information required for drawing conclusions on these matters. The directors should also be satisfied that proper systems to provide them with regular and prompt information are in place."*

[ICAEW Members Handbook 2009 Sec 8.1 paras 69-72].

See also paragraph 8.78 below.

**8.28** A company's normal books of account include:

- Cash books.
- Sales day book.
- Sales returns book.
- Purchase day book.
- Purchase returns book.
- Creditors ledger.
- Debtors ledger.
- Transfer journal.
- General ledger.

**8.29** These books may be retained in book form, or on computer or in any other suitable readable form. Other books of account may be used to assist directors in preparing management accounts. These may include, for example, stock books to record continuous stock records used in a company's costing systems.

### Auditors' duties and rights

**8.30** In addition to the requirement that a company must keep accounting records, the company has a duty to appoint an auditor, unless it is a company within the small companies regime, which may be exempt from this requirement. Small companies that meet the total exemption requirements set out in section 249A (section 477 of the 2006 Act) are exempt from having their financial statements audited. Under the 1985 Act small companies that are charities are required instead to obtain the report of a reporting accountant. This special provision regarding small charitable companies is not carried forward in the 2006 Act but reference should be made to the relevant charities legislation for the requirements post April 2008. The 2006 Act introduces a new exemption from audit for public sector companies. These organisations are exempt from an audit under Part 16 if they are not profit making and subject to a public sector audit. [CA06 Secs 482, 483]. In addition, dormant companies that meet the exemption requirements in section 249AA of the 1985 Act (section 480 of the 2006 Act) are exempt from having their financial statements audited.

**8.30.1**  Apart from the exemptions for small companies and dormant companies, a company's auditors must normally examine the company's financial statements to be sent out to the members or, for a public company, to be laid before the company in its general meeting. The auditors must also report to the members on those financial statements. This report must include the auditors' opinion on those financial statements and as referred to in paragraph 8.25.3.3, the 2006 Act places a requirement on auditors to take the directors' overarching duty for their financial statements to give a true and fair view into consideration when giving that opinion. [CA85 Sec 235(1); CA06 Secs 393(2), 495(1)]. In addition, the auditors are required to report on whether the information in the directors' report is consistent with those financial statements. [CA85 Sec 235(3); CA06 Sec 496]. Furthermore, where a directors' remuneration report is prepared by quoted companies, the auditors are required to report to the members on the auditable part of that report. [CA85 Sec 235(4); CA06 Sec 497].

**8.31**  A company's auditors have a duty, in preparing their report, to carry out investigations that will enable them to form an opinion both on whether the company has kept proper (1985 Act)/adequate (2006 Act) accounting records and on whether they have received returns adequate for their audit from those branches they did not visit. [CA85 Sec 237(1)(a); CA06 Sec 498(1)(a)]. The 2006 Act restates the requirements of the 1985 Act, but refers to 'adequate accounting records' and 'returns adequate for their audit' rather than 'proper accounting records' and 'proper returns adequate for their audit'. The government's intention in restating this requirement was not to change the obligations of either the company or its auditors in respect of accounting records, but to provide consistency in the wording of those obligations; the company must keep 'adequate accounting records' and auditors must investigate whether the company has kept 'adequate accounting records'. However, as indicated in paragraph 8.10.1 there is some concern that the restatement has altered the obligations.

**8.31.1**  The auditors should also form an opinion on whether the company's financial statements are in agreement with the accounting records. [CA85 Sec 237(1)(b); CA06 Sec 498(1)(b)]. Also, in the case of a quoted company, the auditors should form an opinion on whether the auditable part of the company's directors' remuneration report is in agreement with the accounting records and returns. [CA85 Sec 237(1)(c); CA06 Sec 498(1)(c)]. If the company has not kept proper (1985 Act)/adequate (2006 Act) accounting records (including returns from branches), or if the financial statements are not in agreement with those records, or if in the case of a quoted company the auditable part of its directors' remuneration report, is not in agreement with the accounting records and returns, then the auditors must state that fact in their report. [CA85 Sec 237(2); CA06

Sec 498(2)]. However, the auditors need make no reference to these items in the audit report if there are no deficiencies to report.

**8.31.2** A new requirement under the 2006 Act applies where the directors have prepared financial statements and reports in accordance with the small companies regime or have taken advantage of the small companies exemption in preparing the directors' report. Here the auditor has to consider whether the directors were entitled to do so and, if in the auditor's opinion they were not, then the auditor has to state this in the audit report. [CA06 Sec 498(5)].

**8.31.3** In addition:

- if the disclosure required by Schedule 6 to the 1985 Act (Schedule 3 to SI 2008/409 for a company in the small companies regime or Schedule 5 to SI 2008/410 for all other companies) of directors' benefits (remuneration, pensions and compensation for loss of office and, under the 1985 Act only, other transactions that benefit directors) is not made in the financial statements: or

- in the case of a quoted company, the information forming the auditable part of the directors' remuneration report does not comply with Part 3 of Schedule 7A to the 1985 Act (Part 3 of Schedule 8 to SI 2008/410) in that report,

the auditors must include in their report, so far as they are reasonably able to do so, a statement giving the required particulars. [CA85 Sec 237(4); CA06 Sec 498(4)].

**8.32** Auditors have a right of access, at all times, to the company's books and accounting records. They also have a right to require such information and explanations from the company's officers or employees, any person holding or accountable for the company's books and accounting records and any person who previously held any of these positions, as they believe they need to perform their duties as auditors. Any such person commits an offence who knowingly or recklessly makes to the company's auditors an oral or written statement that conveys or purports to convey any such information or explanations that are misleading, false or deceptive. Furthermore there is an additional offence if any person fails to comply with the auditors' requests without delay. [CA85 Secs 389A, 389B; CA06 Secs 499, 501].

**8.32.1** A parent company's auditors are also entitled to require information and explanations directly from UK incorporated subsidiary undertakings, their officers, employees, auditors, persons holding or accountable for their books and accounting records and any person who previously held any of these positions, as they think necessary for the performance of their duties as auditors. [CA85 Secs 389A, 389B; CA06 Sec 499(1)(b), (2)(c)(d)]. In respect of overseas subsidiary undertakings, the auditors may obtain the necessary information and explanations indirectly by requiring the parent company to get them from those undertakings, their officers, employees, auditors, persons holding or accountable for their books and accounting records and any person who previously held of any of these positions. The parent company must take all such steps as are reasonably open to it to obtain the required information or explanations from the person concerned. For UK subsidiary undertakings and their personnel, they can be held to have committed either offence in a similar manner to the parent company's own personnel (see para 8.32). In the case of an overseas subsidiary undertaking, it is the parent company and all of its officers that commit an offence if the parent company fails to comply with the auditors' request. [CA85 Sec 389A, 389B; CA06 Sec 500, 501].

*Senior statutory auditor*

**8.32.2**   Section 503 of the 2006 Act specifies that the audit report must be signed by the senior statutory auditor in their own name on behalf of the audit firm and the name of the senior statutory auditor must be stated in every set of published financial statements. The Act says the audit firm identifies this individual according to standards to be issued by the European Commission on implementation of the EU Statutory Audit Directive (2006/43/EC) or if there are no such standards, according to guidance issued either by the Secretary of State or by a body appointed by him. [CA06 Sec 504(1)]. To be identified as a company's senior statutory auditor, an individual must be eligible himself to be appointed as auditor of the company. [CA06 Sec 504(2)]. The nomination of an individual as senior statutory auditor does not change his exposure to liability. [CA06 Sec 504(3)].

**8.32.2.1**   In April 2008, the APB issued such guidance in Bulletin 2008/6, 'The 'Senior Statutory Auditor' under the United Kingdom Companies Act 2006'. This identifies the engagement partner (as defined in auditing standards) for a company's statutory audit as the 'senior statutory auditor' for the purposes of such an engagement.

**8.32.2.2**   The 2006 Act makes provision for the name of the senior statutory auditor (and that of the audit firm) to be omitted from the published financial statements and from the copy delivered to the Registrar of Companies, if the company believes that on publication of the name(s) there are reasonable grounds that the auditor (or audit firm) would be subject to violence or intimidation. [CA06 Sec 506]. The company must apply to the Secretary of State to obtain this relief.

*Criminal offence for auditors*

**8.32.3**   The 2006 Act makes it a criminal offence to knowingly or recklessly sign an audit report that contains any information that is false, misleading or deceptive. [CA06 Sec 507]. The criminal offence extends to omitting from the audit report a statement required in relation to section 498(2)(b) (statement that the company's financial statements do not agree with accounting records and returns), section 498(3) (statement that necessary information and explanations not obtained) or section 498(5) (statement that directors wrongly took advantage of exemption from the obligation to prepare consolidated financial statements). The criminal offence applies to audit reports on financial statements for financial years beginning on or after 6 April 2008; it does not apply to audit reports signed after that date in respect of financial statements for earlier accounting periods.

### *Auditors' limitation of liability agreements*

**8.32.4**   Chapter 6 of Part 16 of the 2006 Act makes it possible for auditors to limit their liability by agreement with the company, but the agreement is only effective to the extent that it is fair and reasonable. Section 534 allows a company to enter into a 'liability limitation agreement' with its auditor that purports to limit the liability owed to a company in respect of any negligence, default, breach of duty or trust occurring in the course of the audit of the company's financial statements. Any such agreement must be approved by the company's members as specified in section 536. Such an agreement is not effective if it attempts to limit the liability to an amount that is not deemed to be fair and reasonable in all circumstances.

**8.32.4.1**   The ICAEW has obtained a legal opinion that confirms that directors can recommend auditor liability limitation agreements to the shareholders without breaching their fiduciary duties. The FRC has issued guidance that sets out factors for directors to consider when assessing the advantages of entering into a limitation of liability agreement and explains which provisions are permitted and the process for obtaining shareholder approval.

**8.32.5** A company that has entered into a limitation of liability agreement will have to disclose details of the agreement either in the notes to the financial statements or in the directors' report. [CA06 Sec 538]. The details to be disclosed are contained in SI 2008/489, 'The Companies (Disclosure of Auditor Remuneration and Liability Limitation Agreements) Regulations 2008', and are:

- The principal terms of the agreement.

- The date of the resolution approving the agreement or its principal terms or, in the case of a private company, the date of the resolution waiving the need for such approval.

[SI 2008/489 Reg 8(1)].

**8.32.6**   The disclosure is required to be made in the notes to the financial statements for the year to which the limitation of liability agreement relates. If the agreement was entered into too late for inclusion in that year's financial statements to be reasonably practicable, then disclosure should be made in the following year's financial statements. [SI 2008/489 Reg 8].

### Form of records

**8.33**   Any register, index, minute book or accounting record that a company is required to keep under the Act may be kept in a bound book or other similar form. If the company maintains any of these items by recording the data otherwise than in a legible form (such as, in the form of a computer record), any duty imposed by the Act to allow the inspection of, or to provide a copy of, that data can be satisfied by reproducing that data in a legible form. But a company must take adequate precautions against falsification of such records. [CA85 Secs 722, 723; CA06 Sec 1135-1138].

**Statutory books and records and their location**

*Accounting records*

**8.34**  A company must keep its accounting records either at its registered office or at such other place as the directors think fit. The records have to be available for inspection by the company's officers at all times. [CA85 Sec 222(1); CA06 Sec 388(1)]. For this purpose, an officer includes a director, or a manager, or the company secretary. [CA85 Sec 744; CA06 Sec 1121].

**8.35**  If the accounting records are kept outside Great Britain (UK under the 2006 Act), then accounts and returns must be sent to and kept at an appropriate place (for example, the registered office) in Great Britain (UK under the 2006 Act), where they should be available for inspection at all times by the company's officers. [CA85 Sec 222(2); CA06 Sec 388(2)]. These accounts and returns should reflect the transactions recorded in the accounting records in order to:

■  Disclose the company's financial position at intervals not exceeding six months.

■  Enable the directors to ensure that the company's financial statements comply with the Act's requirements and, where applicable, Article 4 of the IAS Regulation.

[CA85 Sec 222(3); CA06 Sec 388(3)].

**8.36**  The requirements as regards accounts and returns to be sent to Great Britain (UK, under the 2006 Act) pose no problem for most companies that have branches overseas, because their overseas entities will usually return management accounts to Great Britain (UK) at regular intervals (normally, monthly). These management accounts will generally satisfy the requirements of section 222(3) of the 1985 Act (CA06 Sec 388(3)).

*Statutory books and other records*

**8.37**  The 1985 and 2006 Acts require a company to keep certain statutory books and records and specify where these should be kept. Under the 2006 Act companies are permitted to keep statutory books at either their registered office or any place specified in regulations created under section 1136, which have, at the time of writing, yet to be published. The current rules are considered in the paragraphs that follow, with an indication of those changes known at the time of writing under the 2006 Act.

**8.38** The company's register of directors and register of secretaries (but see para 8.38.1) must be kept at the registered office. Section 1136 of the 2006 Act gives the Secretary of State the power to create regulations specifying other places where these registers may be kept. The register must contain the particulars of the company's directors (including shadow directors) specified by section 289 (sections 163 and 164 of the 2006 Act) and the particulars of the secretaries specified by section 290 of the 1985 Act (sections 277 to 279 of the 2006 Act). Unlike the 1985 Act, from 1 October 2009, the 2006 Act does not require shadow directors to be included in the register of directors. [CA06 Explanatory Notes para 289]. Any changes to the particulars of directors and secretaries must also be notified to the Registrar of Companies. The register must be open to inspection by members for no charge and by others on payment of a fee. [CA85 Sec 288; CA06 Sec 162(5)]. SI 1991/1998, 'The Companies (Inspection and Copying of Registers, Indices and Documents) Regulations 1991', requires a company to make the register, index or document available for inspection for two hours between 9am and 5pm on business days and to permit the person inspecting it to copy any information by taking notes. From 1 October 2008, the fees that the company is permitted to charge for copying documents are limited by SI 2007/2612, 'Companies (Fees for Inspection and Copying of Company Records) Regulations 2007'.

**8.38.1** From 6 April 2008 private companies are no longer required to have a company secretary, although they may continue to have one if they wish. [CA06 Sec 270]. The 2006 Act states that a director or person authorised by the directors can perform anything required to be done by the secretary in the case of a private company that does not choose to appoint a company secretary. [CA06 Sec 270(3)]. Public companies continue to be required to have a company secretary. [CA06 Sec 271].

**8.39** The company's register of charges and copies of all instruments creating such charges must be kept at the registered office or, under the 2006 Act, a place specified in any regulations created under section 1136 of the 2006 Act. [CA85 Sec 407; CA06 Sec 876, 877].

**8.40** The minute books kept at the registered office or, under the 2006 Act, a place specified in any regulations created under section 1136 of that Act, must include minutes of the proceedings of a company's general meetings, decisions of sole members and records of written resolutions. Members are entitled to inspect and request copies of these minutes. [CA85 Secs 382, 382A, 383; CA06 Secs 355, 358].

**8.41** Minutes of meetings of directors must also be entered into minute books, but the Act does not specify a place where these minute books must be kept. [CA85 Sec 382; CA06 Sec 248]. The 2006 Act specifies that minutes should be kept for a minimum of ten years.

**8.42** Under the 1985 Act applicable in Great Britain, the register of members and, where the company has more than 50 members, an index of their names, must be kept at the registered office or can be kept at another location within England and Wales (for companies registered in England and Wales) and Scotland (for companies registered in Scotland) if this location had been notified to the Registrar of Companies. [CA85 Secs 352-354; CA06 Secs 113-115]. Under the 2006 Act, applicable to Great Britain and Northern Ireland, the register of members (and any index) must be kept at the registered office or, at a place specified in any regulations created under section 1136. Members can inspect the register of members at no cost, but others have to pay a fee. [CA85 Sec 356; CA06 Sec 116 and SI 2007/2612]. In addition, the company must provide members and others with a copy of the register if so requested.

**8.43**  If a company keeps a register of debenture holders it must keep this at its registered office or can keep it at another location if this is notified to the Registrar. [CA85 Sec 190; CA06 Sec 743]. Debenture holders have the right to inspect and take copies of the register for no charge, but others are required to pay an inspection fee and a fee to copy the register.

**8.44**  Prior to April 2007, all companies had to maintain a register of directors' interests in shares and debentures of group companies, together with the index. The register and index had to be either kept at the registered office or at the place where the register of members is kept. The Registrar of Companies had to be notified of the place where the register was kept if other than the registered office. [CA85 Sec 325, 13 Sch 25-28]. The register was open for inspection by members without charge and by others on payment of a fee.

**8.44.1**  On 6 April 2007, sections 324 to 326 and 328 to 329 of, and parts 2 to 4 of Schedule 13 to, the 1985 Act were repealed under section 1177 of the 2006 Act. This removed the obligation under the Companies Act to keep the register and, also with the repeal of the requirement under Schedule 7 to the 1985 Act, to make the disclosure of directors' interests in the director's report. However, for companies incorporated in the UK and included on the Official List maintained by the FSA, the UKLA's Listing Rules still require disclosure of directors' beneficial and non-beneficial interests in shares and debentures of group companies. [LR 9.8.6]. In effect, a listed company has to continue to maintain its register of directors' interests and the relief from maintaining such a register lies with unquoted companies.

**8.45**  Shareholders and holders of certain financial instruments are required by the UKLA's DTR to notify companies included on the Official List maintained by the FSA (that is, those companies listed on the Main Market of the LSE or the Plus Market's PLUS-listed market) and those traded on AIM, Plus Market's PLUS-quoted market or other prescribed markets when such holders have control over the exercise of voting rights attached to the shares equal to or more than three per cent of the total voting rights. [DTR 5.1.2]. Such holders also have to notify the company of acquisitions and disposals of shares and qualifying financial instruments (as defined in DTR 5.3) that take the holder across one per cent thresholds above three per cent (for example, four per cent, five per cent etc. up to 100 per cent). Some voting rights are to be disregarded as set out in DTR

5.1.3, such as those attached to shares held by a custodian or a market maker. The rules apply to direct and indirect holdings. A listed public company has to keep the information it receives in a retrievable form as the UKLA's Listing rules require a statement of such holdings to be made in a listed company's annual financial statements. [LR 9.8.6(2)].

**8.45.1**   The 2006 Act gives a public company the ability to investigate holdings of its shares by sending a section 792 notice (previously a 1985 Act section 212 notice) to any person who the company believes or has cause to believe may be interested in its shares or have been so in the previous three years. Similarly, a member may require the company to use its power to serve a notice of information. [CA06 Sec 803]. Public companies must maintain a register of interests disclosed under section 793 of the 2006 Act in the manner required by that section together with an index required by section 810. [CA06 Secs 808, 810]. Listed public companies must make a statement of such information collected under Part 22 of the 2006 Act in its annual financial statements. [LR 9.8.6(2)].

**8.46**   The register required by section 808 of the 2006 Act (and any index) of disclosed interests obtained under section 793 notices must be kept at the registered office or, at a place specified in any regulations created under section 1136. [CA06 Sec 809]. The Registrar of Companies must be informed of the location of the register and any change of that location. [CA06 Sec 809(2)]. Any person can inspect the register at no cost, but copies have to be paid for using the scale prescribed in SI 2007/2612, 'Companies (Fees for Inspection and Copying of Company Records) Regulations 2007'. [CA06 Sec 811]. Persons wishing to avail themselves of the rights to inspect the register and/or obtain copies must apply to the company in the form prescribed in section 811(4) of the 2006 Act.

**8.47**   A company specifies the intended location of its registered office on incorporation, but it may change its registered office by giving notice on the prescribed form to the Registrar. The change of address will take effect on registration of the notice. Documents held at the registered office must be transferred to the new registered office not more than 14 days after the company gives the notice to the Registrar. [CA85 Sec 287(3)(5); CA06 Sec 87].

**Company identification**

*Company name*

**8.48**   A company's name is important not only for identification purposes, but also as a means of informing the public that it has limited liability status. Consequently, the Companies Act contains several requirements regarding disclosure of company names and other details. Other legislation, such as VAT legislation, may require a company to make additional disclosures, like the VAT registration number to be given on certain company documentation.

**8.48.1**   Chapter six of Part 5 of the 2006 Act has replaced the provisions of the 1985 Act relating to company identification and trading disclosures with effect from 1 October 2008. The detailed provisions are included in SI 2008/495, 'The Companies (Trading Disclosures) Regulations 2008'.

**8.49** A company must state its registered name in characters that can be read with the naked eye on all of its business letters, notices and other official publications, order forms, invoices, cheques, receipts, orders for goods, e-mails and other forms of business correspondence and other documents specified in regulation 6 of SI 2008/495. In addition, the company must disclose its registered name on its web site.

**8.49.1** Failure to give the relevant information renders the company and the signatory liable to a fine. Furthermore, if a director or other officer of the company or a person on its behalf signs or authorises the signing of any of the documents referred to below in which the company's name is not mentioned, he is personally liable for the amount specified unless it is duly paid by the company. The documents are a bill of exchange, promissory note, endorsement, cheque or order for money or goods.

**8.49.2** Section 83 of the 2006 Act sets out civil consequences for the company of failure to make the specified trading disclosures required under section 82 of the 2006 Act. The provision for personal civil liability of officers contained in section 349(4) of the 1985 Act is not carried forward.

**8.50** In addition, the following information is required to be stated on all of the company's business letters, order forms and web sites:

- The part of the UK in which the company is registered.

- The company's registered number.

- The address of its registered office.

- For an investment company (as defined in section 833 of the 2006 Act) that it is such a company.

- For a community interest company that is not a public company, the fact that it is a limited company.

- Even if a limited company is exempt under section 30 of the 1985 Act (sections 60 and 61 of the 2006 Act) from the obligation to use 'limited' as part of its name, or a community interest company that is not a public company, the fact that it is a limited company.

[SI 2008/495 Reg 7].

**8.50.1** In the event that a company is being wound up, whether by court or voluntarily – every invoice, order for goods, business letter or order form (whether in hard copy, electronic or any other form) issued by or on behalf of the company, or a liquidator of the company or a receiver or manager of the company's property, being a document on or in which the name of the company appears and all of the company's web sites must contain a statement that the company is being wound up. [Insolvency Act 1986 Sec 188(1)].

**8.50.2** If the business letters, order forms or company web site contain any reference to the amount of the company's share capital, the reference must be to its paid up share capital. [CA06 Sec 82].

**8.51** Business letters on which the company's name appears should not state the name of any of its directors (otherwise than in the text or as a signatory) unless the letter states the names of *all* of the company's individual or corporate directors. [SI 2008/495 Reg 8]. An equivalent provision is expected to be included in the Regulations applicable to overseas companies with a place of business in the UK.

**8.52** A company using the Welsh equivalent of plc or limited (cwmni cyfyngedig cyhoeddus or cyfyngedig) need not state in English that it is a public limited company or a limited company (whichever is appropriate) on all prospectuses, billheads, letter paper, notices and other publications of the company. [Welsh Language Act 1993 Sec 31].

*Memorandum and articles of association*

**8.53** An up to date version of the company's Memorandum and articles of association must be filed with the Registrar of Companies and the directors must ensure that any alteration to it is filed with the Registrar within 15 days of its coming into force. Any alterations to the Memorandum and articles of association must be printed. Where the amendments are minor the Registrar allows, by concession, amendment slips to be inserted, provided these obscure the amended words.

**8.53.1** Under the 2006 Act, the role of the Memorandum is reduced. For companies incorporated after October 2008 it is a historical document reflecting simply the company's formation, with all other matters contained within the company's articles. It will not be possible to amend the company's Memorandum after formation. For existing companies, from October 2008 all provisions contained in the memorandum will be treated as entrenched provisions of the Articles (see para 8.53.2 below). [CA06 Sec 28].

**8.53.2** Under the 1985 Act, companies were able to entrench certain elements of their constitution by including provisions that could not be altered in their Memoranda. Section 22 of the 2006 Act allows companies to provide in their articles that certain provisions may only be amended or repealed if specific conditions are met that are more onerous than a special resolution. Such a provision is known as a *'provision for entrenchment'*. This section of the 2006 Act came into force on 1 October 2008.

**[The next paragraph is 8.55].**

**Annual return**

**8.55**   An annual return gives general information about a company's directors, secretary (where one is appointed), registered office, shareholders and share capital. Under section 363 of the Companies Act 1985 (section 854 of the 2006 Act) every company must deliver to the Registrar at least once in every 12 months an annual return (in the prescribed form) made up to the return date. Part 24 of the 2006 Act restates the provisions of the 1985 Act in relation to the annual return. The commencement date for Part 24 is now 1 October 2009. The return date is a date not later than:

- the anniversary of the company's incorporation; or

- the anniversary of the date of the last return.

**8.55.1**   A company has 28 days from the return date to deliver its annual return to the Registrar. For filing company documents, reference is made in the rest of this chapter to filing at Companies House or with the Registrar. However, it should be noted that the English and Welsh Registries and the Scottish and Northern Irish Registries are mutually exclusive for this purpose and documents sent to the inappropriate Companies House will be rejected.

**8.56**   There are currently two annual return forms: 363a and 363s (the 'Shuttle'). As these forms are named after the relevant 1985 Act section reference, Companies House will issue renamed forms prior to the commencement of the relevant sections of the 2006 Act in October 2009. Where a company has requested a 'Shuttle' annual return, Companies House will, before the company's return date, send out a pre-printed Form 363s. This will be based on information that Companies House already holds on public record, and will include instructions for completion. Most companies use this form. The alternative form 363a, which does not include any pre-printed information, is normally used in connection with secretarial software packages. It is possible to submit an annual return electronically, but approved software is required for this (see para 8.82.9).

**[The next paragraph is 8.60.]**

**8.60**   The company's annual return form, must state the date to which it is made up and contain the following information, (required by section 364) (section 855 of the 2006 Act):

- The name of the company and its company number.

- The address of the company's registered office as currently registered at Companies House.

- The type of company (for example, private company limited by shares), and a description of its principal business activity, by reference to the UK Standard Industrial Classification (SIC 92) Codes.

- The name and address of the company secretary, where applicable.

- Details of each of the company's directors, to include their full name, usual residential address, nationality, date of birth, and business occupation (see also para 8.38).

- The locations of the register of members and the register of debenture holders, if not kept at the registered office.

**8.60.1** The 2006 Act permits directors to file a service address with Companies House for the public record. Home addresses will still need to be supplied to the Registrar; however, they will generally remain confidential. These provisions come into force in October 2009 and the conditions for a service address will be published in due course.

**8.61** A company having a share capital must also give on its annual return:

- Details of the company's issued share capital and each class of shares at the date to which the return is made up.

- The names and addresses of members and their holdings at the return date, the names and addresses of persons who have ceased to be members since the last return date and the number of shares transferred since that date by each member or past member together with the date of registration of the transfers.

**8.61.1** A full list of shareholders is required in the first annual return and then only every third year. In other years, a list of changes in membership and holdings suffices. [CA85 Sec 364A; CA06 Sec 856(5)]. However, companies may provide a full list of shareholders every year. Capital and shareholder information may now be pre-printed on the Shuttle.

**8.61.2** Consistent with other parts of the 2006 Act, from October 2009 the annual return of companies with share capital will be required to contain a statement of capital (CA06 Sec 856(1)).

*Members' lists*

**8.62** The Registrar has specified certain requirements regarding document quality for all documents filed at Companies House. These requirements apply to the lists of shareholders which accompany annual returns as well as to annual financial statements, and are described briefly in paragraph 8.65 below.

*Penalties*

**8.63** A company that does not complete the annual return properly or fails to deliver it to the Registrar within the 28 days of the return date is guilty of a criminal offence. Where the company is guilty of the offence every director and the company secretary will be liable also unless they can show that they took all reasonable steps to avoid committing the offence. [CA85 Sec 363(3)(4); CA06

Sec 858]. Where a public company is late in filing its annual return, it appears that the Registrar may write to its directors at their home address (even if overseas) reminding them of their liability to prosecution.

### Information annexed to annual return

**8.64**  In certain circumstances, a parent company may omit information required by Schedule 5 to the 1985 Act (Schedule 2 to SI 2008/409; Schedule 4 to SI 2008/410) about certain of its subsidiaries, joint ventures and associates if its directors are of the opinion that it would otherwise result in information of excessive length being included its financial statements. [CA85 Sec 231(5); CA06 Sec 410(1)]. Where advantage is taken of this provision, the full information (including that disclosed in the notes to the financial statements and the information excluded from those statements) must be annexed to the company's next annual return. The next annual return is the return delivered to the Registrar after the financial statements in question have been approved under section 233 of the 1985 Act (section 414 of the 2006 Act). In addition, the financial statements themselves must contain a statement that the information is given only in respect of the undertakings whose results or financial position, in the opinion of the directors, principally affected the figures shown in the financial statements (including those undertakings excluded from consolidation). [CA85 Sec 231(6); CA06 Sec 410(2)]. The company and any of its officers who fail to comply with these disclosure requirements are liable to a fine.

### Document quality

**8.65**  All documents that companies are obliged by statute to deliver to the Registrar of Companies (for instance, annual financial statements and lists of members accompanying annual returns and allotment forms) must comply with certain document quality and other requirements. The following requirements remain extant until October 2009 (see para 8.67.1). Each such document must:

■  State in a prominent position the company's registered number. Companies House has requested that the company's registered number is preferably included in bold figures, in the top right hand corner of the document's front page.

■  Comply with the requirements specified by the Registrar, including requirements to enable him to copy or read the document.

[CA85 Secs 706, 707].

**8.65.1**  The Registrar has a duty to make it possible to inspect the information contained in documents delivered to him and for copies to be produced in legible form. As a consequence, the original documents filed must be clear to enable Companies House to scan them to produce an electronic image.

**8.66**  Section 706 of the 1985 Act permits the Registrar to reject documents that cannot be reproduced electronically and to require the company to produce documents that do comply within 14 days. If a replacement complying with the relevant section is not delivered within a further 14 days, the original cannot be treated as having been delivered in time. The following briefly sets out the Registrar's requirements as to document quality:

- Documents should be on A4 size, plain white paper between 80gsm and 100gsm in weight with a matt finish.

- The text should be black, clear, legible and of uniform density.

Further guidance on print requirements and acceptability of documents is available from Companies House.

**8.67** Consequently, as documents should be black on white with a matt finish, glossy annual reports should not be filed at Companies House. Companies House has made it clear that glossy financial statements will be rejected. Companies House considers that a typed version or printer's proof is ideal provided it has been signed, as required, by the company's directors and auditors and, where necessary, by the company secretary.

**8.67.1** Section 1068 of the 2006 Act gives the Registrar the ability to impose requirements as to the form, authorisation and manner of delivery of documents required to be delivered to the Registrar under any enactment. This section of the Act is effective from October 2009, with the exception of sub-section five relating to electronic filing which was brought into force on 1 January 2007 (see para 8.80 onwards below). At the time of writing these requirements have not been created.

### Retention of accounting and other records

**8.68** The Act requires that a private company should keep its accounting records for three years and a public company for six years from the date they are prepared. However, where a company is being wound up, this requirement is subject to any provision with respect to the disposal of records contained in the insolvency rules made under section 411 of the Insolvency Act 1986. [CA85 Sec 222(5); CA06 Sec 388(4)(5)].

**8.69** The period for which companies should keep their business documents in general (including their accounting records) is also governed by various other statutes. These include the Limitation Act 1980, the Latent Damage Act 1986, the Taxes Management Act 1970, the Value Added Tax Act 1994 and the Money Laundering Regulations. These may affect the retention of accounting records in the following ways:

- Limitation Act 1980 (as amended by the Latent Damage Act 1986 and the Consumer Protection Act 1987). This Act limits the time period during which an action can be brought as follows:

- An action on a simple (non-specialty) contract or in tort (other than in respect of personal injuries) — six years from the date when the cause of the action arose, generally the breach.

- An action on a contract under seal (specialty contracts) — 12 years from the date when the cause of the action arose.

- In cases of personal injury, 3 years from:

  (i)   the date the cause of action accrued; or

  (ii)  the date of knowledge (if later) of the person injured.

- In cases of negligence (excluding personal injuries), the time limit for an action for latent damage will be the later of:

  (i)   six years from the date on which the cause of action accrued; and

  (ii)  where the facts are not known at the date the cause of action accrued, three years from the earliest date on which the plaintiff, or any person in whom the cause of action was vested before him, had the knowledge required to bring an action and a right to bring such an action.

- An overriding time limit for actions for negligence (excluding personal injuries) of 15 years is imposed from the date on which there occurred any act or omission:

  (i)   which is alleged to constitute negligence;

  (ii)  to which the damage in respect of which damages are claimed is alleged to be attributable;

- A judgment debt — barred after six years.

- Interest on a judgment debt — not recoverable more than six years after the date on which it accrued due.

- Actions to recover land — 12 years from the date on which the right of action arose.

- Actions to recover trust property, 6 years from the date on which the right of action accrued, save where the claim relates to a fraudulent breach of trust or where the action is to recover trust property from the trustee. In this context, directors are treated as trustees.

- Actions for damages against manufacturers of defective products under Part I of the Consumer Protection Act 1987 — three years from the later of the date of the damage or injury or the date the plaintiff became aware of the cause of the damage or injury (subject to an overall period of ten years from the supply of the product).

- Finance Act 1998, Schedule 18, paragraphs 21, 23 and 27. For corporation tax purposes, a company must keep and preserve its records for a period of six years from the end of the period for which a tax return may be required. Records for these purposes includes records of all receipts and expenses and sales and purchases together with any supporting documents, which includes accounts, books, deeds, contracts, vouchers and receipts. If a company fails to keep and preserve its records, it is liable to a penalty of up to £3,000. HM Revenue & Customs have the power to require a company to produce documents relating to its tax liability.

- Taxes Management Act 1970. HM Revenue & Customs may generally assess within six years of the end of the chargeable period. Where there is fraudulent or negligent conduct, the limit is 20 years. The Taxes Management Act contains two further rules that may be relevant:

  - Production of accounts, books, documents and other information. HM Revenue & Customs may serve notice and require a company to deliver any documents within the company's possession (or power) that contain information relevant to any tax liability.

  - Time limit for recovery of penalties. Recovery of penalties may be commenced at any time within six years after the date on which the penalty was incurred or at any later time within three years of the amount of tax finally being determined on which the penalty is to be ascertained.

- Value Added Tax Act 1994 and VAT regulations. Those companies that are registered for VAT must keep their records and accounts and other related documents for a period of six years unless a shorter period has been agreed with HM Revenue & Customs. These documents must be open to inspection by HM Revenue & Customs at all times. There are special provisions relating to computerised records.

- SI 2003/2682, 'Income Tax (PAYE) Regulations 2003'. For PAYE purposes, employers are under a duty to keep all PAYE records that do not have to be sent to HM Revenue & Customs under the PAYE regulations for not less than three years after the end of the year to which they relate.

- SI 1999/584, 'National Minimum Wage Regulations 1999'. For National Minimum Wage purposes, employers must keep records to establish that an employee is receiving at least the National Minimum Wage. These records must be kept for a minimum period of three years from the end of the pay reference period.

- SI 2000/944, 'Education (Student Loans) (Repayment) Regulations 2000'. For Student Loan purposes, employers must keep a record of all wages sheets, deductions working sheets and other documents and records relating to the calculation and deduction of Student Loan repayments for a period of at least three years after the end of the tax year to which they relate.

- Companies within the scope of the Money Laundering Regulations are required to retain records of the identification of their customers or clients for the duration of the business relationship and for five years after the termination of the business relationship or after an occasional transaction has been completed. Specific transaction records must be retained for five years from the date the transaction was completed, or general transaction records until the business relationship ends.

**8.70** Consequently, the period of time for which a company should keep its accounting records depends primarily on the type of document involved. As a general rule, most accounting records should be kept for a period of at least six years. Some types of document may need to be kept for longer. Further guidance is available in the ICAEW's Practice Assurance Standard 2: Help Sheet 20, entitled 'Document retention' (published in 2007).

**8.71** To overcome the problems of storing paper accounting records, many companies have historically retained them on microfilm, although electronic storage is now more common. For VAT purposes, HM Revenue & Customs generally accepts records stored on microfilm, microfiche or electronically but the company is required to obtain specific permission prior to destroying original documents.

**8.72** In Court proceedings, a Court will normally require the production of the original document. However, where the original document is not available, a court may accept other evidence of the document. A judge has power to admit copies in evidence and to specify the method of authentication. [Civil Evidence Act 1995 Sec 8]. If original company documents are to be copied in hard or electronic format, directors should ascertain that the procedures adopted not only ensure that all records are copied, but also that they are legible, stored safely and capable of being properly authenticated. If accounting records are in a non-legible form any software, etc. necessary to retrieve the information in a usable form should also be retained.

**8.73** As a consequence, before a company destroys any documents that it has microfilmed or stored in digital form, it should consider very carefully whether it should retain the original document. It should remember that certain transactions (for example, a property lease) must be evidenced in writing and, therefore, it should not destroy the original document. Also, before a company destroys any accounting records, it should consult its auditors about whether the microfilmed or digitally stored records will provide them with sufficient audit evidence. The auditors will also want to satisfy themselves that the company imposes adequate controls over the microfilming, or digital recording process.

**8.73.1** Most accounting records are now stored electronically, all but eliminating this problem. However, it is the company's responsibility to ensure the security of their IT systems and that adequate back-up procedures are in place to prevent records from becoming corrupted or destroyed. Further, it is the company's responsibility to ensure that accounting records are accessible when a company changes its accounting software, for example, it will need to ensure that the old software (and hardware, where necessary) is available to enable the historic records to be accessed.

**Penalties**

**8.74** If a company:

- does not keep proper (1985 Act)/adequate (2006 Act) accounting records sufficient to show and explain the company's transactions as required by section 221 of the 1985 Act (section 386 of the 2006 Act); or

- does not keep its accounting records in the places specified in section 222(1) and (2) of the 1985 Act (section 388(1) and (2) of the 2006 Act) or does not keep accounts or returns as required by section 222(3) of the 1985 Act (section 388(3) of the 2006 Act);

then, every officer in default will be guilty of an offence unless he can show that he acted honestly and that the default in question was excusable in the circumstances in which the company's business was carried on. [CA85 Secs 221(5)(6), 222(4); CA06 Secs 389(1)(2), 387]. For this purpose, officer' includes a director, manager or secretary. [CA85 Sec 744; CA06 Sec 1173(1)].

**8.75** Similarly, where an officer fails to take all reasonable steps to ensure that the company keeps these accounting records for the period specified in section 222(5) (section 388(4) of the 2006 Act), (that is three years for private companies and six years for public companies), or intentionally causes any default by the company in observing this obligation, he will be guilty of an offence. [CA85 Sec 222(6); CA06 Sec 389(3)(4)]. Failure to keep accounting records as required by section 221 of the 1985 Act (section 386 of the 2006 Act) may be attributable to negligence, incompetence or poor administration, but in some cases there may be fraudulent intent. Indeed, a number of alleged fraudsters have been convicted of not keeping proper accounting records even if the prosecution failed to convict them on fraud charges.

**8.76** As mentioned in paragraph 8.25, the failure by directors to comply with their obligations to keep accounting records under section 221 of the 1985 Act (section 386 of the 2006 Act) is one of the matters which a Court is required to take into account when considering disqualifying a director for being unfit to be a director. In *Re Firedart Ltd; Official Receiver v Fairall* [1994] 2 BCLC 340, the company's accounting records were held to be deficient in that the cash book, sales day book, the purchase day book and sales and purchase ledgers had not been written up for a period before the winding up order was issued. In addition, there was a lack of supporting vouchers and explanations for the company's expenditure recorded in the cash book. The judge found that failure to make these relevant entries was a breach of section 221 of the 1985 Act and that failure to maintain the evidence sufficient to explain the expenditure was equally a breach of that section.

**8.77** The judge also considered that: *"When directors do not maintain accounting records in accordance with the very specific requirements of section 221, they cannot know their company's financial position with accuracy. There is therefore a risk that the situation is much worse than they know and that creditors will suffer in* *consequence. Directors who permit this situation to arise must expect the conclusion to be drawn in an appropriate case that they are in consequence not fit to be concerned in the management of a company".*

**8.78**  To guard against the possibility of trading whilst insolvent, directors should ensure that not only are proper (1985 Act)/adequate (2006 Act) accounting records kept, but that there are appropriate systems in place to provide the board with up-to-date information about the company's financial position on a regular basis. The absence of up-to-date information will be relevant to whether it was reasonable for directors to allow a company to continue trading at a time when it was unable to pay its debts. [*Re Grayan Building Services Ltd: Secretary of State for Trade and Industry v Gray & Anor* [1995] 3 WLR 1]. Directors may be guilty of wrongful trading if their company continues to trade when it is insolvent and may incur personal liability to compensate the company. [Insolvency Act 1986 Sec 214]. The amount which a director may be liable to contribute is likely to be calculated on the amount by which the company's assets can be seen to be depleted by the director's conduct. [*Re Produce Marketing Consortium Ltd (No. 2)* [1989] BCLC 520 at 553].

**8.79**  Sections 15 to 17 of the Theft Act 1968 impose penalties for obtaining property by deception and false accounting. False accounting includes dishonestly making in an account or record an entry which is misleading, false or deceptive in a material particular or omitting a material particular from such a document. Where a company has committed an offence under section 15, 16 or 17 of that Act with the consent or connivance of any director or other officer, he, as well as the company, will be criminally liable. [Theft Act 1968 Sec 18]. Also, it a criminal offence for any officer of a company to publish, with intent to deceive the company's members or creditors, any written statement or account that he knows is or may be misleading or false on a material point. [Theft Act 1968 Sec 19]. In this connection, any document has to be regarded as a whole. Moreover, even though each part of a statement is strictly true, that statement may be false if it conveys a false impression of the company's position, because material points have been omitted from it.

**8.79.1**  The Financial Services and Markets Act 2000 (FSMA) creates civil penalties for market abuse, which includes insider dealing as one of seven behaviours that can constitute the civil offence. As the level of evidence is lower than in criminal prosecutions. Directors of listed companies are also subject to the Code of Market Conduct issued by the FSA. Criminal offences under the Code of Market Conduct and the FSMA include making a misleading statement and engaging in a misleading course of conduct for the purpose of inducing another person to exercise or refrain from exercising rights in relation to investments. In 2005, two directors of AIT Group Plc received custodial sentences for releasing a misleading trading update statement to the market. This was the first time that the FSA had used its powers to take criminal proceedings under the FSMA.

**Electronic communications with members, others and the Registrar of Companies**

*Introduction*

**8.80**   The 2006 Act permits, as did the 1985 Act, a company to take advantage of electronic communications for:

■   The electronic transmission of financial statements to members and others entitled to receive them (see para 8.117.1).

■   The electronic transmission of summary financial statements to members who have chosen to receive them (see para 8.170.1).

■   The delivery of documents in electronic form to the Registrar (see para 8.82.5).

**8.81**   In addition, the 2006 Act deals with the use of electronic communications in connection with incorporation, sending notices of meetings (see further para 8.253) and the appointment of proxies. It provides for electronic statements to be delivered to the Registrar as an alternative to statutory declarations in specified instances. The overall effect is that the 2006 Act allows any document or information authorised or required by the Companies Acts to be sent or supplied by, or to, a company to be sent electronically. The provisions of the 2006 Act concerning electronic communication are effective from 1 January 2007.

**8.82**   The Institute of Chartered Secretaries and Administrators (ICSA) has produced a booklet, 'ICSA Guidance on Electronic Communications with Shareholders 2007', that provides guidance to companies in the context of the 2006 Act and the FSA rules for companies traded on a regulated market. It sets out 19 points of issues, guidance and recommended best practice. This booklet also deals with the parallel requirements on electronic communications in the UKLA's Disclosure and Transparency Rules (DTR) at DTR 6.1.7 and 6.1.8. Guidance on the interaction between the Companies Act 2006 and the DTR and the transitional provisions for companies with existing electronic communication authorities can be found in the UKLA newsletter, List! 14 (Updated – April 2007).

**8.82.1**   The 2006 Act also permits companies to communicate with their shareholders *via* their web site, provided that the shareholders have agreed to this method of communication. Agreement can be obtained either by passing a resolution or by each member being asked to agree individually. Under the 1985 Act shareholders had to positively opt for this method of communication; under the 2006 Act failure to respond within 28 days can be deemed to be acceptance provided this is made clear to the member in the initial request. Where a member has not agreed to communications in this way, the company may not ask the member again within a period of twelve months. A company must notify its shareholders when it publishes information on its web site, but this notification can be sent by e-mail. Any member of a company or holder of a debenture that has received a document otherwise than in hard copy is entitled to require the company to send a copy of the document in hard copy form. The company may not charge for providing documents in hard copy. [CA06 Sec 1144, 1145 and 5 Sch].

**8.82.1.1** The 'ICSA Guidance on Electronic Communications with Shareholders' 2007' recommends that a company should, where it is aware of the failure in delivery of an electronic communication (and subsequent attempts do not remedy the situation), revert to sending a hard copy of the communication by mail to the recipient's last known postal address. This should be done within 48 hours of the original attempt. The previous version of the guidance also recommended that companies sending their financial statements and reports *via* a web site should, as a precaution, make the documents available on more than one web site through different service providers. This still seems valid advice. The FSA, as the UK Listing Authority, recommends this best practice guide to listed companies.

### *Meaning of electronic communication*

**8.82.2** 'Electronic communication' is defined as a communication transmitted (whether from one person to another, from one device to another or from a person to a device or *vice versa*):

- By means of an electronic communications network (within the meaning of the Communications Act 2003). [CA06 Sec 1259].

- By other means but while in an electronic form.

  'Electronic form' is stated in section 1168 of the 2006 Act to be documents or information sent or supplied in electronic form or electronic copy, that is those sent by 'electronic means' or by any other means while in an electronic form (for example, sending an electronic copy (CD) by post). Documents or information sent in electronic form must enable the recipient to read or see them with the naked eye and retain a copy (and ability only to retain a copy in electronic form, such as sending a text message, is sufficient).

  A document is sent or supplied by 'electronic means' if it is sent initially and received at its destination by means of electronic equipment for the processing (which expression includes digital compression) or storage of data, and entirely transmitted, conveyed and received by wire, by radio, by optical means or by other electromagnetic means. [CA06 sec 1168].

  The glossary to the UKLA's DTR defines 'electronic form' similarly as any means of electronic equipment for the processing (including digital compression), storage and transmission of data, employing wires, radio, optical technology, or any other electromagnetic means.

**8.82.3** 'Communication' includes a communication comprising sounds or images or both and a communication effecting a payment.

**8.82.4** The definitions thus include information provided by the following means:

- Fax.
- CD-ROM.
- E-mail.
- Text message
- On a web site.

### *Delivery of documents generally to the Registrar of Companies using electronic communications*

**8.82.5** Section 1068(5) of the 2006 Act came into force on 1 January 2007 and provides that the Registrar of Companies must secure that electronic communications may be used for the delivery of documents covered by the EU 1st Company Law Directive (68/151/EEC) to the Registrar of Companies. The Registrar of Companies retains the right to reject documents that do not comply with the statutory requirements.

**8.82.6** Companies House has established an electronic filing service that enables the electronic submission of statutory documents by e-mail using specialist software. These documents must comply with the structure approved by the Registrar for electronic submission, as documented in the 'Electronic filing technical interface specification' (copies of which are available from Companies House on request).

**8.83** All documents received *via* the Electronic Filing Service must be authenticated by (or on behalf of) the company with the company authentication code notified to the company by Companies House by post to the company's registered office. It is also possible to incorporate a company electronically.

## Accounting reference periods

### Accounting reference date

**8.84** The accounting reference date of a company is the last day of the month in which the anniversary of incorporation falls. [CA85 Sec 224(3A); CA06 Sec 391(4)]. Its first and subsequent accounting reference periods will, therefore, end on that date, but this date can still be altered in the way permitted by the Act, which is described from paragraph 8.92. Chapter 3 of Part 15 of the 2006 Act restates the provisions of the 1985 Act relating to a company's financial year is in force from 6 April 2008.

**Financial year**

**8.85** The directors of a company must prepare financial statements for each financial year of their company. [CA85 Sec 226; CA06 Sec 394]. A company's first financial year begins on the first day of its first accounting reference period (see para 8.88 below) and ends either with:

■ the last day of the first accounting reference period; or

■ another date determined by the directors that is not more than seven days before or after the end of that period.

[CA85 Sec 223(2); CA06 Sec 390(2)].

**8.86** Subsequent financial years begin with the day immediately following the end of the company's previous financial year and end either with:

■ the last day of its next accounting reference period; or

■ a date determined by the directors not more than seven days before or after the end of that period.

[CA85 Sec 223(3); CA06 Sec 390(3)].

**8.86.1** This permits a company to end its financial year on the same day in the week rather than on the same date, if it wishes to. As a result, although a company's accounting reference period cannot exceed a period of 18 months, a financial year (and consequently the financial statements) may cover a slightly longer period. [CA06 Sec 392(5)].

**8.87** A parent company's directors should ensure that, except where they consider there are good reasons for it, the financial year of any subsidiary undertakings coincides with the parent company's financial year. [CA85 Sec 223(5); CA06 Sec 390(5)]. The financial year of an undertaking that is not a company formed and registered under the Act refers to any period in respect of which a profit and loss account is required to be drawn up either by its constitution or by the law under which it is established. [CA85 Sec 223(4); CA06 Sec 390(4)].

**First and subsequent accounting reference periods**

**8.88** A company's first accounting reference period starts on the date of incorporation and ends on the accounting reference date (which is determined as set out in para 8.84). This period must not be less than six months (but see para 8.98) and must not exceed 18 months. [CA85 Sec 224(4); CA06 Sec 391(5)].

**8.89** Subsequent accounting reference periods will be for successive periods of 12 months. They will start immediately after the end of the previous accounting reference period and will end with its accounting reference date. [CA85 Sec 224(5); CA06 Sec 391(6)]. However, a company may alter its accounting reference date and shorten or lengthen its accounting reference period if it satisfies certain conditions (see para 8.94 below).

**8.90** If a company's financial statements are not made up to its accounting reference date, or a date which is not more than seven days before or after this date, they will be rejected by the Registrar of Companies. The period for laying and delivering the financial statements to the Registrar is calculated by reference to the end of the relevant accounting reference period. [CA85 Sec 244; CA06 Sec 442]. The date a company chooses for its accounting reference date in the first year after incorporation can alter the accounting requirements considerably. The following three examples illustrate this:

**Example 1**

Company A is incorporated on 1 April 20X2 and the company *did not* inform the Registrar of Companies of a change in accounting reference date. The company's accounting reference period, therefore, starts on the date of incorporation (that is, 1 April 20X2), and ends 13 months later on 30 April 20X3. [CA85 Sec 224(3)(b); CA06 Sec 391(4)].

**Example 2**

Company B is incorporated on 1 April 20X2 and the company *did* notify the Registrar of Companies in accordance with section 225 of the 1985 Act (section 392 of the 2006 Act) of a change in its accounting reference date to 31 December, stating that the accounting reference period is to be shortened. Its first accounting reference period starts on the date of incorporation (that is, 1 April 20X2), and it ends nine months later on 31 December 20X2. It cannot extend the period so that it ends on 31 December 20X3 as this would mean a first accounting reference period of more than 18 months. The next accounting reference period is for 12 months, and it ends on 31 December 20X3. [CA85 Sec 224(5); CA06 Sec 391(5)(6)].

**Example 3**

Company C is incorporated on 1 April 20X2 and the company *did* notify the Registrar of Companies in accordance with section 225 of the 1985 Act (section 392 of the 2006 Act) of a change in its accounting reference date to 31 August, stating that the accounting reference period is to be extended. The company's first accounting reference period, therefore, starts on the date of incorporation (that is, 1 April 20X2), and ends 17 months later on 31 August 20X3. If the notice under section 225 (section 392 of the 2006 Act) had stated that the period was to be shortened, it would have ended on 31 August 20X2 (see further para 8.98).

**[The next paragraph is 8.92.]**

*Change of accounting reference date by a listed company*

**8.92** In addition to complying with the requirements of the Companies Act, a company listed in the Official List of the FSA that changes its accounting reference date must notify a Regulated Information Service as soon as possible of any change in its accounting reference date and the new date. [LR 9.6.20R]. If the effect of the change is to extend the accounting reference period to more than 14 months, the company must prepare and publish a second interim or half yearly report. [LR 9.6.21R]. This report must cover either the period up to the old accounting reference date or the period up to a date not more than six months prior to the new accounting reference date. [LR9.6.22G]. The contents of half-yearly or interim reports are dealt with in chapter 31 of the Manual of Accounting – IFRS for the UK.

### Change of accounting reference date by an AIM or PLUS-quoted company

**8.93** The AIM rules require an AIM company that changes its accounting reference date to notify a Regulatory Information Service without delay. [AIMR 17]. The company is then required to contact AIM to discuss the revised reporting table.

**8.93.1** The PLUS-markets rules require a PLUS-quoted company to announce, as soon as possible, any decision to change its accounting reference date. [PLUS-markets rule 49].

### Current and previous periods

**8.94** A company may give notice to the Registrar that it wishes to alter its accounting reference date in relation to the company's current and subsequent accounting reference periods or its previous accounting reference period and subsequent periods. 'Previous accounting reference period' means the period immediately preceding its current accounting reference period. [CA85 Sec 225(1); CA06 Sec 392(1)]. The period may be shortened or extended, but while it can be shortened any number of times without restriction it cannot be extended more than once in five years unless one of the following applies:

- The company is a subsidiary or parent of another EEA undertaking and the new accounting reference date coincides with that of the other undertaking or, where that undertaking is not a company, with the last day of its financial year.

- An administration order is in force under Part II of the Insolvency Act 1986.

- The Secretary of State directs that a company can extend its accounting reference period more often. He can do this in respect of a notice which has been given or which may be given.

[CA85 Sec 225(4); CA06 Sec 392(3)].

**8.94.1** An 'EEA undertaking' means an undertaking established under the law of any part of the UK or the law of another EEA state. [CA85 Sec 225(7); CA06 Sec 392(6)]. An EEA state includes all Member States of the EU and Norway, Iceland and Liechtenstein.

**8.95** The company must state on the notice given to the Registrar to alter the current or previous accounting reference date whether the accounting reference period is to be treated as shortened or extended. However, a company cannot

8037

extend an accounting reference period to make it exceed 18 months, unless the company is subject to an administration order under Part II of the Insolvency Act 1986. [CA85 Sec 225(6); CA06 Sec 392(2)(5)].

**Previous periods**

**8.96**  A notice may not be given to change the accounting reference date in relation to a previous accounting reference period if the period allowed by section 244 of the 1985 Act (CA06 Sec 442) for laying and delivering financial statements in relation to that period has already expired. [CA85 Sec 225(5); CA06 Sec 392(4)]. (The usual period under the 1985 Act within which a company must deliver is ten months for a private company and seven months for a public company, calculated from the end of the accounting reference period.)

**8.96.1**  Section 442 of the 2006 Act shortens the period allowed for filing financial statements with the Registrar. For financial years beginning on or after 6 April 2008, the period within which financial statements must be filed for a private company is nine months and six months for a public company from the end of the accounting reference period.

**8.97**  The timing of the notice a company gives to the Registrar of a change in its accounting reference date is crucial to the acceptance of that new date, as the notice must reach the Registrar within the period allowed. Consider the following example, which is based on the filing date requirements of the 2006 Act:

**Example**

A private company's accounting reference date is 31 December. The company last completed and filed its financial statements for the 12 month period ended 31 December 20X1. On 27 September 20X3, the company gives notice to the Registrar that it wishes to change its accounting reference date to 30 June in relation to its previous accounting period ended 31 December 20X2.

The company would then appear to have two choices: it may give notice either to lengthen its accounting reference period and prepare financial statements for the 18 month period to 30 June 20X3 provided the notice is not ineffective under section 225(4) (section 392(3) of the 2006 Act) (see para 8.94). Alternatively, it may seek to shorten its accounting reference period and prepare financial statements for the six month period to 30 June 20X2. However, if it does the latter, the company will have only three months from the date that the statutory form 225 is filed with the Registrar to lay the financial statements before the members in general meeting and file them with the Registrar (see para 8.144). [CA85 Sec 244(4); CA06 Sec 442(4)].

If the facts in the example given above remained the same, except that the company gave notice of the change of accounting reference date to the Registrar on 1 October 20X3, then this notice would not take effect. The reason for this is that the period for filing is on the basis of the existing accounting reference date in relation to the previous accounting reference period (that is, 31 December 20X2), would have already expired on 30 November 20X3 (being nine months from the accounting reference date) (see para 8.96 above).

**8.98** A company's first accounting reference period cannot be less than six months [CA85 Sec 224(4); CA06 Sec 391(5)]. However, the company's accounting reference date set at incorporation is one year (see para 8.84.1) and the Act does permit the company to reduce it by giving notice to the Registrar under section 225(1) of the 1985 Act (section 392(1) of the 2006 Act). The procedure is illustrated in the following example, which is based on the filing date requirements under the 1985 Act:

**Example**

Company D, a private company, is incorporated on 1 April 20X2, and its first accounting period will end on the last calendar day of the month in which the first anniversary of its incorporation falls, that is 30 April 20X3, 13 months later. It then decides that seasonal factors require an accounting reference date of 30 June. The company may, at any time within the period to 1 January 20X4 (that is, the earlier of 21 months from the date of incorporation (see para 8.142) and nine months from the default accounting reference date), give notice to the Registrar that it wishes to alter its current accounting reference date to end on 30 June 20X2, which gives a reference period of three months. The financial statements for 30 June 20X2 would then fall due for filing on either 30 April 20X3 (that is, nine months from the period end) or three months after the filing of statutory form 225, whichever is the later (see para 8.144).

## Preparing and approving financial statements

### Directors' duty

**8.98.1**   The directors have a duty to prepare their company's individual financial statements each financial year in accordance with the general requirements of the Companies Act and either in accordance with International Accounting Standards as adopted by the EU ('IAS individual accounts') or section 226A of the 1985 Act (section 396 of the 2006 Act) ('Companies Act individual accounts').

**8.98.2**   The formats and contents for Companies Act individual financial statements are set out in Schedule 8 to the 1985 Act for companies in the small companies regime and Schedule 4 to the 1985 Act for all other companies except banks and insurance companies. The formats for the latter two types of company are set out in Schedules 9 and 9A to the 1985 Act respectively, For accounting periods commencing on or after 6 April 2008, the format and contents for companies in the small companies regime is set out in Schedule 1 to SI 2008/409, 'The Small Companies and Groups (Accounts and Reports) Regulations 2008'. Similarly, the format and contents for other companies, banks and insurers are set out in Schedules 1, 2 and 3 respectively to SI 2008/410, 'The Large and Medium-sized Companies and Groups (Accounts and Reports) Regulations 2008'. Where the provisions of the 2006 Act are consistent with the 1985 Act, dual references have been given in the paragraphs that follow. Any changes introduced by the 2006 Act are included where relevant. All references to the 2006 Act or its supporting regulations are effective for financial statements for financial years beginning on or after 6 April 2008, unless otherwise stated.

**8.98.3** 'Companies Act individual accounts' (financial statements) must comply with UK accounting standards issued by the ASB. Companies subject to the small companies regime may use instead the Financial Reporting Standard for Smaller Entities (FRSSE) issued by the ASB.

**8.99** The form and content of 'IAS individual accounts' (financial statements) must be consistent with IAS 1 as adopted by the EU and comply with the requirements of IFRSs and IASs adopted by that body (see further chapter 2 of the Manual of Accounting – IFRS for the UK).

*Company individual financial statements*

**8.100** In preparing 'IAS individual accounts' (financial statements), the directors must ensure that:

■ They comply with the general requirements of the Act, including the requirement that they give a true and fair view of the assets, liabilities, financial position and profit or loss. [CA06 Sec 393]. The general requirements of the Act that continue to apply to companies preparing IAS accounts are set out in 'Guidance for British Companies on proposed changes to the accounting and reporting provisions of the Companies Act 1985 issued by the DTI (now known as BERR) in November 2004 and revised in 2005. For periods commencing on or after 6 April 2008, 'Guidance for UK companies on accounting and reporting: requirements under the Companies Act 2006 and the application of the IAS Regulation', published by BERR in June 2008. (See further chapter 2 of the Manual of Accounting – IFRS for the UK.)

■ They comply with IFRS and IASs as adopted by the EU.

■ The information concerning related undertakings (CA85 section 231; CA06 section 409), details of off-balance sheet arrangements (CA06 section 410A), particulars of staff (CA85 section 231A; CA06 section 411) and emoluments and other benefits of directors (CA85 section 232; CA06 section 412) is given in the notes to the financial statements.

**8.100.1** In preparing 'Companies Act individual accounts' (financial statements), the directors must also ensure that:

■ They comply with the general requirements of the Act, including the requirement that they give a true and fair view of the assets, liabilities, financial position and profit or loss. [CA06 Sec 393]. (See further chapter 2 of the Manual of Accounting – UK GAAP).

■ The company's individual financial statements comply with Schedules 4, 9 or 9A to the 1985 Act (Schedules 1, 2 or 3 to SI 2008/410) (as appropriate for companies, banks or insurers respectively) or, for companies in the small companies regime, with Schedule 8 to the 1985 Act (Schedule 1 to SI 2008/

409) as to the form and content of the balance sheet and profit and loss account and the additional information to be provided by way of notes.

■ The information concerning related undertakings (CA85 section 231; CA06 section 409), details of off-balance sheet arrangements (CA06 section 410A), particulars of staff (CA85 section 231A, CA06 section 411) and emoluments and other benefits of directors (CA85 section 232; CA06 section 412) is given in the notes to the financial statements. Companies subject to the small companies regime or that qualify as medium-sized company have full or partial exemptions from these disclosures.

■ If compliance with the provisions of that Schedule and the other provisions of the Act would not be sufficient to give a true and fair view, the necessary additional information is included in the financial statements or in a note to them. [CA85 Sec 226A(4); CA06 Sec 396(4)].

■ If, in special circumstances, compliance with any of those provisions is inconsistent with the requirement to give a true and fair view, they must depart from that provision to the extent necessary to give a true and fair view. However, if they do so, the particulars of the departure, the reasons for it and its effect must be given in a note to the financial statements (see further chapter 2 of the Manual of Accounting – UK GAAP). [CA85 Sec 226A(5); CA06 Sec 396(5)].

[CA85 Secs 226(2)-(6); CA06 Sec 396].

The form and content of financial statements are discussed in more detail in chapter 4 of the Manual of Accounting – IFRS for the UK and the Manual of Accounting – UK GAAP.

### Company consolidated financial statements

**8.101** Where at the end of a financial year a company is a parent company, its directors must prepare consolidated financial statements for the company and its group. Like individual financial statements, these must be prepared in accordance with the general requirements of the Act and either in accordance with International Accounting Standards as adopted by the EU ('IAS group accounts') or section 227A of the 1985 Act (section 404 of the 2006 Act) ('Companies Act group accounts'). In the latter case, this means complying with the form and content of Schedules 4 and 4A, or 9 or 9A to the 1985 Act (Schedule 1 and Part 1 of Schedule 6, or Schedule 2 and Part 2 of Schedule 6, or Schedule 3 and Part 3 of Schedule 6 to SI 2008/410) for companies, banks or insurers. [CA06 Secs 399, 404].

**8.101.1** In preparing consolidated financial statements, directors must ensure that they comply, as appropriate, with the matters outlined in paragraphs 8.100 (for IAS group accounts) and 8.100.1 (for Companies Act group accounts).

**8.101.2** Directors of companies in the small companies regime have the option to prepare group accounts. [CA06 Sec 398]. Companies Act group accounts must follow the form and content prescribed in Schedule 6 to SI 2008/409. IAS group accounts must be consistent with the requirements of EU-adopted IAS 1.

**8.101.3**  Directors of medium-sized companies that are parent companies at the end of a financial year must prepare consolidated financial statements for the company and its group for financial years beginning on or after 6 April 2008. The financial statements must include comparative numbers for the group for the previous financial year, even though consolidated financial statements were not required for that year. For example, the consolidated financial statements for the year ending 31 December 2009 must include comparative consolidated numbers for the year ended 31 December 2008. Companies Act group accounts must follow the form and content prescribed by Schedule 6 to SI 2008/410 as modified by Regulation 4(2) of that SI. [SI 2008/410 6 Sch para 1(1)]. IAS consolidated financial statements must be consistent with the requirements of EU-adopted IAS 1.

**8.101.4**  The form and content of consolidated financial statements is considered further in chapter 4 of the Manual of Accounting – IFRS for the UK or the Manual of Accounting – UK GAAP. A parent company's individual profit and loss account may be omitted from its published consolidated financial statements in certain situations (see para 8.106 below).

### Approval, signing, publishing and filing

**8.102**  The board of directors has to approve the company's financial statements and they must be signed on the board's behalf by a company director signing the company's balance sheet. [CA85 Sec 233(1)(2); CA06 Sec 414(2)]. There is no legal requirement for the consolidated balance sheet to be signed in the same way, but this procedure is regarded as good practice. Every copy of the balance sheet laid before a company in general meeting, or otherwise circulated, published or issued, must state the name of the person who signed the balance sheet on behalf of the board. [CA85 Sec 233(3); CA06 Sec 433(1)].

**8.102.1**  The copy of the company's balance sheet that is delivered to the Registrar of Companies must state the name of the person who signed it on behalf of the board and must be signed on behalf of the board by a director of the company. [CA85 Sec 233(4); CA06 Secs 444(6), 445(5), 446(3), 447(3)]. These provisions apply irrespective of whether the company is a small company filing abbreviated or shorter-form financial statements. Companies House has stated that a photocopy or faxed signature is not acceptable in any circumstances. The requirement for signature is expected to be repealed with effect from 1 October 2009 and Companies House will, in due course, issue rules for the authentication of documents after that date.

**8.102.2**  For companies entitled to the small companies exemption in relation to the directors' report, section 444A (inserted by Regulation 6 of SI 2008/393 'The Companies Act 2006 (Amendment)(Accounts and Reports) Regulations 2008') has no requirement for a physical signature on the balance sheet in the copy of the company's annual accounts filed with the Registrar. The copy of the balance sheet must state the name of the person who signed it on behalf of the board. [CA06 Sec 444A(3)].

**8.103** In addition to the legal requirements in section 233 of the 1985 Act (section 414 of the 2006 Act) mentioned above, IAS 10, 'Events after the balance sheet date', and FRS 21, 'Events after the balance sheet date', both require that the financial statements should disclose the date on which the financial statements were authorised for issue and who gave this authorisation. [IAS 10 para 17, FRS 21 para 17]. The date of authorisation will normally be the date on which the board of directors formally approves a set of documents as the financial statements. The date of approval for consolidated financial statements is the date on which the board of directors of the parent company formally approve them.

**8.104** The requirements of both the Act and IAS 10 or FRS 21 will be satisfied if the minutes of the board meeting at which the financial statements are considered record the directors' approval of the financial statements. The financial statements would then include, at the foot of the balance sheet, a note along the following lines:

**Example**

The financial statements on pages X to Y were approved by the board of directors on (date) and are signed on its behalf by:

(Name)

Director

**8.105** The pages of the financial statements that are approved would normally include, where applicable, any supplementary accounts or other financial statements (such as a value added statement or current cost information). The reason for this is that the directors should acknowledge their responsibility for all of the financial information that is presented at the meeting.

**8.106** Where a parent company prepares consolidated financial statements in accordance with the Act (whether they are 'IAS group accounts' or 'Companies Act group accounts'), it is not required to include its own profit and loss account in the group's published consolidated financial statements. Although not published, the company's individual profit and loss account must be prepared and then approved by the board of directors and signed on behalf of the board by a director of the company in accordance with section 233(1) of the 1985 Act (section 414(1) of the 2006 Act). This should occur at the same time as the rest of the financial statements are approved. Also the financial statements must disclose that the exemption applies. [CA85 Sec 230; CA06 Sec 408]. The notes to these financial statements need not contain the information on the parent company's employee numbers and costs. [CA06 Sec 408(2)]. In addition, for Companies Act group accounts, the notes to the consolidated financial statements need not contain the information specified by paragraphs 65 to 69 of Schedule 1 to SI 2008/

8043

410 (information supplementing the company's individual profit and loss account). [SI 2008/410 Reg 3(2)].

**8.106.1** Omission of the company's individual profit and loss account from a set of published IAS financial statements through use of the publication exemption seemingly causes a tension with the requirements of IAS 1 and the compliance statement required by that standard and also section 227B of the 1985 Act (section 406 of the 2006 Act). The EC and BERR have stated that the omission as provided for by European Company Law Directives and UK domestic company law does not breach IAS 1 or the company law requirement. BERR says that the accounting framework that has been used is IAS as adopted by the EU as applied in accordance with the provisions of the 1985 Act (2006 Act).

### Liability for approving defective financial statements

**8.107** All financial statements (including consolidated financial statements) that are approved by the board must comply with the requirements of the Act and, where applicable, Article 4 of the IAS Regulation (see para 8.98.1 onwards). If the financial statements do not comply with the Act, every director of the company who is party to their approval and who knows that they do not comply, or is reckless as to whether they comply, is guilty of an offence. For this purpose, every director of the company at the time the financial statements are approved is taken to be a party to their approval unless the director shows that he took all reasonable steps to prevent their approval. [CA85 Sec 233(5); CA06 Sec 414(4)(5)].

**8.108** There is, however, a statutory procedure (discussed in para 8.214) under which the directors can voluntarily revise any financial statements that they subsequently discover do not comply with the Act. This procedure also applies to a defective directors' report and to a defective directors' remuneration report.

### Liability if balance sheet is unsigned

**8.109** The company and each of its officers that are in default will be guilty of an offence if either of the following applies:

■ A copy of the balance sheet delivered to the Registrar has not been signed by a director as required by section 233 (section 414 of the 2006 Act) (see para 8.102).

■ A copy of the balance sheet has been laid before the company in general meeting or is otherwise circulated, published or issued:

  ■ without the balance sheet being signed as required by section 233 (section 414 of the 2006 Act) (see para 8.102); or

  ■ without the required statement of the signatory's name being included (see para 8.102).

[CA85 Sec 233(6); CA06 Sec 433].

**8.110** In addition to the liabilities described in the paragraph above, delivering the financial statements to the Registrar of Companies without a signature on the balance sheet is likely to trigger a late filing penalty if the directors cannot rectify the omission before the filing deadline.

**8.111** The inclusion of a directors' responsibility statement in a company's financial statement was first recommended by the Cadbury Report in 1993 and subsequently included in the Combined Code for listed companies. The Cadbury recommendation to include a directors' responsibility statement has been effectively extended to unlisted companies by ISA (UK & Ireland) 700, 'The auditor's report on financial statements'. This requires the auditors' report to distinguish between the auditors' responsibilities and those of the directors. Where a company's financial statements or directors' report do not include an adequate description of directors' relevant responsibilities, the auditors' report should include a description of those responsibilities. Directors' responsibility statements are dealt with further in chapter 4 of this Manual.

**Directors' duties regarding their directors' report**

*Preparation*

**8.112** The directors must prepare a directors' report for each financial year. The content of the directors' report is dealt with in chapter 3.

**8.113** It is an offence for the directors' report not to comply with the Act's provisions regarding its preparation and content. In this respect, each person who was a director immediately before the end of the period for laying and delivering the financial statements is guilty of an offence, unless he can show that he took all reasonable steps in trying to secure compliance with the Act's provisions. [CA85 Sec 234(5); CA06 Sec 415(4)].

**8.113.1** It is also an offence to make a false statement about disclosure to the auditors and every director is liable who knew it was false, or was reckless as to whether it was false and failed to take reasonable steps to prevent the report from being approved. [CA85 Sec 234ZA(6); CA06 Sec 418(5)].

*Approval and signing*

**8.114** The directors' report must be approved by the board of directors and be signed on the board's behalf by a director or by the company secretary (where one is appointed). [CA85 Sec 234A(1); CA06 Sec 419]. The approval and signing of directors' reports are considered further in chapter 3.

**[The next paragraph is 8.116].**

**8.116** If the directors' report is either laid before the company (or otherwise circulated, published or issued) without having been signed or without the signatory's name being stated, or delivered to the Registrar without being signed, the company and every officer who is responsible is guilty of an offence. [CA85 Sec 234A(4); CA06 Sec 433(4)]. However, the directors may revise any report they discover to be defective under the procedure for the revision of defective financial statements (see para 8.214).

**Directors' duties regarding directors' remuneration report**

*Preparation*

**8.116.1**   The directors of a quoted company (as defined in section 262(1) of the 1985 Act (section 385 of the 2006 Act) must, for each financial year, prepare a directors' remuneration report. A quoted company does not included companies admitted to trading on the LSE's AIM or Plus Market's PLUS-quoted market. The scope and content of the remuneration report is dealt with in chapter 5.

**[The next paragraph is 8.116.5.]**

**8.116.5**   It is an offence for the directors' remuneration report not to comply with the Act's provisions regarding its preparation and content. In this respect, each person who was a director of the quoted company immediately before the end of the period for laying and delivering the financial statements and reports is guilty of an offence, unless he can show that he took all reasonable steps for securing compliance with the requirements in question. [CA85 Sec 234B(3),(4); CA06 Sec 420(2)].

**8.116.6**   It is the duty of any director of a company, and any person who has at any time in the preceding five years been a director of the company, to give notice to the company of such matters relating to himself as may be necessary for the purposes of Parts 2 and 3 of Schedule 7A to the 1985 Act (Parts 2 and 3 of Schedule 8 to SI 2008/410). A person who does not comply with this requirement, commits an offence and is liable to a fine. [CA85 Sec 234B(5)(6); CA06 Sec 421].

*Approval and signing*

**8.116.7**   The directors' remuneration report must be approved by the board of directors and be signed on its behalf by a director or by the company secretary. [CA85 Sec 234C(1); CA06 Sec 422(1)].

**8.116.8**   In addition, every copy of the directors' remuneration report that is laid before the company in general meeting, or that is otherwise circulated, published or issued, must state the name of the person who signed it on the board's behalf. The copy of the directors' remuneration report that is delivered to the Registrar must be signed on the board's behalf by a director or the company secretary. [CA85 Sec 234C(2)(3); CA06 Secs 433(1)(3), 447(3)].

**8.116.9**   If the directors' remuneration report is either laid before the company (or otherwise circulated, published or issued) without having been signed or without the signatory's name being stated, or delivered to the Registrar without being signed, the company and every officer who is responsible is guilty of an offence. [CA85 Sec 234C(4); CA06 Sec 433(4)(5)].

**Directors' 'safe harbour' provision for directors' reports and remuneration reports**

**8.116.10** With effect from 20 January 2007, the 2006 Act introduced a new statutory liability regime for directors in respect of narrative reporting. [CA06 Sec 463]. This effectively incorporates a 'safe harbour' for information in the directors' reports (including the business review) under section 417 of the 2006 Act, the directors' remuneration reports under section 420 of the 2006 Act and any summary financial statement, so far as it is derived from either of these reports. A director is not subject to any liability to a *person other than the company* resulting from reliance, by that person or another, on information in such a report. A director is liable to compensate the company for any loss suffered by it as a result of any untrue or misleading statement in such a report, or the omission from such a report of anything required to be included in it. However, the director is liable only if he knew the statement to be untrue or misleading, or was reckless as to whether it was untrue or misleading, or he knew the omission to be dishonest concealment of a material fact. An explicit statement is not required in the annual report for the 'safe harbour' protection to be invoked.

**8.116.11** Under the transitional provisions in the SI 2006/3428 'Companies Act 2006 (Commencement No 1, Transitional Provisions and Savings) Order 2006', the 'safe harbour' also covers directors' reports, directors' remuneration reports and summary financial statement published on or after 20 January 2007 under the Companies Act 1985. [SI 2006/3428 5 Sch para 3].

**Persons entitled to receive financial statements**

**8.116.12** Every member of the company, every debenture holder of the company and every person who is entitled to receive notice of general meetings is entitled to receive a copy of each of the following documents for the financial year:

- any person nominated by a member under a power in its articles of association. [CA06 Sec 145]; or

- for public companies whose shares are admitted to trading on at least one regulated market, those persons that have been nominated by registered shareholders to enjoy information rights, such as indirect investors whose investments are held through intermediaries. [CA06 Sec 146],

is entitled to receive a copy of each of the following documents for the financial year:

- The company's annual financial statements (which per section 262 of the 1985 Act (section 471 of the 2006 Act) comprise the individual financial statements (see para 8.98.1) and, if applicable, consolidated financial statements (see para 8.101)).

- The directors' report.

- In the case of a quoted company, the directors' remuneration report.

■ The auditors' report on those financial statements and the directors report and, in the case of a quoted company, on the auditable part of the directors' remuneration report.

[CA85 Sec 238(1),(1A); CA06 Sec 423(1)].

**8.116.13** For a public company, a copy must be sent to them not less than 21 days before the date of the general meeting at which the financial statements and reports are to be laid. [CA85 Sec 238(1); CA06 Sec 424(3)].

**8.116.14** Under the 2006 Act, private companies have no statutory requirement to hold an AGM and lay financial statements before a general meeting. They are required to send out their financial statements and reports to every member, debenture holder and other entitled persons no later than the earlier of the actual date of delivery to the Registrar and the filing deadline. [CA06 Secs 423(1), 424(2)].

**8.117** In the case of both public and private companies, certain persons do not need to be sent copies and they are specified in section 238(2) and (3) of the 1985 Act (section 423(2) of the 2006 Act).

### Financial statements transmitted electronically

**8.117.1** Companies are permitted to send copies of the documents listed in paragraph 8.116.13 (referred to as 'financial statements and reports') electronically (instead of sending paper copies) to members, debenture holders and others entitled to receive them (referred to collectively as 'members'). [CA85 Sec 239(2A); CA06 Sec 1144(2), 5 Sch 5 Part 3]. Thus a company may either:

■ use electronic communications to send a copy of the full financial statements and reports to the address notified to the company by a member for that purpose; or

■ make a copy of the full financial statements and reports available to a member on a web site provided:

  ■ the company and the member have agreed to his having access to the financial statements and reports in question *via* a web site (instead of being sent in paper form); and

  ■ that member is notified, in the manner agreed with the company of:

    ■ the publication of the financial statements and reports on the web site;

    ■ the address of that web site; and

    ■ where and how on the agreed web site they may be accessed (for example, the format of the documents and the software required to read them).

**8.117.1.1** The 2006 Act introduces a new provision to require quoted companies to publish their financial statements on a web site. [CA06 Sec 430]. The financial statements and reports must be made available until the financial statements and reports for the company's next financial year are made available in accordance with this section.

**8.117.2** 'Address' means any number or address used for the purposes of electronic communications. Electronic communication will include information provided by fax, CD-ROM, e-mail, text message or from a web site (see para 8.82.3 for the definition).

**8.117.3** Where a company's financial statements and reports for financial years beginning before 6 April 2008 are accessed from a web site, they will only be treated as 'sent' as required by section 238 of the 1985 Act if the following conditions are satisfied:

■ they are published on the web site throughout the period beginning at least 21 days before the company's general meeting and ending with the conclusion of that meeting; and

■ the members are notified as mentioned in paragraph 8.82.1 above not less than 21 days before the meeting.

However, the proceedings of the meeting will not be invalidated if the failure to publish in this way is wholly attributable to circumstances that it would not be reasonable to have expected the company to prevent or avoid.

**8.117.3.1** Where a company's financial statements and reports for financial years beginning on or after 6 April 2008 are accessed from a web site, they will only be treated as 'sent' (as required by section 423 of the 2006 Act) if they are published on the web site throughout the period beginning at least 28 days following the notification to members of their availability (see para 8.117). However, the proceedings of the meeting will not be invalidated if the financial statements and reports were published in this way for part of the required period and the failure to publish for the remainder of the period is wholly attributable to circumstances that it would not be reasonable to have expected the company to prevent or avoid. [CA06 5 Sch 14].

**8.117.3.2** In addition to the right that a member has to be sent a copy of the annual financial statements and reports (as mentioned in para 8.117 above), every member and debenture holder of the company is entitled (on demand and without charge) to be given or sent by electronic communication, within seven days, a further copy of the company's last financial statements and reports. [CA85 Sec 239(1)-(3); CA06 Sec 432(1)(2)]. The electronic communication must be sent to the address the member or debenture holder has notified to the company for that purpose. [CA85 Sec 239(2A); CA06 Sec 1144(2) and 5 Sch Part 3].

**8.117.3.3** Failure to comply with the provisions of section 238 of the 1985 Act (CA06 Secs 423, 424) to send a copy of the financial statements and reports to members will render the company and every officer who is in default guilty of an offence. [CA85 Sec 238(5); CA06 Sec 425]. Failure to supply a member on request with an additional copy of the financial statements and reports within the seven days, will render the company and every officer who is in default guilty of an offence. [CA85 Sec 239(3); CA06 Sec 432(4)].

**8.117.3.4**  Sections 423 (duty to circulate annual reports and accounts) and 424 (time allowed for sending out copies of annual accounts and reports) of the 2006 Act provide similar timing as indicated in paragraph 8.117.3. However, these sections need to be read in conjunction with the new company communications provisions in sections 1143 to 1148 of, and Schedules 4 and 5 to, the 2006 Act. These sections and schedules make new general provision about communications, including electronic and web site communications for the Companies Acts as a whole, primarily for communications with or from companies, typically with their members but also with debenture holders and others.

**8.117.4**  A company's ability to use electronic communications to send its financial statements and reports or its summary financial statements is not restricted by a contrary provision in its articles. Electronic communications are discussed further from paragraph 8.80.

**Listing, Disclosure and Transparency Rules and electronic communications**

**8.117.6**  The UKLA Listing Rules and Disclosure and Transparency Rules (LR and DTR) also permit issuers to send, circulate or otherwise despatch certain documents to holders of its listed securities electronically. LR 1.4.9 and DTR 6.1.7 and 6.1.8 impose requirements that are similar to the statutory requirements mentioned from paragraph 8.117.1 onwards for sending copies of financial statements and reports to shareholders.

**8.117.7**  Where an issuer uses electronic communications to communicate with its shareholders, it must also have available for holders of its listed securities a sufficient number of the documents in printed form and free of charge. These must be available during normal business hours at the places mentioned below for a period of not less than 21 days from the date of communication or notification or, if later, the conclusion of any general meeting to which the documents relate. These places are:

- The issuer's registered office in the UK.
- The offices of any UK paying agent that the issuer has.

**8.117.8**  The FSA has indicated that issuers also have to comply with existing requirements for copies of documents to be submitted to the UK Listing Authority – to be made available at the document viewing facility.

**8.118**  A copy of all such notices and other communications relating to general meetings must be given to the company's auditors. [CA85 Sec 390(1); CA06 Sec 502]. In addition, the company's bankers may require that they should receive copies of the company's annual financial statements, and, although non-statutory, this requirement could be an enforceable term of either a loan or facility agreement. If all of the members who are entitled to vote at the general meeting are in agreement, the annual financial statements and reports may be sent to members and others less than 21 days before the general meeting. This applies only to public companies under the 2006 Act. [CA85 Sec 238(4); CA06 Sec 424]. See paragraph 8.117 regarding provisions applicable to private companies under the 2006 Act. If the company is listed on the Main Market of the LSE or Plus Market's PLUS-listed market, the annual financial statements and reports must be sent to the members within four months of the end of the financial period to which they relate. Companies traded on AIM and the PLUS-quoted marked are required to send their annual reports to members within six and five months respectively from the end of the financial period to which they relate. [DTR 4.1.3; AIMR 19; PLUS Rules for issuers 31].

**[The next paragraph is 8.121.]**

**Public companies — presentation of financial statements at general meetings**

**8.121** The directors of a public company have a duty to present the annual financial statements and reports (for contents see para 8.117) of the company before the shareholders each year at a general meeting of the company. [CA85 Sec 241(1); CA06 Sec 437]. These financial statements and reports must be laid before the company and filed with the Registrar of Companies before the end of the period allowed for doing so. This period is described in paragraph 8.140.

**8.122** The annual financial statements and reports of a public company do not necessarily have to be laid before the shareholders at the AGM; another general meeting will suffice. This is acknowledged in section 437(1) of the 2006 Act and such a meeting is referred to as an 'accounts meeting'. [CA06 Sec 437(3)]. In practice, however, most public companies do lay their annual financial statements and reports before the shareholders at their AGM. The financial statements presented at that meeting should include the documents listed in paragraph 8.98.1, together with the directors' report, the auditors' report on the financial statements and, for quoted companies, the directors' remuneration report and the auditors' report on the auditable part of the directors' remuneration report.

*Private companies — dispensation from AGMs and laying financial statements*

**8.123** Under the 1985 Act a private company may (by elective resolution passed in accordance with section 379A), elect to dispense with certain formalities, such as the holding of an AGM and laying its financial statements before the company in a general meeting. [CA85 Secs 366A, 252]. The 2006 Act makes this the default position for all private companies for financial years commencing on or after 6 April 2008 so that, not only will private companies no longer be required to hold an AGM or lay financial statements before a general meeting, they will not have to make an election to that effect either. This will have effect subject to any provisions in the company's Articles. This does not remove the requirement to send the financial statements to members under section 423 of the 2006 Act.

**Private companies – 1985 Act elective regime for AGMs transitional provisions**

**8.124**  Where such an election under the 1985 Act has been made and is in force until April 2008, the following sections of the 1985 Act that refer to laying financial statements and other statements before members, should be read as meaning *sending* those financial statements to members, debenture holders and other people who are entitled to receive notice of general meetings:

■ Section 235(1) — financial statements on which auditors are to report.

■ Section 270(3) and (4) — financial statements by reference to which distributions are to be justified.

■ Section 320(2) — financial statements relevant for calculating a company's net assets for the purpose of determining whether approval is required for certain transactions.

■ Section 271(4) — statement made by the auditor where his opinion has been qualified and the company is proposing to pay a dividend.

[CA85 Sec 252(3)].

**8.125**  For instance, section 235(1) of the 1985 Act above refers to the requirement for auditors to report on all annual financial statements that are to be laid before the company in general meeting. Where an election is in force this would be read as still requiring the auditors to report on all annual financial statements that are to be sent to members.

**8.126**  The 1985 Act sets out the period during which the election applies. In the year that the election is made it applies to the financial statements for that year and to all subsequent years until the relevant provisions of the 2006 Act come into force. [CA85 Sec 252(2)]. If the election is revoked, the financial statements for the year in which the election ceases to have effect and subsequent financial years must comply with normal requirements for the laying and delivering financial statements under section 241 of the 1985 Act. [CA85 Sec 252(4)].

**8.127**  Where an election under section 252 of the 1985 Act is in force, copies of the financial statements must be sent to shareholders and others entitled to receive them, not less than 28 days before the end of the period allowed for laying and delivering financial statements. Where they are sent to a member of the company, they should be accompanied by a notice informing him of his right to require the financial statements to be laid before a general meeting. If a default is made in complying with these requirements, the company and every officer who is in default is guilty of an offence. [CA85 Sec 253(1)].

**8.128**  A member or the company's auditor has the right, by giving notice at the company's registered office or by electronic communication, to require that a general meeting be held in order to lay the financial statements before the company. The notice must be sent to the company within 28 days beginning with the day on which the financial statements are sent out. [CA85 Sec 253(2)]. The electronic communication must be transmitted to such address as the company has specified for the purpose. [CA85 Sec 253(2A)].

**8.129**  If the directors do not proceed to convene a meeting within 21 days from the date the notice is deposited with, or the receipt of the electronic communication by, the company, the member or auditor may proceed to call a meeting themselves. [CA85 Sec 253(3)]. Where a meeting is convened by the member or auditor it should be held within three months from the date the notice was deposited and should be convened in a similar manner as meetings convened by directors. [CA85 Sec 253(4)].

**8.130**  Where the directors do not convene a meeting, the person who gave the notice may recover any reasonable expenses incurred in convening the meeting from the company. The company can recoup such expenses from the remuneration of the defaulting directors. [CA85 Sec 253(5)].

**8.131**  The directors are deemed not to have duly convened a meeting if the date chosen is more than 28 days after the date of the notice convening it. [CA85 Sec 253(6)]. Effectively this appears to give the directors 49 days in which to hold the meeting, since they have 21 days in which to proceed to convene a meeting after the notice is deposited or given by a shareholder or auditor.

*Liability for public companies for not laying financial statements*

**8.132**  The directors of public companies must ensure that they lay copies of the annual financial statements and reports (see para 8.117) for each financial year at a general meeting of the company (an accounts meeting) within the period allowed for delivering financial statements to the Registrar of Companies (see section 244 of the 1985 Act and para 8.140 below). If they do not, every person who was a director of the company immediately before the end of that period may be guilty of an offence. [CA85 Sec 241]. The penalty applies to those persons who had been directors of the public company immediately before the end of the six month filing period. [CA06 Secs 437, 438].

**8.133**  It is a defence for a director in this situation to prove that he took all reasonable steps to ensure that the requirements would be complied with before the end of the period allowed. [CA85 Sec 241(3); CA06 Sec 438(1)(2)]. However, it is not a defence that the financial statements and reports had not been prepared. [CA85 Sec 241(4); CA06 Sec 438(3)].

**Quoted companies — members' approval of directors' remuneration report**

**8.133.1**  Where a company is a quoted company as defined in section 262(1) of the 1985 Act (section 385 of the 2006 Act) immediately before the end of a financial year, it must give notice to members, prior to the general meeting at which financial statements and reports are laid, of an ordinary resolution to approve the directors' remuneration report for the year. [CA85 Sec 241A(1)-(3); CA06 Sec 439].

**8.133.2** No entitlement of a person to remuneration is made conditional on the resolution being passed by reason only of the requirements in section 241A of the 1985 Act (section 439 of the 2006 Act). [CA85 Sec 241A(8); CA06 Sec 439(5)]. In other words, the success of failure of the resolution to approve the directors' remuneration report does not affect the entitlement of the directors to the remuneration disclosed in the report. This is because remuneration will already be the subject of contracts that cannot be overturned. However, any 'no vote' or significant opposition is likely to indicate that the company has difficulties with its investor relations.

**8.133.3** In the event of default in complying with the requirement to give notice of the ordinary resolution to approve the directors' remuneration report, every officer of the company who is in default is liable to a fine. [CA85 Sec 241A(9); CA06 Sec 440].

**8.133.4** The existing directors must ensure that the resolution is put to the vote at the meeting. 'Existing director' means a person, who immediately before the meeting, is a director of the company. If the resolution is not put to the vote of the meeting, each existing director is guilty of an offence and liable to a fine, although it is a defence for the director to prove he took all reasonable steps for securing that the resolution was put to the vote of the meeting. [CA85 Sec 241A(6), (10)-(12); CA06 Sec (3)].

**Delivery to the Registrar of Companies**

*Filing obligations for quoted and unquoted companies*

**8.134** In addition to sending out to members and/or laying the annual financial statements and reports before the company in a general meeting, the company's directors also have a duty for each financial year to file a copy of the company's annual financial statements and reports with the Registrar of Companies. [CA85 Sec 242; CA06 Sec 441]. Companies that qualify as small (see paras 8.134.2 to 4) or medium-sized (see paras 8.134.5 to 6) may file less than a complete copy of the annual financial statements and reports sent to their members.

The annual financial statements and reports for filing must comprise the following:

■ A copy of the company's individual financial statements required by section 226 (section 395 of the 2006 Act) and any consolidated financial statements required by section 227 (section 399 of the 2006 Act). Where the company's consolidated financial statements are included, the company's individual profit and loss account may be omitted and the notes need not include information on the company's employee numbers and costs provided that the annual financial statements disclose that advantage has been of the exemption. [CA06 Sec 408]. This applies irrespective of whether the consolidated financial statements are Companies Act financial statements or IAS financial statements. The balance sheet must state the name of the person who signed it on behalf of the board under section 414 of the 2006 Act and must be signed by a director on behalf of the board. [CA06 Secs 446(3), 447(3)].

- A copy of the directors' report. It must state the name of the person who signed it on behalf of the board under section 419 of the 2006 Act and must be signed by a director or company secretary (where appointed). [CA06 Secs 446(3A), 447(3B)].

- In the case of a quoted company, a copy of the directors' remuneration report. It must state the name of the person who signed it on behalf of the board under section 422 of the 2006 Act and it must be signed by the company secretary. [CA06 Sec 447(3A)].

- A copy of the auditors' report on those financial statements and that directors' report and, in the case of a quoted company, on the auditable part of the directors' remuneration report. The copy must state the name of the auditor (and where the auditor is a firm) the name of the person who signed it as senior statutory auditor and be signed by the auditor or (where the auditor is a firm) in the name of the firm by a person authorised to sign on its behalf. In circumstances where the auditor's name can be omitted under section 506 of the 2006 Act (for years commencing on or after 6 April 2008), it must state that the necessary resolution of the company has been passed and notified to the Secretary of State. [CA06 Sec 447(4)].

[CA85 Sec 242; CA06 Secs 446, 447].

The requirements for signature are expected to be repealed with effect from 1 October 2009 and Companies House will, in due course, issue rules for the authentication of documents after that date.

**8.134.1** Financial statements in a language other than English must be accompanied by a translation certified in the prescribed manner. However, financial statements in Welsh may be filed without an accompanying certified translation by unquoted companies whose registered office is in Wales. [CA85 Sec 710B(6); CA06 Sec 1104]. This provision of the 2006 Act came into force on 1 January 2007.

*Filing obligations of companies subject to the small companies regime*

**8.134.2** The directors of a company subject to the small companies regime *must* deliver at a minimum to the Registrar of Companies for each financial year a copy of the balance sheet and its notes from the annual financial statements sent to its members. [CA85 Secs 242(1), 246(5); CA06 Secs 444(1)(a) and 472]. The directors must also deliver a copy of the auditors' report on the accounts (and any directors' report) that it delivers, unless the company is exempt from audit and the directors have taken advantage of that exemption. [CA85 Secs 242(1)(d), 249E(1)(b); CA06 Sec 444(2)]. The directors *may* also deliver a copy of the company's profit and loss account and/or the directors' report for that year (but see para 8.134.5 below). [CA85 Secs 242(1)(b), 246(5); CA06 Sec 444(1)(b)(i)(ii)].

They may, of course, deliver a copy of the complete set of the annual financial statements and reports sent to members.

**8.134.2.1**  If complete sets of the annual accounts and reports sent to members are not filed with the Registrar because the profit and loss account and the directors' report have been omitted, as permitted by section 246(5) of the 1985 Act (section 444(1) of the 2006 Act), the balance sheet must contain a statement in a prominent position that the company's annual accounts and reports have been delivered in accordance with the provisions applicable to companies subject to the small companies regime. [CA85 Sec 246(8); CA06 Sec 444(5)]. This applies irrespective of whether the annual accounts are Companies Act financial statements or IAS accounts.

**8.134.3**  The copies of the balance sheet and of any director's report delivered to the Registrar under section 242 of the 1985 Act (section 444 of the 2006 Act) must state the name of the person that signed it on behalf of the board under sections 233 and 234A of the 1985 Act (sections 414 and 419 of the 2006 Act) and must be signed by a director of the company or, in the case of the directors' report, by the company secretary (where appointed). [CA06 Secs 444(6), (6A)]. Similarly, the copy of the auditors' report delivered under section 444 of the 2006 Act must state the name of the auditors and (for years commencing on or after 6 April 2008, where the auditors are a firm) the name of the person who signed it as senior statutory auditor and be signed by the auditor and (where the auditors are a firm) in the name of the firm by a person authorised to sign on its behalf. [CA06 Sec 444(7)]. (The requirement for signature is expected to be repealed with effect from 1 October 2009 and Companies House will, in due course, issue rules for the authentication of documents after that date.) However, the auditors' names may be omitted if the conditions in section 506 of the 2006 Act are met. In that case there must be a testament that a resolution has been passed and notified to the Secretary of State in accordance with that section. [CA06 Sec 447(7)].

**8.134.4**  Where the company prepares 'Companies Act accounts' for its members the directors may deliver 'abbreviated accounts' to the Registrar instead of the copy extracts from, or the complete set of, its annual financial statements and reports sent to members described above. These financial statements must consist of a balance sheet, a profit and loss account and notes drawn up in accordance with Regulation 6 of, and Schedule 4 to, SI 2008/409. [CA85 Sec 246(5); CA06 Sec 444(3)(a)(b)]. The copy balance sheet must contain a statement in a prominent position that it has been prepared in accordance with the provisions applicable to the small companies regime companies. [SI 2008/409 4 Sch para 1(2)].

**8.134.4.1**  Where abbreviated accounts are delivered to the Registrar they must be accompanied by the special auditors' report required by section 247B of the 1985 Act (section 449 of the 2006 Act), unless the company is exempt from audit and the directors have taken advantage of that exemption. [CA06 Secs 444(4), 449(1)(b)]. The special auditors' report must be signed by the auditor (or where the auditor is a firm) by a person authorised to sign on its behalf. [CA06 Sec 449(4A)(a)]. (The requirement for signature is expected to be repealed with effect from 1 October 2009 and Companies House will, in due course, issue rules for the authentication of documents after that date). In circumstances where the auditor's name can be omitted under section 506 of the 2006 Act it must state that the necessary resolution of the company has been passed and notified to the Secretary of State. [CA06 Sec 449(4A)(b)]. See also paragraphs 8.160 to 161 below.

### Filing obligations for companies subject to the small companies regime

**8.134.5**  A company that qualifies for the small companies regime or would do so but for being a member of an ineligible group, is entitled to the small companies exemption in relation to the directors' report under section 415A of the 2006 Act. The directors of such a company must deliver to the Registrar of Companies a copy of the company's annual financial statements (that is, the company's individual profit and loss account and balance sheet with supporting notes to both primary statements) [CA06 Secs 444A(1)(a), 471 and 472]. Unless the company is exempt from audit and advantage has been taken of that exemption, the directors must also deliver a copy of the auditor's report on those financial statements (and any directors' report) [CA06 Sec 444A(2)]. They may also deliver a copy of the directors' report prepared with the benefit of the exemption in section 415A. [CA06 Sec 444A(1)(b)].

**8.134.5.1**  The copies of the balance sheet and any directors' report delivered to the Registrar of Companies must state the name of the person who signed it on behalf of the board. [CA06 Sec 444A(3)].

**8.134.5.2**  The copy of the auditor's report must state the name of the auditor and (where the auditor is a firm) the name of the person who signed it as senior statutory auditor and must be signed by the auditor or (for years commencing on or after 6 April 2008, where the auditor is a firm) in the name of the firm by a person authorised to sign it on its behalf. [CA06 Sec 444A(4)]. In circumstances where the auditor's name can be omitted under section 506 of the Act, the report must state that the necessary resolution of the company has been passed and notified to the Secretary of State [CA06 Sec 444A(5)]. The requirement for signature is expected to be repealed with effect from 1 October 2009 and Companies House will, in due course, issue rules for the authentication of documents after that date.

### Filing obligations of medium-sized companies

**8.134.6**  The directors of a medium-sized private company *must* deliver to the Registrar of Companies for each financial year a copy of the annual accounts and reports sent to members. The directors must also deliver a copy of the auditors' report on those accounts (and on the directors' report). [CA06 Sec 445(1)(2)].

**8.134.7**  Alternatively, where the company prepares 'Companies Act accounts' the directors may deliver 'abbreviated accounts'. These financial statements must consist of the company's balance sheet as sent to members and a profit and loss account drawn up in accordance with Regulation 4(3) SI 2008/410, 'The Large

8057

and Medium-sized Companies and Groups (Reports and Accounts) Regulations 2008'. [CA06 Sec 445(3)]. If abbreviated accounts are delivered to the Registrar they must be accompanied by the special auditors' report required by section 449 of the 2006 Act, unless the company is exempt from audit and the directors have taken advantage of that exemption. [CA06 Secs 444(4), 449(1)(b)]. See also paragraphs 8.160 to 161 below.

**8.134.8** The content of abbreviated accounts is dealt with in chapter 32 of the Manual of Accounting — UK GAAP. Medium-sized companies that prepare IAS financial statements are not permitted to file abbreviated accounts.

**8.134.9** Unlike the 1985 Act, the 2006 Act does not grant medium-sized companies that are parent companies any exemption from the requirement to file consolidated financial statements. They may, however, omit the company's individual profit and loss account in the same way as other parent companies may. This applies whether they are preparing Companies Act or IAS financial statements (see further chapter 4 of the Manual of Accounting — IFRS for the UK and the Manual of Accounting — UK GAAP).

*Consolidated financial statements not prepared*

**8.135** Where a company is exempt under section 228 or 228A of the 1985 Act (sections 400 and 401 of the 2006 Act) from preparing consolidated financial statements, a copy of the consolidated financial statements of the ultimate parent undertaking in whose consolidated financial statements the company is included must be appended to the company's financial statements delivered to the Registrar. The exemptions from the requirement to prepare consolidated financial statements are explained further in chapter 24 of the Manual of Accounting – IFRS for the UK and the Manual of Accounting – UK GAAP.

**[The next paragraph is 8.139.]**

*Period allowed for sending out, laying and filing*

**8.139** As stated above, the directors of any private company not subject to the 1985 Act elective regime and of all public companies must lay the company's annual financial statements and reports before the company in general meeting and must file them with the Registrar of Companies. (See paragraph 8.117 for private companies that are subject to the 1985 elective regime or, from April 2008, the 2006 Act default regime) These financial statements and reports must be laid and filed before the end of the allowed period. [CA85 Sec 242(2); CA06 Sec 442]. However, an unlimited company does not have to file its financial statements and reports with the Registrar under certain conditions (see para 8.146 below).

**8.140** The 2006 Act sets out the requirements for filing of financial statements and reports for financial years starting on or after 6 April 2008; the 1985 Act sets out the requirements for earlier periods. The usual period allowed for filing financial statements and reports with the Registrar is:

■ Under the 1985 Act, ten months after the end of the relevant accounting reference period for a private company. Under the 2006 Act, nine months after the end of the relevant accounting reference period for a private company.

■ Under the 1985 Act, seven months after the end of that period for a public company. Under the 2006 Act, six months after the end of that period for a public company.

[CA85 Sec 244(1); CA06 Sec 442].

However, this period may be extended or shortened in the situations outlined in the paragraphs that follow.

**8.141** If a company's *first* accounting reference period exceeds 12 months, the period allowed is the last to expire of the following:

■ Ten months for a private company or seven months for a public company from the first anniversary of the company's incorporation. Under the 2006 Act these periods are shortened to nine months for a private company and six months for a public company.

■ Three months from the end of the accounting reference period (see para 8.88 for the meaning of 'accounting reference period').

[CA85 Sec 244(2); CA06 Sec 442(3)].

**8.142** The effect of this is that a new private company under the 2006 Act has to deliver its first financial statements within 21 months of incorporation and that a new public company will normally have 18 months (unless the company shortens its accounting period as set out in para 8.98 above). Under the 1985 Act these periods were one month longer. The example below is based on the filing date requirements of the 2006 Act.

**Example**

A public company is incorporated on 1 August 20X2, and its first accounting reference period ends on 31 December 20X3 (that is, 17 months later). The company must deliver its financial statements to the Registrar by 31 March 20X4. This is because the period allowed is the later of 3 months after the end of the accounting reference period, that is 31 March 20X4, and 6 months from the first anniversary of the inception of the company, that is, 31 January 20X4.

**[The next paragraph is 8.144].**

**8.144** A company may shorten its accounting reference period by notifying the Registrar under section 225 of the Act (section 392 of the 2006 Act) (see para 8.94 onwards). Where a company takes advantage of section 225 of the 1985 Act (section 392 of the 2006 Act) and shortens its accounting reference period, it must file its financial statements for this shorter period before the last to expire of the following:

- The period applicable under the relevant provision of section 244(1) to (2) of the 1985 Act (section 442(2) of the 2006 Act) described in paragraphs 8.140 to 8.142 above.

- Three months after the date on which the notice was given to the Registrar to change the accounting reference date.

[CA85 Sec 244(4); CA06 Sec 442(4)].

**8.145**  In exceptional circumstances the Secretary of State may extend the time for filing if application is made to Companies House before the expiry of the period allowed for filing the company's financial statements. Any such application will, however, need to give good reasons why the extension should be granted. [CA85 Sec 244(5); CA06 Sec 442(5)].

*Filing exemption for unlimited companies*

**8.146**  The directors of an unlimited company are not required under section 254 of the 1985 Act (section 448 of the 2006 Act) to file a copy of the company's financial statements with the Registrar of Companies provided the company was *not*, at any time during the relevant accounting reference period, any one of the following:

- A subsidiary company of a limited undertaking.

- A parent company of a limited undertaking.

- Subject to rights exercisable by or on behalf of two or more limited undertakings which, if exercised by one of them, would have made the company its subsidiary.

- A banking or insurance company or the parent company of a banking or insurance group.

- A qualifying company under SI 1993/1820,'Partnerships and Unlimited Companies (Accounts) Regulations 1993' (1993 Regulations). An unlimited company will be a qualifying company if each of its members is a limited company, or is another unlimited company, each of whose members is a limited company or Scottish partnership, each of whose members is a limited company. References to a limited company, another unlimited company or Scottish partnership include a comparable undertaking incorporated in or formed under the law of a country or territory outside the UK. Section 448(3)(b) of the 2006 Act (as amended by SI 2008/393) re-enacts these provisions of SI 1993/1820.

- A company carrying on a business as the promoter of a trading stamp scheme (under the Trading Stamps Act 1964) (for financial years beginning before 6 April 2008 only).

[CA85 Sec 254(1)(2)(3); CA06 Sec 448].

**8.147** Where an unlimited company is exempt from filing its financial statements under section 254 of the 1985 Act (section 448 of the 2006 Act), its statutory financial statements will be those prepared in accordance with Part VII of the 1985 Act (Part 15 of the 2006 Act) and approved by the board of directors. If it publishes non-statutory financial statements, those financial statements must include a statement that the company is exempt from the requirement to deliver statutory financial statements. [CA85 Sec 254(4); CA06 Sec 488(4)]. See paragraph 8.155 where the meaning of publishing financial statements is explained.

*Exemption for qualifying undertakings*

**8.147.1** A partnership will be a qualifying partnership if each of its members is a limited company (including a limited company incorporated overseas). The members of a qualifying partnership are required to prepare annual financial statements and have those financial statements audited as if the partnership were a company. Each member is then required to append a copy of these financial statements to its own financial statements delivered to the registrar. Non-UK or EU members of a qualifying partnership will be required to make the partnership's latest financial statements available for inspection at its head office. [SI 1993/1820 Regs 4 to 6]. However, the members of the qualifying partnership are exempt from these requirements if the partnership is dealt with either by consolidation, proportional consolidation or equity accounting in the consolidated financial statements prepared by:

■  a member of the partnership which is established under the law of an EU Member State; or

■  a parent undertaking of such a member which is established under the law of an EU Member State.

**8.147.2** This exemption is conditional upon:

■  The consolidated financial statements being prepared and audited in accordance with the provisions of the EU 7th Directive.

■  The notes to those financial statements disclosing that advantage has been taken of the exemption.

[SI 1993/1820 Reg 7].

*Rejection of documents by the Registrar*

**8.147.3** Companies House is entitled to (and does) reject documents (including financial statements) that fail to comply with the law. Rejected financial statements are treated as unfiled and may result in a company failing to meet its filing deadline (see further para 8.139). The most common reasons for rejection of financial statements are:

- Non-compliance with accounting standards or the Companies Act.

- Incorrect references to the Companies Act 1985 (or the Companies Act 2006).

- Unsigned audit reports.

- Unsigned balance sheets and directors' reports.

- Photocopy signatures. These are not acceptable in any circumstances. (The accounts must have manual signatures throughout, that is, at least one director on the balance sheet, the company secretary conventionally on the directors' report and the firm's name signed by the partner on the audit report.)

- Missing pages.

- Figures in the notes failing to agree with the primary statements.

- Typographical errors in figures in the primary statements.

- Casting errors in the primary statements and/or the notes.

- Company number is missing or does not match company name (see further para 8.65).

- Dormant companies/audit-exempt accounts and directors' statement. Rejection occurs because the required directors' statement has not been made, has not been made correctly or has been placed somewhere other than on the balance sheet.

- Accounting reference periods and dates. A change of accounting reference date requires submission of the necessary forms to the Registrar.

- Duplicate financial statements. These will be returned unless they are meant to replace previously submitted financial statements and comply with the defective accounts provisions.

- Financial statements not capable of being reproduced electronically (see further paras 8.65 to 8.67.1).

### Company's liability for late filing

**8.148**  Where a company does not deliver its annual financial statements and reports to the Registrar within the period allowed, the Registrar has authority to require the company to pay a penalty. The penalties, are set out in section 242A of the 1985 Act and, for documents filed on or after 1 February 2009, in SI 2008/497, 'The Companies (Late Filing Penalties) and Limited Liability Partnerships (Filing Periods and Late Filing Penalties) Regulations 2008'. They are based on a sliding scale depending on the length of time between the date permitted by section 244 of the 1985 Act (section 441 of the 2006 Act) for filing and the actual date of delivery to the Registrar. The penalties are higher for public companies. Under SI 2008/497, if a company files late for a second consecutive year, the fine for that second year is doubled.

**8.148.1**  The provisions of SI 2008/497 apply to all financial statements and reports that are filed late on or after 1 February 2009, regardless of the company's period end or the Act under which the financial statements are prepared. It should be noted that the fines under SI 2008/497 are considerably higher and the penalty periods shorter than those set out in the 1985 Act.

**8.149**  The Registrar of Companies applies late filing penalties rigorously and imposes them even if the company is just over the filing deadline. Also, it is the date the financial statements are received by the Registrar of Companies that counts, not the date of posting. The 1985 Act did not specify how the exact filing deadline was to be calculated. The general rule the Registrar has used to calculate the period is based on the House of Lords decision in *Dodds v Walker* [1981] 1 WLR 1441. Thus, the period ends upon the corresponding date in the appropriate month (that is, not necessarily the end of the month) or, where there is no corresponding date, the last day of that month. Consequently, a company with an accounting reference date of 30 September must file its financial statements with the Registrar of Companies by 30 April for a public company or by 30 July (not 31 July) for a private company.

**8.149.1**  Section 443 of the 2006 Act specifies how the period for filing is to be calculated for periods commencing on or after 6 April 2008. This section states that the deadline is the last day of the appropriate month (whether or not that is the corresponding date). This overturns the rule from *Dodds v Walker* above.

**8.150**  Where the deadline falls on a weekend or on a bank (public) holiday, the annual financial statements and reports must be posted or be delivered by hand to arrive at Companies House on or before the last working day before the deadline. Companies House advise that financial statements and reports should be delivered at least three days before the deadline.

**8.151**  The Registrar considers that the late filing penalties extend to the situation where the court has declared that the striking of a company off the register is void and that the company is deemed to continue in existence as if it had never been struck off. The annual financial statements and reports of a company restored to the Register at Companies House may, therefore, be liable to late filing penalties for the period during which the company was dissolved.

*Directors' liability for late delivery*

**8.152**  The late filing penalties mentioned above are quite separate from any offence of which the directors may be guilty for not delivering the annual financial statements and reports to the Registrar before the end of the period allowed (see para 8.140). It is a defence for a director to prove that he took all reasonable steps for securing that the requirements to deliver the annual financial statements and reports would be complied with before the end of the period allowed. It is not a defence that the documents were not in fact prepared.

**8.153**  In addition, if a company has not complied with the filing requirements within the period allowed for laying and filing annual financial statements and reports, any member, or any of the company's creditors, or the Registrar may serve notice on the company requiring it to comply with the filing requirements. If the company's directors fail to make good the default within 14 days after this notice has been served, then the person who served the notice may apply to the court to make an order instructing the directors to comply with the filing requirements within a time the court specifies. The court order may also require the directors to bear the cost of the application. [CA85 Sec 242(3); CA06 Sec 452(1)(2)].

**8.154**  The Company Directors (Disqualification) Act 1986 provides that if a director is persistently in default in filing any returns, financial statements or other document with the Registrar, he may be disqualified. Default may be conclusively proved if he has been adjudged guilty of three or more defaults in the five years ending with the application date. [The Company Directors (Disqualification) Act 1986 Sec 3(2)].

# Exemptions from audit of financial statements

### Small companies and groups

**8.154.1**  Certain small companies (including dormant companies) are exempt from the obligation to have their financial statements audited if they comply with certain size criteria and if the circumstances where the exemption is not available do not apply. [CA85 Secs 249A(1), 249A(6A); CA06 Sec 477]. The audit exemption specifically for dormant companies is discussed in paragraph 8.154.13. Part 16 of the 2006 Act replaces the 1985 Act's legislation on audit of financial statements and applies to financial years starting on or after 6 April 2008.

**8.154.2**  A company qualifies as small under section 246 of the 1985 Act (for periods commencing before 6 April 2008) and may be exempt from the need to have an audit for that financial year if it complies with the following conditions:

- Its annual turnover and balance sheet total for the year (unless is it a charitable company) are not more than £5.6 million and £2.8 million respectively.

- For a small charitable company, instead of the turnover total mentioned above, a total of £250,000 for gross income is substituted. However, an accountant's report, prepared by an independent reporting accountant in accordance with section 249C of the Companies Act 1985, will be required where gross income is in the range £90,000 to £250,000. The 2006 Act does not carry forward the provision above regarding small charitable companies.

[CA85 Sec 249A].

**8.154.2.1**   A company qualifies as small under section 477 of the 2006 Act (for periods commencing on or after 6 April 2008) and may be exempt from the need to have an audit for that financial year if its annual turnover and balance sheet total for the year (unless is it a charitable company) are not more than £6.5 million and £3.26 million respectively. Unlike the 1985 Act, the 2006 Act does not make provisions in this area for small companies that are charities, which must comply with charity law rather than company law to determine whether an audit is required.

**8.154.2.2**   A company qualifies as small or medium-sized in relation to a financial year if the qualifying conditions are met:

- In the case of the company's first financial year, in that year.

- In the case of any subsequent financial year:

    - in that year and the preceding year;

    - in that year and the company qualified as small in relation to the preceding financial year; or

    - were met in the preceding financial year and the company qualified as small in relation to that year.

[CA85 Sec 247; CA06 Secs 382, 465].

In practice, this means that a company is small or is medium-sized if it meets the size tests for two consecutive years and it is not small or medium-sized if it fails the size tests in two consecutive years.

**8.154.3**   The audit exemption is available to all qualifying small companies, regardless of whether they report in accordance with UK GAAP or IFRS. Note, however, that charitable companies are not permitted to prepare their financial statements in accordance with IFRS. [CA85 Sec 226(3); CA06 Sec 395(2)]

**Small companies ineligible for audit exemption**

**8.154.4**   The circumstances where companies that meet the size exemption criteria but are still prevented from obtaining an audit exemption are set out in sub-sections (1) to (1C) of section 249B of the 1985 Act (section 478 of the 2006 Act). This indicates that a company will not be entitled to the audit exemption conferred by section 249A (section 477 of the 2006 Act) if at any time during a financial year ending on or after 31 December 2006 it was one of the following:

- A public company. (A public company that is dormant may be entitled to the audit exemption for dormant companies (see para 8.154.14).)

- A small company that is an authorised insurance company, a banking company, an e-money issuer, a MiFiD investment firm or a UCITS management company (as defined by the Financial Services and Markets Act 2000).

- A company that carried on an insurance market activity.

- A special register body as defined in section 117(1) of the Trade Union and Labour Relations (Consolidation) Act 1992 or an employers' association as defined in section 122 of that Act or Article 4 of the Industrial Relations (Northern Ireland) Order 1992 (SI 1992/807 (N15)).

- A group company (that is, a parent company or a subsidiary undertaking unless:

  - throughout the period in the financial year during which it was a subsidiary undertaking, the company was dormant; or

  - the company is a parent company or a subsidiary undertaking in a small group that meets the following conditions:

    - the group qualifies as small under section 249 of the 1985 Act (section 383 of the 2006 Act) for the financial year, or, if all bodies corporate in the group were companies, would so qualify, and the group is not, and was not at any time within that year, an ineligible group within the meaning of section 248(2) of the 1985 Act (section 384(2) of the 2006 Act);

    - the group's aggregate turnover in that year, where the company is a charity (under the 1985 Act only), is not more than £350,000 net or £420,000 gross, or where the company is not a charity, is not more than £5.6 million net or £6.72 million gross (section 249B of the 1985 Act) (£6.5 million net or £7.8 million gross (section 497(2)). The provision regarding a charitable company is not carried forward into the 2006 Act, but reference should be made to SI 2008/629, 'The Charities (Accounts and Reports) Regulations 2008'; and

    - the group's aggregate balance sheet total is not more than £2.8 million net or £3.36 million gross (£3.26 million and £3.9 million respectively under the 2006 Act).

The group in relation to a group company means that company together with all its associated undertakings. For this purpose undertakings are associated if one is a subsidiary undertaking of the other or both are subsidiary undertakings of a third undertaking. [CA85 Sec 249B(1)-(1C); CA06 Secs 478, 479].

**8.154.5** Members of a small or dormant company have the right to require the company to obtain an audit of its financial statements and so prevent it from taking advantage of the exemption. Under section 249B(2) of the 1985 Act (section 476 of the 2006 Act) members holding 10 per cent or more of the company's nominal share capital or ten per cent of a particular class of share may deposit at the company's registered office after the start of the financial year to which it relates and not later than one month before the year end a notice requiring an audit for that year. If the company does not have share capital, the notice must be given by 10 per cent or more of members. If such a notice is deposited, the company will not be entitled to the audit exemption for the year to which the notice relates.

**8.154.6** The disclosures listed below are required for small and dormant companies. A qualifying small company will not be entitled to the audit exemption in sub-section (1) or (2) of section 249A of the 1985 Act (section 477(1) of the 2006 Act) and a dormant company will not be entitled to the audit exemption in sub-section (1) of section 249AA of the 1985 Act (section 480(1) of the 2006 Act) unless its balance sheet includes three statements by the directors to the effect that:

- For the year in question the company was entitled to the exemption:

  - under section 249A(1) of the 1985 Act (section 477 of the 2006 Act) (in the case of a small company or small charitable company qualifying for the total exemption under the 1985 Act. The provisions relating to small charitable companies are not carried forward into the 2006 Act);

  - under section 249A(2) of the 1985 Act (in the case of a charitable company claiming partial exemption with gross income of more than £90,000 but not more than £250,000) (this provision is not carried forward into the 2006 Act);

  - under section 249AA (1) of the 1985 Act (section 480 of the 2006 Act) (in the case of a dormant company); or

  - under section 482 of the 2006 Act (no equivalent provision in the 1985 Act) (in the case of a non-profit-making company subject to public sector audit).

- Members have not required the company to obtain an audit of its financial statements for the financial year in question in accordance with section 249B(2) of the 1985 Act (Section 476 of the 2006 Act) (see para 8.154.8 below).

- The directors acknowledge their responsibilities for:

  - Ensuring that the company keeps accounting records as required by the legislation.

  - The preparation of accounts that give a true and fair view of the state of affairs of the company as at the end of the financial year, and of its profit or loss for the financial year, in accordance with the requirements of section 226 of the 1985 Act, and which otherwise comply with the requirements of the Companies Act relating to financial statements, so far as applicable to the company. Section 475(3)(b) of the 2006 Act shortens this to an acknowledgement of their responsibilities for complying with the requirements of the Act for the preparation of accounts.

[CA85 Sec 249B(4); CA06 Sec 475(2)-(4)].

**8.154.7** The requirements above apply both to companies that take advantage of the total exemption from audit and to those charitable companies, under the provisions of the 1985 Act, claiming partial exemption that require a report by reporting accountants. The provisions relating to charitable companies are not carried across into the 2006 Act. The required statements must appear above the director's signature on the balance sheet. [CA85 Sec 249B(5); CA06 Sec 475(4)]. The unaudited financial statements can be full financial statements, but as the company will be a small company under the 1985 Act or 2006 Act, it may, if it prepares 'Companies Act individual accounts' (financial statements) (that is, in accordance with UK GAAP), it may choose to take advantage of the special provisions of section 246 of the 1985 Act (section 444 of the 2006 Act) concerning abbreviated or shorter-form financial statements.

**8.154.8** The ICAEW has issued Technical Release Audit 02/04, 'Chartered accountants' report on the compilation of financial statements of incorporated entities'. The Technical Release provides guidance to accountants who assist in the compilation of financial statements where a company does not have to have its financial statements audited.

**8.154.9** Technical Release Audit 02/04 paragraph 31 states that where the financial statements are unaudited, the financial statements should contain a reference to the fact that they are unaudited, either on the front cover or on each page of the financial statements.

**8.154.10** Where the directors of a company have taken advantage of the exemption from audit either because it is a qualifying small company (see para 8.154.2) or a dormant company (see para 8.154.14):

- The financial statements sent to members under sections 238 or 239 of the 1985 Act (section 423 of the 2006 Act) need not contain an auditors' report.

- No copy of the auditors' report need be sent to the registrar or laid before the company in general meeting.

- Sub-sections (3) to (5) of section 271 of the 1985 Act (section 837 of the 2006 Act) (accounts by reference to which distribution is to be justified) will not apply.

[CA85 Sec 249E(1); CA06 Secs 444(2), 445(2)].

A company that qualifies for audit exemption as a small company or a dormant company will also be exempt from the obligation in section 384 of the 1985 Act to appoint auditors. [CA85 Sec 388A(1); CA06 Sec 485]. This is worded in section 485(1) of the 2006 Act as *"An auditor or auditors of a private company must be appointed for each financial year of the company, unless the directors reasonably resolve otherwise on the grounds that audited accounts are unlikely to be required"*.

**8.154.11** If, however, a company ceases to qualify for an audit exemption for any reason during the year, and section 385 of the 1985 Act applies (appointment of auditors at general meetings at which financial statements are laid) the directors may appoint auditors at any time before the next meeting at which financial statements prepared under section 226 of the 1985 Act (that is either 'IAS individual accounts' or 'Companies Act individual accounts') (section 394 and 395 of the 2006 Act) are laid. Where this applies, those auditors appointed shall hold office until the conclusion of that meeting. [CA85 Sec 388A(3)].

**8.154.11.1** Under the 2006 Act only public companies are required to hold general meetings, thus, if under the 2006 Act, a dormant public company ceases to qualify for an audit exemption during the year, the directors may appoint auditors at any time before the next 'accounts meeting' at which financial statements prepared under section 394 of the 2006 Act are laid. [CA06 Sec 489].

**8.154.12** Where under the 1985 Act section 385A applies (appointment by private company not obliged to lay financial statements) the directors shall appoint auditors at any time before the end of the period of 28 days beginning with the day on which copies of the company's financial statements for the previous financial year are sent to members under section 238 of the 1985 Act or, if notice is given under section 253(2) of the 1985 Act requiring that the financial statements be laid before the company in general meeting, the conclusion of that meeting. [CA85 Sec 388A (24)].

**8.154.12.1** Under the 2006 Act, if a small or dormant private company ceases to qualify for an audit exemption for any reason during the year, the directors shall appoint auditors at any time before the next period for appointing auditors. The period for appointing auditors is no later than 28 days after the period allowed for sending out copies of the company's financial statements for the previous financial year or if earlier the date on which the financial statements for the previous financial year are sent out. [CA06 Sec 485(2)(3)(b)].

**8.154.13** If the directors fail to exercise their powers of appointment in either of the above cases, the powers may be exercised by the company's members. [CA85 Sec 388A(4); CA06 Secs 485(4), 489(4)].

**Dormant companies**

**8.154.14** A dormant company is exempt from the requirement to have its financial statements audited, irrespective of the accounting framework used to prepare its financial statements, if all the following apply:

- It has been dormant since its formation or since the end of the previous financial year and it:
    - is entitled to prepare individual financial statements for the year under section 246 of the 1985 Act (that is, as a small company) (sections 381 to 384 of the 2006 Act), or would be if it were not a public company or a member of an ineligible group (see para 8.154.6);
    - and is not required to prepare group financial statements for that year.

- It is not (and was not at any time in the year in question) an authorised insurance company, a banking company, an e-money issuer, a MiFiD ISD investment firm or a UCITS management company (as defined by the Financial Services and Markets Act 2000).

- No notice under section 249B(2) of the 1985 Act (section 476 of the 2006 Act) has been given to the company requiring an audit of its financial statements for that year. More details of this notice are contained in paragraph 8.154.6.

- Its balance sheet for the year contain the disclosures required by section 249B(4) and (5) of the 1985 Act (section 475(2)(3) of the 2006 Act). The disclosures required are referred to in paragraph 8.154.6.

[CA85 Sec 249AA; CA06 Secs 480, 481].

**8.154.15**   A company that ceases to be dormant during a year may still be able to take advantage of an audit exemption if it satisfies the size criteria and conditions for the small company exemption (see para 8.154.2 above). If not, it will no longer be exempt from the obligation to appoint auditors (see para 8.154.11).

*Effect on financial statements*

**8.154.16**   Where the directors of a dormant company have taken advantage of the exemption from audit in section 249AA of the 1985 Act for a financial year beginning before 6 April 2008 (section 480 of the 2006 Act for a financial year beginning on or after 6 April 2008):

- The company is entitled to prepare its financial statements under section 246 of the 1985 Act (sections 381 to 384 of the 2006 Act) (as a small company), or it would be so entitled but for having been a member of an ineligible group or for having been a public company and is not required to prepare group accounts. [CA85 Sec 249AA(2)(b), Sec 249E(IA); CA06 Sec 480(2)(a)(b)].

- Under the 1985 Act, for financial years beginning before 6 April 2008, the following statements and reports are not required:

  - The statements that would be required under section 246(8) of the 1985 Act to be included in the financial statements and directors' report, that the financial statements are prepared in accordance with the special provisions of Part VII of the 1985 Act relating to small companies. [CA85 Sec 246(9)].

  - The special report of the auditors that would be required by section 247B(2) of the 1985 Act. [CA85 Sec 247B(1)(b)].

- Under the 2006 Act, for financial years beginning on or after 6 April 2008, the following statements are required:

- A statement required under section 475(2) of the 2006 Act that it is exempt from audit as a dormant company under section 480 of the 2006 Act.

- A statement required under section 475(3) of the 2006 Act that the members have not required the company to obtain an audit of its accounts for the year in question in accordance with section 476 of the 2006 Act; and that the directors acknowledge their responsibilities for complying with the requirements of this Act with respect to accounting records and the preparation of accounts. [CA06 Sec 480(3)].

**8.154.17** The previous year's figures must be shown alongside for comparison, even if there are no items of income or expenditure for the current year. In addition, certain notes to the balance sheet must be included. Companies House has produced model balance sheets and notes for dormant companies in its booklet 'Accounts and accounting reference dates' (version 19 — April 2008 for financial years beginning before 6 April 2008, version 3 — May 2008 for financial years beginning on or after 6 April 2008).

## Definition of 'dormant company'

**8.154.18** Under section 249AA of the 1985 Act (section 1169 of the 2006 Act), a company is 'dormant' during any period in which it qualifies as a small company in accordance with section 246 of the 1985 Act (sections 381-384 of the 2006 Act) and has no significant accounting transaction. A 'significant accounting transaction' means a transaction that is required by section 221 of the 1985 Act (section 386 of the 2006 Act) to be entered in the company's accounting records, but excluding the following:

- A transaction arising from the taking of shares in the company by a subscriber to the memorandum as a result of his undertaking in the memorandum.

- The payment of a fee to the registrar of companies on a change of name.

- The payment of a fee to the registrar on the re-registration of a company.

- A penalty under section 242A (section 453 of the 2006 Act) for the failure to deliver financial statements to the registrar.

- The payment of a fee to the registrar for the registration of an annual return.

[CA85 Sec 249AA(4) to (7); CA06 Sec 1169].

## Examples of significant accounting transactions

**8.154.19** Any transaction by a non-trading company, such as the payment of distributable reserves to its parent, will constitute a significant accounting transaction. Section 221 of the 1985 Act (section 386 of the 2006 Act) requires, for example, a company's accounting records to contain entries on a daily basis of all money received and expended, a record of its assets and liabilities and a statement of goods sold and purchased. Any such transaction will prevent the company from taking advantage of the dormant company audit exemption. However, if the company qualifies as a small company it may be entitled to the exemption from audit under section 249A(1) of the 1985 Act (section 477 of the 2006 Act) (see para 8.154.2).

**8.154.20** Another difficulty arises when companies, wishing to qualify as dormant and thereby avoid the need to appoint auditors, dispose of assets to other companies in their group in order to facilitate this. Sometimes, particularly where land is concerned, it is only the beneficial interest that is transferred, the company intending to retain only the legal interest or bare legal title. Such transfers are frequently conducted with the minimum of formality and paperwork. However, since 26 September 1989, with regard to land the legal position is that any contract for the sale or other disposition of an interest in land can only be made in writing and only by incorporating, in one document, all the terms which the parties to the transaction have expressly agreed. This document must be signed by or on behalf of each party to the contract. Transfers not complying with these provisions may not be legally effective to transfer land or the beneficial interest in such land. If the 'dormant' company will retain the land and, should that land generate income or incur costs, those will be transactions of the company. Thus, it may not be held to have been dormant during the periods in question.

### Additional disclosure to be made by dormant agency company

**8.154.21** An additional disclosure requirement applies where the directors of a company are taking advantage of the audit exemption for dormant companies in section 249AA of the 1985 Act (section 1169 of the 2006 Act) and the company has during the financial year acted as an agent for any person. In these circumstances the notes to the financial statements must include a statement that the company has so acted. [CA85 4 Sch 58A, 8 Sch 51A and 8A Sch 9A; SI 2008/ 409 1 Sch 63, SI 2008/410 1 Sch 71].

## Publication of financial statements

### Definition of publication

**8.155** Section 240 of the 1985 Act (section 434 of the 2006 Act) sets out the requirements that companies have to comply with when they 'publish' their financial statements. A company will be regarded as 'publishing' financial statements if it publishes, issues or circulates them, or otherwise makes them available for public inspection in a manner calculated to invite members of the public (or any class of members of the public) to read them. [CA85 Sec 240(4); CA06 Sec 436(2)]. The provisions of the 2006 Act in this area come into force on 6 April 2008.

**8.156**   A company may publish the following categories of financial statements:

- Statutory financial statements:
    - Full financial statements.
    - Abbreviated Companies Act accounts for small and medium-sized companies.
    - Shorter-form Companies Act accounts for small companies.
    - Balance sheet and notes for small companies.
    - Financial statements in euros.
- Summary financial statements.
- Non-statutory financial statements.
- Voluntary preliminary statements of annual results (for example, from companies listed on the Main Market of the LSE) for companies with accounting periods commencing on or after 20 January 2007 complying with the DTR and amended Listing Rules.
- Half-yearly financial reports of quoted companies.

The definitions and the rules for publication of these categories of financial statements are discussed in the paragraphs that follow.

### Statutory accounts

#### *Full financial statements*

**8.157**   Full financial statements are referred to in section 240(1) of the 1985 Act (section 434 of the 2006 Act) as a company's 'statutory accounts'. 'Statutory accounts' in that section means the company's individual financial statements or consolidated financial statements for a financial year, as required to be delivered to the Registrar under section 242 of the 1985 Act (section 441 of the 2006 Act). [CA85 Sec 240(5); CA06 Sec 434(3)]. Statutory accounts are referred to in the paragraphs that follow and throughout this book as statutory financial statements.

**8.158**   A company that publishes any of its statutory financial statements must include:

- The relevant auditors' report under section 235 of the 1985 Act (section 495 of the 2006 Act) or the report of a reporting accountant (on a company which is a charity) made for the purposes of section 249A(2) of the 1985 Act. [CA85 Sec 240(1); CA06 Sec 434(1)]. For accounting periods commencing on or after 6 April 2008, companies that are charities are governed by charity law and do not fall under the 2006 Act.

■ Its statutory consolidated financial statements for the same year with its statutory individual financial statements, if it is required to prepare statutory consolidated financial statements by section 227 of the 1985 Act (section 399 of the 2006 Act). [CA85 Sec 240(2); CA06 Sec 434(2)].

**8.159** If any of these requirements of section 240 of the 1985 Act (section 434 of the 2006 Act) are not complied with, the company and any officer of it who is in default will be guilty of an offence. [CA85 Sec 240(6); CA06 Sec 434(4)].

## Abbreviated Companies Act accounts

**8.160** Abbreviated accounts are not full financial statements; they are a special form of financial statements as defined by legislation. They may be prepared by some small and medium-sized companies that wish to take advantage of the special provisions for such companies for filing financial statements with the Registrar of Companies. [CA06 Secs 444(3), 445(3)]. These provisions permit a company that qualifies as small for a financial year to *file* abbreviated Companies Act individual accounts instead of full or shorter-form individual Companies Act accounts with the Registrar (CA85 section 246(5) for financial years beginning before 6 April 2008; CA06 section 444(3) and Regulation 6 of SI 2008/409 for financial years beginning on or after 6 April 2008). Such financial statements must be prepared in accordance with Schedule 8A to the 1985 Act (Schedule 4 to SI 2008/409).

**8.160.1** A company that qualifies as medium-sized may also file a form of abbreviated Companies Act individual accounts under the provisions for medium-sized companies.[CA85 Sec 246A(3); CA06 Sec 445(3) and Regulation 4(3) of SI 2008/410]. Such financial statements must be prepared in accordance with Schedule 4 to the 1985 Act as modified by section 246A(3) of that Act for financial years beginning before 6 April 2008 (Schedule 1 to SI 2008/410 as modified by Regulation 4(3) of SI 2008/410 for financial years beginning on or after 6 April 2008).

**8.160.2** The directors of a medium-sized company that is a parent company at the end of a financial year beginning on or after 6 April 2008 must prepare consolidated financial statements. The consolidated financial statements form part of the company's annual accounts (section 471 of the 2006 Act) that the directors must file with the Registrar of Companies (sections 446 of the 2006 Act). However, the annual accounts filed with the Registrar may comprise the company's abbreviated Companies Act individual and group accounts. The abbreviated Companies Act group accounts are prepared in accordance with Schedule 6 to SI 2008/410 as modified by Regulation 4(3) of SI 2008/410. [SI 2008/410 6 Sch para1(1)].

**8.160.3** The intention of these provisions is to provide small and medium-sized companies with a degree of privacy rather than to reduce the burden on them. A small or medium-sized company that files abbreviated accounts must still prepare full financial statements, including consolidated financial statements where required, for its members.

**8.161** Abbreviated financial statements in the prescribed form that are filed with the Registrar are the company's 'statutory accounts' for the purposes of section 240 of the Act (section 434(3) of the 2006 Act). In this case the reference in section 240 of the 1985 Act (section 435 of the 2006 Act) to the auditors' report is to be read as a reference to the special auditors' report referred to in section 247B of the 1985 Act (section 449 of the 2006 Act). [CA85 Sec 247B(5); CA06 Sec 449(5). The provisions relating to abbreviated financial statements are dealt with fully in chapter 32 of the Manual of Accounting – UK GAAP.

### Shorter-form Companies Act accounts for small companies

**8.162** The directors of a company that qualifies as a small company for a financial year are entitled under section 246(2) of the 1985 Act (section 396(3) of the 2006 Act and Regulation 3 of SI 2008/409) to *prepare* its Companies Act individual accounts in one of the two special formats included in Schedule 8 to the 1985 Act for financial years beginning before 6 April 2008 (Schedule 1 to SI 2008/409 for financial years beginning on or after 6 April 2008). Section 246(3) and (4) of the 1985 Act permits certain information required by section 231A of and Schedules 5, 6 and 7 to the 1985 Act to be omitted from these financial statements. Equivalent reliefs are found in sections 411(1), 416(3) and 417(1) of the 2006 Act.

**8.162.1** If at the end of a financial year a small company is a parent company its directors may also prepare consolidated financial statements under section 248A of the 1985 Act for financial years beginning before 6 April 2008 (section 398 of the 2006 Act for financial years beginning on or after 6 April 2008). Where that company's individual accounts are Companies Act accounts and its consolidated financial statements are Companies Act group accounts the latter must be prepared in accordance with Schedule 8 to the 1985 Act as modified by section 248A of that Act (Regulation 8 of, and Part 1 of Schedule 6 to, SI 2008/409) for the relevant financial year.

**8.163** If the directors prepare shorter-form financial statements for their company under section 246(2) of the 1985 Act (section 396(3) of the 2006 Act and Regulation 3 of SI 2008/409), they will be the company's annual financial statements. As a consequence, they must be authorised by the board of directors, sent to members (after having laid them before the company in general meeting if the election has not been made under the 1985 Act to dispense with laying financial statements) and filed with the Registrar. The company may, however, instead of filing the shorter-form financial statements prepare abbreviated financial statements specifically for filing and file these instead (see paras 8.134.3 and 8.160 above).

**8.164** Shorter-form financial statements that are filed with the Registrar are the company's statutory financial statements for the purposes of section 240 of the 1985 Act (section 434(3) of the 2006 Act). The formats provided for shorter-form financial statements do not reduce greatly the number of items to be shown compared with full financial statements.

**8.165** The accounting requirements concerning shorter-form financial statements are considered in detail in chapter 32 of the Manual of Accounting – UK GAAP.

## *Balance sheet and notes*

**8.166** A company subject to the small companies regime may file with the Registrar of Companies just a copy of the balance sheet and notes from the annual financial statements prepared for its members together with, where appropriate, a copy of the auditor's report sent to members. [CA06 Secs 444(1)(a), (2) and 472(2)]. This option is available to all qualifying companies irrespective of whether the financial statements prepared for their members are Companies Act or IAS financial statements. A company that takes this option may also file with its balance sheet and notes, the profit and loss account (and notes) and/or the directors' report sent to its members. [CA06 Secs 444(1)(b), 472(2)].

**8.167** The balance sheet and notes (and, where relevant, the profit and loss account and notes) filed with the Registrar are the company's 'statutory accounts' for the purposes of section 240 of the 1985 Act (section 434(3) of the 2006 Act).

**[The next paragraph is 8.170.]**

## Summary financial statements

## *Background*

**8.170** Both the 1985 Act and the 2006 Act permit companies, subject to certain conditions, to send summary financial statements to members in place of full financial statements. [CA85 Sec 251; CA06 Secs 426–429]. The provisions of the 2006 Act relating to summary financial statements are in force for financial years beginning on or after 6 April 2008. The 2006 Act contains little of the detailed requirements surrounding summary financial statements: instead this is the subject of SI 2008/374, 'The Companies (Summary Financial Statement) Regulations 2008'.

**8.171** Companies may send summary financial statements by electronic communication to members. The Act imposes the same conditions for sending summary financial statements to those who wish to receive them electronically, as mentioned in paragraphs 8.117.1 onwards above in connection with the electronic transmission of full financial statements. Sections 1143 to 1148 of, and Schedules 4 and 5 to, the 2006 Act govern a company's sending or supplying documents or information.

**8.172** Where summary financial statements are accessible on a web site to persons other than those entitled to receive the full financial statements (entitled persons), the summary financial statements should include the wording required by section 240(3) of the 1985 Act (section 435(1) of the 2006 Act). This is because they are not the company's statutory financial statements and are accessible to a wider audience than the entitled persons (see further para 8.196).

**8.173** Section 426(5) of the 2006 Act makes new provision for persons nominated to enjoy information rights under section 146 of the 2006 Act (indirect investors). Such persons may be provided with summary financial statements rather than the full accounts and reports.

**8.174** Summary financial statements have also been used by building societies, that are allowed to send such summaries to their members under the Building Societies Act 1986.

**8.175** Although summary financial statements have been issued by an increasing number of companies, the potential benefits must be set against the extra cost of preparing an additional set of financial statements and reports and their audit. The provisions relating to preparing and issuing summary financial statements are described below.

### General conditions

**8.176** A company is prohibited from sending summary financial statements to a member instead of full financial statements and reports in the following circumstances:

■ Where the company is prohibited from doing so by any provision in its memorandum or articles of association (for periods beginning on or after 6 April 2008, its constitution) or (where the member is a debenture holder) in any instrument governing the company's debentures. [SI 1995/2092 Reg 3; SI 2008/374 Reg 4(1)].

■ Where no auditors' report has been issued on the full financial statements under section 235 of the 1985 Act (section 495 of the 2006 Act). [SI 1995/2092 Reg 3; SI 2008/374 Reg 4(2)(a)].

**8.176.1** Where the member or other entitled person has indicated a wish to receive full financial statements and reports, they should receive them in addition to the summary financial statement. [CA85 Sec 251(2); CA06 Sec 426(2)].

**8.177** In addition, the company must not send summary financial statements for any financial year in place of copies of the full financial statements and reports, unless both the following conditions are satisfied:

■ The period allowed for laying and delivering full financial statements and reports under section 244 of the 1985 Act (section 442 of the 2006 Act) for that year has not expired.

- The summary financial statements have been approved by the board of directors and the original statements have been signed on the board's behalf by a director of the company.

[SI 1995/2092 Reg 4(4); SI 2008/374 Reg 4(2)].

**8.178** Summary financial statements must be derived from the company's annual accounts and reports, and, in the case of a quoted company, the directors' remuneration report (together referred to above and below as 'full financial statements and reports') and comply with the requirements of section 251 and the regulations made under it (sections 427 and 428 and the regulations made under those sections). [CA85 Sec 251(1); CA06 Secs 427, 428]. Provided that the summary financial statements sent to members comply with those requirements, the normal rules relating to publishing statutory and non-statutory financial statements in section 240 of the 1985 Act (sections 434 and 435 of the 2006 Act) do not apply. [CA85 Sec 251(7); CA06 Secs 434(6), 435(7)]. However, where they are accessible from a web site section 240 of the 1985 Act (section 435 of the 2006 Act) is likely to apply (see para 8.170.2).

**8.179** The requirements of section 251 of the 1985 Act (sections 426 to 429 of the 2006 Act) fall into the following categories:

- The manner in which the wishes of members to receive full financial statements and reports are to be ascertained. These provisions are set out in regulation 4 of SI 1995/2092 (regulations 5-8 of SI 2008/374).

- The statements to be included in the summary financial statement. [CA85 Sec 251(4); CA06 Secs 427(4), 428(4)].

- The form and content of summary financial statements. [SI 1995/2092 Regs 7-10, SI 2005/2281; SI 2008/374 Regs 9-11].

Unless these requirements are complied with, a company cannot send out summary financial statements. These requirements are discussed in more detail below.

**8.180** In addition to the above information, the UKLA's Listing Rules require companies with securities admitted to trading on a regulated market (that is, the main market of the LSE or Plus Market's PLUS-listed market) to disclose the earnings per share in summary financial statements. [LR 9.8.13].

### Ascertaining wishes of members

**8.181** A company cannot send summary financial statements to a member in place of its full financial statements and reports, unless it has ascertained that the member does not wish to receive the full financial statements and reports. A company has to ascertain whether a member wishes to receive full financial statements and reports for a financial year (and future years) from one of the following.

- From a relevant notification in writing expressly given to the company by the member as to:

  - whether the member wishes to receive the full financial statements and reports; or

  - whether, instead of full financial statements and reports, the member wishes to receive summary financial statements.

  A notification will be a relevant notification for a financial year if it relates to that year (whether given at the company's invitation or not) and is received by the company not later than 28 days before the first date on which copies of the full financial statements and reports are sent out to members under section 238(1),(1A) of the 1985 Act (sections 423(1) and 424(1) to (3) of the 2006 Act).

- Failing any express notification (that is, if a member has not replied to a consultation by notice or has not otherwise informed the company of a wish to receive full financial statements and reports), from a member's failure to respond to an opportunity to elect to receive copies of the full financial statements and reports in response to one of the following:

  - To the company's consultation by notice.

  - As part of a relevant consultation by the company of his wishes.

[SI 1995/2092 Reg 4(1)-(3); SI 2008/374 Reg 5].

### Consultation by notice

**8.182**   This procedure is a simple procedure by which companies may ascertain whether members wish to receive full financial statements and reports or summary financial statements. It enables a company to send to a member by post (or in any other manner authorised by the company's articles or under the company communications provisions of sections 1143 to 1148 of, and schedules 4 and 5 to, the 2006 Act an advance notice that must comply with all the following. The notice must:

- State that for the future the member will be sent summary financial statements for each financial year, unless notification is received by the company in writing of a wish to receive full financial statements and reports.

- State that the summary financial statements will contain a summary of the company's or group's profit and loss account, balance sheet and (in the case of a quoted company) the directors' remuneration report for that year and may contain additional information delivered from the directors' report or (in the case of a quoted company for years beginning before 6 April 2008) the operating and financial review for the year.

- State that the printed card or form accompanying the notice must be returned by the date specified in the notice. This date must be at least 21 days after the notice is sent out and not less than 28 days before the first date on which copies of the full financial statements and reports for the next financial year are to be sent out to members under section 238(1) of the 1985 Act (sections 423(1) and 424(1) — (3) of the 2006 Act).

■ Include in a prominent position a statement that a summary financial statement will not contain sufficient information to allow as full an understanding of the results and state of affairs of the company (or group, as applicable) as would be provided by the full financial statements and reports and that members and debenture holders requiring more detailed information have the right to obtain, free of charge, a copy of the company's last full financial statements and reports.

■ State that the summary financial statements will contain a statement by the company's auditors as to whether:

   ■ The summary financial statements are consistent with the annual financial statements and the directors' report (if information derived from that report is included) for the year in question.

   ■ In the case of a quoted company, the summary financial statements are consistent with the directors' remuneration report and (for financial periods beginning before 6 April 2008, the operating and financial review for the year in question).

   ■ The summary financial statements comply with either the requirements of section 251 of the 1985 Act and of SI 1995/2092, 'The Companies (Summary Financial Statement) Regulations 1995' for financial years beginning before 6 April 2008 or the requirements of section 427 (for unquoted companies) or section 428 (for quoted companies) and SI 2008/374, 'The Companies (Summary Financial Statement) Regulations 2008' for financial years beginning on or after 6 April 2008.

   ■ Their report on the financial statements was unqualified or qualified.

[SI 1995/2092 Reg 5(1), CA85 Sec 251; SI 2008/374 Reg 6, CA06 Secs 427 to 428].

**8.183** The printed card or form accompanying the notice (mentioned above) must be worded so as to enable a member, by marking a box and returning the card or form, to notify the company of a wish to receive full financial statements and reports for the next financial year and for all future financial years. Postage for the return of the printed card or form must be borne by the company, unless the member or debenture holder is outside the European Economic Area. [SI 1995/2092 Reg 5(2),(3); SI 2008/374 Reg 8(2),(4)].

*Relevant consultation*

**8.184** A 'relevant consultation' is an alternative option which companies may use to establish whether a member wishes to receive summary financial statements and also to establish whether any member who has chosen to receive full financial statements and reports would like to change and receive summary financial statements instead. A relevant consultation of the wishes of a member is a notice given to a member by post (or in any other manner authorised by the company's articles or under the company communications provisions of the 2006 Act (sections 1143 to 1148 of, and schedules 4 and 5 to, the 2006 Act) which complies with all the following:

- It states that in future the member will be sent a summary financial statement instead of full financial statements and reports, unless the company is notified in writing that the member wishes to *continue* to receive the full financial statements.

- It accompanies a copy of the full financial statements and reports.

- It accompanies a copy of the summary financial statements for the same financial year and this is identified in the notice as an example of the statement the member will receive in the future, unless the company is notified otherwise.

- It is accompanied by a printed card or form which is worded so as to enable the member, by marking a box and returning the card or form, to notify the company of a wish to receive full financial statements and reports for the next financial year and for all future financial years. Postage on the return of the card or form must be paid by the company unless the member or debenture holder is outside the European Economic Area.

[SI 1995/2092 Reg 6, SI 2008/374 Regs 7, 8(2)(3)].

### *Statements to be included in all summary financial statements*

**8.185**   All summary financial statements must:

- State that they are only a summary of information in the company's annual financial statements and, in the case of a quoted company, the directors' remuneration report.

- State whether they contain additional information derived from the directors' report and, if so, state that they do not contain the full text of that report or review.

- State how an entitled person can obtain a copy of the full financial statements.

- Contain a statement by the company's auditors as to whether the summary financial statements:

  - Are consistent with the annual financial statements, the directors' remuneration report and, where information derived from the directors' report is included, with that report.

  - Comply with the requirements of section 251 of the 1985 Act and SI 1995/2092 (section 427 (in the case of unquoted companies) or section 428 (in the case of quoted companies) of the 2006 Act and SI 2008/374).

■ State whether the auditors' report on the annual financial statements (and, in the case of a quoted company, the auditable part of the directors' remuneration report) was unqualified or qualified and, if it was qualified, set out the report in full together with any further material required to understand the qualification.

■ State whether, in the auditors' report on the annual financial statements the auditors' statement under section 235(3) of the 1985 Act (section 496 of the 2006 Act) (whether the directors' report is consistent with accounts) was qualified or unqualified. If it was qualified, the qualified statement should be set out in full, together with any additional information needed to understand the qualification.

■ State whether the auditors' report contained a statement concerning proper accounting records or inadequate returns under section 237(2) of the 1985 Act (section 498(2) of the 2006 Act), or failure to obtain certain necessary information and explanations under section 237(3) of the 1985 Act (section 498(3) of the 2006 Act). If so, the statement will have to be set out in full.

[CA85 Sec 251(4); CA06 Secs 427(4), 428(4)].

■ State the name of the director who signed them on behalf of the board.

■ Include, where the company is required to prepare consolidated financial statements, a statement in a prominent position that the summary financial statements do not contain sufficient information to allow as full an understanding of the results of the group and state of affairs of the company or of the group and of their policies and arrangements concerning directors' remuneration as would be provided by the full financial statements and reports; and that members and debenture holders requiring more detailed information have the right to obtain, free of charge, a copy of the company's last full financial statements and reports.

■ Where a company is not required to prepare consolidated financial statements, a similar statement appropriately amended to refer solely to the company must be included in the summary financial statements.

■ Contain a clear, conspicuous statement of how members and debenture holders:

  ■ can obtain, free of charge, a copy of the company's last full financial statements and reports; and

  ■ may elect in writing to receive full financial statements and reports in place of summary financial statements for all future financial years.

[SI 1995/2092 Reg 7, SI 2008/374 Reg 9].

**[The next paragraph is 8.185.2.]**

**8.185.2**  As noted above, the summary financial statements must state whether the auditors' report on the annual financial statements (and, in the case of a quoted company, the auditable part of the directors' remuneration report) was unqualified or qualified and, if it was qualified, must set out the report in full together with any further material required to understand the qualification. APB Bulletin 1999/6, 'The auditors' statement on the summary financial statement', expands on this and states that if the auditors' report on the full annual financial statements includes an explanatory paragraph dealing with a fundamental uncertainty, the auditors should refer to the uncertainty in their statement on the summary financial statement in sufficient detail for the reader to obtain a proper understanding of the issue or issues involved. For periods commencing on or after 6 April 2008, APB Bulletin 1999/6 has been superseded by APB Bulletin 2008/3, 'The auditors' statement on the summary financial statement', which provides similar guidance and states that, if the auditors' report on the full annual financial statements includes an 'emphasis of matter' paragraph that includes a reference to a note to the financial statements, unless that note is included in the summary financial statements, the information contained in it should be reproduced in the auditors' statement.

### Form and content of summary financial statement

**8.186**  For periods beginning before 6 April 2008, Schedule 1 to SI 1995/2092 specifies slightly different forms for summary financial statements that can be prepared by companies and by groups that prepare their annual financial statements in accordance with UK GAAP. Schedule 3A to the those regulations specifies the form and content of summary financial statements of companies and groups that prepare their annual financial statements in accordance with EU-adopted IFRS. (Schedules 2 and 3 deal with the forms that apply to banking and insurance companies preparing financial statements under Schedule 9 and 9A to the 1985 Act). For periods beginning on or after 6 April 2008, Schedules 1 and 4 to SI 2008/374 specify the forms for summary financial statements prepared by companies and groups respectively that prepare their annual financial statements in accordance with UK GAAP. Schedules 7 and 8 of those regulations apply to companies and groups respectively that prepare their annual financial statements in accordance with EU-adopted IFRS. The remaining schedules apply to banking and insurance companies and groups.

**8.187**  The paragraphs that follow outline the form and content of summary financial statements that are applicable to companies that prepare consolidated financial statements in accordance with UK GAAP or EU-adopted IFRS (except banking, and insurance, companies and groups to which different rules apply).

**8.188**  Summary financial statements must contain the information prescribed by the relevant schedule (see para 8.186) to the regulations in such order and under such headings as the directors consider appropriate. In addition, any other information necessary to ensure that the summary financial statements are consistent with the full financial statements and reports for the financial year in question must be given.

*Secretarial matters*

***Summary directors' emoluments and remuneration report information***

**8.189**   For periods beginning before 6 April 2008, the summary financial statements must include:

- That portion of the notes to the financial statements for the year in question that sets out the information on the aggregate amount of directors' emoluments and other disclosures required by paragraph 1(1) of Part 1 of Schedule 6 to the Act.

- To the extent that the company is required to produce a directors' remuneration report, those portions of the report for the year in question that set out the statement of the company's policy on directors' remuneration (paragraph 3 of Schedule 7A to the 1985 Act) and the performance graph (paragraph 4 of Schedule 7A to the 1985 Act).

[SI 1995/2092 Sch 1 para 2A, Sch 3A para 2].

**8.189.1**   For periods on or after 6 April 2008, the summary financial statements must include:

- The whole or a summary of the notes to the financial statements for the year in question that sets out the information on the aggregate amount of directors' emoluments and other disclosures required by paragraph 1 of Schedule 3 to SI 2008/409, 'The Small Companies (Accounts and Directors' Report) Regulations 2008', or paragraph 1 of Schedule 5 to SI 2008/410, 'The Large and Medium-sized Companies (Accounts and Reports) Regulations 2008', as the case may be.

- To the extent that the company is required to produce a directors' remuneration report, those portions of the report for the year in question that set out the statement of the company's policy on directors' remuneration (paragraph 3 of Schedule 8 to SI 2008/410) and the performance graph (paragraph 4 of Schedule 8 to SI 2008/410).

- Where, at the end of the year, the company has securities carrying voting rights admitted to trading on a regulated market (for example, the main market of the LSE or the Plus Market's PLUS-listed market), the information required by paragraphs 13 and 14 of Schedule 7 to SI 2008/410 to be included in the directors' report that derives from the EU Takeovers Directive. (This may be sent together with the summary financial statements, rather than included within them).These requirements are considered further in chapter 3.

[SI 2008/384 Regs 9, 10].

***Summary profit and loss account***

**8.190**   The format of the summary consolidated profit and loss account will depend the format the company has adopted in its full financial statements.

**8.191**  For companies or groups preparing their annual financial statements in accordance with UK GAAP, the summary profit and loss account is required to contain the following line items:

- Turnover.

- Income from interests in associated undertakings.

- The net of other interest receivable and similar income and interest payable and similar charges.

- Profit or loss on ordinary activities before tax.

- Tax on the profit or loss on ordinary activities.

- Profit or loss on ordinary activities after tax.

- Extraordinary items (although these have been all but eliminated by FRS 3).

- Profit or loss for the financial year.

- Earnings per share (for listed companies).

[SI 1995/2092 Sch 1 para 3; SI 2008/374 Sch 1 para 1; LR 9.8.13].

**8.191.1**  For companies or groups preparing their annual financial statements in accordance with EU-adopted IFRS, the summary profit and loss account (which is shown in the illustration below) is required to include each of the headings and sub-totals included in the full profit and loss account, although aggregation of such headings and sub-totals is permitted where they are similar in nature and the directors consider it appropriate. In addition, as mentioned in paragraph 8.180, listed companies must disclose of earnings per share. As illustrated, the summary profit and loss account will not add up from top to bottom.

| Summary consolidated profit and loss account | |
| --- | --- |
| Turnover | X |
| Operating profit | X |
| Other interest receivable and similar income and interest payable and similar charges | X |
| Share of post tax income from associates | X |
| Profit or loss on ordinary activities before tax | X |
| Tax on profit or loss on ordinary activities | X |
| Profit or loss on ordinary activities after tax | X |
| Profit or loss attributable to minority interest | X |
| Profit or loss attributable to equity shareholders | X |
| Earnings per share      – basic | X |
| – diluted | X |

*Summary balance sheet*

**8.191.2**   Summary financial statements must include a summary balance sheet.

**8.192**   For companies or groups preparing their annual financial statements in accordance with UK GAAP, the summary balance sheet is required to show, under such headings as the directors consider appropriate, a single amount for each heading to which letters are assigned in the format used for the full balance sheet in the order set out in that balance sheet. Balance sheet formats are discussed in chapter 4 of the Manual of Accounting – UK GAAP.

**8.192.1**   For groups preparing their annual financial statements in accordance with EU-adopted IFRS, the summary balance sheet is required to show each of the headings and sub-totals included in the full balance sheet, although such headings and sub-totals may be combined where they are similar in nature and the directors consider it appropriate. An illustrative summary balance sheet is shown below.

| Summary consolidated balance sheet | | |
|---|---|---|
| Fixed assets | | |
| Tangible fixed assets | | X |
| Intangible fixed assets | | X |
| Current assets | X | |
| Current liabilities | (X) | |
| Net current assets/(liabilities) | | X |
| Total assets less current liabilities | | X |
| Long-term liabilities | | (X) |
| | | X |
| Capital and reserves | | X |
| Minority interests | | X |
| | | X |

**8.193**   Whether a group prepares UK GAAP or IFRS financial statements, the order of the line items included in the summary balance sheet must be consistent with the order of the line items included in the annual financial statements.

*Dividends*

**8.193.1**   The summary financial statements are also required to contain the information concerning recognised and proposed dividends that is included in the notes to the annual financial statements. [SI 1995/2092 Sch 1 para 3A, Sch 3A para 3(2); SI 2008/374 Sch 1 para 2, Sch 7 para 1(2), Sch 8 para 1(2)].

## Comparative information

**8.193.2** For both the summary profit and loss account and the summary balance sheet. Comparative information must be disclosed for the immediately preceding financial year. This information must be prepared on the same basis as the comparative information included in the group's annual financial statements.

## Penalties

**8.194** Default in complying with section 251 of the 1985 Act (sections 426 to 428 of the 2006 Act) or SI 1995/2092 (SI 2008/374) renders the company and every officer of it who is in default, guilty of an offence and liable to a fine. [CA85 Sec 251(6); CA06 Sec 429].

## Non-statutory accounts

**8.195** Non-statutory accounts are not full financial statements. A company must comply with the provisions of section 240(3) (section 435(1),(2) of the 2006 Act) when it *publishes* non-statutory accounts. 'Non-statutory accounts' means any balance sheet or profit and loss account of the company or the group that either relates to, or purports to deal with, a company's or group's full financial year, otherwise than as part of the company's statutory financial statements. [CA85 Sec 240(5)(a),(b); CA06 Sec 435(3)]. This means that where a full year's figures and a narrative explanation of those figures are recognisable as either a balance sheet or a profit and loss account of the company or the group, the rules that relate to non-statutory accounts are likely to apply. 'Publication' and 'statutory accounts' are discussed in paragraphs 8.155 and 8.157.

**8.196** Where a company publishes non-statutory accounts, those accounts must be accompanied by a statement indicating:

- That the accounts are not the company's statutory accounts.

- Whether or not the statutory accounts have been delivered to the Registrar for the same year.

- Whether or not the auditors have reported under section 235 of the 1985 Act (section 495 of the 2006 Act) on the statutory accounts for that year.

- Whether or not the auditors' report was qualified or unqualified or contained a statement:

  - Drawing attention by way of emphasis to any matters without qualifying the report.

  - Under section 237(2) (section 498(2) of the 2006 Act), where accounting records or returns have been inadequate, or the financial statements have not agreed with the records or returns.

  - Under section 237(3) (section 498(3) of the 2006 Act), where necessary information and explanations have not been received.

- Where no auditors' report has been made and the company falls into the category of a small company, which is exempt from being audited under section 249A of the 1985 Act, whether the company's reporting accountant has made a report (on a small charitable company) for the purposes of section 249A(2) of the 1985 Act on its statutory financial statements for that year. Under the 2006 Act, the specific rules governing small charity audits from the 1985 Act are not carried forward. From April 2008 small companies that are charities will be governed by charity law as to the degree of scrutiny required on their accounts.

- Where no auditors' report has been made, whether any report made for the purposes of section 249A(2) of the 1985 Act (on a charitable company) was qualified. (See above about small charitable companies under the 2006 Act.)

[CA85 Sec 240(3); CA06 Sec 435(1)].

**8.197** Where a company publishes non-statutory accounts dealing with one financial year and the company's full financial statements are subject to audit, a statement along the lines of one or other of the following examples (as appropriate) should be included in the non-statutory accounts. (See para 8.199 for the statement where there is comparative information.)

### Example 1

The figures and financial information for the year 20XX do not constitute the statutory financial statements for that year. Those financial statements have been delivered to the Registrar and included the auditors' report which was unqualified and neither drew attention to any matters by way of emphasis nor contained a statement under either section 237(2) of the 1985 Act (section 498(2) of the 2006 Act) (accounting records or returns inadequate or accounts not agreeing with records and returns), or section 237(3) (section 498(3) of the 2006 Act) (failure to obtain necessary information and explanations).

### Example 2

The figures and financial information for the year 20XX do not constitute the statutory financial statements for that year. Those financial statements have not yet been delivered to the Registrar, nor have the auditors yet reported on them.

**8.198** When a company publishes non-statutory accounts and the company is exempt from audit, but is subject to the requirement for a reporting accountant's report under section 249A of the 1985 Act (on a charitable company), a statement along one or the other of the following lines (as appropriate) should be included in the non-statutory accounts. Under the 2006 Act, the specific rules governing small charity audits from the 1985 Act are not carried forward. From April 2008 small companies that are charities are governed by charity law as to the degree of scrutiny required on their accounts.

**Example 1**

The figures and financial information for the year 20XX do not constitute the statutory financial statements for that year. Those financial statements have been delivered to the Registrar and included the reporting accountant's report for the purposes of section 249A(2) of the 1985 Act which was unqualified.

**Example 2**

The figures and financial information for the year 20XX do not constitute the statutory financial statements for that year. Those financial statements have not yet been delivered to the Registrar, nor has the reporting accountant made a report for the purposes of section 249A(2) of the 1985 Act.

**8.199**   Where published non-statutory accounts deal with more than one year (for example, voluntary preliminary statements of the annual results of listed companies that must include comparative figures for the previous year), the one document may contain two sets of non-statutory accounts. Where this applies, the wording of the appropriate statement in paragraph 8.197 should be adapted to cover both sets of accounts.

**8.200**   A company that does not comply with the requirements for the publication of non-statutory accounts outlined above and any officer who is in default will be guilty of an offence. [CA85 Sec 240(6); CA06 435(5)].

**8.201**   Published non-statutory accounts must not include the auditors' report made in connection with the company's annual financial statements in accordance with section 235 of the 1985 Act (section 495 of the 2006 Act) or any report by a reporting accountant made for the purposes of section 249A(2) of the 1985 Act on the individual financial statements of a charitable company which is exempt for the requirement to have an audit. See paragraph 8.198 relating to provisions of the 2006 Act relating to small companies that are also a charity. [CA85 Sec 240(3); CA06 Sec 435(2)].

## Additional rules for listed companies

### Preliminary announcements

**8.202**   For accounting periods commencing on or after 20 January 2007, preliminary statements of annual results of companies admitted to trading on a regulated market (for example, the main market of the LSE or Plus Market's PLUS-listed market) are no longer required under the UKLA's Listing Rules and, thus, *voluntary*. However, if a listed company issues a voluntary preliminary statement of annual results it must comply with LR 9.7A.1 and be published as soon as possible after it has been approved by the board. Despite the rule change, preliminary announcements are expected to continue to be produced as they are generally considered to play a key part in the annual financial reporting cycle as they are the first public communication of companies' results for the whole year.

Preliminary announcements of listed companies (including those traded on AIM and the PLUS-quoted market) are considered in more detail in chapter 31 of the Manual of Accounting – IFRS for the UK.

**[The next paragraph is 8.204.]**

### Half-yearly reports

**8.204** For accounting periods beginning on or after 20 January 2007, issuers of any shares and debt (denominated in units of less than 50,000 euros) admitted to trading on a regulated market (for example, the main market of the LSE and Plus Market's PLUS-listed market) must publish half yearly reports within two months of the period end. [DTR 4.2.2] Further details on the content and publication requirements are dealt with in chapter 31 of the Manual of Accounting – IFRS for the UK.

### Interim management statements

**8.205** For accounting periods beginning on or after 20 January 2007, the FSA's DTR require companies with listed shares that do not already report quarterly (either voluntarily or to meet regulatory requirements) to prepare interim management statements (IMS). See further chapter 31 of the Manual of Accounting — IFRS for the UK.

**[The next paragraph is 8.207.]**

### AIM Companies

**8.207** The AIM Rules provide that AIM companies must prepare a half-yearly report and issue it within three months of the end of the relevant period. The half-yearly report should cover the six month period from the date of the financial information disclosed in the admission document and at least every subsequent six months thereafter (apart from the final period of six months preceding its accounting reference date for its annual audited financial statements). [AIMR 18]. The guidance notes to the Rules state that the LSE will suspend AIM companies that are late in publishing their half-yearly report or annual financial statements. The content of interim reports for AIM companies is dealt with the chapter 31 of the Manual of Accounting – IFRS for the UK.

### PLUS-quoted Companies

**8.207.1** The PLUS Markets Rules provide that PLUS-quoted companies must prepare an interim report for the first half of each financial period and issue it as soon as possible, but no later than three months after the end of the relevant period. The interim report should contain a statement by the Board, the profit and loss account and a statement of whether or not the information has been reviewed by the company's auditor. [PLUS markets Rules 30-31].

**Status of half yearly reports, preliminary announcements and other statements**

**8.208** Half yearly reports are considered to be non-statutory accounts, because they contain comparative financial information for the last full financial year. Consequently, the provisions of the Companies Acts 1985 and 2006 that relate to non-statutory accounts (mentioned in para 8.195 above) apply. Half yearly reporting (interim reporting) is dealt with more fully in chapter 31 of the Manual of Accounting – IFRS for the UK.

**[The next paragraph is 8.210.]**

**8.210** Preliminary statements of annual results that listed companies may issue are *prima facie* considered to be non-statutory accounts. This is because the preliminary results either relate to, or purport to deal with, a company's full financial year. Furthermore, the information that paragraph 9.7A of the UKLA's Listing Rules (for voluntary preliminary announcements) require companies to give on a preliminary basis is capable of being recognised as a balance sheet or a profit and loss account. Consequently, where a listed company publishes a preliminary statement of annual results, the rules in the Companies Acts 1985 and 2006 that relate to non-statutory accounts apply. The ASB's statement, 'Preliminary Announcements', states that the preliminary announcement should contain a statement that satisfies the provision of section 240 of the 1985 Act (section 435 of the 2006 Act) regarding the publication of non-statutory accounts. [PA para 50]. The requirements for preliminary announcements are discussed more fully in chapter 31 of the Manual of Accounting – IFRS for the UK.

**8.210.1** Where a company publishes preliminary statements of annual results or half-yearly reports they must comply with the rules for non-statutory financial statements and include the appropriate wording referred to in paragraphs 8.197 and 8.198 above.

**8.211** Another possible example of non-statutory accounts is the special reports that some companies prepare for employees. Much depends on whether the report either relates to, or purports to deal with, the company's activities during a full financial year, and also on whether it takes the form of a recognisable balance sheet or a profit and loss account. Where the report meets the non-statutory accounts criteria, the rules for such accounts must be followed and the appropriate wording used.

**8.212** The five year or ten year summaries of financial information provided by listed companies are not considered to be non-statutory accounts. The reason for this is that the purpose of such a summary is not to deal with a company's activities for any particular year. Rather its purpose is to put the company's current position in a larger perspective and to provide pointers for the future.

**Compensation for false statements in reports and financial statements**

**8.213.1**   With effect from 8 November 2006, the 2006 Act inserted specific provisions into the Financial Services and Markets Act 2000 (FSMA) concerning liability of listed companies for false and misleading statements in their annual financial statements, half yearly reports or interim management statements required under the EU Transparency Obligations Directive (2004/109/EC), as implemented in the UK through the UKLA's DTR. [FSMA Sec 90A(1)(a); CA06 Sec 1269]. The provisions also extend to any preliminary statement of results that may be given voluntarily under Listing Rule 9.7A. [FSMA Sec 90A(1)(b)]. Listed company in this respect generally means a UK incorporated public company that has any of its securities traded on a regulated market situated or operating in, or outside, the UK. [FSMA Sec 90A(2)].

**8.213.2**   The listed company is liable to pay compensation to a person who has acquired any of its securities and has suffered a loss in respect of them as a result of any untrue or misleading statement in the publications referred to in paragraph 8.213.1, or as a result of an omission of a matter required to be included in the relevant publication. A loss is not regarded as having been suffered as a result of the statement or omission in the relevant publication, unless the person suffering the loss acquired the relevant securities in reliance on the information in the publication, and at the time when, and in circumstances in which, it was reasonable for him to rely on that information. Furthermore, the listed company is liable only if a person discharging managerial responsibilities (for example, a director) within the company responsible for the relevant publication knew the statement to be untrue or misleading, or was reckless as to whether it was untrue or misleading, or knew the omission to be dishonest concealment of a material fact. A person other than the listed company (for example, a director) is not subject to any liability, other than to the listed company, in respect of such loss.

# Revision of defective financial statements

**8.214**   The Companies Act 1985 contains provisions (which have been carried forward to the 2006 Act) that:

- Permit directors to prepare revised financial statements, a revised directors' report or a revised directors' remuneration report where it appears to them that the annual financial statements, the directors' report or the directors' remuneration report did not comply with the Act or, where applicable, Article 4 of the IAS Regulation ('voluntary revision'). [CA85 Sec 245; CA06 Sec 454].

- Permit the Secretary of State (in the absence of a satisfactory explanation from the company's directors as to the question of whether the annual financial statements comply with the Act), to apply to the court for an order that revised financial statements, directors' report or directors' remuneration report should be prepared. Such an application can only be made by the Secretary of State or a person authorised by the Secretary of State ('compulsory revision'). [CA85 Sec 245(A),(B),(C); CA06 Sec 455, 456, 457]. The FRRP is authorised for this purpose. By agreement with BERR, the normal ambit of the FRRP is public and large private companies, BERR dealing with all other cases.

**8.214.1** Chapter 11 of Part 15 of the 2006 Act restates the provisions under the 1985 Act in relation to revision of financial statements. This part of the Act applies to revisions of financial statements or reports for accounting periods commencing on or after 6 April 2008. The 2006 Act states the broad principles allowing revision of financial statements, but the detail is found in SI 2008/272, 'The Companies (Revision of Defective Accounts and Reports) Regulations 2008'.

**Voluntary revision**

**8.215** The detailed regulations governing preparing, auditing and issuing revised financial statements and directors' reports for years commencing before 6 April 2008, where the revision is voluntary, are contained in SI 1990/2570, 'The Companies (Revision of Defective Accounts and Report) Regulations 1990'. For periods after that date, the detailed regulations are contained in SI 2008/373, 'The Companies (Revision of Defective Accounts and Reports) Regulations 2008'. The content of the regulations are described below. References to 'Regulations' covers both SI 1990/2570 and SI 2008/373, unless otherwise stated.

**8.216** If it appears to the company's directors that the financial statements, the directors' report or the directors' remuneration report did not comply with the requirements of the Companies Act 1985 (or the Companies Act 2006, where appropriate), they may prepare revised financial statements or a revised report or review. [CA85 Sec 245(1); CA06 Sec 454(1)]. Where copies of the previous financial statements or report have been laid before the company in general meeting or delivered to the Registrar, the revisions are required to be confined to:

■ Correcting those aspects in which the previous financial statements did not comply with the requirements of the Act or, where applicable, Article 4 of the IAS regulation.

■ Making any necessary consequential alterations.

[CA85 Sec 245(2); CA06 Sec 454(2)].

It appears, therefore, that if the directors wish to revise the financial statements, directors' report or directors' remuneration report after the financial statements are sent out to members, but before they are laid before the company in general meeting, the revisions do not have to be confined to the matters listed above.

**8.217** Revision of the financial statements, directors' report or directors' remuneration report may be made either by preparing replacement financial statements or directors' reports or by preparing a supplementary note indicating the corrections to be made to the original documents.

**8.218** Where a decision has been made to replace the original financial statements or directors' report or directors' remuneration report, they should be prepared in the normal way in accordance with the Act's provisions that were in force at the date on which the original financial statements and directors' report were approved. (And not, as might have been expected, the provisions in force at the company's year end date.) There could, therefore, be additional consequential amendments to be made as a result of changes in the Act between the company's year end and the date of approval of the original financial statements.

**8.219**  The regulations state that the Act's provisions relating to the matters to be included in a company's annual financial statements shall apply to the revised financial statements (whether prepared in accordance with UK GAAP or IFRS) as if the revised financial statements were prepared and approved by the directors as at the date of approval of the original financial statements. [SI 1990/2570 Reg 3(1); SI 2008/373 Reg 3(1)]. Similar provisions for directors' reports and directors' remuneration reports are contained in regulation 3(4) of SI 1990/2570 (regulation 3(4) of SI 2008/373). The purpose of this is to exclude from consideration events that occur between the date of approval of the original financial statements and the date of approval of the revised financial statements, directors' report or directors' remuneration report.

### *Approving and signing revised financial statements*

**8.220**  The regulations provide that the revised financial statements must be approved by the board and signed by a director on the board's behalf. In the case of revision by supplementary note the signature should appear on the supplementary note.

**8.221**  Where the original financial statements have been sent to members, laid before the company in general meeting, or delivered to the Registrar, all the following must be stated in the financial statements that are revised by replacement.

- That the revised financial statements replace the original financial statements for the financial year (specifying it).

- That they are now the company's statutory financial statements for that financial year.

- That they have been prepared as at the date of the original annual financial statements (that is, the date on which the original financial statements were approved) and not as at the date of revision (that is, the date of approval of the revised financial statements) and, accordingly, do not deal with events between those dates.

- The respects in which the original financial statements did not comply with the Act's requirements.

■ Any significant amendments made as a consequence of remedying the defects.

[SI 1990/2570 Reg 4(2)(a); SI 2008/373 Reg 4(2)(a)].

**8.222** Where the financial statements are revised by supplementary note the following statements must be made in the note:

■ That the note revises in certain respects the company's original annual financial statements and is to be treated as forming part of those financial statements.

■ That the annual financial statements have been revised as at the date of the original financial statements and not as at the date of revision (see point three in para 8.221) and, accordingly, do not deal with events between those dates.

[SI 1990/2570 Reg 4(2)(b) ; SI 2008/373 Reg 4(2)(b)].

**8.223** The date of approval of the revised financial statements must be given in those financial statements. In the case of revision by supplementary note, the date should be given in the note itself. [SI 1990/2570 Reg 4(2); SI 2008/373 Reg 4(2)].

*Approving and signing revised directors' report or directors' remuneration report*

**8.224** Similar considerations apply to a revised directors' report or revised directors' remuneration report. The revised report must be approved by the board and signed on its behalf by a director or, or in the case of a revised directors' report, by a director or the company secretary. In the case of revision by supplementary note the note must be signed. Where the original directors' report or original directors' remuneration report has been sent to members, laid before the company in general meeting, or delivered to the Registrar of Companies, all the following must be stated in the report that is revised by replacement:

■ That the revised report replaces the original report for the financial year (specifying the year).

■ That it has been prepared as at the date of approval of the original directors' report or original directors' remuneration report and not as at the date of approval of the revision and, accordingly, does not deal with any events between those dates.

■ The respects in which the original directors' report or original directors' remuneration report did not comply with the Act's requirements.

■ Any significant amendments made as a consequence of remedying the defects.

[SI 1990/2570 Reg 5(2)(a); SI 2008/373 Regs 5(2)(a), 6(2)(a)].

**8.225** Where the report is revised by supplementary note the note must state the following:

- That the note revises in certain respects the original directors' report or directors' remuneration report of the company and is to be treated as forming part of that report.

- That the directors' report or directors' remuneration report has been revised as at the date of approval of the original report and not as at the date of approval of the revision and, accordingly, does not deal with events between those dates.

[SI 1990/2570 Reg 5(2)(b), 5A(2)(b); SI 2008/373 Regs 5(2)(b), 6(2)(b)].

**8.226** The date of approval of the revised report must be given in the revised report (or in the supplementary note, if revision is made by supplementary note). [SI 1990/2570 Reg 5(2), 5A(2); SI 2008/373 Regs 5(2), 6(2)].

*Auditors' report*

**8.227** The report on the revised financial statements should be made by the company's current auditors. If, however, there has been a change of auditors between the date of the original financial statements and the date of the revised financial statements the directors of the company may resolve that the report will be made by the former auditors. In this case, the former auditors will have to agree to do so and be qualified for appointment as the company's auditors. [SI 1990/2570 Regs 6(1), 7(1); SI 2008/373 Regs 7(1), 7(2)].

**8.228** Whether the auditors' report as present or former auditors, the contents of the report must be the same. It must deal with all of the following matters:

- Whether in the auditors' opinion the revised financial statements have been properly prepared in accordance with the Act's provisions (and, where applicable, those of article 4 of the IAS regulation) as they have effect under the regulations.

- Whether in their opinion a true and fair view, seen as at the date when the original financial statements were approved, is given by the revised financial statements of the state of the company's affairs at the end of the financial year, and of the profit or loss of the company for the financial year (or, in the case of consolidated financial statements, of the state of affairs of the company and the group at the end of the financial year and of the profit or loss of the group for the financial year).

- Whether in the auditors' opinion the original annual financial statements failed to comply with the Act's requirements (and, where applicable, those of article 4 to the IAS regulation) in the respect identified by the directors:

  - in the situation where the revision is made by replacement, in the statement the directors are required to make in the revised financial statements (see the fourth point in para 8.221 above); and

- in the situation where the revision is made by supplementary note, in the supplementary note.

[SI 1990/2570 Reg 6(3); SI 2008/373 Reg 7(3)].

**8.229** The auditors must also state whether the information in the original directors' report or, if this has been revised, the revised report, is consistent with the revised financial statements. [SI 1990/2570 Reg 6(4); SI 2008/373 Reg 7(4)].

**8.230** Where the financial statements are not being revised, but the directors' report or directors' remuneration report is, the present or former auditors (as the directors decide) are not required to report on the financial statements. They must, however, report on the revised report and state the period covered by the financial statements with which it is consistent.

**8.230.1** Where the directors' remuneration report has been revised, the auditors' report must state whether, in the auditors' opinion, any auditable part of that revised report has been properly prepared. [SI 1990/2570 Reg 6(3B); SI 2008/373 Reg 9(4)].

### Reporting accountant's report

**8.231** For financial years beginning before 6 April 2008, small companies that are charities are, as a condition of the exemption, required to obtain a reporting accountant's report under section 249A(2) of the 1985 Act in respect of their individual financial statements. Where a reporting accountant has made a report for the purposes of section 249A(2) on a charitable company's original financial statements, they have to make another report to the company's members on any revised financial statements. Alternatively, the directors may decide that the report should be made by someone who was not the original reporting accountant, but nevertheless is qualified to act as the company's reporting accountant. [SI 1990/2570 Reg 6A(1)(2)]. The 2006 Act does not carry forward the specific provisions of the 1985 Act in relation to small companies that are charities.

**8.232** Where a company that was exempt from audit and a reporting accountant's report, but since requires a reporting accountant's report, it must obtain such a report on the revised financial statements in accordance with section 249C of the 1985 Act. Similarly, it is not eligible to obtain an accountant's report, it must have the revised financial statements audited. [SI 1990/2570 Reg 6B(1)(2)].

**8.233** On being signed by the reporting accountant, the replacement report substitutes the report on the original financial statements. [SI 1990/2570 Reg 6A(4)]. The accountant's report or the auditors' report must be delivered to the Registrar within 28 days after the date on which the financial statements were revised. [SI 1990/2570 Reg 6B(3)].

### Effects of revision

**8.234** As soon as the revised financial statements, revised directors' report or revised directors' remuneration report are approved by the directors, they become the annual financial statements, directors' report or directors' remuneration report of the company in place of the original financial statements or report for all Companies Act purposes. For instance, regarding publishing statutory financial statements, the provisions in section 240(5) of the 1985 Act (section 434(3) of the 2006 Act) (see para 8.157 above) will then apply to the revised financial statements.

**8.235** If the original financial statements, directors' report and (where applicable) directors' remuneration report have already been sent to members and others entitled to receive copies, the directors must send copies of the revised financial statements and report(s) review together with the auditors' report, to those persons. The revised copy has to be sent not more than 28 days from the date of the directors' approval of the revised financial statements and report. Where, however, the revision has been made by supplementary note the directors need only send the supplementary note and the auditors' report on the revised financial statements (or, as the case may be, on the revised report). The directors must also send a copy of the revised financial statements or report, together with the audit report within 28 days of approval of the revision to each person who, at the date on which the revised financial statements or report are approved, is:

■   A member of the company.

■   A holder of the company's debentures.

■   A person who is entitled to receive notice of general meetings.

[SI 1990/2570 Reg 10; SI 2008/373 Reg 12(3)].

Some of these people will not have been entitled to receive the financial statements at the time the original financial statements were sent out.

**8.236** Where the original financial statements, directors' report and, where appropriate, directors' remuneration report have already been laid before members, the company will have to lay the revised financial statements, report(s) and (where applicable) review, together with the auditors' report, before the next general meeting at which annual financial statements are laid, unless they choose to lay them before an earlier general meeting. [SI 1990/2570 Reg 11; SI 2008/373 Reg 13].

**8.237** Where the original financial statements, directors' report and, where appropriate, directors' remuneration report have already been delivered to the Registrar of Companies, the directors must deliver the revised financial statements and report(s), together with the auditors' report to the Registrar within 28 days of the date of their approval of the revised financial statements and report. Where the revision has been by supplementary note, only that note and the auditors' report on the revised financial statements (or as the case may be on the revised report) need be delivered. [SI 1990/2570 Reg 12; SI 2008/373 Reg 14].

*Abbreviated financial statements*

**8.238** The regulations provide for the revision of abbreviated financial statements where these are affected by the revision of a company's full financial statements. In this case *either* the revised abbreviated financial statements should be delivered to the Registrar of Companies within 28 days with a statement as to the effect of the revisions made *or* the company must deliver a copy of the revised financial statements and directors' report together with the auditors' report. The latter alternative must be adopted, if, as a result of the revision, the company is no longer entitled to file abbreviated financial statements. Where abbreviated financial statements are not affected by the revision to the full financial statements, a note stating that the full financial statements have been revised in a respect that has no bearing on the abbreviated financial statements, together with a copy of the auditors' report on the revised financial statements, must be delivered to the Registrar. [SI 1990/2570 Reg 13; SI 2008/373 Reg 15]. Regulation 13A of SI 1990/2570 (regulation 16 of SI 2008/373) provides for the revision of abbreviated accounts which do not comply with the Act for reasons other than the revision of the full financial statements.

*Companies exempted from audit*

**8.239** A small or dormant company that is exempt from audit by virtue of section 249AA of the 1985 Act (section 480 of the 2006 Act) can apply the regulations as if they omitted any reference to an auditors' report. [SI 1990/2570 Reg 15; SI 2008/373 Reg 18].

**8.240** Where a small charitable company that is exempt from audit by virtue of section 249A(2) of the 1985 Act has obtained a report of a reporting accountant, regulations 10 to 13 of SI 1990/2570 have effect as if the references to an auditors' report were references to the report of the reporting accountant and references to the auditors' report, revised directors' report, revised directors' remuneration report were omitted. [SI 1990/2570 Reg 14A]. The provisions of regulations 10 to 13 are described above and relate to sending the revised financial statements to members and others who received copies of the original financial statements (see para 8.235), and delivering the revised financial statements (paras 8.236 and 8.237) and revised 'abbreviated accounts' of small and medium-sized companies (para 8.238). The provisions relating to charitable companies in the 1985 Act have not been carried forward into the 2006 Act: instead charitable companies must refer to charities legislation.

**8.240.1** Under the 2006 Act, where, as a result of revisions to its financial statements, a company is no longer entitled to exemption from audit, an auditors' report on the revised financial statements must be prepared and delivered to the registrar within 28 days of the date of the revision. [SI 2008/373 Reg 8].

## Summary financial statements

**8.241**  Where a company has sent summary financial statements to members, the company is permitted to prepare revised summary financial statements, or a supplementary note indicating the corrections required, if one of the following applies:

- The summary financial statements did not comply with the requirements of the Act or supporting regulations (see para 8.170).

- The contents of the summary financial statements are affected by the revision of the annual financial statements, such that they no longer comply with the requirements of the Act or supporting regulations.

[SI 1990/2570 Reg 14(2); SI 2008/373 Reg 17(2)].

**8.241.1**  Where the company prepares a supplementary note, that note is required to state that it revises the summary financial statements and is to be treated as part of those statements. [SI 1995/2570 Reg 14(3B); SI 2008/373 Reg 17(5)].

**8.241.2**  The company must send the revised summary financial statements or the supplementary note to all those who received the original summary financial statements and to any person to whom the company is entitled, as at the date of the revised summary financial statements, to send summary financial statements for the current year. [SI 1995/2570 Reg 14(2) ; SI 2008/373 Reg 17(2)].

**8.242**  If the revision by the company of the annual financial statements or directors' report, directors' remuneration report does not affect the summary financial statements, the company must send a note stating that the annual financial statements, directors' report or directors' remuneration report for the year have been revised in a respect that has no bearing on the summary financial statement for that year. This note should be sent to the same persons as mentioned in paragraph 8.241.2 above. If the auditors' report on the revised financial statements, directors' report or directors' remuneration report has been qualified, a copy of that report must also be sent attached to the note. [SI 1990/2570 Reg 14(4); SI 2008/373 Reg 17(6)].

**8.243**  The revised summary financial statement or note must be sent within 28 days of the date of approval of the revised financial statements or directors' report.

### Compulsory revision

**8.244**  Responsibility in connection with the compulsory revision of defective financial statements is shared between the FRRP and BERR. The FRRP's ambit is in respect of the financial statements of public and large private companies. BERR remains responsible for all other companies. The FRRP operates under the aegis of the FRC. Its role is to examine the directors' report (including the business review) and annual accounts of unquoted and quoted public, and large private, companies to determine departures from the accounting requirements of the Companies Act. The FRRP also has remit over the half yearly reports of listed companies, but not the Interim Management Statements required by paragraph 4.3 of the UKLA's DTR. In respect of quoted companies, the FRRP derives part of its authority from the FSA.

**8.244.1**   Within this framework, the FRRP's main concern is stated to be material departures from accounting standards (UK and EU-adopted IFRS) where such a departure results in the financial statements in question not giving a true and fair view as required by the 1985 and 2006 Acts. In practice, the FRRP concerns itself with a variety of matters within the framework. Where a company's financial statements are defective the Panel will endeavour to secure their revision by *voluntary* means, but if this approach fails it has the power to make an application to the court under section 245B of the 1985 Act (section 456 of the 2006 Act) for an order compelling a revision.

**8.244.2**   The FRRP's role does not extend to considering whether the business review complies with the non-mandatory, but best-practice, ASB 'Reporting statement: Operating and financial review'. However, where a company states that it has voluntarily complied with the statement, the Panel will take this into account in its review.

**8.245**   Since its inception in 1991 to the end of 2007, the FRRP has issued public statements in respect of its findings on over 100 companies. To date no court application has been pursued as the companies concerned have all agreed to make revisions on a 'voluntary' basis in line with the FRRP's opinion. Although such revisions are 'voluntary' in the terms of the 1985 and 2006 Acts, in practice some of the 100-plus companies went along with the FRRP's wishes very reluctantly, on the basis that doing so is preferable to being taken to court. The operations of the FRRP are discussed further in chapter 2 of the Manual of Accounting – IFRS for the UK and chapter 2 of the Manual of Accounting – UK GAAP.

**8.246**   There are no regulations governing preparing, auditing and issuing financial statements and directors' reports that are compulsorily revised, as the court is empowered to give directions as to these and other matters as it thinks fit.

## Meetings and resolutions

### Directors' meetings

**8.247**   The board of directors will generally have power to manage the company's business (see Table A Reg 70). As a result of the Companies Act 2006, 'The Companies (Tables A to F) Regulations 1985' have been amended and enshrine the directors' responsibility for the management of the company's business. On the question of how they should conduct their meetings, Table A provides, *"Subject to the provisions of the articles, the directors may regulate their proceedings as they think fit"*. [Table A Reg 88]. One of the factors in deciding how often the board should meet would be the nature of the company's business. Any of the company's directors can call a board meeting and the company secretary also has to call such meetings if he is requested to do so by a director. The company's articles usually specify the number of directors required to constitute a quorum at such meetings. There are amendments under the 2006 Act but, at the time of writing, revised model articles have not been issued. They are expected to take effect from 1 October 2009.

**8.248** No specific notice period is necessary to call a board meeting provided the notice period is, in the circumstances in question, a reasonable one and the notice has been given to all directors. If some directors do not receive proper notice of a board meeting, the decisions taken at it will be invalid. A board meeting can be held informally, but a casual meeting will not be sufficient if all parties do not agree to treat it as a meeting.

**8.249** The question sometimes arises as to whether the directors can hold a board meeting by telephone or other electronic means. The issue as to whether a meeting will be properly constituted if it is held by means of a conference call or video conferencing has not been tested in the English courts. It is, however, thought that provided there is a carefully worded provision permitting telephone meetings in the articles and the meeting is duly convened, the meeting would be valid. The articles of association of many companies now incorporate powers to permit telephone board meetings to occur. The proposed new Model Articles regulations are expected to make clear that directors do not have to be in the same place nor have to communicate using the same means of communication for directors to participate in a directors' meeting.

**General meetings**

**8.250** A public company can hold the following types of shareholder meetings: AGMs; general meetings; and class meetings. One of a public company's general meetings each year must be an 'accounts meeting' at which it lays its annual accounts and reports (see para 8.122). This will generally be its AGM. The concept of an extraordinary meeting is not carried forward in the 2006 Act. With effect from 1 October 2007, the 2006 Act abolished the requirement for private companies to hold an AGM. All shareholder meetings of private companies are now termed general meetings. These meetings are regulated partly by statute and partly by a company's articles. The directors may call general meetings (as permitted by section 302 of the 2006 Act). If the directors are required to do so by the company's members in accordance with the Act, they must immediately convene a general meeting to be held no later than 28 days after the date of the notice convening the meeting. [CA06 Sec 304]. For a private company limited by shares or guarantees having only one member, the quorum required to be present at the meeting, subject to any provision in the Articles, is one qualifying person. In other cases two qualifying persons are generally a quorum. A qualifying person is a member of the company, a person authorised under section 323 of the 2006 Act (representation of corporations at meetings) or a person appointed as proxy of a member. [CA06 Sec 318].

**8.250.1**  The directors must call a general meeting once the company has received requests from the required percentage of members. The required percentage is one tenth of paid up capital having voting rights unless, in the case of a private company, more than twelve months has elapsed since the end of the last meeting called under this section, when the required percentage is five. For this purpose, any of the company's paid up capital held as treasury shares should be disregarded. The requisition by the members for such a meeting must state the general nature of the business to be dealt with at the meeting and may include the text of the resolution intended to be moved at the meeting. [CA06 Sec 303(4)]. If the directors do not call a meeting within 21 days (to be held not more than 28 days thereafter) the requisitionists may do so themselves within three months and claim expenses of holding the meeting from the company. [CA06 Sec 305].

*Annual general meetings*

**8.251**  Since October 2007, public companies' AGMs, must be held within six months of the year end. [CA06 Sec 336(1)]. Under the 1985 Act, a company was required to hold an AGM each calendar year and not let more than 15 months elapse between one AGM and the next. A public company must specify that the meeting is an AGM in the notices calling it. A public company's annual financial statements, including the directors' report and auditors' report, are usually, but do not have to be, laid before the company at its AGM. However, if this is not the case the annual financial statements and reports must be laid at a general meeting designated as an 'accounts meeting' (see para 8.122 above).

**8.252**  It is the directors who usually convene the AGM. [CA06 Sec 302]. If the company fails to hold an AGM, the company and every director who is in default will be guilty of an offence. [CA06 Sec 336(4)].

**8.252.1**  Section 527 of the 2006 Act introduced a new right for shareholders of quoted companies from April 2008. The members may require the company to publish on its web site a statement setting out any matter relating to the audit of the company's financial statements that are to be laid before the company in the next accounts meeting, or circumstances in relation to the auditor ceasing to hold office since the last accounts meeting. [CA06 Sec 527]. A company is required to comply once requests have been received from members holding five per cent of the voting rights or when 100 member each holding a minimum of £100 of shares. There is no requirement to include any of the matters raised in the agenda for the accounts meeting. If the directors choose to respond to the matters raised, they may wish to consult with the auditors prior to doing so.

*Notice*

**8.253**  The directors are required to give at least 21 days notice in writing to call an AGM. [CA06 Sec 307(2)]. Notice of general meetings can be given in hard copy, in electronic form or *via* a web site. [CA06 Sec 308]. This is covered by the company communications provisions found in sections 1143 to 1148 of, and Schedules 4 and 5 to, the 2006 Act. This provision of the 2006 Act on the form of notice of meetings came into force on 1 January 2007. For company meetings other than AGMs (including all private company general meetings) or meetings at which special resolutions are being proposed, 14 days notice in writing is required (or 7 days notice for an unlimited company), subject to any provisions in a company's articles of association. It is possible to call company meetings on shorter notice if all members who are entitled to attend and vote at the meeting agree to the short notice. [CA06 Secs 307(4), 337(2)]. The notice should state the time, place and date of the meeting and the general nature of the business to be transacted. For public companies' AGMs the notice must specify that it is an AGM. [CA06 Secs 311, 337(1)]. Business ordinarily conducted at AGMs comprises: receiving or adopting the financial statements; declaring a dividend; appointing and reappointing directors; and reappointing auditors and fixing their remuneration.

**8.254**   More detailed information should be given in the notice of the proposals to be considered at the meeting if business other than ordinary business is to be placed before shareholders. In relation to the notice convening the AGM of a listed company, if business other than ordinary business (see para 8.253) is included, an explanatory circular must accompany the notice. The explanation may be included in the directors' report if it is to be considered at the AGM. Any circular should comply with the requirements of the content requirements of the UKLA's Listing Rule 13.3.1. [LR 13.8.9G].

**8.255**   The notice periods required to be given for meeting often cause confusion in practice. The notice periods for shareholders' meetings must be 'clear' days. This means that it is necessary to disregard both:

■   the date on which the notice is served or deemed to be served. Companies must consult their articles of association, but the notice period is usually 24 or 48 hours after posting; and

■   the date of the meeting itself.

**8.256**   The notice period rules work in the way illustrated in the table below.

|  | '24 hour' articles Day | '48 hour' articles Day |
|---|---|---|
| Notices despatched | 1st | 1st |
| Notices deemed to be received | 2nd | 3rd |
| First day of the notice period | 3rd | 4th |
| Twenty-first day of the notice period | 23rd | 24th |
| AGM can take place on or after | 24th | 25th |

**8.257**   Also, the Combined Code (2006) and the Combined Code (2008) recommend that AGM notices should be sent to shareholders 20 working days before the meeting. [CC D.2.4]. Refer to chapter 4 of this Manual for further details.

**[The next paragraph is 8.259.]**

*Single member companies*

**8.259** Private companies limited by shares or guarantee with only one member should comply with the usual formalities relating to meetings with the necessary modifications for a single member company. For instance, when the single member takes a decision, which is of the nature that may be taken by a company in general meeting, that member must provide the company with a written record of that decision. [CA85 Sec 382B]. If the decision is taken by way of a written resolution, the resolution must be recorded in the same way as minutes of the proceedings of a general meeting (see para 8.275). [CA85 Sec 382A].

**[The next paragraph is 8.262.]**

*Class meetings*

**8.262** Where a company's share capital is divided into different classes of shares, meetings of the different classes have to be held where required by the Act, the company's articles or the shares' terms of issue. Class meetings are most frequently required when it is proposed to vary the rights attached to a particular class of shares. [CA06 Sec 334].

**Resolutions**

**8.263** Resolutions of a private company may be passed as a written resolution or in a general meeting of the members. Resolutions of public companies must be passed in a meeting of the members. [CA06 Sec 281(1)(2)]. Section 281 of the 2006 Act states that where, the members or the articles of association do not specify the type of resolution required, an ordinary resolution is required. Ordinary and special resolutions are defined in the 2006 Act, but the concept of extraordinary resolutions has not been retained. Regulation 46 of Table A (as amended in 2007) provides that a resolution is to be decided on a show of hands, unless a poll is demanded on or before the result of the show of hands is declared. The articles may not require the number of members required to demand a poll to be greater than five members entitled to vote at the meeting. [CA06 Sec 321]. The procedure for a poll is usually set out in the articles. [CA06 Sec 321]. On a poll, every member shall have one vote for each share he holds. [CA06 Sec 284].

**8.263.1** Under section 341 of the 2006 Act, quoted companies have to disclose the results of all polls taken during a general meeting on their web site.

**8.264** Companies' articles of association frequently make it easier for shareholders to demand a poll by reducing the number of members or the proportion of shares below the maximum set out in section 321 of the 2006 Act. Also the articles must be consulted to see whether they specify such matters as:

*Secretarial matters*

- Format of proxy cards.

- Adjournment of meetings.

- The chairman's right to demand a poll.

- Provisions concerning where and when any validly demanded poll can be conducted and the results announced.

**8.264.1**   It should be noted that the Combined Code on corporate governance contains additional recommendations regarding proxy voting and proxy forms (see further chapter 4).

**8.265**   There are often circumstances where it would be advisable for companies to appoint independent scrutineers, for example, if a close result is expected or where perhaps the resolution is particularly contentious. In certain situations a scrutineers' report is required, for example, at meetings held at the request of a court. The scrutineers need not be the company's auditors, unless the company's articles say they should be, which is rare.

**8.265.1**   The 2006 Act gives members of a quoted company the right to require an independent report of any poll taken or to be taken at a general meeting. The minimum threshold for the demand is 5 per cent of the voting rights or 100 members each holding a minimum of £100 of paid up capital. [CA06 Sec 342(2)]. The members request must be made within one week of the meeting at which the poll was taken.

*Ordinary resolutions*

**8.266**   An ordinary resolution is defined in the 2006 Act as a resolution that is passed by a simple majority. [CA06 Sec 282(1)]. An ordinary resolution is passed as a written resolution, or in a meeting on a poll, if it is passed by members representing a simple majority of the total voting rights. It is passed on a show of hands if passed by a simple majority of members entitled to vote. The Act requires an ordinary resolution, for example, for the removal of a director from office (section 168 of the 2006 Act with special notice); to approve directors' service contracts for over two years (section 188(2) of the 2006 Act); to approve loans, quasi-loans and credit arrangements for directors and their connected persons (sections 197 to 203) and to approve substantial property transactions that the company enters into with its directors (section 190 of the 2006 Act).

**[The next paragraph is 8.268.]**

*Special resolutions*

**8.268**   A special resolution is required by the Act for certain important transactions, for instance, alteration of a company's objects or articles (sections 4, 9 of the 1985 Act, section 21 of the 2006 Act), reduction of share capital (section 135 of the 1985 Act, section 641(1) of the 2006 Act), and off-market purchase of its own shares (section 164 of the 1985 Act, section 694(2) of the 2006 Act). A special resolution requires a majority of not less than three quarters of the members entitled to vote. Under the 2006 Act, the notice period for a special resolution is the same as an ordinary resolution. Under the 1985 Act, a resolution is not passed as a special resolution unless the notice stated that the proposed resolution was a special resolution. [CA06 Sec 283(3)(6)]. The intention to propose a resolution as a special resolution and the resolution itself must be given in the notice of the meeting. A copy of every special resolution must be sent to the Registrar of Companies within 15 days after it is passed. A copy of all such resolutions must also be attached to every copy of the articles subsequently issued. [CA85 Sec 380; CA06 Sec 30].

**[The next paragraph is 8.271.]**

*Written resolutions*

**8.271** Section 288 of the 2006 Act sets out a procedure where by a private company may pass a written resolution in place of an ordinary or special resolution. Under the 1985 Act, a written resolution of a private company required unanimity; the 2006 Act changes this. A written resolution may now be passed with the same majority as if it were an ordinary or special resolution proposed in a general meeting. The date of the resolution is when the resolution is signed by or on behalf of the required majority of eligible members. [CA06 Sec 296(4)].

**8.272** Under the 2006 Act written resolutions no longer have to be notified to the company's auditors, although an appropriate record book of written resolutions (including the signatures) must be kept in the same way as minutes of general meetings. [CA06 Sec 355].

**8.272.1** A copy of the proposed written resolution must be sent to every member eligible to vote on the resolution. The copy must be accompanied by a statement explaining how to signify approval and the date by which the resolution must be passed if it is not to lapse.

**8.273** A written resolution may be proposed by either the directors or members of a company. A company is required to circulate a resolution from the members, within 21 days of the request, if the request is received from members representing at least 5 per cent of the voting rights. [CA06 Secs 292, 293.] The expenses of the circulation are to be met by the members who requested the resolution. [CA06 Sec 294]. A member signifies agreement to a proposed written resolution when the company receives an authenticated document identifying the resolution to which it relates and indicating agreement to the resolution. A proposed written resolution will lapse if it is not passed within the period specified for this purpose in the Articles or if none is specified a period of 28 days beginning with the circulation date. [CA06 Sec 297].

**8.274** There are two situations where written resolutions cannot be used: to remove a director before the expiration of his period of office; and to remove an auditor before the expiration of his term of office. [CA06 Sec 288(2)].

### Records of meetings

**8.275** The Act requires companies to keep records comprising copies of all resolutions passed otherwise than at a general meeting, minutes of all proceedings of a company's general meetings, meetings of its directors and managers to be entered into books kept for that purpose and provides for penalties on default. [CA06 Secs 248, 355]. The 2006 Act states that these records should be kept for a minimum of ten years. Where minutes have been kept and have been signed by the chairman of the meeting or the next succeeding meeting they are evidence of those proceedings. Once those minutes have been signed, if any mistakes are found in them they should be rectified only by a further minute passed at a subsequent meeting.

**8.276** The books containing the records of resolutions passed otherwise than at a general meeting and minutes of the proceedings of general meeting must be open to inspection by members at either the registered office or another place permitted by regulations created by the Secretary of State under section 1136 without charge. A member is entitled on payment of the prescribed fee to be provided with a copy of any such minutes within fourteen days of his request. Failure to do so by the company and any officer is an offence. In addition, the Court may compel immediate inspection. [CA06 Sec 358]. The place where minute books can be kept is dealt with in paragraph 8.37 above.

# Index

Locators are:
  paragraph numbers: 11.149, for Chapter 11, paragraph 149

Entries are in word-by-word alphabetical order, where a group of letters followed by a space is filed before the same group of letters followed by a letter, eg 'capital structure and treasury policy' will appear before 'capitalisation'. In determining alphabetical arrangement, initial articles, conjunctions and small prepositions are ignored.

**Abbreviated financial statements**
  publication, 8.160—8.161
**Accountability**
  audit committee, 4.84—4.87
  financial reporting, 4.76—4.78
  internal controls, 4.79—4.83
**Accounting policies**
  operating and financial review, and, 2.164—2.166.1
**Accounting records**
  accounting records, and
    criminal offence, 8.32.3
    generally, 8.30—8.32.1
    limitation of liability agreements, 8.32.4—8.32.6
    senior statutory auditor, 8.32.2—8.32.2.2
  form, 8.33
  introduction, 8.6—8.8
  location, 8.34—8.36
  penalties for failure to comply, 8.74—8.79.1
  proper records
    annual financial statements, 8.25.2—8.25.7
    assets and liabilities, 8.22
    auditors' duties and rights, 8.30—8.32.6
    directors' duty, 8.26—8.29
    disclosure of financial position 'at any time', 8.16—8.20
    disqualification orders, and, 8.25—8.25.1
    duty to keep records, 8.13—8.15
    financial statements, 8.25.2—8.25.7
    general obligation, 8.9—8.10.1
    goods sold and purchased statements, 8.24
    guidance statement, 8.11
    individual financial statements, 8.25.2—8.25.7
    penalties, 8.25—8.25.1
    place of keeping, 8.34—8.36
    'proper records', 8.9—8.10.1
    record of assets and liabilities, 8.22
    requirement to prepare financial statements, 8.25.2—8.25.7
    senior statutory auditor, 8.32.2—8.32.2.2
    statements of goods sold and purchased, 8.24
    statements of stock, 8.23
    sums of money, 8.21
  retention period, 8.68—8.73.1
  statutory books and records, 8.37—8.47
**Accounting reference date**
  change by AIM company, 8.93—8.93.1
  change by listed company, 8.92
  generally, 8.84
**Accounting reference periods**
  accounting reference date
    change by AIM company, 8.93—8.93.1
    change by listed company, 8.92
    generally, 8.84
  current periods, 8.94—8.95

financial year, 8.85—8.87
generally, 8.88—8.90
introduction, 8.84
previous periods, 8.96—8.98
**Acquisition of own shares**
  assignment of rights, 7.87—7.88
  authority for market purchase, 7.69—7.71
  authority for off-market purchase, 7.72—7.77
  cancellation, 7.23
  capital, from
    accounting requirements, 7.47—7.62
    capital maintenance, 7.55—7.62
    generally, 7.19—7.20
    legal procedures, 7.93—7.106
    liability of winding up, 7.107—7.108
    nominal value less than PCP and proceeds of fresh issue, 7.59—7.62
    permissible capital payment, 7.49—7.54.2
    shares to be purchased at a premium in excess of the original premium, 7.62.1—7.62.2
    transfer to capital redemption reserve, 7.56—7.58
  capital maintenance, and
    general rules, 7.36—7.39
    introduction, 7.22
    nominal value less than PCP and proceeds of fresh issue, 7.59—7.62
    private companies, 7.55—7.62
    shares to be purchased at a premium in excess of the original premium, 7.62.1—7.62.2
    transfer to capital redemption reserve, 7.56—7.58
  checklists, 7.Annex
  closed periods, during, 7.114—7.114.2
  conditions, 7.13
  consent of priority shareholders, 7.25
  consideration, 7.14—7.15
  contingent purchase contracts, 7.89—7.92
  contracts, 7.83—7.85
  directors' report, and
    generally, 3.75—3.76
    introduction, 7.42—7.43
    listed companies, 3.142.1
  disclosure requirements
    directors' reports, 7.42—7.43
    introduction, 7.41
    Listing Rules, under, 7.128
    notes to financial statements, 7.46—7.46.1
  discount from proceeds of new issue, at
    accounting requirements, 7.40
    generally, 7.17—7.18
  distributable profits, from
    accounting requirements, 7.27—7.30
    charging purchase cost, 7.29—7.29.2
    expenses of acquisition, 7.30
    generally, 7.17—7.18

effect, 7.26
failure to acquire, 7.109—7.111
financial assistance for
  effect of contravention, 7.141—7.144
  private companies, by, 7.132.1—7.132.4
  public companies, by, 7.133—7.138
funding requirements
  assignment of rights, 7.87—7.88
  capital maintenance, 7.22
  distributable profits, 7.17—7.18
  introduction, 7.16
  payment out of capital, 7.19—7.20
  proceeds of new issue, 7.17—7.18
  summary, 7.21
initial considerations, 7.12
insider dealing
  generally, 7.81—7.81.2
  legal procedures, 7.114.3
institutional shareholders, and, 7.131—7.132
introduction, 7.1—7.4.1
issue of further shares, 7.24
legal procedures
  acquisitions from capital, 7.93—7.106
  assignment of rights, 7.87—7.88
  contingent purchase contracts, 7.89—7.92
  contracts, 7.83—7.85
  definition of 'off-market', 7.64—7.67
  insider dealing, 7.81—7.81.2
  introduction, 7.63—7.63.1
  private company purchases, 7.79—7.80
  public company purchases, 7.68—7.78
  returns, 7.82—7.86
legal procedures for public company purchase
  authority for market purchase, 7.69—7.71
  authority for off-market purchase, 7.72—7.77
  introduction, 7.68
  variation of existing contract, 7.78
Listing Rules, under
  closed periods, during, 7.114—7.114.2
  insider trading, 7.114.3
  introduction, 7.112—7.113
  market abuse, 7.114.3
  prohibited periods, during, 7.114—7.114.2
  purchase from related parties, 7.115
  purchase of equity shares, 7.116—7.122
  purchase of non-equity shares, 7.123—7.126
  redemption of redeemable shares, 7.128
  Treasury shares, 7.126.1—7.126.3
Major Shareholding Notification Rules, 7.130
market abuse, 7.114.3
notes to financial statements
  IFRS, 7.46.1
  UK GAAP, 7.46
payment out of capital, by
  accounting requirements, 7.47—7.62
  capital maintenance, 7.55—7.62
  generally, 7.19—7.20
  legal procedures, 7.93—7.106
  liability of winding up, 7.107—7.108
  permissible capital payment, 7.49—7.54.2
  shares to be purchased at a premium in excess of
    the original premium, 7.62.1—7.62.2
  transfer to capital redemption reserve, 7.56—7.58
premium from proceeds of new issue, at
  accounting requirements, 7.32—7.34
  generally, 7.17—7.18
private company purchases, 7.79—7.80
prohibited periods, during, 7.114—7.114.2
public company purchases, 7.68—7.78
purchase from related parties, 7.115
purchase of equity shares, 7.116—7.122

purchase of non-equity shares, 7.123—7.126
redeemable shares, 7.8—7.11
redemption of redeemable shares, 7.128
reduction of share capital, and
  court confirmation, 7.146—7.153
  generally, 7.145
  solvency statement, 7.154—7.159
regulatory requirements
  institutional shareholders, of, 7.131—7.132
  Listing Rules, under, 7.112—7.128
  Major Shareholding Notification Rules, 7.130
requirements
  accounting requirements, 7.16—7.20
  cancellation of shares, 7.23
  conditions, 7.13
  consent of priority shareholders, 7.25
  consideration, 7.14—7.15
  funding requirements, 7.16—7.22
  initial considerations, 7.12
  introduction, 7.5—7.6
  issue of further shares, 7.24
  redeemable shares, 7.8—7.11
returns, 7.82—7.86
Treasury shares
  accounting treatment, 7.111.17
  cancellation, 7.111.12—7.111.13
  conditions, 7.111.5—7.111.9
  delivery of returns, 7.111.14—7.111.16
  introduction, 7.111.1
  qualifying shares, 7.111.2—7.111.4
  sale, 7.111.10—7.111.11
variation of existing contract, 7.78

**Aggregation of emoluments**
benefits in kind, 5.42—5.46
generally, 5.32—5.41
introduction, 5.27—5.31
long-term incentive plan receivables, 5.47—5.55
pension contributions, 5.58—5.71
readily ascertainable, 5.72—5.73
share option gains, 5.47—5.55
**AIM companies**
disclosure of directors' remuneration, and
  generally, 5.118—5.120
  share option gains, 5.47—5.49
half-yearly reports, 8.207
substantial property transactions, and, 6.113—6.114
**Alteration of accounting reference date**
current periods, 8.94—8.95
introduction, 8.93—8.93.1
listed company, by, 8.95.1—8.98
previous periods, 8.94—8.95
**Alternate director**
directors' loans, and, 6.16—6.17
**Annual financial statements**
compensation for false statements, 8.213.1—8.213.2
generally, 8.25.2—8.25.7
**Annual general meetings**
corporate governance, and, 4.91—4.92
introduction, 8.251—8.252.1
notice, 8.253—8.257
single member companies, 8.259
**Annual return**
generally, 8.55—8.61.2
information annexed, 8.64
members' lists, 8.62
penalties for failure to comply, 8.63
**Appointments to board**
corporate governance, and, 4.54—4.61
**Approval of directors' report**
generally, 3.153—3.157
secretarial matters, and, 8.114—8.116

**Approval of remuneration report**
disclosure of remuneration, and, 5.222—5.223
secretarial matters, and, 8.116.7—8.116.9
**Articles of association**
directors' transactions, and, 6.170
secretarial matters, and, 8.53—8.53.2
**Assets and liabilities, record of**
proper accounting records, and, 8.22
**Assignment of rights**
acquisition of own shares, and, 7.87—7.88
directors' loans, and
general prohibition, 6.54—6.56
value, 6.57
**Associated company**
directors' loans, and, 6.25.1
**Associated with body corporate**
control of shares or votes, 6.21
generally, 6.19—6.20
interests in shares, 6.22
limits on aggregation, 6.23—6.24
**Audit committee**
corporate governance, and, 4.84—4.87
**Audit requirements**
disclosure of directors' remuneration, and,
5.224—5.231
**Auditors**
accounting records, and
criminal offence, 8.32.3
generally, 8.30—8.32.1
limitation of liability agreements, 8.32.4—8.32.6
senior statutory auditor, 8.32.2—8.32.2.2
directors' reports, and
directors' disclosure statements, 3.127.5—3.127.7
general position, 3.158—3.159.3
re-appointment, 3.128
generally, 4.84—4.87
re-appointment, 3.128
review of compliance
generally, 4.171—4.173
Listing Rule Requirement, 4.166—4.168
**Auditors' report**
secretarial matters, and
introduction, 8.6
voluntary revision, 8.227—8.230.1

**Balance of board**
corporate governance, and, 4.50—4.53
**Balance sheet**
summary statements, 8.191.2—8.193
value of land, and, 3.48—3.49
**Banking companies, loans by**
disclosure requirements
from 6 April 2008, 6.161—6.162
pre-6 April 2008, 6.147—6.156
disclosure requirements (pre-6 April 2008)
financial statements, in, 6.147—6.149
register of transactions, 6.155
special statement for members, 6.156
statement of transactions, 6.150—6.154
introduction, 6.133—6.136
liability for contravention, 6.162
loans on beneficial terms for house purchase, 6.141
loans on commercial terms, 6.137—6.140
**Beneficial loans for house purchase**
directors' loans, and, 6.141
**Benefits in kind**
aggregation, and, 5.42—5.46
compensation for loss of office, and, 5.102
**Board of directors**
appointments, 4.54—4.61
balance, 4.50—4.53

Chairman, 4.47—4.49
chief executive officer, 4.47—4.49
generally, 4.45—4.46
**Body corporate**
directors' loans, and, 6.25.2
**Business review**
*and see* **Operating and finanical review**
ASB's views, 2.21—2.24
background, 2.5—2.8
contents, 2.10—2.17
introduction, 2.1—2.4
location in annual report, 2.25—2.26
requirements, 2.10—2.34
**Business transactions**
directors' loans, and, 6.53—6.53.1

**Cadbury Committee report**
corporate governance, and, 4.9—4.11
**Cancellation of shares**
acquisition of own shares, and, 7.23
**Capital maintenance**
general rules, 7.36—7.39
introduction, 7.22
nominal value less than PCP and proceeds of fresh
issue, 7.59—7.62
private companies, 7.55—7.62
shares to be purchased at a premium in excess of the
original premium, 7.62.1—7.62.2
transfer to capital redemption reserve, 7.56—7.58
**Capital structure**
operating and financial review, and, 2.167—2.171.1
**Cash flow**
operating and financial review, and, 2.172—2.176
**Chairman**
corporate governance, and, 4.47—4.49
**Charitable donations**
directors' report, and
accounting period from 6 April 2008,
3.121—3.121.2
accounting period pre-6 April 2008, 3.118—3.120
**Chief executive officer**
corporate governance, and, 4.47—4.49
**Class meetings**
secretarial matters, and, 8.262
**Combined Code**
accountability and audit
audit committee, 4.84—4.87
financial reporting, 4.76—4.78
internal controls, 4.79—4.83
additional guidance, 4.100
annual general meeting, 4.91—4.92
application, 4.20
approval, 4.19
audit committee
generally, 4.84—4.87
requirement, 4.100.2—4.100.3
auditors' review
generally, 4.171—4.173
Listing Rule Requirement, 4.166—4.168
background
Cadbury Committee report, 4.9—4.11
Combined Code (1998), 4.14—4.15
Combined Code (2003), 4.19—4.20.1
Combined Code (2006), 4.20.1—4.20.3
Combined Code (2008), 4.20.3—4.20.4
Hampel Report, 4.11—4.13
Higgs Report, 4.17—4.19
balance of board, 4.50—4.53
board of directors
appointments, 4.54—4.61
balance, 4.50—4.53

# Index

Chairman, 4.47—4.49
chief executive officer, 4.47—4.49
generally, 4.45—4.46
Cadbury Committee report, 4.9  4.11
Chairman, 4.47—4.49
chief executive officer, 4.47—4.49
Combined Code (1998), 4.14—4.15
Combined Code (2003)
  background, 4.16—4.19
  introduction, 4.19—4.20
  review, 4.20.1
Combined Code (2006)
  adoption, 4.38.12
  background, 4.38.8—4.38.10
  compliance statement, 4.110.1—4.110.2
  introduction, 4.20.1—4.20.3
  overview, 4.39—4.40
  review, 4.38.13—4.38.14
Combined Code (2008)
  background, 4.38.13—4.38.14
  generally, 4.110.13—4.100.14
  introduction, 4.20.3—4.20.4
  modifications, 4.100.15
compliance statement
  Combined Code 2008, and, 4.110—4.110.1
  generally, 4.101—4.104
  non-compliance with Code, 4.105—4.109
corporate governance statements, 4.100.4—4.100.11
development, 4.34—4.38.12
directors
  appointments, 4.54—4.61
  board balance, 4.50—4.53
  generally, 4.44
  performance evaluation, 4.64—4.65
  professional development, 4.62—4.63
  re-election, 4.66—4.67
  remuneration, 4.68—4.75
directors' remuneration
  compensation, 4.72
  generally, 4.68
  policy, 4.69—4.71
  procedure, 4.73
  recommendations, 4.74—4.75
  service contracts and compensation, 4.72
financial reporting, 4.76—4.78
FRC assessment and review, 4.38.1—4.38.8
FSA Rules, and, 4.100.12
format, 4.19
good practice reporting, 4.155
Hampel Report
  background, 4.11—4.13
  'box ticking', 4.26—4.27
  listed companies' objectives, 4.28—4.29
  objectives, 4.22—4.24
  recommendations, 4.31—4.33
  stakeholders position, 4.30
Higgs Report, 4.17—4.19
institutional shareholders, 4.93—4.97
internal controls, 4.79—4.83
introduction, 4.1—4.8
listed companies' requirements, 4.41—4.43
non-listed organisations, 4.157—4.159
objective, 4.34—4.38
overview, 4.39—4.43
performance evaluation, 4.64—4.65
professional development, 4.62—4.63
relations with shareholders
  dialogue, 4.88—4.90
  use of AGM, 4.91—4.92
re-election of directors, 4.66—4.67
remuneration of directors

compensation, 4.72
generally, 4.68
policy, 4.69—4.71
procedure, 4.73
recommendations, 4.74—4.75
service contracts and compensation, 4.72
reporting on going concern
  form of disclosure, 4.114—4.123
  generally, 4.111—4.113
  groups, and, 4.124
  foreseeable future, 4.127—4.130
  procedures, 4.125—4.126
reporting on internal control
  board's role, 4.144—4.147.11
  generally, 4.131—4.134.1
  groups, and, 4.154
  internal audit, 4.147.12
  Turnbull guidance (2005), 4.138—4.143
schedules, 4.98—4.99.1
shareholder relations
  dialogue, 4.88—4.90
  use of AGM, 4.91
smaller listed companies, 4.156
statements of compliance with 2006 Code,
  4.110.1—4.110.2
statements of non-compliance, 4.105—4.110
Turnbull guidance, and
  board's role, 4.144—4.147.11
  generally, 4.131—4.134.1
  groups, and, 4.154
  internal audit, 4.147.12
  Turnbull guidance (2005), 4.138—4.143
**Commercial terms, loans on**
  directors' loans, and, 6.137—6.140
**Company identification**
  articles of association, 8.53—8.53.2
  memorandum of association, 8.53—8.53.2
  name, 8.48—8.52
**Compensation for loss of office**
  benefits in kind, 5.102
  disclosure in financial statements, 5.110—5.112
  disclosure to members of company, 5.108
  ex gratia payments, 5.103
  introduction, 5.97—5.98
  pension scheme top ups, 5.100—5.101
  post-retirement payments, 5.104—5.107
  readily ascertainable from other information, 5.99
**Compensation for past directors**
  quoted companies, 5.209—5.214
**Compliance statement**
  operating and financial review, and, 2.215
**Connected persons**
  directors' loans, and, 6.18
  directors' reports, and, 3.137.7—3.137.10
**Connected with body corporate**
  control of shares or votes, 6.21
  generally, 6.19—6.20
  interests in shares, 6.22
  limits on aggregation, 6.23—6.24
**Consent of priority shareholders**
  acquisition of own shares, and, 7.25
**Consideration**
  acquisition of own shares, and, 7.14—7.15
**Consolidated financial statements**
  *and see* **Directors' remuneration reports**
  *and see* **Directors' reports**
  *see also* **Individual financial statements**
  abbreviated statements, 8.160—8.161
  accounting records, and, 8.25.2—8.25.7
  approval, 8.102—8.106.1
  balance sheet and notes, 8.166—8.167

compulsory revision, 8.244—8.246
consolidated statements, 8.101—8.101.4
delivery
  company's liability for late filing, 8.148—8.151
  consolidated statements not prepared, 8.135
  directors' liability for late delivery, 8.152—8.154
  euros, in, 8.166
  filing, 8.134—8.135
  qualifying undertakings, 8.147.1—8.147.2
  time limits, 8.139—8.145
  unlimited companies, 8.146—8.147
directors' duties
  approval, 8.102—8.106.1
  filing, 8.102—8.106.1
  preparation, 8.98.1—8.101.4
  publication, 8.102—8.106.1
  signature, 8.102—8.106.1
dormant companies
  additional disclosure, 8.154.21
  definition, 8.154.18
  effect, 8.154.16—8.154.17
  generally, 8.154.14—8.154.15
  significant accounting transactions,
    8.154.19—8.154.20
exemptions from audit requirements
  dormant companies, 8.154.14—8.154.21
  small companies, 8.154.1—8.154.13
filing
  directors' duties, 8.102—8.106.1
  medium-sized companies, 8.134.6—8.134.9
  qualifying undertakings, 8.147.1—8.147.2
  quoted companies, 8.134—8.134.1
  small companies, 8.134.2—8.134.5.2
  unlimited companies, 8.146—8.147
  unquoted companies, 8.134—8.134.1
full statements, 8.157—8.159
individual statements, 8.100—8.100.1
introduction, 8.6—8.6.1
liability for
  defective statements, 8.107—8.108
  unsigned balance sheet, 8.109—8.111
non-statutory accounts, 8.195—8.201
operating and financial review, and
  complementing, 2.70—2.72.1
  supplementing, 2.65—2.68
persons entitled to receive, 8.116.12—8.117
preparation
  generally, 8.101—8.101.4
  introduction, 8.98.1—8.99
presentation
  election to dispense, 8.123—8.131
  introduction, 8.121—8.122
  liability for failure to comply, 8.132—8.133
proper accounting records, and, 8.25.2—8.25.7
publication
  abbreviated statements, 8.160—8.161
  balance sheet and notes, 8.166—8.167
  definition, 8.155—8.156
  euros, in, 8.166
  full statements, 8.157—8.159
  introduction, 8.102—8.106.1
  non-statutory accounts, 8.195—8.201
  short-form statements, 8.162—8.165
  summary statements, 8.170—8.194
revision of defective
  compulsory, 8.244—8.246
  introduction, 8.214—8.214.1
  voluntary, 8.215—8.243
short-form statements, 8.162—8.165
signature, 8.102—8.106.1
small companies, 8.154.1—8.154.13

summary financial statements
  background, 8.170—8.175
  balance sheet, 8.191.2—8.193
  comparative information, 8.193.2
  conditions, 8.176—8.180
  directors' remuneration report, 8.189.1
  directors' report, 8.189
  dividends, 8.193.1
  form and content, 8.186—8.188
  general conditions, 8.176—8.180
  members' wishes, 8.181—8.184
  penalties for failure to comply, 8.194
  profit and loss account, 8.190—8.191.1
  relevant statements, 8.185—8.185.2
voluntary revision, 8.215—8.243
**Contingent purchase contracts**
acquisition of own shares, and, 7.89—7.92
**Corporate governance**
accountability and audit
  audit committee, 4.84—4.87
  auditors, 4.84—4.87
  financial reporting, 4.76—4.78
  internal control, 4.79—4.83
additional guidance, 4.100
annual general meeting, 4.91
appointments to board, 4.54—4.61
audit committee
  generally, 4.84—4.87
  requirement, 4.100.2—4.100.3
auditors, 4.84—4.87
auditors' review
  generally, 4.171—4.173
  Listing Rule Requirement, 4.166—4.168
background
  Cadbury Committee report, 4.9—4.11
  Combined Code (1998), 4.14—4.15
  Combined Code (2003), 4.19—4.20.1
  Combined Code (2006), 4.20.1—4.20.3
  Combined Code (2008), 4.20.3—4.20.4
  Hampel Report, 4.11—4.13
  Higgs Report, 4.17—4.19
balance of board, 4.50—4.53
board of directors
  appointments, 4.54—4.61
  balance, 4.50—4.53
  Chairman, 4.47—4.49
  chief executive officer, 4.47—4.49
  generally, 4.45—4.46
'box ticking', 4.26—4.27
Cadbury Committee report, 4.9—4.11
Chairman, 4.47—4.49
chief executive officer, 4.47—4.49
Combined Code
  accountability and audit, 4.76—4.87
  additional guidance, 4.100
  audit committee requirement, 4.100.2—4.100.3
  auditors' review, 4.171—4.173
  auditors' review of compliance, 4.166—4.168
  background, 4.13—4.21
  compliance statement, 4.101—4.110.1
  corporate governance statements,
    4.100.4—4.100.11
  development, 4.34—4.38.12
  dialogue with institutional shareholders, 4.88—4.92
  directors, 4.44—4.67
  FSA Rules, and, 4.100.12
  institutional shareholders, 4.93—4.97
  listed companies' requirements, 4.41—4.43
  non-listed organisations, 4.157—4.159
  objective, 4.34—4.38
  overview, 4.39—4.40

relations with shareholders, 4.88—4.92
remuneration of directors, 4.68—4.75
reporting on going concern, 4.111—4.130
reporting on internal control, 4.131—4.153
schedules, 4.98—4.99.1
smaller listed companies, 4.156
statements of non-compliance, 4.105—4.110
Combined Code (1998), 4.14—4.15
Combined Code (2003)
  background, 4.16—4.19
  introduction, 4.19—4.20
  review, 4.20.1
Combined Code (2006)
  adoption, 4.38.12
  background, 4.38.8—4.38.10
  compliance statement, 4.110.1—4.110.2
  introduction, 4.20.1—4.20.3
  overview, 4.39—4.40
  review, 4.38.13—4.38.14
Combined Code (2008)
  background, 4.38.13—4.38.14
  generally, 4.110.13—4.100.14
  introduction, 4.20.3—4.20.4
  modifications, 4.100.15
compliance statement
  compliance with 2006 Code, 4.110.1—4.110.2
  generally, 4.101—4.104
  non-compliance with 2003 Code, 4.105—4.110
corporate governance statements, 4.100.4—4.100.11
development
  Cadbury Committee report, 4.9—4.11
  Combined Code (1998), 4.14—4.15
  Combined Code (2003), 4.19—4.20.1
  Combined Code (2006), 4.20.1—4.20.3
  Combined Code (2008), 4.20.3—4.20.4
  Hampel Report, 4.11—4.13
  Higgs Report, 4.17—4.19
directors
  appointments to board, 4.54—4.61
  balance of board, 4.50—4.53
  board of directors, 4.45—4.46
  Chairman, 4.47—4.49
  chief executive officer, 4.47—4.49
  independence, 4.50—4.53
  introduction, 4.44
  performance evaluation, 4.64—4.65
  professional development, 4.62—4.63
  re-election, 4.66—4.67
  remuneration, 4.68—4.75
directors' remuneration
  compensation, 4.72
  generally, 4.68
  policy, 4.69—4.71
  procedure, 4.73
  recommendations, 4.74—4.75
  service contracts and compensation, 4.72
directors' reports, and, 3.139
EU Action Plan, 4.176—4.182
EU Directives
  generally, 4.183—4.186
  UK implementation, 4.186.1
European Corporate Governance Forum,
  4.187—4.189
FEE's activities, 4.190—4.192
financial reporting, 4.76—4.78
going concern, reporting on
  foreseeable future, 4.127—4.130
  form of disclosure, 4.114—4.123
  groups, 4.124
  introduction, 4.111—4.113
  procedures, 4.125—4.126

good practice reporting, 4.155
Hampel Report
  background, 4.11—4.13
  'box ticking', 4.26—4.27
  listed companies' objectives, 4.28—4.29
  objectives, 4.22—4.24
  recommendations, 4.31—4.33
  stakeholders position, 4.30
Higgs Report, 4.17—4.19
Higgs 'Suggestion for Good Practice', 4.100
independence of directors, 4.50—4.53
institutional shareholders
  dialogue with, 4.93—4.97
  generally, 4.93—4.97
internal control
  generally, 4.79—4.83
  reporting, 4.131—4.153
internal control reporting
  board's role, 4.144—4.147.11
  generally, 4.131—4.134.1
  groups, and, 4.154
  internal audit, 4.147.12
  Turnbull guidance (2005), 4.138—4.143
international matters
  EU Action Plan,—4.182
  EU Directives, 4.183—4.186.1
  European Corporate Governance Forum,
    4.187—4.189
  FEE's activities, 4.190—4.192
  IASB, 4.193
introduction, 4.1—4.8
listed companies' requirements, 4.41—4.43
non-listed organisations, 4.157—4.159
performance evaluation of directors, 4.64—4.65
professional development of directors, 4.62—4.63
re-election of directors, 4.66—4.67
relations with shareholders
  annual general meeting, 4.91
  dialogue with institutional shareholders, 4.88—4.90
  institutional shareholders, 4.93—4.97
remuneration of directors
  compensation, 4.72
  generally, 4.68
  policy, 4.69—4.71
  procedure, 4.73
  recommendations, 4.74—4.75
  service contracts and compensation, 4.72
reporting on going concern
  foreseeable future, 4.127—4.130
  form of disclosure, 4.114—4.123
  groups, 4.124
  introduction, 4.111—4.113
  procedures, 4.125—4.126
reporting on internal control
  board's role, 4.144—4.147.11
  generally, 4.131—4.134.1
  groups, and, 4.154
  internal audit, 4.147.12
  Turnbull guidance (2005), 4.138—4.143
Sarbanes-Oxley Act, and, 4.194—4.196
service contracts, 4.72
shareholder relations
  annual general meeting, 4.91
  dialogue with institutional shareholders, 4.88—4.90
  institutional shareholders, 4.93—4.97
smaller listed companies, 4.156
Smith Guidance on Audit Committees, 4.100
stakeholders position, 4.30
statements of non-compliance, 4.105—4.110
Turnbull guidance, and
  board's role, 4.144—4.147.11

generally, 4.131—4.134.1
groups, and, 4.154
internal audit, 4.147.12
Turnbull guidance (2005), 4.138—4.143
US listed companies, 4.194—4.196
**Corporate reporting**
generally, 1.1—1.7
international developments, 1.8—1.12
**Credit transactions**
business transactions, 6.53—6.53.1
conditions, 6.49.1—6.51
definition, 6.48
exceptions, 6.52—6.53.1
minor transactions, 6.52—6.52.1
value, 6.49
**Creditor payment policy**
directors' report, and, 3.83—3.89
**Criminal sanctions**
directors' loans, and, 6.68

***De facto* director**
directors' loans, and, 6.15.1—6.15.4
**Declaration of interest**
directors' transactions, and, 6.163—6.178
**Delivery of financial statements**
company's liability for late filing, 8.148—8.151
consolidated statements not prepared, 8.135
directors' liability for late delivery, 8.152—8.154
euros, in, 8.166
filing
directors' duties, 8.102—8.106.1
medium-sized companies, 8.134.6—8.134.9
qualifying undertakings, 8.147.1—8.147.2
quoted companies, 8.134—8.134.1
small companies, 8.134.2—8.134.5.2
unlimited companies, 8.146—8.147
unquoted companies, 8.134—8.134.1
time limits, 8.139—8.145
**Directors**
*and see* **Directors' report**
alternate director, 6.16—6.17
appointments, 4.54—4.61
board balance, 4.50—4.53
de facto director, 6.15.1—6.15.4
definition, 6.9—6.10
details of, 3.50—3.51
directors' loans, and, 6.9—6.10
generally, 4.44
interests in contracts, 3.69
performance evaluation, 4.64—4.65
professional development, 4.62—4.63
re-election, 4.66—4.67
remuneration
*and see* **Directors' remuneration**
compensation, 4.72
disclosure requirements, 5.1—5.248
generally, 4.68
policy, 4.69—4.71
procedure, 4.73
recommendations, 4.74—4.75
service contracts and compensation, 4.72
responsibility statements, 3.127—3.127.2.5
shadow director, 6.11—6.14
**Directors' business expenditure**
directors' loans, and, 6.64—6.67.6
**Directors' details**
directors' reports, and, 3.50—3.51
**Directors' emoluments**
*and see* **Directors' remuneration**
corporate governance, and, 4.68—4.75
disclosure requirements, 5.1—5.248

**Directors' interests**
contracts, in
generally, 3.69
disclosure, 3.137.1—3.137.6
**Directors' loan transactions**
alternate director, 6.16—6.17
assignment of rights
general prohibition, 6.54—6.56
value, 6.57
associated company, 6.25.1
associated with body corporate
control of shares or votes, 6.21
generally, 6.19—6.20
interests in shares, 6.22
limits on aggregation, 6.23—6.24
banking companies, and
*and see* **Banking companies, loans by**
disclosure requirements, 6.147—6.161
introduction, 6.133—6.136
liability for contravention, 6.162
loans on beneficial terms for house purchase, 6.141
loans on commercial terms, 6.137—6.140
body corporate, 6.25.2
business transactions, 6.53—6.53.1
civil remedies, 6.68
company, 6.26
connected persons, 6.18
connected with body corporate
control of shares or votes, 6.21
generally, 6.19—6.20
interests in shares, 6.22
limits on aggregation, 6.23—6.24
credit transactions
business transactions, 6.53—6.53.1
conditions, 6.49.1—6.51
definition, 6.48
exceptions, 6.52—6.53.1
minor transactions, 6.52—6.52.1
value, 6.49
criminal sanctions, 6.68
*de facto* director, 6.15.1—6.15.4
definitions
alternate director, 6.16—6.17
associated company, 6.25.1
associated with body corporate, 6.19—6.24
body corporate, 6.25.2
company, 6.26
connected persons, 6.18
connected with body corporate, 6.19—6.24
de facto director, 6.15.1—6.15.4
director, 6.9—6.10
holding company, 6.27
introduction, 6.8
members of a director's family, 6.18.1
relevant company, 6.25
shadow director, 6.11—6.14
subsidiary, 6.27
director, 6.9—6.10
directors' business expenditure, 6.64—6.67.6
disclosure requirements
beginning and ending pre-6 April 2008, 6.70—6.83
from 6 April 2008, 6.83.3—6.83.8
introduction, 6.69—6.69.2
straddling 6 April 2008, 6.83.1—6.83.2
disclosure requirements (pre-6 April 2008)
credit transactions, in, 6.79
excluded transactions, 6.81—6.82
exemptions, 6.80
financial statement, in, 6.70—6.73
guarantees or securities, for, 6.77—6.78
intra-group loans, for, 6.80

introduction, 6.70—6.73
loans, for, 6.75
penalties for failure to comply, 6.83
quasi-loans, for, 6.79
relevant information, 6.74
exceptions
  business transactions, 6.53—6.53.1
  directors' business expenditure, 6.64—6.67.6
  general, 6.62
  inter-company group loans, 6.39, 6.47
  minor transactions, 6.52—6.52.1
  other loans, 6.40—6.41.1
  small loans, 6.33—6.38, 6.46
  transaction between subsidiary and parent, 6.63
holding company, 6.27
indirect arrangements
  general prohibition, 6.58—6.60
  value, 6.61
inter-company group loans
  generally, 6.39
  quasi-loans, and, 6.47
introduction, 6.1—6.7
invalidity of
  effect of contravention of rule, 6.122—6.125
  general rule, 6.121
loans
  definition, 6.30
  eligible member, 6.32.3—6.32.4
  exceptions, 6.33—6.41.1
  general prohibition, 6.32
  inter-company group loans, 6.39
  member approval, 6.32.1—6.32.2
  other loans, 6.40—6.41.1
  small loans, 6.33—6.38
  value, 6.31
members of a director's family, 6.18.1
minor credit transactions, 6.52—6.52.1
money-lending companies, and
  *and see* **Money-lending companies, loans by**
  disclosure requirements, 6.143—6.144
  introduction, 6.133—6.136
  liability for contravention, 6.162
  loans on beneficial terms for house purchase, 6.141
  loans on commercial terms, 6.137—6.140
prohibited transactions
  assignment of rights, 6.54—6.57
  credit transactions, 6.48—6.53.1
  exceptions, 6.62—6.67.6
  indirect arrangements, 6.58—6.61
  introduction, 6.29
  loans, 6.30—6.41.1
  quasi-loans, 6.42—6.47
  sanctions and remedies, 6.68
quasi-loans
  definition, 6.42
  exceptions, 6.46—6.47
  general prohibition, 6.44—6.45.1
  inter-company group loans, 6.47
  small loans, 6.46
  value, 6.43
relevant company, 6.25
shadow director, 6.11—6.14
small loans
  loans, 6.33—6.38
  quasi-loans, 6.46
sanctions and remedies, 6.68
subsidiary, 6.27
transaction between subsidiary and parent, 6.63
validity of
  effect of contravention of rule, 6.122—6.125
  general rule, 6.121

**Directors' meetings**
secretarial matters, and, 8.247—8.249
**Directors' remuneration**
compensation, 4.72
disclosure of
  *and see below*
  generally, 5.1—5.248
generally, 4.68
policy, 4.69—4.71
procedure, 4.73
recommendations, 4.74—4.75
service contracts and compensation, 4.72
**Directors' remuneration, disclosure of**
*and see* **Directors' remuneration report**
aggregation of emoluments
  benefits in kind, 5.42—5.46
  generally, 5.32—5.41
  introduction, 5.27—5.31
  long-term incentive plan receivables, 5.47—5.55
  pension contributions, 5.58—5.71
  readily ascertainable, 5.72—5.73
  share option gains, 5.47—5.55
AIM companies
  generally, 5.118—5.120
  share option gains, 5.47—5.49
all companies, by
  aggregate emoluments, 5.27—5.73
  general rules, 5.9—5.126
approval of remuneration report, 5.222—5.223
audit requirements, 5.224—5.231
benefits in kind
  aggregation, and, 5.42—5.46
  compensation for loss of office, and, 5.102
Combined Code
  compensation, 4.72
  generally, 4.68
  policy, 4.69—4.71
  procedure, 4.73
  recommendations, 4.74—4.75
  service contracts and compensation, 4.72
"company", 5.6.4
compensation for loss of office
  benefits in kind, 5.102
  disclosure in financial statements, 5.110—5.112
  disclosure to members of company, 5.108
  ex gratia payments, 5.103
  introduction, 5.97—5.98
  pension scheme top ups, 5.100—5.101
  post-retirement payments, 5.104—5.107
  readily ascertainable from other information, 5.99
compensation for past directors
  quoted companies, 5.209—5.214
ex gratia payments, 5.103
excess retirement benefits
  quoted companies, 5.204—5.208
  unquoted companies, 5.93—5.96
general rules
  auditors' duties, 5.9—5.10
  directors' duties, 5.9—5.10
  other rules, 5.24—5.26
  payment for services, 5.11—5.15
  year in which receivable, 5.16—5.23
Greenbury Report, 5.1
group situations, 5.233—5.248
highest paid director's emoluments
  'accrued pension', 5.87—5.90.2
  ascertaining the director, 5.78—5.82
  comparative figures, 5.92—5.92.4
  disclosure, 5.83—5.86.1
  introduction, 5.75—5.77
  readily ascertainable from other information, 5.91

information subject to audit
  approval of remuneration report, 5.222—5.223
  compensation for past directors, 5.209—5.214
  excess retirement benefits, 5.204—5.208
  individual emoluments, 5.163—5.169
  long-term incentive schemes, 5.180—5.192
  pensions, 5.193—5.203
  share options, 5.170—5.179
  sums paid to third parties for directors' services,
    5.216—5.220
information not subject to audit
  compensation for past directors, 5.152—5.154
  composition of remuneration committee,
    5.130—5.133
  performance graph, 5.143—5.148.5
  service contracts, 5.149—5.151
  statement of consideration of conditions within
    company or group, 5.142
  statement of policy on remuneration, 5.134—5.141
introduction, 5.1—5.5
long-term incentive plan, sums receivable under
  AIM companies, 5.47—5.49
  definitions, 5.51—5.55
  information subject to audit, 5.180—5.192
  quoted companies, 5.47—5.49
  unquoted companies, 5.50
past directors, compensation for, 5.152—5.154
pension contributions
  quoted companies, 5.193—5.203
  unquoted companies, 5.58—5.71
pension scheme top ups, 5.100—5.101
performance graph, 5.143—5.148.5
quoted companies
  "company", 5.6.4
  definition, 5.6.3—5.6.3.1
  information subject to audit, 5.163—5.223
  information not subject to audit, 5.130—5.154
  remuneration report, 5.121—5.129
  share option gains, 5.47—5.49
remuneration committee, 5.130—5.133
scope of requirements, 5.6—5.8
service contracts, 5.149—5.151
share option gains
  AIM companies, 5.47—5.49
  definitions, 5.51—5.55
  quoted companies, 5.47—5.49
  unquoted companies, 5.50
share options, 5.170—5.179
statement of consideration of conditions within
  company or group, 5.142
statement of policy on remuneration, 5.134—5.141
third parties for directors' services, sums paid to
  quoted companies, 5.216—5.220
  unquoted companies, 5.113—5.117.3
unquoted companies (including AIM companies)
  compensation for loss of office, 5.97—5.112
  excess retirement benefits, 5.93—5.96
  highest paid director's emoluments, 5.75—5.92.4
  introduction, 5.74
  share option gains, 5.47—5.49
  sums paid to third parties for directors' services,
    5.113—5.117.3
**Directors' remuneration report**
approval
  directors' duties, 8.116.7—8.116.9
  generally, 5.222—5.223
Combined Code, and, 5.155
directors' duties
  approval, 8.116.7—8.116.9
  preparation, 8.116.1—8.116.6
  safe harbour provisions, 8.116.10—8.116.11

introduction, 8.6
members' approval, 8.133.1—8.133.4
preparation, 8.116.1—8.116.6
safe harbour provisions, 8.116.10—8.116.11
summary statements, 8.189.1
signature, 3.153—3.157
**Directors' reports**
acquisition of own shares, 3.75—3.76
approval, 3.153—3.157
auditors
  directors' duties, 8.114—8.116
  directors' disclosure statements, 3.127.5—3.127.7
  general position, 3.158—3.159.3
  re-appointment, 3.128
business review
  generally, 3.23—3.27.4
  interaction with OFR, 3.31—3.32
  key performance indicators, 3.28—3.30
charitable donations
  accounting period from 6 April 2008,
    3.121—3.121.2
  accounting period pre-6 April 2008, 3.118—3.120
connected persons, 3.137.7—3.137.10
consolidated financial statements, 3.12—3.13
corporate governance, 3.139
creditor payment policy, 3.83—3.89
directors' details, 3.50—3.51
directors' duties
  approval, 8.114—8.116
  introduction, 8.6
  preparation, 8.112—8.113.1
  safe harbour provisions, 8.116.10—8.116.11
  summary statements, 8.189
  voluntary revision, 8.224—8.226
directors' interests in contracts
  generally, 3.69
  significance, of, 3.137.11
directors' service contracts, 3.136—3.137
disabled employees, 3.80
disclosure
  directors' disclosure statements, 3.127.5—3.127.7
  directors' interests, of, 3.137.1—3.137.6
  overseas branches, 3.126
  qualifying third party indemnity provisions,
    3.128.1—3.128.3
dividends, 3.43
employee information
  disabled persons, 3.80
  generally, 3.79
employee involvement, 3.81—3.82
employee numbers
  disabled persons, 3.80
  generally, 3.79
enforcement, 3.160—3.161
environmental and social matters, 3.42.4—3.42.6
financial instruments, 3.122—3.125
future developments, 3.42.1—3.42.3
IFRS, and, 3.11
interaction with OFR, 3.31—3.32
introduction, 3.1—3.5
listed companies, and
  additional matters, 3.42.12—3.42.18
  connected persons, 3.137.7—3.137.10
  corporate governance, 3.139
  directors' interests in contracts of significance,
    3.137.11
  directors' service contracts, 3.136—3.137
  disclosure of directors' interests, 3.137.1—3.137.6
  introduction, 3.129.7.1
  major interest in company's shares, 3.130—3.132
  purchase of own shares, 3.142.1

special business, 3.142
transactions with controlling shareholder,
    3.135—3.135.2
waiver of dividends, 3.138
major interest in company's shares, 3.130—3.132
operating and financial review, and, 2.16—2.19
overseas branches, 3.126
overview, 1.2
political donations
    definitions, 3.101—3.101.4
    director's liability, 3.109—3.111
    disclosures from 6 April 2008, 3.117.1—3.117.5
    disclosures pre-6 April 2008, 3.112—3.117
    exemptions, 3.106
    introduction, 3.100
    non-EU political parties, 3.114
    prohibition, 3.102—3.105
    subsidiaries incorporated in GB, 3.107—3.108
post balance sheet events, 3.44
preparation, 8.112—8.113.1
principal activities, 3.16—3.21
publicly traded companies, and
    additional matters, 3.129
    agreements affected by change of control, 3.129.7
    control and share structures, 3.129.1—3.129.6
purchase of own shares, 3.142.1
qualifying third party indemnity provisions,
    3.128.1—3.128.3
re-appointment of auditors, 3.128
research and development activities, 3.45—3.47
responsibility statements, 3.127—3.127.2.5
safe harbour provisions
    directors' duties, 8.116.10—8.116.11
    generally, 3.143
sale of Treasury shares, 3.75—3.76
seriously prejudicial, 3.42.10—3.42.11
signature, 3.153—3.157
small companies, 3.147—3.149
special business, 3.142
third party indemnity provisions, 3.128.1—3.128.3
transactions with controlling shareholder,
    3.135—3.135.2
value of land, 3.48—3.49
waiver of dividends, 3.138
**Directors' responsibility statements**
directors' reports, and, 3.127—3.127.2.5
**Directors' service contracts**
directors' reports, and, 3.136—3.137
**Directors, transactions involving**
articles of association, and, 6.170
banking companies, and
    *and see* **Banking companies, loans by**
    disclosure requirements, 6.147—6.161
    introduction, 6.133—6.136
    liability for contravention, 6.162
    loans on beneficial terms for house purchase, 6.141
    loans on commercial terms, 6.137—6.140
civil consequences, 6.176—6.179
criminal sanctions, 6.175—6.175.1
declaration of interest, 6.163—6.178
invalidity of
    effect of contravention of rule, 6.122—6.125
    general rule, 6.121
loans, etc.
    *and see* **Directors' loan transactions**
    assignment of rights, 6.54—6.57
    credit transactions, 6.48—6.53.1
    definitions, 6.8—6.27
    disclosure requirements, 6.69—6.83.8
    general exemptions, 6.62—6.67.6
    indirect arrangements, 6.58—6.61

introduction, 6.1—6.7
loans, 6.30—6.41.1
quasi-loans, 6.42—6.47
sanctions and remedies, 6.68
material interest transactions
    *and see* **Material interest transactions**
    disclosure requirements, 6.88—6.99.1
    introduction, 6.84—6.87
money-lending companies, and
    *and see* **Money-lending companies, loans by**
    disclosure requirements, 6.143—6.144
    introduction, 6.133—6.136
    liability for contravention, 6.162
    loans on beneficial terms for house purchase, 6.141
    loans on commercial terms, 6.137—6.140
notification to board, 6.163—6.178
penalties for failure to disclose, 6.171—6.174
sole members, who are, 6.126—6.128
substantial property transactions
    *and see* **Substantial property transactions**
    disclosure requirements, 6.112—6.114
    introduction, 6.100
    penalties for contravention, 6.110—6.111
    shareholders' approval, 6.100.1—6.109
**Disabled employees**
directors' reports, and, 3.80
**Disclosure requirements**
acquisition of own shares, and
    directors' reports, 7.42—7.43
    introduction, 7.41
    Listing Rules, under, 7.128
    notes to financial statements, 7.46—7.46.1
banking company loans, and
    from 6 April 2008, 6.161—6.162
    pre-6 April 2008, 6.147—6.156
banking company loans (pre-6 April 2008), and
    financial statements, in, 6.147—6.149
    register of transactions, 6.155
    special statement for members, 6.156
    statement of transactions, 6.150—6.154
directors' loans, and
    beginning and ending pre-6 April 2008, 6.70—6.83
    from 6 April 2008, 6.83.3—6.83.8
    introduction, 6.69—6.69.2
    straddling 6 April 2008, 6.83.1—6.83.2
directors' loans (pre-6 April 2008), and
    credit transactions, in, 6.79
    excluded transactions, 6.81—6.82
    exemptions, 6.80
    financial statement, in, 6.70—6.73
    guarantees or securities, for, 6.77—6.78
    intra-group loans, for, 6.80
    introduction, 6.70—6.73
    loans, for, 6.75
    penalties for failure to comply, 6.83
    quasi-loans, for, 6.79
    relevant information, 6.74
material interest transactions, and
    exemptions, 6.98
    financial statements, in, 6.94—6.97
    introduction, 6.93
    penalties for failure to comply, 6.99
money-lending company loans, and, 6.143—6.144
officer-related transactions, and
    from 6 April 2008, 6.132.1
    pre-6 April 2008, 6.129—6.122
officer-related transactions (pre-6 April 2008), and
    exemptions, 6.131
    introduction, 6.129—6.129.1
    penalty for failure to comply, 6.132
    relevant information, 6.130

operating and financial review, and
  detailed guidance, 2.101—2.190
  generally, 2.96—2.100
substantial property transactions, and
  AIM Rules, under, 6.113—6.114
  Companies Act 1985, under, 6.112
  Listing Rules, under, 6.113—6.114
**Discount from proceeds of new issue**
accounting requirements, 7.40
generally, 7.17—7.18
**Distributable profits**
acquisition of own shares, and
  accounting requirements, 7.27—7.30
  charging purchase cost, 7.29—7.29.2
  expenses of acquisition, 7.30
  generally, 7.17—7.18
**Dividends**
directors' reports, and, 3.43
**Document quality**
secretarial matters, and, 8.67.1—8.67
**Dormant companies**
financial statements, and
  additional disclosure, 8.154.21
  definition, 8.154.18
  effect, 8.154.16—8.154.17
  generally, 8.154.14—8.154.15
  significant accounting transactions,
    8.154.19—8.154.20

**Electronic communications**
'communication', 8.82.3
financial statements, of, 8.117.1—8.117.4
general entitlement, 8.82.5—8.83
introduction, 8.80—8.82.1.1
Listing Rules, and, 8.117.6—8.118
meaning, 8.82.2—8.82.4
**Employee information**
disabled persons, 3.80
generally, 3.79
**Employee involvement**
directors' report, and, 3.81—3.82
**Employee numbers**
directors' reports, and
  disabled persons, 3.80
  generally, 3.79
**Environmental and social issues**
directors' report, and, 3.42.4—3.42.6
**EU Action Plan**
corporate governance, and, 4.176—4.182
**EU Directives**
corporate governance, and
  generally, 4.183—4.186
  UK implementation, 4.186.1
**European Corporate Governance Forum**
corporate governance, and, 4.187—4.189
**Ex gratia payments**
directors' remuneration, and, 5.103
**Excess retirement benefits**
quoted companies, 5.204—5.208
unquoted companies, 5.93—5.96
**Extraordinary resolutions**
secretarial matters, and, 8.267

**Fédération des Experts Comptables Européeans (FEE)**
corporate governance, and, 4.190—4.192
**Filing financial statements**
directors' duties, 8.102—8.106.1
medium-sized companies, 8.134.6—8.134.9
qualifying undertakings, 8.147.1—8.147.2
quoted companies, 8.134—8.134.1
small companies, 8.134.2—8.134.5.2

unlimited companies, 8.146—8.147
unquoted companies, 8.134—8.134.1
**Financial assistance for acquisition of own shares**
effect of contravention, 7.141—7.144
private companies, by, 7.132.1—7.132.4
public companies, by, 7.133—7.138
**Financial instruments**
directors' reports, and, 3.122—3.125
**Financial position**
operating and financial review, and
  accounting policies, 2.164—2.166.1
  capital structure, 2.167—2.171.1
  cash flows, 2.172—2.176
  general, 2.159—2.163
  going concern, 2.188—2.190
  introduction, 2.158
  liquidity, 2.177—2.187
  treasury policies, 2.167—2.171.1
**Financial reporting**
corporate governance, and, 4.76—4.78
**Financial statements**
*and see* **Directors' remuneration reports**
*and see* **Directors' reports**
abbreviated statements, 8.160—8.161
accounting records, and, 8.25.2—8.25.7
approval, 8.102—8.106.1
balance sheet and notes, 8.166—8.167
compulsory revision, 8.244—8.246
consolidated statements, 8.101—8.101.4
delivery
  company's liability for late filing, 8.148—8.151
  consolidated statements not prepared, 8.135
  directors' liability for late delivery, 8.152—8.154
  euros, in, 8.166
  filing, 8.134—8.135
  qualifying undertakings, 8.147.1—8.147.2
  time limits, 8.139—8.145
  unlimited companies, 8.146—8.147
directors' duties
  approval, 8.102—8.106.1
  filing, 8.102—8.106.1
  preparation, 8.98.1—8.101.4
  publication, 8.102—8.106.1
  signature, 8.102—8.106.1
dormant companies
  additional disclosure, 8.154.21
  definition, 8.154.18
  effect, 8.154.16—8.154.17
  generally, 8.154.14—8.154.15
  significant accounting transactions,
    8.154.19—8.154.20
exemptions from audit requirements
  dormant companies, 8.154.14—8.154.21
  small companies, 8.154.1—8.154.13
filing
  directors' duties, 8.102—8.106.1
  medium-sized companies, 8.134.6—8.134.9
  qualifying undertakings, 8.147.1—8.147.2
  quoted companies, 8.134—8.134.1
  small companies, 8.134.2—8.134.5.2
  unlimited companies, 8.146—8.147
  unquoted companies, 8.134—8.134.1
full statements, 8.157—8.159
individual statements, 8.100—8.100.1
introduction, 8.6—8.6.1
liability for
  defective statements, 8.107—8.108
  unsigned balance sheet, 8.109—8.111
non-statutory accounts, 8.195—8.201
operating and financial review, and
  complementing, 2.70—2.72.1

# Index

supplementing, 2.65—2.68
persons entitled to receive, 8.116.12—8.117
preparation
  consolidated, 8.101—8.101.4
  individual, 8.100—8.100.1
  introduction, 8.98.1—8.99
presentation
  election to dispense, 8.123—8.131
  introduction, 8.121—8.122
  liability for failure to comply, 8.132—8.133
proper accounting records, and, 8.25.2—8.25.7
publication
  abbreviated statements, 8.160—8.161
  balance sheet and notes, 8.166—8.167
  definition, 8.155—8.156
  euros, in, 8.166
  full statements, 8.157—8.159
  introduction, 8.102—8.106.1
  non-statutory accounts, 8.195—8.201
  short-form statements, 8.162—8.165
  summary statements, 8.170—8.194
revision of defective
  compulsory, 8.244—8.246
  introduction, 8.214—8.214.1
  voluntary, 8.215—8.243
short-form statements, 8.162—8.165
signature, 8.102—8.106.1
small companies, 8.154.1—8.154.13
summary financial statements
  background, 8.170—8.175
  balance sheet, 8.191.2—8.193
  comparative information, 8.193.2
  conditions, 8.176—8.180
  directors' remuneration report, 8.189.1
  directors' report, 8.189
  dividends, 8.193.1
  form and content, 8.186—8.188
  general conditions, 8.176—8.180
  members' wishes, 8.181—8.184
  penalties for failure to comply, 8.194
  profit and loss account, 8.190—8.191.1
  relevant statements, 8.185—8.185.2
  voluntary revision, 8.215—8.243
**Financial year**
  secretarial matters, and, 8.85—8.87
**Full financial statements**
  secretarial matters, and, 8.157—8.159
**Funding requirements for acquisition of own shares**
  assignment of rights, 7.87—7.88
  capital maintenance, 7.22
  distributable profits, 7.17—7.18
  introduction, 7.16
  payment out of capital, 7.19—7.20
  proceeds of new issue, 7.17—7.18
  summary, 7.21

**General meetings**
  annual
    introduction, 8.251—8.252.1
    notice, 8.253—8.257
    single member companies, 8.259
  generally, 8.250—8.250.1
  introduction, 8.25
  records, 8.275—8.276
  single member companies, 8.259
**Going concern**
  corporate governance, and
    foreseeable future, 4.127—4.130
    form of disclosure, 4.114—4.123
    groups, 4.124
    introduction, 4.111—4.113

    procedures, 4.125—4.126
    operating and financial review, and, 2.188—2.190
**Good practice reporting**
  corporate governance, and, 4.155
**Greenbury report**
  corporate governance, and, 4.10
  directors' remuneration, and, 5.1
**Groups**
  disclosure of directors' remuneration, and,
    5.233—5.248
  reporting on going concern, and, 4.124
  reporting on internal controls, and, 4.153

**Half-yearly reports**
  AIM companies, 8.207
  compensation for false statements, 8.213.1—8.213.2
  generally, 8.204
  interim management statements, 8.205
  PLUS-quoted companies, 8.207.1
  status, 8.208—8.212
**Hampel Report**
  background, 4.11—4.13
  'box ticking', 4.26—4.27
  listed companies' objectives, 4.28—4.29
  objectives, 4.22—4.24
  recommendations, 4.31—4.33
  stakeholders position, 4.30
**Higgs**
  generally, 4.15—4.17
  'Suggestion for Good Practice', 4.100
**Highest paid director's emoluments**
  'accrued pension', 5.87—5.90.2
  ascertaining the director, 5.78—5.82
  comparative figures, 5.92—5.92.4
  disclosure, 5.83—5.86.1
  introduction, 5.75—5.77
  readily ascertainable from other information, 5.91
**Holding company**
  directors' loans, and, 6.27

**IFRS**
  directors' report, and, 3.11
  introduction, 1.1
**Independence of directors**
  corporate governance, and, 4.50—4.53
**Indirect arrangements**
  general prohibition, 6.58—6.60
  value, 6.61
**Individual financial statements**
  *and see* **Directors' remuneration reports**
  *and see* **Directors' reports**
  abbreviated statements, 8.160—8.161
  accounting records, and, 8.25.2—8.25.7
  approval, 8.102—8.106.1
  balance sheet and notes, 8.166—8.167
  compulsory revision, 8.244—8.246
  consolidated statements, 8.101—8.101.4
  delivery
    company's liability for late filing, 8.148—8.151
    consolidated statements not prepared, 8.135
    directors' liability for late delivery, 8.152—8.154
    euros, in, 8.166
    filing, 8.134—8.135
    qualifying undertakings, 8.147.1—8.147.2
    time limits, 8.139—8.145
    unlimited companies, 8.146—8.147
  directors' duties
    approval, 8.102—8.106.1
    filing, 8.102—8.106.1
    preparation, 8.98.1—8.101.4
    publication, 8.102—8.106.1

signature, 8.102—8.106.1
dormant companies
    additional disclosure, 8.154.21
    definition, 8.154.18
    effect, 8.154.16—8.154.17
    generally, 8.154.14—8.154.15
    significant accounting transactions,
        8.154.19—8.154.20
exemptions from audit requirements
    dormant companies, 8.154.14—8.154.21
    small companies, 8.154.1—8.154.13
filing
    directors' duties, 8.102—8.106.1
    medium-sized companies, 8.134.6—8.134.9
    qualifying undertakings, 8.147.1—8.147.2
    quoted companies, 8.134—8.134.1
    small companies, 8.134.2—8.134.5.2
    unlimited companies, 8.146—8.147
    unquoted companies, 8.134—8.134.1
full statements, 8.157—8.159
individual statements, 8.100—8.100.1
introduction, 8.6—8.6.1
liability for
    defective statements, 8.107—8.108
    unsigned balance sheet, 8.109—8.111
non-statutory accounts, 8.195—8.201
operating and financial review, and
    complementing, 2.70—2.72.1
    supplementing, 2.65—2.68
persons entitled to receive, 8.116.12—8.117
preparation
    generally, 8.100—8.100.1
    introduction, 8.98.1—8.99
presentation
    election to dispense, 8.123—8.131
    introduction, 8.121—8.122
    liability for failure to comply, 8.132—8.133
proper accounting records, and, 8.25.2—8.25.7
publication
    abbreviated statements, 8.160—8.161
    balance sheet and notes, 8.166—8.167
    definition, 8.155—8.156
    euros, in, 8.166
    full statements, 8.157—8.159
    introduction, 8.102—8.106.1
    non-statutory accounts, 8.195—8.201
    short-form statements, 8.162—8.165
    summary statements, 8.170—8.194
revision of defective
    compulsory, 8.244—8.246
    introduction, 8.214—8.214.1
    voluntary, 8.215—8.243
short-form statements, 8.162—8.165
signature, 8.102—8.106.1
small companies, 8.154.1—8.154.13
summary financial statements
    background, 8.170—8.175
    balance sheet, 8.191.2—8.193
    comparative information, 8.193.2
    conditions, 8.176—8.180
    directors' remuneration report, 8.189.1
    directors' report, 8.189
    dividends, 8.193.1
    form and content, 8.186—8.188
    general conditions, 8.176—8.180
    members' wishes, 8.181—8.184
    penalties for failure to comply, 8.194
    profit and loss account, 8.190—8.191.1
    relevant statements, 8.185—8.185.2
voluntary revision, 8.215—8.243

Insider dealing
    acquisition of own shares, and, 7.81—7.81.2
Institutional shareholders
    acquisition of own shares, and, 7.131—7.132
    corporate governance, and, 4.93—4.97
Interim management statements
    compensation for false statements, 8.213.1—8.213.2
    generally, 8.205
Internal control
    generally, 4.79—4.83
    reporting
        board's role, 4.144—4.147.11
        generally, 4.131—4.134.1
        groups, and, 4.154
        internal audit, 4.147.12
        Turnbull guidance (2005), 4.138—4.143
Intra-group company transactions
    directors' loans, and
    generally, 6.39
    quasi-loans, and, 6.47
Invalidity of directors' transactions
    effect of contravention of rule, 6.122—6.125
    general rule, 6.121

Key performance indicators
    operating and financial review, and
        flexibility of choice, 2.199
        group, 2.198
        introduction, 2.192—2.193
        key indicators, 2.194—2.196
        number, 2.197
        reliability, 2.200—2.202
        reporting, 2.203—2.206.1
        segmental, 2.198

Land values
    directors' report, and, 3.48—3.49
Liquidity
    operating and financial review, and, 2.177—2.187
Listing Rules
    acquisition of own shares
        closed periods, during, 7.114—7.114.2
        insider trading, 7.114.3
        introduction, 7.112—7.113
        market abuse, 7.114.3
        prohibited periods, during, 7.114—7.114.2
        purchase from related parties, 7.115
        purchase of equity shares, 7.116—7.122
        purchase of non-equity shares, 7.123—7.126
        redemption of redeemable shares, 7.128
        Treasury shares, 7.126.1—7.126.3
    electronic communications, 8.117.6—8.118
    half-yearly reports
        AIM companies, 8.207
        compensation for false statements, 8.213.1—8.213.2
        generally, 8.204
        interim management statements, 8.205
        PLUS-quoted companies, 8.207.1
        status, 8.208—8.212
    interim management statements
        compensation for false statements, 8.213.1—8.213.2
        generally, 8.205
    preliminary announcements, 8.202
    purchase of equity shares, 7.116—7.122
    purchase of non-equity shares, 7.123—7.126
    redemption of redeemable shares, 7.128
    secretarial matters, and
        electronic communications, 8.117.6—8.118
        half-yearly reports, 8.204—8.212
        preliminary announcements, 8.202
    substantial property transactions, 6.113—6.114

Treasury shares, 7.126.1—7.126.3
**Loan for acquisition of own shares**
  effect of contravention, 7.141—7.144
  private companies, by, 7.132.1—7.132.4
  public companies, by, 7.133—7.138
**Loan, etc., transactions involving directors**
  alternate director, 6.16—6.17
  assignment of rights
    general prohibition, 6.54—6.56
    value, 6.57
  associated company, 6.25.1
  associated with body corporate
    control of shares or votes, 6.21
    generally, 6.19—6.20
    interests in shares, 6.22
    limits on aggregation, 6.23—6.24
  banking companies, and
      *and see* **Banking companies, loans by**
    disclosure requirements, 6.147—6.161
    introduction, 6.133—6.136
    liability for contravention, 6.162
    loans on beneficial terms for house purchase, 6.141
    loans on commercial terms, 6.137—6.140
  body corporate, 6.25.2
  business transactions, 6.53—6.53.1
  civil remedies, 6.68
  company, 6.26
  connected persons, 6.18
  connected with body corporate
    control of shares or votes, 6.21
    generally, 6.19—6.20
    interests in shares, 6.22
    limits on aggregation, 6.23—6.24
  credit transactions
    business transactions, 6.53—6.53.1
    conditions, 6.49.1—6.51
    definition, 6.48
    exceptions, 6.52—6.53.1
    minor transactions, 6.52—6.52.1
    value, 6.49
  criminal sanctions, 6.68
  de facto director, 6.15.1—6.15.4
  definitions
    alternate director, 6.16—6.17
    associated company, 6.25.1
    associated with body corporate, 6.19—6.24
    body corporate, 6.25.2
    company, 6.26
    connected persons, 6.18
    connected with body corporate, 6.19—6.24
    de facto director, 6.15.1—6.15.4
    director, 6.9—6.10
    holding company, 6.27
    introduction, 6.8
    members of a director's family, 6.18.1
    relevant company, 6.25
    shadow director, 6.11—6.14
    subsidiary, 6.27
  director, 6.9—6.10
  directors' business expenditure, 6.64—6.67.6
  disclosure requirements
    beginning and ending pre-6 April 2008, 6.70—6.83
    from 6 April 2008, 6.83.3—6.83.8
    introduction, 6.69—6.69.2
    straddling 6 April 2008, 6.83.1—6.83.2
  disclosure requirements (pre-6 April 2008)
    credit transactions, in, 6.79
    excluded transactions, 6.81—6.82
    exemptions, 6.80
    financial statement, in, 6.70—6.73
    guarantees or securities, for, 6.77—6.78
    intra-group loans, for, 6.80
    introduction, 6.70—6.73
    loans, for, 6.75
    penalties for failure to comply, 6.83
    quasi-loans, for, 6.79
    relevant information, 6.74
  exemptions
    business transactions, 6.53—6.53.1
    directors' business expenditure, 6.64—6.67.6
    general, 6.62
    inter-company group loans, 6.39, 6.47
    minor transactions, 6.52—6.52.1
    other loans, 6.40—6.41.1
    small loans, 6.33—6.38, 6.46
    transaction between subsidiary and parent, 6.63
  holding company, 6.27
  indirect arrangements
    general prohibition, 6.58—6.60
    value, 6.61
  inter-company group loans
    generally, 6.39
    quasi-loans, and, 6.47
  introduction, 6.1—6.7
  invalidity of
    effect of contravention of rule, 6.122—6.125
    general rule, 6.121
  loans
    definition, 6.30
    exemptions, 6.33—6.41.1
    general prohibition, 6.32
    inter-company group loans, 6.39
    other loans, 6.40—6.41.1
    small loans, 6.33—6.38
    value, 6.31
  members of a director's family, 6.18.1
  minor credit transactions, 6.52—6.52.1
  money-lending companies, and
      *and see* **Money-lending companies, loans by**
    disclosure requirements, 6.143—6.144
    introduction, 6.133—6.136
    liability for contravention, 6.162
    loans on beneficial terms for house purchase, 6.141
    loans on commercial terms, 6.137—6.140
  prohibited transactions
    assignment of rights, 6.54—6.57
    credit transactions, 6.48—6.53.1
    exemptions, 6.62—6.67.6
    indirect arrangements, 6.58—6.61
    introduction, 6.29
    loans, 6.30—6.41.1
    quasi-loans, 6.42—6.47
    sanctions and remedies, 6.68
  quasi-loans
    definition, 6.42
    exceptions, 6.46—6.47
    general prohibition, 6.44—6.45.1
    inter-company group loans, 6.47
    small loans, 6.46
    value, 6.43
  relevant company, 6.25
  shadow director, 6.11—6.14
  small loans
    loans, 6.33—6.38
    quasi-loans, 6.46
  sanctions and remedies, 6.68
  subsidiary, 6.27
  transaction between subsidiary and parent, 6.63
  validity of
    effect of contravention of rule, 6.122—6.125
    general rule, 6.121

**Long-term incentive plan, sums receivable under**
AIM companies, 5.47—5.49
definitions, 5.51—5.55
information subject to audit, 5.180—5.192
quoted companies, 5.47—5.49
unquoted companies, 5.50

**Major interest in company's shares**
directors' report, and, 3.130—3.132
**Major Shareholding Notification Rules**
acquisition of own shares, and, 7.130
**Material interest transactions**
beginning after 6 April 2008, 6.99.1
beginning pre-6 April 2008
definition of 'material interest', 6.88—6.92
exemptions under CA 1985, 6.98
financial statements, in, 6.94—6.97
introduction, 6.84—6.87
penalties for failure to comply, 6.99
requirements, 6.93—6.99
**Meetings**
annual general
introduction, 8.251—8.252.1
notice, 8.253—8.257
single member companies, 8.259
class, 8.262
directors', 8.247—8.249
general, 8.250—8.250.1
records, 8.275—8.276
resolutions
extraordinary, 8.267
introduction, 8.263—8.265
ordinary, 8.266
special, 8.268
written, 8.271—8.274
single member companies, 8.259
**Memorandum of association**
secretarial matters, and, 8.53—8.53.2
**Minor credit transactions**
directors' loans, and, 6.52—6.52.1
**Money-lending companies, loans by**
disclosure requirements, 6.143—6.144
introduction, 6.133—6.136
liability for contravention, 6.162
loans on beneficial terms for house purchase, 6.141
loans on commercial terms, 6.137—6.140

**Name of company**
secretarial matters, and, 8.48—8.52
**Narrative reporting**
operating and financial review, and, 2.1
**Non-listed organisations**
corporate governance, and, 4.157—4.159
**Non-statutory accounts**
secretarial matters, and, 8.195—8.201
**Notes to financial statements**
acquisition of own shares, and
IFRS, 7.46.1
UK GAAP, 7.46
**Notification to board**
directors' transactions, and, 6.163—6.178

**Officers, transactions involving**
disclosure requirements
from 6 April 2008, 6.132.1
pre-6 April 2008, 6.129—6.122
disclosure requirements (pre-6 April 2008)
exemptions, 6.131
introduction, 6.129—6.129.1
penalty for failure to comply, 6.132
relevant information, 6.130

**Operating and financial review**
accounting policies, 2.164—2.166.1
background, 2.5—2.8
balanced and neutral, 2.92
business analysis through the Board's eyes, 2.46—2.47
business review
*and see* **Business review**
ASB's views, 2.21—2.24
background, 2.5—2.8
contents, 2.10—2.17
introduction, 2.1—2.4
location in annual report, 2.25—2.26
requirements, 2.10—2.34
business' nature, objectives and strategies,
2.101—2.119
capital structure, 2.167—2.171.1
cash flows, 2.172—2.176
comparable, 2.93—2.95
complementing financial statements, 2.70—2.72.1
comprehensive and understandable, 2.79—2.91
definitions, 2.36—2.39
development and performance in the year,
2.120—2.134
disclosure framework
detailed guidance, 2.101—2.190
generally, 2.96—2.100
financial position
accounting policies, 2.164—2.166
capital structure, 2.167—2.171.1
cash flows, 2.172—2.176
general, 2.159—2.163
going concern, 2.188—2.190
introduction, 2.158
liquidity, 2.177—2.187
treasury policies, 2.167—2.171.1
financial statements, and
complementing, 2.70—2.72
supplementing, 2.65—2.68
focus on matters relevant to interests of members,
2.48—2.52
forward looking, 2.53—2.63
going concern, 2.188—2.190
guidance
business' nature, objectives and strategies,
2.101—2.119
development and performance in the year,
2.120—2.134
financial position, 2.158—2.190
principal risks and uncertainties, 2.138—2.145
relationships, 2.146—2.157
resources, 2.135—2.137
international developments, 2.222—2.226
introduction, 2.1—2.4
key performance indicators
flexibility of choice, 2.199
group, 2.198
introduction, 2.192—2.193
key indicators, 2.194—2.196
number, 2.197
reliability, 2.200—2.202
reporting, 2.203—2.206.1
segmental, 2.198
liquidity, 2.177—2.187
narrative reporting, and, 2.1
non-statutory financial information, 2.73—2.78
objective, 2.41
other performance indicators
introduction, 2.207—2.208
'seriously prejudicial', 2.209—2.214
principal risks and uncertainties, 2.138—2.145
principles

# Index

balanced and neutral, 2.92
business analysis through the Board's eyes,
2.46—2.47
comparable, 2.93  2.95
complement and supplement financial statements,
2.64—2.78
comprehensive and understandable, 2.79—2.91
focus on matters relevant to interests of members,
2.48—2.52
forward looking, 2.53—2.63
introduction, 2.44—2.45
"quoted company", 2.37
relationships, 2.146—2.157
Reporting Statement (RS(OFR))
definitions, 2.36—2.39
disclosure framework, 2.96—2.100
guidance, 2.101—2.190
international developments, 2.222—2.226
key performance indicators, 2.192—2.206.1
objective, 2.41
other performance indicators, 2.207—2.214
principles, 2.44—2.95
scope, 2.36—2.39
statement of compliance, 2.215
resources, 2.135—2.137
scope, 2.36—2.39
statement of compliance, 2.215
supplementing financial statements, 2.65—2.68
treasury policies, 2.167—2.171.1
**Ordinary resolutions**
secretarial matters, and, 8.266
**Overseas branches**
directors' report, and, 3.126

**Past directors**
directors' remuneration, and, 5.152—5.154
**Payment out of capital, acquisition of shares by**
accounting requirements, 7.47—7.62
capital maintenance, 7.55—7.62
generally, 7.19—7.20
legal procedures
acquisition, 7.101—7.103.1
auditor's report to directors, 7.100
introduction, 7.93—7.94
public of notice of acquisition, 7.104—7.106
statutory declarations, 7.95—7.99
liability of winding up, 7.107—7.108
nominal value less than PCP and proceeds of fresh
issue, 7.59—7.62
permissible capital payment
available profits, 7.50—7.54
generally, 7.49
no available profits, 7.54.1—7.54.2
shares to be purchased at a premium in excess of the
original premium, 7.62.1—7.62.2
transfer to capital redemption reserve, 7.56—7.58
**Pension contributions**
directors' remuneration, and
quoted companies, 5.193—5.203
unquoted companies, 5.58—5.71
**Pension scheme top ups**
directors' remuneration, and, 5.100—5.101
**Performance evaluation of directors**
corporate governance, and, 4.64—4.65
**Performance graph**
directors' remuneration, and, 5.143—5.148.5
**Performance indicators**
key performance indicators
flexibility of choice, 2.199
group, 2.198
introduction, 2.192—2.193

key indicators, 2.194—2.196
number, 2.197
reliability, 2.200—2.202
reporting, 2.203—2.206.1
segmental, 2.198
other performance indicators
introduction, 2.207—2.208
'seriously prejudicial', 2.209—2.214
**Place of keeping books and records**
accounting records, 8.34—8.36
statutory books, 8.37—8.47
**PLUS-quoted companies**
half-yearly reports, 8.207.1
**Political donations**
definitions, 3.101
director's liability, 3.110—3.111
disclosures from 6 April 2008
stand-alone company not wholly owned by GB
parent, 3.117.1—3.117.2
subsidiaries not wholly owned by GB parent,
3.117.3—3.117.4
subsidiaries wholly owned by GB parent, 3.117.5
disclosures pre-6 April 2008
introduction, 3.112
stand-alone company not wholly owned by GB
parent, 3.113—3.114
subsidiaries not wholly owned by GB parent,
3.115—3.116
subsidiaries wholly owned by GB parent, 3.117
exemptions, 3.106
introduction, 3.100
non-EU political parties, 3.114
parent company of non-GB subsidiary, 3.109
prohibition, 3.102—3.105
subsidiaries incorporated in GB, 3.107—3.108
**Post balance sheet events**
directors' report, and, 3.44
**Preliminary announcements**
generally, 8.202
status, 8.208—8.213
**Premium from proceeds of new issue**
accounting requirements, 7.32—7.34
generally, 7.17—7.18
**Presentation of financial statements**
election to dispense, 8.123—8.131
introduction, 8.121—8.122
liability for failure to comply, 8.132—8.133
**Principal activities**
directors' report, and, 3.16—3.21
**Professional development of directors**
corporate governance, and, 4.62—4.63
**Profit and loss account**
summary statements, 8.190—8.191.1
**Proper accounting records**
annual financial statements, 8.25.2—8.25.7
assets and liabilities, 8.22
auditors' duties and rights
criminal offence, 8.32.3
generally, 8.30—8.32.1
limitation of liability agreements, 8.32.4—8.32.6
senior statutory auditor, 8.32.2—8.32.2.2
directors' duty, 8.26—8.29
disclosure of financial position 'at any time',
8.16—8.20
disqualification orders, and, 8.25—8.25.1
duty to keep records, 8.13—8.15
financial statements, 8.25.2—8.25.7
form, 8.33
general obligation, 8.9—8.10.1
goods sold and purchased statements, 8.24
guidance statement, 8.11—8.12

individual financial statements, 8.25.2—8.25.7
introduction, 8.6—8.8
location, 8.34—8.36
penalties, 8.25—8.25.1
penalties for failure to comply, 8.74—8.79.1
place of keeping, 8.34—8.36
'proper records', 8.9—8.10.1
record of assets and liabilities, 8.22
requirement to prepare financial statements,
    8.25.2—8.25.7
retention period, 8.68—8.73.1
senior statutory auditor, 8.32.2—8.32.2.2
statements of goods sold and purchased, 8.24
statements of stock, 8.23
sums of money, 8.21
**Publication of financial statements**
abbreviated statements, 8.160—8.161
balance sheet and notes, 8.166—8.167
conditions, 8.176—8.180
definition, 8.155—8.156
euros, in, 8.166
full statements, 8.157—8.159
introduction, 8.102—8.106.1
non-statutory accounts, 8.195—8.201
short-form statements, 8.162—8.165
summary statements, 8.170—8.194
**Purchase of own shares**
*see* **Acquisition of own shares**

**Quasi-loans**
definition, 6.42
exceptions, 6.46—6.47
general prohibition, 6.44—6.45.1
inter-company group loans, 6.47
small loans, 6.46
value, 6.43
**Quoted companies**
directors' reports, and
    additional matters, 3.42.12—3.42.18
    connected persons, 3.137.7—3.137.10
    corporate governance, 3.139
    directors' interests in contracts of significance,
        3.137.11
    directors' service contracts, 3.136—3.137
    disclosure of directors' interests, 3.137.1—3.137.6
    introduction, 3.129.7.1
    major interest in company's shares, 3.130—3.132
    purchase of own shares, 3.142.1
    special business, 3.142
    transactions with controlling shareholder,
        3.135—3.135.2
    waiver of dividends, 3.138
disclosure of directors' remuneration, and
    information subject to audit, 5.163—5.223
    information not subject to audit, 5.130—5.154
    remuneration report, 5.121—5.129
    share option gains, 5.47—5.49
operating and financial review, and, 2.37

**Re-appointment of auditors**
directors' report, and, 4.66—4.67
**Redeemable shares**
acquisition of own shares, and, 7.8—7.11
**Reduction of share capital**
court confirmation, 7.146—7.153
generally, 7.145
solvency statement, 7.154—7.159
**Regulatory Information Service**
acquisition of own shares, and
    equity shares, 7.113
    non-equity shares, 7.123

**Relations with shareholders**
annual general meeting, 4.91
dialogue with institutional shareholders, 4.88—4.90
institutional shareholders, 4.93—4.97
**Relevant company**
directors' loans, and, 6.25
**Remuneration committee**
directors' remuneration, and, 5.130—5.133
**Remuneration of directors**
*and see* **Director's remuneration**
corporate governance, and
    compensation, 4.72
    generally, 4.68
    policy, 4.69—4.71
    procedure, 4.73
    recommendations, 4.74—4.75
    service contracts and compensation, 4.72
disclosure, 5.1—5.248
**Reporting accountant's report**
voluntary revision, 8.231—8.233
**Reporting on going concern**
foreseeable future, 4.127—4.130
form of disclosure, 4.114—4.123
groups, 4.124
introduction, 4.111—4.113
procedures, 4.125—4.126
**Reporting on internal control**
generally, 4.79—4.83
reporting
    board's role, 4.144—4.147.11
    generally, 4.131—4.134.1
    groups, and, 4.154
    internal audit, 4.147.12
    Turnbull guidance (2005), 4.138—4.143
**Reporting Statements**
operating and financial review (RS(OFR))
    definitions, 2.36—2.39
    disclosure framework, 2.96—2.100
    guidance, 2.101—2.190
    international developments, 2.222—2.226
    key performance indicators, 2.192—2.206.1
    objective, 2.41
    other performance indicators, 2.207—2.214
    principles, 2.44—2.95
    scope, 2.36—2.39
    statement of compliance, 2.215
**Research and development activities**
directors' report, and, 3.45—3.47
**Resolutions**
extraordinary, 8.267
introduction, 8.263—8.265
ordinary, 8.266
special, 8.268
written, 8.271—8.274
**Returns**
acquisition of own shares, and, 7.82—7.86
**Revision of defective financial statements**
compulsory, 8.244—8.246
introduction, 8.214—8.214.1
voluntary
    abbreviated financial statements, 8.238
    approval and signature, 8.220—8.226
    auditors' report, 8.227—8.230.1
    companies exempt from audit, 8.239—8.240.1
    effects, 8.234—8.237
    introduction, 8.215—8.219
    reporting accountant's report, 8.231—8.233
    summary financial statements, 8.241—8.243

# Index

**Safe harbour**
directors' remuneration reports, and,
  8.116.10—8.116.11
directors' reports, and
  generally, 8.116.10—8.116.11
  introduction, 3.143
**Sale of Treasury shares**
directors' report, and, 3.75—3.76
generally, 7.111.10—7.111.11
**Sarbanes-Oxley Act**
corporate governance, and, 4.194—4.196
**Secretarial matters**
abbreviated financial statements
  publication, 8.160—8.161
  voluntary revision, 8.241—8.243
accounting records
  annual financial statements, 8.25.2—8.25.7
  assets and liabilities, 8.22
  auditors' duties and rights, 8.30—8.32.6
  directors' duty, 8.26—8.29
  disclosure of financial position 'at any time',
    8.16—8.20
  disqualification orders, and, 8.25—8.25.1
  duty to keep records, 8.12—8.15
  financial statements, 8.25.2—8.25.7
  form, 8.33
  general obligation, 8.9—8.10.1
  goods sold and purchased statements, 8.24
  guidance statement, 8.11—8.12
  individual financial statements, 8.25.2—8.25.7
  introduction, 8.6—8.8
  location, 8.34—8.36
  penalties, 8.25—8.25.1
  penalties for failure to comply, 8.74—8.79.1
  place of keeping, 8.34—8.36
  'proper records', 8.9—8.10.1
  record of assets and liabilities, 8.22
  requirement to prepare financial statements,
    8.25.2—8.25.7
  retention period, 8.68—8.73.1
  senior statutory auditor, 8.32.2—8.32.2.2
  statements of goods sold and purchased, 8.24
  statements of stock, 8.23
  sums of money, 8.21
accounting reference date
  change by AIM company, 8.93—8.93.1
  change by listed company, 8.92
  generally, 8.84
accounting reference periods
  accounting reference date, 8.84
  current periods, 8.94—8.95
  financial year, 8.85—8.87
  generally, 8.88—8.90
  introduction, 8.84
  previous periods, 8.96—8.98
alteration of accounting reference date
  current periods, 8.94—8.95
  introduction, 8.93—8.93.1
  listed company, by, 8.95.1—8.98
  previous periods, 8.94—8.95
annual financial statements, 8.25.2—8.25.7
annual general meetings
  election to dispense, 8.257—8.258
  introduction, 8.251—8.252.1
  notice, 8.253—8.256
  single member companies, 8.259
annual return
  document quality, 8.67.1—8.67
  generally, 8.55—8.61.2
  information annexed, 8.64
  members' lists, 8.62

penalties for failure to comply, 8.63
approval of financial statements, 8.102—8.106.1
articles of association, 8.53—8.53.2
auditors' report
  introduction, 8.6
  voluntary revision, 8.227—8.230.1
balance sheet
  summary statements, 8.191.2—8.193
class meetings, 8.262
company identification
  articles of association, 8.53—8.53.2
  memorandum of association, 8.53—8.53.2
  name, 8.48—8.52
comparative information, 8.193.2
consolidated financial statements
  approval, 8.102—8.106.1
  delivery, 8.134—8.154
  exemptions from audit, 8.154.1—8.154.21
  filing, 8.102—8.106.1
  introduction, 8.6—8.6.1
  persons entitled to receive, 8.116.12—8.117
  preparation, 8.98.1—8.101.4
  presentation at general meeting, 8.121—8.133
  publication, 8.155—8.201
  revision of defective, 8.214—8.246
  signature, 8.102—8.106.1
delivery of financial statements
  company's liability for late filing, 8.148—8.151
  consolidated statements not prepared, 8.135
  directors' liability for late delivery, 8.152—8.154
  euros, in, 8.166
  filing, 8.134—8.135
  qualifying undertakings, 8.147.1—8.147.2
  time limits, 8.139—8.145
  unlimited companies, 8.146—8.147
directors' meetings, 8.247—8.249
directors' remuneration report
  approval, 8.116.7—8.116.9
  introduction, 8.6
  members' approval, 8.133.1—8.133.4
  preparation, 8.116.1—8.116.6
  safe harbour provisions, 8.116.10—8.116.11
  summary statements, 8.189.1
directors' report
  approval, 8.114—8.116
  introduction, 8.6
  preparation, 8.112—8.113.1
  safe harbour provisions, 8.116.10—8.116.11
  summary statements, 8.189
  voluntary revision, 8.224—8.226
dividends, 8.193.1
document quality, 8.67.1—8.67
dormant companies
  additional disclosure, 8.154.21
  definition, 8.154.18
  effect, 8.154.16—8.154.17
  generally, 8.154.14—8.154.15
  significant accounting transactions,
    8.154.19—8.154.20
electronic communications
  'communication', 8.82.3
  financial statements, of, 8.117.1—8.117.4
  general entitlement, 8.82.5—8.83
  introduction, 8.80—8.82.1.1
  Listing Rules, and, 8.117.6—8.118
  meaning, 8.82.2—8.82.4
exemptions from audit of financial statements
  dormant companies, 8.154.14—8.154.21
  small companies, 8.154.1—8.154.13
extraordinary resolutions, 8.267
filing

directors' duties, 8.102—8.106.1
  medium-sized companies, 8.134.6—8.134.9
  qualifying undertakings, 8.147.1—8.147.2
  quoted companies, 8.134—8.134.1
  small companies, 8.134.2—8.134.5.2
  unlimited companies, 8.146—8.147
  unquoted companies, 8.134—8.134.1
financial statements
  approval, 8.102—8.106.1
  delivery, 8.134—8.154
  exemptions from audit, 8.154.1—8.154.21
  filing, 8.102—8.106.1
  introduction, 8.6—8.6.1
  persons entitled to receive, 8.116.12—8.117
  preparation, 8.98.1—8.101.4
  presentation at general meeting, 8.121—8.133
  publication, 8.155—8.201
  revision of defective, 8.214—8.246
  signature, 8.102—8.106.1
full financial statements, 8.157—8.159
general meetings
  annual, 8.251—8.259
  introduction, 8.250—8.250.1
  records, 8.275—8.276
  single member companies, 8.259
half-yearly reports
  AIM companies, 8.207
  compensation for false statements, 8.213.1—8.213.2
  generally, 8.204
  interim management statements, 8.205
  PLUS-quoted companies, 8.207.1
  status, 8.208—8.212
individual financial statements
  approval, 8.102—8.106.1
  delivery, 8.134—8.154
  exemptions from audit, 8.154.1—8.154.21
  filing, 8.102—8.106.1
  introduction, 8.6—8.6.1
  persons entitled to receive, 8.116.12—8.117
  preparation, 8.98.1—8.101.4
  presentation at general meeting, 8.121—8.133
  publication, 8.155—8.201
  revision of defective, 8.214—8.246
  signature, 8.102—8.106.1
interim management statements
  compensation for false statements, 8.213.1—8.213.2
  generally, 8.205
introduction, 8.1—8.5
Listing Rules requirements
  half-yearly reports, 8.204—8.207
  preliminary announcements, 8.202
meetings
  annual general, 8.251—8.259
  class, 8.262
  directors', 8.247—8.249
  general, 8.250—8.250.1
  records, 8.275—8.276
  single member companies, 8.259
memorandum of association, 8.53—8.53.2
name of company, 8.48—8.52
non-statutory accounts, 8.195—8.201
ordinary resolutions, 8.266
persons entitled to receive financial statements
  electronic transmission, 8.117.1—8.118
  introduction, 8.117
place of keeping books and records
  accounting records, 8.34—8.36
  statutory books, 8.37—8.47
preliminary announcements
  generally, 8.202
  status, 8.208—8.213

preparation of financial statements
  generally, 8.101—8.101.4
  introduction, 8.98.1—8.99
presentation of financial statements
  election to dispense, 8.123—8.131
  introduction, 8.121—8.122
  liability for failure to comply, 8.132—8.133
profit and loss account
  summary statements, 8.190—8.191.1
proper accounting records
  annual financial statements, 8.25.2—8.25.7
  assets and liabilities, 8.22
  auditors' duties and rights, 8.30—8.32.6
  directors' duty, 8.26—8.29
  disclosure of financial position 'at any time',
    8.16—8.20
  disqualification orders, and, 8.25—8.25.1
  duty to keep records, 8.13—8.15
  financial statements, 8.25.2—8.25.7
  form, 8.33
  general obligation, 8.9—8.10.1
  goods sold and purchased statements, 8.24
  guidance statement, 8.11—8.12
  individual financial statements, 8.25.2—8.25.7
  introduction, 8.6—8.8
  location, 8.34—8.36
  penalties, 8.25—8.25.1
  penalties for failure to comply, 8.74—8.79.1
  place of keeping, 8.34—8.36
  'proper records', 8.9—8.10.1
  record of assets and liabilities, 8.22
  requirement to prepare financial statements,
    8.25.2—8.25.7
  retention period, 8.68—8.73.1
  senior statutory auditor, 8.32.2—8.32.2.2
  statements of goods sold and purchased, 8.24
  statements of stock, 8.23
  sums of money, 8.21
publication of financial statements
  abbreviated statements, 8.160—8.161
  definition, 8.155—8.156
  euros, in, 8.166
  full statements, 8.157—8.159
  non-statutory accounts, 8.195—8.201
  short-form statements, 8.162—8.165
  summary statements, 8.170—8.194
reporting accountant's report
  voluntary revision, 8.231—8.233
resolutions
  extraordinary, 8.267
  introduction, 8.263—8.265
  ordinary, 8.266
  special, 8.268
  written, 8.271—8.274
revision of defective financial statements
  compulsory revision, 8.244—8.246
  introduction, 8.214—8.214.1
  voluntary revision, 8.215—8.243
short-form statements, 8.162—8.165
special resolutions, 8.268
statutory books and records, 8.37—8.47
summary financial statements
  background, 8.170—8.175
  balance sheet, 8.191.2—8.193
  comparative information, 8.193.2
  conditions, 8.176—8.180
  directors' remuneration report, 8.189.1
  directors' report, 8.189
  dividends, 8.193.1
  form and content, 8.186—8.188
  general conditions, 8.176—8.180

members' wishes, 8.181—8.184
penalties for failure to comply, 8.194
profit and loss account, 8.190—8.191.1
relevant statements, 8.185—8.185.2
voluntary revision of defective financial statements
abbreviated financial statements, 8.238
approval and signature, 8.220—8.226
auditors' report, 8.227—8.230.1
companies exempt from audit, 8.239—8.240.1
effects, 8.234—8.237
introduction, 8.215—8.219
reporting accountant's report, 8.231—8.233
summary financial statements, 8.241—8.243
written resolutions, 8.271—8.274
**Senior statutory auditor**
generally, 8.32.2—8.32.2.2
**'Seriously prejudicial' exemption**
operating and financial review, and, 2.209—2.214
**Service contracts**
directors' remuneration, and
compensation, 4.72
disclosure, 5.149—5.151
unquoted companies, 5.113—5.117.3
**Shadow director**
directors' loans, and, 6.11—6.14
**Share option gains**
AIM companies, 5.47—5.49
definitions, 5.51—5.55
quoted companies, 5.47—5.49
unquoted companies, 5.50
**Share options**
directors' remuneration, and, 5.170—5.179
**Shareholder approval to property transactions**
exemption, 6.109
generally, 6.104—6.108
**Shareholder relations**
annual general meeting, 4.91
dialogue with institutional shareholders, 4.88—4.90
institutional shareholders, 4.93—4.97
**Short-form statements**
secretarial matters, and, 8.162—8.165
**Signature**
directors' reports, and, 3.153—3.157
**Single member companies**
annual general meetings, and, 8.259
**Small companies**
directors' reports, and, 3.147—3.149
financial statements, and, 8.154.1—8.154.13
**Small loans**
loans, 6.33—6.38
quasi-loans, 6.46
**Smaller listed companies**
corporate governance, and, 4.156
**Smith Guidance on Audit Committees**
corporate governance, and, 4.100
**Sole members**
directors' transactions, and, 6.126—6.128
**Special business**
directors' report, and, 3.142
**Special resolutions**
secretarial matters, and, 8.268
**Statement of compliance**
operating and financial review, and, 2.215
**Statement of directors' responsibilities**
corporate governance, and, 3.127—3.127.2.5
**Statement of non-compliance**
corporate governance, and, 4.105—4.110
**Statement of policy**
directors' remuneration, and, 5.134—5.141
**Subsidiary and parent, transaction between**
directors' loans, and, 6.63

**Subsidiary undertakings**
directors' loans, and, 6.27
**Substantial property transactions**
approval by shareholders
exemption, 6.109
generally, 6.100.1—6.108
disclosure requirements
AIM Rules, under, 6.113—6.114
from 6 April 2008, 6.112.1
Listing Rules, under, 6.113—6.114
pre-6 April 2008, 6.112
introduction, 6.100
liability for contravention, 6.110—6.111
transaction value, 6.102—6.103
**Summary financial statements**
background, 8.170—8.175
balance sheet, 8.191.2—8.193
comparative information, 8.193.2
conditions, 8.176—8.180
directors' remuneration report, 8.189.1
directors' report, 8.189
dividends, 8.193.1
form and content, 8.186—8.188
general conditions, 8.176—8.180
members' wishes
consultation by notice, 8.182—8.183
generally, 8.181
relevant consultation, 8.184
penalties for failure to comply, 8.194
profit and loss account, 8.190—8.191.1
relevant statements, 8.185—8.185.2
voluntary revision, 8.241—8.243

**Third parties for directors' services, sums paid to**
quoted companies, 5.216—5.220
**Third party indemnity provisions**
directors' report, and, 3.128.1—3.128.3
**Transactions with controlling shareholder**
directors' report, and, 3.135—3.135.2
**Treasury policy**
operating and financial review, and, 2.167—2.171.1
**Treasury shares**
accounting treatment, 7.111.17
cancellation, 7.111.12—7.111.13
conditions, 7.111.5—7.111.9
delivery of returns, 7.111.14—7.111.16
introduction, 7.111.1
Listing Rules, and, 7.126.1—7.126.3
qualifying shares, 7.111.2—7.111.4
sale
directors' report, 3.75—3.76
generally, 7.111.10—7.111.11
***Turnbull* guidance**
board's role, 4.144—4.147.11
generally, 4.131—4.134.1
groups, and, 4.154
internal audit, 4.147.12
Turnbull guidance (2005), 4.138—4.143

**Validity of directors' transactions**
effect of contravention of rule, 6.122—6.125
general rule, 6.121
**Value of land**
directors' report, and, 3.48—3.49
**Voluntary revision of defective financial statements**
abbreviated financial statements, 8.238
approval and signature
directors' remuneration report, 8.224—8.226
directors' report, 8.224—8.226
generally, 8.220—8.223
auditors' report, 8.227—8.230.1

companies exempt from audit, 8.239—8.240.1
effects, 8.234—8.237
introduction, 8.215—8.219
reporting accountant's report, 8.231—8.233
summary financial statements, 8.241—8.243

**Waiver of dividends**
directors' report, and, 3.138
**Written resolutions**
secretarial matters, and, 8.271—8.274